NATURAL GOD

NATURAL GOD

DEISM IN THE AGE
OF INTELLIGENT DESIGN

BETH HOUSTON

New Deism Press ⃞ Florida

Beth Houston, MA, MFA, has taught creative writing, literature, and/or composition at San Francisco State University; University of California, Berkeley; University of California, Santa Cruz; Eckerd College; University of Central Florida; University of South Florida; University of Tampa; Polk State College; and State College of Florida. She has published six poetry books and nearly three hundred works in literary and professional journals. Her spiritual memoir, *Born-Again Deist*, was published in 2009. She is a Deist minister with a Doctor of Divinity (DD) and Doctor of Metaphysics (DM).

Cataloging Record – Created 10.01.12 (First Edition)

Houston, Beth.
   Natural God: Deism in the age of intelligent design / second edition / Beth
   Houston. – Florida : New Deism Press, c2012.
      486 p. ; 22 cm.
Includes selected bibliographical references (p. 477-486).
      ISBN 978-0-9719190-9-9

         1.   Deism. 2. Evolution (Biology). 3. Intelligent design (Teleology). 4.
         Darwin, Charles ‡d 1809-1882. I. Houston, Beth. II. Title.

BL224.4 .O68 2012

      First edition published in 2012
         ISBN 978-09719190-8-2

For Cheryl

Hibiscus blossoms—
Fig fragrance laced with jasmine—
Tanned hands sorting seeds...

CONTENTS

CHAPTERS

PART I: DEISM NOUVEAU

1   New Deism: The Golden Mean . . . 11
2   Deist Democracy: The Higher Ground . . . 49
3   Transcending the "Historical Jesus" Meme . . . 79

PART II: THE INTELLIGENT DESIGN SHUFFLE

4   The Origin and Evolution of Charles Darwin . . . 123
5   Darwin's Descent . . . 159
6   Calculated Construction: The Science of Intelligent Design . . . 183
7   Neo-Darwinism on Steroids . . . 219
8   The Tinkering Watchmaker: The Deology of Intelligent Design . . . 261

PART III: SLOUCHING TOWARDS DEISM

9   Hogtied . . . 293
10   Logos Lost . . . 333
11   Soror Mystica . . . 369
12   Aesthetic Transfiguration . . . 409
13   The Big *Other*: Sex, Diversity, and the Meaning of Life . . . 441

Selected Bibliography . . . 477

PART I

DEISM NOUVEAU

CHAPTER 1

NEW DEISM: THE GOLDEN MEAN

Survival of the fittest; kill or be killed; look out for Number One: Most of us accept these axioms as facts of life. Or do we? What about cooperation, love, compassion? Clearly these two sets of assumptions contradict each other. How is it, then, that most people today do believe both sets?

Humans are born with an innate conscience, and very early on kids heed the intrinsic urge to do the right thing, to be good, to not hurt others or themselves. Even preschoolers know when someone else does the wrong thing and is bad towards them: It *hurts*. We humans *feel* moral violation, whether perpetrated by us or upon us. We wise up early to the necessity of looking out for Number One, yet we also instinctively know, and quickly learn to deeply appreciate, the virtue of—virtue.

The philosophical discrepancy between do-unto-others and stick-it-to-others as valid worldviews starts for most of us in grade school when we're taught to accept Darwin's *theory* of evolution as verified *fact*. As adults we think we see kill-or-be-killed quite naturally played out every day, just for starters on TV nature shows and front-page battle fronts, and less transparently in college classrooms and corporate offices, on football fields and playgrounds, in advertising and political campaigns and hedge fund banking, really in every competitive environment (and what *isn't* competitive). So what choice is there but to concur with science that at least at some level, a survival-of-the-fittest approach to life is valid, necessary, and perfectly natural, if not good, even though it contradicts other moral, social, and experiential facts that we also accept as true.

But what if Darwin's theory has been *disproven*? Would it change how you look at the world if you discovered that although minor lateral change within a species group, or *micro*evolution, is accepted by everyone, scientists now concede that the fossil record—Darwin's Big Proof Number One—provides absolutely no evidence of Darwinian *macro*evolution, the smooth upward transitioning from one primeval ancestral organism to all other life-forms? In fact, after years of digging, paleontologists have not found a single fossil definitively linking any two major organism types.

But neo-Darwinians, notorious for squeezing fossils into boxes labeled "*a priori* assumptions," still fabricate textbook pictures depicting jagged, quantum leap "transition" based on a few fossil fragments that do not actually demonstrate lineage, much less smooth transition from one universal ancestor via "natural selection," science's bowtie jargon for survival of the fittest.

Would it change your philosophy of life to learn that Darwin's theory has been debunked, that microbiologists have recently discovered that at the deep level of DNA—Darwinians' Big Proof Number Two—life is not inherently a *struggle* for survival, that all living systems are inherently *cooperative*, that the molecular factory of life itself is composed of workers performing specific functions for the production of healthy growth within the whole system? Separate fields of science have confirmed that the principle of survival of the fittest, kill or be killed, look out for Number One is not the driving structural feature of living systems or of the universe finely tuned to produce and sustain them. All the rich diversity of life is composed of the same shared star-stuff perpetually manifesting purposeful (Darwinians prefer "directional") uniqueness via the exact same, though extraordinarily differentiating—and not fundamentally power-over generating—DNA. Throughout nature, mutual accommodation among life-forms is far more prevalent and profoundly creative and procreative than "eat or be eaten."

Surely this knowledge could benefit the world. Why then, if it has been disproven, is kill-or-be-killed Darwinism still taught as fact? Because invested Darwinians have not only dismissed the data, they have also persuaded academia and the government that if Darwin isn't valid, then creationism (or biblical *Genesism*, as I call it), i.e., religious fundamentalism, must be right. Genesists agree. Unfortunately, the possibility that this either-or might be a fallacy has been largely overlooked.

Atheist biologist Richard Dawkins calls biology "the study of complicated things that give the appearance of having been designed for a purpose," stressing that "the evidence of evolution reveals a universe without design." Of course, even Darwinians' *stylized* Tree of Life—make that *Trees*, because they can't agree upon one—depicting a *well-designed, logically ordered* evolutionary process, real or imagined, contradicts the bar-God, ban-design naturalism of both Dawkins and Darwin. Though extrapolation of Darwinian macro from micro has proven to be invalid, "fundamentalist" Darwinians like Dawkins continue to assert their hypothesis that an original organism somehow (they know not how) randomly erupted into existence by chance and somehow knew to, and knew *how* to, exist and survive and even reproduce itself—all very sophisticated processes—and that all subsequent fully-functioning, highly-complex life-forms somehow randomly accidently mutated or otherwise erupted into their own existence by some as yet unexplained, seemingly logical but really illogical mechanism that caused each discrete life-form to know to, and know how to, exist and reproduce itself in such a way that its entire life-form type would survive due to some random but inherently superior trait that seemingly logically but really illogically allowed it to kill rather than be killed. As I'll show in later chapters, atheist physicists' multiverse theory just inflates x-God Darwinism *ad absurdum*.

Meanwhile, to exorcize anti-design extremism with biblical literalism, while accommodating the overwhelming scientific verdict that Earth was not created in six days, radical "young earth" Genesism asserts that contrary to what the Bible *seems* to say, the "days" of the Creation story are actually "eras" that are longer than a literal day, and that God *really* created Creation in less than ten thousand years, not in six days. Never mind that the scientific consensus is that Earth is about 4.6 billion years old and the universe somewhere upward of 10 billion years old. Never mind that the Bible says nothing about these fabricated "eras." When back in the late '80s an international sampling of genes tracked a DNA trail to "mitochondrial Eve," the woman whose mtDNA was ancestral to that in all living people, researchers estimated that she lived in Africa 100,000 to 200,000 years ago, to which young earthers cried, "See, the biblical Creation story is right," give or take another 90,000 to 190,000 years or so. Never mind the rib, the apple, the talking snake, the god walking in the Garden asking questions…

The Deist view is that the young earth theory is as made-up as the original biblical Creation myth itself, which is as made-up as the random-chance natural-selection Creation myth of neo-Darwinism.

Recently, Deism has reemerged as the voice of common sense ensuring that both science and religion are demystified, myths and superstitions deconstructed, mistakes and misinterpretations corrected, lies and white lies and "noble lies" shelved with other relics of the past so that truth—the whole truth and nothing but the truth—can prevail. Unlike ever before, the survival of the planet depends on it.

We Deists consider it fitting that the artificial dichotomy between science and religion is best transcended, and the fallacies of both domains best rebutted, by the same Deism that guided America's most illustrious Founders. From the time of the ancient Greeks, and especially since the eighteenth century, scientists and humanists have laid the foundation of truth-centered Deism by instituting its most fundamental tenet: Nature alone, not special revelation, reveals equally to everyone the supremely intelligent and creative Creator. We still hold these truths to be self-evident, that in this *natural* way, all of us are created equal and are endowed by our Creator with certain unalienable rights, such as life, liberty, and the pursuit of happiness. Deistic natural revelation, unlike special revelation dictated by organized religion, does not violate one's freedom to choose. The Deist perspective simply appeals to each person's own reason and other inherent faculties, those same faculties that have caused so many people to doubt both scientific and religious fundamentalism.

The progress from theism to deism (a perspective) to Deism (a bona fide religion) has been slow but sure. Deists have always been a minority, but in this day and age of intelligent design, Deism is leaping into the foreground. In 2001, the American Religious Identification Survey (ARIS) reported that between 1990 and 2001, the number of self-identified Deists grew at a rate of 717 percent, making it by far the fastest growing religious classification in the U.S. Since then, other surveys with limited, predefined categories (which do not include Deism) show the greatest growth to be the category of those who believe in a supreme being but have no direct religious affiliation, which makes those people at least philosophically deist.

Recent science proving intelligent design has added momentum to the enduring Deist revolution that gained steam during the Enlightenment. Although fundamentalism and scientific determinism both challenge

Deism, they are more formidable opponents of each other. While these two armies battle it out, Deism peacefully persuades on the sidelines, where the God of ordinary people manifests through a universe of small things far more significant than religion or science or the sum of their concerns.

TOUCHSTONE TRUTH

All of us—fundamentalists, Darwinians, and Deists—would surely agree that *truth* is the solution to evolution confusion spotlighting today's science/religion dichotomy. But how can we know what's true? How can we know what's really real?

Deism argues that although logically it is incontestable that reality exists, clearly reality transcends what we perceive it to be—*we* including scientists and religionists. As I explain more fully in Chapter 8, what and how we perceive are limited, and being finite and temporal, human perception is subject to best guesses, which, let's face it, sometimes add up to misinterpretations. Unlike Darwinism and fundamentalism, Deism willingly revises its stance as it considers all possible angles in its search for truth. But it avoids blind acceptance of hearsay, including hearsay glorified as tradition: Deism is the "show me" religion. The touchstone of Deism is truth accessed via God-given common sense—common sense being the consensus of all our inherent faculties, including reason, conscience, intuition, experience, aesthetic, emotion, volition, and spirit.

While Deism acknowledges the necessity of a Designer/Creator God, it advocates a humble, open-minded approach to theology and maintains a skeptical stance toward absolutism, both religious and scientific. Deism seeks to end the Great War between absolutist factions, especially between people who contend *absolutely* that reality is spiritual and physical existence as most of us know it is illusion or evil, vs. people who insist that physical existence is *absolutely* the only reality and the so-called spiritual realm is illusion, and even evil. Modern Deism prefers secular holism and religious integration, ultimately seeking an ideal synthesis of science and religion, knowing, of course, that seeking is a perennial process of revision.

We humans are a passionate species, and that's a good thing, until crude fervor transmutes our natural cooperation into uncivilized competition. Deism encourages friendly disagreement as a means to truth. But disagreement escalated into kill-or-be-killed is a moral failure at best, at worst the tragic flaw that will destroy us all. Deism notes that the most evolved science and religion both affirm that egalitarian cooperation benefits, brute competition harms. Deist ethics in a nutshell is: That which benefits. Or put another way in this age of situational ethics: Maximum benefit with minimum harm. Why the easy road to ultra-beneficial concord is so hard for us humans remains the great spiritual query.

It's not the classic mind/body (or mind/matter) dichotomy, today couched as religion vs. science, but rather the aggressive misinterpretation of the dichotomy as *us vs. them* that pits extremist spiritual/material binaries against each other, creating either-or fallacies that lead to invalid and dangerous conclusions. Soulless capitalists exploiting their own grandmothers; tormented religionists flagellating themselves for their sins; suicide, world hunger, unemployment, crime, global warming, lynching, crusades, inquisitions, pogroms, terrorism, wars, nations blowing up nations—multitudes of woes we humans have brought upon ourselves as civilizations and as individuals are deeply rooted in fallacies translated into extremist choices established by this dichotomy. Deism rejects the assumption that exploiting the choice of us vs. them is a natural necessity.

Creation, both noun and verb, embodies the source and sustenance of our existence and of our truth. Truth is *natural.* Nature, holistically apprehended and understood, embodies truth, both scientific and religious.

In contrast, the unnaturally polarized creationist visions, Genesism and neo-Darwinism, represent the crux of spiritual bisection. Each contender claims to be the purveyor of absolute truth. The Genesist insists that creationism is true because the Bible says so and the Bible is God's Word, i.e. God. The neo-Darwinian insists that science continues to prove as incontrovertible fact its version of creationism, Darwin's theory of descent via natural selection—or these days, random variation (mutation) shaped by natural selection. Ironically, each contender plays God by assuming an authority that transcends nature and the Creator of Nature. Just as ironically, Genesism doesn't prove, and Darwinism doesn't disprove, the existence of a Creator. Deism, however, demonstrates that Nature itself reveals the necessary and self-evident Creator.

Though neither fundamentalism nor Darwinism is exactly correct, each view contains some measure of truth. The Bible is easily proven to be a manmade miscellany of mythic, literary, and pseudo-historical material that contains many profound representations of truths along with mistakes, propaganda, and superstitious absurdities assumed by fundamentalist believers to be absolute fact. Although the Genesis story of Creation is mythic, the impulse to understand and explain the origin and meaning of Creation, literally and via poetic representation, is valid and good. At the same time, recent science demonstrates that core Darwinian assumptions regarding bottom-up macroevolution are just plain wrong, although the fundamental concept of microevolution remains unchallenged. New propositions include the *way* change occurs and the degree to which change demonstrates *rational purpose.*

If Darwinian evolution were true, Deism would accommodate it just as easily as it would any other version of intelligently designed creation. Deists accept as valid whatever has been most convincingly substantiated. Our common sense insists that elegantly designed existence necessitates a transcending designer. Because creation is an ongoing process, some Deists, myself included, believe that the designer is immanent as well as transcendent. Having assimilated recent knowledge, our evolved common sense concludes that that designer God can be neither Darwinian nature nor the God of fundamentalism.

Technically for Christian fundamentalism, that's *Gods.* Fundamentalist factions of various religions have their own versions of God or Gods. Christian fundamentalists have one God who is really three Gods, that are really two Gods, since God the Spirit is a manifestation of God the Father, and Jesus is a human sub-God child of God the Father/Spirit. Deists believe that there is one God, or one unified entity, the Designer/Creator and Sustainer of existence as we know it.

The latest theory of intelligent design has already superseded Darwinism and Genesism, and though many scientists and religionists and culture in general are dragging behind like a comet's tail, ever-progressive Deism asserts that intelligent design is a current scientific and religious fact, and that any version of intelligent design, whether prewired or programmed on the fly, necessitates an intelligent designer of Nature who operates well beyond the catechisms of either religion or science. Even Darwinism logically necessitates a rational designer. The Darwinist's quandary is that because he doesn't like that designer personally, he must preserve the ersatz scientific theory that discredits design. Ironically, this parallels exactly the fundamentalist's quandary in preserving biblical literalism to discredit Darwin.

Even progressive Darwinians are as militantly closed-minded in their zeal to impose the anti-intelligent design dogmas of natural selection as other religionists are to impose their own theologies. Religious fundamentalists (Christian, Jewish, Islamic, etc.) worship their manmade texts as God-breathed; biology fundamentalists venerate their manmade text (Darwin) as nature-breathed. Stark nature—as interpreted and defined via their profoundly limited human perception—is their equivalent god. Neo-Darwinians ignore validated facts to uphold their faith in chance/random emergence, as if that would disprove intelligent design, just as religious fundamentalists deny the multitude of contradictions in their sacred texts, as if those texts prove an intelligent Designer.

Though both hard-line Genesist and Darwinist beliefs have been debunked, each side continues to lionize its dogma. Each side claims to uphold the truth while ignoring and even denying the truth. Religion accuses Darwinism of inciting ruthlessness. Darwinism ties the score by stressing how red in tooth and nail competing religions can be.

To some extent, each side defends its extremist view in reaction to the extremist view of the opposing side: Darwinists hate the evil and irrationality perpetrated by religious superstition; the religious hate the total denial of a supreme being, dehumanization, and theology of ultimate meaningless. Neither side will admit that its own view is just as extremist as the other—and just as wrong. Neither side will admit that there is *some* truth, or some *kind* of truth, to the competing position. Neither side will even truly *listen* to the other. Worst of all, when they feel threatened, both sides attack any challenge to their authority. It's tragic that in our modern world, wars are fought, societies destroyed, Earth itself ravaged over colliding ideological fallacies of these two "civilized" worldviews.

Not that every battle is between religion and Darwinism. But intentionally or not, atheistic Darwinism and religious fundamentalism sanctify any worldview of militant extremism that foments eradication of opposing ideologies. Even calling Darwinism secular can be misleading, since Darwinism has become an anti-theistic natural religion, and the vocal apologetics of its more passionate defenders disclaiming a Creator other than nature is at present most certainly a theology condemning the idolatry of scientists not bowing to natural selection.

Most Americans reside uncomfortably in a murky compromise between those two extremist ideologies. Though historical movers and shakers and those who benefit from their upheavals often support extremist principles that privilege their power, many philosophers, poets, and ordinary folk have felt that truth lies deep below the historical, sociopolitical, science-culture "real world" bustle of everyday life. Most people are equally distressed by religious terrorism and the spiritual deicide committed by atheism. Society has tried to average out the insufficient and contradictory answers provided by religion and science to our most primal metaphysical concerns: the origin and purpose of life. That attempt has failed. Ours is an age of spiritual angst.

CULTURAL-SPIRITUAL SCHIZOPHRENIA

Thanks to scientific indoctrination, most people today accept, albeit tentatively, Darwinian survival-of-the-fittest evolution as a fact, kill-or-be-killed as a necessity, look-out-for-number-one as common sense. Sanitized clichés of healthy competition make it easy even for us progressives to ignore that Darwinian convictions endorse the ruthless self-interest impelling most of the gravest evils threatening the survival of the modern world. "Natural selection acts by life and death, by the survival of the fittest, and by the destruction of the less well-fitted individuals," Darwin informed his often scandalized audiences. "Extinction and natural selection go hand in hand." His truth, embraced by atheists and magnates of British Imperialism, forced another *mysterium* upon Christians and a serious quandary upon secular humanists. In the twentieth century, extinction of enemies became an outright global agenda of dictators, of the most vicious forms of communism, socialism, and Nazism, and even of Christian, Muslim, and other religious fundamentalism that today sanctifies terrorism.

From time to time, in spite of, or perhaps because of, our education, common sense defers to misinformation. But the shock of brutality does prompt our reflection. Though natural selection has been taught as fact in science classes for generations and is a fundamental assumption in every other field, most of us deep down don't really *believe* it. Though, of course, we do accept it "intellectually." It makes perfect sense, right, that grandma was an ape, and great-grandpa, a worm?

Certainly academia's tacit obligation is to uphold Darwinism, if only as the most viable antidote to Genesism and to fundamentalist extremism in general. But this is a mistake, both logically and politically. Besides competing with the almost universal conviction that humans are not just animals, endorsement of humanism on the one hand plus survival-of-the-fittest evolution on the other appears contradictory even to freshmen. The political Right exploits the misunderstanding, misleadingly positioning itself as the exclusively *Christian* (Genesist) "Right" pitted against the *atheist* (Darwinist) "wrong," the Left. Leading fundamentalists and Darwinians amplify the confusion by publicizing their polarized ultimatum: You either trust Darwinism or have faith in Genesism. The either-or is as dishonest as it is fallacious. Leaders on both sides know perfectly well that there are other choices, but they allow, even propagate, the two-option-only fallacy.

But though academia, the government, and the media authorize Darwinism, usually at the exclusion of competing theories, including any that posit intelligent design, recent statistics show that the majority of Americans don't fully embrace all the tenets of Darwinian evolution. That doesn't mean they consider the creation myth of Genesis, or any other creation myth, to be literal fact; most people don't. According to recent Gallup polls, no more than thirty percent of Americans interpret the Bible literally. But polls show that at least ninety percent of Americans believe in God or some form of supreme being, and that percentage includes many liberals and agnostics that the Christian Right and Darwinians have both stereotyped as atheist. About half of the population believes that God created humans in their present form; an additional quarter-plus percent think that God guided the process. Only about thirteen percent (not all of whom are atheist) believe that a supreme being had no role in evolution.

That thirteen percent is significant. As much as Darwinians deny it, Darwinism is a religion. One of its fundamental doctrines is that anything supernatural is superstition, and superstition must be cleared away before real science can take place. It's true that superstition must be replaced with truth. Many of us believe that the survival of the planet depends on it. But is *anything* supernatural necessarily *superstition*?

Perhaps more to the point, does the supernatural really fall under the jurisdiction of science? Several atheist scientists believe that it does, and they've explicitly stated that they construct scientific theories specifically for the purpose of disproving the existence of a supreme being. Richard Dawkins, perhaps the most outspoken of the many atheist scientists writing books and lecturing on the evils of theism, has publically avowed that his goal as a scientist is to "kill religion." By frontally attacking God, Dawkins and crew have stepped outside the arena of pure science and beyond the realm of metaphysics into the domain of theology—the very God-centered theology their arguments incessantly rant against allowing into any discourse concerning reality, especially in the field of science. Meanwhile, fundamentalists accuse those scientists of tossing out the kill-God red herring because their attempt to scientifically prove Darwinian evolution has miserably failed.

Darwinists condemn fundamentalists for believing in the special revelation of a "God-breathed" Bible and for worshipping Jesus as a divinity or as Divinity itself. But Darwinian scientists regard Darwinism as an even more special revelation disclosed to their consecrated prophet, Charles Darwin. Darwinism, like Christianity, is a theory named for the human being who synthesized it. Just as many Christians conflate the four divergent gospels into "The Gospel," and often call the entire Bible and even all of Christendom "Christ," or "Jesus," Darwin devotees often refer to evolution, implying *every* version of evolution, as simply "Darwin."

Darwinians criticize fundamentalists for worshipping as Christ a person who cannot be proven to have existed, and for selectively choosing only Bible verses and stories they like while utterly ignoring all the rest because it contradicts their wishful beliefs. Yet even lauded disciples of Darwin betray surprisingly little acquaintance with, or remembrance of, or concern about, the biographical and autobiographical details of their prophet's life. And their reverence for his great gospel, *The Origin of Species*, doesn't prevent them from extracting only skewed minutia to support the theory of bottom-up, simple-to-complex macroevolution that even Darwin himself doubted.

The actual human being that synthesized the religious theory—Christ or Darwin—no longer exists; his dust has evolved into a motif, and his life into a myth. The theory lives on in all its mutant incarnations pretending to be a unified whole asserting itself as a religion. (Darwinians might prefer "philosophy.")

Each generation thinks it has reached the pinnacle of knowledge. It has moved past the myths and mistakes of the past and has at last arrived at the ultimate truth. Some people today see the ancients as ignorant, superstitious primitives whose brains were less evolved than our own. (The Neanderthal brain was even bigger than ours, but of course Neanderthals don't count, being extinct, and not an ancestor of us superior *Homo sapiens.*)

The reality is that humans today have the same brains as our cave-cozy ancestors and can be just as ignorant and superstitious as ever. The main difference is that advances in technology allow us to spread ignorant, superstitious assertions at viral speed.

Darwinists want you to agree that they have saved the world from blind faith in the supernatural by the grace of bald-eyed Darwinian confidence in scientifically proven mechanistic determinism. Old equals ignorant equals supernatural; new equals enlightened equals evolution.

DEISM RISING

People want truth. People embrace truth when it's presented to them directly, in clarifying, detailed terms. But when the trusted authorities of faith lie, believers defend the lie they have been indoctrinated to believe is truth. Even so, truth always finds a way to seep through any subterfuge, as it did here in America, for instance, with the rise of Deist democracy, right around 1776.

By the mid-eighteenth century, the Enlightenment had enlightened the multitudes. Church crusades no longer directed attacks toward infidels of other religions, like Jews and Muslims, but toward the multitude of backsliders. New inquisitions were mounted, not against witches and other heretics, but against humanist intellectuals, especially those most dangerous heretics, those treacherous truth-tellers, Deists.

The so-called quest for the historical Jesus (the topic of Chapter 3), groping for any beam to prop up the crumbling basilica, gleaned not one shred of proof that such a man-god or man Jesus had existed, and a heap of evidence that he had not. When Darwin's ape stepped on stage in 1859, properly dressed in tails and top-hat, the excommunicated seized his hairy hand and announced that here was the new Messiah. Just off stage right, fundamentalism was born.

Darwinism spawned the fundamentalist backlash, which spawned yet another backlash, neo-Darwinism, a truly fundamentalist sect of science. Both breeds of fundamentalism murder truth for the sake of their absolutist cause, and at their worst, their deceptions sanctify war and other atrocities. Evil is one short step down from ignorance.

The Good News of Deism today is that science is right now proving as true what many people have intuited since the birth of humanity: The exquisitely intelligent universe was and is still being perfectly designed by an intelligent designer. The Creator, the God of existence, is none other than the natural God affirmed by Deism. Just like our ancestors, we seek for the meaning, purpose, and origin of our life. Just like them, we make guesses based on the latest available information. Their guesses were no more primitive than our own; ours are just informed by new information made available via the latest technology. In Darwin's time, or in the era of our Founders, or even two or five thousand years ago, our ancestors would have been no more open or resistant to verified truth than we are today.

From the Deist's perspective, truth is not indoctrination by either science or religion; truth is eloquently expressed through Nature, the true, rational Word of God, offered democratically to everyone. As I will show, there's plenty of evidence from science and religion that hope and joy and meaning and purpose are profoundly illuminating realities embedded in the material structure of existence. God is astounding, and so is the natural realm so conspicuously created for a reason. Common sense guides us to self-evident truths taught by Nature, truths that constitute the essence of Deism, the religious philosophy of choice of many of our democracy's most seminal Founders, like Thomas Jefferson, John Adams, George Washington, Benjamin Franklin, and Thomas Paine, to name but a few.

Deists believe that the Creator reveals truth, including spiritual truth, to *everyone* through our space-time existence, or Nature, via innate, God-given faculties, not just to a chosen elite via special revelation. Contrary to the fundamentalist and Darwinist claim, naturalism is not atheism. Nor is Deism the religion of an absent-father God who wound up the universe and left it to run on its own like a ticking clock. Some Deists believe that, but certainly not all, or even most, and certainly not the originators of Deism. Most Deists accept William Paley's famous watch analogy to intelligent design, dating back to the eighteenth century—if you stumbled upon a watch out on a heath, you'd know it was designed by an intelligent person; likewise, Nature is clearly designed by an intelligent Mind. Paley's analogy follows Robert Boyle's comparison of the universe to the Great Clock of Strasbourg, a century earlier. Even the pre-Socratic Greeks understood that Nature is structured. But many Deists, today as in the past, reject the false correlation of an intelligent First Cause to a *checked-out* watchmaker/clockmaker God. Exquisitely designed Creation necessitates a transcending Intelligent Designer that is immanently engaged in the perpetual process of creating novelty sustained within the secure margins of natural laws. Even granting chance, free will, and cause-effect, because Creation of novelty is an ongoing process, God is necessarily immanent as well as transcendent, and immanent means *present.*

Most people don't mind that scientists are human beings with religious or philosophical interest in the source and purpose of our existence. From earliest antiquity, people included spiritual considerations in their investigations of the natural realm. With the advent of the scientific revolution, the subject of scientific study narrowed to the specifically material realm, but at the same time, almost all great scientists in Europe, America, and the Middle East prior to the nineteenth century were theists: they believed in a transcendent God. Many European scientists were ostensible Christians with deistic leanings in an era when it was dangerous to contradict the Church.

Although today mixing the fields of science and religion is generally censured by both scientists and religionists, traditionally both domains fell under the authority of the Church, and nonconformist views from either domain were typically condemned only by religious oligarchs. Most scientists were religious and saw no contradiction between religion and science. Copernicus, for instance, sought to uncover "the mechanism of the universe, wrought for us by a supremely good and orderly Creator." But one consequence of this honest inquiry was that for centuries many scientists who agreed with Copernican cosmology were branded heretics by the Inquisition.

All scientists seek to discern the mechanisms of existence; not all scientists today agree that those mechanisms were wrought by a Creator. And very few scientists in the nineteenth century of Darwin and even fewer today consider the biblical creation myth to be literal fact. In the late nineteenth century, fundamentalism came into being to fight skepticism toward religion, especially toward biblical literalism, but in doing so it alienated large numbers of theists, including not-fundamentalist Christians. In the twentieth and twenty-first centuries, fundamentalists still falsely accuse Deists and agnostics of atheism. Ironically, the kill-religion assumption of anti-design Darwinian evolutionists is exactly the stamp-out stance taken by radical fundamentalists of any religion toward competing religions and non-religious critics, even those that believe in God.

The elegantly simple truth Copernicus deciphered within his domain of the material realm revolutionized our thinking about our place in the universe, and like many great scientific discoveries, the Copernican insight informed our spiritual understanding as well. Materialists ever since have concluded that because Earth is not in any way the center of the universe, humanity is insignificant, life has no ultimate meaning, existence is utterly devoid of inherent purpose.

Copernicus didn't take that radical leap of non-faith. He merely highlighted the obvious immensity of God's discernible Creation, a matter-of-fact gesture that humbled man and elevated God. But the cosmic decentering caused by the impact of his calculations knocked the Church into orbit along with the planet. Threatened by this challenge to its central position as divine authority, organized religion burrowed deeper into denial, buttressing its myths of elected superiority with persuasive arguments like inquisitions, crusades, pogroms, and, perhaps even worse than torture and death, excommunications, those precious tickets to eternal hell. These tactics were only ostensibly religious; their chief purpose was to bolster Church authority by controlling wealth, and more importantly knowledge, especially stubbornly candid science, which "transcended" religious dogma and monopolized new wealth-generating technologies.

Today the Church agenda is executed by fundamentalists trying to hijack the science of intelligent design to support biblical literalism, or at least to shore up the superior validity of their religion. The strategies used by fundamentalists to force-fit science into proofs for biblical fact-claims—most significantly misrepresentation of facts (lying) and intellectual/moral coercion—are quite similar to force-fit tactics used by the Church of the Inquisition, which ironically are quite similar to force-fit tactics used by kill-religion atheists today to disprove a transcending Designer. (Today, of course, we don't usually bodily kill our fellow citizens who disagree with us, just their souls, though citizens of enemy nations are still fair game.)

It's perversely ironic that until the modern era of materialist determinism, religion squelched spiritual knowledge far more aggressively than science did. Copernicus and his theist-deist progeny such as Galileo, Kepler, and Newton exemplified the most fundamental spiritual principle of human existence: Truth must be embraced; or put negatively: Truth must not be shunned. Armed with his telescopes and a pen, Galileo fought with and ridiculed the pope even while under house arrest for heresy;

Kepler, a sometime Christian astrologer, hid his un-Aristotelian elliptical orbits in obscure Latin treatises circulated quietly; Newton spent far less time on science than he expended interpreting alchemical and biblical texts that to him were clearly not literal fact, and those forbidden metaphysical manuscripts, the bulk of his life's work hidden out of fear, were only discovered after his death.

The annals of history are replete with the names of leaders and groups who boldly risked everything, including their lives, to assert the rights of their truth. But more often than not, fear prevented the heretic from making his views public.

Newton is a classic example. Best known for his advances in physics and mathematics that centuries later are still revolutionizing civilization's quality of life, the name Isaac Newton often conjures the portrait of a cold rationalist responsible for our mechanistic determinism. Most people are unaware that Newton's work in physics and mathematics simply built on discoveries he made very early in his life, in 1665-1666, or that he also secretly wrote over 100,000 pages of heretical ideas on alchemy, astrology, and the occult, unorthodox commentaries on Revelations and the prophecies of Daniel, and essays that debunked the traditional doctrine of the Trinity, just for starters—only recently have we gained access to the sealed trunk of voluminous papers he left behind at his death.

John Maynard Keynes, a British intellectual with early access to those papers, made this amendatory observation:

> In the eighteenth century and since, Newton came to be thought of as the first and greatest of the modern age of scientists, a rationalist, one who taught us to think on the lines of cold and untinctured reason. I do not see him in this light. I do not think that anyone who has poured over the contents of that box which he packed up when he finally left Cambridge in 1696 and which, though partly dispersed, have come down to us, can see him like that. Newton was not the first of the age of reason. He was the last of the magicians, the last of the Babylonians and Sumerians, the last great mind which looked out on the visible and intellectual world with the same eyes as those who began to build our intellectual inheritance rather less than 10,000 years ago. Isaac Newton, a posthumous child born with no father on Christmas Day, 1642, was the last wonder-

child to whom the Magi could do sincere and appropriate homage.

Newton sealed that trunk to protect his good name both as a scientist and a Christian, and he certainly had just cause to fear revealing his mysticism. Not only did the scientific method itself challenge church authority, Newton's radical conclusions also contradicted accepted interpretations of biblical truth and therefore threatened clerical power. In 1553 another important contributor to science, Spanish physician Miguel Serveto, author of *On the Error of the Trinity*, was burned at the stake for repudiating the tripartite personality of God, one of his more radical views shared by Newton. Better to seal up those pages in a trunk than have them stoke a bonfire.

But Newton was a man in love with Creation, and that love, fueled by a kind of inner integrity that strove for truth, drove his genius. He once said about himself: "I do not know what I may appear to the world; but to myself I seem to have been only like a child playing on the seashore, and diverting myself in now and then finding a smoother pebble or a lovelier shell than ordinary, while the great ocean of truth lay all undiscovered before me." As Newton's great admirer, Einstein, understood, "The most beautiful thing we can experience is the mysterious. It is the source of all true art and science." Einstein felt a profound affinity with his fellow rebel against the status quo, especially with Newton's appreciation of the intricate, aesthetic order of Creation.

Rational observation and experimentation within the material realm—the scientific method—is the tradition of science as a field of study. Atheist scientists today don't just explore the material realm; they claim that the material realm is all there is: The mechanisms of the universe weren't created by a transcending Creator; they either "just are" as a result of random chance and mechanistic determinism, or they are self-created, meaning the mechanistic/deterministic universe itself is God. Many of these scientists today believe that nothing is beyond their ken. That's right: Elite members of a species spawned by a crap shoot of blind chance driven by the rational irrational god natural selection are able to grasp the myriad nuances of all existence—some would go so far as to say control and even retroactively create existence (more on that in Chapter 7). At the very least they are very close to constructing a unified theory of everything, even reconciling Einstein's theory of relativity with quantum physics, which at the moment remain incompatible. They are very close to creating life and building artificial intelligence. They are on the brink of grasping the fundamental essence that unifies all existence.

Hard to believe, isn't it, that a tiny, albeit complicated speck of dust can vanquish the complex immensity of existence. Their boast is *meta physical*: metaphysical. They perpetuate the ancient tradition of creating gods in their own image and think their knighted evolution is a uniquely enlightened concept. Yet the walking shadow they worship as their god, by their own admission ultimately signifies nothing: That's the heart and soul of atheism.

INTELLIGENT DESIGN AND THE GOLDEN MEAN OF DEISM

Whether the challenge of Darwinism intensifies or fades, conservative believers must still grapple with mounting proofs that the Bible, like Darwin (as I'll show in Chapters 4 and 5), is a defective authority. Believers realize that it is untruthful to deny that its pages are packed with incongruities, with false and contradictory histories, with obvious myths and superstitions lifted from far more ancient religions. Scholars know— though many downplay or conveniently "forget"—that the books collected in what we now call the Bible were understood at the time they were written and compiled to be largely conjectural and evolving, most being based on fluid oral transmissions that were later written down by various individuals, and then rewritten, edited, and compiled by many more people who had heard different versions or had different understandings and agendas. Even early Christians understood that it had taken the various Jesus religions a very long time to consolidate into a relatively stable religion, eventually christened Christianity, which by that point had become the property of an elite controlling body, the Church. Even within the Church itself, battles over faith definition and ownership raged for centuries, among the bloodiest clashes being the Inquisition and the Reformation, each of which took the lives (and according to the Church, the souls) of millions.

For the last century, fundamentalism has thrived because academic theologians and freelance evangelicals, threatened by the intellectual honesty that culminated during the Enlightenment, have herded believers into a retro Dark Ages. Rather than reveal the facts to believers, scholars and their schooled priests and preachers have chosen to perpetuate a Noble

Lie of blind faith, a practice still enshrined today. Operative word: Lie.

As the absurd, dishonest battle between Darwinians and fundamentalists rages on, Deists, myself included, must once again challenge the Ignoble Lie of the status quo with straightforward, commonsense explanations supporting the *fact* of intelligent design—a hip concept that's older than Darwin's grandmother.

In reality, smart theists have critiqued religious superstition for millennia. The challenge has always been to persuade believers to step back and recognize their irrational belief in primitive magic. Do religionists still, in the twenty-first century in America, really believe that a talking snake seduced a woman into eating a piece of fruit that caused all subsequent newborns to be guilty as hell of sin? Do they really believe that an antediluvian man built a boat that could hold two of literally all animals, including snakes, elephants, polar bears, kangaroos, whales, eels, mosquitoes, and germs (there are a quarter million species of beetles alone, and who knows how many species of microorganisms, which leads to questions of collection process, not to mention food gathering, storage, and distribution, and then there's the nasty job of poop scooping)? Do they really believe that a stick turned into a snake, or that a man lived forty days in the belly of a whale deep under the sea? Do they really believe that their God impregnated a virgin with his son, and do they really believe that that impregnation process is qualitatively different from, say, Zeus raping Leda, or from men "possessing" women as chattel? Do they really believe that their man-god had to cast demons into swine because he couldn't or wouldn't just destroy them? Do they really believe that a man ascended into heaven in a flaming chariot, that a woman was turned into a pillar of salt, that a voice out of heaven spoke through a bush that burned without burning up or out? Do they really believe those ten black-magic plagues of Egypt more brutal than Inquisition torture devices where inflicted upon innocent people whose king was trying to repent but couldn't because God wouldn't let him? Do they really believe that manna rained down daily in the desert, that Balaam's donkey spoke, that a dead man's bones revived the dead, that the sun stood still one day, and moved backward another? Do they really believe that a very dead rabbi came back alive, which insiders claimed was a hoax? Or that Satan tricked God into tormenting Job. Or that God demanded rape, murder, plunder, slavery, bigotry, hate, or lies?

Do Christians really believe that their superstitious beliefs are literally or even symbolically *real* but the superstitious beliefs of other religions are—well, superstitions?

Many scientists acknowledge that something that *appears* to be miraculous could have happened naturally. We Deists agree that we must seek the facts and evaluate all the evidence. Las Vegas swarms with masters of "believable" magic tricks. And today's health craze has made everyone aware that thought, emotion, visualization, breathing, herbs, nutrition, and other natural techniques can cure—really help the body itself cure—illness and disease. Someone not privy to the tricks and trade secrets might judge them to be supernatural.

We know that the Bible is not a reliable source of facts; we know that it is steeped in magical stories that derive from or resemble stories of other ancient religions; we know that people are gullible; we know that religious dogma can short-circuit reason, whether the believer accepts its magical elements willingly or has been brainwashed. Common sense and education concur that there never could have been a talking snake or a stick that turned into a snake. Even children raised on Harry Potter don't buy that shtick for very long.

But do Darwinians really expect fundamentalists to give up their faith in biblical magical realism for an esoteric claim that their grandpa was an ape that randomly mutated from a bacterium by the grace of the mindless god "selection"?

Most of us look at apes...look at humans...shake our heads. Even on a purely organic level we humans are clearly a discrete category. Darwinians make much ado about the "identical" DNA we share with chimps, while ignoring that every life form is composed of the same DNA, and brushing aside the tried-and-true typological view of nature first illustrated by Aristotle and still used today with only minor tweaks. Thanks to microbiology it's even more obvious today that living beings can be grouped together according to major defining categories of shared biological characteristics that correspond with morphological classifications. Each discrete group is what it is. Clearly there are characteristics that define a group—species, genus, family, order, class, phylum, kingdom, domain, life—and that make that group not any other group. It's no surprise to fundamentalists that paleontologists have never located transitional missing links between major types that would substantiate Darwin's theory of macroevolution.

Today most Christians have settled upon some form of "God created evolution," though Darwinians on the one side and strict fundamentalists on the other still decry any such compromise. Darwinism continues to dominate academia and the government, but during the last decade or so, as paleontologists systematically disconfirmed Darwinian macroevolution, shrewd fundamentalists have stepped in to appropriate the new secular science of intelligent design to support biblical creationism.

The truth is that intelligent design supports neither Darwinian evolution nor biblical creationism. Darwinism is obsolete, though it's taking awhile for some textbooks to catch up. Genesism is a bit harder to demystify, if only because religion privileges faith, even blind faith, over fact.

But reality doesn't just vanish. As fundamentalist leaders shroud the truth in smokescreens, academics and ordinary truth-seekers continue exposing the facts. This might sound very progressive, very contemporary, but this exposé was going on long before your great-grandparents started courting. Fundamentalism, a late conservative development, which originated during the mid- to late-nineteenth century as a reaction to Darwinism and to the far more dangerous deconstruction of the Bible and the historical Jesus, has lately found itself in the uncomfortable position of needing to evolve.

To divert attention away from the devastating dismantling of biblical infallibility and Christian authority, prominent fundamentalists toss out their latest red herring, intelligent design, outrageously naming one of their own, Phillip E. Johnson, the "father of ID." Johnson—a lawyer, not a scientist—might have used the phrase "intelligent design" in his 1991 book *Darwin on Trial*, but he derived his concept and research from scientists already writing on the subject, like agnostic microbiologist and medical researcher Michael Denton, author of the groundbreaking book *Evolution: A Theory in Crisis,* published in 1985, well before Johnson's book. Conferring titles like "father of ID" smacks of elitist self-promotion, if not outright deception. As most educated people know, including Johnson and his cronies, intelligent design itself has a rich philosophical and scientific history reaching back well over two millennia, and just stirring in the latest scientific data confirming the ancient theory doesn't change that fact that the theory is ancient. Nor does dousing fundamentalism with a little science scientifically validate fundamentalism.

Certainly the grandparents of intelligent design were our ancient ancestors, who realized that our amazing life in our amazing cosmos had to have been created by a transcending, supra-natural Creator—god, gods, goddesses, immanent spirits: Whatever the representation, the understanding was that some higher power was clearly in control of designing, generating, and sustaining existence. The real progenitors of intelligent design, at least in the West, were the Greek philosophers. Being the first critics of religious myths and the first teleological naturalists, those ancient questers were the sires of deism. Deism is a more legitimate heir to intelligent design than is fundamentalism. My vote for father of ID would not be a person, but rather a synthesis of the meta-physical naturalism of Plato and Aristotle, whose rational philosophies explicated nature far better than the often mocked pre-Socratic Greek materialists, sires of Darwinism, and pre-pre-Socratic mythology, sire of fundamentalism. In essence, Deist religion is an updated synthesis of Platonic and Aristotelian metaphysics with an added dose of contemporary ethics.

Deism has always been theism with a conscience. Truth and love—*philos*, brotherly love—are two fundamental pillars of Deism; deception and hate, in all their permutations, are anathema to a Deist. Surely it would change the way civilization functions if most of us believed that compassion and creativity, truth and justice, liberty and the pursuit of happiness really were inherent truths within the grasp of us all.

Aristotle observed that between two extremist positions there is usually a better position, which he called the Golden Mean. Not a watered-down gray between black and white, the Golden Mean transcends the extremes and is a positive between two negatives. Courage, for example, is a Golden Mean between the polar extremes of cowardice and rashness. Intelligent design is a Golden Mean between Genesism and Darwinism. Deism is a Golden Mean between fundamentalism and atheism.

Deist religion respects differing perspectives sustained by common sense. But even in the name of open-mindedness, the Deist version of intelligent design cannot support Genesism, which contradicts common sense. The entire Bible, not just the Old Testament account of Creation, has been so thoroughly deconstructed that to continue lifting it up as God's Word in this day and age displays not so much profound ignorance as much as unconscionable dishonesty.

Nor does Deism align with Darwinian or neo-Darwinian definitions of evolution. As a matter of conscience, New Deism embraces scientifically evidenced intelligent design and rejects disproven Darwinian macroevolution. Darwin's theory of evolution begins with similarities between, say, humans and apes, and attempts to establish a smooth transition between their separate distinguishing features. We now know that no smooth transition exists. While the similarities between humans and apes might prove *something*, they don't prove Darwinian evolution.

In contrast to Darwinism, Deism stresses similarities within specific categories of distinctive difference. Humans and apes are currently classified as primates; humans are *very much* not apes. How we are like apes is certainly an important point in any consideration of what it means to be a living being on Planet Earth. But whether we evolved from apes or not, being a human is categorically different from being an ape, and the distance between us—and I don't mean brain size—is astronomical. If we are not evolved from apes, we might have more in common with our Cro-Magnon ancestors than we suspect.

Deism critiques the random chance natural selection of neo-Darwinian-materialist atheism, and endorses the version of life coming-to-be confirmed by very recent scientific discoveries in biology and mathematics, specifically genetic information systems and probability. Should a mechanism proving some version of macroevolution be discovered, we Deists will gladly accept it as an aspect of an intelligently designed Creation. Deism understands that any valid version of coming-into-being, including Darwinian evolution, would be rational creation that requires a transcending designer.

FROM EVOLUTION CONFUSION TO INTELLIGENT DESIGN

Since the time of the pre-Socratic Greeks, science, or natural philosophy, has always been far less engaged in proving theories than in falsifying them. It's not just the perpetual waterfall of new information that forces scientists to constantly adapt and adjust even those theories marketed as facts. All of us who rely upon pronouncements of science must be vigilant in also considering a scientist's motives, which even these days tend to be philosophical more than academic or monetary. The stated objective of science is to ascertain facts. In reality, though, the goal of many scientists is to metaphysically *interpret* ascertained facts.

Comparing contradictory conclusions by two scientists explaining the exact same fact illustrates the subjectivity of ostensibly objective science. For instance, in an essay titled "Dawkins, God, and the Scientific Enterprise: Reflections on the Appeal to Darwinism in Fundamentalist Atheism," theology professor and writer Alister McGrath compares two empirically equivalent statements describing the MO of genes interpreted via radically conflicting *a priori* ontological and teleological assumptions. The first statement is from Richard Dawkins' *The Selfish Gene*, the second from *The Music of Life* by noted physiologist and systems biologist Denis Noble. The book titles themselves already blare interpretative difference. First Dawkins: "[Genes] swarm in huge colonies, safe inside gigantic lumbering robots, sealed off from the outside world, communicating with it by tortuous indirect routes, manipulating it by remote control. They are in you and me; they created us, body and mind; and their preservation is the ultimate rationale for our existence." Now Noble: "[Genes] are trapped in huge colonies, locked inside highly intelligent beings, moulded by the outside world, communicating with it by complex processes, through which, blindly, as if by magic, function emerges. They are in you and me; we are the system that allows their code to be read; and their preservation is totally dependent on the joy that we experience in reproducing ourselves. We are the ultimate rationale for their existence." That's two theologies.

In spite of its reputation for minute precision and objective facts, at times science confuses more than it clarifies. It isn't the seemingly complex semantics of DNA as much as the skewed semantics of basic scientific jargon that causes probably the biggest source of evolution confusion among laypersons. Even scientists have to deal with the "species problem," as they call their inability to define a species: There are over two dozen distinct definitions of the word species used among biologists, because no one definition applies to all organisms or contexts.

If a couple dozen contradicting definitions of this important scientific term weren't enough to muddy our understanding of a species and its origin, just add common dictionary meanings, like class, type, kind, sort, genus, variety, group, order, and so on. Many people think of humans and apes as separate species. Cats and dogs are species, as are bats and butterflies. But in a scientific context, cats, dogs, butterflies, and bats, aren't all technically species. There are 14,000 (some experts say 28,000, others 100,000) species of butterflies belonging to the order Lepidoptera, but most of us, who know a butterfly when we see one but probably can't identify or name many species, and even some scientists who can, call the butterfly group a species. Darwin himself used the word species in different and sometimes conflicting ways, and in the *Origin of Species* laments that "No one definition has satisfied all naturalists; yet every naturalist knows vaguely what he means when he speaks of species. Generally the term includes the unknown element of a distinct act of creation. The term 'variety' is almost equally difficult to define." He adds, "I look at the term species as one arbitrarily given, for the sake of convenience, to a set of individuals closely resembling each other...it does not essentially differ from the term variety, which is given to less distinct and more fluctuating forms. The term variety, again, in comparison and with mere individual differences, is also applied arbitrarily, for convenience sake."

When most of us talk about the human species, what we really mean is *Homo* (genus) *sapiens* (species). The international nomenclature system always assigns a new species a two-part name of genus + species. This all sounds very cut-and-dry, but even at the level of genus, categorization is not an exact science, only a convenient way to group together into taxa life-forms sharing a few similar, mostly external physical characteristics. And which characteristics define the genus and its species, like interbreed ability and hypothetical ancestry of species within a genus, are matters of contention. We Deists might ask biologists why *physical* aspects are privileged in the first place.

Microbiology, with its subatomic examination of organisms, further complicates species identification. Some scientists now use terms like phylum, form, group, class, or type to designate discrete, self-contained morphological entities—really discrete containers with well-defined borders, which often contain other smaller self-contained containers. Think nested Russian dolls or Chinese boxes.

Species definition is especially frustrating for Darwinians, who approach species changes as links in their theoretical evolutionary chain from first organism to all subsequent organisms. For them, a species serves as proof of evolution. Whatever *that* means; evolution is just as hard to define as species. Nobody contests the obvious reality of change within a species group—say, a butterfly type developing orange or yellow wings; and after a series of such changes, which scientists call "trivial," the butterfly type can justifiably be given a separate species name, which could change with addition of new data. But those adaptations or any other kinds of trivial changes occur because the potential for such change is already programmed in the butterfly type's DNA. A butterfly can become a different version of butterfly. A butterfly might laterally microevolve, but a butterfly doesn't macroevolve into a bat or a bird or any other not-butterfly. The butterfly container contains many varieties of butterfly but no varieties of bat or bird. The butterfly container doesn't transmute, suddenly or slowly, into a bat or bird container.

Anatomists and other ordinary observant people realized early on, and certainly knew in Darwin's day, that even considering unique characteristics of species within a group, there was, as Michael Denton puts it, "an underlying unity in design of each group of organisms," and furthermore that "the distribution of these characteristics conformed to a highly ordered pattern which permitted the species to be classified into a hierarchy of increasingly inclusive classes": Containers within containers. Darwin's microevolution simply restates speciation within a class (or type, or group, or container, call it what you will), which even the Greeks understood. Microbiology has proven, and each new finding further proves, that Darwin's extrapolation of macroevolution from microevolution is a fallacy.

It's still the case that species can evolve into new species within a species class. Selective breeding can generate new varieties so different from each other that they are classified as new species. But even aggressive genetic modification and cloning only prove what scientists already knew, that there are limits to breeding possibilities. There is always a threshold beyond which a species type can't be altered. We understand maximum capacity and thresholds intuitively and through experience: This jar can hold only so much water; that runner can run only so fast. A species type can only evolve in so many ways. In this age of microbiology, the old Greek discrete-container typology turns out to be an accurate template.

A class, or type, is a complex whole. You can't just tweak one part of a regular watch and get a digital watch—a new type of watch; you'd need to make other simultaneous changes so that all the components still function together in a coherent and integrated manner. This is even more the case for an organism, even a teeny tiny minor one, which is not only far more complex than a watch, its complexity is alive.

Because organisms are complex, it took awhile for the old anatomists to sort the various species into their respective containers. One problem was that there are very different kinds of resemblances. According to the so-called "analogous" resemblance, species in different containers share similar structures, like the whale flipper and the fish fin, or the forelimbs of a mole and a mole cricket. The "homologous" resemblance shows that species in different containers have essentially the same organ or structure that serves very different functions, like the forelimbs of terrestrial vertebrates. One might ask the Darwinian how a very few, totally unrelated species—humans, certain snails, the octopus, a group of jellyfish called the box jellies—developed the same kind of very complex eye—the "camera eye," as opposed to, say, the compound eye found in insects—via very different evolutionary routes in order to accomplish the exact same function, to see, but to see in very different ways in very different environments requiring very different adaptations. How and why could a pair of human camera eyes be constructed like the camera eyes on the tentacles of primitive animals that don't even really have a brain, just a nervous system? Although Darwinians point to this odd occurrence as proof of "punctuated equilibrium" macroevolution, in fact it simply highlights that there are discrete containers containing life-forms that have been designed intelligently according to similar sophisticated blueprints.

Until molecular biology began comparing organisms biochemically, there was no mathematical way to measure the morphological complexity of life-forms or the difference between, say, cat and dog compared to cat and mouse. During the 1960s, as scientists began cataloguing protein sequences, it became clear that molecules wouldn't provide evidence of sequential arrangements in nature, as required by Darwin, but rather further reaffirmed "a highly ordered hierarchic scheme from which all direct evidence for evolution is emphatically absent." And what a scheme! Denton notes, "The division turned out to be more mathematically perfect than even the most diehard typologists could have predicted."

Once molecular biologists had created the "percent sequence difference matrix" to classify species into groups, it became clear just how precisely molecular and morphological groups correspond. Even each identifiable subclass of sequences is isolated and distinct, and transitional or intermediate classes are completely absent.

"The almost mathematical perfection of the isolation of the fundamental classes at a molecular level is astonishing!" Denton exclaims. "There is not a trace at a molecular level of the traditional evolutionary series: cyclostome to fish to amphibian to reptile to mammal. Incredibly, man is as close to lamprey as are fish!"

The mathematical exactness in the degree of isolation means that the amphibia are not intermediate between fish and other terrestrial vertebrates; in fact, their molecular makeup is as far from fish as from any group of reptiles or mammals. "To those well acquainted with the traditional picture of vertebrate evolution," Denton muses, "the result is truly astonishing."

Although human and chimp sequences differ on average at only one base in a hundred, and every gene identified in the human genome has its counterpart in the chimpanzee genome, the *percent sequence difference matrix* comparing protein, DNA, and RNA sequences of primates shows that the classes of monkeys, apes, and humans are entirely non-overlapping. Besides, genes take up only about five to ten percent of our DNA. Many latent genes are just waiting to perform functions accommodating some future need—or in humans, desire. Latent potential might have something—but not everything—to do with the enormous difference between human and chimp.

It's not unusual that morphologically different organisms are very closely related at the building block level of DNA. We're all constructed according to "a basically identical genetic architecture," as paleobiologist Simon Conway Morris puts it. A multitude of very different structures have been constructed using the exact same building materials. The difference between a human and a chimp is greater than the difference between a picture created by Michelangelo and one painted by a five year old in the same room using the same canvas, brushes, and paints.

Recently, some scientists have proposed a top-down version of evolution, which starts with the blueprints of major phyla that came into existence all at once during the Cambrian explosion. The blueprints include features allowing for adaptation, like longer beaks developed by birds in order to lunch on larger seeds. Intra-type microevolution happens all the time. There are 14,000 species of butterflies (again, some reference books say 28,000, some 100,000 species) belonging to four families, which along with moths (150,000 species) and skippers (3,000 species) make up the order Lepidoptera. But inter-type Darwinian evolution doesn't happen. Butterflies don't become bats or birds.

Since molecular intermediates that cross over between classes are as absent as fossil missing links, scientists now refer to organism relationships as "sisterly" (I prefer "lateral"); no organism is "ancestral" or more "primitive" or "advanced" than its relatives. The extraordinary orderliness of the discrete divisions made up of the exact same molecular building blocks—some scientists liken a gene to a Lego—is persuasive evidence of intelligent design.

All of this, of course, has spiritual implications. Here are a few slivers of the *natural* miracle sanctioned by Deism: Matter exists (a mindboggling fact, if you really think about it); every *thing* exists, embodies the same existence, and is composed of the same space-time matter, therefore we are one; but each thing is a discrete entity unlike each other entity, therefore each of us is unique; collectively all of us unique beings are many and one. *Life*—now that's a miracle. Life exists; every organism exists, embodies the same life, and is composed of the same life matter, therefore we are one; but each organism is a discrete entity unlike each other entity, therefore each of us is unique; collectively all of us unique living beings are many and one.

The case against Darwin becomes more and more convincing the closer scientists peer through their ever-thickening lenses. Darwin assumed that the smaller the building block, the less complex, in descending order down to the primal building block, the cell. Looking through his nineteenth-century microscope, the cell looked like a simple little blob of Jello that didn't do a whole lot. Today we can see that cells are structurally enormously complex and perform elegantly elaborate functions; even at the tiny atomic level, primeval doesn't mean simple.

As if to dazzle us with artistic cunning, the Builder has assembled wildly diverse organisms using the same DNA molecule. The genetic information in every life-form is coded in a universal language of four letters, A, G, C, T (adenine guanine, cytosine, and thymine), the four chemical compounds that comprise the DNA double helix. As a substance, DNA doesn't vary among species; only the order of its letters changes. The individual letters are meaningless in themselves, but they combine into meaningful words, sentences, paragraphs, books—whole libraries of discrete organisms. Typed out on a page, the code of our particular DNA would look similar to computer code written by programmers. By definition, *code*, which translates into a *message*, is never random. The code of DNA is vastly more elaborate than computer code, not to mention, it's alive.

And if it's truly code, what is its message? Code isn't code unless it *means* something. Code is language. Language conveys meaning. What is the message, the meaning of life, of *your* life? The answer demands teamwork; deciphering the code requires a synthesis of science and religion, which is the task of Deism, which assumes that God is a Natural God articulating truth intelligently through Nature: That's naturalism; that's Deism.

The neo-Darwinian's Little Bang theory starts with a simple little genome that randomly slithers up the slippery slope to the first mutant human being—whose genetic information is written as three billion letters along a single DNA filament! In some places, the filament winds around itself, forming twenty-three more segments, the chromosomes. Since we each inherit a complete set of chromosomes from each of our parents, we each have twenty-three pairs of chromosomes. Our genetic story is written in six billion pairs, or twelve billion letters (that we thus far know of). And the plot thickens: Where did the idea of reproduction come from; why two of a kind to tango? Where did number *two* come from (or the *number* two, or numbers)?

Two separate languages—DNA constructed from a four letter alphabet, and proteins from a twenty letter alphabet (the twenty amino acids)—communicate via one translation mechanism to form the paragraphs of our bodies, our cells. Does that sound randomly not-really-designed to you?

All those living building blocks perform amazingly sophisticated, perfectly choreographed predetermined tasks with atomic precision at astronomical speeds. Add to consistent form a cell's structural efficiency, and you've got a good case for intelligent design.

As deterministic as all this wonder seems to the Darwinian materialist, the predetermined, always pragmatic purposes of DNA and proteins can't explain the wildly innovative creations of the human spirit yearning to transcend itself. All Nature down to our subatomic core provides us unique humans with the most fantastic form through which we can express the rich poetic essence of ourselves.

Darwin must be rolling over in his grave. The recent discovery that even the organism's molecular building blocks themselves are not only complex, they're also self-contained is but the latest catch-22 for random

Darwinian materialist determinism. Michael Katz coined the term "irreducible complexity" for this atomic dilemma: "Contemporary organisms are quite complex, they have a special and an intricate organization that would not occur spontaneously by chance. The 'universal laws' governing the assembly of biological materials are insufficient to explain our companion organisms: one cannot stir together the appropriate raw materials and self-assemble a mouse."

Or even a mousetrap, a simple illustration often used by geneticist Michael Behe, though his more compelling examples include five cellular systems (which I discuss more fully in Chapter 6). As Behe describes it in his influential book, *Darwin's Black Box: The Biological Challenge to Evolution*, an irreducibly complex system is "composed of several, well-matched interacting parts that contribute to the basic function, wherein the removal of any one of the parts causes the system to effectively cease functioning." For example, the DNA molecule, which excels at stockpiling and duplicating information, can't build itself without the help of proteins. But proteins are incapable of reproducing themselves without the information provided by DNA. Even the elaborate system of the miniscule cell was created as a fully functioning whole.

An organism type is an irreducibly complex system. There could not possibly have been a sudden random addition of one magical part that made it a new type; changing one part would require simultaneously changing millions and possibly billions of other perfectly interlocked gears in the organic watch if it's to continue ticking, especially ticking the correct time. An organism, being alive, consists of a multitude of precisely integrated materials and processes that allow it not just to *be*, but to be *alive*. Every cell is an engineering masterpiece beyond anything the human pea brain can comprehend. Clearly a transcending intelligence must have designed and constructed Nature in a way that ensured that its *stability of form* would be perpetually maintained in a way that ensured *perpetual change*. Now that's a bunny from a hat that makes a Deist clap.

DNA microbiology has made classification immensely more complicated because it sees that life is characterized by surprising "discontinuities"—as scientists call those discrete containers—that contradict the obsolete Darwinian model of smooth evolutionary continuity. Conflation of the terms discontinuous and discontinuity seems inaccurate enough to be a bit unfair. In Darwin's mind, it seems, continuous macroevolution fit the *a priori* scientific assumption of absolute natural continuity, even though he knew that old-fashioned typology could also exemplify continuity. Even in the nineteenth century, science offered the Great Chain of Being as emblematic of its version of continuity, even though a chain is composed of discrete, "discontinuous" links. Continuity literally means permanence, stability, connection, link. One dictionary definition is "uninterrupted duration or continuation, esp. without essential change," and "the property of being mathematically continuous." Geometrical forms, for instance, can come in many shapes, yet each shape conforms to its discrete form's definition. All triangles are equidistant from any quadrilaterals. All triangles have three sides, although the lengths of the sides and corresponding angles can vary according to the "species" (so to speak): equilateral, acute, obtuse, scalene, isosceles, right triangle. The abstract containers triangle and quadrilateral are both contained within a larger container, polygon. Containers are absolute forms, or archetypes. Each form can be defined and named because it is decidedly this, not that: Each ideal form has its own defining essence. And we're back to Plato meets Aristotle.

Missing links are—links. Darwin knew as well as neo-Darwinians today know that nature is "discontinuous," that its *continuity* consists of discrete, nested, "Euclidian" containers. Even neo-Darwinism's newfangled punctuated equilibrium popularized by Niles Eldredge and Stephen Jay Gould is just another way of "explaining" those discontinuous containers, which is just another way of reframing unexplainable, necessarily creative, intelligent, and purposive engineering. But really, wouldn't Darwin's notion of transitional evolution also be a way of reframing unexplainable, necessarily creative, intelligent, and purposive design? Science seeks *first and natural causes* of physical phenomenon—an entirely deistic agenda. Science, which deems itself super-intelligent, is inherently vested in the *intelligibility* of the material realm. Need I say more? What's amazing is that, yes, we do need to spell out the obviously necessary first and abiding cause of intelligibility: God. Darwinians spend so much time dissecting the brain that they've no time left to study their own minds. Brain, mind: two very discrete containers.

Darwin posited that species very gradually evolved from the bottom up, starting with a very simple cell and building up from there. Microbiology revised the description of a cell from simple to astoundingly complex. Either model necessitates an intelligent organizational blueprint. Even neo-Darwinians admit this;—well, they say it only *appears* to be a blueprint.

It's become increasingly clear that life that exists today began all at once (in geological time) during the Cambrian explosion as discrete phyla types that changed from the top down. I'm not a scientist; I accept this view, but frankly, I can't see that the top-down model solves the bottom-up model's central problem of transition; it doesn't eliminate a necessary divine first-cause intervention for every type of first cause. All models fail to show the incremental steps or a mechanism that makes even microevolution possible. All start with the extraordinary complexity of the tiniest building blocks and the irreducible complexity of discrete building materials and their final product—but even that's incomplete. The problem isn't just forms, but how forms gel. Maybe it's time for biologists to throw out universal ancestry and start with a fresh paradigm, like, say, extraordinary potential within constant form. Replace either-or with a synthesis of transition and boundary, freedom and conformity, individual and type; start with a broader definition of *essence*.

The fact is that the more we discover, the less we can explain the origin of life, not to mention its perpetual flowering. I believe that future study will uncover more and more profoundly ordered complexity. God, after all, is infinite in a way and to a degree that transcends space-time. ("Infinite" so to speak—because infinite is a space-time term, and again, God transcends space-time.) We know that Zeno's arrow crosses infinite subunits of space—a foot, an inch, a quarter inch and so on infinitum. But we can never know how the finite traverses the infinite; we can never even really fully know what finite and infinite are, or what we are, or what anything is in any absolute sense of knowing. We get glimpses, very real and in a way, very comprehensive traces, but ultimate reality never fully discloses itself to us. We instinctively accept more on faith than most people realize and most scientists will admit. Atheist determinists might feel frustrated and even angry at the tiny dimensions of their pea brain. But throughout all the ages, many of us geniuses—and that's what *Homo sapiens* are—have stood in awe, sometimes ecstatic, sometimes humble, before the manifest Creator of Nature. And we naturally intuit that each trace of reality presents a vital clue to the purpose of our being here.

Whether life evolved top down or bottom up or sideways or inside out, scientists now know that even the simplest life-forms function according to elaborate blueprint specifications. So do the most complex life-forms, like us.

The interminable "kill religion" Richard Dawkins, never one to shave with Ockham's razor, offers his ironically named Mt. Improbable as his solution to the Darwinian quandary: Life is like a mountain; on one side the smooth cliff face appears unscalable, but on the not-seen back side of the mountain lie materials built up step by step into the mountain. Life only *appears* to be intelligently designed, he argues; really Darwinian evolution obviously works via some not yet discovered Darwinian-esque mechanism that's…unintelligent? Putting aside the invalidity of his mountain analogy (for example, complex life is categorically different from simple inanimate matter, even a mountain of it), even if Dawkins were right that evolution is bottom up, that would not eliminate complex purpose executed step-by-step according to a logical plan to accomplish a logical end via logical means, i.e., intelligent design.

The point that finally pops the neo-Darwinian bubble is that you can't randomly assemble DNA code into a coherent complex organism any more than you can mindlessly toss out alphabet letters and get *Romeo and Juliet*. Not ever. Not once, much less trillions of times to get trillions of different "plays," or complex wholes. Not even just the letters on the page, not to mention their meanings and the overall significance of the play. It's ridiculous to argue that a DNA letter, which alone means nothing by itself (and where did the letter come from; and why) could meaningfully "attach" by random selection to another (and why select; what intelligence decides that that selection is best) and so on, giving rise to an intelligible play of life written in poetry rich with metaphoric connotations, significance, and beauty. And where do analogy and symbolism come from?

Even though die-hard Darwinians know these facts, they still assert that the "essentially identical" DNA in chimps and humans "proves" that chimps and humans are essentially identical.

Really? I picture Darwin Jr. walking down the aisle with a chimp—a lovely, stylish chimp, but still. No, my friend, chimps don't write poetry, don't engineer spacecraft, don't weep at the movies, don't kill over love, don't implode from ennui or explode with the angst of injustice or suffer such excruciating despair over the meaningless of life that they jump off bridges. Chimps are categorically different from humans, and that great gulf of difference lies not in quantity of DNA strands but in quality of spirit. What's truly astounding is not that we are so quantitatively close to chimps and all other organisms in terms of our DNA and other corporeal raw materials, but that there is that humungous extra something about us that is qualitatively "other" than our material make-up. It's time to stop privileging the material as a starting point of anything.

The neo-Darwinist angrily grumbles that Zeno's arrow has somehow hit the target. As a Deist, my whole being ripples with delight at the inexplicable miracle of existence. Descartes was right, but the mind/body dichotomy is really a distinction between spirit and matter, and more broadly, between the spiritual and the materialistic worldviews. If matter is created by God, it could be infused by God with spirit, the way Shakespeare infused *Romeo and Juliet* with poetic beauty and meaning. But the self-evident necessity of God could as easily escape the atheist-materialist Darwinian mind as could the theme of any great play.

Personally, it makes no difference to me whether Darwinian macroevolution is a fact or not. Creation for me is a work of literary art. (And how does one understand metaphor?) I study the imagery (which scientists call facts) and then work to interpret, appreciate, and enjoy the meanings they represent. Scientists agree that any version of the coming into existence of life describes extraordinarily sophisticated interconnecting mechanisms, apparatuses, functions, and material "stuff," not to mention informational instructions and the near-perfect execution of the instructional information, all of which obviously comes from somewhere—really some*one*, since a *where* isn't intelligent, isn't creative, couldn't engineer or program or orchestrate even the tiniest component of our immensely elegantly calibrated universe and its awesomely exquisitely complex life, a structure that even includes wiggle room where chance and free choice can take place. In later chapters I will discuss scientifically verified intelligent design in more detail, including some atheist scientists' amazingly ludicrous alternatives to the eloquently simple "Creator."

All scientists know that science is wrong far more often than it is right, that the inside history of science is a chronicle of fact checks, adjustments, corrections, and starting from scratch. Both Darwinian and scientific infallibility are cultural memes. The truth is that Darwinism has never identified a mechanism by which natural selection could bring about changes at all. There is no soft tissue, genetic, or embryonic evidence verifying causal Darwinian relationships among types, or direct connection to a common ancestor. But there are multitudes of examples of attributes shared—oddly, unpredictably—by life-forms not genetically related. The baffling yin/yang fusion of dissimilarity and similarity is one very painful thorn in the side of Darwinism. Concurrently, and perhaps not coincidentally, difference as oneness is a thorny ache civilization is currently trying to resolve.

A scientist is not a brain in a jar. Even the great Charles Darwin was a human being with proclivities, emotions, and agendas. In Chapters 4 and 5, I demystify Darwin the man in order to expose his very human motivations for promoting a theory he deeply doubted and quite possibly disbelieved. It's not my concern to negate Darwinian evolution for its own sake, but rather to show that science, like religion, can be steered by presupposition, ignorance, closed-mindedness, and personal weakness.

WARP-SPEED EVOLUTION

What is humanity, then, if neither apish nor fallen? What are you if you could *know* that God truly is the God of love? How would it change you if you knew you were free—truly *free*—to choose your own self-definition?

By synthesizing natural religion and science of nature, Deism seeks to discover the purpose of our being here. Science helps to objectively verify religious truth; religion helps decipher the deep meaning encoded in scientific discoveries. Science and religion together help us understand purpose to be a dimension of existence itself—of Nature perpetually created by the God of Nature. All of us, even atheists (when they're honest), begin with the understanding that Nature is intelligible *because* it is intelligently designed.

Science demonstrates qualitatively that the major systems with which we and all things are made are by necessity designed. Science becomes religious when it asks who or what has done (and is doing) the designing. And why.

This book begins with *why*, represented by the incredible instance of American democracy (Chapter 2), then builds on the deconstruction of fundamentalism begun in *Born-Again Deist* with a critique of the so-called quest for the historical Jesus (Chapter 3). Part II (Chapters 4-8) deconstructs Darwinism, including neo-Darwinism (bear with me, for that deconstruction will be *thorough*), delineates the basic science of intelligent design, and outlines a working *deology* (Deist philosophy/theology) of intelligent design. Part III (Chapters 9-13) demonstrates some contemporary dangers resulting from fallacious Darwinian and fundamentalist absolutism and offers solutions with a confidently optimistic grin.

Whenever I refer to Deism as new, I am simply distinguishing my personal version from that of old-school Deists, like, say, Edward Herbert, the early seventeenth century British philosopher and poet credited with initiating bona fide Deism, and brother of metaphysical poet George Herbert. Deism has always welcomed differences of opinion. New Deism is simply traditional Deism in the fresh context of the present.

My version of Deism differs from that of other Deists writing today in that it is rooted not in reason alone, but in common sense, which as I mean it is the consensus of our faculties, including reason, conscience, intuition, experience, emotion, aesthetic, volition, and spirit. Though our faculties are inherent and rational, they must be constructively educated and exercised. Amazingly, high-level engagement of our faculties can shift our paradigms at warp speed. High-level engagement is the Deist challenge.

As far as I can tell, all Deists believe in one Creator God, in transcendental truth manifested in Creation, and in the primacy of reason, or of common sense, in apprehending truth. Like all Deists, I believe in the inviolable laws of nature that constitute the structural integrity of existence and therefore reject miracles that violate natural law. But as I discuss especially in Chapter 8, I also affirm wiggle rooms where chance and choice can take place. Personal preference, or individual free will, is an ancient understanding confirmed by recent scientific conclusions of non-determinism based on several key concepts centered on randomness—most recently chaos theory, following Gödel's incompleteness, Heisenberg's uncertainty, Turing's uncomputability, Shannon and Weaver's entropy as disorder, Chaitin's randomness and chaos, and the information theory revolution.

Deists accept the latest scientific interpretations of intelligent design, knowing that science is rarely absolute and is perpetually under reconstruction; we appreciate Creation myths as not-literal representations subject to literary analysis and interpretation.

Though I share many beliefs with fellow Deists of the past and today, I take full responsibility for this book's assertions and arguments.

To give you a sense of where you're headed, below I list Eighteen Premises of New Deism that I substantiate throughout this book.

EIGHTEEN PREMISES OF NEW DEISM

1) Truth is absolute.
2) Human apprehension of truth is limited and tentative.
3) Humans apprehend truth via common sense.
4) Common sense is the consensus of human faculties.
5) God exists.
6) God is transcendent and immanent.
7) God is good.
8) Existence is intelligently designed by God.
9) Existence consists of perpetual transformation within constant form.
10) Existence embodies more than matter and forces.
11) Existence has purpose.
12) Existence has meaning.
13) Humans are moral, spiritual beings.
14) Humans have free will.
15) Good *being* manifests as good *doing*.
16) The Good consists of unselfish benefit.
17) In relationships and in society, ideal benefit is reciprocal.
18) Good humans transcend throughout this life and on into an afterlife.

For me, writing a book is a process of discovery. I've assembled the thoughts herein for myself, for fellow Deists, and for those interested in Deism. (I only dimly hope to unbolt the brains of the closed-minded.) At their best, books provide portals to paradigm shifts. This book's paradigm is Deism, in my experience the best all-natural antidote for spiritual disenchantment.

Ultimately, my intent is to honor the amazing Creator that designed this intelligible universe for the amusement and edification of our intelligent minds (among other reasons, I'm sure), and to warn my fellow global citizens against dishonoring Creator and Creation with our selfishness and our stubborn ideological wars. I hope to persuade every reader that replacing the dangerous matrix of misunderstanding with a more adult vision of God and each other can ultimately benefit us all.

CHAPTER 2

DEIST DEMOCRACY: THE HIGHER GROUND

Within the limits of real world possibilities, what would an ideal society look like?

Like our Deist Founders, Deists today assume that the best society is a highest-functioning democracy, and that each of its citizens is an exemplary democrat—not specifically a member of the Democratic Party, but an eager, principled participant in the democracy.

What if I suggested that the exemplary democrat is by necessity the Golden Mean between doormat and despot? If you're a good Democrat, or even a good Republican, and certainly if you're a good Independent, you might think seating doormat and despot together on the same couch would spell trouble at even the most cordial party thrown by the most exemplary democrat.

Remember, the Golden Mean is not the winner of a competition; nor is it a compromise between competing interests: It's not a watered-down average, but the transcending positive between two opposite negatives, like courage is the Golden Mean between cowardice and rashness.

Despot, you think, is certainly negative, but despot seems more the antithesis of democrat than of doormat. Isn't it a bit unfair to put doormat on a par with despot as the negative opponent of democrat, as if doormat could or would oppose a highest-functioning democracy? How is it just to blame doormat equally with despot? Isn't holding the poor, helpless doormat responsible for anything simply a case of blaming the victim?

Deism posits that if the best society, the highest-functioning democracy, is run by consensus of exemplary democrats, at its highest level of operation it would produce no doormats or despots: no victims, no victimizers.

Furthermore, in a democracy like ours still striving toward ideal fulfillment, a Golden Mean democrat stands midway between, yet entirely above, doormat and despot. By "above" I mean in a position to help cure the democracy of doormat and despot, of victim and victimizer.

By victim—in the Golden Mean model, the negative opposite of the negative victimizer—I do *not* mean an *un*willing victim. I mean willing, or at least unable to be unwilling.

Does anyone really *want* to be a victim? Perhaps not. But in America, easy targets abound, and in a democracy, easy targets must be taught survival tactics, first because it's the right thing to do, but also because the only implacable enemy of a democracy is the predator, and predators need victims: despots need doormats.

"Don't feed the animals" here is no joke. Most of us Americans—even the strongest Darwinian and most prayerful fundamentalist—have been thrown to the wolves in one way or another. The planet itself bleeds from wolf tooth and nail—and by *wolf* I mean human. There are copious concrete reasons why this might be so. But in the abstract, there is really one root cause. Victimization, predation, exploitation, oppression, despotism—it's all the same problem. And that problem is the antithesis of a democracy "of, by, and for the people": It is elitism, in the broadest sense.

Despots come in many flavors, from tyrannical, abusive fathers to child-molesting priests to control-freak bosses who force you to lie, cheat, fraud, and "handle" insider trading. Every despot rules from his/her elite position of control. In the broader context of a democracy, specifically in America, the currently ruling one-percent elite is the despot, and the ninety-nine percent allowing this despot to rule is the doormat. Well, technically the one-percent elite is Dr. Frankenstein, and his monstrous projection, Frankenstein (junior), is the psychopathic corporate "person" terrorizing the global village, the ninety-nine percent.

THE NATURAL URGE FOR DEMOCRACY

Although many credit Plato for inspiring an ideal republic and Aristotle for inventing democracy, both were elitists who repudiated democracy or a republic of free and equal citizens. It's understandable that in a tiny haven populated by both aristocrats and uneducated peasants surrounded by barbarians and warmongers, two of antiquity's greatest geniuses advocated rule of the many by an elite class of philosopher-kings. If they lived today, Plato and Aristotle might join the ranks of later geniuses who favored modern representative democracies. But like Thomas Jefferson, they would insist that government be fully transparent and all citizens well-educated; the politically savvy majority, Jefferson believed, would rein-in despots, elites, predators, victimizers—any individuals or groups that might jeopardize the rule of, by, and for the people.

Our Declaration of Independence, Constitution, and system of just, equitable laws were largely influenced by the Roman Stoics, who argued that an inherent spark of reason endowed every human being with the capacity to apprehend a universal natural law to which we could harmoniously align our behavior. Once people understood that conformity to the natural law of mutual cooperation most benefited each individual as well as the whole of society, the majority of people would naturally abide by those laws. Governments were created to check the selfish exploitation of the "unnatural" minority, whether a solo psychopath or an elite aristocracy.

Generally speaking, political philosophers throughout the ages have either believed that mankind is essentially good and that a minimum of laws could be created to restrain the not good, or assumed that mankind is essentially selfish and that an elite minority of the enlightened or otherwise superior should rule in order to maintain order and security.

Our Founders, inspired by thinkers like the Roman Cicero, envisioned a commonwealth that served as an association of friendly parties seeking various ends within the overall harmonious structure, and they believed that this association, rightly constructed, would be held together by laws that reflected universal natural laws that constituted the cosmic, God-given order. The Romans never achieved the ideal commonwealth envisioned by Stoic political philosophy. Dictators flourished in the midst of wars and assassinations, plunder and rape. America's Founders took a quantum leap closer to an ideal commonwealth: "rule by the people" (the definition of democracy)—an extraordinary intellectual and practical feat many Americans today take completely for granted.

The fundamental principles of deist naturalism and democratic possibilities emerged thousands of years ago, but as conquests by both State and Church took the human spirit hostage and instituted a dark-age denial of Nature's Prime Mover, mediated obedience to elite-controlled institutions obliterated natural communion with God along with individual freedom. Humans economically controlled were further reduced to spiritual serfs by divine-right autocrats.

Chiseled by centuries of struggle, at the dawn of the Enlightenment Deism's definition of human had evolved, and so had its position to the God held hostage by organized religion. After years excavating the Self from the rubble of antiquated religion and science, Deists blew the dust off the book of life only to discover the pulsating unified organism that is Creation, both noun and verb. "We hold these truths to be self-evident..." The self-evidence of truth was a radical concept, a revolutionary humanist stance that simply recognized that we don't need otherworldly priests conferring truth any more than we need political masters barking orders. Creation, Deists insisted, is rational and can be understood by our rational minds. Humans are *meant* to understand. Humans understand *because* we have been intelligently designed to intelligently understand. Furthermore, it is *rational* to believe that all the highest values of humanity have been rationally bestowed.

The assumption that the power of the religious and political aristocracy constitutes the framework of civilization had become so entrenched by the eighteenth century that it's remarkable that America's Founders even thought to, much less fought to, segment power by establishing a democracy with separate branches of government, and within that framework to allow independent state governments, and at the same time limited religious monopoly by codifying separation of church and state to protect freedom of conscience.

The Founders themselves recognized their remarkable position in history and acknowledged the guidance of Providence. Democracy came into existence in America because of a belief in God, the necessary Cause, the obvious Designer of the massive, elegant design of existence, a benevolent Creator that willed the good of naturally free humanity. God was the Good of Nature; "super-nature" described God's active, transcendent benevolence in creating Nature.

The Stoic assumption of a transcendent constitution of ordered, fixed equality manifested through the laws of nature was echoed in Thomas Jefferson's eminent words, "We hold these truths to be self-evident, that all men are created equal, that they are endowed by their Creator with [inherent and] certain unalienable Rights, that among these are Life,

Liberty and the pursuit of Happiness.—That to secure these rights, Governments are instituted among Men, deriving their just powers from the consent of the governed."

It's worth noting that Jefferson's original version included the words "inherent and," which I've indicated with brackets. Congress struck those words, which in my view diluted the intended meaning that our rights are ours at birth and are not conferred upon us or earned by us at a later date. In the final version, the ambiguous "certain" could mean definite, which Jefferson surely meant, or particular, which needed qualification as to what those rights might be, and which could be limited by the qualification.

In theory, at least, the principle of responsible liberty equally enjoined was and is the requisite bedrock of our democracy. Unlike the social contract of the European Enlightenment, expounded by Thomas Hobbes, John Locke, and Jean-Jacques Rousseau as a sacred covenant legally enacted for the common good, the sacredness of our contract was ascribed by its authors not to a Christian God but to a universal Creator equally available to all. This truly democratic religious vision is decidedly Deistic. Although there were forerunners (most notably Roger Williams) to our refusal to be exploited either by state (in that case, the monarchy of King George III) or by religion (the Anglican Christianity that supported it), the best-selling works of Thomas Paine, especially *Common Sense, The Rights of Man*, and *The Age of Reason*, were most central to Americans' understanding of humanity's place in the universe and the role of government in securing every person's God-given right to liberty and equality.

The Founders responsible for authoring our seminal Declaration of Independence and the Constitution drew upon their extensive knowledge of great thinkers, especially Enlightenment philosophers. Jefferson, a confirmed Deist, is known to have consulted in addition to books both ancient and modern, dozens if not hundreds of pamphlets, manifestos, and other writings circulating at the time. The Founders infused their texts with Deist theism popularized especially by Paine, whose writings enjoyed unprecedented international success. The merging of revolution and Deism ushered the world into a truly new era characterized by a belief that equally endowed individual rights, epitomized by life, liberty, and the pursuit of happiness, could best be protected within a society of cooperative democracy. Deism inspired revolution and revolution animated Deism, which more than any other religion truly represented "love your neighbor as yourself" and the spirit of reciprocity.

Deists, not religious authoritarians, codified the clear separation of church from state in addition to the division of powers within the state. Deists, not the Continental philosophers, established our democratic republic upon uniquely radical interpretations of constitutional and procedural stability, representation, accountability, and transparency. Deists, not autocrats, formed a more perfect Union that preserved equally for each individual the universal civil liberties inscribed in the Bill of Rights. It was Deists who stood up for Everyman by instituting true equality and freedom for all.

From the very beginning, we the people debated the definition of equality and freedom. Some argued that slavery and denial of women's rights violated our understanding that all people are created equal and are equally endowed with the inherent, unalienable right to liberty. But others countered that overturning the institutions of slavery and women-as-chattel violated a white Judeo-Christian aristocrat's freedom to make money, retain property, and maintain the traditional male-dominated household. To allow slaves and women their liberty would not only diminish the competitive edge of the aristocracy and the personal power of the individual male, it would defy the hierarchy of organized religion and would therefore lead to the collapse of civilization. Today blacks, Hispanics, feminists, gays, liberals, and Muslims continue the long tradition of perceived threats to aristocratic power-over. A leftist-multiracial-Muslim lesbian mother is tantamount to spiritual castration and a sign from heaven that the End Times are near.

We Americans revere life, liberty, equality, and justice as the most fundamental principles upon which our nation was founded. Our happiness depends on our possessing these conditions. As individuals and as a society, we value freedom from the restraints of others; we warrant universal freedom from exploitation, which constitutes the essence of equality; and we demand that exploiters be brought to justice. In our society, the greatest crime is murder, and close behind are violating forms of assault, like rape and molestation, that while leaving the victim physically alive, torture ("murder") the *psyche* (self, soul). Even most Darwinians agree that plundering the freedom of others to enhance ones chances of survival is immoral, much more immoral if it would not in any way contribute to survival. Even Darwinians would likely agree that cold-blooded murder and rape do not contribute to survival, do not enhance superiority, and do not define the fittest. Why, then, do they not also agree that socioeconomic slavery and capitalist serfdom neither benefit humanity nor ensure its survival? Oh right, because agreeing wouldn't fatten their 401k.

Darwinians view Nature as the kill-or-be-killed province of natural selection, like many fundamentalists view it as the treacherous province of Satan. But the growing congregation of enlightened Deists equates Nature with Creation intelligently designed by a benevolent Creator, who has built human freedom and responsibility into the structure of Nature itself. Human nature is part of Nature; moral integrity conforms to the structural integrity of Nature; willing conformity to moral integrity contributes to authentic happiness of the individual and of humanity.

Natural law as our Founders understood it is natural, and even the pragmatist's understanding included a conviction of innate *philos*. Brotherly goodwill in any form contradicts the fundamental principles of Darwinism, including cutthroat capitalism whitewashed as free enterprise. Just as rape is never love, the enterprise of exploitation is never truly free; to equate "free enterprise" with freedom as our Founders meant it is intentional deception spun by the ultra-greedy pretending to be righteous Americans. Authentically righteous Americans promoting the freedom of our Founders are labeled "socialists" by these traitors. The most insidious hucksters mask their greed with a godly persona, Bible in hand, accusing their critics of atheism. Pure red herring.

What exploiters don't grasp is that violent destruction is ultimately self-destruction at every level, including the spiritual level, where morality resides. In a society established on civilized principles of beneficence, or at least mutual benefit, rather than on obsolete theories of unnatural competition, secular or religious, everyone benefits, even the rich and powerful, who are only harmed by their own greed and hubris and are ultimately consumed by their selfishness.

If people didn't exploit one another, we wouldn't need governments. But we do need governments—of, by, and for the people, not of, by, and for the rich, those ultimate controllers of power-over.

On the other hand, sometimes governments fail us. Then what? Our Founders concluded, in words we all learned in grade school: "When in the

Course of human Events, it becomes necessary for one People to dissolve the Political Bands which have confined them with another, and to assume among the Powers of the Earth, the separate and equal Station to which the Laws of Nature and Nature's God entitle them, a decent Respect to the Opinions of Mankind requires that they should declare the causes which impel them to the Separation."

It is a necessity, they believed, that people shuck off the shackles that confine them to another. In America today, the "political bands" that shackle us to another are more subtle, more Machiavellian than the British monarchy and the Anglican religion that legitimized its rule in the eighteenth and nineteenth centuries.

OF PSYCHOPATHS AND KINGS

If you think about what a democracy embodies, it's everything a psychopath is not. For starters, every psychopath is an incorrigible liar. For a democracy to succeed, it must be built upon a solid foundation of truth— in government, that's "transparency," in the press, that's not giving "equal time" but rather documenting facts. It's interesting that in America, what is a *kind* of lying—identity theft, fraud, robbery, slander—is illegal, but except under oath in a legal proceeding, lying itself is not. That's part of the problem. Even a society like ours that glorifies free speech still needs to guard against deception; otherwise fast-talking predators will gobble up free speech and every other expression of liberty. And everything good, including truth, hinges upon personal and collective liberty. Your personal liberty—your Self being itself—and the blessings of your liberty by which you enjoy and express your Self—your stuff—are what the predator stalks. The predator lies to steal, you and yours.

Among the many breeds of predators threatening our maturing democracy, those superlative villains, psychopaths—clinically, exploiters without conscience—are the only inexorable enemy.

In the opening of his book, *Without Conscience: The Disturbing World of the Psychopaths Among Us*, Dr. Robert Hare, a foremost authority on psychopathy, describes psychopaths as "social predators who charm, manipulate, and ruthlessly plow their way through life...Completely lacking in conscience and in feelings for others, they selfishly take what they want and do as they please...without the slightest sense of guilt or regret." Should we be letting these people run our relationships, our workplaces, our churches, our banks, our schools, our governments, our militaries, our lives? Of course not! Yet we do. The news trumpets examples of our failure to resist, to reign in, to reckon with predators, and those headlines represent just a sliver of actual instances. Can't we do more? Are we doormats? Willing victims? Unwilling victims? How much responsibility should good democrats—good human beings—assume?

Of the roughly two million psychopaths currently living in North America, only a minority are gruesome serial butchers splashed by the media. Most psychopaths slip under the skin of individuals or groups like a deadly undiagnosed parasite. Many spread like incurable plague, destroying individuals, institutions, nations, potentially the world.

Though psychopaths are by nature narcissistic and self-absorbed and therefore greedy isolationists who hide their hoard (be it stashed cash or stockpiled frozen penises a la Jeffrey Dahmer), solo predators at times join a hunting party to boost their game. Think Holocaust. Think gang rape. Think Carlyle Group. Think Spanish Inquisition. Think smiley-face "helluva good job" back-patting in the face of Katrina's worsening catastrophe. Think cocktail party ego-enriching dilettantism. Think politicians. Psychopaths relish catastrophe as business as usual with a twist of lime.

Every variety of psychopath comes packaged in lies. These are the pimps who charm their way close enough to pick your pocket, seduce your wife, and "recruit" your daughter to their sex trade. These are banksters who "appropriate" your house and pilfer the treasury of your tax dollars for their overseas expenditures. These are insurance vampires who suck the blood of the dying pleading for transfusions. These are political traitors who represent the corporate nation's "extraction-war" with America. These are religious terrorists parading in the pomp and circumstance of obscene wealth, passing the collection plate for coins to damn gays and infidels and feminists but actually to sequester their cult of child molesters and rapists and mammonites. These are the dragons spewing poison in the air, excreting your next meal. These are the tribal chieftains shaking their spears tipped with nuclear warheads.

Like individual psychopaths, an aristocracy, including the corporate oligarchy currently sacking America, is self-centered, callous, and remorseless, is profoundly lacking in empathy, and functions without the restraints of conscience. "What is missing in this picture [of the psychopath] are the very qualities that allow human beings to live in social harmony." Social harmony—highest-functioning democracy—does not include the Darwinian exploitation of one class by another that currently defines America. But aristocrats try to persuade you that it does. The most insidious hierarchs wrap themselves in designer robes of "free" market rectitude that you yourself paid for. That self-righteous, holier-than-thou aristocrat you shelled out to elect as your representative?—He's the repair roofer who cut a bigger hole in your roof and ripped off even your kitchen sink right under your nose.

Killing is a form of lying, because the killer asserts that the person killed had to be killed for a legitimate cause, even if that's just the killer's power and pleasure. In our democracy, "had to do it" is the reigning justification for every evil brought to light. It's true that not all CEOs and lobbyists and political gofers are necessarily psychotic killers, except, at times, indirectly. But even when they're not bombing Bagdad, even when they're not sending coal miners back into half-collapsed mines, even when they're not yachting in Dubai to escape their oil rig slicks, even when they're not tanning in the Cayman Islands to escape their stacks' soot and taxes, their acts still gush from a crude "cold, calculating rationality combined with a chilling inability to treat others as thinking, feeling human beings." Social thugs, their mugs fit Dr. Hare's depiction to a T. Not deranged, disoriented, or distressed, these cheap chump chatters are just plain wicked, charming though they might be.

Darwinian and religious psychopaths share this feature: They claim that they "have to" hurt others, like the rich "have to" hurt the lower classes to stay rich, like insurance companies "have to" deny care when it's not profitable, like inquisitors "have to" torture and kill heretics, like men "have to" beat their wives into submission, like factories "have to" spew poisons to make their products profitable, like real men "have to" bash gays, like Christians "have to" destroy Islam, like CEOs "have to" ship American jobs overseas, like politicians "have to" represent the corporate elite, like Americans "have to" blow up nations to get to their oil, like rapists "have to" rape.

Some cunning psychopaths argue that they are the victims. They'll tell you that people are messing with them, trying to rip them off, attacking them, like CEOs asked to pay themselves less, like the rich expected to contribute their fair share of taxes. After claiming that he was a warm, caring guy, one psychopath sulking in the slam for kidnapping, rape, and extortion, was asked if he felt bad when he hurt someone. "Yeah, sometimes. But mostly it's like…uh…[laughs]… how did you feel the last time you squashed a bug?"

Many experts believe that psychopaths are born that way. In other words, they are what they are from the very beginning. Psychopaths tend to exhibit their true colors even as young children. Horrified parents are unable to control the ruthless self-gratification that runs the gamut from lying and stealing to rape of other children to torture and butchery of animals as practice for future hunts, which, by their twenties, comes as easy as plugging Alaskan moose from a chopper.

How do they get their dark knowledge, their evil skills? They're not the victims that they claim to be; they use that line to victimize victims. No, they seem to be born to be what they manifest themselves to be. Is this free will? Yes, because they choose to be what they are, as do we all. It's hard to believe that we start choosing from the moment we're born. Negative experiences and harsh treatment can take its toll. But "I can find no convincing evidence that psychopathy is the direct result of early social or environmental factors," Dr. Hare tells us. Although negative socio-environmental influences can be reversed and deep emotional damage can be healed in not-psychopaths, psychopaths have no inner ability to want healing, or to even know they need it. Unlike sociopaths, psychopaths can't be cured, only trained to pursue evils less pinching on the scale of social consequences.

Not that psychopaths really care about consequences. They are fearless to the point of absurdity, risking their own and other people's lives without so much as a blink. But they like the game, and they *must* win.

Though anti-social at heart, if psychopaths could be said to have a heart, being masters of disguise they shape-shift at will, molding their persona to fit the conquest.

"Unlike psychotic individuals," like, say, schizophrenics, "psychopaths are rational and aware of what they are doing and why. Their behavior is the result of *choice*, freely exercised." Italics, Dr. Hare's.

In a democracy, doesn't it make sense to subject our elected officials to thorough psychological evaluations and lie detector tests, not to mention exams on citizenship, history, the Constitution, economics, sociology, etc.? Technically our representatives are our employees. How is it, then, that they're telling *us* what to do? The political purpose has become a lie. Well okay, it does make sense that they're telling us what to do, because they don't know what *they're* doing, other than that they're pulling the wool over our heads while they tax us broke so we'll work cheaper to make them richer and subsidize them for the honor. I'm overgeneralizing about politicians; but the point is that the *system itself* is becoming psychopathic, which forces even honorable politicians to get in the game with the psychopaths. The game, of course, has already been won, thanks to a marked card: In the land of the free, each American like Pavlov's dog drools for a job that leashes him to serfdom.

Isn't it important to understand what makes a psychopath tick, to become savvy about a psychopath's characteristics and MOs in order to protect ourselves as individuals and as a society, and to prevent our government from becoming full-blown psychopathic? Surely an authentic democracy depends, as our Founders understood, on due diligence on the part of its citizens.

We should care—really, really care—that the psychopath's portrait looks way too familiar, like famous con artists we see on TV that run much of our country and too many of its institutions and the corporations that pilfer them.

Psychopaths have many traits in common, but anyone who looks closely will notice right away that psychopaths are notoriously *superficial* liars. Dr. Hare quotes from the chilling *The Mask of Sanity*, in which psychiatrist-author Hervey Cleckley describes the psychopath in terms that probably sound a lot like a politician, CEO, or TV evangelist in your neighborhood. "The [psychopath] is unfamiliar with the primary facts or data of what might be called personal values and is altogether incapable of understanding such matters." Psychopaths only understand how to manipulate your values by charming their way into your heart and your bank account. "It is impossible for him to take even a slight interest in the tragedy or joy or the striving of humanity as presented in serious literature or art." Which is why we should keep a close eye on bored politicians who push math and science but slash funding for educational and other programs in the arts and humanities.

Of course, the psychopath, a master of disguise, can easily fake interest and knowledge. That good-looking fast-talking charmer with the gift of bull that makes everyone laugh knows all about literature and art. He's an expert on biology and politics and psychology and religion. Hell, he'll talk your ear off. But the real experts in the room roll their eyes at this humbugger's humdingers that no one else seems to notice. Those no one elses are the doormats and victims that make an ideal democracy impossible and a hobbling democracy painfully expensive.

In truth, the psychopath is, as Cleckley warns us, "indifferent to all these matters in life itself. Beauty and ugliness, except in a very superficial sense, goodness, evil, love, horror, and humor have no actual meaning, no power to move him." It's all for display; it's bait in the trap. In one, this indifference to depth is atrophy, the willful erasure of meaning and purpose. In another, indifference fulfills a predatory nature, climaxing in absolute emptiness. The essence of the fulfilled predator is his absence. What appears to consume is self-consuming, spiritually speaking.

HOW THE EXPLOITATION OF JESUS THREATENS DEMOCRACY

Fundamentalists will tell you that Jesus was the opposite of a psychopath. His authentic goodness transcended that of all other humans. As hopeful as the protagonist Jesus makes us feel, the Jesus narrative is fiction; that much we know (as I'll show in Chapter 3). Whether the original narrative was inspired by an actual person, we will never know. Regardless, the character Jesus merges qualities derived from protagonists of Greek tragedy, heroes who were "ourselves but better than ourselves," as Aristotle would have it, blessed and cursed of the gods and often born of them, who represented concretely, with the high seriousness of loftiest thought and conscience, humanity's deepest striving for meaning and purpose. The hero's fate, always suffering and usually death, displayed the judgmental mystery that controlled human destiny. Submission to fate was considered spiritually noble. Doormats of the gods, needless to say, tend toward pessimism.

The god-man status of Jesus clearly derives as well from the great Homeric and other epic traditions of warrior-kings with the blood of one or another divinity in their veins. Jesus' wise sage teaching style, which borrowed from existing archives of parables and wise sayings and continued a long dialogue tradition that culminated with the Greeks, plus the similarity between the itinerate rabbinic Jesus and Plato's Socrates suggests that Jesus was the brainchild of a Greek-educated rabbi.

The character Jesus is certainly "better than ourselves." We might be tempted to imagine that the author himself was a man of the highest moral character, but that can't be proven, nor should it be assumed. The author had a reason for representing high moral and spiritual qualities in his Jesus, but we can't know that reason. Perhaps the author himself passionately believed that humans should aspire to live up to the Jesus ideals. Perhaps the author was instructed by an elite Roman or Jewish official to create a hero that could serve as a model to the masses, aiding the official's efforts to subdue rebels while extracting property and taxes. Perhaps the character Jesus emerged as the best aesthetic choice of an author with serious literary intention.

Whatever the motivation, the author's character succeeded in gripping its audience by the collar and holding it spellbound for two millennia. Even if the Jesus character were the reigning king of longevity, which it isn't—many mythic gods and man-gods and heroes have survived much longer—that doesn't prove that it's literally true. What's interesting is that the Christians who most loudly argue that the story's longevity is proof of its literal authenticity are the very Christians who most brazenly pervert and exploit the character Jesus.

It's true that the god qualities in Jesus contribute to the mass appeal. A miracle man who promises healing, blessings, and eternal life is going to be as big a hit as Zeus and Venus, as Krishna and Buddha, as twilight vampires and Harry Potter. But it's the moral wisdom of Jesus that explains the god-man's survival into the twenty-first century. Because that wisdom is so impressive, and because that wisdom is part of the god-man package, many believers force themselves to believe the god part of the god-man narrative in order to honor the man and his wisdom—never realizing that the wisdom of Jesus is entirely derivative and the god-man package older than mud, a fact that honest scholars have been documenting for centuries.

Extracting the man from the god-man, as many have done—Jefferson, for instance, in his cut-and-paste *Jefferson Bible*, as it's now called—exposes a moral philosophy that is rooted in love of God and benevolence toward one's neighbor as equal to oneself. This is a moral philosophy found in many ancient religions and philosophies. Love of God expressed through benevolence toward all humanity is the foundation of the Deist democratic ideal.

What most fundamentalists ignore is that the aspect of loving God and humanity most highly accentuated by Jesus is the absolute rejection of mammon-lust. Selfishness, manifested as greed and its Siamese sibling hubris, is the antithesis of love of God and benevolent love of one's neighbor and oneself. This embodies the heart and soul of Christianity; this does not embody the heart and soul of most Christians.

Through a mythic principle of blanket grace that has been spread over Christianity like a magic shroud over a corpse to make it appear alive, mammon-lust has become justified and sanctified as a form of rightfulness. In the perverting minds of the greedy self-righteous, it is actually the will of Jesus that you be rich—if you believe hard enough. The original wisdom narrative has been torqued into the very opposite of what it actually says. Compassionate giving and sharing have been replaced with an accounting spreadsheet that allows you to calculate how much you have to invest in the Church or your favorite TV evangelist to force God to cough up a huge dividend.

From the humble beginnings of the Jewish rabbi Jesus preaching against mammon has sprung a Christian aristocracy operating a lucrative wealth-generating politicized franchise preaching a morality of mammon in the name of their anti-mammon Savior. You see, they say, "because Jesus died for our sins," we no longer have to be poor. We can be rich, because it's God's will that all his children be rich—his children being those born-agains who belong to the right club. God's job is to make you rich—because he promised. And God can't break his promise. All this is contained in the legal contract known as the Bible. Thus saith the TV evangelists and rightwing politicians. Oh yeah, and anyone who isn't on board with this deserves punishment and death in this life and hell in the next.

I have thoroughly deconstructed many spiritual frauds in *Born-Again Deist*, and have demonstrated there and in less depth in later chapters of this present book that the Bible is packed with factual errors and logical incongruities in addition to its pervasive fictive mythic and superstitious elements. I have documented what others have proven, that the god-man Jesus is a myth. Yet like many nonbelievers, including many of our Founders, I do deeply respect the ethical wisdom conveyed by the author of the Jesus literature. What's amazing to me is that the people who still claim that the Bible and Jesus are absolute literal truth are the very people who most contradict the moral code of Jesus by perverting his anti mammon morality with their own pro mammon-lust. We who don't believe the Jesus myth literally aren't doing that. The "believers" are. Evangelists preaching the love, caring, and compassion of Jesus shroud his risen body in the gilt of selfish greed and self-righteous hubris. Jesus was poor so we don't have to be poor: This is the essence of their message. These mammonites succeed in becoming filthy rich by seducing filthy-rich wannabes into the net of willing victims. The spiritual doormats only wake up when exhausted with keeping the faith they realize they've been filched. In a fully realized Jeffersonian democracy of well-educated citizens, this level of foolishness could not exist.

To illustrate my point, let me add one more case study to the long list of wolves in sheep's clothing. Please bear in mind that this specific description of one TV evangelist could generally apply to any genre of psychopath. Think of the psychopathic evangelist as a metaphor for one of the most deadly diseases afflicting democracy.

There's a Sucker Born Again Every Day

Like other "prosperity gospel" evangelists, Robert Tilton promises magical quick fixes for everything from cancer to alcoholism to credit card debt to job layoffs, anything for those who "vow" $1,000 donations. Watchdog groups have documented that he spends at least 68% of his airtime asking for money (so he, the high-priest middleman, can persuade God to give *you* money). As with other shearers of the flock, Tilton's tastes have always run toward the extravagant—the usual luxury vehicles, yachts, and mansions in San Diego, Dallas, and Miami, compliments of the shorn.

In the 1990s, Robert Tilton's *Success-N-Life* show appeared in all 235 U.S. television markets for 5,000 air hours, pulling in $80 million a year. Tilton registered his tax-free Word of Faith World Outreach Center Church, Inc. in Florida, but the registration was inactive as of November 21, 1991, when ABC's *PrimeTime Live* ran an exposé, prompted by Ole Anthony's watchdog organization, the Trinity Foundation. During its six-month investigation, ABC learned that Tilton had used twelve addresses in one decade, three of them in Fort Lauderdale, but two were commercial mail drops. His traffic tickets handed out in Broward County indicated that he at least hung out in Florida.

As it turned out, Tilton was one of several "seed faith" evangelists that raked in a fortune via a post office box in Tulsa, Oklahoma. Like most TV evangelists, Tilton promised to pray over each miracle request sent to him.

When ABC pulled thousands of requests and letters from garbage dumpsters in Tulsa—minus the food stamps, wedding rings, and money deposited at a nearby bank—a state fraud investigation and further investigations by the FBI and Postal Service followed. As ripped-off sheep filed lawsuits, Tilton insisted that the trashed requests were part of a plot against his "church."

During her divorce from Tilton in 1996, Leigh Valentine testified:

> Bob's mail ministry is a lie and a total deception. He does not write those [mass-mailed] letters. He did not even proofread them during our marriage. He makes it sound like [he's] writing to you right now, this is what God spoke to me for your life, Jesus will appear to you tonight; if you sleep with this little red cord under your pillow, you will prosper. He doesn't even know what's going out to those people, and he doesn't care, as long as they send their money in. One time he said in one of the letters that was sent, I will be taking these to the East Coast to pray for you by the ocean where Jesus prayed for his people. So we flew to Fort Lauderdale and we checked into a four- or five-star hotel on the beach and got a nice penthouse view...That is stealing from people. Most of those people are on welfare. They're little Hispanics and blacks. And he even said, what I do is I look at a map and we go after the ghettoes, we go after those on welfare, we go after those that don't read, those that are lower socioeconomic backgrounds. That's who we send our letters to.

Suits, countersuits, and public humiliation didn't stop Tilton. The year after his divorce, the "prophet of prosperity," as he calls himself, began recycling taped versions of his old shows on cable's Black Entertainment Television (BET), though he himself is white. He sold his Dallas church in 1999 for $6.1 million and started preaching new prosperity shows on BET, pitching his latest "free" books, *How To Be Rich and Get Anything You Want* and *How To Pay Your Bills Supernaturally*, building his already huge mailing list by offering to send you his "free" Faith Aid Miracle Healing Kit with anointing oil, prayer cloth, and prayer of agreement, not to mention the large poster of Tilton in the prayer-grimace position.

In 2001, Tilton was still dumping unread prayer requests, stripped of money, food stamps, and other offerings, in the exact same dumpsters he was using when busted in 1991. Patricia Morrow, one of a dozen employees of Tilton's Mail Services Inc. expected to produce a quota of at least $1,000 per hour from the opened letters, quit in disgust when she realized the extent of exploitation of what she described as lonely, homebound people from rural Florida and Georgia sending apologies with their offerings of small amounts, sometimes including coins. At last report, Brother Bob was raking in $30 million a year and living in a $4 million Miami mansion. He has formed additional non-profits to supplement his tax-free takings.

Entirely subsidized by "good" Christians, Robert Tilton and his seed-faith cronies are exactly the kind of hypocritical moneychangers that the biblical Jesus drove from the temple, a fact apparently lost on the sheep, if not the shepherd.

TV evangelists get rich easily because religious indoctrination has already trained adherents to be trusting and obedient toward any authority figure that solicits them in the name of God. If told that, say, a "gay agenda" threatens our "Christian America," millions of couch potato sheep will gladly send money to help eradicate that threat, especially if the donation will also reap an immediate "seed faith" reward from God. Plant a seed in faith, and God will reward your seed with growth. Translated, send me money [sucker], and God will reward you with answers to your prayers and a monetary "increase" greater than the interest rate [on nothing] at your local bank. You don't have to work for it. You don't even have to get up off your duff. Just pull out your wallet and pick up the phone. God and I will do the rest.

Ironically, it's the flamboyantly nontraditional TV evangelists, with their Christ-mocking rich-and-famous lifestyles and doctrines of biblically contradictory superstitions, who most loudly exploit biblical "truth." Add the handful of rightwing Republicans they underwrite—who strive for a rewrite of the consummate neocon/dominionist Bush administration—and that's a powerful, unchallenged core group that exploits for huge profits the Islamic feminazi socialist anti-white communist pedophilic gay menace concealed behind illegal immigration terrorism. Yes, folks, we have much to fear, right here in River City.

Who's jumping out from behind the bush to scare the sheep isn't even the manufactured terrorist; it's the proverbial wolf in the wool, the evangelist himself, or herself, who terrorizes the fold. Evangelists' lust for sheepskin—or seed, as the seed-faith evangelists put it (perhaps spilling the Freudian beans on their other repressed desires)—is supported by the rightwing herders they in turn support in a perfect symbiotic waltz of mutual sheering for profit: You give me no-tax status, I give you votes. To continue the con game, the wolves must pull the wool over the sheep's open eyes. Thus far, no shepherd has successfully pulled back the wool and exposed the wolves' game, at least not to the conned sheep themselves. Even seeing wool, they still send money, they still vote far-Right.

Robert Tilton and all the other exploiting TV evangelists, like Pat Robertson, Benny Hinn, and Jim Bakker, to name but a few mega-rich sheep-fleecers, operate by the same principles, but on a larger scale.

GOT TRUTH?

Exploitation of Jesus is only possible because scholars and their protégé who know better continue to perpetuate the myth that the Bible is God's Word and that Jesus is a historical person. People are longing for spiritual truth—real truth, not empty myths and disappointing superstitions. If those scholars refuse to tell the truth, if those scholars promote the suffering of the longing, we Deists have no choice but to expose their deception and to deconstruct their assertions.

Pursuit of truth—no, *insistence* on truth is as critical today as it was when our Deist Founders voted to reject political myths in favor of a bold new government founded upon natural, self-evident, universal truths. "We hold these truths to be self-evident…" Other countries struggle to establish governments upon those same fundamental truths—truths designed by intelligently derived Deism.

Self-evident truth is the absolute foundation of Deism. It is the bedrock of reason, conscience, intuition, experience, aesthetic, emotion, and every other human faculty. Individually, it is the grounding of spirituality. Collectively, it is the keystone of democracy.

Upholding truth begins by filing myths in the folder labeled Myth. From a Deist perspective, the intellectual battle today between neo-Darwinian materialist atheism and religious fundamentalism is as mythic as their respective tenets, but those myths, parading as truth, jeopardize a democracy based on truth. Though academically their differences amount to a local feud between two clans sniping with rusted muskets, because profiteers continue to wage sophisticated wars constructed upon genocidal ideals promoted by those two feuding clans, the feud must be ended.

If perpetuation of those myths—lying—by intellectuals who know better could light the fuse of horrendous oppression and suffering worldwide that even children know could explode into nuclear holocaust, if it doesn't first obliterate Earth's ecosystem, isn't it the responsibility of those intellectuals to tell the truth, loudly, articulately, so the whole world can hear? Shouldn't intellectuals critical of their deliberately misleading colleagues out them with the truth?

The fact is that not all scientists are neo-Darwinian, materialist, or atheist; not all the religious are fundamentalist or submissively allegiant to any organized religion. Many scientists and religionists are technically deists—they believe that a transcending intelligence created our intelligently designed universe and are open-minded if not skeptical about the unproven tenets of science and religion.

The timidity of this silent majority is due in part to legal actions taken against many professors and schoolteachers, who as public employees are currently denied their right to free speech (unlike those *really* loud-mouth public employees, politicians), thanks to a distorted interpretation of the constitutional clause forbidding promotion of religion by the state. The Left has protected the distortion to prevent fundamentalist intrusion into education. But the hands-off hush-hush don't push religion stance toward Darwinians and religionists mystifies and validates those myths. Allowing open debate and expression of opinion in a classroom is not the same as promoting religion. Discussion of the merits of Darwinism and fundamentalism would promote truth, which would certainly benefit the open-minded truth-seeking of commonsense democracy.

Deists seek to critique deception for the sake of truth and the peace truth naturally fosters. Simply by speaking up, Deists can muster allies to truth and peace, in and beyond academia. The truth I'm speaking of is of course a metaphysical concern, a matter of universal morality that can be advocated objectively and is experienced subjectively. Peace is simply the state of moral people getting along—both cause and effect of a working democracy. Obviously not everyone is motivated by truth, peace, or any version of morality. Ideally, laws protect the morally motivated from the perverted morals of sociopaths and nonexistent morals of psychopaths, who according to the experts have no conscience at all.

Outside the walls of academia, Deism appeals to many people these days because it avoids the defensive emotionalism of authoritarian absolutism that even in polite society gags its children at sunrise and pelts the neighbors before lunch. Although materialism and fundamentalism have succeeded in establishing themselves as monolithic institutions, their truth-claims and methods of conveying them are challenged more and more by ordinary people, as much for the sake of common decency as in the spirit of old-fashioned honest freethinking.

Materialists and fundamentalists continue to spar, each side asserting its thoroughly *disproven* theories as absolute fact. Although the terms *theory* and *fact* are not synonymous, under the thumb of absolutism, custom has legitimized conflation of those terms if they represent concepts within the domains of science or religion. Deism, on the other hand, stresses the critical distinction between theory and fact.

The theory of Darwinism and religious doctrines today are accepted as truth not because people arrived at those conclusions after careful thought. They are traditions received from certain scientists or clerics who presented those assumptions as fact. We're taught to trust those authorities to be correct, or at least honest, but scientists and clerics are human beings, and even neo-Darwinian and fundamentalist professionals and scholars can be, as we'll see in later chapters, neither correct nor honest. Deism leads the way in making this point, because it has no problem abandoning disproven theories and recalibrating its facts, and it doesn't balk at exposing fallacies and lies. Deism is fully invested in truth, not in perpetuation of received traditions. We Deists like our education to stress critical thinking, not indoctrination.

Fundamentalists sometimes argue that truth transcends mundane fact—truth meaning *their* truth. I've heard people say, "If God said that 2+2=5, I would believe God." Leaving behind the issue of how one would know that God *said* something, if the Creator God is the source of truth and the source of reality understood as fact, how can truth and fact contradict each other? They can't. Even God can't cook the books, not even for TV evangelists or rightwing politicians. Though transcendent truth might supersede mundane fact (as in, spiritual afterlife superseding physical death), it can never *contradict* it. Transcendental truth and space-time truth are always part of Truth. One never excludes the other— evidence, in fact, that God is a natural God who is good in being consistent.

Like fundamentalists, Darwinians pretend that the theories they posit as facts are the truth, the whole truth, and nothing but the truth. Period. And by truth they mean reality. One might ask, which is more arrogant, the proclamation of fundamentalism: "Our truth is *the* truth because God said so, directly to us," or the assumption of scientific materialism: "Our facts *are* reality which is *the* truth, because we said so"?

Deism is a religion that pursues truth-as-such, meaning all the facets of facts and their nuanced implications, physical, mental, and spiritual. Deists acknowledge that theories are not facts, even if they might in time prove to be factual; that accepted facts (like, the sun revolves around the earth) are not necessarily truth; that sometimes new evidence necessitates tweaking or abandoning a cherished theory or established fact. We humans can ask whether a fact is true because there is a difference between fact and truth. An accepted fact can be tentative, like the *theory* that space-time is curved, or that the speed of light is the absolute speed limit of the universe; or an accepted fact can be self-evident, like 2+2=4, or yes does not equal no. Truth is the goal of the open-minded. Deist freethinkers, who are not afraid to change their minds, are those truly seeking objective truth. In fact, we Deists relish changing our minds, because that means we have discovered new facts or have been persuaded of new perspectives that move us closer to the truth. Deists, not religious authoritarians, truly seek God, the God of truth, not the God of 2+2=5. Being static, authoritarianism atrophies. Organic and alive, Deism perpetually grows.

Being open-minded doesn't mean giving equal time to absurdities. 2+2 will never equal 5; exploitation will never elevate society. It's irrational to sanction any form of uncritical faith in Darwinian natural selection or in biblical literalism and the so-called historical Jesus (or other god), if only because the intense, sustained efforts to support such claims, scientific or religious, remain utterly fruitless. Extremist dogmas of Darwinian atheism and religious myth are equally ludicrous. Even a staunch freethinker cannot in good conscience tolerate egregious error in deference to Everyman's right to his own preposterous opinion.

We Deists never attempt to enforce our beliefs—with this one caveat: Each person is entitled to his or her opinion as long as it is sensible, i.e., not nonsensical. Permitting nonsense presented as fact empowers a lie. Our motto is: Truth must be embraced; or, truth must not be shunned. We counteract nonsense not with violence but with rational discourse. We prefer that debates be friendly, but when opponents won't permit that, we insist that they be honest. Deism upholds truth for its own sake, but also for the sake of that high level of freedom that facilitates individual self-actualization, and for the sake of protecting each other from the injury of lies.

Deism as philosophy and practice provides the simplest, surest means to anyone's essential authenticity. Our fundamental ethic is simple: That which benefits is good, that which harms is not good to varying degrees, the greatest degree of harm being evil. Within that definition there is wiggle room for discussion—the Deist's forte. But a Deist is not an exclusionary rationalist. We are multi-rational in that we consult all our faculties, not just reason, in our quest for truth, and of course it's our duty to act ethically upon our findings.

Unlike traditional religion, Deism is a multi-rational naturalism rooted in the inherent and acquired knowledge of the transcendent, immanent Creator, the Natural God—transcendent in being necessarily outside Creation and immanent in being actively engaged ("present") in the perpetual process of creation. As with other religionists, for us, space-time reality includes a spiritual dimension. How pervasive that dimension is and what it consists of is subject to debate. We relish debate. Debate engages us in rigorous thought, and thought leads to wisdom. We don't believe in the lazy dogmatic "special revelation" of traditional religion or "received truth" of New Age science. God's Creation, Nature itself, perpetually reveals truth that imparts knowledge that matures into wisdom, spiritual and secular. Some revelations come easy; others require hard work. But for those of us who love the quest for truth, work is play. Deists try to ask the right questions. Why are we alive? What is the meaning and purpose of life, and of *my* life? Is there an afterlife?

THE SPIRIT OF LIBERTY

For as long as we humans have been asking ourselves profound questions, we've been proposing answers. Some say that life is meaningless, and when you're dead, you're dead. Others assume that life is a test. Still others see life as a series of reincarnations that take us toward some ultimate transcendence (to *what* is subject for speculation). Many people sense that life is a practice of soul creation, or perhaps soul refinement. The truth is that we just don't know for sure. But that doesn't mean we can't guess correctly, or that rational speculation isn't itself meaningful.

Like many, I believe that life is a process of self-creation that is really self-manifestation. The process of self-creation is fostered best in a highest-functioning democracy, where people are free to explore the most beneficial possibilities for themselves in the most nurturing environment.

Perhaps the greatest revelation is our revealing ourselves to ourselves through our overt choices and our natural proclivities that express our innate decisions to be what we are. What's interesting to me is how difficult it is for many people to believe in themselves as free self-creations. We are so aware of how profoundly our experience and environment mold us that we find it hard to accept that we have anything substantial to do with our being what we are. Most people find it easier to have faith in impossible miracles and "the devil made me do it" than to believe in their own freedom.

But there have always been enough strong-willed freethinkers shaking their shackles that most of the rest of us must admit the possibility that we do have at least that much free will. I find it a compelling proof of free will that even many of those who don't believe in it will fight to the death to preserve the least semblance of it.

Deists believe in free will. Our freedom is limited, clearly, but often the limitation strengthens the will to be free. The extent to which we are free is one measure of our humanness. I can be shackled and still exert my free will mentally, emotionally, and spiritually. I can be crushed via mind control and torture without succumbing to the quality of evil that crushes me. And even if I can be forced to succumb, my programmed "will" is against my will.

Ultimately, freedom is a spiritual imperative. A person who passively conforms to external pressure is not a free spirit. Is such a doormat even fully human? Isn't a fundamental difference between humans and other animals our freedom to choose in accordance with our common sense, the consensus of all our innate faculties?

And doesn't it make sense that only those choices that are reasonable are truly free and good? There is no freedom and no authentic goodness in accepting what others program you to accept. Why be a mockingbird when you can be a free, creative spirit? It might seem reasonable to choose evil to benefit oneself, but such a choice isn't ultimately reasonable if one's selfish attainments weaken the infrastructure that makes selfish attainment possible, as in, say, exploiting workers or subjugating nations. The benefits of evil are always tentative and transitory and carry their own inherent harms; the wealthy, for instance, live in fear of losing their wealth and never know for sure who loves them just for their money or who would stab them in the back for a crumb of the pie. If there is a God who is good and just, if there is even the remote possibility that there is an afterlife, then choosing evil is never ultimately rational.

The ideal human is free in rationally choosing the good. This is the definition of a purely natural human according to Deism as I understand it. A democracy functions as the highest level of association among responsible humans whose rights of life, liberty, pursuit of happiness, and truth are legally ensured and in every way protected. A citizen has the right to own property and even great wealth, but not at the expense of others. A healthy democracy differentiates between wealth and exploitation; a failing democracy conflates them, and greed prevails.

What does it say about an individual human life, what does it reveal about the human *spirit*, when mankind's history highlights war and political intrigue, power-over and greed? What does it say about collective humanity when history records civilization's perennial struggle to shuck the shackles of selfishness embodied by religious and economic overlords? Why is it that even for us noble animals nothing ever changes? Still the struggle continues; we are forever driven to be free of our oppressors.

It's an ancient strategy for religious and secular elites to join forces, even to merge into one divine-right regime, in order to subjugate and exploit humanity's exuberance that naturally freely manifests through advancements in the humanities, arts, and sciences. Remarkably, despite eons of outrageous oppression, the human spirit could never be quashed. Instead, we adaptable creatures have settled as comfortably as possible into the million tiny rooms that constitute the larger institutional edifice. The evil irony has always been that without the oppressive edifice, the rooms—our homes, our lives—would not exist. But even though we have successfully adapted to the limits on our freedom, we know there's a better way to exist than to subsist at the mercy of power-lords. We Deists believe that it is every human being's sacred duty to bring about that progress.

PROMOTING THE COMMON GOOD: THE SACRED DUTY OF DEMOCRACY

We Deists accept that God exists, that God creates, that Creation is a perpetual process, that humans were created to be a distinct species, whether all at once or over a long period, and that among our distinctive features are our sophisticated faculties and the free will to use them.

We also recognize that moral conscience is clearly a faculty as natural as reason or intuition. We assume that moral conscience was bestowed by a transcendently good God and that the natural, healthy growth of the individual includes moral progress developed through pursuit of the good.

But what is good? Philosophers have argued over a definitive definition for eons, but there has always been a consensus about certain features. Sadism, for instance, is never morally good, even in the minds of most sadists. The opposite of sadism is benevolence, the impetus and essence of moral good in the opinion of most people. From a practical Deist perspective, the good is that which most benefits, which includes that which most eliminates suffering. Benefit is the consequence of benevolence and unnecessary suffering the consequence of cruelty (unnecessary suffering as opposed to, say, the pain of surgery and side-effects of chemo).

Our Founders believed in a Creator that entitles us to an equal station in life, separate from oppressors. This principle, they asserted, is encoded in the laws of nature. Today we understand that the principle of cooperation is even encoded in our DNA. Existence *is* the perfectly choreographed yet perpetually fluid interconnection of all things. Human society works best when every person has a truly equal opportunity to achieve life, liberty, and the pursuit of happiness to the fullest. This is a spiritual, not a mercenary, agenda.

Although mechanistic Darwinism and authoritarian religion appear to be mortal enemies, under the surface their fusion constitutes a perverse church-state regime that enforces the worship of one unnatural, tyrannical god. Yes, one god—the god that sneers at human beings. We are windup dolls at the mercy of our materialistic makeup or are fallen clay dolls at the mercy of our ancestors' shattering. It doesn't make much difference which worldview you subscribe to: Human beings aren't good. But if we aren't good because there is no inherent goodness (Darwinism) or because we are built with an inherent design flaw that makes us necessarily not good (religion), doesn't that contradict the Darwinist's claim that life is good, so good it's worth struggling for, doesn't that contradict any religious claim that Providence is consistently benevolent in *not* creating innocents bad? Darwinists and religionists agree that human beings should be good. Why? Even Darwinists agree that the rape, torture, and murder of a child is evil.

We know this because conscience tells us that this is so. Is conscience learned or inherent? Clearly it's inherent, except perhaps in a psychopath. Is good behavior also inherent? Deism says the potential for good behavior is inherent, but the good is something one must choose. The potential for good in people and the freedom to choose are both evidence of a good Creator of that good.

God's goodness is of course categorically different than our own. God's goodness is perfect and absolute, or so we assume, because goodness exists as goodness; abstract goodness exists as concrete goodness, which could only be created by a moral being of transcending goodness.

Human goodness is derivative. We don't create goodness, we choose it—we choose to embrace it or shun it. In order to be good we have to choose to be good. A good God would not create us evil; a good God would not even create us necessarily good. Either way, we would be automatons. A truly good God would create us *free to choose* to be good or to be evil. A creature that is self-propelled to create itself—now that's an impressive creation! It is the gift of our perpetual freedom to choose rationally to be *not that but this* that makes us seem at least a little created in the image of God.

Who doesn't think that freedom to choose is good?

Well, Darwinists and fundamentalists. Darwinists think there's no good at all, just temporary survival for the sake of propagation, and fundamentalists think humans can never be good, just co-dependently reliant on a good God.

While Darwinian materialists and religious fundamentalists paint themselves into their stuffy fatalistic corners, Deism steps outside into the awesome perfection of an intelligently designed universe. Deism is the *real* Good News. Even Nature's seeming imperfections contribute to the perfection that nurtures human free will. Because this makes sense, throughout the ages we humans have acknowledged the good God's involvement in the meaning and purpose of our lives. Many people have sought to get to know that God better, some motivated by respect, some by curiosity, some by a sensate awareness of connection experienced as oneness or emotional bond registered as love. This is the impetus of religion before it becomes organized and misrepresented as myths and superstitions. This is also the catalyst of democracy.

The concept of a personal relationship with God is a perfectly natural emergence. Some people pray to that God to get things, like security or money. But many people pray because they sense the Presence of God, by whatever name, and want a more intimate connection.

Some Deists don't believe in the efficacy of prayer, which in their view is irrational and unnatural. Many Deists do believe in Providence—in the vein of, say, Deist George Washington—and see no reason why prayers can't be answered in a form that doesn't violate God-ordained laws of nature. Answers to prayer could occur in the wiggle rooms (the "gaps" of "freedom" per recent mathematics and physics) where chance and choice and change take place, especially that square footage reserved for human free will. I might, for instance, get guidance on a career choice, but if I ask for the power to step out my front door and walk to the moon, it's not going to happen. Too often people throw hissy fits when God fails to grant all the requests—aka "promises"—on the prayer list taped to the fridge. That's the kind of disrespectful, ignorant, arrogant entitlement that makes a Deist sneeze.

Frustrated pray-ers respond in a way that manifests their true Self. Some try to get what they want anyway, by taking matters into their own hands. The consequence could be good or evil depending on the person's motives and goals. Good people strive for the good. Selfish people strive to exploit the good via tyranny, on a grand or minute scale.

Our Founders believed that any form of tyranny unnaturally transgresses Providential benevolence expressed through Nature. History records that many of the Founders prayed to Providence for guidance in securing freedom from British rule and in establishing a nation that ensured freedom, equality, and justice. A Deist prayer today could be this simple: "God bless America and all the world. May we live in peace."

Our commonsense Founders understood that progress of humanity involves progress of societies of progressing individuals. If they were alive today, the authors of America would surely warn us that Darwinist and fundamentalist ideologies, which justify elitist despotism, necessarily thwart progress of individuals and societies. Any individual or group— king, dictator, church, or corporate oligarchy—seeking to destroy progressive, creative development of universal human potential is as clinically psychopathic as Ted Bundy or Jim Jones. Ruthless violence or subtle brainwashing—the goal is always power-over, the method always spiritual terrorism. Collective human happiness is not on their to-do list, even if they pretend that it is.

At the heart of every crisis is the spiritual imperative to benefit humanity and the world that sustains us. This imperative is truly spiritual, even for those who consider themselves agnostic or atheist or utterly disinterested in or even disgusted by anything smacking of religion. It's the centrality of spirituality, our profound sense of core inner Self vested with value and purpose, that has allowed the feuding atheist and fundamentalist clans to convince the masses that their myth of either-or ideals divides the whole world into two camps, Darwinists or fundamentalists, and that the other side is fully responsible for all the falsehoods and unrest. But each side and the battle between them are equally guilty as charged.

A cloud of psychosis has settled over the Earth. Too many people in charge are psychotic, too many of their machines programmed to attack with ice-cold precision, too many of their institutions, assuming a life of their own, calculate the next assault with the empty, heartless gaze of the predator. American wars today are fought not for democratic ideals, but for the corporate aristocracy, a cartel of self-centered, callous, remorseless gold-gluttons who glibly disregard the moral bonds that promote social harmony. Aristocrats recruit idealistic serfs for their armies, making the aristocrats themselves indirect killers hidden from blame. The aristocrats' battle plans are brute, calculating, rational conquest of fellow human beings. Because that looks bad, which is unacceptable to any psychopath ego worth its salt, the aristocrats lie, brazenly, breezily spinning their fables, shamelessly gloating behind their smiley-face masks.

I picture the whole apparatus that feeds psychopaths as a giant octopus, the classic Leviathan perhaps, its long preying arms lined with suckers tightly grasping everything in its path. With its every move, each discrete arm participates in one coordinated task of ruthless selfishness. Its complex coldblooded eyes glare from a head only slightly demarcated from the body of arms joined at the center, the mouth, where sharp horny beaks drill shells and file-like radula rasp away flesh. When the body squirts ink, each arm is shielded. This diabolical god of the dark watery underworld of our nightmares represents any entity—from psycho killer to the Corporate Nation—that embodies the antithesis of "love your neighbor as yourself," the essence of Deist democracy.

Who can escape such a monster? The answer, of course, is that *we* can. But slaying such a beast means slaying the predatory impulse within ourselves, within each other, and that takes effort, that takes an overhaul of human culture parading as human nature.

Thus far in our evolution, democracy has emerged as the ultimate maximizer of benefit and minimizer of harm, at least in theory. No democracy is ever perfect, because the morals of individual citizens range from righteous to wicked. America's democracy has always been deficient, because there have always been morally deficient citizens who elbow their way to positions of power for the purpose of accommodating their selfishness.

Individual or group self-interest isn't a social problem unless it violates the rights of others. Democracy protects us all from violations. Deism proposes true democracy as the surest route away from exploitation, the defining sin of elitism.

Overt psychopaths inflict damage like a bullet to the head. But covert psychopathy grows like a cancer, at times even spreads like a lovely poisonous wildflower blossoming in the garden. Evil interpreted as good is far more dangerous to society than a blatantly treacherous psycho-killer. But though society provides a sophisticated apparatus for coping with the overt psychopath, it barely addresses the dangers wreaked by covert psychopathy.

A true democracy is the only safe haven that can equally protect us all from psychopathy. It is the duty of Deist democrats, therefore, to shine the light on the feuding dark lords covertly thwarting democracy: Darwin's noble savage, and the reactionary fundamentalist hunting him down.

CHAPTER 3

TRANSCENDING THE "HISTORICAL JESUS" MEME

Remember when you believed in Santa Claus? Not the scary parade Santa; the *real* Santa Claus, with awesome, magical benevolence grander than a great-grandpa of Superman or Harry Potter. The Santa Claus even grownups revered with extended, very expensive celebrations of their own.

Early on, Mom assured you that the grubby fake Santa at the mall was really a stand-in elf—no wait, elves were short and had pointy ears; he was a human stand-in, the middle-school music teacher to be exact, because it being so near the delivery date, the real Santa Claus and his elves were very busy in the North Pole putting the psychedelic decals on your new Schwinn bike. Oh, you were getting a bike, not the telescope you'd put at the top of your list (a bike wasn't even on the list). That's because, Dad explained later as you unwrapped your helmet, the telescope went to a starving child in Africa to help him search for food. (Mom groaned.) But couldn't Santa give you both telescopes? Guess you weren't good enough, Grandma chimed in with a (you thought rather sadistic) wink.

Though a lesser god, perhaps, your god was no less genuine than the great deities of classical mythology. It's no coincidence that the festival commemorating the god Santa—or if you prefer, the godlike Santa—coincides with another god's holiday. More than a thousand years before Christ, the Italians honored Saturn (for whom the planet Saturn and Saturday were named), god of sowing and seed, with the seven-day Saturnalia, which traversed the solstice and concluded on December 25, the beginning of the new year. From the Saturnalia came Christmas feasting, candle burning, gift exchanges, and halls decked with garlands of holly, which the Romans considered sacred to sun gods as a symbol of good will and joy, and additionally to Saturn, of health and happiness. Christmas lights and ornaments derived from the Roman custom of placing decorative candles in live trees and hanging small masks of Bacchus, god of wine, fruitfulness, and vegetation, on pine trees during the festival.

Many people today assume that the ancient primitives naively believed in a literal god Saturn. As a whole, the ancients, of course, were no more or less naïve than we moderns. Many of our spiritual ancestors did believe in a literal Saturn, but at least by the time of the Greeks, many ancients, especially the well-educated, understood the named gods and their celebrations to be representational—of *what* being as subject to speculation as such queries remain today. But like Saturn, pretty much every god everywhere was a natural god—a god embedded in nature and usually controlling some jurisdiction of natural phenomenon. Just like today, enlightened ancients understood the gods to be poetic, fictional, analogous representations of the fundamental human quest to understand and explain the profound mysteries of nature—if they weren't created just for entertainment value. Now as then, manmade deities aesthetically express our intuited awareness of the spiritual dimension of existence and its connection to us humans. Now as then, some people take those representations literally. Now as then, high priests exploit religious representations for power and profit.

Because belief in deities, mythic or otherwise, has always been a core human value, it's not surprising that a god like Santa has persisted into the twenty-first century. In America, at least, the myth of the jolly old North Pole toymaker who bestows gifts under Christmas trees of the good and deposits coal in chimney stockings of the bad provides parents with an empowering conduct-control device that makes the Santa story "good for kids." It makes sense that most parents want their brood to believe in a real Santa for as long as possible. Besides, the clockwork gaiety allows adults a guaranteed yearly escape into the nostalgia of childhood.

Back when you were six or nine years old, no-Santa was a hard concept to wrap your mind around. Maybe you even engaged in verbal combat with opponents of the Santa fact-claim. There was a Santa, all right, you were absolutely sure of that, and you substantiated your faith convincingly.

But then one day, the big moment of revelation, a trusted friend or big sister or grandpa persuasively announced: There's no Santa Claus. You were stunned. Or maybe you already had your suspicions—the stash of presents in the basement closet, sightings of Mom and Dad arranging the doll house and football under the tree.

Weren't you lied to? Not exactly, you were told. The Santa story embodied the Christmas spirit of righteous giving. But Santa was kid stuff. No-Santa ushered you through the firewall between childhood and the coveted rank of adolescence. If you were Christian, the focus shifted to the Baby Jesus.

Eventually you were embarrassed by manger scenes—still too kid-stuff, even your wellness art project, *Still Life with Smoking Camels*, for which you received an A. You moved on to virgin birth, miracles, resurrection, the end of the world, and if you were Catholic, rosary beads and saints.

You questioned, you doubted: Were you really guilty of an original sin? Were the wafer and wine really transmuted into the literal body and blood of Christ? Was blasphemy really an unforgivable sin that your beloved drunken uncle had recently committed? Were people who had never heard of Christ really going to burn in hell for all eternity? Were people who doubted that the world was flat really once hanged as heretics? Were women with moles really tortured and burned as witches who copulated with devils—millions of witches, for centuries?

Once you learned that Christmas was a calculated blend of manger scene and Santa legend spiced with elements from the Roman Saturnalia and other ancient religious festivals, you wondered, what *wasn't* just childish superstition? As a twenty-first century adult, you've been politely admonished by people you respect to Question Authority. You've been tutored to use your own God-given noggin. You've observed firsthand the dangers of imprudent belief. Now, at the crossroads, a seductive whisper sings: Imagine there's no Jesus.

I wonder if you can.

Many Americans can't. And even if they can, they're trying hard not to. And these aren't just Baby-Jesus fundamentalists, a minority of Americans. Even progressive Christians assume that the human Jesus existed, though he might not have been a miracle-working, grave-busting God. Your priest or preacher doesn't seem to think that Jesus was just an addition to the pantheon of more ancient gods and heroes. They believe—

they *want* to believe—that unlike Saturn or Santa, Jesus was an actual historical person who was born and lived at a specific time and place. That's easy enough to prove, right?

Well, not really. The very experts who teach the historical Jesus don't actually posit a historical Jesus as established *fact*. The reason is quite simple: There is absolutely no data that proves that Jesus ever lived.

Hard to believe, isn't it? I know it has been for me. I, too, want there to have been a Jesus. What person, actual or fictional, has surpassed him in spiritual wisdom and integrity? The deep human need to believe that such a heroic figure could exist makes it difficult to let go of, or even to closely scrutinize, the Jesus meme.

But for the sake of truth, we must. Regardless of what you've been told, the *fact* is that there is absolutely no proof that the actual human Jesus ever existed. There's not even much circumstantial evidence, and none that is reliable.

Of course, there's plenty of evidence that a Jesus *myth* existed, and still exists. Because there is no information about Jesus dating from the era in which Jesus supposedly lived, Jesus scholars resort to working their way backward from much later mythic material about Jesus, mainly the four Gospels, to the "historical Jesus," which, as it turns out, is like working backward from *The Odyssey* to Helen of Troy or the goddess Athena, or like proving macroevolution with the fossil record.

FAITH, OR BLIND FAITH, IN JESUS

But then people who believe in a talking snake, people who accept that a woman turned into a pillar of salt, people who are positive that a man lived in the belly of a whale, that a stick turned into a snake, that the sun stood still and moved backward; believers who never doubt that God impregnated a virgin with a human-god or a just-god, or that a man ascended into the clouds in a flaming chariot, or that God spoke through a perpetually burning bush; the faithful who smile knowing that their good God inflicted sorcerous plagues on innocent subjects of a pharaoh whose repentance God himself blocked so He could harden the pharaoh's heart, the same beneficent God who commanded his most faithful servant to murder his own son, and only pulled him back at the last moment, and called this sadistic trick a "test"; Bible believers who never blink asserting that food rained down daily from the desert sky, that a man's donkey spoke, that a dead man's bones revived other dead people, or that dead men were called back from tombs and even ascended bodily into heaven—these people, schooled by teachers who know better, find it easy to believe in a tenuously hypothetical historical Jesus.

A lot of these believers, instructed by satellite evangelists or some knuckle-rapping nun, want Santa Claus and his sled of elves tossed from Christmas because they're as "pagan" as the witchcraft of Harry Potter is demonic.

These are the faithful unruffled by brain teasers such as: If Jesus was born of Mary, then Mary is his mother. If God is One, and if God (the Holy Spirit) is the father, and if Jesus is God, then Mary is both "wife" (concubine, "handmaid") and mother of Jesus and of God, making her the originating God. But if Jesus is God and if God is the Father of all mankind, then Mary is Jesus' daughter. If Mary is the daughter of God and if Jesus is the son of God, then Mary is Jesus' sister.

If Jesus is God, then the son is the father and the father is the son, which by definition is impossible, since the father is the source of the son and the son the offspring of the father. The son must be younger than the father, in which case they could not be equal, or equally eternal. Even in a realm that transcends our space-time universe, surely if God is One, God cannot be two. Here on Earth, surely if God cannot die, and if Jesus died, then Jesus cannot be God. It doesn't help most of us in the twenty-first century to call it a miracle. If God is God and Jesus is the spawn of God, Christianity is not monotheism, but another version of "pagan" polytheism.

But believers don't seem to care that logically Jesus and God cannot be the same person. Throw these contradicting verses from the Gospel of John their way (3:17; 3:34; 3:35; 5:19-20; 5:24; 6:29; 6:38; 6:57; 7:16-18; 7:28-29; 8:18; 8:28-29; 8:42-43; 8:54-55; 8:58; 10:14; 10:17; 10:18; 10:34-36; 10:38; 13:20; 15:1,5; 16:26-28; 17:20-23), and they will smile and wave as the train pulls out hauling you off to hell.

The faithful refuse to grasp that if Jesus were a manifestation, aspect, or "person" of God, then God is the supreme egomaniac, giving birth to himself, praying to himself, worshipping himself, glorifying himself, even committing suicide for himself. (It's even worse if he murdered his innocent "Son.")

If God is the father of Jesus, why do the literally-perfect Gospels offer human genealogies that include the line of Joseph? And why are they different? Matthew 1:17 says, "So all the generations from Abraham to David are fourteen generations; and from David to the deportation to Babylon, fourteen generations; and from the deportation to Babylon to the Messiah, fourteen generations." That's a total of forty-two generations. Luke's list goes all the way back to Adam, the son of God, but from Abraham forward, Luke lists fifty-seven generations, not forty-two. Matthew and Luke are close in their list, starting with Abraham and ending with David, but Luke lists fifteen generations, not fourteen. The first fourteen for each are the same except that from Hezron to Boaz, Matthew lists Aram, Aminadab, Nahshon, and Salmon, but Luke lists Arni, Admin, Amminadab, Nahshon, and Sala. From that point on, the genealogies are completely different.

The Gospels are steeped in self-contradictions to which believers in a God-breathed Bible pay no mind. For instance, the Gospel of John claims that "No one has ascended into heaven except the one who descended from heaven, the Son of Man," but the Old Testament says in 2 Kings that "Elijah ascended in a whirlwind into heaven," and Genesis claims that "Enoch walked with God; then he was no more, because God took him," and Hebrews adds, "By faith Enoch was taken so that he did not experience death; and 'he was not found, because God had taken him.'" And if Jesus was born in a manger, did he really "descend" from heaven in a unique way? What kind of guy was Joseph to buy his fiancé's story that she was still a virgin and that God was the father of her child? Or maybe to save face for his own indiscretion, *he* spread that rumor.

All Christians know about the significant moment when Jesus tells his disciples that he will suffer and die. Christians consider the Transfiguration to be another extraordinary, one-time-only event, which, according to Matthew and Mark, occurs six days after Jesus foretells his suffering, or was that eight days after Jesus foretells his suffering, as Luke claims?

The presence of Jesus' betrayer is revealed *during* the Last Supper according to Matthew and Mark but *after* the Last Supper in Luke. Mark says that Jesus is tempted in the wilderness and later John is arrested, but in Luke, John is arrested and later Jesus is tempted in the wilderness. Jesus begins his ministry after the arrest of John the Baptist according to Mark but before the arrest of John the Baptist per the gospel writer's narrative voice, "John" (the gospel writer's real name is unknown).

After the feeding of the 5000, do Jesus and the disciples go to Gennesaret as Mark claims, or to Capernaum, as it says in John? Answering that Jesus fed 5000 twice, or that he went to both Gennesaret and Capernaum, doesn't help if each gospel is read as a whole or melded into a single narrative. Laying out the Gospels side by side reveals a mountain of contradictory chronology and logistics that simply cannot be logically resolved unless Jesus lived (lives) in parallel universes, which I suspect will be apologists' next line of defense.

For Christians, the crucifixion is one of the most important events in the Bible. Maybe believers in a literal Bible don't care whether Jesus' robe was scarlet as per Matthew, or purple as it says in Mark and John. Does it matter whether the robe was put on Jesus during his trial (John) or after Pilate delivered him to be crucified (Matthew and Mark)? Mark says that Jesus was crucified at the third hour, Luke says it was before the sixth hour, and John says it was after the sixth hour. They can't all be right.

Who first arrived at the empty tomb after the resurrection? Was it Mary Magdalene and the other Mary (Matthew)? Mary Magdalene, Mary the mother of James, and Salome (Mark)? "The women" (Luke)? Mary Magdalene alone (John)?

When did she/they first arrive at the tomb? When it was still dark (John), as day was dawning (Matthew), at early dawn (Luke), when the sun had already risen (Mark)? Again, they can't all be right.

Who first sees Jesus? Mary Magdalene and the other Mary (Matthew), Mary Magdalene alone (Mark and John), or Cleopas and another follower of Jesus, and possibly Peter at the same time (Luke)?

The betrayal of Jesus by Judas is one of the most widely explicated stories in the Gospels. But what happens to Judas after the betrayal? According to Matthew, Judas returns to the priests the thirty pieces of silver he got for turning Jesus over to the authorities, then hangs himself; the priests use the silver to buy the potter's field as a place to bury foreigners, hence its name Field of Blood (Matt. 27:3-10). But according to the Acts account, Judas buys the field with the silver; and falling headlong on the field, he bursts open in the middle and all his bowels gush out, hence the name Field of Blood (Acts 1:16-20). Preachers pick the version that suits their sermon.

Preachers quote Jesus as if his words were absolute fact, never mentioning that those exact words taken from one gospel are a bit different in another. Theologies are built upon the exact wording of simple Jesus sayings, and upon those systems of belief, thought is dictated, feeling manipulated, natural spirituality quashed because of an interpretation of the precise meaning of a sentence or phrase that might be presented with different wording and meaning in another text. Do preachers really believe there were stenographers meticulously writing down Jesus' conversations word for word at all, much less with a hundred percent accuracy? Yet congregants are taught to fear misquoting as if that were tantamount to driving in the crucifixion nails. Superstitious reverence for magical words substitutes for sacred reverence for God's Creation; text worship replaces worship of God; blind faith transgresses responsible common sense. Congratulations: your congregants are now dummied down, ripe for your exploitation, or someone else's.

These very few examples of incongruities from among the multitudes highlight one very significant problem for serious scholars: With so many different versions of when and where and under what circumstances critical events occurred, how can we know for certain which ones if any are accurate? If early Christians didn't even know the easy particulars concerning the birth and crucifixion of Jesus, why should we trust the far-fetched magical aspects as facts? The inaccuracy of significant historical details does not definitively prove that Jesus never existed. But scholars have proven beyond a shadow of a doubt that the aura surrounding him was airbrushed in by generations of believers who never even met the man. And the list of fallacies, contradictions, and erroneous facts, not counting apologists' contorted exegeses, is longer than Pinocchio's nose.

RESURRECTING THE JESUS MYTH

For centuries, very sensible intellectuals and ordinary folk have doubted the Christian stories of a miracle god-man who rose from the dead. Even the Gospel of Matthew notes that in tandem with reports of resurrection there were rumors already circulating that followers of Jesus had stolen the body. The Greco-Roman philosopher Celsus insinuates that because Jesus was born a bastard, which wasn't very noble, the writer of Luke tossed in the virgin Mary census/manger story with its overkill peasant-pleasing details of magi led by a magical star and shepherds awestruck by angels, all particulars lifted from popular regional myths. Miracles, divine incarnation, even the existence of someone named Jesus were disputed right and left. Governments—the Romans, for instance—early on outlawed Christian superstitions along with all the others. Challenges to the veracity of Christianity continued throughout the centuries, though in many quarters, the heresy of doubt was viciously repressed. Though many great thinkers prior to the Dark Ages assumed that a teacher named Jesus had existed, many considered the subsequent Jesus religion to be part of the folkish tradition of myths, legends, and superstitions prevalent among the masses. To correct this "misconception," bishops devised creeds instituting their magical God-Jesus, who was tortured and executed and who rose from the dead. After centuries of coping with doubting Thomases, Dark-Age inquisitors were forced to torture and execute detractors.

There had always been critics of the Church's assumption of divine authority. But as the Church allied and sometimes fused with State, begging to differ with orthodoxy led to dire consequences that forced many critics to bite their tongues. But the rumblings continued.

When critics are silenced, abuse runs rampant. Symbols of spiritual perfection, the clergy became infamous for the multitude of their sins. Eventually Luther challenged corrupt clerical power by suggesting that the Bible, as God's Word, was the ultimate religious authority. Luther's innocuous presumption sparked the bloodbath we now refer to as the Reformation. For centuries, defenders of the Church as Christ on earth clashed with advocates of the divinely inspired Bible, each camp claiming divine right until Church and Bible each became God in the minds of their respective believers. These twin Bible-as-God, Pope-as-God idolatries held sway until both Church and Bible lost considerable credibility during the Enlightenment. Twentieth century fundamentalism had to be created to reestablish the authority of the "God-breathed" Bible. Conservative propaganda succeeded in generating Christian faith in the divine Word despite continuation of the ongoing commonsense critique reaching back to the genesis of the primitive Jesus-religion itself.

THE CURRENT QUEST TO EXCAVATE JESUS FROM THE RUBBLE OF MYTH

For many of us ex-believers today, serious skepticism about the Santa Jesus—the one that performed miracles and rose from the dead—commenced once we could no longer trust the ultimate authority on the matter, the Bible. With the exception of a few teachers at fundamentalist colleges, all scholars associated with seminaries and university religion departments the world over agree that the Bible is not literally word-for-word perfect. In fact, it's steeped with inaccuracies. There are hundreds if not thousands of discrepancies within the texts themselves, besides numerous incongruities between the biblical historical accounts and external historical records and scientific facts.

To protect their preconceived cherished assumptions that Jesus existed and that the Gospels are admissible evidence, God-breathed Bible apologists torque the facts to "explain" how their sacred book was indeed divinely dictated, directly or telepathically. Progressive Jesus scholars instead try to untangle a few strands of "probable" facts about Jesus from the wildly incongruous Gospel narratives.

But it doesn't work. There are no probable facts. On the contrary; considering all the Gospel materials with the requisite scrupulous objectivity, critical-historians concede that the existence of any person resembling any version of the Jesus presented in the Gospels is *extraordinarily improbable*. Yet those same scholars persist in their quest for the historical Jesus as if that Jesus were a demonstrable fact.

For example, in *The Historical Jesus: The Life of a Mediterranean Jewish Peasant*, prominent Jesus scholar John Dominic Crossan begins his Prologue with this startling disclaimer: "Historical Jesus research is becoming something of a scholarly bad joke." He chooses to view as positive "the number of competent and even eminent scholars producing pictures of Jesus at wide variance with one another." In the Prologue's second paragraph, Crossan offers an illustration of the "present problem": an address by Daniel J. Harrington to the Catholic Biblical Association that included "a short description of seven different images of Jesus that have been proposed by scholars in recent years," namely, Jesus as a political revolutionary, as a magician, as a Galilean charismatic, as a Galilean rabbi, as a Hillelite or proto-Pharisee, as an Essene, and as an eschatological prophet.

In the third paragraph, Crossan acknowledges that "the plurality is enough to underline the problem," and "that stunning diversity is an academic embarrassment. It is impossible to avoid the suspicion that historical Jesus research is a very safe place to do theology and call it history, to do autobiography and call it biography."

Crossan then notes that the "problem of multiple and discordant conclusions" requires an updated theory and method. The continuation of "cultural looting" by contemporary Jesus scholars that has ignored "scientific stratigraphy" has led to a big problem with archeological research: at the very least, the absence of the "detailed location of every item in its own proper chronological layer," meaning that "almost any conclusion can be derived from almost any object," and that gives "the distinct impression that the researcher knew the result before beginning the search." Crossan then assures the reader that he will not "add to the impression of acute scholarly subjectivity in historical Jesus research" but will "raise most seriously the problem of methodology" and follow his chosen method "most stringently."

Next, Crossan explains that his methodology will attempt an "effective synthesis" of anthropological, historical, and literary levels, acknowledging that "weakness in any element imperils the integrity and validity of the others." He promises to address "the interweaving of retention, mutation, and creation within the Jesus tradition."

He notes the books he will use as models for his study, then provides us with a list of primary texts he'll use to make his case for a historical Jesus: not surprisingly, just the four Gospels, which he calls "biographies" by "individuals all directly or indirectly connected with him and all composing within, say, seventy-five years after his death." He says "within, say," because no one knows for sure when those works were first written, and seventy-five years is a *long* time in an era of no media, printing press, or quick and easy transport, not to mention short lifespan of persons. No one knows whether any one gospel was the work of one person, or whether the gospels were written accounts taken from decades of various mutating oral traditions (the singular "oral tradition" here is misleading in that it implies a single seminal story). No one knows whether the writers were even of the same era or from the same region as Jesus. Many scholars believe that the links between Jesus and the Gospels are many and tenuous. Crossan asks offhandedly if these four sources are not better than sources for other ancient biographies. He asks rather than states, because the honest answer would be "no."

In paragraph nine, Crossan admits that "that fourfold record [the four canonical Gospels]…constitutes the literary problem." Readers who read the four texts "vertically" from beginning to end, one after another, "get a generally persuasive impression of unity, harmony, and agreement." But read horizontally, or comparatively, with similar "units" laid side by side, what "strikes one most forcefully" is the "disagreement," a wooly word often used by Jesus scholars to underplay "contradiction" and "incongruity." Then Crossan makes an astonishing admission: "By even the middle of the second century, pagan opponents, like Celsus, and Christian apologists, like Justin, Tatian, and Marcion were well aware of those discrepancies." One solution to this problem was "to reduce that plurality to unity" by either eliminating all gospels but one (take your pick) or blending them into one narrative (take your pick of unit elements).

During the last two hundred years, other gospels have been found, and rather than clarifying a portrait of Jesus, they have only added to the collection of divergent units and their elements. Studies of the four canonical Gospels admittedly do not add up to a cohesive total collection or a random sampling; they were works selected deliberately for specific reasons. Scholars have concluded that differences and discrepancies among the various gospel accounts are due to "deliberate theological interpretations of Jesus." Brazenly begging the question, Crossan takes an enormous leap of blind faith when he adds that "the continuing presence of the risen Jesus and the abiding experience of the Spirit gave the transmitters of the Jesus tradition a creative freedom we would never have dared postulate were it not forced upon us by the evidence." Even the writers of the four Gospels "are unnervingly free about omission and addition, about change, correction, or creation in their own individual accounts...subject to their own particular interpretation of Jesus. The Gospels are neither history nor biographies" but are "some individual's or community's opinion or interpretation." I.e., fiction.

Searching for an actual person named Jesus is fair enough, as fair as searching for an actual Krishna or King Arthur, but presenting Jesus *as* historical rather than hypothetical is technically dishonest. Even the ethical biblical Jesus says it's unconscionable for anyone, especially a scholar—a scribe, a Sadducee, a Pharisee—to sacrifice truth on the altar of religion.

Every biblical scholar knows that the Bible is an unreliable source of raw factual data. That doesn't mean that there are no facts in the Bible; it means that much that is in the Bible is not factual. By not factual I don't mean that it hasn't been proven to be true, or that it is symbolic; I mean that there is much biblical material presented as fact that has been *proven to be false*. I have provided a multitude of examples in *Born-Again Deist*, following the lead of the many authors writing on the subject over the course of centuries, so I won't belabor that point here. The point that I do want to stress is that the people who teach us about the Bible—from seminary professors to preachers in the pulpit to Christian bookstore apologists—know the truth about the falseness of the biblical texts yet perpetuate among the masses the "noble lie" of a true and valid Bible. From there it's easy to maintain the "pious fiction" of an actual historical Jesus.

Of course, no lie is noble, and there's nothing pious about fiction presented as fact.

Perhaps Jesus scholars don't think they are deceiving any more than Mom thought she was lying about Santa Claus. But really, do you want to be treated like a child, or do you want to know the truth? I believe that most people want truth, and that's why multitudes are ditching the church for alternative forms of spirituality, and many more are just staying with the "church club" safe-zone because it offers positive social connections for themselves and moral instruction for the kids.

As mentioned in Chapter 1, according to the 2001 American Religious Identification Survey (ARIS), between 1990 and 2001, the number of self-identified Deists grew at a rate of 717 percent, making it the fastest-growing religious classification in America. By 2008, 12 percent of Americans identified as Deist, but this figure is misleading, since surveys define Deist as someone believing in a higher power but not in a personal God. Many Deists—myself included—do believe in a personal God, but not a God of nature-violating miracles or special revelation in the Christian sense.

Since 1990 there has been a significant exodus from churches and denominations. The number of people who still considered themselves spiritual or who believed in God but not in a particular religion rose from 14.3 million or 8 percent in 1990 to 34.2 million or 15 percent by 2008. Some surveys showed even higher increases.

During the same time frame, the number of respondents who identified as Christian dropped by ten percent. No doubt that trend will accelerate as more and more Christians learn the facts, or lack of facts, about the historical Jesus. Of course, many Christians prefer to remain in denial.

Scholars who beg the question by assuming that Jesus existed, for instance, spend their time trying to dig up proof to substantiate their claim that Jesus existed. Every scholar knows that a statement begs the question when it assumes as given what it is in fact trying to prove; such circular reasoning slyly supports an assertion with the assertion itself. Among scholars, fallacies are generally proscribed, yet academia assumes the same hands-off approach toward theological distortion that the legal system until recently assumed toward clerical child molestation.

Jesus scholars' only source material is contained in the Bible, specifically the Gospels. This begs the question further in that the Gospels are contained in a book that is qualitatively unreliable and in that the Gospels themselves, being subjectively theological rather than objectively historical, are unreliable as source material for any academic contention that Jesus was a historical person. Luke is sometimes considered to be historical. But at the beginning of that gospel, the author explains up front that he is attempting to construct some kind of chronology based on numerous conflicting accounts of Jesus circulating at the time, which was long after the events supposedly occurred. Even my college undergrads know they can't use sources that are not authoritative and unbiased. Yet Jesus scholars do just that, basing their conclusions on the invalid premises that Jesus existed and that the Gospels are factual, or at least historically valid sources of facts about Jesus.

Not only are they part of an unreliable source (the Bible), the Gospels as independent sources are also more generally unreliable for several reasons: They were written long after the events recorded in the Gospels occurred and by people who were not present when and where the events took place; they were based on oral tradition, which like any oral tradition is subject to typical human interpretation and embellishment; they were written down by people intent on making faith-claims; they were written to make faith-claims not about Jesus so much as about particular "denominations," or cults, of a diffuse Jesus-religion that had evolved over decades; they were written to establish the primacy of specific faith-claims of particular Christian groups among the many Christian groups that existed at the time of writing; in order to convert nonbelievers, they incorporated entrenched beliefs: myth, legend, folklore, ritual, and wise sayings, which made Christianity more familiar and allowed converts to retain prior beliefs; they were written, edited, rewritten, revised, and rewritten over and over; the original *autographs*, the actual original written versions, no longer exist and have not existed probably since the decade when they were written; the original autographs were likely transcriptions of oral narratives and other preexistent, malleable materials; the original autographs of each of the four Gospels did not all exist at the same time; out of the many different versions circulating back in the mid- to late-fourth century C.E., a few centuries after Jesus supposedly died, only four gospels were chosen to be included in what we now call the Bible; "a few centuries after Jesus supposedly died" is a very long lapse of time in an era of camel express, no media or local libraries, and "paper" of papyrus or other volatile materials that disintegrated in less than ten years (far less if they were regularly handled); disintegrating texts were copied by the educated elite that knew how to read and write and edit and tweak; the gospels chosen out of the many circulating represented the faith-claims of elite bishops; those faith-claims were put forward to establish, by order of Roman Emperor Constantine, one orthodox position distilled from the chaos of conflicting positions; even the faith-claims of the elite bishops varied, in some respects greatly, and the selection, sometime in the distant-from-Jesus fourth century, was not unanimous or even friendly, which no doubt explains the compromise that allowed tremendous variations—aka contradictions—among the four Gospel accounts; the embarrassing contradictions were kept under wraps by maintaining the texts in languages only understood by priests and a few scholars (until very recently, Catholic Mass was still performed in Latin to protect believers from this truth of contradictions and to enhance the aura of priestly authority).

It's true that an actual Jesus *might* have existed. But there is *no reason to assume* that the Gospel accounts were based on actual events or that the people mentioned in the accounts were actual people. The Gospels *could* be versions of an entirely fictional story that was told or written. Many similar fictions—which Christians dismiss as pagan myths despite their striking resemblance to the Jesus story—were circulating at the same time, and the content of those stories changed at the whim of each storyteller just like the Bible stories were altered when the need or desire to alter arose. We all know that Greek myths transformed over time and were further renovated by the Romans. We know that there were many—possibly hundreds or even thousands—of Jesus gospels circulating during the first few centuries C.E. and that it was just luck that a handful remained intact and in the hands of the fourth-century elite who decided what material would make it into what we now call The Bible. And of course those four Gospels vary hugely.

Amazingly, perhaps desperately, some Jesus scholars actually argue that the *variation* among the four Gospels is the *very quality* that indicates their validity, because the early believers really only cared about the central fact of Jesus' miracle-working life, his message, and his resurrection, not minor details like Jesus' miracle-working life, his message, and his resurrection. Other scholars assert that the real autographs, or one real autograph, was the authentic source, and the task is to try to reconstruct the original (or originals) from cut-and-paste excerpts from the four existing Gospels, and maybe even the non-canonical gospels, all to locate the real Jesus. One might as plausibly cut-and-paste elements from the various myths of Zeus to uncover the real Zeus.

Jesus scholars know that just as the Greek/Roman god Zeus/Jupiter mutated, so did the Hebrew/Greek/Roman god Messiah/Christ. We all know that no god, no goddess, no hero, no religion has not transfigured in the forge of human imagination. And unlike the Egyptians, as Edith Hamilton reminds us in her *Mythology*, the Greeks and the Romans created their gods in their own image. Jesus Christ was one of those Greco-Roman gods, whether or not he began as a human. Excavating a human Jesus from ruins of mythic proportions is not going to happen. Much less a human who is God.

THE JESUS COLLAGE

The multitude of "textual problems," as scholars today nonchalantly refer to the internal contradictions, is most pronounced in the four Gospels. Regular readers of the Bible balk at this assertion because they usually peruse particular passages of the Gospels, often their favorite excerpts, over and over again, or they read a Gospel vertically from beginning to end, or all the Gospels vertically, one after another, and they see no problem. But again, comparing the texts horizontally, arranging the same units—events, sayings, etc.—side by side, one can't but be struck by the massive "disagreement" between and among the accounts. Apologists argue, "What they *really* said," or "What they *really* meant," or "What *really* happened," or "Back then they didn't care about *chronology*," or "Back then they didn't care about *accuracy*," or "Back then the *oral tradition* was more important than anything written," or "Those grammatical errors just prove that the followers of Jesus were *regular guys*," or... But why go on? The critical contortionism of apologists only proves the point they're trying to confute: The Bible is manmade. In fact the Bible is an ancient miscellany of manmade texts that even edited retains numerous species of flaws and creative flourishes.

The Gospels don't agree on the basic facts of the years that Jesus was born or died or who his ancestors were, data that was extremely important to the Jews of that era. The letters of Paul, which are supposedly the earliest Jesus material, say nothing about Jesus the man; Paul's writings are purely apologetic symbolic theology. Since Jesus scholars can't ignore the historical inaccuracies of the Gospels, they cite their choice of them, or cut-and-paste excerpts from among them, to "prove" that Jesus existed. Cherry-picking from illegitimate texts is like citing the smoking gun to prove the innocence of the defendant with the smoking gun in his hand. What's truly astounding is that even many Jesus scholars who should know better still celebrate pagan-steeped Christmas and Easter to commemorate a savior-God born of a virgin who was crucified for our sins, rose from the dead, and ascended into the clouds. On the basis of absolutely no conclusive evidence—a position they themselves have substantiated—almost all Jesus scholars still believe in a seminal historical Jesus. They believe because—just like Darwinians who believe in macroevolution—they *want* to believe; they want to *believe* rather than to *know*.

Because various circular explanations cannot resolve the variant Gospels problem, uncomfortable scholars search for puzzle pieces outside the Gospels. But the external sources have been deemed unreliable, too, because they were written decades after Jesus would have lived, and for the most part they speak not of Jesus but simply note that unorganized Jesus-followers with ill-defined beliefs (sometimes referred to as "superstitions") were floating about, along with followers of other gods and goddesses.

Incongruities between the Gospels and external historical materials are just as striking as discrepancies between the Gospels themselves. In Jesus' era, the Romans, meticulous record-keepers and vigilant overlords, never mention the birth, activities, trial, or crucifixion of Jesus. Not a peep about the radical multitudes that supposedly turned out to be healed or to hear their Lord's message or to lay palm fronds under his treasonous feet upon his kingly Triumphal Entry into Jerusalem. The earliest mention of Jesus, written by a Roman governor, Pliny the Younger, in 112 C.E., nearly a century after the death of Jesus, records that a cult calling themselves Christians were meeting illegally. Shortly after that, in 115 C.E., the Roman historian Tacitus mentions the "superstition" of Christianity that had spread to Rome, and notes that Nero had allegedly blamed Christians for the fire he set in Rome in 64 C.E., an event that took place half a century before Tacitus recorded it. That Nero blamed Christians is doubted by most scholars today. Regardless of whether Nero did blame Christians or whether later Christians blamed Nero for persecution they later experienced, there are *no* records of any kind from the era of Jesus that mention Jesus or his followers.

The four canonical Gospels were written decades, possibly many decades, after Jesus supposedly died, and they were written in Greek by foreigners in foreign lands, not in Aramaic, which was the language of the time and place of Jesus. Luke 3:1 mentions the joint high priesthood of Annas and Caiaphas, for example, when there could be only one high priest at a time; there were never two high priests at the same time. The writer of Luke (the gospel lifted up as "history") doesn't know that, because he was writing at a time and place and culture far removed from Jesus-era Jerusalem. Luke also locates the birth of Jesus during the reign of Herod at the time of the famous census of Quirinius, which necessitated lodging for out-of-towners Mary and Joseph that wound up being a manger. But Quirinius was not the legate of Syria while Herod was alive.

Jesus' crucifixion is also a problem. John says the execution occurred on Friday, 14 Nisan (Nisan is the name of a month according to the Jewish calendar), the Friday when the Passover lambs were sacrificed (Passover was on the 14th day of the first full moon of spring). The other three Gospels date the execution on Friday, 15 Nisan. But there was no year in the late twenties or early thirties, the range of years during which Jesus could have died, in which 15 Nisan fell on a Friday. It's worth noting that John is considered the least authentic gospel, yet Christians make much ado about Jesus being sacrificed on Passover and even refer to him as the Passover Lamb, a concept that doesn't jive if Jesus was executed on the date reported in Matthew, Mark, and Luke.

The only external source taken seriously by some is a brief paragraph attributed to Josephus written half a century after the death of Jesus—that late date being sufficient to dismiss it, yet this text is typically discredited because it is a hearsay source that relied on other unreliable sources and was later edited by a Christian monk (Christian monks "owned" the text); some scholars assert that it was actually written by the Christian monk, because it puts Christian faith-claims in the mouth of Josephus, a decidedly Jewish priest. It should be noted that Josephus himself was not a consistent historian. Furthermore, details of Josephus's early life, like his being consulted by high priests when he was fourteen and his three-year sojourn in the wilderness undertaken when he was sixteen, suggest possible material incorporated into subsequent Jesus stories.

Archeology doesn't prove that Jesus existed, either. At best it only confirms that a couple places and rulers mentioned in the Gospels actually existed, but what scholar doubted those in the first place? Though perhaps based on archeologically verifiable people, places, and events, the Gospel's characters, settings, and plots might be no more literally actual than similar references in Homer's mythic *Iliad* and *Odyssey* or Hesiod's *Theogony* and *Works and Days*. Looked at through a literary lens, elements of myth, legend, and folktale in the Gospels are as obviously imaginative as those same elements found in the tragedies of Aeschylus, Sophocles, and Euripides, the odes of Pindar, the ancient mythographies of Callimachus and Euphemerus, Ovid's poetic *Metamorphosis*, Virgil's epic the *Aeneid*, and the legend of Santa Claus. Viewed through the lens of historical methodology, the Gospels are no more historical than Chrétien de Troyes' Arthurian romances or, three centuries later, Thomas Malory's *Le Mort Darthur*, and are no more historically exact than the history plays of Shakespeare or more recent historical novels and movies. Texts like the Dead Sea Scrolls give us a narrow glimpse of worldviews and practices of the era but never mention anything about Jesus or Jesus-followers.

The truth is that there is no authoritative, unbiased source that proves that Jesus existed. Even if we surmise the possibility that someone named Jesus actually existed, we have absolutely no idea who or what he actually was, or even when he lived; in fact, there is no way we *could* know. Scholars searching for proof of the historical Jesus have groped as futilely as Darwinians scouring fossil beds for missing links.

HISTORY AS CREATIVE WRITING

Even college students know (or should know) that good research in any field requires not only sources that are authoritative and unbiased, but also rational, on-point analysis of the data and coherent, fallacy-free presentation of valid conclusions. Common sense is the ultimate authority, truth the ultimate data. Why, then, do religious scholars who point out all those biblical discrepancies and incongruities and other textual problems at the same time cite the Bible as a legitimate—really, the only—source of information about the historical Jesus?

Much depends on what is meant by "information" and by "historical Jesus." If you're researching ancient *beliefs about* Jesus, yes, the Bible could be a valuable source of information. But if you're researching the *existence of an actual person* named Jesus who is represented as such in the Bible, not so much.

Some scholars seem unable or unwilling to distinguish between these two agendas. Not only is their fact-claim that Jesus was an actual person based on sources that are neither authoritative nor unbiased, the fact-claim itself is based on a *prior assumption* that Jesus was (and is) actual; in other words, the "fact" of Jesus is an *a priori bias*. The concluding fact-claim drawn from this invalid premise is invalid. The syllogism falls apart, the research begs the question, and the presentation of a living, breathing "historical Jesus" is necessarily incoherent and fallacious. Put another way, scholars work backward from the Gospels' Jesus myths, legends, and folktales toward a bias-created "real Jesus" that is based on nothing but the Gospels' Jesus myths, legends, and folktales. In any other academic field (except perhaps Darwinian biology), this "methodology" would be laughable.

Even college freshmen understand the fundamental difference between content taught in Creative Writing and in straightforward Exposition or Argument. Yet Jesus scholars downplay the obvious fact that the books of the Bible, and certainly the Gospels, are creative writing. Even if a historical Jesus existed, the Gospels paint imaginative, divergent, often contradictory portraits of that person. Once creative enters into the writing, the actual person Jesus disappears.

Rarely is writing not creative. Even a scholarly historical account of a well-documented famous person is by necessity part speculation, part interpretation, part gap-guessing, and part cherry-picking hearsay, which is another way of saying part fiction. Did George Washington really cut down the cherry tree? How articulate was George verbally? What were his passions, his fears, his authentic religious convictions, his opinions about John Adams and Thomas Jefferson? What did he have for dinner on the fifth of July, 1776? Did someone assist him in writing his First Presidential Address? We know almost nothing about George's life, much less about the actual person. We know he attended church (which was required by law) but skipped communion as a matter of conscience. We know he had wooden teeth, but don't know if he was ever madly in love or had ever cussed at his horse—and which is more important in getting to know the real man? Yet we think we know all about George Washington. We know virtually nothing. We don't even know much about George Bush or Barak Obama, though the image-crafting media makes us believe that we do.

Historians take tremendous liberties when painting portraits of people and events, filling in massive gaps, omitting almost everything surrounding those people and events, because almost everything is unknown. And those "scholarly" creative renderings become established "facts" that are peer-reviewed by other creative scholars, which perpetuates the fiction as "fact." (Virginia Woolf's *Orlando*, a "fictional autobiography" of her closest friend, Vita Sackville-West, is a dazzlingly brilliant exemplum of this process.) When doing research, we must scrutinize not only the scholarship but also the scholar. Historians are human individuals with their own proclivities, agendas, and aesthetic inclinations. History is as subjective as what is more frankly called myth, legend, and folktale; history just mixes in more objectively verifiable details. Presenting history, especially ancient history, as pure objective fact is just plain dishonest.

A teacher named Jesus might have inspired the original story of Jesus, but that *story* (or album of stories) was a fiction that even during the first few decades C.E. evolved into further fictions. Jesus scholars who claim that they know that Jesus was or did this or that are citing biases conjured in their own imaginations. That a bias is rooted in a two-thousand year tradition does not excuse the academic dishonesty of presenting the bias as fact. Most scholars understand their biases; therefore, they knowingly lead people astray.

Why assume that a real-person Jesus existed when the only accounts of Jesus that we have are the four Gospels of the Bible, which religious scholars know were not intended to present a history or biography of Jesus but were rather crafted to inspire faith, to explain faith-positions, and to create and maintain coherence within a wildly diffuse Jesus-religion? Nonetheless, the plodding pedants meander through the dusty terrain of their so-called Quest for the Historical Jesus, arguing over sources and dates of composition, criticizing each other's research and interpretative methodologies, perpetually begging the question in that no one has moved an inch closer to locating any actual person named Jesus.

I find this remarkable, if not scandalous. They could as justly assume the scholarly task of determining if Santa Claus always wore the red suit and if only eight reindeer could have pulled the sleigh. Locating the historical Jesus in the Gospels is like deducing the sex appeal of Cleopatra from analysis of the character played by Liz Taylor. Jesus questers are scholars of skimpy assumptions no less than Darwinian biologists I dissect in Part II of this book.

If Jesus existed, who, or rather what he was is anybody's guess. Some speculate that he was a wise rabbi or peasant rebel living roughly at the time scholars have settled on. At the other extreme, some argue that since Jesus proclaimed the imminent end of the world, which of course never happened, perhaps he was a fraud (like end-of-the-world cult leaders today), or at least a failed prophet, and therefore not a legitimate "messiah," certainly not a god or God. Scholars who pontificate about the eschatology of Jesus being spiritual rather than literal have neither addressed the *fact* that the biblical Jesus himself considered the imminent end of the world to be a literal fact nor proven that Jesus ever existed.

Even if Jesus had been an actual person, the Jesus of the Bible is not that person. The Jesus of the Bible is the protagonist of a story that has been created, edited, and recreated into the fiction we now have. Even if that fiction was based on seminal facts about an actual person, we have no way to know that or even to assume that. All we have is the fragmented Jesus material known as the Gospels, a miscellany of references to Jesus in other New Testament books, and a few inadmissible artifacts. What we have is literature.

THE JESUS LITERATURE

Whether an actual teacher named Jesus existed or not, the *biblical* Jesus is simply a literary character, like King Arthur of the Round Table, like the gods and goddesses and heroes of ancient Greece or Rome, like the George Washington who chopped down the cherry tree of American legend—a fabricated fiction, it should be noted, inserted into the fifth edition (1806) of *The Life and Memorable Actions of George Washington* by Mason Locke Weems, aka Parson Weems, an Anglican clergyman and itinerant book hawker for the publisher Mathew Carey.

Though perhaps modeled on some actual person or persons, the character Jesus of the written texts was created, just like other gods, goddesses, and heroes, by some imaginative literary writer or writers. Only some of the uneducated masses, the "children" of society, believed in those obvious fictions about gods and goddesses and heroes handed down via oral tradition and then written down by poets, dramatists, philosophers, and historians. Some of those myths, like Apuleius's *Psyche and Cupid*, were creative writing that never pretended to be literally true. Apuleius ends his tale, "So all came to a most happy end. Love and the Soul (for that is what Psyche means) [parenthesis his] had sought and after sore trials had found each other; and that union could never be broken."

The story of Jesus bears a striking similarity to the story of his contemporary Galilean, the Pythagorean teacher Appolonius of Tyana. Like Jesus, he was a divine incarnation; like Jesus his miraculous conception was announced before his birth; like Jesus he possessed in childhood the wisdom of a sage; like Jesus he is said to have led a blameless life; like Jesus his moral teachings were declared to be the best the world had known; like Jesus he remained a celibate; like Jesus he was averse to riches; like Jesus he purified the religious temples; like Jesus he predicted future events; like Jesus he performed miracles, cast out devils, healed the sick, and restored the dead to life; like Jesus he died, rose from the grave, ascended to heaven, and was worshiped as a god. Christians reject the miraculous in Apollonius because it is preposterous; rationalists reject the miraculous in Christ for the same reason.

Motivations to create Jesus/Apollonius fictions are similar to motivations to perpetuate the fiction of Santa Claus or Zeus or cherry-tree George or any other myth, legend, or folktale. Instead of trying to prove the historical truth of myths, legends, and folktales, or pursuing some provable tidbit of source material as if it were the Grail, wouldn't it be more productive to examine our perfectly rational reasons for creating religious fictions and our non-rational motives for perpetuating them as historical truths? Once we wipe away the whitewash, we can more fully appreciate the ethical and spiritual insights of the Jesus literature, just as we appreciate the writings of Sophocles and Shakespeare, Homer and Dante, Tolkien and George Bernard Shaw.

Like many creative writers throughout the ages, the creators of the

Jesus/Apollonius fictions borrowed from prior sources. To some extent, borrowing from other texts is part of the tradition of creative writing. Without literary cherry-picking, very little of the canon of narrative literature would exist. There would be almost no Shakespeare, Milton, or Chaucer, almost no Greek or Roman drama or epic, almost no Jewish, Christian, Islamic, Hindu, or Buddhist scripture. Great literature surpasses history like the quest of the human spirit transcends the treadmill of day-to-day survival. Literature always embodies symbolism, meaning, and representation even when it incorporates facts. Religion is a genre of literature, and as such, the scholar must consider the creative intentions that generated the religion.

Certainly in many of its details and in the scope of its symbolic intent, the Jesus myth retains conspicuous features derived from far more ancient Greco-Roman, Middle-Eastern, and other regional myths that circulated along trade routes. There is virtually no element of Jesus' life, teachings, divine incarnation, death, and resurrection that were not also present entirely or in large part in myths of Krishna, Buddha, Zoroaster, Mithra, Osiris, Horus, and a host of other gods, goddesses, and prophets. The Eucharist continued Bacchanalian and Eleusinian feasts suppressed by the Roman government. Christmas continued the Saturnalia and other pagan holidays. Angels, devils, incarnate semi-human sons and daughters, wizard-prophets, magicians, and other supernatural beings were present in virtually every religion of the East and West.

One could easily imagine a Jesus-religion arising from a myth created by a single ingenious Homer able to amalgamate circulating versions of myths, parables, fables, legends, and wisdom-sayings into one relatively cohesive wise-man or god-man hero.

Even if the story was not generated as a single literary work, the stories that propelled the original Jesus-religion evolved into monolithic Christianity not because an actual historical Jesus existed, but because a compelling Jesus myth gripped the imaginations of people for whom fear required mitigation, injustice demanded restitution, and collectively concurrent rectitude merited enshrinement in legends, parables, and wise sayings. It's easy to understand the emotional evolution from appreciation of a story to reverence of God's man to worship of a god-man as God—a creative, archetypal evolution present in a multitude of religious and other literary traditions. Fantasy representations in literature allow us to explore possibilities of transcendental realities, like soul, karma, divine intervention, and the afterlife, and to creatively contemplate good and evil.

Even believers in an actual historical Jesus must still quote him the way we would quote the Virgil of *The Inferno*, or perhaps the way we quote Plato's Socrates; we should not quote Jesus as if he is God or the Bible is God. Why does this deification of Jesus and the Bible continue even among scholars who know better?

Driving religion is humanity's insatiable quest for truth, meaning, purpose, and everlasting life with the Creator of life. Who are we? How did we get here? Why are we here? Where are we going? Deep philosophical questions propel religion, even more than does fear, that great archenemy of rational reflection.

LITERARY TRADITION OF PHILOSOPHIZING

Assessing whether Aristotle sported a beard, the badge of the philosopher's profession, or whether he shaved, as an ancient biographer noted, Jonathan Barnes points out in *The Cambridge Companion of Aristotle* that "ancient biographies are not cordon blue concoctions of fact—they are crude stews, the rare gobbets of fact swimming in a sauce of dubious inference and unreliable anecdote…we know very little about [Aristotle's] body and very little about his soul." We do, however, know that Aristotle lived and wrote, because he left behind an immense body of work (though less than a third of his opus survives intact), because a host of prominent people traveled to his Lyceum to learn from him, because he was a prominent figure in other notable lives—he was Alexander the Great's tutor, for instance—and because he and his work were referenced in works written by his peers and students and by a multitude of philosophers and students in the years and decades following his death. Official government records of the era also validate his historical existence.

Even the writings that do survive are likely not Aristotle's published works, which were known throughout the region to be literary and eloquent; the surviving works read more like his working drafts and lecture notes. Even so, Aristotle's influence on philosophy is second to none. What we do know from a great deal of valid evidence is that Aristotle himself lectured and wrote in Athens and elsewhere, and we do have proof of that from the era in which he lived. Perhaps more importantly, Aristotle's thought gripped the imaginations of a host of the world's greatest thinkers and changed forever the *way* we think and the *objects* of our thoughts.

A generation earlier, Plato, Aristotle's teacher, also taught and wrote, and it appears that all his writing has survived. Plato's texts present other problems. We don't know exactly in what order he wrote his works; we aren't sure about the authorship of a few works, though all his major and most of his minor works are certain; and most challenging, we can't know the accuracy of his dialogues, which involve real people but were written years or decades after the supposed discussions took place, or which use real people as characters through which he articulates his own philosophy.

Scholars usually divide his work into three groupings, but because Plato didn't begin writing until after Socrates' death, even his early dialogues with Socrates as the central figure are far from literally accurate. We suppose that Plato made every effort in the early works to convey the actual words and positions of his teacher, who himself wrote nothing. Literary analysis of Plato's later work shows extreme shifts in both discourse style and philosophical ideas. Plato was working to produce a system of thought, but Socrates was known to have been uninterested in any such system. Plato took liberties in using the beloved and revered Socrates as the leading character in his dialogues, which are essentially closet dramas (plays meant to be read, not performed) expressing philosophical concepts via the so-called Socratic Method of Q&A rather than dramatizing events. But Plato uses mythmaking and other conventions utilized by poets and playwrights, although Plato always makes it obvious that the myths are myths. In fact, in his Republic, poets are banned for misleading the naïve masses and especially youth into thinking that the mythic representations of anthropomorphic gods are real entities and valid role-models. Misleading, of course, was and is not the goal of poets any more than it was Plato's goal in presenting his Socrates "as is."

Although Socrates was a real person, the representation of Socrates that we get through Plato and other writers of the era is not the actual historical person Socrates—who, it should be noted, bore a remarkable similarity to the later Jesus. Socrates became a template for many writers in the years following Plato; the character Jesus is in many respects quite similar to the Socrates prototype. The "Socratic dialogue" tradition evolved over three centuries into a genre including various discourse styles, including those employed by the gospel writers.

The people reading the works of Plato and subsequent Socratic writers knew perfectly well that those representations of Socrates were just that. Some, especially the early Plato dialogues, were approximations of what Socrates said, but everyone knew that the writer of the representation had his own agenda and did not have a photographic memory regarding anything or anyone, including Socrates. Historical accuracy was not Plato's objective.

The tradition of generating creative works to represent philosophical and theological speculations dates back hundreds of years B.C.E. Literary forms like dialogue, with a Socrates-type sage at the center of the discussion, as well as myth-stories, fables, hero legends, and proverbs (or what today we might call quotable quotes), had been entrenched in Greek culture for centuries. It's not surprising that during the first century C.E., the Jesus story, with all the typical literary trimmings, would be written by a Greek Jew.

Nor is it surprising that the story caught fire. Great epics by poets like Homer and Hesiod, who didn't originate their material but lithified it by writing it down, were commonplace artifacts in the Greco-Roman culture and psyche. In the centuries before and after the era of the Jesus story, multitudes gathered to hear recitations of the great epics and to view the great plays. Stories were a common form of entertainment. And literature—essays, dialogues, plays, poetry, proverbs, epics—were common vehicles for philosophical ideas. The famous ethics of Jesus are derived from already existing ethical ideas and systems generated by the Greeks, Romans, Persians, Jews, and earlier Assyrians and Babylonians, as well as the Chinese. Pointedly articulating ethical ideals was itself a literary genre. The originator of the Jesus story brought together common literary elements, including a variety of popular regional myths, the dialogue form with its central sage engaging in teaching and debating, proverb recitation, and archetypal motifs.

Most of the Gospels' philosophical concepts were lifted right out of philosophical traditions of the Greeks of Plato's Academy and Aristotle's Lyceum, with some pre-Socratic morsels mixed in. From Greek speculations regarding logos and epistemology and arguments for immortality, to Greco-Jewish messianic eschatology and concepts of prophecy fulfillment—all propositions embodied by Jesus were already centuries old and widely utilized. The Gospel's ethics fused especially

Greek, Roman, and Jewish ideals, distilling from them the essence of what the creative Jesus author thought was ultimately real, good, and sensible. The presentation of the ethical essence was simple enough for the uneducated to understand, and that pedagogical style has been a major reason for the story's perpetual appeal.

LITERARY REPRESENTATION IS MORE FUNDAMENTAL THAN HISTORY

A literary work's longevity is not a proof of historical authenticity or of divine providence. It is an indication of engaging form and compelling content. It's important to study the Gospels as didactic literary works and to ask why the content of the Jesus story is still so spiritually forceful. Is Christian zeal simply the result of indoctrination, or does Jesus impart a deep message we long to hear? Does the story represent a transcendental truth we can't always quite consciously grasp? Is the portrait of the spiritual wise man consistent with an inherent ideal? Does the philosophy represented speak to our needs and desires? In terms of civilization as a whole, all of the above.

Jesus scholars know this; scholars have known this for centuries. In fact, the process of myth generation was understood by the Greeks centuries before the Jesus myth was even created. Whether it began as oral mythmaking that eventually was written down or originated as a written work that was continually revised is something we will likely never know. What we do know is that miracles and resurrection were common literary elements, not literal truths. Common sense tells us that Santa Claus won't be driving his sleigh over our rooftops now or ever. Scholars, like children, need to grow up and start acknowledging the truth—the whole truth and nothing but the truth.

Adults understand that representation is just that. Children, not adults, believe in twilight vampires, wiccan spellbinding, and Santa Claus. Children believe in a virgin-born, human baby-God. Children believe in myths, fairytales, and superstitions. Children accept that the impregnating Father is also magically the Son, and that the Son is sacrificed by the Father like an animal for unknown, inherited crimes of children—a belief perhaps easier to hold by adults who were abused as children by their fathers.

Do the puerile imagination and emotion that propel the mutant Jesus religion also propel most Jesus scholars? What other explanation is there? Projection? Academic or spiritual codependency? Are scholars *really* searching for the man Jesus? Or are they desperately hoping against hope to locate the man-God at the center of their prefab religion? Pursuit of the man named Jesus is valid, though perhaps futile, but seeking the man to authenticate a weed-patch religion that only *might have* sprung up in a garden, not to mention distorting a few artifacts to establish causality, and to pervert that causality into proof of miracles, is not only morally wrong, it's dangerous. Once Jesus was deified to certify The One True Faith, the Bible had to be deified to confirm the God Jesus. Many have documented the anti-Christ atrocities committed by the authority of the God-breathed Bible. "Even the devil can cite scripture for his purpose," Shakespeare long ago reminded us. As his friend John Selden concluded, "*Scrutamini scriptura* [search the scriptures]. These two words have undone the world."

Every religion, including New Age self-help theologies, claims to have The Big Secret through which you can have and be anything you choose. To the extent that they worship the Unholy Trinity—*selfishness* manifested as *greed* and *pride*—those religions are false. I would go so far as to call them evil.

Don't most of us deep down believe that the center of religion must be God, the Natural God of Creation? Don't most of us deep down believe that real worship consists of ethical behavior and gratitude centered in the God of all that is considered to be The Good? Personally, I think it's just that simple. Complicating the matter causes doubt, anxiety, fear, and bloodbaths. Stepping outside the simple truth leads one down the crooked path of elitism, prejudice, hate, and self-loathing.

If discovering core truth is an inherently joyous occasion—and I believe it is—surely Jesus scholars are as unhappy as Darwinian atheists. Seeking truth, finding truth, accepting truth, assimilating truth—it's all a joyous process. Perpetuating delusions must be a disappointing profession. Certainly, any version of Jesus, biblical or historical, would not recommend lying in defense of religion.

STEPPING OFF THE JESUS MERRY-GO-ROUND

It might seem surprising that the Jesus myth sprang up centuries after the Athenian renaissance of great rationalists like Socrates, Plato, and Aristotle. But contemporaries of Jesus were no more philosophical or educated than the typical citizen of ancient Greece or the average person today. Despite technological advancement, the human species itself hasn't evolved much in the last couple millennia. People today are no more likely to prefer enlightenment to entertainment than they ever were. Even many people seeking truth shun truth that jolts them out of their comfort zone. So it makes sense that after centuries of critique, the quest for the myth-validating historical Jesus continues on into the twenty-first century.

Why does superstition prevail? In grade school we learn that the religious worldview dramatically changed with the discovery of the New World and the scientific discoveries by Copernicus, Kepler, and Galileo. Once the world and the universe got a whole lot bigger; once the Age of Reason rescued humanity from Dark Age constriction that followed Roman expansionism; once newly-established universities launched humanist challenges to the brutalities of the Inquisition and the Reformation; once the eighteenth century Enlightenment resurrected Greek reason to usurp authority from blind tradition embodied by Church and State; once civilization shucked off the shackles of religious superstition and political tyranny; once the authority of rational inquiry into the laws of nature displaced divine revelation, we just naturally stepped into the far more evolved worldview, Deism. By "we" I mean, of course, a few humanists in history books juxtaposed alongside your average Jack and Jill and the usual dictators, aristocrats, oligarchs, and instigators of war and exploitation who have cloaked themselves in the robes of any available religion—Christianity, Judaism, Islam, capitalism. Fusion of Church and State is still the world's most dangerous fuse.

There had always been a better way, but Deists mainstreamed enlightenment. Borrowing from the Greco-Roman philosophy, Deism posited a supremely rational Creator God whose Creation was structured upon inviolable laws available to anyone's inspection. Humanist ethical principles inherent in nature promoted a more progressive, humane society.

Seventeenth century British and French Deists paved the way to concerted biblical criticism with their critique of divine revelation and miracles. British philosopher Edward Herbert, the Father of Deism, presented the first fleshed-out system of Deist thought early in the seventeenth century. Herbert's seminal works on the nature of truth, the bedrock of Deism, include *De Veritate* (On Truth), *De Causis Errorum* (On the Causes of Errors), *De Religione Laici* (On the Religion of the Laity), *De Religione Gentilium* (On the Religion of the Gentiles), and his

Autobiography. In his treatises, Herbert proposes that all humans since the beginning of time have held five innate, God-given religious ideas: belief in God, in the need for worship, in virtue as the ultimate form of worship, in the need for repentance, and in rewards and punishments in the afterlife. How these five concepts expressed as private beliefs and the fundamental beliefs of institutionalized religions determined whether the religion would be humane or barbarous.

Subsequent Deist thinkers—the list includes Charles Blount, John Toland, Anthony Collins, Conyers Middleton, Matthew Tindal, Thomas Chubb, Thomas Woolston, Voltaire, Hermann Samuel Reimarus, Elihu Palmer, and Thomas Paine—modified and expanded Herbert's ideas. Considerations by skeptics like Montaigne, Pierre Bayle, Montesquieu, and many other freethinking philosophers and poets further legitimized Deism.

Though some Deists and political philosophers such as John Locke argued that Deism need not contradict basic Christian beliefs, conservative Christianity begged to differ, and seeing it a grave threat, set about discrediting Deism, deeming it unorthodox, if not heretical. Though equated with paganism, the intelligent, progressive naturalistic theology quickly spread.

Skepticism toward the Gospels gave rise to the historical-critical method of evaluating the validity or non-validity of biblical texts. In his book published in 1738, British Deist Thomas Chubb presented the intractable Jesus as a Deist sage of reason and natural religion.

Challenging the status quo like many thinkers before him, Enlightenment Deist Hermann Samuel Reimarus applied the scientific method even to biblical texts and to Jesus himself and announced the important distinction between the Jesus presented in the Gospels and Jesus as an actual historical person. Although Reimarus disputed miracles and the resurrection, rather than reject Jesus altogether, he proposed that the very human Jesus was wrong in assuming the coming kingdom of God through military force that would establish him as Messiah, and that therefore Jesus was misguided in his urgent call to repentance on the brink of the end of the world—the so-called eschatological worldview. After his death, Jesus' loyal disciples were forced to perpetuate the fraud of a divine savior of the world to ensure that the ethical and spiritual teachings of their beloved rabbi would thrive. Reimarus pointed out that history did not control doctrine, but that doctrine created history, therefore both history and doctrine were fallacious.

Reimarus's critique is credited with initiating the quest for the historical Jesus. But it really got off the ground around 1835, when David Friedrich Strauss published *The Life of Jesus Critically Examined*. Though Strauss thought that the Jesus story could have been generated by a historical event, the miraculous elements did not arise from the historical events of Jesus' life but rather from the faith-based worldview of the gospel writers. Not exactly outright fraud, Jesus followers unconsciously incorporated into their stories mythic elements that best represented their belief in Jesus' divinity. The Jesus myth could not then be considered history but must rather be viewed as the spontaneous, unreflective, uncensored "sacred legend" of creative imagination. Only twenty-seven when he published his book, Strauss was spurned by academics and lost his opportunity for a promising university teaching career. In the end, after a life of ostracism while relentlessly pursuing truth, Strauss, like many Deists, completely disavowed his Christian faith. But his unflinching, deliberate unmasking and amplification of mythic elements, such as New Testament fabrications incorporating Old Testament elements, gave rise to form criticism as a permanent methodology in subsequent Jesus studies.

Strauss also introduced explicit, metacritical self-consciousness as a condition of historical studies. Because any methodology is necessarily motivated and guided by presuppositions that could lead to biased conclusions, reason and fact must supersede dogma.

Bruno Bauer took Strauss's point a step further. According to his Christ-Myth theory, Jesus was not an actual person in history; the "historical Jesus" was all myth.

The First "Liberal" Quest for the Historical Jesus, spawned by Reimarus and Strauss, viewed the Gospels skeptically; no longer divinely revealed, the Gospels were now considered to be merely human witnesses to revelation that could only be understood in their original historical and cultural contexts. Jesus scholars published many portraits of Jesus as they sought to disentangle original historical elements about the human Jesus from later Church embellishments that included miracles and doctrines of Jesus' divinity.

Ironically, the Jesus portraits of the nineteenth century, such as Ernest Renan's extremely popular Romantic-era *The Life of Jesus*, which portrayed the human Jesus as a great moral teacher, were as steeped as the Gospels themselves in interpretative fictional embellishments. Some scholars argued that Jesus escaped the crucifixion, got married to Mary Magdalene, and had kids and grandkids. Some claimed to have found the bones of Jesus in the Jesus family gravesite. In some accounts, he traveled to Asia and returned a kind of Buddhist magi. Some "proved" that Jesus was really the apostle Paul. Some scholars rejected the divinity of the just-human Jesus; some rejected his humanity altogether.

Ironically, Jesus scholars themselves serve to illustrate the point that people unrestrainedly elaborate or concoct details to create fictions that embody their presuppositions, all the while believing that they are representing the truth. It is this tendency to creatively adlib that Deist rationalism has always critiqued.

Source criticism emerged to pump up some historical credibility for the Gospels deflated under the pressure of skepticism. Because the Gospels were mutually contradictory, source critics posited a two-source solution to the "synoptic problem." Mark, in their view the earliest Gospel, and a second source, Q (from the German *Quelle*, meaning source), which is not a tangible text but just a speculative abstraction, together provided the source material for Matthew and Luke. The John material, being qualitatively different from the other Gospels, presented its own set of problems.

Scholars of the era decided that Mark was the earliest written gospel, an opinion of convenience still widely held today. The agenda of Mark and subsequent gospels was to pass on traditions from oral preaching, which meant that although there were specific writers, there were many contributors to the oral tradition leading to the written versions. Furthermore, the oral tradition, which perpetuated after-the-fact faith-claims, did not necessarily include much or any accurate historical information about Jesus. The sequence of events in the Gospel narratives were also arranged differently, included contradictory information, and presented conflicting and subjective portraits of Jesus and his message that included assumptions of an imminent end of the world that didn't happen.

Albert Schweitzer accused Jesus scholars of projecting what they wanted the Gospels to be into their interpretations, creating their God in their own image. Following the lead of Johannes Weiss, Schweitzer portrayed Jesus as a liberal social reformer and teacher of love who was swept up in the end-times fervor, and who, in the end, believed that his own suffering was pivotal to the culmination of this world. Because Jesus predicted an end of the world that never happened, he was a failed apocalyptic prophet, but we can still embrace his message of love even as we reject the obsolete Jewish end-times worldview.

Scholars like Rudolph Bultmann, attempting to demythologize the Gospels, concluded that the historical Jesus could not be excavated and that it didn't matter because the "Christ of faith" was more important than the "Jesus of history." Being a Lutheran, he privileged Luther's privileging of Paul's salvation by grace through faith accomplished through Jesus' death and resurrection. Martin Kähler raised a theological objection to the quest, arguing that all the various historical Jesuses concealed the living Christ. Following World War I, Neo-orthodox scholars like Karl Barth and Paul Tillich maintained a reserved stance toward the historical questing.

After the First Quest petered out in the nineteenth century, the Second Quest for the Historical Jesus reconvened in Germany after World War II. (One might think of its impetus as the Quest for a Redeemer of Edenic German reason and tradition fallen under the satanic spell of nationalized Nazi-Christianity.) The seminal theoretical concept was that whoever and whatever the historical Jesus was, and as little as we can excavate about him from the Gospels, a person named Jesus was important enough that his followers told and wrote stories about him. Of course, the same could be said about any god or legendary hero or about any of the great myths, epics, and philosophical dialogues spontaneously generated the world over; in fact, the same could be said for urban myths and legends and ordinary gossip. Even minor literary characters can take on a life of their own via the creative imagination of good storytellers—and few of us human beings aren't good storytellers.

Scholars began to apply the rules of historicity as they systematically sieved the Gospels to uncover some authentic morsel of Jesus data. They advanced the rule of "discontinuity," the principle that assumed that when the Gospel Jesus did or said something that differed from prior Jewish tradition or later Church teaching, those elements are likely authentic— although the writers' tradition was *Greek*, and later teaching was, well, *later*. Scholars reasoned that the Jesus tradition must have arisen from a unique, memorable, compelling personality. Of course, literature is steeped in fictional characters that are unique, memorable, and compelling, so discontinuity doesn't really indicate historical accuracy.

Other scholars thought Jesus was better understood not as an exception to but as a product of Jewish culture, and their portraits privileged that assumption. But again, the Gospel writers were products of Greek culture.

Even seeking to reconstruct a plausible Jesus based on occurrences and events that typify his teachings and conduct, these scholars engage in the same Jesus-mythmaking process as the generators of the myth itself; the Quest movement itself exemplifies the process by which the Jesus myth evolved.

Looking even outside the canon for continuities that best represent a plausible portrait of Jesus, the Third Quest is plagued by their generation's multitude of possible portraits, none of them substantially plausible. Attempting to purify the quest with a more rigorous historical methodology, the scholarly conclusion remains that "Jesus is inaccessible by historical means," as William Hamilton put it succinctly. Amazingly, the resolution to this problem is, as William Arnal sums it up, "The historical Jesus does not matter…The Jesus who is important to our day is not the Jesus of history, but the symbolic Jesus of contemporary discourse."

The quest for the historical Jesus is theologically unnecessary. Jewish scholar Jacob Neusner commented, "And since when do matters of fact have any bearing on the truths of faith?"

Scholars today, like those belonging to the Jesus Seminar, grapple with the obvious problem of their own subjectivity while groping toward every tenuous mirage that might miraculously materialize into concrete reality. All of their approaches smack of rationalized justification. "Multiple independent attestation" is self-defeating; the more the sources don't match, the *less*, not the more likely they are to be authentic. "Embarrassment"? Here, too, the more embarrassingly inconsistent the less likely the authenticity. Embarrassingly "creative" stories aren't more plausible just because they're fantastic. Just ask any kid. "Historical plausibility"? To date, there isn't any. "Characteristic Jesus"? What Jesus?

THE POSSIBLE, IMPROBABLE, PREPOSTEROUS HISTORICAL JESUS

For the past three centuries, numerous books have been written about the absence of an actual historical Jesus. Of course that doesn't keep the professors from speculating; bookstores and libraries are flooded with their books advancing one or another theory of the historical Jesus. And why not? Even though Jesus *probably* never existed, that doesn't rule out the remote *possibility* that he did.

Once they establish possibility, they can also entertain the possibility that Jesus performed miracles and that he was God, even though those scholars themselves have demonstrated those possibilities to be extremely unlikely.

In fact, the possibility that there ever existed anyone remotely resembling the biblical Jesus is as *improbable* as the possibility that Darwinian evolution is a fact (a "fact" I deconstruct in the next four chapters). In other words, it's almost, or even essentially, impossible. Yet seminary-trained pastors continue to preach "the risen Lord" because resurrection is possible—remotely possible, almost impossible, probably impossible, but still. A living Jesus, real or symbolic (does it really matter?), is good for us.

The Christian elite—seminary trained pastors, professors, theologians, Christian writers—only admit the possibility that Jesus existed because they can. Academia respectfully grants them this license. As improbable as they know the historical Jesus to be, as far removed as that Jesus must be from the Gospel representation, the Christian elite perpetuate the Santa myth as fact.

Whoops. Did I say Santa?

But really, doesn't the Christian elite continue the traditional myth because they think we "children" can't handle the truth and can benefit from the fiction? Didn't the tradition likely arise in the first place to entice the hope that good behavior would result in gifts and bad behavior in a lump of coal (hell, or worse, extinction)? Or perhaps it alleviates the fear of death. Some Jesus scholars have called the perpetuation of the possibility of a historical Jesus embarrassing. More pointedly, it's insulting at best, dishonest at worst.

Like Darwinians, Christians hang their hats on the flimsy hook of astronomically remote possibility.

It's possible or it's probable. Or it's improbable. In academia, you're not supposed to call a colleague's theory strictly impossible; the moon *could* be made of blue cheese, mushrooms *could* mutate into muskrats, humans *could* evolve from bacteria. Probable, possible, improbable, a drug trip—those are the choices offered by the methodology of responsible history, of good science, of cordial theorizing.

But do these choices suffice? In the spirit of intellectual rectitude, I'd like to add a new option to the list: *Preposterous*. (I prefer impossible, but I'll settle for preposterous.)

I'm sure many Jesus scholars have considered this concept before, but the keepers of the keys of the kingdom suppress (or repress) this antidote to ignorance to save their jobs in the ministry or seminary, or to maintain academic politeness among the peers they must cite, or to protect the gullible "children" of the world, or to prevent civilization from chucking traditional values for the slippery slope joyride to barbarism, or to exploit the passive sheep, or to enhance their own power, or to honor the traditions of their ancestors, or to explain an ineffable numinous experience, or to shore up their own fears and righteous indignation, or to mummify the prophets of their area of expertise—but why go on? In the quest for truth, the claim *preposterous* trumps presumptuous propaganda.

A CASE STUDY: A SPIRITUAL MANIFESTO

In 1862, three years after Darwin's *The Origin of Species* shocked the British Empire, an Anglican mathematician and the Bishop of Natal in South Africa, John William Colenso, D.D., published a work of biblical criticism far more disturbing than Darwin's ape. The dust stirred up by Chubb, Reimarus, Strauss, and other scholarly troublemakers had been quietly swept under the academic carpet, but the timing of Colenso's courageous commentary, prefaced with confessions of doubt, juxtaposed against Darwin's cocky convictions triggered an uproar that couldn't quite be squelched. Allow me to crank up the amplifier.

The controversy began when Colenso's pious intention to translate the Bible into Zulu led him to closely examine the text word by word. By the time he completed the Pentateuch and the Book of Joshua, he realized that the Bible was neither scientifically nor historically accurate, and felt it was his duty to systematically present his findings. By today's standards, the thesis of this first of his books seems quite tame: "proving the *unhistorical character*, the *later origin*, and the *compound authorship*, of the five books usually attributed to Moses." Because Colenso "desired to place, in a clear and intelligible form, before the eyes of the general reader, the main arguments which have been advanced," and published his writings in a book available not just to scholars but to every believer, all Christendom reeled under the weight of the truth.

Though most people today (other than lit. and religion majors) have never heard of John William Colenso, his spirit still haunts the alleys and cafes of Main Street. Many of us can "relate" to Colenso's spiritual crisis if not the indignant accusations of heresy and insanity and worse launched by both his academic peers and threatened laymen. Despite his genuine humility, Colenso boldly asserted that religious belief should not conflict with historical scholarship or scientific fact or be shackled to outdated myths and superstitions. For his honest insights regarding the historical "forgery" and logical absurdity of the Old Testament, plus his opposition to the doctrine of eternal punishment and his toleration of polygamy among the Zulus, Colenso was tried for heresy, deposed as bishop, and excommunicated by his superior in Cape Town; later he was reinstated by the church Privy Council in England due to a legal technicality; later still he was deposed again, this time by the English bishops. Nonetheless, Colenso continued in his post, ministering to his dwindling congregation, and there wrote commentaries, a New Testament translation in Zulu, a grammar, and a dictionary.

The forthright self-scrutiny Colenso includes in the Preface to his book is worth reexamining for three important reasons: His indictment of his own conscious sidestepping of the truth gives notice to scholars still lying today; his description of submitting to the truth encourages believers undergoing the same process; and although he probably wouldn't think to call himself a Deist, Colenso's fundamental belief is decidedly Deist: "The Law of Truth must be obeyed." He writes,

> Engrossed with parochial and other work in England, I did what, probably, many other clergymen have done under similar circumstances,—I contented myself with silencing, by means of the specious explanations, which are given in most commentaries, the ordinary objections against the historical character of the early portions of the Old Testament, and settled down into a willing acquiescence in the general truth of the narrative, whatever difficulties might still hang about particular parts of it. In short, the doctrinal and devotional portions of the Bible were what were needed most in parochial duty. And, if a passage of the Old Testament formed at any time the subject of a sermon, it was easy to draw from it practical lessons of daily

life, without examining closely into the historical truth of the narrative...But, on the whole, I found so much of Divine Light and Life in those and other parts of the Sacred Book, so much wherewith to feed my own soul and the souls of others, that I was content to take all this for granted, as being true in the main, however wonderful [fanciful], and as being at least capable, in an extreme case, of *some* sufficient explanation.

Here, however, as I have said, amidst my work in this land, I have been brought face to face with the very questions which I then put by. While translating the story of the Flood, I have had a simple-minded, but intelligent, native,—one with the docility of a child, but the reasoning powers of mature age,—look up, and ask, "Is all that true? Do you really believe that all this happened thus,—that all the beasts, and birds, and creeping things, upon the earth, large and small, from hot countries and cold, came thus by pairs, and entered into the ark with Noah? And did Noah gather food for them *all*, for the beasts and birds of prey, as well as the rest?" My heart answered in the words of the Prophet, "Shall a man speak lies in the name of the LORD?" Zech. xiii.3. I dared not do so. My own knowledge of some branches of science, of Geology in particular, had been much increased since I left England; and I now knew for certain, on geological grounds, a fact, of which I had only had misgivings before, viz. that a *Universal* Deluge, such as the Bible manifestly speaks of, could not possibly have taken place in the way described in the Book of Genesis, not to mention other difficulties which the story contains...Knowing this, I felt that I dared not, as a servant of the God of Truth, urge my brother man to believe that, which I did not myself believe, which I knew to be untrue, as a matter-of-fact, historical, narrative. I gave him, however, such a reply as satisfied him for the time, without throwing any discredit upon the general veracity of the Bible history.

But I was thus driven,—against my will at first, I may truly say,—to search more deeply into these questions; and I have since done so, to the best of my power, with the means at my disposal in this colony. And now I tremble at the result of my enquiries,—rather, I should do so, were it not that I believe firmly in a God of Righteousness and Truth and Love, who both "IS, and is a rewarder of them that diligently seek him." Should all else give way beneath me, I feel that His Everlasting Arms are still under me. I am sure that the solid ground is there, on which my feet can rest, in the knowledge of Him, "in whom I live, and move, and have my being," who is my "faithful Creator," my "Almighty and most Merciful Father." *That* Truth I see with my spirit's eyes, once opened to the light of it, as plainly as I see the Sun in the heavens. And that Truth, I know, more or less distinctly apprehended, has been the food of living men, the strength of brave souls that "yearn for light," and battle for the right and the true, the support of struggling and sorrow-stricken hearts, in all ages of the world, in all climes, under all religions...

Our duty, surely, is to follow the Truth, wherever it leads us, and to leave the consequences in the hands of God...After reading that article [by Ernst Wilhelm Hengstenberg on the Pentateuch, which deliberately dismisses biblical discrepancies and opposes the historical-critical method], I [Colenso] felt more hopelessly than ever how hollow is the ground upon which we have so long been standing, with reference to the subject of the Inspiration of Scripture. I see that there is a very general demand made upon the clerical authors of "Essays and Reviews," that they should leave the Church of England, or, at least, resign their preferments. For my own part, however much I may dissent, as I do, from some of their views, I am very far indeed from judging them for remaining, as they still do, as ministers within her pale,—knowing too well, by my own feelings, how dreadful would be the wrench, to be torn from all one has loved and revered, by going out of the Church. Perhaps, they may in time feel it to be their duty to the Church itself, and to that which they hold to be the Truth, to abide in their stations, unless they are formally and legally excluded from them, and to claim for *all* her members, clerical as well as lay, that freedom of thought and utterance, which is the very essence of our Protestant religion, and without which, indeed, in this age of advancing science, the Church of England would soon become a mere dark prison-house, in which the mind both of the teacher and the taught would be fettered still with the chains of past ignorance, instead of being, as we fondly believed, the very home of religious liberty, and the centre of life and light for all the land.

In my view, John Colenso is one of Deism's great spiritual heroes, even though he never ceased being, in a sense, a Christian, and a Christian priest at that. He was *beginning* to understand what many believers of his era were beginning to understand, but unlike most scholars and believers then and today, Colenso was honest in his insights, doubts, and skepticism. Well over a century after Colenso wrote his popular books, we have, even in democratic America, aggressive challenges to religious liberty and God-given common sense from far-right fundamentalists, from dominionists, from TV evangelists, from the Tea Party, from self-righteous wannabe spiritual dictators like Rick Santorum and Sarah Palin. There's a good reason why Jesus called the devil "the father of lies." The *lie* is the real root of all evil.

The Deist position remains quite clear: Preposterous religion denigrates truth and defaces God. Our agenda today is centuries old: *Stop lying.*

"The Law of Truth must be obeyed," Colenso proclaimed. Now *that* would bring salvation.

CODA: THE END IS THE BEGINNING

For some of us, Colenso's confession of doubt resounds like a mighty bell calling us to join the congregation of Truth. Relinquishing our cherished assumptions might sting like a painful divorce, might pinch like outgrowing an old friend with whom we still share fond memories and to whom we owe a debt of gratitude for helping us become who we are. But the aches of growing up, of crossing those thresholds that mark life's shifts into higher paradigms of ourselves—even those sometimes excruciating pangs register catalysts that only hurt as we pass through them.

Who doesn't want to grow up? What adult still needs Santa Claus, or spiritual codependence? Maturity requires a little suffering, or a lot, but if the midwife causes pain, it's to hand us the joy of new life—*our* life.

I know very intimately what relinquishment feels like. Leaving your religion can feel like a death, but it's only a death that brings you to your senses—to the reality of yourself, your wiser Self, and to a transcending knowledge of the reality of God as God.

We are perpetually dying in order to live. In fact, death *is* life, is perpetually new life. And we humans are built to know this, which is so amazing it's exciting.

If you really think about it, death as life is an extraordinary paradox. Resurrection didn't happen to one man in one place at one moment in history. Resurrection is everlasting. Imagine: Every moment dies, and in each departing moment a part of you "dies," yet *you* never die—*you* continue on into the fullness of your constantly coherent Self coming into being.

Isn't it irresponsible to take such an intelligently designed miracle completely for granted?

Certainly it's reasonable to assume that the big Death is but another threshold, just another paradigm shift into the better angels of ourselves. Understanding death as life alleviates fear of Death in its myriad incarnations and defuses the fallout of that fear.

John William Colenso, like many soul-searchers throughout the ages, like me, like you perhaps, understood the necessity of embracing reality *in spite of*. Living in a fiction has its perks. But Truth is the source of genuine happiness, regardless of the pain it takes to get there. The reality of God is the ultimate source of joy. What is joy really but the experience of being truly alive in your authentic Being, as your most real and true Self in relationship with the literally real and true God? Isn't *that* the religion we're all searching for?

PART II

THE INTELLIGENT DESIGN SHUFFLE

CHAPTER 4

THE ORIGIN AND EVOLUTION OF CHARLES DARWIN

Sometimes even respected scholars forget that theories aren't sacred tomes from heaven crashing on consecrated heads of prophets sitting under Bodhi trees. Theories might seem to spring full-grown like Athena from the head of Zeus, hence the mythic representation. But in truth, theories sprout in the brains of ordinary humans whose thoughts reverberate with mix-and-match thoughts of other humans, multitudes of humans, entire milieus of humans: Even the thoughts of the dead pace and chatter in the brains of the living.

Theories aren't facts. Synonyms of theory include: hypothesis, supposition, conjecture, speculation, premise, presumption, guess. A theory is an opinion, a belief. It's common sense that theories need to be weeded and the best cultivated and hybridized. But because theories are often steeped in agendas that relegate reason, brilliant deductions can flare and fizzle while absurdities infest and mutate like a plague for millennia.

Theories are thoughts evolving. A theory gets a name once it gels in a brain capable of transcribing it into published words that make enough sense that the theory's name stands for something recognizable, even if only vaguely understood: How many people really understand Einstein's $E=mc^2$? How many people can accurately define Darwinian evolution?

Theories evolve, and so do the brains that devise them. Because the official theory of evolution emerged from Darwin's evolving brain, and because that theory remains controversial, it's fair, perhaps even essential, to assess Darwin the theory in light of Darwin the man.

Darwinians, of course, as much as they revere *evolution*, prefer to assert Darwinism as a not-evolving absolute fact, and they certainly don't want you to know that *The Autobiography of Charles Darwin* candidly reveals that Charles Darwin did indeed evolve, and even devolve—though using a different term, Darwin referred to it as the *atrophy* of faculties beginning early in adulthood.

The term "evolve," of course, means many things. It means change; it means grow up; it indicates macroevolution, and microevolution, and the current demand to distinguish between the two.

For Darwin, even the term itself evolved: In the first edition of *The Origin of Species by Means of Natural Selection; or, the Preservation of Favoured Races in the Struggle For Life*, published in 1859, he uses only forms of the word "descent" rather than "evolution." Not until the sixth edition, published in 1872, does he use the word evolution.

Most people aren't taught that the theory of evolution via natural selection was not a Darwin original. Darwin, being at the right place at the right time in the right income bracket, was naturally selected by his peers to be the prophet to facilitate the theory's evolution into "fact." The basis of this so-called fact has always been challenged, even by Darwin himself. The self-avowed inadequacies in Darwin's personal evolution over the course of his lifetime perhaps reveal more about the insufficiencies of his theory than does the theory itself.

That Darwin would be the fittest to survive the race to the title Father of Evolution probably could not have been predicted early on. Far from being a child prodigy, Darwin admits, "I was considered by all my masters and by my father as a very ordinary boy, rather below the common standard in intellect." He did, however, master the fine art of telling tall tales and spreading false rumors. Though morally disgusted by the failures of amateur con artists, he appreciated the talent of skilled hoodwinkers—unless he himself was a victim. He takes considerable time in his *Autobiography* to describe several notorious scientific hoaxes, which interested him immensely, and chuckles at some of his own juvenile successes.

Darwin maintained that even as an adult he was not a superior thinker. "I have no great quickness of apprehension or wit which is so remarkable in some clever men, for instance, Huxley," referring to Thomas Henry Huxley, his great friend and his theory's greatest advocate, for which Huxley was nicknamed "Darwin's Bulldog." Lacking the acute, quick perception of his intelligent friends, Darwin tells us, "I am therefore a poor critic: a paper or book, when first read, generally excites my admiration, and it is only after considerable reflection that I perceive the weak points. My power to follow a long and purely abstract train of thought is very limited; and therefore I could never have succeeded with metaphysics or mathematics."

Since Darwin was a poor critic of the works of others, we could justly ask whether we should trust his objective, critical evaluation of his own work, especially given that *The Origin of Species* was researched and written and rewritten over the course of twenty-plus years, during which time he was often unable to work due to illness—and written while he worked concurrently on other projects, which could well have been confusing. The only reason he published the *Origin* at all was that his peer, Alfred Russel Wallace, had already just publicly announced his own discovery of the principle of natural selection. In truth, the theory that eventually became known as evolution had been explored by many other scientists of the era and earlier. Darwin notes some of those scientists and other thinkers in the introduction to the sixth edition of the *Origin*, though in the *Autobiography* he brusquely stakes his claim to originality. (Ironically, Wallace, an accomplished naturalist and a theist who believed the spirit survived after death, would be one of the pallbearers that would carry Darwin not to his family plot in the local churchyard where he wanted to be buried, but to Scientists' Corner in Westminster Abbey.)

In an era when science was exploding with new discoveries and information, not to mention ensuing controversies, but that had no computers or typewriters, surely the long-term, drawn-out composition of the *Origin* would require a sharp memory and data filing system. But Darwin confesses, "My memory is extensive, yet hazy: it suffices to make me cautious by vaguely telling me that I have observed or read something opposed to the conclusion which I am drawing, or on the other hand in favour of it; and after a time I can generally recollect where to search for my authority. So poor in one sense is my memory, that I have never been able to remember for more than a few days a single date or a line of poetry."

His confession of poor memory alone recommends our caution as we consider the validity of his monumental theory, especially since it is enormously dependent on research data.

Commenting on his critics who complained that "he is a good observer, but he has no power of reasoning," Darwin notes that his book, "one long argument," has convinced more than a few illustrious scientists, proving to him that he has at least some power of reasoning. Yet again he admits, "I have a fair share of invention, and of common sense or judgment, such as every fairly successful lawyer or doctor must have, but not, I believe, in any higher degree…With such moderate abilities as I possess, it is truly surprising that I should have influenced to a considerable extent the belief of scientific men on some important points."

Darwin's Ambition/Competition Inherited by Natural Selection

Perhaps Darwin's ambition more than anything else accounts for his success. It certainly explains his rush to publish the *Origin*—after twenty years, still in progress—once Wallace arrived on the scene.

It is also conceivable that the central role of survival-of-the-fittest competition in his theory of natural selection was a projection of his own ambitious nature.

Though he doubted his intellectual agility, he considered his talent for observation and collection of facts to be superior, and his love of natural science, "steady and ardent." One might conclude that he was a natural naturalist, but by his own admission, his love of nature was "much aided by the ambition to be esteemed by my fellow naturalists." While at Cambridge, his reading of a couple books by naturalists "stirred up in me a burning zeal to add even the most humble contribution to the noble structure of Natural Science."

During his famous voyage on the HMS *Beagle*, he worked not only from the pleasure of investigation, but also from his "strong desire to add a few facts to the great mass of facts in Natural Science…I was also ambitious to take a fair place among scientific men." Some of the letters he wrote to a friend during the voyage were read and copies distributed among members of the Philosophical Society of Cambridge, and the fossil collection he sent along was examined by paleontologists. When he learned from a return letter that one of his mentors, Professor Adam Sedgwick, had noted that Darwin could become an important man of science, the young Charles "clambered over the mountains of Ascension with a bounding step, and made the volcanic rocks resound under my geological hammer. All this shows how ambitious I was."

Darwin well knew that his one shot at an important contribution would only be his theory of natural selection. Despite his own grave doubts, by the time the *Origin* was published and barked by his Bulldog, Darwin was fully invested, if not in his theory's validity, then in the *need* for it to be valid and true, or at least highly esteemed. That need itself evolved.

Early on, Darwin was less than intellectually inclined. Ambitious as he was, his years at Cambridge were, in his words, a waste of time. He pursued only what interested him, and his academic interests were quite limited and his performance well below par. He hired a tutor and slogged his way through enough algebra to pass the required course for his B.A.; geometry he found more interesting. But in his Classics course, he "did nothing except attend a few compulsory college lectures." The only schoolwork he considered to be worth his time was his careful study of arguments William Paley presented in *A View of the Evidence of Christianity* and *The Principles of Moral and Political Philosophy*, as well as *Natural Theology*, a work based on the seventeenth-century work by John Ray, *Wisdom of God Manifested in the Works of the Creation*. At this point in his life, Darwin was a religious young man, so it is not surprising that he was fully convinced by Paley's famous watch analogy proving that Creation was clearly as intelligently designed as a watch one might stumble upon out on a heath. Paley's proof ticked in the back of Darwin's evolving mind for the rest of his life.

Once he returned from his voyage on the *Beagle*, Darwin was most strongly influenced by Sir Charles Lyell, a science mentor who "was very kind-hearted, and thoroughly liberal in his religious beliefs, or rather disbeliefs; but he was a strong theist." Perhaps more than anything else it was Lyell's encouragement, advice, and example that most ignited Darwin's aspiration to prove specifically a theory of origin—a topic very much in the air, and one that was sure to impress the impressive Lyell.

Despite his tendency toward self-deprecation, Darwin's ambition fueled his vanity and triggered defensiveness toward his "original" theory of natural selection. Though his goal was to impress a few select people, he did relish the fame that came with success.

Is ambition vain or humble if the writer cares not about the readers who made him famous? In Darwin's case, perhaps a bit of both: "I think that I can say with truth that in after years, though I cared in the highest degree for the approbation of such men as Lyell and Hooker, who were my friends, I did not care much about the general public." On the other hand, he notes that the continued public success of his first work, the *Journal of Researches*, which recorded his observations on volcanic islands visited during the *Beagle* voyage, "always tickles my vanity more than that of any of my other books." Vain or not, the fundamental force that drove his work was desire for that high esteem among fellow naturalists that can only be attained by an important contribution to "the noble structure of Natural Science."

DARWIN THE COLLECTOR/CATALOGUER: THE SURFACE DATA OF NATURAL SELECTION

Throughout his life, Darwin had a passion for three things: collecting (his obsession being beetles), dissecting, and hunting—especially hunting, or shooting, as the Brits call it.

It should not be surprising that Darwin supported a scientific theory established on the principle of kill or be killed (the phrase itself coined by economist Herbert Spencer), being himself a person who enjoyed the pleasure of killing for its own sake, collecting life forms for the pleasure of displaying conquest and perfecting his own superiority, and dissecting to objectify life for the satisfaction of voyeuristic perusal.

Darwin was aware of the implications of a well-developed "taste" and ardor for collecting that "leads a man to be a systematic naturalist, a virtuoso, or a miser."

But his dominant passion was shooting. He reminisces that once, to his "deep mortification," his kindly, beloved father scolded him, "You care for nothing but shooting, dogs, and rat-catching, and you will be a disgrace to yourself and all your family." Darwin admits,

> I do not believe that any one could have shown more zeal for the most holy cause than I did for shooting birds. How well I remember killing my first snipe, and my excitement was so great that I had much difficulty in reloading my gun from the trembling of my hands. This taste long continued, and I became a very good shot. When at Cambridge I used to practice throwing up my gun to my shoulder before a looking-glass to see that I threw it up straight. Another and better plan was to get a friend to wave about a lighted candle, and then to fire at it

with a cap on the nipple, and if the aim was accurate the little puff of air would blow out the candle. The explosion of the cap caused a sharp crack, and I was told that the tutor of the college remarked, "What an extraordinary thing it is, Mr. Darwin seems to spend hours in cracking a horse-whip in his room, for I often hear the crack when I pass under his windows."

Darwin's competitive perfectionism was so acute that he kept an exact record of each bird he shot. One time while hunting with a couple friends, each time Darwin killed a bird, one of the friends pretended to have shot the bird himself, and only hours later confessed the joke. But it was no joke to Darwin, "for I had shot a large number of birds, but did not know how many, and could not add them to my list, which I used to do by making a knot in a piece of string tied to a button-hole. This my wicked friends had perceived." Darwin felt so ashamed of his zeal for gunning down birds that eventually he tried to persuade himself that shooting was an intellectual skill.

Gradually his love of shooting succumbed to the pleasure of observing and reasoning, but not before his rich father, who worried that his son was turning into an idle sporting man, suggested that Darwin embark on a career. Darwin had already proven his distaste for medicine, which he had been studying at Edinburgh. Though not a religious man himself, Darwin's father thought perhaps Charles might consider becoming a country clergyman. Although he liked the idea of the semi-idle life of a parson, Charles had scruples regarding some of the dogmas of the Church of England. After reading a few books on divinity, he persuaded himself that he must fully accept the Creed. At that point, he believed wholeheartedly in the "strict and literal truth of every word in the Bible." All was decided. Those plans, however, quickly vanished when a fresh opportunity knocked: An invitation to accompany a gentleman captain on his voyage on the HMS *Beagle*.

THE COLD-BLOODED SIDE OF DARWIN/ISM

Given his early religious convictions, we might well believe Darwin's claim that he was a humane boy. Yet he admits, "I owed this entirely to the instruction and example of my sisters. I doubt indeed whether humanity is a natural or innate quality." He substantiates this startling claim with personal anecdote: "I was very fond of collecting eggs, but I never took more than a single egg out of a bird's nest, except on one single occasion, when I took all, not for their value, but from a sort of bravado." Yet he did always take *one* from each nest. Perhaps he left the rest to hatch into birds for future shooting. Coming from a shooter, his comment that he never took more than a single egg implies that this qualified him as a good boy by his sisters' standards. Taking all the eggs as an act of bravado evidently was equivalent to sin.

It's fair to ask the future Father of Evolution how he decided which single egg to choose. Was his selection the not-fittest and therefore the one targeted for non-survival? Did that make him a pawn of the demigod, natural selection? Certainly if humanity is not innate or natural, and if the thoroughly modern Darwin considered himself and all *Homo sapiens* to be just animals, a position antagonistic to any form of spirituality traditionally assumed to be the source of the humane in human, Darwin the nest-bandit shooter likely tangled with Darwin the devout Christian.

It's not uncommon for a person to greatly evolve over the course of a lifetime. Ideally, personal evolution manifests the authentic inner self. But sometimes, as in Darwin's case, personal evolution regurgitates psychic glitches in a widening loop. Discrepancies in Darwin's theory are not surprising coming from a man whose nature accommodated rather than resolved self-contradiction. For instance, his intense passion for dogs made him "adept in robbing their love from their masters," yet he "acted cruelly" in beating a puppy "simply from enjoying the sense of power." Though he says the "crime" he committed "lay heavily on my conscience," we might assume this to be the conscience he owed "entirely to the instruction and example of [his] sisters" rather than to innate or natural humanity. What is the source of his or any boy's sadistic power-lust? It's easiest, of course, to blame evolution.

Darwin's autobiographical confessions highlight the dualism in his nature, which represents the schism in human nature translated into great metaphysical puzzles such as life vs. death, good vs. evil, sacred purpose vs. meaninglessness, God vs.—not, for Darwin, atheism, but natural selection, the surrogate "Christ" representing the Word (logos), the brute force of life emerging from cold material existence.

Ironically, evolutionary theory justified the natural evils that horrified the still religious young Charles Darwin during his famous five-year expedition with the *Beagle*. The predatory nature of life, exemplified by every link of the food chain from civilized savages to the parasitic ichneumon wasp that farmed living caterpillars as food for its grubs, provided sufficient evidence against beneficent design. The paragon of animals, *Homo sapiens* was created in the image of no god but *Animalia*.

Darwin observed that the "difference between savage & civilized man is.—It is greater between a wild & domesticated animal," noting that even the civilized practiced genocide and slavery. Without rejecting God outright, where the South American jungle paradise exposed its heart of darkness, Darwin settled upon his compromise of natural selection. Only a divinely created mechanism that ran on its own steam could explain the gruesome savagery that led to extinctions of the less than fittest as the natural means of advancement.

Certainly his Unitarian pedigree would have made Darwin comfortable with radical ideas of friends like Charles Babbage, inventor of the calculating machine, who viewed God as a divine programmer that had preordained life via natural law. Darwin could understand morality as the current culmination of social instincts of troop animals, could view love of deity as an effect of the brain's structure, could accept that fierce competition and struggle up the food chain and the heaps of dead in the wake of the victor simply conformed to mechanistic law laid down by the ultimate calculator of the universe.

But what kind of God would create such a cold-blooded mechanism? And why?

Darwin couldn't say. Nor did he try.

His not trying still matters. In the twenty-first century, extinction of life itself would be but the most extreme collective consequence of bowing to a radical tradition of survival of the fittest when even our own inherent faculties, like reason, conscience, and intuition, cry *No!* Many of us simply don't accept that kill-or-be-killed is the fundamental mindless/purposive mechanism of nature. Isn't *mindless*—or chance, or random (as neo-Darwinians put it)—and *purposive*—proceeding with consistent intent for a specific outcome—self-contradictory? And murder as the means of "improvement" strikes some of us as incongruous and unnatural.

But extinction—as in rendering something extinct—is life, according to proponents of natural selection. Time passes; five minutes ago is dead except in our memory. Space itself is perpetual change. New technology renders the old ways extinct. Species come and go. Competition, as natural as apple pie, forces us to kill or be killed, figuratively and literally. Rights, freedoms, cultures, values, individual souls are regularly exterminated not only by ruthless dictators but also by power-mongers as conventional as corporate aristocrats and self-righteous evangelists. Survival of the fittest consecrates elite entitlement to our means of existence, physical and spiritual and everything in between.

Granted, similar precepts were driving civilization long before Darwin convinced us we descended from apes. But though selfishness in the nineteenth century was not a new insight, Darwin unwittingly provided a rationale for Everyman to compete with the power players for the means to exploit. Although theoretically this leveled the battlefield, the cost was high: Humanist arguments for do unto others on grounds of conscience and reason were shredded by tooth and nail of scientific fact. God was dead, Nietzsche proclaimed. Angels evolved into animals.

From the very beginning, not everyone agreed with Darwin and his naturalist progeny, and even many scientists refused to forfeit humanist values or to sacrifice God on the altar of science. The Christian mutant, fundamentalism, emerged to thwart ape descent with even more primitive Genesism. But eventually Darwinian evolution theory mainstreamed, enforced by academia backed by law, partly in resistance to Genesist extremism but mainly because many of Darwin's assumptions appeared to be true.

Darwin pointed out, for instance, the remarkable similarities among living organisms. How true, we exclaimed, although great philosophers and ordinary people had been noting the resemblances for millennia. Beginning in the 1960s, molecular biology enormously amplified knowledge of our genetic connectedness. No scientist disputes these connections among living things. But just because we are all constructed of the same building materials and have similar features does not prove that one distinct type did or can descend from another. Even Darwin fretted, "Why, on the theory of Creation, should there be so much variety and so little real novelty?" and, "Why should similar bones have been created to form the wing and the leg of a bat, used as they are for such totally different purposes?" These cases, he lamented, are "inexplicable...on the ordinary view of creation!" He quickly realized that they certainly aren't explained by evolution.

Few doubt that distinguishable differences *within* a species are due to modifications in successive generations; and yes, we call this evolution. But since the time of Darwin, the theory of cross species-type evolution—the macroevolution of one major type into another—has continued to be challenged by at least one very persuasive argument: There is no scientific evidence that individual types originated in other preexisting types, but there is massive scientific evidence that they did not.

DARWIN'S FLAWED RESEARCH: MALTHUS AND POPULATION SURVIVAL

Darwin's theory of large-scale evolution was profoundly influenced by Thomas Malthus's views on population trends, which Darwin first learned about indirectly while he was on the *Beagle*, by reading Malthusian pamphlets written and sent to him by his friend Harriet Martineau. Soon after he arrived home, he read Malthus's *Essay on the Principle of Population*.

Malthus believed that population increases exponentially while the means of production increases only linearly, so the population must be limited via birth control, starvation, disease, or war (for animals, predation). For Darwin, the limited means of survival created a struggle for existence through competition that led to the fittest surviving, reproducing, and gradually evolving.

But Darwin, like Malthus, was wrong in assuming that populations always outpace resources. Researchers have found that populations are held in check not by starvation, disease, or predation but by intrinsic forces; there is no overarching "struggle for existence," no natural selection that preserves the strong and destroys the weak. This doesn't mean that there is no struggle, only that some cosmic fundamental struggle is not the core motivation for life; life is not created and sustained by a struggle for food. Even in times of catastrophe, such as extreme drought, species survive by adapting or moving on, and geneticists now know that the ability to do either is already preprogrammed in the species.

During the hard times, reproduction rates adjust to the new environment. Plants, for instance, maintain equilibrium by sensing density; when growth is dense, they produce less seeds; when growth is sparse, they produce more seeds. Animals reproduce at a rate that can be accommodated by available natural resources. Plants and animals almost always stop increasing long before they exhaust their habitat. Humans, the glaring exception, who express love, hate, and a great many other things through sex, reproduce at the drop of a hat, not just "in season," and our prolific species must *choose* to control our birth rate. Our population explosion is uniquely unnatural among species because our *failure to choose* is unnatural within our choosy species.

Evidently, choice as a natural aspect of human was/is programmed by a programmer expecting us to choose. We come specially programmed with the facility—the expectation, the natural demand—to act responsibly; to act irresponsibly is unnatural. Responsible choice benefits the individual, the species, the whole planet of living beings. Responsible cooperation, not selfish competition, is most natural for us humans, if by natural we mean contributing to survival.

EVOLUTION VIA ADAPTATION WITHIN A SELF-CONTAINED SYSTEM

Darwinians are right that nonrandom small-scale evolution can occur, but it occurs when a new need arises due to a change in the organism's behavior to adapt to a change in its environment. This isn't a process of natural selection in the sense of survival of the fittest. Usually survival isn't at stake; usually it's a matter of adaptive fine tuning for the sake of convenience.

Scientists have observed that rodents, for instance, sample new foods, and when they find a food they like, they continue eating that food. The whole rodent community joins in the food fest, and they pass on their preference for that food to their young. The preference is inherited culturally rather than genetically. If, let's say, the new food is a large, hard seed, the rodent's jaw and tooth structure abruptly change, but not due to mutation or natural selection; the whole rodent community has accommodated its new large-seed diet; it has adapted to its new environment.

In rare instances when there is a need to struggle for survival, the consequence is that some survive. It's not even necessarily the strong that survive. Usually the individual organism that best adapts survives, and yes, sometimes it's just luck that you find that extra seed you need to stay alive. The struggle for survival is about survival, not about evolution. Survival is one thing, evolution another.

Adaptation is called evolution, but because it is a nonrandom change in phenotype (meaning how you purposely change as an individual) and not a random change in genotype (meaning an accidental molecular change that is passed on genetically), it is not evolution in the Darwinian sense. In fact, many biologists today point out that the missing links in the fossil record consist solely of adapted teeth and bones, which are not links *between* species types at all. Nor is this evolution according to the neo-Darwinian theory of random chance mutation. As W.H. Ho and P.T. Saunders note, "It stretches credulity to imagine, for example, that the woodpecker first got a long beak from some random mutation followed by other random mutations that made it go in search of grubs in the bark of trees."

MODERN ANCIENT INTELLIGENT DESIGN: PALEY'S WATCH AND MENDEL'S PEAS

Although even the ancients assumed the necessity of a First Cause or Prime Mover or Creator of the universe, today's notion of intelligent design derives from the eighteenth century phrase "argument from design" coined by William Paley, who reasoned that a very complex object must have been designed and therefore there must be a designer. It made sense to Darwin the college student that if you found a watch out on the heath, for instance, you wouldn't assume that it had come into being by chance. Someone must have deliberately designed and constructed it as an integrated whole that performed a specific function, unlike, say, a rock, which could have resulted from natural processes and didn't have any functional work to do. There was a time (no pun) when Darwin was impressed and fully convinced by Paley's argument.

It is common sense that if the simplest organism is far more complex than a watch (it is), an intelligent Creator must have created life. This self-evident fact had been one of the fundamental tenets of Deism since it was transplanted to Britain by Edward Herbert in the early seventeenth century. For the Deist of the late eighteenth century, Watchmaker God referred to Paley's assumption of intelligent design, not to an absent father who wound up the universe and left it to run on its own with no child support, the intentional misinterpretation conferred upon Deism by maligning Christian critics.

In order to buttress his theory of evolution, Darwin the theory-proving adult countered that the watch argument doesn't work for living beings, because a species—like, say, pigeons—could evolve by natural means. Of course this begs the question, because Darwin and his followers have never shown how or why or that evolution by natural selection exists; a "trivial" change (as scientists call it) within a species type (a change possible because its potential is already programmed in the species' DNA—think of it as English language possibilities allowed by its alphabet and grammar rules) is not a macroevolution transition.

Even if Darwin's version of evolution did work, it could only work because it was designed to work. The intricate mechanism that allows any version of evolution to work—the laws of nature—must have been designed in order to consistently exist at all, not to mention as an elegant, rational entity. Existence itself, and the continued existence of existence, must have been designed.

Back in Darwin's era, science itself demonstrated that even in terms of small-scale evolution, Darwin got it wrong. He thought he understood that inherited traits would be mixed and diluted, that breeding black and white pigeons would produce gray pigeons, or pigeons with both black and white patterns; he assumed that a tall father and short mother would result in a medium sized daughter. Logically, though, blending would not cause a "going beyond" which defined macroevolution but more of a self-contained averaging out, a lessening, a diluting. On this point, Darwin's theory was self-contradictory.

A mere six years after the original publication of the *Origin of Species* in 1859, Gregor Mendel reached conclusions regarding natural selection that undermined Darwin's fundamental assumption. Mendel's experiments showed that mixing a yellow pea and a green pea does not result in a yellowish-green pea. The offspring would be either yellow or green. The daughter of a blue-eyed father and brown-eyed mother would have either blue eyes or brown eyes, not eyes of bluish brown.

Mendel's peas made sure Darwin's pigeon breeders didn't stop Paley's watch from ticking. A watch and a pigeon are both as complexly designed as two peas in a pod.

So where did blue eyes come from? How does difference emerge? That's the "mystery of mysteries," as Darwin's friend astronomer John Herschel put it. Even today Darwinians can't explain how less could produce true more—a complex cell consisting of complex integrated cell stuff from a bacteria, say—or how less creates true other, like a new species type, or even a trivial difference like blue eyes. Spontaneous generation, the emergence of life from not-life, is utterly beyond us. That mystery of mysteries alone confutes atheistic naturalism; hence Darwin's agnosticism.

For Darwin's freethinker grandfather, Erasmus Darwin, and for other thinkers of that era, like Malthus and Paley, higher creatures evolving from lower and all from one common ancestor didn't in any way negate, and in fact affirmed, a Creator God. But nobody could explain how evolution could exist at all in the first place. Evolution, really, is a form of natural supernatural creationism. Even if some natural mechanism could be located, where did that possibility come from? The "it just is" of neo-Darwinians is an admission that the mystery of mysteries is actually the miracle of miracles. Why not embrace the miracle of naturalism, the Deist asks. That would certainly challenge the creationism of fundamentalist myth.

Nobody contests the obvious occurrence of "trivial" change within a species group—say, the human type developing blue and brown eyes. What agnostic Darwin didn't know, and what stubbornly staunch neo-Darwinians do know, is that potential for that kind of trivial change was already programmed in that species' DNA. Like neo-Darwinians today, Darwin was well aware of the underlying, cohesive unity of design that defined each organism type, each container (as you'll recall from the first chapter). Extrapolation of macroevolution from microevolution is just as fallacious in Darwin's day as it is today. Yes, pigeons can be bred for variation. And variations can be multiplied to the extent that eventually versions of the overarching type will be given, for convenience's sake, a new species name. But breeding can't exceed the threshold boundary of the container; you can't breed something that escapes its container. Genetically modify wheat all you want and you might get wheat obese with new gluten protein chains but you will never get cabbage. Even if you could get cabbage it would only be because nature's blueprint allows for such design tweaks. Any mechanism that allows for any version of evolution works because it was designed to work, and to work within a far vaster network of complementary design elements.

Biologists now know that pigeons can be bred for variation because the laws of nature governing the process of breeding are "given," and the information/instructions governing variation are already present in the pigeon; the information/instructions needed to bring out certain traits are already encoded in the pigeon's DNA; the latent information/instructions can be activated by environmental triggers. In other words, within the inexorable parameters of a specific structure, there is preprogrammed potential for great—but not infinite—variation. For the Deist, the wiggle room of bounded *potential* supports the possibility of free will and of mind existing independently of brain; it indicates a bridge between material manifestation and transcending creativity—and I'm talking about you, the spiritual creator, not God, the ultimate Spirit Creator of your potential creativity. This view is entirely anti determinist-Darwinian.

We now know that Darwin was even wrong about small-scale microevolution. And he was certainly wrong in assuming that large-scale macroevolution was a series of very small steps guided by natural selection—an intellectual leap that is especially strange given his assumptions about mixing for averages, a form of watering down, not creating newness. Although it's true that mutations can result in small-scale changes, because no *heritable* information/instructions are added to the organism—in fact, information is almost always lost, usually resulting in degeneration and disease or even death—the process would not result in long-term, large-scale evolution.

DARWIN'S FLAWED RESEARCH: EMBRYOS

Even though Darwinism today contradicts the confirmation rules embodied by the scientific method; despite the marked absence of evidence and reasons to validate Darwin's natural selection; despite evolving coherence, completeness, and correctness of fossil record assessments that conflict with Darwin's theory of very long, drawn-out origin of species; despite the conspicuous lack of necessary and sufficient conditions to substantiate his fundamental claim; even though neo-Darwinism violates the fundamental rules of formal logic, not to mention everyday common sense—all of which the next few chapters of this book will confirm—Darwin's theory, or a neo-Darwinian version of it, continues to be the only theory of origin taught.

In fact, Darwinian *theory* is presented as absolute, scientifically verified fact. For example, Encyclopedia Britannica (2008 Ultimate Reference Suite DVD) states:

> The virtually infinite variations on life are the fruit of the evolutionary process. All living creatures are related by descent from common ancestors. Humans and other mammals descend

from shrewlike creatures that lived more than 150 million years ago; mammals, birds, reptiles, amphibians, and fishes share as ancestors aquatic worms that lived 600 million years ago; and all plants and animals derive from bacteria-like microorganisms that originated more than 3 billion years ago. Biological evolution is a process of descent with modification. Lineages of organisms change through generations; diversity arises because the lineages that descend from common ancestors diverge through time.

The grammar school textbook description that every organism evolved from a single common ancestor as a result of natural selection acting on random variation was never presented as a theory; it was truth: We descended from worms—like those worms we were forced to dissect. Many of us recall the surprise, if not horror we felt on first viewing the family portrait depicting our descent from our more recent ancestor, apes. (Perhaps you, too, wondered why it wasn't called *ascent*.) Most of us remember the picture of Darwin's Tree of Life, the evolved modern version, with protists branching up and outward into various types, and the other more contemporary trees of life, all depicting universal descent, our genesis, from one common ancestral form, the single-celled, atom-small Adam. Nobody bothered to mention that those representations were purely speculative, that those convenient ways of showing relationships were not in any way demonstrations of lineage. The branching, we were told, took millions or billions of years, because it took that long for enough differences to accumulate into a completely different species—multiplied by millions and billions of species. Our little elementary bodies, crippled by the weight of scientific authority, flocked to the lunchroom food-fight with renewed animalistic zeal, or fled to the depressive isolation of a clique honing the skills of escapism. We cracked books with monkey minds, we aped apes. Spawn of Darwin, we evolved into Victorians, nakedly insignificant now as cold metal gears in a mammoth machine.

As if the Tree of Life would not suffice to terrorize us back into our furs, our advanced biology textbooks treated us to the lovely nineteenth-century depictions of embryonic stages of some species drawn by Ernst Haeckel. A classic Victorian, Haeckel dutifully obtained a practical medical degree before his father would agree to allow him to study art in Italy. Although he considered pursuing art as a career, Haeckel (pronounced *heckle*) eventually settled upon the more responsible profession as professor of zoology.

After reading Darwin's *On the Origin of Species by Means of Natural Selection* in 1859, Haeckel embraced Darwin's theory as the precious unification Grail sought by many scientists to explain nature *in toto* in terms that soundly defeated the first and final causes confirmed by the Church.

Inspired by rumors that certain structureless organisms had been discovered in deep-sea dredgings, Haeckel concluded that the lowest creatures were protoplasm without nuclei that had spontaneously sprung into existence through combinations of carbon, oxygen, nitrogen, hydrogen, and sulfur. Even when scientists announced that the rumors were in error, Haeckel brushed off the facts and continued to convince his audiences that animal, vegetable, and neutral protista had evolved from the monera that had colonized his creative imagination. Eagerly informing his audiences that both inorganic and organic nature could be explained by the same physical laws, Haeckel embellished his popular Darwinian writings and lectures with his own theory that life originated spontaneously from inorganic matter by a kind of crystallization, a concept that occurred to him as he studied certain members of the one-celled protozoan group *Radiolaria*, which appeared to his artist eye as crystalline.

Artist that he was, Haeckel drew up numerous genealogical trees in his quest for ideal symmetries. Always grappling with the problem of heredity, at one point he speculated that the cell nucleus had something to do with inheritance. To further unify nature, Haeckel envisioned embryos as microcosms of the macrocosmic process of evolution. At the time it was assumed that humans evolved from fish, so Haeckel reasoned that the human embryo would develop as a fish before passing through the rest of the evolving stages prior to developing specifically human characteristics. In order to demonstrate his theory, Haeckel worked on various drawings depicting embryos of different species looking almost identical in early stages but growing different as they develop. Haeckel's theory didn't emerge from scrupulous assessment of research findings. Haeckel *created* art works that depicted a theory of life he *created* in his own imagination. It might have been art, but it definitely was not science.

Even in Haeckel's day it was known that he had cherry-picked and exaggerated his examples and that his drawings did not accurately represent early embryos. In 1894, distinguished embryologist Adam Sedgwick complained that the doctrine of early similarity and later difference was "not in accordance with the facts of development." Haeckel's Darwinian embryos were freaks and his presentation a carnival show. (Robert Louis Stevenson's *Strange Case of Dr. Jekyll and Mr. Hyde* might well be read Haeckel and Hyde.)

Yet even in the late twentieth century, our male teachers were gleefully telling us girls that someday we would be pregnant with fish. When photos of actual embryos were published in 1997 by embryologist Michael Richardson and a team of international experts, Richardson told an interviewer at *Science* magazine, "It's turning out to be one of the most famous fakes in biology." In 2000, Stephen Jay Gould remarked that "Haeckel had exaggerated the similarities by idealizations and omissions. He also, in some cases—in a procedure that can only be called fraudulent—simply copied the same figure over and over again," and exclaimed, "We do, I think, have the right to be both astonished and ashamed by the century of mindless recycling that has led to the persistence of these drawings in a large number, if not a majority, of modern textbooks!"

Staunch neo-Darwinians have shrugged off the obvious fraud. Biologist Jerry Coyne claims that Haeckel's drawings were merely "doctored." Anthropologist Eugenie Scott, perhaps the most outspoken advocate of Darwinian education today, admits that Haeckel "may have fudged his drawings somewhat." Textbook author Douglas Futuyma pooh-poohs that Haeckel "did improve his drawings." Why should we trust these guys? Why should we accept that reptiles evolved from amphibians when the eggs of reptiles and amphibians are as different as omelet and caviar?

Darwinians ignore the significant *fact* that both Haeckel and Darwin relied on the research of embryologist Karl Ernst von Baer to bolster their creation myths—the myths they *created*. Several decades before Darwin published his *Origin of Species*, von Baer showed that embryos of some vertebrates look similar at a certain stage of development. Von Baer knew of many exceptions of this, and he did not consider embryology as evidence for evolution. After rejecting Darwin's proposal of his theory based on what had become known as "von Baer's law," Von Baer himself criticized Darwinists, including Darwin, for having "already accepted the Darwinian evolutionary hypothesis as true before they set to the task of observing embryos."

Even knowing that "von Baer's law" was misleading, Darwin still maintained that "the embryos of the most distinct species belonging to the same class are closely similar, but become, when fully developed, widely dissimilar." Even after von Baer himself explained that this was wrong, Darwin insisted that von Baer's law was "by far the strongest single class of facts in favor of" his theory of descent. "It seems to me, the leading facts in embryology," meaning von Baer's observations, "which are second to none in importance, are explained on the principle of variations in the many descendants from some one ancient progenitor." Deliberately distorting the facts, Darwin claimed that early embryos "show us, more or less completely, the condition of the progenitor of the whole group in its adult stage." Darwin knowingly relied on a complete falsification of von Baer's observations to prop up his theory of descent. Haeckel trumped Darwin's falsifications with falsifications of his own, resulting in fraudulent distortions of distortions codified as textbook definitions of Darwinism dogmatically enforced today by the academic police.

It's shocking if not absurd and more than a bit ironic that atheist scientists accept their state of psychological denial in order to deny Divinity—or as Richard Dawkins puts it today, to "kill religion." Of course, atheists are "free" to assert their opinions, as wrong as their scientific guesses might be. But should we listen?

Humans have always tried to arrive at a palatable version of truth. Six centuries before Christ, the Greek Thales of Miletus attempted to find a scientific answer to the question, "What is the world made of?" His search for the permanent, unchanging substance beneath all change led him to guess that the primal substance was water. We no longer listen to someone who asserts this antiquated opinion, though we acknowledge the view itself as historically meaningful.

Thales' student Anaximander thought the primal substance was a formless lump of matter that was always in motion. He called his version of Chaos "The Unlimited," a perpetual battlefield where opposites—hot and cold, wet and dry—fought and separated themselves out. As heat dried up the wet to form land, our world began to evolve. Life, which first appeared in the ocean, resulted from the action of heat on moisture. We and other land animals evolved from fish that adapted to dry land.

Sounds familiar, doesn't it. It's a tune of "new" Darwinian science with the lyrics of very old creation myths. Such theories are important historically, but we no longer accept them as scientific fact.

Darwin was never confident that natural selection answered the riddle of how we had come to be. At the urging of his friends, divine intervention had to be ruled out. Evolution was the only viable alternative.

DARWIN'S EXPLODING RESEARCH: THE MISSING FOSSILS PROVING DESCENT

Darwin believed that his best evidence came not from fossils, but from embryos. Fossils, however, were necessary to document the process of species types morphing into other types. The crucial component that Darwin's theory lacked, and still lacks, is the actual glue that binds discrete types together into one long smooth ascending road from the first primal cell to the first human being. We have massive evidence that a vast diversity of species have existed. What we don't have are the so-called missing links, those intermediate steps that indicate the process of macroevolution from one major species type to a completely different type. All we have are indications of small-scale microevolution within a species type.

The truth is that no fossil, embryonic, or molecular links between major types have ever been found—not to mention that the differences between discrete types is so marked that there would need to be humungously many links between any two types. Those links simply don't exist. As discussed in Chapter 1, there is no gradual gradation between apes and humans, or between any two types. There is no macroevolution—a species type morphing into another species type; there is only microevolution—a species type changing within itself, like humans developing blue, green, and brown eyes.

This is not new information. The ancient Greeks—Aristotle in particular—long ago quantified the clear demarcation between types. Darwin himself admitted this major problem with his theory: "One, namely, the distinctness of specific forms and their not being blended together by innumerable transitional links, is a very obvious difficulty."

In all fairness, it's pretty much *the* difficulty. On the basis of this "difficulty" alone, Darwinism should not be taught as the only viable theory of species origin, if at all.

It's odd that a newsflash from the 1890s—*Darwinism Exploded by Fossils,* for instance—could still be news today. It's odd that it was a newsflash in the 1890s.

To his last breath, Darwin remained puzzled by the complete absence of fossils showing transitions between specific forms—the necessary missing links. What's particularly puzzling about Darwin is his persistent advocacy of natural selection when it had already become clear to him, as it had to many other scientists, that this critical data was conspicuously missing, which cast a deep shadow of doubt over any theory of macroevolution. Darwin's theory of natural selection was no more factual, therefore no less speculative, than the theories of Thales and Anaximander, or any of the world's creation myths.

For well over a century, paleontologists have known that during the Cambrian explosion, a vast array of phyla suddenly appeared during a very brief moment of creation. Darwin knew about this, too. In 1831, when he was fresh out of college, and three months before embarking on his expedition with the HMS *Beagle,* 22-year-old Charles Darwin assisted the geologist Reverend Adam Sedgwick (not to be confused with his grandnephew, Adam Sedgwick the embryologist), an advocate of Providential design in the animal world, with his excavation of Cambrian fossils from rock strata in Northern Wales. Already it was apparent that in a very brief moment of geologic time, complex animals first began to appear all at once, in what scientists call a "radiation," an explosion of different life forms, an enormous diversification, an inexplicably abrupt appearance of amazing biological complexity. This fireworks of diversity was not a long drawn-out process of evolution driven by natural selection.

So why, decades after the Wales excursion, did Darwin continue to promote a theory of natural selection?

Darwin was a man of many theories, almost all of which were debunked by researchers in his own day. For instance, Darwin hypothesized that an organism's tissues dispersed tiny "gemmules" to sex organs by means of pangenesis, a process by which tissues permitted copies of themselves to be inherited. When experiments performed by Darwin's cousin Francis Galton failed to find evidence of gemmules, that theory was abandoned.

(It is worth noting that pangenesis was not a new concept. Aristotle, for instance, the first person to classify animals into genus and species, wondered whether animals were fully formed in their embryo at conception, or whether the different parts developed as the embryo grew. Aristotle correctly maintained the latter. Interestingly, despite his theories of dynamic change, Aristotle rejected Empodocles' theory of evolution.)

Darwin published in the *Philosophical Transactions* another of his failed theories, a paper he later called "a great failure," so great he added, "I am ashamed of it." He attributed the parallel lines in the elevated land of South America to the action of the sea, a theory discredited by Alexander Agassiz's glacier-lake theory. Darwin excuses his mistake: "Because no other explanation was possible under our then state of knowledge, I argued in favour of sea-action; and my error has been a good lesson to me never to trust in science to the principle of exclusion." Of course, Darwinians trust in Darwinism to the exclusion of all other theories, especially ignoring if not ridiculing the well-documented proofs for intelligent design.

Darwin's failed theories continue to pile up. For instance, the recent "giraffe gaff," as it's referred to. Darwin believed that the giraffe's elongated neck and whole frame were "beautifully adapted for browsing on the higher branches of trees." During droughts, he argued, giraffes with shorter necks would have died off, and the taller giraffes with the competitive edge able "to reach even an inch or two above the others, will often have been preserved…those individuals which had some one part or several parts of their bodies rather more elongated than usual, would generally have survived." That's Darwinian evolution in a nutshell. But in the twentieth century, researchers Robert E. Simmons and Lue Scheepers documented that "females spend over 50% of their time feeding with their necks horizontal" and that "both sexes feed faster and most often with their necks bent." Giraffes spend the dry season feeding on low Grewia bushes and migrate up to 200 miles to feed on the tall Acacia trees during the wet season, when new leaves are plentiful and no competition is expected. The researchers concluded, "Long necks did not evolve specifically for feeding at higher levels." No competition, no natural selection.

In his *Autobiography*, Darwin candidly confesses his poor track record on theories: "With the exception of the Coral Reefs, I cannot remember a single first-formed hypothesis which had not after a time to be given up or greatly modified. This has naturally led me to distrust greatly deductive reasoning in the mixed sciences. On the other hand, I am not very skeptical,—a frame of mind which I believe to be injurious to the progress of science."

Given Darwin's track record on failed hypotheses and disinclination to be skeptical about his own work or the work of those upon which his theory of natural selection rests, it seems necessary to ask: Why trust his theory of evolution?

Darwin begs us to ask this question with his apologetic disclaimers in the *Origin of Species* itself: "This abstract, which I now publish, must necessarily be imperfect." Why, one asks, *necessarily*? His answer would not fly in a typical undergraduate college class: "I cannot here give references and authorities for my several statements…No doubt errors will have crept in…I can here give only the general conclusions at which I have arrived, with a few facts in illustration…" That's lame enough. But now the clincher: "For I am well aware that scarcely a single point is discussed in this volume on which facts cannot be adduced, often apparently leading to conclusions directly opposite to those at which I have arrived."

By the time the reader of the *Origin* reaches Chapter VI, titled "Difficulties of the Theory," Darwin sheepishly acknowledges, "Long before the reader has arrived at this part of my work, a crowd of difficulties will have occurred to him. Some of them are so serious that to this day I can hardly reflect on them without being in some degree staggered." Even today Darwinians distort these "difficulties" as cold, hard scientific fact. I don't hear neo-Darwinian assertions as honest as Darwin's admission, "We are profoundly ignorant of the cause of each slight variation or individual difference." His excuse still echoes today: "We are far too ignorant to speculate on the relative importance of the several known and unknown causes of variation."

"No one ought to feel surprise at much remaining as yet unexplained in regard to the origin of species and varieties," he assures us to our surprise, "if he make due allowance for our profound ignorance in regard to the mutual relations of the many beings which live around us." Darwin taught Darwinians how to shrug off profound ignorance and the much unexplained as if facts were not contingent upon knowledge and proofs. "Who can explain why one species ranges widely and is very numerous, and why another allied species has a narrow range and is rare?" The point, of course, is that his theory of evolution claims to explain this. Is natural selection just another of Darwin's failed hypotheses?

Right up front in Chapter VI, Darwin lists a few of the "difficulties and objections" that disconfirm, or show strong evidence of disconfirming, his theory: "Difficulties of the theory of descent with modification—Absence or rarity of transitional varieties—Transitions in habits of life—Diversified habits in the same species—Species with habits widely different from those of their allies—Organs of extreme perfection—Modes of transition—Cases of difficulty—Natura non facit saltum [nature makes no leap]—Organs of small importance—Organs not in all cases absolutely perfect—The law of unity of type and of the conditions of existence embraced by the theory of natural selection."

A list like this from Darwin himself should be sufficient to give us pause when asserting Darwinism as scientific fact.

FAILED QUEST FOR THE HOLY GRAIL

Keenly aware that the lack of evidence for the progression of one distinct species type into another was a problem, Darwin decided that announcing the problem would stave off the criticism that he was purposely hiding the problem. In Chapter X of the *Origin*, "On the Imperfection of the Geological Record," Darwin again lists some of the more glaring problems right up front: "On the absence of intermediate varieties at the present day—On the nature of extinct intermediate varieties; on their number—On the lapse of time, as inferred from the rate of denudation and of deposition number—On the lapse of time as estimated by years—On the poorness of our paleontological collections—On the intermittence of geological formations—On the denudation of granitic areas—On the absence of intermediate varieties in any one formation—On the sudden appearance of groups of species—On their sudden appearance in the lowest known fossiliferous strata—Antiquity of the habitable earth."

What but his desire to impress the impressive Lyell and his other intellectual heroes could have led Darwin to develop a theory he suspected might well be false? The anxious contradiction he reveals in the *Origin* is far from trivial: "We do not find infinitely numerous fine transitional forms closely joining [species] all together. The sudden manner in which several groups of species first appear in our European formations, the almost entire absence, as at present known, of formations rich in fossils beneath the Cambrian strata, are all undoubtedly of the most serious nature."

Although the lack of transitions might well have been sufficient cause for Darwin to reconsider his theory, he not only glosses over these, he presumes to transcend even the experts: "We see this in the fact that the most eminent palaeontologists, namely, Cuvier, Agassiz, Barrande, Pictet, Falconer, E. Forbes, etc., and all our greatest geologists, as Lyell, Murchison, Sedgwick, etc., have unanimously, often vehemently, maintained the immutability of species."

Then, no doubt with relish, he notes: "But Sir Charles Lyell now gives the support of his high authority to the opposite side, and most geologists and paleontologists are much shaken in their former belief." Though "most" being "much" shaken no doubt overstates Lyell's influence, Darwin would have interpreted Lyell's minor tremor as a significant event for him personally. Now that he had his coveted pat on the back from Lyell, Darwin had no choice but to honor the endorsement by accepting his own shaky theory of evolution as absolute fact.

Never mind the absence of the most important evidence for his theory. His excuse argues fallaciously: "Those who believe that the geological record is in any degree perfect," which of course is no one, "will undoubtedly at once reject my theory." Yes, but leading scientists who did *not* believe the record to be perfect also rejected his theory. Still, Darwin reveals the source of his confidence in his theory to be a metaphor. Not actual hard scientific evidence—a metaphor, offered by none other than Sir Charles Lyell, the one named "high authority" who switched his support to Darwin's side. "For my part," Darwin affirms with bravado, "following out Lyell's metaphor, I look at the geological record as a history of the world imperfectly kept and written in a changing dialect." Histories and dialects, it's important to note, are products of intelligent, rational creatures, not of mindless blind forces of nature. "Of this history we possess the last volume alone, relating only to two or three countries. Of this volume, only here and there a short chapter has been preserved, and of each page, only here and there a few lines. Each word of the slowly-changing language…" Wait a minute: the "language" of geology never changes, only our interpretation of it, "…more or less different in the successive chapters, may represent the forms of life, which are entombed in our consecutive formations, and which falsely appear to have been abruptly introduced"? Lyell, clueless that his metaphor has broken down, continues confidently, "On this view the difficulties above discussed are greatly diminished or even disappear."

Not so, of course. Difficulty obtaining proof does not diminish the necessity of proof.

Darwin himself notes: "But I do not pretend that I should ever have suspected how poor was the record in the best preserved geological sections, had not the absence of innumerable transitional links between the species which lived at the commencement and close of each formation, pressed so hardly on my theory." What he is admitting here is his *lack of knowledge about the fossil record* that developed his theory of evolution, a theory that depended utterly upon the fossil record for its confirmation. "Pressed so hardly on my theory" was a quaint way to admit that his theory was being crushed by the weight of its own inadequacy.

"Some of the most ancient [pre-Cambrian] animals...do not differ much from living species; and it cannot on our theory be supposed, that these old species were the progenitors of all the species belonging to the same groups which have subsequently appeared, for they are not in any degree intermediate in character." The absence of necessary intermediate links between any two discrete species groups disconfirms his theory. Furthermore, the vast number of species that must have evolved before the Cambrian period to give rise to all subsequent species is a problem. As Darwin admits, regarding his theory, "Here we encounter a formidable objection; for it seems doubtful whether the earth, in a fit state for the habitation of living creatures, has lasted long enough" for the vast menagerie of living creatures to have come into existence.

Not only that, there is no evidence of that presumed multitude of originating forms. The common assumption was and is that the fossil record does not reveal those multitudinous creatures because there was no multitude. Darwin doesn't accept that answer. His answer? "To the question why we do not find rich fossiliferous deposits belonging to these assumed earliest periods prior to the Cambrian system, I can give no satisfactory answer." His answer is that he has no answer. But he'll stick to his theory, by gosh, because without it he'll have no claim to fame and will wind up the embarrassed, disgraced failure that his father had predicted. "Nevertheless," he admits, "the difficulty of assigning any good reason for the absence of vast piles of strata rich in fossils beneath the Cambrian system is very great." He acknowledges that erosion or "metamorphic action" cannot be used as an explanation, because geologists would have found fragments. Furthermore, he says, older formations are not always the ones to suffer from erosion and metamorphism.

Remarkably, he admits, rather dryly: "The case at present must remain inexplicable; and may be truly urged as a valid argument against the views

[Darwin's theory] here entertained."

Darwin himself pointedly asserts that the utter absence of fossil evidence is a valid argument against his theory of evolution. But that didn't keep him or his fellow Darwinians from affirming his theory as fact.

Darwin's theory of natural selection relied upon future excavations digging up links showing the gradual progression from one species type to another.

But subsequent fossil finds have only widened the gap between types. When in 1886 geologist R. G. McConnell excavated the Mount Stephen shale bed in British Columbia, he uncovered billions of fossils and collected hundreds of new species specimens. In 1907, Charles Doolittle Wolcott, an expert on Cambrian paleontology, excavated a site fifteen miles north of McConnell's dig. This new site, the Burgess Shale, a massive reef that geological upheaval displayed 7,000 feet above sea level, revealed thousands of soft-bodied specimens that had been buried alive, so well preserved that one could see a Morella crab's lunch of shellfish undecayed in its gut.

Darwin's assertion, "No organism wholly soft can be preserved," was wrong, in more ways than one: Those well-preserved soft-bodied specimens contributed to the disconfirmation of his theory.

Even the delicate geological process exquisitely embalming all those extraordinarily "not-preservable" life forms and transporting them from the ocean depths to mountaintops neatly stratified like a museum exhibit so we humans could discover them in an era when these findings are most pertinent looks suspiciously like the directional immanence of a purposive Creator.

The Present Future Disconfirmation

Over a century ago it was already clear that so many new phyla with their own discrete major body plans appearing all at once—all of a sudden, with no intermediate steps to be found—had not evolved slowly via natural selection acting on random variation as Darwin predicted. There was no abundance of transitional forms leading back to a common ancestor. No incremental steps have ever been found. Although one could believe that God created evolution in the Darwinian sense, such a stance would be misguided.

Darwin himself knew that "The abrupt manner in which whole groups of species suddenly appear in certain formations, has been urged by several paleontologists—for instance, by Agassiz, Pictet, and Sedgwick, as a fatal objection to the belief in the transmutation [evolution] of species." Darwin himself explicitly concurs: "If numerous species, belonging to the same genera or families, have really started into life at once, the fact would be fatal to the theory of evolution through natural selection."

Darwin *knew* that numerous species types really started into life all at once. There was no "If." The Cambrian explosion was fact, and Darwin knew it. And he knew that fact was "fatal to [his] theory." As if that were not crushing enough, "There is another and allied difficulty" to the absence of transitions in the fossil record "which is much more serious. I allude to the manner in which species belonging to several of the main divisions of the animal kingdom suddenly appear in the lowest known fossiliferous rocks." It is not just *that* species types appeared all at once; the *manner* in which they appeared is much more serious, because it implicates the immanent hand of an active Creator in the act of creating.

In the very book in which Darwin supposedly proves his theory for evolution, he disproves that theory. What is truly astounding is that Darwinian scientists today continue to argue for Darwin's theory while further disproving his theory. This shocking disconnect between fact and belief among Darwinian "fundamentalists" is the exact type of disconnect between fact and belief for which Darwinians criticize religious fundamentalists.

Numerous excavations by universities and scientific organizations on every continent throughout the last century have only further verified the magnitude and global scope of the Cambrian explosion, and paleontologists have confirmed with a near-collective sigh the complete absence of missing links between major species types. The missing link meme is fast becoming a cultural artifact. Yet desperate Darwinians continue screeching against God, now usually referred to as "the God of the gaps." They want believers to dismiss God, too, but get really angry when believers won't dismiss those pesky gaps. No wonder they're angry: The fissure in their theory is evolving before their eyes into an enormous, ever-widening chasm.

The 1984 discovery of the amazing fossil site, the Chengjian Fauna, in Yunnan, China, provided scientists with more diverse, better preserved, and even older fossils from the Cambrian explosion, some of which are older yet anatomically more complex than those excavated from the

Burgess Shale. A similar fossil site has been discovered in Greenland. What this means is that the Cambrian explosion not only occurred, it occurred simultaneously at different locations throughout the world and produced the same life forms. By the 1990s, when even perfectly preserved embryos had been discovered and studied down to their molecular composition, it had become all but impossible to uphold Darwin's antiquated theory of evolution. The Cambrian explosion was a sudden worldwide phenomenon.

Recent analysis of drill cores from oil wells, of radioactive minerals, and of changes in the earth's magnetic field have led scientists to acknowledge the unlikelihood of ever locating any missing links predating the sudden emergence of Cambrian life forms.

Pre-Cambrian, Cambrian, or post-Cambrian missing links simply aren't there because they never existed.

Furthermore, paleontologists today point out that fossils found from eras subsequent to the Cambrian fit into groups already established. In other words, the Cambrian explosion provided all known body plans, including biologically complex structures like heads, compound eyes, skeletons, spinal cords, the nervous system, and fully articulated limbs that have existed since the explosion and still exist today.

All these consistent features have continued to exist, albeit in many cases in different final designs: Exuberant design differentiation is a fundamental quality of nature. But differentiation within a species is not the same as evolution into a completely different species type.

Exuberant design differentiation is characterized by discontinuities— discrete containers—like those produced by the Cambrian explosion, not by long, drawn-out continuity predicted by Darwin's evolution. The internet is full of deceptive claims of transitions between species types that turn out to be discrete species with a few minor features similar to those found in the species to which it supposedly links. Instead of transitional creatures, what we actually find in nature is what Michael Denton calls a "mosaic" of fully developed traits within the respective classes. We find mix-and-match, such as animals that have some organs from one taxon and some from another, but we never find organ systems that are intermediate stages between the higher taxa.

Blueprints and Building Materials

The unity sought by scientists like Darwin and Haeckle exists, but it doesn't disprove God; it further substantiates the miraculous elegance of Creation. Each animal species is built of the same materials, but no two animal species are exactly alike. Scientists point out that discrete species types are like different styles of house made of the same materials. Wood, nails, stone, and concrete result in structures as diverse as a Southwest adobe and the Taj Mahal. But we recognize a building and its style when we see one. We know an organism when we see one, be it an amoeba or an asp.

Humans have become so adept at classification that far too often we can't see the trees for the forest. We're *Homo sapiens*, yes, but we're also people. When pragmatism pooh-poohs aesthetic sensibility, when materialism denudes our intuitive awe, we murder that innate faculty we used to boldly call the human spirit. When science desiccates muscle and marrow and mind into mechanistic diagrams, and tracks the source of humanity to fossils that can't even be found, it's time for science to go back to school for a few courses in the arts and humanities.

The kids I know, and even most adults, are amazed that though all snowflakes are crystals, and almost all are hexagons, no two snowflakes are alike. Yet even a preschooler knows a snowflake when he sees one. Most of us can see that no two humans are alike, yet humans are human. No two apes are alike, yet apes are apes. Snowflakes are not humans any more than humans are apes. A human is no more an ape than a spiral galaxy is a nautilus shell. There's a similarity, but we know the difference. It is the category of difference and each category's unique features that define each specific category. Which is amazing.

During the Cambrian explosion, new styles of life were constructed out of the same materials, generating species types of animals as unique as the examples within the species themselves: humans are not apes; no two humans are exactly alike. Yet in spite of seemingly infinite variation within a species type, there's a continuity of form: apes are apes; humans are human. Humans are human, despite our myriad differences. Humans with blonde hair and blue eyes are as recognizably human as humans with black hair and brown eyes.

Not only are types uniquely themselves, each discrete type displays what scientists call *stability*: Despite small changes *within* the species type, the type remains identifiably itself forever—for as long as it survives.

And within types, species don't really *ever* change (or microevolve) all that much, contrary to Darwin's theory of gradual but radical change over time. As Stephen J. Gould puts it in his 1993 book, *Natural History*, "Stasis, or nonchange, of most fossil species during their lengthy geological lifespans was tacitly acknowledged by all paleontologists, but almost never studied explicitly because prevailing theory treated stasis as uninteresting nonevidence for nonevolution...The overwhelming prevalence of stasis became an embarrassing feature of the fossil record, best left ignored as a manifestation of nothing (that is, nonevolution)." Even so, many scientists note this dilemma in their books and papers. Species do change; they aren't exact facsimiles tossed from a cosmic photocopy machine. Every discrete member of a species is unique, but the species itself remains its own discrete, unique type.

So-called living fossils, which are very ancient species that have members living today, are evidence against Darwin's evolution. For instance, scientists thought fossils of the prehistoric coclacanth fish had small fin bones that could have evolved into fingers that eventually became our fingers, then subsequently discovered coclacanth fish swimming in the Indian Ocean that looked exactly like the fossils of the prehistoric coclacanth, hence the name "living fossils." Is it really likely that just one rebellious coclacanth fish developed fingers, or rather almost-fingers, and then just one rebellious almost-coclacanth fish developed the more literal fingers, and then another rebellious fingered not-really-coclacanth fishy thingy added some transitional partial feature, and on and on through the zillions of other transitional features that would eventually resemble humans, when absolutely no evidence of those transitional thingys exists yet we have fossils of the prehistoric coclacanth fish in a box and the modern coclacanth fish trashing on the end of a hook? And how would a new species type reproduce when species aren't supposed to be able to successfully mate outside their own species type?

Even if evolution *has* proceeded from a common ancestor on up to the higher species types like us *Homo sapiens*, isn't each transition just as miraculous as any one-time act of Creation in the biblical sense? Any Creation myth is just an aesthetic representation of the mystery of mysteries, the miracle of miracles, actual natural Creation, organic and material. We Deists see the miracle of Creation as an ongoing process.

One has to wonder what kind of intelligent designer cares enough to maintain the magnitude of perfect equilibrium between stability and flux, between stasis and creation that constitutes our universe. And cares enough to create us able to perceive that.

But instead of being impressed, by the time of the *Descent*, Darwin &co. ascribed this creative feat to a mindless mechanism.

Darwin assumed that nature takes no sudden leaps. So how many links would it take to provide the smooth transition between species types that Darwin anticipated? Five? Fifty? Infinite?

But there are *none*. The more scientists discover about the structures of animals, the clearer it becomes that stable animal forms that exemplify distinct phyla never blend imperceptibly into one another. There was no smooth ascent from some primitive life-form to us. Yet we continue to teach Darwinian evolution as absolute fact.

What *is* fact is that the history of life was an extremely long period of very minute life creation and almost no change, disrupted by one huge creative blast, the Cambrian explosion. And despite the few very minor eruptions since, the body plans that burst into being during the Cambrian era are the exact body plans that exist today. The building blocks are the same, though new kinds of buildings are being built.

"EXPLOSION" IS NO EXAGGERATION

To get a sense of how fast the Cambrian explosion took place, consider that the first life form, single-celled bacteria, appeared about 3½ billion years ago. Over a very long time these cells gathered into clusters to form blue-green algae. For three billion years, life changed very little. Multi-celled organisms appeared right before the Cambrian period; some larger organisms arose, as if God were warming up, then they disappeared. Following their extinction, in the biological Big Bang, the Cambrian explosion, the basic blueprints for almost all species types that have ever existed came into being.

Biologists' classic example of one clock day of life puts the first life, appearing about 3.8 billion years ago, at the beginning of the day. For almost the entire clock day, nothing appeared but those simple single-celled organisms. Then about 500 million years ago, at about nine p.m., in the space of about two minutes, or roughly ten million years, the full spectrum of all the major animal forms exploded into being in the forms they have had down to the present.

These animal forms didn't evolve from the bottom up, branching up and outward, as Darwin assumed. Each form appeared suddenly, fully intact from day one, and evidently, from there each species developed and evolved its variations, like our blue and brown eyes, and blonde and black hair. Each species type diversified—evolved—from the top down; it produced variations on the same original theme: Each species type is its own tree sprouting its own branches and leaves. And this same process continues today.

The major body plan—the blueprint, the "top"—for each species type was present at its Cambrian beginning. With any complex design, the theme—the blueprint—comes first. The first car was built according to a blueprint for that car; the fundamental design comes before the first car is built. Every variation on the car theme is a car, as differentiated as a platinum Rolls-Royce is from a staid black hearse is from a psychedelic stretch Beetle is from a lipstick-red Spitfire convertible. There is one kind of diversity between species—a human is a human, an ape is an ape—and another level of diversity within species—you and me and the wacky guy next door.

Again: Life emerged in a way that is clearly contrary to Darwin's slow evolution model, and life continued for eons to exist in the same, essentially unchanged phyla forms, those escaping extinction still remaining today. Those species types weren't evolving according to Darwinian predictions; in fact, there is no evidence that any type originated from another type.

Although Darwin's ambition would suffice to drive his theory forward, it took other conditions to plow him deeper into that high degree of denial that allowed him to willfully perpetuate scientific fraud Conditions similar to his exist today among Darwinian scientists. Correction might save us from far more than the nuisance of misinformation.

What's the Problem With Creation?

Darwin acknowledges that many of the "difficulties and objections...urged against the theory...are serious." His solutions to the problems come in two forms: self-contradiction, and reliance upon future discoveries, the latter of which, as we have seen, has only further disconfirmed his theory.

Darwin's problems begin "In the beginning" in the biblical sense. "I think in the discussion light has been thrown on several facts, which on the belief of independent acts of creation are utterly obscure." What renders creationism obscure is the clarifying theory of natural selection. Never mind that his theory is not clarifying because it is obscured by not-proven and even disproven "facts." Creation by a Creator doesn't make sense in Darwin's mind not because the "facts" he's working with suggest his version of evolution, but because his version only makes sense if he can rule out a Creator creating "independent" species.

Darwin tries desperately to explain away the absence of evidence for his version of evolution. "We have seen that species at any one period are not indefinitely variable," which proves nothing, because species having aspects in common does not prove evolution; in fact, it suggests "independent" creation of similar aspects in animals not genetically related. Darwin argues that species types "are not linked together by a multitude of intermediate gradations, partly because the process of natural selection is always very slow, and at any one time acts only on a few forms; and partly because the very process of natural selection implies the continual supplanting and extinction of preceding and intermediate gradations." Please note that he says that species "are not linked together," not that they "appear to be not linked together." If species are not linked together, lowest to highest, encompassing the entire realm of life-forms, then they have not evolved according to his theory. Also, remember that he himself pointed out that there has not been enough time in the history of the planet for the slow process of evolution, even if all species were evolving at the same time; and here he says that evolution only acts on a few forms at a time, in which case Darwin's version of evolution would take an even astronomically longer time than his basic theory predicts.

His next explanation for the absence of links (or the apparent absence of links) is the continual supplanting and extinction of preceding and intermediate gradations. Yet he just said that evolution only acts on a few forms at a time, not on all forms continually. Furthermore, the supplanting and extinction process would still leave many traces in the fossil record. But there are no such traces.

"We have seen that a species under new conditions of life may change its habits, or it may have diversified habits." But again, adaptation is not Darwinian macroevolution.

"Many large groups of facts are intelligible only on the principle that species have been evolved by very small steps." This is neither accurate nor valid. The "facts" Darwin is referring to are not actually facts. The actual facts, even the facts that Darwin was himself aware of (like the absence of fossil evidence for macroevolution) are intelligible on principles other than evolution by small steps.

"Although very many species have almost certainly been produced by steps not greater than those separating fine varieties," he asserts against the evidence, or lack of it, "yet it may be maintained that some have been developed in a different and abrupt manner." Development in an abrupt manner is an admission of Creation. This he concedes because there is no choice. The obvious fact of the Cambrian explosion he could not deny. Instead, he cautions against believing all that massive fossil evidence for it. "Such an admission, however, ought not to be made without strong evidence being assigned." Yes, but by his own admission, there is strong evidence for Creation, and by his own admission, as we saw in his previous chapter, there is no hard evidence for macroevolution.

As Darwin well knows, that strong evidence was documented and presented to him while he was still a student. Granted, he wasn't necessarily a good student. Even so, he was well aware of the evidence, and so were all scientists of the era. "One class of facts, however, namely, the sudden appearance of new and distinct forms of life in our geological formations supports at first sight the belief in abrupt development." Ah, so it only *appears* to be an abrupt development. All those scientists are mistaken; all their fossils prove nothing. This is classic Darwin in denial. "If the record is as fragmentary as many geologists strenuously assert, there is nothing strange in new forms appearing as if suddenly developed." The record of the abrupt appearance of discrete species types was not as fragmentary as Darwin implies, and it has only gotten far less fragmentary in recent years. Furthermore, there surely is something strange from a Darwinian perspective in new developed forms suddenly appearing at all, not to mention that it is even stranger to observe that if the record is fragmentary.

"But against the belief in such abrupt changes, embryology enters a strong protest." Ah yes, the fraud of embryology.

Fraud upon fraud to save face, to fulfill his ambition.

Fraud today deified to prove the impossibility of a divine Creator, the grandest of Darwin's failed hypotheses.

CHAPTER 5

DARWIN'S DESCENT

DARWIN'S DIS-EASE

Though Darwin's long life was replete with abandoned theories—most scientists' lives are—he never abandoned his assumption that species originated via the process of natural selection, despite his grave doubts; in fact, it could be argued that he willingly force-fit false data into his pet theory, much like Freud (now famously) force-fit bogus clinical data into his theory of hysteria.

Perhaps Darwin's stubborn persistence was a matter of filial loyalty. Like many freethinkers of the time, his grandfather and his father both believed in descent through natural selection, as did many other intellectuals who frequented the same soirees. In his youth, Charles had been a ne'er-do-well and a drifter (his five-year excursion on the HMS *Beagle* was as a self-financed gentleman companion to the young captain, Robert Fitzroy, himself an aristocrat), and yet Charles always lived a privileged life thanks to the great wealth he inherited. Perhaps he felt obliged to his genetic patrons to propagate the seeds of their philosophy, if only to rationalize his family's entitlement to the easy life of the gentry, and to justify his inherited elitist position: Despite any potential for "improvement" ("taming") among even the "lowest" races, Charles maintained that non-whites, "primitive" classes, and women were his natural inferiors; this was his explicit, typically Victorian position despite his abolitionism, concern for the poor, and dependence upon women throughout his life (his doting older sisters raised him, his doting wife nursed him through decades of illness).

One might dismiss Darwin's self-contradictions as typical of the era. One could even imagine Darwin as the protagonist of an Oscar Wilde satire. But though in his later years Darwin could afford to be the sweet, affable, grandfatherly old man that codified his ancestors' faith in "the deity Natural Selection" (by which Darwin reportedly swore), the world that survived him could not afford Darwinian eugenics practiced by the Nazis or cost-benefit exploitation of nature, including humans, perfected by modern corporations.

There is no indication that Darwin himself expected such malevolent outcomes. Early in life he became a devout Christian, influenced more by his years at the Anglican Shrewsbury School and Christ's College, Cambridge, than by his two years at Edinburgh University or his Unitarian family. But soon, appalled by Christian myths of eternal torment and by the sadistic side of humanity observed on the Continent and in the field abroad, Darwin became a self-proclaimed agnostic—a term he borrowed from Huxley. Motivated less by all-out rebellion (a la Nietzsche or Freud) against the cosmic Father figure who would allow profound and perennial suffering—for instance, the profound suffering Darwin experienced with the deaths of his promising young brother, two of his children in infancy, and his beloved daughter Annie—Darwin and his agnostic colleagues offered evolution and natural selection as the rational, scientific alternative to the mythic absurdity of divine, "benevolent" creation.

But does Darwinism really erase the possibility of a transcendent or even an immanent Creator? Does evil in the world necessarily rule out the possibility of a benign Creator? Darwin tried to think it did. Which makes sense, if by "sense" one is content to indicate superficial justification. If the Romantic poets or transplant essayists like Friedrich Engels accurately portrayed the Blakeian underworld that was London, the stench and blinding assault of poverty, abuse, and hopeless agony would have slugged any proper chap in the chop. Any squire with cash in his coffers would be well aware of the savage exploitation that defined British Imperialism.

Psychologically it makes sense that a rich white male heir to the British Empire would need to rationalize his rank when faced with the sins committed by the power of his own superiority. Although Darwin loathed philosophy, he embodied the Noble Lie inherited from another wealthy elitist, the ancient Greek philosopher Plato, whose ideal Republic necessitated stratification of society into three classes. "This myth," Plato asserted, "would have a good effect making them more inclined to care for the state and one another."

For most of his mature years, Darwin led a double life. Outwardly he enjoyed his relaxed station as an immensely wealthy respectable gentleman, and eventually the ambitious careerist achieved the position of a highly successful natural scientist who commanded the respect of numerous devotees, in large part thanks to the aggressive promotion of evolution by Bulldog Huxley's "X Club." But Darwin worked guardedly as he developed his theory of transmutation, which he learned about very early from his freethinking grandfather and family friend Robert Grant, among others, and later refined as evolution through the influence of his inner circle of fellow dissident materialists, mostly Whig reformers repelling the tight control of Anglican clerics, with their conservative morality and religious myths of divine Providence.

Early, when he kept his scientific theories and writing secret from almost everyone, even his wife, a devout Unitarian Christian, he did confide to Kew Gardens botanist Joseph Dalton Hooker, a close friend, that believing in evolution was "like confessing to a murder." While outspoken evolutionists were jailed for blasphemy, Darwin, nervous and nauseous, internalized his fear. Darwinism, which atheist Daniel Dennett recently called a "universal acid" that "eats through just about every traditional concept," was eating Darwin alive. It's not surprising that his sickness grew more and more intense the harder he hacked away at religion's views on Creation. Surely he knew he destroyed, for better or for worse, the ordered moral foundation upon which he and civilization precariously perched.

As society threw off the shackles of Anglican oppression, eventually with the help of Darwin's theory expressed through his writings, Darwin the man embodied the new malaise that filled the vacuum where the soul had been. Reduced to talking apes, humanity was no longer the crown of creation designed by a present and loving God.

The giver of ultimate laws of randomness and destructiveness, God was reduced to the father-savage created in the darkest image of man. Such an anti-vision might well lead to a sickness unto death for the anti-hero created by its image; one could at least theorize that Darwin's heart and stomach problems were an illness of angst. It is not without irony that in that age when the death of God the Father and the ascent of the *Ubermench* (superman) was proclaimed by Nietzsche—the "father of postmodernism," an underling plagued his whole life by sickness who died poor and alone, a ranting, syphilitic madman—the sickly Darwin could not attend his father's funeral or act as one of his executors.

But Darwin was no atheist. He simply could not reconcile the dark side of nature with any religious vision of a loving or just God. He never considered that the presence of both good and evil might have some higher purpose, like the opportunity for humans to freely choose the constitution of their own souls, as a number of philosophers had suggested. Choosing might involve giving up one's inherited wealth and status.

It's not surprising that the Darwin who loathed his classical education and failed in the fields of both religion and medicine would ultimately interpret the organized chaos of the world, and even the most beautifully ordered structures, as the work of a cold, distant taskmaster, an abstract Watchmaker God that wound up the universe and left it to run (amok) on its own, instead of as the free creation of an avant-garde Artist, or an Inventor tinkering at his workbench.

THE BLIND AESTHETE AND HIS MURDERED MUSES

Darwin was a man of contradictions. He loved his dogs and his beetles, but he also loved killing and collecting trophies. Early on he believed in God and the Bible and even fervently defended his religion against the taunting crew of the *Beagle*; later his religion gave way to agnosticism which gradually slipped toward atheism. Darwin evolved—he grew up, he changed.

Adapting to his new environment of questioning scientists, of religious doubters and political rebels, Darwin sought to fulfill his ambition the best way he could. And he succeeded. But in spite of his fame and place beside the great scientists of the age, Darwin was aware that something profound and natural in him had been sacrificed: first and foremost, the faculty of aesthetic sensibility.

During his Cambridge years, Darwin was, as he put it in his *Autobiography*, "inoculated" by his friends and professors with a taste for quality art. He frequented the Fitzwilliam Gallery and the National Gallery in London, and the intense pleasure he got from the art of Sebastian del Piombo excited in him "a sense of sublimity." He acquired a taste for music from his musician schoolmates. But though he regularly listened to the daily anthems in King's College Chapel and even hired the chorister boys to sing in his rooms, he admitted, "I am so utterly destitute of an ear, that I cannot perceive a discord, or keep time and hum a tune correctly; and it is a mystery how I could possibly have derived pleasure from music."

Can someone tone deaf who can't discern pitch or melody or harmony or rhythm be said to truly *hear* the music? Can he be said to hear the *actual work* itself? Can he *appreciate* that actual work? Wouldn't such a person be existing on a plane far removed from musical experience? The flat, one-dimensional plane would not be the same rich, multi-dimensional musical plane experienced by Chopin or the conductor and musicians of a professional orchestra, or even by someone of modest schooling who had an acute musical sensibility. If Darwin's aesthetic faculty was so severely handicapped, what is the quality of pleasure he derived from flat, distorted sound not actually discerned as *music*? What is the quality of pleasure deprived of the depth and meaning of genuine appreciation? Was Darwin only pretending to "derive pleasure" from music?

In his early years, he says, art brought him "intense pleasure" and sometimes "excited" in him a "sense of sublimity." Though he was informally taught to appreciate art and probably did derive pleasure from it, given his disconnect from music it's fair to ask whether by looking at art he was actually *seeing* and *appreciating* the work itself. While on the *Beagle*, he also delighted in reading metaphysical books and the poetry of Wordsworth, Coleridge, and Milton, his favorite at that time and most famously the poet of *Paradise Lost*. But his love of metaphysics and poetry waned during his twenties.

Even if Darwin's aesthetic sensibilities were not refined, his pleasure was evidently genuine. It is no mere coincidence that as Darwin's theory of evolution developed, his spiritual and aesthetic faculties atrophied. His own assessment of the demise of his personal aesthetics is worth quoting in full:

> I have said that in one respect my mind has changed during the last twenty or thirty years. Up to the age of thirty, or beyond it, poetry of many kinds, such as the works of Milton, Gray, Byron, Wordsworth, Coleridge, and Shelley, gave me great pleasure, and even as a schoolboy I took intense delight in Shakespeare, especially in the historical plays. I have also said that formerly pictures gave me considerable, and music very

great delight. But now for many years I cannot endure to read a line of poetry: I have tried lately to read Shakespeare, and found it so intolerably dull that it nauseated me. I have also almost lost my taste for pictures or music. Music generally sets me thinking too energetically on what I have been at work on, instead of giving me pleasure. I retain some taste for fine scenery, but it does not cause me the exquisite delight which it formerly did. On the other hand, novels which are works of the imagination, though not of a very high order, have been for years a wonderful relief and pleasure to me, and I often bless all novelists. A surprising number have been read aloud to me, and I like all if moderately good, and if they do not end unhappily— against which a law ought to be passed. A novel, according to my taste, does not come into the first class unless it contains some person whom one can thoroughly love, and if a pretty woman all the better. This curious and lamentable loss of the higher aesthetic tastes is all the odder, as books on history, biographies, and travels (independently of any scientific facts which they may contain), and essays on all sorts of subjects interest me as much as ever they did. My mind seems to have become a kind of machine for grinding general laws out of large collections of facts, but why this should have caused the atrophy of that part of the brain alone, on which the higher tastes depend, I cannot conceive. A man with a mind more highly organized or better constituted than mine, would not, I suppose, have thus suffered; and if I had to live my life again, I would have made a rule to read some poetry and listen to some music at least once every week; for perhaps the parts of my brain now atrophied would thus have been kept active through use. The loss of these tastes is a loss of happiness, and may possibly be injurious to the intellect, and more probably to the moral character, by enfeebling the emotional part of our nature.

It strikes me as a peculiar tragedy worthy of Shakespeare or Milton or any of the great Romantics that the man most responsible, nominally at least, for the sacrifice of the human spirit on the altar of mechanistic determinism could admit nonchalantly that he had in essence willfully programmed his mind into a machine—a computer—that resulted in loss of happiness, injury to moral character, emotional enfeeblement, and, ironically, severe mental atrophy. Darwin the man created the theory that symbolizes the absurd predicament, perhaps even the tragic flaw, of modern humanity.

Darwin's faith in his theory of evolution reached the pitch of religious conviction even while he expressed his doubts about the theory's validity. The passionate naturalist, cannibalized by the dark lord kill-or-be-killed, leaned toward mechanistic atheism. As if on auto-pilot, Darwin describes the objects and processes that his close observation once reckoned as beautiful, yet his stance now seems aloof and flat, as if his enjoyment of nature was like his tone-deaf "enjoyment" of music or his atrophied pleasure in art and poetry. Something was missing. That "something" was exactly that which could be registered directly as spiritual, or even fully real. The dimension that gives life lived to the fullest its zing always seemed to be missing, an absence, fully realized, that verged on extinction. By the time he finished the *Origin*, and certainly his later *Autobiography*, beauty had ceased to be beauty at all. Darwin objectified nature into a kind of intellectual pornography for scientific voyeurs; beauty was observed and used like a prostitute for a distant satisfaction of an immediate need, never for love of beauty for its own sake, never for the pleasure of intimate contact.

Darwin, like some neo-Darwinians today, could state the facts of elegance and beauty in an objective, abstract tone even while the descriptions themselves betray the inherent vitality of their own inherent elegant beauty. Beauty is in the eye—or rather, the spirit—of the beholder. Atheists and mechanistic agnostics like Darwin—and I really can see no important distinction between the two—know intellectually that nature is beautifully constructed while emotionally denying that it is. The aesthetic atrophies when the spirit does, or when the spirit lies dormant and inactivated. It is not the death of God but rather the fear or hate of God that inevitably leads to a kill religion/death of God theology of mechanistic determinism and Darwinian natural selection. There is never any death of God, only the murder or suicide of the killer's own God-given faculties.

DARWIN'S SPIRITUAL DISSOCIATION

Far from being scientific treatises proving natural selection, Darwin's writings betray the psychological angst of a man plagued by self-doubt, contradiction, and denial. Read closely, his work becomes a casebook exposing the consequences of spiritual dissociation that has infected modern thought. The atrophy of the aesthetic faculty and its subsequent flattening of perception is a crucial symptom of spiritual dissociation rarely considered when assessing declarations of scientific theory as fact.

Darwin realized that his mind had become a machine for grinding out abstractions from collections of facts, but because he had repressed his spiritual faculty and erased the possibility of a spiritual dimension from Nature, he was unable to understand why his aesthetic faculty had atrophied. What he acknowledges as "the higher tastes," so intimately connected with meaning and appreciation, are at their highest, spiritual experiences. That profound awareness of connection to that "something more" conveyed via the deep meaningfulness of beauty—the beauty of beauty—is akin to the sensation of spiritual Presence experienced via religious rituals, or feeling "one" with Nature, or that intimate "oneness" felt by lovers passionately in love. These experiences of touching transcendence are different facets of the same numinous sensation of touching the finger of God, as it's often represented figuratively, aesthetically. What Darwin *knew about* he could not truly *know*.

Yet the flat, objective, abstract observation of nature's beauty and design left Darwin uncomfortable with his theory. When on his *Beagle* voyage, he realized that differences among species "could only be explained on the supposition that species gradually become modified; and the subject haunted me." This "supposition" was only necessary because he had ruled out the possibility that species had been *created* and became modified, in the sense of microevolution, by the engagement of innate potentials responding to environmental cues. "But it was equally evident that neither the action of the surrounding conditions, nor the will of the organisms (especially in the case of plants) could account for the innumerable cases in which organisms of every kind are beautifully adapted to their habits of life…" Please note his use of the haunting word "beautifully" and his beautiful examples: "for instance, a woodpecker or a tree-frog to climb trees, or a seed for dispersal by hooks or plumes. I had always been much struck by such adaptations, and until these could be explained it seemed to me almost useless to endeavor to prove by indirect evidence that species have been modified" via macroevolution. He spent the rest of his life trying to prove that species types have been modified into new types. He never succeeded. To an artist, transcending modifications are perfectly natural. Darwin was unable to process the *creation* in Creation. As any true artist knows, creation is a generous act of love, even if the representation must be as "ugly" as Picasso's *Guernica*.

Darwin decided early on that nature was brutal and selfish: "Natural selection cannot possibly produce any modification in a species exclusively for the good of another species; though throughout nature one species incessantly takes advantage of and profits by the structures of others." Like Anaximander, Darwin considered life to be a battleground where opposites fight and separate themselves out, but Darwin's "good" was brute selfishness, the antithesis of anyone else's definition of *good*. His theological vision had no choice but to conclude, "But natural selection can and does often produce structures for the direct injury of other animals, as we see in the fang of the adder, and in the ovipositor of the ichneumon, by which its eggs are deposited in the living bodies of other insects." In Darwin's world of fangs and ovipositors, good equals harm successfully inflicted on another. In other words, benefit exists only through harm. Isn't that like saying that good is evil, evil is good? Darwin knew that his theory was dependent upon the inherent ruthlessness of Nature, not upon something reminiscent of the benevolent God of his abandoned religion. "If it could be proved that any part of the structure of any one species had been formed for the exclusive good of another species, it would annihilate my theory, for such could not have been produced through natural selection."

It seems logical to assume that a species, or an individual member of a species, has not been created for the *exclusive* good of another species or individual. Even theists agree that nothing has been created to masochistically serve the sadistic selfishness of another. But that doesn't mean that a species or individual does not serve *any* good of another. An artist produces art for his own good and for the good of the viewer. In fact, producing art is only ultimately good for the artist when it is good for the viewer. (Art that serves as therapy is not the high art appealing to the "higher tastes" that Darwin referred to and that I refer to here.) Mutual benefit is a given in the processes of living things. Yes, there is a brutal aspect to animal existence. But it is not *exclusively* brutal. Just because nature is not masochistic does not prove that it is exclusively driven by brutally selfish natural selection. Furthermore, as we have seen, Darwin's version of natural selection itself has never been proven; in fact, it has been disproven.

Perhaps Darwin's insistence that natural selection is ultimately brutal is a projection of shame for the brutal side of his own nature. Natural selection justifies brutality and sanctifies guilt. The brutal cannot face a God who might not condone brutality. Therefore, religions create their gods in the image of their own brutality to justify and sanctify brutality, and science creates its god, natural selection, the shadow of civilized man, for the same purpose.

The cooperative goodness produced by the God proclaimed by every major religion and recognized by the vast majority of people who have ever lived is an abstract construct to the tone-deaf, spiritually myopic Darwin. Intellectually, abstractly, Darwin understands the facts. Yet he never sees their multidimensional actuality, their transcending depth. He never even sees the glass half full, like, say, Anaximander or the vast majority of souls ever since. For Darwin, the glass is entirely empty. Life exists only to reproduce itself in an endless loop of brute survival for its own sake. One might ask the Victorian Darwin if marriage is *knowing about* a person or *knowing* that person. Is living knowing about life or knowing life? If one does not know life, can one know God, and vice versa? Yes, this is a metaphysical query, and one scientists often pose, if only negatively by denying its validity. There is the knowledge of the collector and the knowledge of lovers, madmen, and poets. To know *about* like a collector is not to *know* like a lover of art. Darwin and neo-Darwinians and atheists and many agnostics don't *know*. They can't know what they refuse to believe exists—God and the spiritual dimension that animates everything.

Darwinians are like people who visit art museums but are never deeply moved by the art. For them, Nature is a picture of life, a still life produced with paints on a two-dimensional canvas. Nothing more. What escapes them is depth, representational meaning, the correspondence between one world and another. Their faculties are not fully engaged. Reason is diluted by reductive scansion; intuition, emotion, and aesthetic exist like phantom limbs. Conscience rests upon self-congratulation, which looks suspiciously like a smokescreen masking the worship of brutality.

Darwin had already provided proof of natural cooperation for mutual benefit in the few pages preceding his assertion that natural selection never modifies to benefit another, and offers yet more proof in the pages following. For instance: "Seeds are disseminated by their minuteness, by their capsule being converted into a light balloon-like envelope, by being embedded in pulp or flesh, formed of the most diverse parts, and rendered nutritious, as well as conspicuously colored, so as to attract and be devoured by birds, by having hooks and grapnels of many kinds and serrated awns, so as to adhere to the fur of quadrupeds, and by being furnished with wings and plumes, as different in shape as they are elegant in structure, so as to be wafted by every breeze." The fact is that things exist for each other: Seeds are nutritious to birds; they are the food, the sustenance of the birds' existence. Birds assist a plant's survival, and even participate in the reproductive process. The profound beauty of the symbiosis of living seems completely lost on Darwin.

At first glance, it appears that seeds merely exploit available means of dissemination. It's fair to ask right off how seeds know how to exploit. Ah, Darwinians respond, seeds don't know this. Natural selection knows this. That would be a satisfactory response for someone whose answer to the mystery of Creation is a drawer of seeds and a few stuffed birds and quadrupeds. Darwin doesn't seem to realize that natural selection is a knowing intelligence, a god. He also dismisses the fact that birds *do* benefit from seeds. Have seeds been formed for the exclusive good of birds? Well, have birds or quadrupeds been formed for the exclusive good of seeds? The good is not exclusive if it is reciprocal. Good is good only if it is *not* exclusive. Nature is democratic with its goodness. Darwin misses the point that there is as much good for birds in seed dissemination as there is bad for the victim of the adder's fang. Darwin avoids dualism and "unifies" Nature by making it exclusively selfish.

INTELLIGENT CREATION

Darwin never asks how natural selection, or Nature, got so smart. For instance, "pollen does not spontaneously fall on the stigma, some aid is necessary for their fertilization. With several kinds this is effected by the pollen-grains, which are light and incoherent, being blown by the wind through mere chance on to the stigma; and this is the simplest plan which can well be conceived." Who drew up this complex "simplest" plan? Who put the plan into action? "An almost equally simple, though very different plan occurs in many plants in which a symmetrical flower secretes a few drops of nectar, and is consequently visited by insects; and these carry the pollen from the anthers to the stigma." If the first plan worked, why create another? Ask any artist why she paints picture after picture. Nature isn't a mere plan; it's a humungous gallery continuously stocking new works displaying exuberant creativity.

When aesthetic atrophies, when amazing feats of nature are reduced to flat facts on a spreadsheet, reason, too, flattens. The flat reason of Darwinian biology takes the formation and processes of life for granted and fails to notice that their existence is no more scientifically necessary than Picasso's Blue Period *Old Guitarist* or his controversial *Les Demoiselles d'Avignon* or the Analytical Cubism he developed with Braque. Creativity spreads outward, always pregnant with something new; reductionist science squeezes the life out of life.

Reductionists can't answer why, if natural selection is so smart, does fertilization need to take place at all? And why is it such an elaborate process? Darwin continues to describe the amazingly beautifully elaborate natural process, but he does so coolly, dispassionately, as one unable to aesthetically *feel* what is witnessed:

> From this simple stage we may pass through an inexhaustible number of contrivances, all for the same purpose and effected in essentially the same manner, but entailing changes in every part of the flower. The nectar may be stored in variously shaped receptacles, with the stamens and pistils modified in many ways, sometimes forming trap-like contrivances, and sometimes capable of neatly adapted movements through irritability or elasticity. From such structures we may advance till we come to such a case of extraordinary adaptation as that lately described by Dr. Cruger in the Coryanthes. This orchid has part of its labellum or lower lip hollowed out into a great bucket, into which drops of almost pure water continually fall from two secreting horns which stand above it; and when the bucket is half-full, the water overflows by a spout on one side. The basal part of the labellum stands over the bucket, and is itself hollowed out into a sort of chamber with two lateral entrances; within this chamber there are curious fleshy ridges. The most ingenious man, if he had not witnessed what takes place, could never have imagined what purpose all these parts serve. But Dr. Cruger saw crowds of large humble-bees visiting

the gigantic flowers of this orchid, not in order to suck nectar, but to gnaw off the ridges within the chamber above the bucket; in doing this they frequently pushed each other into the bucket, and their wings being thus wetted they could not fly away, but were compelled to crawl out through the passage formed by the spout or overflow. Dr. Cruger saw a "continual procession" of bees thus crawling out of their involuntary bath. The passage is narrow, and is roofed over by the column, so that a bee, in forcing its way out, first rubs its back against the viscid stigma and then against the viscid glands of the pollen-masses. The pollen-masses are thus glued to the back of the bee which first happens to crawl out through the passage of a lately expanded flower, and are thus carried away. Dr. Cruger sent me a flower in spirits of wine, with a bee which he had killed before it had quite crawled out, with a pollen-mass still fastened to its back. When the bee, thus provided, flies to another flower, or to the same flower a second time, and is pushed by its comrades into the bucket and then crawls out by the passage, the pollen-mass necessarily comes first into contact with the viscid stigma, and adheres to it, and the flower is fertilized. Now at last we see the full use of every part of the flower, of the water-secreting horns of the bucket half-full of water, which prevents the bees from flying away, and forces them to crawl out through the spout, and rub against the properly placed viscid pollen-masses and the viscid stigma.

This wildly exotic orchid-bee choreography far exceeds the creativity of any dance conceived by Twyla Tharp. Granted, this process might not be a mass orgy of mutual benefit. Then again, who's to say the bees don't enjoy this trip to the baths? And it was Dr. Cruger who killed the bee preserved in the spirits of wine (now the bee's spirit has mixed with the wine's). Perhaps more to the point, Mr. Darwin, is such an elegant art work as the fertilization of an orchid really an example of ruthless, to-the-point natural selection?

But this sticky point persists: Why not stick to the finished product, if it works? Why embellish?

The construction of the flower in another closely allied orchid, namely, the Catasetum, is widely different, though serving the same end; and is equally curious. Bees visit these flowers, like those of the Coryanthes, in order to gnaw the labellum; in doing this they inevitably touch a long, tapering, sensitive projection, or, as I have called it, the antenna. This antenna, when touched, transmits a sensation or vibration to a certain membrane which is instantly ruptured; this sets free a spring by which the pollen-mass is shot forth, like an arrow, in the right direction, and adheres by its viscid extremity to the back of the bee. The pollen-mass of the male plant (for the sexes are separate in this orchid) is thus carried to the flower of the female plant, where it is brought into contact with the stigma, which is viscid enough to break certain elastic threads, and retain the pollen, thus effecting fertilization.

I can't help but feel that God is messing with Darwin's mind. Darwin simply muses, "How, it may be asked, in the foregoing and in innumerable other instances, can we understand the graduated scale of complexity and the multifarious means for gaining the same end." We can't, unless we accept that Creation is the opus-in-progress of a wildly ingenious Creator.

Early on Darwin wondered why the world teemed with beautiful creatures and objects, most of which no human had ever witnessed. He was quick to assure himself and us that beauty was not God's gift to humanity. It never occurred to him that God might want to create beauty for its own sake rather than to impress humans. Dismissing any notion of divine art for art's sake, never considering an innate human aesthetic faculty for the sake of aesthetic appreciation—whatever "god" existed was certainly not a personal God—by the time he published his *Descent of Man, and Selection in Relation to Sex* in 1871, Darwin had reduced beauty to a means for sexual selection, never considering why *beauty* as a means would be necessary or even possible from a reductive standpoint.

Eventually, in the fullness of his atrophied brain, Darwin decided that beauty, like creation itself, was simply a byproduct of a mechanical process. The beauty of orchids was a result of *selection* that led to petals' construction to attract bees and guide them to nectar, where pollen sacs could be deposited and extracted, transporting the pollen from flower to flower...Why orchids should be beautiful to *humans* who are not involved in the orchids' blossoming sexuality at all he never resolved. By the time of his *Descent*, Darwin believed that nature created nature, even beautiful nature, and that nature was simply the function of natural laws. Darwin's agnosticism had evolved into absolute reverence for the mechanistic god, natural selection.

Selection *is* a god, for what *selects* if not a willful intelligence? And are laws, which in themselves are abstract, that rational, that smart, that creative to produce even one flower? Nothing about the elaborate, beautiful process of an orchid could have been implemented by irrational intent, because intent is rational, intent has foresight, and even beauty—if beauty exists—is the culmination of aesthetic decisions. And even that culmination isn't static but is perpetually coming into being as unique form. Orchids *are* elegantly orchestrated complexity. Only an intelligence—not a mindless, will-less "mechanism" devoid of aesthetic—could design and implement such a plan as the blueprint *orchid*, much less the innumerable variations on the orchid theme.

And an orchid isn't the blueprint; it's a realized *process* of existing—a process of becoming and being an absolutely unique *version* of an absolutely fixed *form*. Isn't it impossible for mindless mechanisms to maintain the integrity of discrete form while promoting its perpetual transformation? Just contemplating this reality abstractly, much less its myriad concrete manifestations, confounds the human mind, including Darwin's.

While reading Darwin's long description of the orchid I couldn't help but notice the many words he used to describe the intelligent, willful creation of such an organism: aid, plan, contrivances, purpose, effected, entailing changes, etc.; not to mention the incredibly intricate apparatuses and complicated procedures of pollination—plural because nature, be that God or some blind mechanism, likes to tinker with his/her/its inventions; not to mention the breathtaking beauty of the general order orchid (Orchidales, consisting of four families, the largest of which consists of approximately 1,000 genera and 20,000 species); not to mention any of the utterly unique concrete examples of orchid. None of this was lost on the astute naturalist, Mr. Darwin. Yet something was very, very lost.

Though time echoed in the back of his mind, Darwin could no longer hear Paley's watch ticking on the heath. Intelligent design was reduced to mindless natural selection brutally mindful of anything that would assure survival. Well, even that's not quite right. Wouldn't natural selection be mindful of the survival of all species? And wouldn't natural selection therefore prefer a plan of cooperation that ensured protection of otherwise victim species? Darwin's god isn't concerned with mere survival; his god wants superior predators with hearty appetites and big muscles.

The Darwin who could not see the self-contradiction of mindless mindfulness ruled out a Creator and therefore divine, or natural, art for art's sake. Darwin makes a startling admission of the limitations of scientific observation when he says, "If green woodpeckers alone had existed, and we did not know that there were many black and pied kinds, I dare say that we should have thought that the green color was a beautiful adaptation to conceal this tree-frequenting bird from its enemies; and consequently that it was a character of importance, and had been acquired through natural selection." If Creation that he had observed alone existed, if he did not know that there was much more to Creation, like say DNA, and if he did not know that there was a designer of the ticking watch or wildly diverse ticking life forms, from his self-contained, reductionist, limited, elitist, privileged, narcissistic vantage he would have no choice but to observe, "As it is, the color is probably in chief part due to sexual selection." *Probably*. He has no solid evidence that this is a fact. *In chief part*. And the rest? Darwin's theory is a flat, one-dimensional, reductionist assumption. His perception was distorted by his belief that certain obvious realities did not exist, therefore other realities had to be constructed. He stopped his ears to the ticking until his hearing atrophied. He made himself deaf.

So deaf that he sometimes couldn't hear his own contradictions. For example, he acknowledges that "Some naturalists [argue] against the utilitarian doctrine that every detail of structure has been produced for the good of its possessor. They believe that many structures have been created for the sake of beauty, to delight man or the Creator (but this latter point is beyond the scope of scientific discussion), or for the sake of mere variety... Such doctrines, if true, would be absolutely fatal to my theory." In other words, if some details of structure did not simply serve utilitarian purposes, his theory would fall flat. Yet he continues, "I fully admit that many structures are now of no direct use to their possessors, and may never have been of any use to their progenitors; but this does not prove that they were formed solely for beauty or variety." This might not prove beauty or variety as the *sole* purpose, but it does not disprove beauty or variety as *a* purpose, and nonutility certainly *dis*proves necessary utility of natural selection.

If Darwin has not reached the point of atheism, if his agnosticism dislocates God to a transcendent realm utterly dislodged from life, Earth, and the universe, then beauty has absolutely no purpose beyond the procreation of beautiful creatures (which still begs the question: why something as convoluted as beauty), and there is no reason why creatures utterly disconnected from the sexual process of that species should register that same beauty as beautiful. Humans have always wondered why things should strike us as beautiful. Even atheist scientists wonder why we register beauty when it serves no utilitarian purpose.

Darwin offered a typically flat scientific explanation, which doesn't really *explain* the purpose of beauty, or the faculty of beauty. He pronounces, "With respect to the belief that organic beings have been created beautiful for the delight of man—a belief which it has been pronounced is subversive of my whole theory—I may first remark that the sense of beauty obviously depends on the nature of the mind, irrespective of any real quality in the admired object; and that the idea of what is beautiful, is not innate or unalterable."

Darwin skirts the issue, of course. Humans are delighted by the beauty of organic beings, and shrugging it off by arguing that this human delight isn't natural, it's only a human construct, doesn't make sense if humans have always been delighted by the beauty of organic beings. Even small children choose certain colors just because they *like* them. Their preference expresses a budding, innate aesthetic.

Darwin has ruled out *a priori* the possibility that a Creator is involved in Creation, so the idea that anything, including beauty, has been created for our delight is impossible. Most of us believe on the basis of common sense that a Watchmaker might well have created a watch for more than utilitarian purposes, and that life's beautiful embellishments might well have been created for our joyful appreciation. Those of us whose aesthetic has not atrophied feel a deep intuitive connection to the Source of beauty.

That the sense of beauty depends on the nature of the mind only supports the point that the mind has been designed to register beauty as *beauty*, not as a red light flashing in Hooker Alley. The mind has been constructed to apprehend and appreciate beauty. Darwin asserts that beauty is somehow disconnected from any quality of inherent beauty. But how could we register any beauty at all if there were not some objective condition that could be perceived as beautiful? It's true that people differ in their tastes and preferences. But above the varieties of beauty, there is some reality of beauty. I might prefer a French garden to a New Mexico cactus garden, but I don't think anybody would argue that either inherently lacks beauty. Issues of quality aside, most people understand that preference for a version of beauty is a matter of personal taste. For a mechanistic determinist, taste, which depends on free choice, isn't even an actuality.

Darwin believes that the idea of what is beautiful is not innate or unalterable. It is true that the aesthetic sensibility can be honed, just like reason can be schooled and experience can be enlarged. We are born with potentials, but they must be activated and cultivated. Use it or lose it. Even our bodies must be exercised and nutritiously fed to grow normally. But normal growth is possible and is perfectly natural. Growth of all our faculties depends upon normal, natural functioning. Darwin is right that the *idea* of beauty is not innate or unalterable. But even Darwin naturally responded to beauty as a child. His beetles were beautiful. The many objects that he collected were to him beautiful. Nature was beautiful, and he intuitively, instinctively *felt* its beauty emotionally. The aesthetic faculty to register and experience beauty is innate, but taste—the conceptual *idea* of beauty—results from one's own preferences choosing a "style" as well as from enculturation. One's taste might change as one experiences new forms of beauty. One's preferences might change as one apprehends and assimilates, discerns and distinguishes and decides. This is possible because the Creator of beautiful has given us in addition to the aesthetic faculty the even more amazing facility of free will

Even when the adult Darwin doubted his own childhood experience of beauty, he could still recognize beauty when he saw it. But his *a priori* bias against a Creator and against any possibility that beauty was a matter of art for art's sake diverted him from logical conclusions. His research and observations, tangled in self-contradiction, prevented him from really seeing what he was looking at. Although he could ask the right questions, he could not see that asking those questions in itself confirmed the rational basis of reality, including beauty. "Few objects are more beautiful than the minute siliceous cases of the diatomaceae: were these created that they might be examined and admired under the higher powers of the microscope?" he asks. Of course he cannot entertain the possibility of *Yes*.

Yet he does not and cannot prove his implied *No.* "The beauty in this latter case, and in many others, is apparently wholly due to symmetry of growth." Symmetry might explain some versions of beauty, but of course asymmetry could as easily explain the beauty of windswept cypresses on the craggy cliffs of costal Monterey. "Flowers rank among the most beautiful productions of nature; but they have been rendered conspicuous in contrast with the green leaves, and in consequence at the same time beautiful, so that they may be easily observed by insects." Of course, being easily observed and being beautiful are two very different qualities of reality. Now we have contrast, and perhaps color: the beginning of a very long list of what we humans might register as beautiful. Do other creatures also register at least some of these aspects of beauty as beauty?

Symmetry. Contrast. Color. That's *smart*. Who decided to make "easily observed" easy? Who decided to make it easy in a billion different ways that are beautiful? Who made us humans, at least, register symmetry and contrast and color as beauty?

"That the gaily-colored fruit of the spindle-wood tree and the scarlet berries of the holly are beautiful objects—will be admitted by everyone." Such universal admitting contradicts his earlier assertion that beauty is not innate or unalterable. "But this beauty serves merely as a guide to birds and beasts, in order that the fruit may be devoured and the matured seeds disseminated." Why should birds and beasts need beauty to guide them to fruit and seeds? The gaily-colored fruit and scarlet berries could beckon like a lighthouse beacon without their colors registering as beautiful either to animals or to us humans on the sidelines. The registering of beauty goes well beyond recognition of the object. It exists on its own plane of existence; it is a separate dimension that transcends the object as object; it is a reality that exists both as a quality of the object and as a quality of perception in our minds. Beauty is one of the aspects of existence that connect things to one another for the sake of connection, not for any utilitarian purpose on the flat plane of Darwinian nature.

"On the other hand, I willingly admit that a great number of male animals, as all our most gorgeous birds, some fishes, reptiles, and mammals, and a host of magnificently colored butterflies, have been rendered beautiful for beauty's sake." Did I hear "beautiful for beauty's sake"? Ah, "But this has been effected through sexual selection, that is, by the more beautiful males having been continually preferred by the females, and not for the delight of man." First, beauty for the sake of sexual selection isn't beauty for beauty's sake. Second, even if it wasn't created for us voyeur humans, it still is delightfully beautiful to us. Why is that? Why this instinctual response to beauty? Third, why are animals attracted to beauty? How is this attraction to beauty in any way an aspect that makes a creature fittest to survive? How does beauty contribute in any way to survival? It could even be argued that all that beauty draws extraordinary attention to the animal, making it an easier target for predators and therefore much *less* fit to survive.

"So it is with the music of birds," the tone-deaf Darwin continues. "We may infer from all this that a nearly similar taste for beautiful colors and for musical sounds runs through a large part of the animal kingdom." This taste for art surely does not directly contribute to a creature's survival, though it may make him or her sexy. But *why* is that sexy? Taste gives pleasure. Beauty gives pleasure. Pleasure exists to motivate behavior but it also exists for its own sake, which is one reason dieting is so hard and birth control so necessary. Most people don't visit art museums or attend operas just to pick up one night stands or even life partners. Limiting the aesthetic faculty of humans to sexual function is absurd.

Darwin has locked himself into a dark cellar in his brain where the remarkable elegant designs of nature are reduced to pin-up girls and dudes displayed for masturbatory perusal. Without God, the multitude of wondrous depth and dimension of which we are composed shrivels up and dies. This is the experience of atrophy from which Darwin suffered.

He asks, "Can instincts be acquired and modified through natural selection? What shall we say to the instinct which leads the bee to make cells, and which has practically anticipated the discoveries of profound mathematicians?" This is quite a claim coming from a man who barely passed algebra.

What shall we say to the lack of instinct that leads a man to perceive so much profoundly intelligently designed beauty with a clinical eye devoid of any insight that most of us call spiritual? The answer to the deepest mystery of life's origin is staring him in the face, eyeball to eyeball. Does he really believe that the sense of beauty is nothing more than habit, and instinct a mindless accident? What shall we say, he asks almost rhetorically, yet I sense in his recognition of the profoundly exquisite cell-making of bees the longing of a shriveled old man seeking a comb of honey.

"How the sense of beauty in its simplest form—that is, the reception of a peculiar kind of pleasure from certain colors, forms and sounds—was first developed in the mind of man and of the lower animals, is a very obscure subject. The same sort of difficulty is presented if we enquire how it is that certain flavors and odors give pleasure, and others displeasure. Habit in all these cases appears to have come to a certain extent into play; but there must be some fundamental cause in the constitution of the nervous system in each species."

The fundamental cause must be God. But he argues, "Have we any right to assume that the Creator works by intellectual powers like those of man?" Perhaps the habit of trying to prove his theory to fulfill his personal ambition has blinded him to the truth that he might have sensed in his youth, beginning with "the Creator," a Freudian slip here, a confession of his unwillingness to let go of the concept.

Clearly he senses a Creator; he just wants to recreate God in the image of his own theory. Natural selection is his god, a lesser god, I think even Darwin would admit.

"We must suppose that there is a power, represented by natural selection or the survival of the fittest, always intently watching each slight alteration in the transparent layers; and carefully preserving each which, under varied circumstances, in any way or degree, tends to produce a distincter image." What but a god is always intently *watching*? "We must suppose each new state of the instrument to be multiplied by the million; each to be preserved until a better is produced, and then the old ones to be all destroyed. In living bodies, variation will cause the slight alteration, generation will multiply them almost infinitely, and natural selection will pick out with unerring skill each improvement." What but a god picks at all; what but a god picks out with unerring skill? "Let this process go on for millions of years; and during each year on millions of individuals of many kinds; and may we not believe that a living optical instrument [the eye] might thus be formed as superior to one of glass, as the works of the Creator are to those of man?"

The logic here is that the god of natural selection can produce a complex eye—a part of the works usually attributed to the Creator—that is as superior to a glass eye as the works of the Creator are to man. More simply put, the Creator (in the guise of natural selection) can produce nature that is superior to the devices created by humans. Natural selection is, in other words, God, or the working of God. Why not just admit that Nature is the intelligently designed creation of the Creator we all know and love?

Because then his precious theory fails, and all his glory is one of those ingenious scientific hoaxes he so admired in childhood. But hoaxes don't cut it in old age. The possibility of discovery of this magnitude makes a vain man's integrity sick. Literally. I feel sorry for the man. I feel sorry for all the drawers of collected objects that represent a life not lived.

Oh, for the good old days of collecting beetles.

Not art, not music, certainly not academic studies were pursued at Cambridge "with nearly so much eagerness or gave me so much pleasure as collecting beetles. It was the mere passion for collecting, for I did not dissect them, and rarely compared their external characters with published descriptions, but got them named anyhow."

> I will give a proof of my zeal: one day, on tearing off some old bark, I saw two rare beetles, and seized one in each hand; then I saw a third and new kind, which I could not bear to lose, so that I popped the one which I held in my right hand into my mouth. Alas! It ejected some intensely acrid fluid, which burnt my tongue so that I was forced to spit the beetle out, which was lost, as was the third one...I was very successful in collecting, and invented two new methods; I employed a labourer to scrape during the winter, moss off old trees and place it in a large bag, and likewise to collect the rubbish at the bottom of the barges in which reeds are brought from the fens, and thus I got some very rare species. No poet ever felt more delighted at seeing his first poem published than I did at seeing, in Stephens' *Illustrations of British Insects*, the magic words, "captured by C. Darwin, Esq."

Darwin was, in a sense, a lost soul. And that childhood zeal was the soul he lost.

Throughout his life Darwin discussed his theological concerns with his wife Emma. Shortly before he proposed to her, Darwin confessed the dwindling of his faith. A Unitarian, Emma didn't accept all the dogmas of traditional Christianity, such as the Trinity or certain miracles, but she did believe in the love represented by the Christ of John's Gospel and in the afterlife. The couple supported their local church, and sacrificed time and money to its charitable causes, some of which were so progressive that they drew heated controversy and resentment from at least one of their pastors. Emma was well known for her personal generosity toward the poor and the sick. Being a loving person and a devoted wife, she agonized over the fate of Charles' soul.

What drives a man who seemingly has every good gift that matters in life to reject the personal God of love—for his denial was rejection. Could he not sense that depression and perennial illness were symptoms of a soul slipping into an abyss—red flags of his living being devolving? Even before they married, Emma made no secret of her fear that the great spiritual chasm between them would persist throughout their marriage. She cherished spiritual love as the highest expression of the highest level of human potential. Their spiritual disconnect was the cross she bore.

Surely Darwin didn't will his dislocation from the burnished ideals and numinous ecstasies he had cherished in his youth. What happened to the Fern Hill joy of innocence? Perhaps Darwin felt, as Dylan Thomas would a century later, that even young and easy in the mercy of Nature's means, time held him green and dying as he sang in his chains like the sea.

Spiritual dissociation; spiritual depression: These seem to me to be masculine frailties expressed in both men and women. Emma's spiritual love-ness and confidence in afterlife certainly exude life-force, whereas natural selection grunts its joyless hopelessness. Darwin would never grasp the mysterious mechanism of life. He would never join his deceased parents or beloved children. Death would remove him from Emma forever.

If that's evolution, who wants it, who needs it? Why would Darwin choose to believe it even when he *knew* conclusive evidence was blatantly lacking? Isn't Darwin's tragic flaw his *frustration* at *not knowing*? If only he could have relaxed into Keatsian *negative capability*, "of being in uncertainties, Mysteries, doubts, without any irritable reaching after fact and reason" so that "the sense of Beauty overcomes every consideration, or rather obliterates all consideration." Emma would surely agree with Keats, "I am certain of nothing but of the holiness of the heart's affections and the truth of Imagination—what the imagination seizes as Beauty must be truth—whether it existed before or not—for I have the same Idea of all our Passions as of Love: they are all in their sublime, creative of essential Beauty." I can hear Emma, exasperated with Charles, "O for a Life of Sensation rather than Thoughts!"

It's not farfetched to assert that delusions of mindless creation result from privileging fossilized husks of reason over common sense, which includes all our inherent faculties, like intuition, aesthetic—and yes reason, but reason that's vibrant and juicy. Scientists who get their hands dirty with the loam of life are too often content to simply catalogue their discoveries instead of reaching deeper to touch life's dynamic source. Even their dirty hands must ultimately look abstract to them.

And it's this tendency to abstract the concrete into subservient caricatures of reality that allows an otherwise decent man to push a button and blow up a point on a map that abstractly represents millions of "enemies." Oh for the day when we had to look our target in the eye. Instead we pin our little flags to a map, like butterflies to a corkboard.

Nothing Darwin hypothesized or proved *disproved* the possibility—or even necessity—of a creating Mind. But science decided that that Mind could not be a transcendent or even immanent Creator but rather had to be an impersonal "mechanism" like natural selection. If humans were just smart apes, why couldn't a mechanical messiah "direct" the windup universe, even if part of that universe breathed? Remarkably, this notion was not considered absurd by Darwin and his cronies.

Darwin continued to work on his theology—er, theory, for the rest of his days. It is not without irony that the mighty Darwin concluded his life with the publication of *The Formation of Vegetable Mould, Through the Action of Worms.* When he died of a heart attack (symbolism noted), his union with lowly worms was a consummation devoutly wished, and he considered "Down graveyard as the sweetest place on earth." Alas, he will spend eternity embalmed in marble, immortalized in his corner of Westminster Abbey, estranged from his beloved family buried in their local churchyard plot.

To the end, Darwin hoped that future excavations would dig up links showing the gradual progression from one species to another—a kind of last ditch nod toward a materialist's version of eternal life.

Darwin became a scientific hero by being a victim of his age. Perhaps the felt sense of divine immanence so potent in childhood was more than his repressed Victorian reason, oppressed by ambition, could accommodate.

CHAPTER 6

CALCULATED CONSTRUCTION: THE SCIENCE
OF INTELLIGENT DESIGN

Intelligent design, the ancient wisdom introduced by Greco-Roman philosophers, and later energized by humanists from the Renaissance through the Enlightenment, and then modernized by Paley's watchmaker motif, and now touted as "new" and "exciting" by the sages of cutting-edge science, is making a huge comeback, and so is the timeless natural religion it scientifically confirms. Deism is the fastest growing religion in America in part because of the growing popularity of today's rendition of intelligent design.

Meanwhile, fundamentalists, scrambling to shore up biblical creationism with each new discovery that demonstrates design, equivocate using cherry-picked data, skewed logic, and bogus exegesis starting with "What the Bible *really* says is…"

The truth is that intelligent design confirms neither religious creation myths not the creation myth of Darwinian evolution and its mutant brainchild, mechanistic determinism.

Meanwhile, nervous neo-Darwinians ramp up their assertion that Darwin proved and knew he had proven the fact of evolution via natural selection, even as more and more scientists disagree with the claim that evolution is a *fact* or even a valid theory. At issue today is not that category of evolution we now call microevolution, or evolution within a species type. What is disputed is macroevolution, or the metamorphosis of Gregor Samsa into a giant cockroach.

The truth is not just that macroevolution has not been proven; the glaring reality is that it has been *disproven*. Furthermore, Darwinians from Bulldog Huxley to Rottweiler Dawkins have been well aware that even in their holy scripture, *The Origin of Species*, Darwin indicates profound anxiety about the validity of his theory of evolution *by Means of Natural Selection of the Preservation of Favored Races in the Struggle for Life*.

Darwin himself establishes the criteria that would disconfirm his theory; on the basis of those criteria, his theory has been disconfirmed. But Darwinians have always been adept at selective science. They know that in the *Origin*, Darwin, a man of contradictions, contradicts himself and a great many leading scientists of the era as well. Darwin's rhetorical fallacies alone demand a skeptical stance toward his theory, but Darwinians treat them like trivial incidentals. Neo-Darwinians transcend science with their special brand of mysticism centered in their material Creator, natural selection, eschatologically driven by blind chance. Recent scientific discoveries that have disproven fundamental Darwinian assumptions are skewed or skewered in the sacred name of atheism.

Meanwhile, Darwinians scramble semantics in order to index circus animals found in cloud formations they can add to their box of embarrassing proofs of macroevolution. Take the fish fossil *Panderichthys*, back in 2005 the celebrated mascot of evolution, the clincher (i.e., only) transitional fossil demonstrating our transition from sea to land, specifically from fish to tetrapod, due to its pectoral fins' radial bones that proved that fingers evolved from distal radials of fish. Then in 2006, a new fish fossil, *Tiktaalik*, arrived in science's small in-box of fossil fragments, and suddenly almighty *Panderichthys* was abandoned as not really revealing "tetrapod synapomorphies" or evidence of transition after all. Whoops. But *Tiktaalik* rocked. It was the premier fossil fragment that proved transition. The National Academy of Science's 2008 "Science, Evolution, and Creationism" booklet called it "a notable transitional form." Even PBS tooted its horn in the special, "Judgment Day: Intelligent Design on Trial." But then by fall 2008, someone gave the little *Panderichthys* fossil fragment a CT scan, and thought a few radial bones in its pectoral fins did look an awful lot like something that could evolve into fingers. And really, *Tiktaalik* wasn't such a good specimen after all. In fact, the quality of the specimen was now classified as "poor." Whoops. But *Panderichthys* rocked. Until evolutionary biologist Michael Coates, a Darwinian, noted that radials aren't really finger-like, aren't really precursors to fingers at all. In fact, the fragments that kinda sorta maybe looked like future fingers could well be just fragments of damaged bones, which is the current consensus. Whoops. Of course he still believes in X-God humans-evolved-from-fish. And here we have the fruits of Darwinian speculation, carefully crated and cataloged under "I think I see a fish crawling ashore in that cloud over there." And thus fish evolved into birds. Really. Just ask any authority on ancient mythology.

On the Discovery Institute website, biologist Jonathan Wells frames his critique of absurd Darwinian assertions as questions aimed at producers of school textbooks. For instance, "Why do textbooks use pictures of peppered moths camouflaged on tree trunks as evidence for natural selection—when biologists have known since the 1980s that the moths don't normally rest on tree trunks, and all the pictures have been staged?" "Why do textbooks claim that beak changes in Galapagos finches during a severe drought can explain the origin of species by natural selection—even though the changes were reversed after the drought ended, and no net evolution occurred?" "Why do textbooks use fruit flies with an extra pair of wings as evidence that DNA mutations can supply raw materials for evolution—even though the extra wings have no muscles and these disabled mutants cannot survive outside the laboratory?" "Why are artists' drawings of ape-like humans used to justify materialistic claims that we are just animals and our existence is a mere accident—when fossil experts cannot even agree on who our supposed ancestors were or what they looked like?" I might not agree with Wells' theology, but I respect his insistence that Darwinian proselytizers explain their misrepresentations, which are required reading for schoolchildren.

As Keats might have said, axioms in philosophy-as-science are not axioms until they are proved upon our pulses. He might well have wondered if progress might be better served by leaving scientific fact-gathering to scientists and assigning interpretation of facts to the literati.

It makes me sad that I, who grew up loving and trusting science, must join the growing ranks of increasingly diligent science skeptics. But I'm excited by the prospect of redefining science as a representational genre and subjecting it to the rigors of literary analysis. (I dream of a science course titled Fun with Fallacies.)

Academics know not what they do, at least not fully, when they bow to the authority of scientists who bow to the authority of "Darwin," when even Darwin himself had grave doubts about his own conclusions; when science itself has disallowed Darwin's theory of natural selection; when the Darwinian worldview is rigorously advanced by people and groups bent on exploiting it.

Most people never actually see a neo-Darwinian defiantly shake his clenched fists at the empty sky, stubbornly poised to make that final leap of faith into the abyss of personal extinction, some on their way down slashing their wrists on the blunt edge of pseudo-science. Most of us never see the neo-Darwinian world devoid of any hope of an afterlife, of any inherent meaning or ultimate justice, of any God, of any reason to go on living other than to shove their beliefs down the gullets of the gullible.

Neo-Darwinians know perfectly well that Darwin consciously and willingly pressed a theory that relied on biased and bogus research concluding with a "crowd of difficulties" ranging from the inaccurate bottom-up design assumption of his great Tree of Life to Haeckel's falsified embryonic depictions that were fraudulent distortions of von Baer's observations. Darwin's cool disregard for the hard facts of the Cambrian explosion and the complete absence of transitional links in the fossil record, his disagreement with his own agreement with Paley's watchmaker design argument, his reliance on Malthus' fallacies regarding population growth, and his ignorance (or ignoring) of Mendel are Darwin's frauds, frauds of the past, frauds we know to be frauds. Yet this "crowd of difficulties" is the basis of neo-Darwinism upon which today's atheism has been propped.

It's true that neo-Darwinians rely less on fossil and embryonic evidence and more on molecular proof of evolutionary mutation. Unfortunately for them, the fact is that beneficial mutations that would promote evolution are extremely rare and are biochemical in nature; and contrary to Darwin's assumption, most mutations are harmful or fatal, or they don't produce any noticeable effects, and few mutations are reproducible anyway. But even beneficial mutations only add very minor changes (wondrous minor-key jazz riffs called "trivial" by underwhelmed, anti-design scientists); even if reproducible they result from latent adaptation potentiality triggered by the environment. As scientists like Jonathan Wells point out, mutate DNA of, say, a fruit fly in every possible way and you can only get a normal fruit fly, a defective fruit fly, or a dead fruit fly. Mutations never radically transform the species. Per Wells et al, they certainly never change the species type (those discrete "containers" explained in Chapter 1) into another species type: That has *never* happened. Sax improv is still sax.

Even if beneficial large-scale molecular changes could occur, even Darwinian biologists (and atheist physicists like Stephen Hawking) agree that the number of steps from the earliest living form—a bacterium, say—to any one contemporary species would take hundreds of trillions of times more time than the lifespan not just of Earth but of the entire universe. And that's just for one major species type to another. Even admitting this, even *knowing* this, they stubbornly assert Darwinism (and its neo *idée fixe*, multiverse) as *fact*. Their self-contradiction is consistent with the self-contradiction of Darwin's theory and with Darwin the man.

Abstractly, one might be able to imagine one species gradually morphing into a different genus, or a genus morphing into an order into a class. But even Darwin understood that for many reasons incremental change cannot possibly explain the appearance of a complex organ. "Although the belief that an organ so perfect as the eye could have been formed by natural selection, is enough to stagger anyone; yet in the case of any organ, if we know of a long series of gradations in complexity..." But we do not know of any process of gradations in complexity that leads to the formation of so perfect an organ as a fully developed, unified eye. I will discuss this more fully later; suffice it to note here that Darwin himself in his next breath argues against himself by admitting that "we know of no intermediate or transitional states." Yet those states must exist or Darwin's theory is disconfirmed, because as Darwin himself states, "On the theory of natural selection we can clearly understand the full meaning of that old canon in natural history, 'Natura non facit saltum [nature makes no leap].'"

Darwin's explanation to this conundrum is but another contradiction. [Patient reader, please bear with just a few more quotes as I drive these last couple nails in Darwin's coffin: The man has been dead, after all, for quite some time.] He asserts, "It is generally acknowledged that all organic beings have been formed on two great laws—Unity of Type, and the Conditions of Existence. By unity of type is meant that fundamental agreement in structure which we see in organic beings of the same class, and which is quite independent of their habits of life. On my theory, unity of type is explained by unity of descent."

Problem One: Only an intelligence could recognize, much less create, much less create organically, any kind of structural unity. Designing, implementing, and maintaining unity of type is an intellectual, aesthetic component of the creation process. Unity of type among untold millions and billions of species types and their discrete species and their individual members requires aesthetic intelligence well beyond human comprehension. It takes a personality who loves creating orchids and butterflies. It takes a God.

Problem Two: Darwin claims that each species type, or discrete container, consists of structures that are specific to the species type, or even a single species within the type, that are not dependent upon habits of life, meaning they do not depend upon and did not emerge from environmental cues. But throughout nature we see a huge variety of genetically unrelated species that possess the same structures—legs, eyes, skin, brains, and bright colors, for instance. If they did not emerge naturally when triggered by environmental cues, then they were spontaneously created by God, or, as neo-Darwinians assert, emerged randomly. But can anything truly unique, even if practical—especially if practical—*not* have been created by design?

In the same passage in which Darwin makes his point of species differentiation, he acknowledges, "The common rule throughout nature is infinite diversity of structure for gaining the same end; and this again naturally follows from the same great principle."

Again, diverse species possess the same structures. Furthermore, the very fact that species seek the same end (survival and procreation) and follow this naturally (something in them drives them) and they seek and are driven by a great principle (a rational directive inherent in all species) is a way of saying that an intelligent mind willfully created (past tense)—or creates and drives (present tense)—natural selection. That which would confirm Darwin's theory is exactly that which disconfirms it: intelligent design.

When Darwin tries to explain why species have unity of type independent of their conditions of existence, he inadvertently reveals the hand of God once again: "In many other cases, modifications are probably the direct result of the laws of variation or of growth, independently of any good having been thus gained." Laws of variation for its own sake (independent of any good gained) contradict the law of unity of type. Variation suggests creative design—art for art's sake.

As we saw earlier, Darwin maintained that the fundamental and only purpose of natural selection is the good gained by the species, so he has just contradicted himself. "But even such structures have often, as we may feel assured, been subsequently taken advantage of, and still further modified, for the good of species under new conditions of life." This suggests that something, whether the species itself or something outside the species, made (makes) the conscious decision to take advantage of purposeless (independent of any good gained) structures (which aren't supposed to happen in the first place, according to Darwin's theory) and modified (modifies) them for the good of the species.

"Modified" means changed. A thing changes to serve a purpose (the good of the species) because something changes it, whether it be something within the thing itself or something outside the thing itself. In either case, the thing causing the change causes it—meaning willfully changes it to serve the purpose: in this case, causes it for the good of the species—meaning creates the change in order to benefit the species. That *It* that is causing the good must know what will be good. That means it must have the intelligence to discern the good and the foresight to predict the future good outcome. It also must have some motivation to benefit the species and to promote its continued existence. It's absurd to think that "nothing," or some random and/or mindless non-entity called a "principle," could or would do that. But neo-Darwinians follow Darwin in believing just that.

Darwin knew that most people wouldn't buy a theory that ran so counter to common sense, including his own. Chapter VII of the *Origin*, titled "Miscellaneous Objections to the Theory of Natural Selection," begins with Darwin's list of what he calls various objections advanced against his views. "Longevity—Modifications not necessarily simultaneous—Modifications apparently of no direct service—Progressive development—Characters of small functional importance, the most constant—Supposed incompetence of natural selection to account for the incipient stages of useful structures—Causes which interfere with the acquisition through natural selection of useful structures—Gradations of structure with changed functions—Widely different organs in members of the same class, developed from one and the same source—Reasons for disbelieving in great and abrupt modifications."

Darwin specifically acknowledges the "serious objection...urged by Bronn, and recently by Broca, namely, that many characters appear to be of no service whatever to their possessors, and therefore cannot have been influenced through natural selection." This is a crucial point, because Darwin understands clearly that non-utilitarian qualities disconfirm natural selection and point to the creative license of a Creator.

The second crucial point is that Darwin himself highlights examples that lend themselves to disconfirmation, perhaps leading the reader to infer that Darwin himself was not fully convinced by his own arguments:

> Bronn adduces the length of the ears and tails in the different species of hares and mice—the complex folds of enamel in the teeth of many animals, and a multitude of analogous cases. With respect to plants, this subject has been discussed by Nageli in an admirable essay. He admits that natural selection has effected much, but he insists that the families of plants differ chiefly from each other in morphological characters, which appear to be quite unimportant for the welfare of the species. He consequently believes in an innate tendency towards progressive and more perfect development. He specifies the arrangement of the cells in the tissues, and of the leaves on the axis, as cases in which natural selection could not have acted. To these may be added the numerical divisions in the parts of the flower, the position of the ovules, the shape of the seed, when not of any use for dissemination, etc.

Nageli's belief "in an innate tendency towards progressive and more perfect development" is the fundamental assumption of both Darwinism and religion. But while Darwinism defines progressive and more perfect development as more efficient means to procreate and survive, religion defines it as spiritual transcending, not just from this life to the next after death, but as a perpetual process occurring in this life. Death is just a door into another room in the same house: another phase of the same process. In every instance, progression is logical: intelligent: designed.

Darwin clearly respects Nageli's opinion and probably agrees with it. In this passage, as in many others, Darwin betrays his doubt via his contradictions. He really isn't sure that natural selection is truth; he has never really entirely abandoned his early religious tendencies. Reading between the lines, it's possible to imagine Darwin grappling with his inherent faith in the spiritual perfectibility contradicted by animal brutality and human evil.

Unlike Nageli and Darwin, Darwinians today contend that the evolutionary progression of purely material life, like the emergence of all existence, is driven by the powerful force of contingency, meaning luck, or what has lately of necessity been dubbed "organizing convergence." Amazingly, these scientists don't have a problem believing that randomness and organization "just are" and that their coexistence is not contradictory. Everything just happens to be the way it is. Super-organization out of seemingly infinite potential isn't for them an amazing display of Intelligence; it's a random and unsupervised "event." To someone literate, the myopic Darwinian scientist might look a bit like a chimp watching *Hamlet*.

Infinite potential within the highly consistent structure that we apprehend as the laws of nature constitutes a worldview we humans have always intuited: Much is given, but within the given there is plenty of wiggle room for creativity and free choice, and yes, even for chance, in the extraordinary process of change. The world's creation myths creatively articulate our primal understanding that there has to be a transcending cause of the overarching structural consistency—a God—and of our ability to choose within the given parameters—free will.

A recent devastating blow to Darwin's unity of types and thus to evolutionary development biology (aka evo-devo, a hip 80s handle for embryology) has been the disconcerting discovery that radically different animals share developmental genes that are so similar that a gene serving as a kind of non-specific switch needed for eye development in, for example, a mouse can induce eye development in, say, a fruit fly embryo, yet the fruit fly develops fruit fly eyes instead of mouse eyes. This contradicts the Darwinian assumption that different organisms have their own sets of genes that very specifically control embryo development, and that any mutations in those genes would change the embryo, which equals evolution: Inheritance of mutation *is* evolution—macroevolution, according to Darwinians.

The problem is that some radically different organisms that do not share a common descent share the same developmental "switch" gene, while other organisms that are in other ways genetically closer do not. It would be like a contractor mixing a special fixative in concrete used for the foundation of an adobe in New Mexico and a cathedral in Spain that he doesn't use when building the split-levels next door to the adobe or the synagogue down the block from the cathedral.

Darwin, of course, didn't know about our astoundingly intricate DNA. Through the best microscopes of the nineteenth century, which magnified cells times seven hundred, a cell's nucleus looked like a simple blob. Magnified by our microscopes times a thousand million, the nucleus becomes about as elegantly complex and sophisticated as a planet or a universe. We aren't even close to unraveling its mysteries. Darwin also didn't have access to the extensive findings of paleontologists that for over a century have only verified the complete absence of any missing links between species.

But neo-Darwinians today do have knowledge of DNA yet continue to promote Darwin's misconceptions. Why? Because science is confirming intelligent design, and that's tantamount to confirming a Creator God. The evidence of God is right there in our genes, and even more irritating, right there in their own genes.

For example, recent discoveries in genetics have revealed that adaptation is possible because there is latent, built-in informational instruction capability that can be activated by environmental cues. Any genetic change comes about after the adaptation has occurred. The organism must have a reserve of extra, latent instructional information that can be accessed as needed. Whether the change occurs in the structure of an organ, in its function, or in the animal's behavior, evolution occurs because evolution is possible, and it is possible because information and instructions—building blocks and instruction manual—for the new form already exist in the animal's molecular structure. The more instructional information programmed in the organism, the greater the potential for change. The potential for evolution is prepackaged; the raw materials of evolution are already inherent in the animal—any animal, from day one.

Darwinism argues change via mutation "from the ground up," a version of making something (adding the extra) from nothing (what does not yet exist). But can one apple plus one apple make a pear, much less a pair of pears (needed to reproduce)? As it turns out, almost all mutations *delete* genetic information rather than add new information.

The quandary for Darwinians today is that species types appear to be self-contained systems that could not possibly have evolved from other types, at least not by any means explained by survival-of-the-fittest Darwinism or random chance neo-Darwinism. (And how can something *random* be mechanistically consistent; how can chance *intend* for the fittest to survive?) Today scientists deduce that species change—evolve—from the top down, meaning a species type begins as itself and then changes varieties within the parameters of its prepackaged potential. New species—like Darwin's finches—still fit within the species-type container.

Neo-Darwinians know this. Yet they still insist that the awesomely intricately fine-tuned universe is the result of blind chance and that human existence is just a lucky throw of the evolutionary dice that resulted in you, the culmination of random genetic mutations that are astronomically more improbable than tossing magnet-poetry letters at the fridge and getting the blank verse of *Paradise Lost.*

HOW TO KNOW HOW

Perhaps the crux of geneticists' critique of classical evolution is the extraordinary fact of irreducible complexity, a concept perhaps most succinctly articulated by Michael Katz in 1986. Katz pointed out that "Contemporary organisms are quite complex, they have a special and an intricate organization that would not occur spontaneously by chance. The 'universal laws' governing the assembly of biological materials are insufficient to explain our companion organisms: one cannot stir together the appropriate raw materials and self-assemble a mouse."

Even a simple, inorganic mousetrap has to be designed and assembled by an intelligence, specifically, a human. Biological designs such as cells, DNA molecules, and proteins are vastly more complex than a mousetrap and need a vastly greater than human intelligence to design and implement them. Katz notes that "There are useful scientific explanations for these complex systems, but the final patterns that they produce are so heterogeneous that they cannot effectively be reduced to smaller or less intricate predecessor components." Humans build with available materials. The designer of complex biological systems creates the materials and the systems.

Katz's simple insight, "These patterns are, in a fundamental sense, irreducibly complex," is as devastating to any current version of macroevolution as an elliptical Earth revolving around the sun was to the sixteenth-century Church.

In his book *Darwin's Black Box*, geneticist Michael Behe describes an irreducibly complex system as one that is "composed of several, well-matched interacting parts that contribute to the basic function, wherein the removal of any one of the parts causes the system to effectively cease functioning." For example, the DNA molecule, which excels at stockpiling and duplicating information, cannot build itself without the help of proteins. But proteins are incapable of reproducing themselves without the information provided by DNA. A species type is an irreducibly complex system. There could not possibly have been a sudden addition of one magical part that made it a new type.

Think of an irreducibly complex system as a discrete, complete whole. A simple mousetrap, to borrow Behe's description, consists of five parts: the flat wooden base on which the other parts are mounted, the metal hammer to crush the mouse, the wire spring connected to the base, and the hammer, a pressure-sensitive catch on which the bait is placed, and the bar connected to the catch, which holds the hammer back when the trap is cocked. Remove any one of these components—base, hammer, spring, catch, or holding bar—and the mousetrap doesn't work; in fact, it is no longer a mousetrap. The materials used are not aspects of the system's irreducible complexity; what's decisive is its design. Substitute a bone for the classic metal bar or metal for the wooden base and you still have a working mousetrap.

Well-designed or not, this mousetrap is an inanimate object that was clearly intentioned by a human being. It's absurd to ask the Darwinian: *What* designed the vastly more creative irreducibly complex *organic* systems? Common sense leads us to phrase the question reasonably: *Who* designed them. A *what* is not intelligent or creative; only a *who* fits the bill.

What most disturbs Darwinists today is not only the discovery that small—say, a strand of DNA—isn't necessarily simple, but also the fact that many tiny structures are irreducibly complex systems within other tiny irreducibly complex systems. The discovery of irreducibly complex organic systems delivered the knock-out blow to Darwinian macroevolution. Irreducibly complex organic systems within systems dragged them out of the ring.

Although Behe likes the easily understood example of a mousetrap, one of his favorite examples of an irreducibly complex whole is the bacterial flagellum, which operates like an outboard motor attached to bacteria. *E. coli*, the intestinal bacterium we hear about now and then on the news, usually has six to twelve flagella protruding from the bacterial cell's body. Flagella are linked to a system that enables the organism to sense and follow chemicals more efficiently than fishermen follow trout. The flagella bundle together to form the cell's rotary engine, operating on a proton motive force drive system that spins up to 100,000 rpm. In addition to its astonishing acceleration capability, the whiplike flagellum sports a sophisticated braking and steering mechanism that includes a bushing with L and P rings, a universal joint, a stator with studs and C ring, a rotor with M and S rings, and a drive shaft. This outboard baby can stop on a shrimp's dime and abruptly twist to reverse direction in quarter turns. Geneticists have discovered that when any protein required for assembly or operation of the flagellum is removed or otherwise rendered inoperable, the cell can't work—at all. It would be the equivalent of a hunk of metal falling off the fisherman's outboard motor and sinking to the Siren song of mermaids.

And remember, the cell's motor is *alive*.

The fact of irreducible complexity complicates a fundamental scientific quandary: How does a system—or anything, for that matter—*know*? How does it know how to function, how to be, how to know?

How would a species know *to* produce, much less know *how* to produce, the blood-clotting cascade? A person with even a minor cut would bleed to death if the body didn't know how to form a clot to stop the bleeding and close the wound. The clot forms only when all of more than a dozen extremely complex protein molecules interact sequentially at just the right time and place. Should the clot form in a blood vessel when it's not needed, the person dies. Because all the molecules must contribute to the clotting, the system is irreducibly complex. The absence of just one molecule, as in the case of hemophilia, crashes the program.

How would an eye know how to become an eye? If an organism had no sight, how would it know what sight would be, how would it decide it needed sight? If the organism isn't deciding, who or what is? Granted, an eye would be beneficial, but building an original eye from scratch step by step by adding incremental levels of sophistication requires a predetermined blueprint of a completed eye. An organism doesn't just randomly stumble upon an eye; nor would or could it incrementally develop such a highly structured organ. An eye isn't just a spongy ball in a socket (and where did the socket come from?). Darwin acknowledged that the gradual evolution of such a complex organ as the human eye was essentially a disconfirmation of his theory.

The eye's elaborate operation begins when light striking the retina is absorbed by a molecule that alters an attached protein. What follows is a cascade—a precisely integrated series of molecular reactions—that transmits a nerve impulse to the brain. The eye is irreducibly complex in that every part of the light-sensing mechanism must function or the person is blind; if a single molecule is missing or defective, no light transmission takes place. Darwin's theory couldn't explain how, much less why, all the necessary component molecules could or would assemble into an intricately constructed, fully functioning eye, much less a pair of eyes.

As if that were not enough of a quandary, neo-Darwinians can't explain how or why many creatures have many different kinds of structural eyes. The so-called camera eye that humans have is the same kind of eye present in only a few other species, which are not genetically related. How could and why would those discrete species develop the same version of the same elaborate organ? Because Darwinians know a close similarity that doesn't result from common ancestry contradicts natural selection, they hide the contradiction behind a fancy scientific name: "convergent evolution." Let me explain.

Darwinians claim to have proven evolution by noting similar, less developed aspects of human eyes in the eyes of other organisms. Michael Shermer describes the long, complex pathway of the eye's evolution: "Initially a simple eyespot with a handful of light-sensitive cells that provided information to an organism about an important source of the light." Shermer doesn't give a clue to why and how the simple eyespot came about, how such a profoundly simple organism could recognize "information," much less how it could process it in such a way as to decide it needed to "create" an eyespot, in Shermer's view apparently by itself. What were the tools, materials, and blueprint that the uneducated blind organism developed and used to "build" such an eyespot? Shermer doesn't say, perhaps because he knows that tools, materials, and "mental" blueprint are a tad beyond the creative intelligence of the simple organism.

Shermer continues: "It developed into a recessed eyespot, where a small surface indentation filled with light-sensitive cells provided additional data on the direction of light." I had to read that twice. This simple organism must have an IQ of at least Shermer's to have designed, manufactured, and implemented such a sophisticated apparatus for processing data about light direction. Even Edison couldn't do that. Shermer adds: "Then into a deep recession eyespot, where additional cells at greater depth provide more accurate information about the environment; then into a pinhole camera eye that is able to focus an image on the back of a deeply-recessed layer of light-sensitive cells; then into a pinhole lens eye that is able to focus the image; then into a complex eye found in such modern mammals as humans." I'd like to meet these creatures, have a conversation over coffee about their creative process, ask them to explain how they thought of fully-developed eyes, or even just a simple eyespot, their having never had or seen them.

Ah, Darwinians don't think the creatures themselves designed the initial or intermediate stages of what became a wondrous organ even in their estimation. No. Natural selection designed the eye, along with all its permutations. Well then, I'd like to chat with natural selection, whoever that is.

In spite of how ingenious an eye is, and how desperately I'd love to have a few moments of focused brain-picking with natural selection, Shermer swears, almost under his breath, that the design is, well, not up to his standards. "The anatomy of the human eye, in fact, shows anything but 'intelligence' in its design." If Shermer in all his glorious brilliance has created something better that had never before been conceived, even abstractly, I could find no evidence of it in the literature. Shermer complains, "It is built upside down and backwards, requiring photons of light to travel through the cornea, lens, aquaeous fluid, blood vessels, ganglion cells, amacrine cells, horizontal cells, and bipolar cells before they reach the light-sensitive rods and cones that transduce the light signal into neural impulses—which are then sent to the visual cortex at the back of the brain for processing into meaningful patterns." What would the aesthetically challenged Dr. Shermer make of Dali's *Melting Time*, or Gaudí's *Sagrada Família*, or Shakespeare's *A Midsummer Night's Dream*? Only a dreadfully boring science accountant would snarl, "For optimal vision, why would an intelligent designer have built an eye upside down and backwards?" My guess is, to make you ask that question. But more to the point, Dr. Shermer, why did Ginger Rogers dance backwards and in high heels?

Darwinians who should know better claim that they have located in other creatures all the intermediate stages of the construction process. Human IT guys have built computer models that have shown that the theory "works." But then, a computer animated game "works" if it's designed to work. Personally, I don't think computer "simulation" proves anything relating to biology. Even though "it" *works,* their proof of evolution is the ineptness of the design and the accidents of blindness, like that caused by brilliantly designed microscopic parasites.

In an essay, "Organs of Extreme Perfection and Complication," Darwin himself worried: "To suppose that the eye, with all its inimitable contrivances for adjusting the focus to different distances, for admitting different amounts of light, and for the correction of spherical and chromatic aberration, could have been formed by natural selection, seems, I freely confess, absurd in the highest possible degree."

What's really absurd is *Bathylychnops exilis,* a sea creature with four eyes, one pair to look outward, another pair to check out what's below. Darwinians consider it a proof of macroevolution. Dr. Daniel Nilsson, an authority on four-eyed fish, put it nonchalantly, "This species has reinvented the lens despite the fact that it already had one. It serves as a good support for the view that lenses are not difficult to evolve." In my view (but granted, I have but one set of eyes), the good doctor's claim that a fish, even a lowly two-eyed fish, could "reinvent" the lens is almost as ludicrous as his assumption that lenses "are not difficult to evolve." Purportedly he added in a letter to Richard Dawkins, "A creative deity, of course, would have been more likely to double the complement of optics in the first place, which would have left us with nothing to wonder about, or to discover."

Nilsson, the expert on what a creative deity would do, no doubt complains to his longsuffering wife that if Leonardo would have inched up Mona Lisa's smile a bit, we wouldn't have to call it "enigmatic"; and if Bach would have just cut out all those laboriously convoluted and repetitive passages from his fugues and chorales, his opus could fit on one CD; and god knows tribal gyrations cannot be updated simply by outfitting preverbal anorexics in tutus and tights. No doubt she complains about her shipshape reductivist brute that makes love with a manual in one hand.

One fatal flaw of Darwinism is that it can't explain how an orgasm—whoops, organism, would know how to construct itself into something greater than itself, or how it would know to know this. A complete bacteria flagellum, a process as complicated as blood clotting, a pair of camera eyes could each only come into existence as an end product of a step-by-step assembly process. If that process is natural selection, it would take an enormously long time, even granting it "intelligence."

But there's a bigger problem for Darwinians. If the result of the assembly process is a flagellum, a blood clot, or a pair of eyes, that result began in the past as a future goal of completed assemblage that would serve a remarkably sophisticated function for the benefit of something, for the benefit of yet another something, greater than itself. A pair of human eyes facilitates sight, which enhances the human's chances of staying alive, which contributes to the endurance of the species, and it also contributes to a quality of meaningful, purposive life for the individual and for the species that far exceeds mere survival.

Nature doesn't just randomly "assemble" anything as elegant, as rationally purposive as a flagellum, a blood clot, or an eye. It doesn't even just randomly assemble the complex units of the less complex first step or second step or third step that "evolved" into the final step. Even that tiny step must serve a purpose. And the purpose can't be served until the structure *functions*, which can't happen until all the structure's parts, all the interconnected units and subunits, are in place. Even an itsy bitsy step would need to serve a future function. How would the organism know this? The ultimate purpose of the flagellum, a blood clot, or an eye transcends the functional assemblage. The flagellum services a cell's life, which services the organism's life; a human life rescued is an actuality that exists above and beyond the blood clot; the eyes see: sight is an "entity" separate from physical eyes. Purpose is always greater than the sum of its functional parts—even its *future* functional parts. Everyone knows this, even Darwinian materialists.

Even the *possibility of creation*—the creation process itself—must be set up by an intelligence—a mind—that possesses an *understanding* of the process that is greater than the process itself. Construction of a factory requires an architectural blueprint drawn by an intelligent mind smarter than a factory; the factory's function requires skilled workers who follow specific instructions to perform specialized tasks using dedicated tools with particular expertise. We can look at a factory manned by human workers and know that humans built it; it didn't just magically appear. But how can a busy factory exist and operate at the molecular level, or even the not-living mechanical level?

If the factory produces, say, computers, an organic mind smarter than a computer—humans—must have designed the hardware and programmed the software. A machine doesn't design and program machines that can function at a higher level than it does. A chimp doesn't design and program computers.

Nothing short of a transcending Creator could design and program irreducibly complex microsystems like the enormously sophisticated bacterial flagellum, or perfectly synchronized waterfalling cascades that constitute the process of blood clotting, or the elegantly cascading mechanisms of the human eye. Each of these amazingly complex structural entities is so efficient and its components so proficient at performing its tasks and even in some cases adlibbing the tasks of other components when needed that they could almost be called talented. These components don't have minds; they were designed and programmed by a super-Mind.

A predetermined theology like atheism can drive even a smart scientist like Francis Crick to board the spaceship of science fiction in search of a non-supernatural explanation for life on Earth. Aliens. That's right. Aliens planted the seeds of life on Earth, according to Crick. Of course, this begs the question: Where did the aliens come from? Aliens from multiverses, the latest jazzed-up scientific version of ancient mythological deities, are as passé clichéd as a Victorian soirée.

Less whimsical but equally fogeyish Darwinians still living in Newtonian outer space of boundless possibilities argue that given an infinite amount of time, space, and mass, anything, even an irreducibly complex system, could come into existence by random chance. But could that "anything" be a chimp computer programmer? Could that "anything" be an elaborately elegant universe composed of a dizzying array of uniquely elegant parts all perfectly choreographed into a dazzling multidimensional symmetry that transcends any human or alien adult's understanding of random?

Not to mention that given the almost universally accepted Big Bang model of a finite universe that's roughly 13.7 billion years old, space-time is nowhere near big or old enough for the probability, or even possibility, that anything, must less everything, just sort of accidently came into being. This according to *all* scientists.

Then there's the Second Law of Thermodynamics, which in effect says that the movie of existence runs in one direction only in what is called a "thermodynamically irreversible process." As the scientists point out, we don't grow younger, ashes don't turn back into logs, broken dishes don't spontaneously reassemble, time flows from past to present. Hmm...Very consistent; very logical. Ordinary people "get" this via common sense; scientists have spent dozens of years and millions of dollars proving it to themselves via elaborate mathematical computation.

Eventually, physicists arrived at their concept of entropy, which measures the degree of disorganization of a system. Left to run on its own, a system trends toward disorganization (entropy) rather than spontaneously organizing. Everything runs down, even time and space themselves, which is why a perpetual motion machine is impossible. Again, very consistent, very logical.

Nonetheless, as if messing with entropy, existence as a whole, its material parts, and all the various systems that define them in terms we call the laws of nature, partake of predictable directionality; life itself and its myriad life-forms within life-forms possess predictable directionality toward functional competence, even if that just means growing up. Perpetual entropy in perfect equilibrium with perpetually blooming existence is a reductionist orgy of random and illogical.

Anybody recognizes compositional order in anything that's organized. As any housewife or secretary will tell you, there's no such thing as random order; accidental organization is a coffee break fantasy. Piaget would note that at an early stage of development—by the concrete operational stage, ages seven to twelve, or at least by the formal operational stage beginning at age twelve—children understand that complex structures don't just magically assemble.

Surprisingly, things not only *are*, they can also be represented by something else, like the housewife and secretary, who aren't examples of organization or disorganization, but who stand as symbols of those conditions by being what understands those conditions via experience. That's a very indirect connection, yet somehow we grasp the connection instantaneously via understanding. Things are, and things are understood to be. Being and knowing are two different things, and being and knowing are two different aspects of the same thing. The thing we know doesn't teach us to know it. We know it because we have been programmed to know how to know it. Once we know something, that knowledge of it becomes part of us. The two become "one" while remaining two. The "how" of existence transcends the mere material aspect of being.

Poets and artists have always intuitively commanded the art of symbol and metaphor. Mathematicians display a symbolic, though less layered equivalence to some material structure, such as two apples plus two oranges equaling four pieces of fruit. Not only is there symmetry between math and matter, there is symmetry within math and within matter. Aspects of existence mirror other aspects of existence; infinitely receding mirrors facing mirrors represents multidimensional intricacies that far transcend mimetic mathematics. Meaning transcends data; aesthetics transcends science; our innate faculties transcend the material stuff they comprehend. Meaning is an aspect of being human; it's a quality of the unique, meta-physical human spirit.

Common sense tells us that the sophisticated program of Nature necessitates a transcending programmer, a superior Mind that exists outside of the program. Common sense itself must have been designed by something that transcends common sense and the things that common sense "just knows." This is an ancient understanding that most of us ordinary folk have never doubted—except perhaps for a few years in college while under the spell of academic dogmatists, like scientists who worship materialist determinism (not even nature, much less a creator) and its requisite atheism; or postmodern philosophers, who worship the narcissistic delusions of anti-thought; or long-haired gurus of fringe philosophies like monism or suicide-angst existentialism.

To call the superior Mind a mind might be misleading. Unlike the human mind, which understands a tittle and creates a tad with available materials, the Designer's Mind truly *creates everything from nothing*. There is no way we can possibly grasp the ultimate reality of the Primal Creator, the Prime Mover. All we can do is stand humbly in awe. We can know *that* the Designer is, even if we can never know exactly *what* or *how* the Designer is.

Some Darwinians think that asking, Where did God come from, or Who created God, proves that God does not exist. But if God transcends space-time, which God necessarily must, then God is not bound by space-time categories or definitions. What but sheer hubris would lead one to think that the Big Bang's transcendent Big Brain could be understood by our miniscule, finite-temporal mind? Just because we mortals aren't privy to the details of God's origin, just because God's "substance" eludes our inspection, that's no proof that God doesn't exist. I don't even fully know what *I* am, but I do know *that* I am.

You can't grasp the origin and essence of God? You can't just joyfully celebrate the creative Mystery that's greater than you? Instead of suffering the humiliation of not-knowing, why not try praising the inexplicable gift of your knowing this much? The tragic flaw of the atheist is ingratitude.

IRREDUCIBLY COMPLEX LIFE

The enormously complicated DNA molecule is irreducibly complex in several ways. For example, as noted earlier, it excels at stockpiling and duplicating information but cannot build itself without the help of proteins, but proteins are incapable of reproducing themselves without the information provided by DNA. A species type, too, is an irreducibly complex system. There could not possibly have been a sudden addition of one magical part that made it a new species type—its own discrete discontinuous container.

Each new invention that magnifies our range of sight intensifies our awareness that existence is far more immensely elegantly complex than we had ever imagined. As our knowledge grows exponentially, so does our sense of smallness in the shadow of so vast a universe, but conversely so does our awareness that at least some structures of existence are clearly intelligently designed. The Deist's sense of awe inspires profound gratitude tempered with responsibility that accompanies the privilege of discerning intelligence.

Darwinists, however, present a different interpretation of the latest discoveries of microbiology. Richard Dawkins defines biology as "the study of complicated things that give the appearance of having been designed for a purpose." The atheist's experience is the anxiety of insignificance. Design is only an *appearance,* an illusion, because "the evidence of evolution reveals a universe without design." There is ample evidence of microevolution, but absolutely no evidence of macroevolution. But atheist Dawkins and peers misrepresent the facts—in other words, they lie—in order to uphold their theology. Which, to be honest, strikes me as a bit masochistic, if not dumb. Certainly their metaphysical bias keeps them from perceiving the obvious reality, the absolute *necessity,* of intelligent design.

Naturalists in the era of Darwin assumed that cells were simple building blocks that evolved into progressively more elaborate structures, with primates, specifically *Homo sapiens*, being the most elaborate. Little did they know that the closer we would observe tiny structures like cells and their molecules and *their* atoms, the more mindboggling intricate and sophisticated the cellular world would prove to be. Darwin's lack of "sight" could excuse his inaccurate insight. But today's Darwinians maintain the traditional insight of the nineteenth century even though it is invalidated by the expanded sight of twenty-first century science.

Let's see: "Throughout 150 years of the science of bacteriology, there is no evidence that one species of bacteria has changed into another," points out bacteriologist Alan Linton. "Since there is no evidence for species changes between the simplest forms of unicellular life, it is not surprising that there is no evidence for evolution from prokaryotic [bacterial] to eukaryotic [plant and animal] cells, let alone throughout the whole array of higher multicellular organisms."

Though molecular biology has rendered Darwinism obsolete, Darwinism still prevails, at least in academia and popular culture. Though it conflicts with the most basic intuitions of most of us, the people classified as most educated and smartest, or at least most knowledgeable, expect themselves and us to accept as fact the *already disproven* determinist Darwinian worldview.

That worldview is a cultural construct, a meme, a zombie lie. We will never arrive at a point of ultimate, comprehensive scientific truth. The ancient axiom perpetually proves its truth: The more you know the more you know you don't know. But we today do still know more. And now we know that the more closely we peer inward to subatomic structures and outward to the farthest reaches of space, the more intricately elegantly designed the universe appears. The more sophisticated our instruments and methods become, the more *dishonestly* we cling to obsolete beliefs and disbeliefs, be they fundamentalist or Darwinist.

GENETICS: REMAPPING THE LANDSCAPE

Scientists on the cutting edge of genetics have recently demonstrated that even on a small scale, evolutionary differentiation does not proceed as per the Darwinian roadmap. This discovery is immensely important, and not just for scientists. For starters, what if the worldview of life as cutthroat competition is patently inaccurate?

Darwin assumed that when you're threatened with diminishment of food supplies or with death, you struggle, and by struggling you become stronger, more fit. The fittest organism survives and mates with other fittest survivors within its own species, thus producing superfit offspring. Serious threats require drastic adaptation. Modifications—neo-Darwinians would say mutations—cause changes that leap beyond mere strengthening. You're not just buffed; you've sprouted wings.

Darwin could see that life was a struggle for survival. We have been so conditioned to believe this as the overarching paradigm of existence that few would challenge its validity. History perennially chronicles humanity's evolution as a series of eruptions between and within competing civilizations. At its best, religion, even if with inquisitional accusation sprinkled with conditional hope, perpetually fights humanity's inherent selfishness, the root of all evil; at its worst, it fights to render extinct everything that sneezes. Every aspect of existence is a struggle of the fittest to survive: Darwinian natural selection confirms an ancient cultural meme: Weakness must be overcome: Use it or abuse it.

But isn't society more than a bloodlust crusade to exploit? Isn't a person more than a blacklist of sin, more than a thorn in the power-monger's skin? It could be argued that Darwin's theory emerged from selective data interpreted by his individual mind—trained for the clergy at the height of the Industrial Revolution and British Imperialism—perverted by a cultural emphasis on the dark side.

Consider again these questions from Chapter 1: How would it change the way you think and behave if scientists could document that life is *not* inherently a struggle for survival? Could it transform the way civilization functions if we ordinary citizens of Earth discovered, as scientists *have* discovered, that at the deep level of DNA, all living systems are inherently cooperative, that the molecular matter of life itself is composed of workers performing specific functions for the production of healthy growth within the whole system? What if it could be scientifically demonstrated that any living system at war with itself is destined for quick extinction?

Darwinians argue that this proves that Darwinism is true: The ultimate goal of any species is to prevent its extinction. Even so, this new scientific perspective does negate the struggle for survival—power—within a species, and it nudges us dangerously close to classic religious morality. The basic structure even of amoral animals is thoroughly beneficial, so logically whatever designed and constructed that structure is likely beneficent.

Neo-Darwinians have had to explain this apparent negation of absolute survivalism just to stay in the metaphysical game. In order to kill any semblance of a beneficent creator God, they have postulated a "new" theory of evolution, the process of *random* mutation *guided* by natural selection. This incongruous theory has proven to be as mythical as Nietzsche's dead God rotting in some parallel universe.

It's odd that as students of natural design, scientists would deny the existence or even possibility of a Designer. Even atheist scientists agree that nature is a structure in motion powered by a system. In fact, they agree that nature is an astoundingly immense, complex, and elegant structural system. Could *so much something*, so much organizational *elegance* that's prewired to function beautifully, just happen to emerge—to be emerging— from *nothing*? Clearly a something (nature as a whole) of seemingly infinite somethings (nature's myriad components) requires a transcendently intelligent, constantly creating meta-creator.

Scientists are well aware of the exceptionalness of our universe. Fred Hoyle observed, for instance, that while explosions throw matter apart, the Big Bang explosion's exquisite magnitude surprisingly produced the opposite effect: matter clumping together in the form of galaxies. Scientists have calculated that the rate of expansion was at the "critical value" at which the universe barely escaped its own gravity, allowing it to expand for billions of years. Had the rate been a bit slower—Stephen Hawking says by even one part in a hundred thousand million million, other scientists say in a trillion trillion trillion—the cosmos would have collapsed; a bit faster, by one part in a trillion trillion trillion, and the spewed material would have quickly dispersed.

Scientists are fully cognizant of the rational, finely-tuned structural equilibrium of the universe that is hypersensitive to even minor alterations; none of them denies that "the seemingly miraculous concurrence of numerical values that nature has assigned to her fundamental constants must remain the most compelling evidence for an element of cosmic design," as atheist Paul Davies put it.

Scientists understand that the mindboggling exactitude of each calibration of every minute detail of the universe—from the precise strength of gravity to the formation of the carbon atom, the essential ingredient for life, to the strong nuclear force with the exact strength to produce hydrogen (if the speed or mass of the electron had been anything but exactly what it is, there could be no life on Earth or anywhere in the universe), and on and on—all the billions and trillions and bazillions of minute constituents have led to life.

The Big Bang revolution is as spiritually charged as the revolution ignited by Copernicus. The discovery that Earth is not the center of the universe or even of our galaxy forced humanity to rethink its worldview, the source of that worldview, and the authority of that source.

In the 1940s science confirmed that the universe was not infinite and eternal as scientists and theologians had believed. About 13.7 billion years ago it exploded from a highly compressed state of extreme heat and density that existed in a single moment at a single point—in fact, the only moment at the only point, both of which had presumably spontaneously emerged simultaneously *ex nihilo*, out of nothing—nothing, because space and time came into existence at the exact moment that the space-time universe came into existence; that "place" and "time" is the Big Bang.

The Big Bang model is based on two principles: Einstein's general theory of relativity, which describes the fixed, perfectly calibrated gravitational interaction of all matter, and on the "cosmological principle," which means that the observer's view of the universe doesn't depend on his location or on the direction in which he looks. Because the Big Bang blasted out in all directions, the universe has no edge because Creation is still in progress: it's still blasting, spewing outward in all directions.

In scientific terms, during the first few seconds of the Big Bang, there were already many types of elementary particles present, and processes that predict proton decay were already causing matter to overcome anitmatter—itself a substance composed of subatomic particles that have the mass, electric charge, and magnetic moment of electrons, protons, and neutrons of ordinary matter but with negative electric charge and magnetic moment. Within a few seconds after the Big Bang, the universe cooled enough to form nuclei and to produce precise amounts of hydrogen, helium, and lithium. After another million years, the universe had cooled enough to form atoms and to allow radiation, which already existed, to travel through space; the residue of that radiation still exists as microwave background radiation.

It's uncanny, if not miraculous, that we today can witness the Big Bang event 13.7 billion light years away, almost as if we're supposed to "get" this moment of Creation as evidence of—well, Creation.

What also existed at the moment of the Big Bang were all the precisely calibrated, perfectly interconnected and mutually facilitating laws of science, even laws that would not be needed for another dozen or so billion years when life would explode into the universe, and for the 3.8 billion years of biosphere expansion, including the accommodation of intelligent consciousness, here on our singularly remarkable planet.

Science has helped us look inward as well as outward. And I mean inward in a purely material sense. The discovery of DNA is another cosmic revolution that has spun the chatting heads of science and theology.

Really, the cell itself is a separate organism, its own universe. Scientists often liken it to a factory, which is a fair analogy for a universe, an organism, or a cell. But this factory builds, among other things, copies of itself. No other factory can do that. The cell's nucleus runs like a human-built factory, except that it's alive. Picture a huge metropolis of Detroit-type assembly lines producing unimaginatively innovative products using a massive multitude of molecular machines. The nucleus warehouses an astonishing assortment of raw materials and cranks out a dazzling array of intricately assembled goods. Parts are freighted to various outlying assembly lines along microtubule tracks using cables, ropes, and pulleys powered by batteries that harness and store particles of light. Like people, these machines literally flip electrical switches, run copy machines, even ingest and digest like workers at a lunch counter. There are machines for every imaginable task, and some of those machines act as managers making split-second decisions. Some are geeks performing feats of nanotechnology that make human devices look like Stone Age flints.

Taking inventory is like trying to count the stars. But all those parts are literally *alive*.

DNA is a sophisticated living machine coded with genetic information. The organism-specific coding of a cell is as logical and patterned and wildly unique as Virginia Woolf's unclassifiable book *The Waves*. "Glory be to God for dappled things," poet Gerard Manley Hopkins hymned in "Pied Beauty," and in another poem, "The world is charged with the grandeur of God" and "There lives the dearest freshness deep down things." Most of us understand.

Scientists have christened the inexorable movement from nothing to us the "anthropic principle," which means that the laws of nature facilitate the appearance of intelligent life.

But for most scientists, the leap from designer universe to Designer is a leap of blind faith into the scary abyss of mystery. Mystery makes a scientist sweat. It's the terror of the small in the presence of enormity, the bravado of the self-aware finite-temporal at the mercy of its own necessary Creator which transcends even the space-time categories of infinite and eternal.

But they've got the solution: The universe is self-created.

DNA: THE IMPOSSIBLE POSSIBILITY OF LIFE

Life comes only from life. Only once did life come from not-life. Mathematicians have demonstrated that it is all but impossible that life could happen at all, and that it is mathematically inconceivable that such a miracle could happen more than once. Furthermore, it is mathematically impossible for a system as intricate as a single organism to have not been intelligently designed.

Despite what the mathematicians say, neo-Darwinian biologists insist that random variation, or chance, is natural—is part of the functional laws of nature. But the cohesive, supra-organized functional laws of nature are by definition anything but random. Nature is a complex system of intricate functions. And every biologist knows that.

Neo-Darwinians argue that life evolved randomly via natural *selection*. One big problem here is that randomness and natural selection are contradictory. Selection is an act or process executed by *will*, a choice responding to a need. Selection is the effect, will the cause. If you *select*, you *choose*. Only an *intelligent will* can choose. Only an intelligent will can choose *intelligently*. Only intelligence can say you (or I) need to choose this to become that.

Intelligent choosing results in an intelligently constructed product. Inert matter and life are highly sophisticated products. The immensity of highly sophisticated products within highly sophisticated products within highly sophisticated products existing in perfect equilibrium necessitates a designer of even higher intelligence and sophistication designing by an act of will.

The structural foundation of microevolution, indeed, of all change, consists of fixed laws (the bones of the universal house) and their adjacent wiggle rooms (the zones of chance, simple choice, and complex free will) that are both intelligently constructed. Intelligently constructed fixed laws and their complementary wiggle rooms are the mechanisms-by-which/tools-with-which life and inert matter are constructed.

Construction is a creative process that increases the complexity of the product while amplifying symmetry. Creative *use* of fixed laws and bordered wiggle rooms as mechanisms/tools organizes and balances the constructed product. Any act or process of construction, certainly any act or process of intelligent construction, is executed by will. Fixed natural laws, including laws governing chance, choice (or "selection"), and free will, always perform a function. A function always serves a purpose. A purpose is a product of higher, willful, purposeful intelligence.

The wiggle room where a human is free to exercise his or her will, that room of true freedom, is a reality that is probably harder to grasp than the existence of a huge complex universe emerging from "nothing." It boggles the mind to contemplate that freedom is built right into immutable structures. The laws of nature, and even our DNA, for instance, seem fixed forever. We are what we were born to become. And that's true, up to a point.

What's interesting, if not disconcerting especially for a Darwinist, is that our DNA appears to enfold wiggle room. Stephen Meyer notes that "Although the sequence of bases on one strand determines the sequence of bases on the second strand, no physical or chemical laws dictate what the sequence will be in an isolated strand of DNA." DNA sequences are like letters and words on a printed page. We have a limited alphabet and only so many dictionary words to relay information that conveys a message that far transcends ink and paper and letters and words and even language itself. DNA, functional proteins, and the cell as a whole all possess coding regions that must be programmed like the software of a computer. Only an intelligent agency can program information. Most of us assume that DNA can't be changed once we're born. But many things can change our specific DNA, both negatively, as with pollutants, and positively, as with certain nutrients. To some extent, even at the level of DNA we are self-created, whether we know it or not.

Scientists now know that the complex, specific information needed to assemble complex protein machines that manufacture the most primitive one-celled organism is already stored in DNA or some equivalent molecule. The computer's hardware and even a sizable package of software are preloaded so the computer is ready to boot and run right out of the box.

But software is information, and information isn't matter, even though the means of transmission of information is material. Brain, lips, vocal cords transmit information, but the information itself is none of these transmission apparatuses. Words on a page aren't the message; words simply *convey* the message. Knowledge isn't a "thing" the way a brain is a thing. DNA processes information that comes from beyond DNA itself. This isn't simply mind/body dualism; this is material/spiritual dualism. (And dual does not mean duel.)

Darwinians, of course, need to kill knowledge-as-language if they are to kill religion. Their agenda mirrors postmodern deconstruction, a term coined by Jacques Derrida, who deconstructs (so to speak) via a process of erasure, usually with a poem as its target. Derrida might tape a poem to the blackboard, and with a large black felt-tip pen mark a bold X through every word or phrase that signifies appeals to concealed or forgotten origins, such as tradition, authority (literary, religious, cultural, or any other), meaning, author intention, or anything else "centered." Or a deconstructionist might simply mark the X through the whole poem, an invasive, violent, reactive gesture of a wannabe that betrays, "Those who can, create; those who can't, deconstruct."

The process is meant to demonstrate that a poem is not an individual creation, but is rather a collage of constructed conventions, cultural and/or collective. A poem, like any other language act, is merely text, and as such, does not belong to the poet but to us all; like the universe, it appears out of the nowhere that has always existed. Deconstructionists appropriate any or all of the text for their own use. Some postmodernists tweak famous poems slightly and called those poems their own to prove their point.

The process of erasure derives from Martin Heidegger, who sometimes wrote out the poem in pencil and erased anything centered, but his erasures showed traces of the word. For him, traces of meaning and truth are truly recoverable. But for Derrida, erasure exposes all the non-present meanings of a word, and its possible *differance*, meaning *anything goes*. Derrida's erasure places under suspicion Heidegger's philosophy, which assumed a metaphysics of presence. Derrida's ultra-relativism deconstructs presence down into non-metaphysical absence.

In the most precise sense, deconstruction is commentary writings about other texts, usually literary, intent on turning those texts against themselves by showing that meaning is contradictory or "undecidable," that the difference between literal and figurative is equivalent to appearance/essence, matter/spirit. The agenda of their work is anti-metaphysical, anti-essentialist, deconstructive.

How startling different from the logos of DNA is deconstruction's bold X's of "erasure" that so desperately, violently *need* to decenter *presence, need* to reject the closures and foundations so obviously beautifully inherent in the rhythms of existence. Why this *need* to foreground absence, to focus on removing what things can have or be? Why this compulsion to prove *differance*, to prove absolutely an unbridgeable gap between any thing and its word, between words and words, things and things...Why this psychotic hatred of meaning, stability, connection? Why this murder of communication, community, communion? It's no coincidence that so many deconstructionists commit suicide, when they've spent their lives X'ing out all possibility of meaning expressed by their own being. At least Heidegger allowed for the recovery of concealed and forgotten being, and the Being of being, by recapturing traces on the page of what had been erased.

DNA: The Word of God to Humanity

Like many Deists, I believe that the thinking God communicates with us thinkers through Nature. I would go so far as to say that God is trying to tell us something right now via DNA that is crucial to our survival.

Francis Crick, the Nobel Prize-winning co-discoverer of the structure of DNA and reportedly an atheist and believer in alien seeding, first observed that DNA *is* language. But then, even the ancients understood that matter *is* logos. Greek philosophers understood logos—from the Greek word for "word," "reason," or "plan"—to mean the divine reason organizing the universe by giving it form and meaning. By ancients I mean, for instance, Heraclitus (6th century B.C.E.); Plato (4th century B.C.E.), for whom logos was both immanent and transcendent; Zeno (4th-3rd century B.C.E.); and Philo of Alexandria, a Jewish contemporary of Jesus from whom the writer of John's Gospel freely borrowed.

Today we understand that the DNA in *each* human cell contains the equivalent of the information contained in 1,500 encyclopedia volumes. One human body contains 1,500 volumes times 100 thousand billion cells.

The massive living library contained in DNA is the part of the "infinite" difference between life and inert matter. To put that difference in perspective, consider atheist Edmund O. Wilson's point that there is more information in one handful of Earth's living soil than there is on the surfaces of all other known planets combined.

Or consider this: DNA is approximately 120 times narrower than the smallest wavelength of visible light, which means a thread of DNA is invisible to us without the help of our most powerful optical microscopes. We need to trust a device well beyond ourselves to see ourselves. Yet we know that the two ribbons of the DNA double helix wrap around each other 600 million times inside the nucleus of a human cell, each of which is about the size of two-millionths of a pinhead. If the DNA thread of one nucleus were stretched out, it would be two yards long and only ten atoms wide—a billion times longer than wide.

Again, that two-yards-long thread fits into a nucleus two millionths the size of a pinhead. By current estimates, the average human being is made up of 100 thousand billion cells. If the DNA from all the cells in one human body were stretched out, they would reach 125 billion miles, long enough to wrap around the earth 5 million times.

Amazingly, the DNA molecule is the same in every species of life—all of which exist here on Earth. The genetic information in every life-form is coded in a universal language of four letters, A, G, C, and T (adenine, guanine, cytosine, and thymine), the four chemical compounds that comprise the DNA double helix.

The living universe is coded like a cosmic Internet. Every living being contains DNA. As a substance, DNA does not vary among species; only the order of its letters changes. The individual letters are meaningless in themselves, but they combine into meaningful words and stanzas that build the poetry of species and individuals. Typed out on a page, the code of our particular DNA would look similar to code written by computer programmers. By definition, *code* is never random. The code of DNA is vastly more elaborate than computer code. Not to mention, it's alive.

Clearly that code was written by a cosmic super-genius. And if we are reading and understanding the code, we have been designed to read and understand the code, and the code has been designed to be read and understood by us. That's the definition of information communication. Yet atheist scientists like Richard Dawkins say that living systems "give the *appearance* of having been designed for a purpose"—*give the appearance*, as if mindless living systems were intelligent enough, and willful enough, to mastermind a grand illusion of such mindboggling magnitude.

The genome, or genetic information of a human being, is written as three billion letters along a single DNA filament. In some places, the filament winds around itself, forming twenty-three more segments, chromosomes. Since we each inherit a complete set of chromosomes from each of our parents, we each have twenty-three pairs of chromosomes. Our genetic story is written in six billion pairs, or twelve billion letters (that we thus far know of).

Although the DNA molecule excels at stockpiling and duplicating information, it cannot build itself without the help of proteins. But proteins are incapable of reproducing themselves without the information provided by DNA. No proteins could exist without DNA, no DNA could exist without proteins. They were created at the same time, as part of the same package.

As mentioned before, the paradox of irreducible complexity is perhaps the ultimate negation of any Darwinian theory of evolution. Again quoting Michael Behe, an irreducibly complex system is "composed of several, well-matched interacting parts that contribute to the basic function, wherein the removal of any one of the parts causes the system to effectively cease functioning." Such a system must have been created as a fully functioning whole.

These two separate languages—DNA constructed from a four letter alphabet, and proteins from a twenty letter alphabet (the twenty amino acids)—communicate via one translation mechanism to form the paragraphs of our bodies, our cells.

Only the sections of the DNA text coded for construction of proteins and enzymes are read by the transcription enzymes. Only a small percent of a genome is included in these passages, or genes. Much of the genome serves other purposes, and much appears to be latent, waiting for an adaptive need—a need that does not yet exist but which might, or will.

Within genes themselves, there are non-coding notations, called introns. Once transcription enzymes have translated a gene, editing enzymes delete the introns with atomic precision and splice together the correct coding segments, called exons. Some genes contain very little genetic information. The function of the remaining percent of introns is unknown.

What is known, however, is that every aspect of every DNA molecule has a precise predetermined function. The most fundamental component of the simplest, most infinitesimal form of life is amazingly elegant in its structural complexity and efficiency. Life did not emerge out of nothing; the very first speck of life came fully equipped with a massive array of fully functioning bells and whistles. Coded text, duplication, transcription, translation, editing—as a writer, I am awed by life's eloquently "written" DNA.

Darwinians argue that life evolved in the sea and that a sea creature crawled up on land to become us land animals. But just because every cell in the world is filled with salt water with the same salt concentration as the ocean doesn't prove that we evolved from fish, just that we are all made of the same stuff. Even if we were evolved from fish, that wouldn't prove that evolution was not by design. Whatever process led to our existence is the elegant design of a supra-intelligent Designer.

By design, every cell is its own ocean filled with the same salt water. DNA's four bases (A, G, C, and T) coil up from the center of the molecule to avoid contact with surrounding water molecules. Due to the arrangement of their atoms, the bases can only pair up A with T, and G with C, which gives rise to the spiral shape of the double helix. The spiral is made up of two ribbons—a main text, and its mirror image, which is usually not read by the transcription enzymes. The backup ribbon enables the repair enzymes to reconstruct the main text if it is "hacked," and provides the mechanism for duplicating the genetic information. The repair enzymes make only one mistake for every ten billion letters they correct. Imagine human copy editors being that accurate! Enzymes are highly skilled at their jobs, and a really smart boss manages the factory.

Enzymes transcribe DNA into RNA, edit out non-coding passages, splice together the final text, construct the machines that read the instructions, and manufacture other enzymes, all at astronomical speed. This profoundly complex orchestration is amazingly precise and efficient.

Again: Every living being contains DNA. As a substance, DNA does not vary among species; only the order of its letters changes.

This fact is nothing short of mind-boggling. As biologist Robert

Pollack pointed out, "The planet's surface has changed many times over, but DNA and the cellular machinery for its replication have remained constant...no stone, no mountain, no ocean, not even the sky above us, have been stable and constant for this long; nothing inanimate, no matter how complicated, has survived unchanged for a fraction of the time that DNA and its machinery of replication have coexisted."

That much stability in a state of flux is almost a case for eternal life.

Almost all the species that have ever lived are extinct. In four billion years, DNA has transformed itself into millions of species, yet it has remained exactly the same, down to the letter. Of course the master of metamorphosis has not bothered to explain to us the mechanism by which she creates her infinite variations out of the exact same four DNA letters, or proteins made of the exact same twenty amino acids.

Computer coding is nothing compared to the dazzlingly intricate coding that spells out *life*.

Life is the consummate miracle in progress. And by miracle I mean the opposite of generically random.

Ironically, scientists themselves, often inadvertently, support the theory of miracle by arguing a good case for the *impossibility* of life. They explain that protein molecules are composed of amino acids linked together in *very specific* order and structure. Specific proteins can have as few as fifty amino acids, or tens of thousands, but each protein is *uniquely itself* because of the *exact order* of amino acids in its molecular chain.

The specific gene of each specific protein is responsible for the correct ordering of the amino acids in each protein molecule. The gene, which is the length of DNA carrying the genetic code for that protein, is coded so that three DNA letters are needed for each amino acid. A DNA strand of three hundred letters would carry the genetic instructions for a protein of a hundred amino acids.

This fundamental biochemical process is extraordinarily complex, and the mathematical possibility of it occurring by chance to give the first primitive protein has often been illustrated with the example of the so-called typing monkey, a clever visual aid created in 1913 by French mathematician Émile Borel.

If the monkey tried to type out the 300-letter word of his single 300-letter gene with the four available letters, the odds against getting the first letter correct are 4-1. The odds against getting the first two letters correct are 16-1, the first three letters are 64-1, and so on x 4 for the remaining 277 letters of the gene code. The odds against getting the gene-word correct are 1 in 10^{130} (10 followed by 130 zeros, a number many billions of times greater than the number of atoms in the observable universe). Even if there were a thousand million monkeys on each square inch of the Earth's surface typing at a rate of a thousand million words per second for a thousand million years, the odds against the correct gene-sequence are still 1 in 10^{80}. To put this in perspective, consider that there are only 10^{65} atoms in our galaxy.

This is for just one gene with a 300-letter code. A simple virus has a 20,000-letter code, bacterium a 4.5 million-letter code, and a human being about a 5,000 million-letter code. The statistical chances of forming such complex genes are almost infinitely minute.

Not only that, in this example for a relatively small protein of 100 amino acids, the chance selection of this correct sequence would have to be made from 10^{130} alternative choices. The organic molecules in the primordial soup would have to undergo 10^{130} trial assemblies over 500 million years to hit on the correct sequence. The probability of such a chance occurrence leading to the formation of just one of the smallest protein molecules is effectively zero.

The chances of that happening twice, of life emerging elsewhere in the universe, is that same zero multiplied astronomically. And this doesn't even take into consideration that the primordial soup exists, that the laws of nature exist to make "formations" possible, that one thing can give rise to another completely unique substance, and so on. And the emergence of every-thing results from this same kind of extraordinary process. And each and every result is utterly unique.

Probability estimates of some mathematicians are even more mindboggling minute. As Stephen Meyer explains in his aptly titled *Signature in the Cell*, according to today's calculations, the odds are 1 chance in 10^{164} of finding a functional protein among the possible 150-amino-acid compounds, the probability being 84 orders of magnitude (or powers of ten) *smaller* than the probability of finding a specific particle in the whole universe. In other words, the probability of finding a functional protein by chance is a trillion, trillion, trillion, trillion, trillion, trillion, trillion times smaller than the odds of finding a single specified particle among all the particles in the universe.

But that's not all. Typical proteins have hundreds of amino acids, many of which require close functional association with other protein chains. The probability of producing all the necessary associated proteins by chance would be far smaller than the odds of producing just the 150-amino-acid protein. Even a simple cell requires many proteins, not just one. Generating the necessary proteins by chance, not to mention the genetic information to produce them, is as close to impossible as it gets.

But wait, it gets more impossible. One simple cell needs a minimum of 250 proteins made of approximately 150 amino acids. Now the probability of getting one simple cell with its necessary proteins by chance is 1 in 10^{164} multiplied by itself 250 times, or 1 in $10^{41,000}$. In the real world where most of us live, it's *impossible*.

Then there is us—all the almost infinite human sperms and eggs that did not result in life, all the chance meetings and matings, all the other factors, the what-if's, the cancelled flights—and yet somehow each one of us human beings has come into existence. The impossible possibility of any two people being at the same place at the same time is incomprehensible and, despite any free decision by either or both parties to meet there, inconceivably outside our control. There should be a religious holiday dedicated to nothing more than the contemplation of this awesome miracle of knowing each other.

CHAPTER 7

NEO-DARWINISM ON STEROIDS

Does Darwinian shape-shift shaman Richard Dawkins really offer anything new? You bet. He and his God-slayer peers are now seeking not just scientific knowledge but also the cutting-edge *unification* of all knowledge, the latest and greatest magical ax that will X God.

Of course, this revolutionary mission dates back at least to the sixth century B.C.E. to the Ionian Thales of Miletus, the first Greek philosopher, and one of the legendary Seven Wise Men, or Sophoi, of antiquity. By offering the first not-mythic, nature-specific study of natural causes, Thales was the first naturalist; two centuries later Aristotle named him the founder of the physical sciences and the first philosopher. By disallowing mythological elements, Thales was the first demythologizer. By establishing rational simplification as the best means of explaining phenomena without X-ing First Cause, he was the first deist.

Thales is often mocked for guessing that the essential ingredient of matter is water, but his theory, much like Darwin's evolution, was based on the discovery of fossil sea animals far inland. Since life requires water, and since the universe itself is an organism, an assumption some scientists today claim is not entirely inaccurate, then the primal material substratum of the cosmos might well be water. Though perhaps wrong in positing water as the primal essence of nature, Thales' conviction that existence is orderly and can be explained by a small number of natural laws has funneled science ever since. Physicist Gerald Holton dubbed this core Greek principle the Ionian Enchantment. One person's enchantment, of course, is another person's common sense.

In the atheist-materialist brain, complete unification would miraculously prove that all the exquisite complexity of the universe is really just simple stuff tossed together into bigger simple stuff, and that all that stuff is the exact same stuff; therefore, the universe is self-contained and simple, a single dunce in a pointy paper hat perpetually constructing simple paper stuff from silly paper stuff he's perpetually shredding: neo-Zeus in his pantheon of one.

Shortly after Thales declared water to be the primordial unifying element of the cosmos, Heraclitus proposed that the original element was not water but fire. Other philosophers thought that air or earth was the primal element. All those ancient naturalists were an early version of monists, who assumed that there was a single essential cosmic element, the fundamental building block of which the universe was constructed. But they weren't necessarily materialists. Only later did monists equate—unfairly—the primal element theory with X-God materialism.

Empedocles, the first pluralist, suggested that rather than just one, there were four building blocks, the primal elements water, fire, earth, and air. Aristotle added that a constant, immutable fifth essence, the quintessence, was needed to cause the flux of the elements to gel. Because the courses of the constellations were constant, Aristotle thought that perhaps the unifying quintessence in some way consisted of star-stuff—a view remarkably modern considering Einstein's discovery that the speed of light is an invariant, immutable number and that light in some way connects and/or explains the emergence of space, time, energy, and matter. Light, of course, emanates from stars. (Or are stars created by light-stuff?)

Theories and perspectives like these are each era's best guesses about the substance of intelligently designed Nature. Scientific interpretation is always metaphysical. Unification is recognition of integrated design. Recognition of design is intrinsic proof of a necessary Designer, a necessarily transcending Designer that by definition can't be the design or an aspect, extension, or function of the design and that designed us capable of recognizing design and Designer as separate entities.

It's worth noting that shortly after Thales disallowed mythological explanations for reality, Xenophanes observed that people made the gods in their own image, and argued that there could be only one Creator God, the eternal ruler of the universe, a view shared by Deists today. A century later Empedocles claimed that the four elements, the "roots of everything," were activated by two perpetual forces, love and hate, love constantly mixing the elements, hate forever separating them. Sometimes mixtures came together in a way that allowed the resulting creations to support and reproduce themselves; hence, species were produced and continued to exist by a simple unifying mechanism, which Darwinians assume is survival of the fittest, but could as justly be interpreted as yin-yang harmonization.

Fast-forward to Einstein, who led the twentieth-century charge toward the unification of physics, specifically space with time with motion, and gravity with electromagnetism with cosmology. Edward O. Wilson pointed out that Einstein displayed signs of enchantment very early, for example when the alignment of the microscopic physics of capillaries with the macroscopic, universe-wide physics of gravity led Einstein to write to his friend Marcel Grossmann, "It is a wonderful feeling to recognize the unity of a complex of phenomena that to direct observation appear to be quite separate things." Einstein whittled the Ionian sentiment to a sharp point when he remarked, "I want to know all God's thoughts; all the rest are just details," and when he even more pointedly remarked, "It was the experience of mystery—even if mixed with fear—that engendered religion." Unlike atheists like Richard Dawkins, who think unification can kill religion, deists like Albert Einstein understood that exquisitely mysterious unity exposes a glimpse of its intelligent Designer.

Wilson betrays his deistic leanings when he interprets the motivation of the Ionian Enchantment this way: "Preferring a search for objective reality over revelation is another way of satisfying religious hunger. It is an endeavor almost as old as civilization and intertwined with traditional religion, but it follows a very different course—a stoic's creed, an acquired taste, a guidebook to adventure plotted across rough terrain. It aims to save the spirit, not by surrender but by liberation of the human mind. Its central tenet, as Einstein knew, is the unification of knowledge. When we have unified enough certain knowledge, we will understand who we are and why we are here." The Deist answers, "Been there, done that. Please catch up."

Trust in Nature's coherence, or what Wilson calls its "consilience," the same intuitive metaphysical faith in intelligent design that fertilized the flowering of Greco-Roman civilization, fueled the Renaissance and the Enlightenment. Philosophically and practically, a scientific revolution had been steaming along for millennia. Today's term "physics" derives from the Greek word *physis*, which means "nature." Scientists are naturalists; Deists are naturalists who locate the originating "quintessence" of intelligently unified Nature in a unifying Originator of transcending intelligence: God.

How can atheists today tout unification, which demonstrates consistent unity across domains of knowledge, as proof of the nonexistence of an intelligent Designer? How can they explain the recurrence of the exact same mathematical proportions of a spiral galaxy and a nautilus shell, or for that matter, explain a mind capable of working out their sequences, as Leonardo of Pisa, aka Fibonacci, did in 1202? How account for self-similarity of fractals, the reiterations of details or patterns at progressively smaller scales: how explain micro repetitions of the macro, such as cross-sections (and cross-sections of cross-sections) of component parts of a cauliflower or sunflower or snowflake or blood cell, that almost identically mirror the whole cauliflower or sunflower or snowflake or blood cell in an infinite regress? These kinds of major design elements, the very objects of scientific scrutiny, simply cannot be interpreted as random results of "just is" any more than can the intricacies of Reims Cathedral or Chantilly lacework, the subjects of aesthetic study, be they representations or "just beauty." All designs in all fields reverberate as aspects of a larger aesthetic design. Unification doesn't demote design, it promotes it.

Neo-Darwinians offer neo-naturalism to support their metaphysical anti-God contention like pickpockets try to sell you your wallet. Biologists calling atheist-materialism "naturalism" is like the processed muffin mix trumpeting its "real artificial blueberries." They select random chaos from their disordered bag of tricks and expect you to accept it just magically changed into that beautiful woman brainchild *Life* conceived of smoke and mirrors. And there's her man. Poof! Unity.

A few hundred years before Jesus performed miracles, Aristotle and other philosophers systematically detailed their observations of an astonishingly ordered Nature as part of their quest to gain knowledge. Aristotle grouped animals into two categories, those with and those without blood, which corresponds closely to our classifications of vertebrate and invertebrate. Even Aristotle understood that each order of animal or plant was its own discrete order.

At about the same time, Hippocrates advised his patients that their diseases and illnesses were due to diet and other physical causes rather than to the meddling of gods. In the second-century C.E., the Roman physician Galen began to use dissection to study the function of animal organs. In the seventeenth century, William Harvey finally theorized that blood flows throughout the body to and from the heart.

From the Middle Ages onward, naturalists expanded Aristotle's system of classification, adding class, order, genus, and species. And from their categorizations, the idea of common descent later codified by Darwin emerged like a leap of faith into the dark abyss of what scientists call a "black box," which is any current object, be it structure or process, just beyond scientific perusal. Scientists in Darwin's era couldn't see the molecular innards of a cell. But it was no black box, but rather myopia that kept Darwinians from seeing intelligent design.

Eyeglass lenses—spectacles—were in use by the fifteenth century, and the first microscope was constructed two centuries later. Galileo, an early owner of a microscope, was amazed by the compound eyes of insects looking back at him. The little world observed in his microscope and the vast cosmos viewed through his infamous telescope revealed both the intricate complexity of life and the majestic order of the astronomical heavens.

In the early nineteenth century, cell theory established similarities between plant and animal cellular structures. But cells were tiny and almost impossible to discern. The nineteenth century's snobbish bias assumed that small meant simple, so cells were considered to be rather insignificant little gelatinous blobs that could have first arisen, in the view of Darwin and others, from "some warm little pond" somewhere, and from that primal life evolved all the life-forms on Earth. By 1885, scientists believed that chromosomes in the cell nucleus carried the information for cell heredity. What scientists at that time couldn't tell was that chromosomes are extraordinarily complex structures composed of extraordinarily complex proteins and DNA.

With the invention of the electron microscope in the late nineteenth century and X-ray crystallography during the early twentieth century, cells could be viewed more closely, albeit indirectly by their pattern of diffraction on photographic film. James Watson and Francis Crick proposed a structural model for DNA in 1953. In 1958, scientists were able to examine the detailed structure of a basic protein, and soon after that, nuclear magnetic resonance, computers, and other instruments made it possible to determine the structures of several proteins and nucleic acids. Those amazing structures impressed even the atheists.

THE GREAT ZIGGURAT: UNITY IN DIVERSITY

We now know that a person, society, or species microevolves in the post-Darwinian sense by the addition of complexity and sophistication within the parameters of given form. Complex creativity within stable form is a core tenet of Deistic intelligent design. For millennia scientists have known that existence consists of discrete wholes that exist unto themselves but also within other wholes, like nested dolls. Open the largest doll, and inside is a smaller doll; open that doll, and inside there is another even smaller doll, and so on, each doll, though distinctly a doll, being unique in design. The human species exists within the Earth world, which exists within a solar system, which exists within a universe, all of which—the whole and its parts—is made up of the same physical stuff.

Over twenty centuries ago Aristotle realized that nature constitutes a hierarchy of discrete whole entities, with quantity being at the bottom and quality culminating at the top, a kind of ziggurat configuration that was later called, among other things, the Great Chain of Being. Some prefer picturing a pyramid, but the ziggurat is a more precise representation, with each step up representing a higher level of quality that contains aspects of everything below it but in smaller quantity. The foundation of the ziggurat is made up of quarks and other particles; above quarks are suddenly atoms (there are more quarks than atoms); above atoms are molecules (there are more atoms than molecules). Quarks, atoms, and molecules constitute inert matter.

That each step—quarks, atoms, molecules—is just that, a step, is a persuasive argument for intelligent design and against Darwinian evolution, as Darwin well knew. Rather than a smooth upward slope posited by Darwinians, Creation is actually composed of a series of discrete steps, or layers, each step up the ziggurat being its own discrete whole layer. The step itself can change somewhat—that's microevolution within a species—but one step doesn't morph into the next step. Not change, but each next step's transcending—a province usually ascribed to Divine intervention—remains the quandary of Darwinism. But how does this fit with the top-down, blueprint version of evolution?

Again, I have no bias for top-down over bottom-up; top-down-from-blueprint currently makes the most sense, but any coming-to-be necessitates transcending intelligent first cause. Personally, I think scientists should be exploring a model of simultaneous top-down and bottom-up—or better yet, a model of simultaneous creations, some generated one way, some another, but all melding into one perfectly integrated whole of perfectly integrated wholes.

Keep in mind that each step is a unique, discrete whole unto itself that is categorically different from all other steps. A molecule is a whole entity: a molecule. All molecules are a whole abstract entity: the category molecule. An atom is a whole entity; the category atom is a whole entity. A quark is a whole entity. Though a molecule contains atoms which contain quarks, a molecule is not an atom or a quark. You are not in essence the components of your material form. Your essence form/container and your material form/container are two different forms/containers. Does material contain essence, or vice versa?

A molecule is its own form/container which contains several instances of the atom form/container. Yet at the same time, each discrete step makes up the composition of the next step: quarks make up atoms make up molecules. But each step up possesses that something extra that makes it uniquely itself. Here's the rub: That something extra must necessarily originate beyond the step itself; something uniquely "other" can't be generated by something that doesn't have within itself—within its reach, at its disposal—something that does not yet exist, like the "spark of life" that made the first life alive. At the same time, each discrete, unique step— quarks, atoms, and molecules—are made of the same space-time materials. And not only each step; each individual instance of each step—each quark, atom, molecule, and each absolutely unique human being is made of the same space-time materials.

We are profoundly all in this together. But at the same time, humans are a quantum leap above anything else. In terms of essence, that huge extra something that transcends the mere animal/material is at least as "beyond" other life-forms as life is beyond inorganic matter. Using the model of the ancient Mesopotamian temple tower, the ziggurat, the shrine at the top represents humanity. (Mesopotamia, you'll recall, was the "cradle of civilization," the area between the Tigris and Euphrates rivers centered at the spot the Bible calls Eden, also known in antiquity as Babylon, today's Baghdad, the city our military shocked and awed with bombs that ripped the temple curtain in half at the start of the Iraq War.)

Again, from Aristotle to Newton to New Age philosophers, thinkers throughout the ages have noted that in every nook and cranny of the universe, reality is composed of wholes, and those wholes are composed of parts that are themselves wholes. Whole particles are part of whole atoms that are part of whole molecules that are part of whole cells that are part of whole organisms. (Have you ever wondered how the ancient Greeks could know about atoms?)

But here's a startling fact: A whole cannot exist without its whole-parts: Molecules cannot exist without atoms. But the whole-parts can exist without the larger wholes that contain them: Quarks can exist without atoms, atoms can exist without molecules. Quarks can exist without atoms, but atoms cannot exist without quarks, and so on up the ladder, the Great Chain of Being, the Great Ziggurat. There's a kind of anti-elitism, anti-hubris quality built right into Nature's structure. Imagine how the world would change if humanity gave that fact its due regard.

Each *whole* is built to maintain its own discrete wholeness, which includes individual *parts*, each of which maintains its own discrete wholeness. Furthermore, the universe isn't just a container of parts but is those parts themselves coming into existence and being. If the parts began to cease to exist and no new parts were created to replace their space in time, the universe would shrink accordingly.

Quarks, atoms, molecules—then suddenly a gigantic, inexplicable quantum leap to radically unique, self-replicating life: early cells, or prokaryotes (there are more molecules than prokaryotes); then advanced cells, or eukaryotes (there are more prokaryotes than eukaryotes); then simple organisms known as the neural net (there are more eukaryotes than simple organisms); simple organisms known as the neural cord; and so on up the ziggurat—reptiles, paleomammals, and—another gigantic quantum leap—conscious, self-conscious organisms: us humans with our complex brain capable of abstract logic, linguistics, and vision-logic. But even that amazing physical brain doesn't explain our transcending propensity for art, morality, spirituality, self-consciousness, or a multitude of other uniquely human preoccupations. We truly have been endowed with a big dose of something "other." That other is what we often call the *human spirit*.

Wholes within wholes within wholes structurally "ziggurats" into a hierarchy of whole-parts. The "biggest" whole contains the most whole-parts; it's the "fullest." A single human contains a lot of cells; each of those cells contains an even greater number of molecules; each molecule contains even more atoms. Each successive whole up the Great Ziggurat is more complex, and that complexity means not only that it's more individuated—meaning that in a sense it's "smallest"—but also that it's more *dependent*.

Atoms contain quarks, but quarks do not contain atoms; atoms are not quarks, quarks are radically different from atoms. Something *created* atoms and quarks; one did not create the other. It's impossible to create a new step—something that does not yet exist at all in any form, something that is categorically greater and smarter and other than oneself. It's equally impossible for the greater to create the lesser, because the greater is already composed of the lesser. All the whole parts must have been created by something with a transcending mind, a someone, the intelligent designer of all Nature, the Creator God. Such a God not only makes the stuff that exists; that God integrates all that stuff. And because all that stuff is constantly coming into being, changing, and ceasing to exist, that God orchestrates all that stuff. And because all that perpetual change occurs within unchanging forms that dance together in perfect concert, that God is actively engaged in meaningful aesthetic creation. And that God engages meaningfully with *us*, hence our ability to have this conversation.

God is not part of Nature's hierarchy, because God is not a whole or a part of or anything like space-time matter; God transcends us and the universe; therefore, God cannot *be* the universe, contrary to the view of pantheists and Christian polytheists. But as the active Creator of the universe, the transcendent God is also necessarily immanent in Creation (the way the author is "immanent" in her book but is not the book).

Molecules contain atoms and quarks, but atoms and quarks do not contain molecules; and so on up the ever-increasingly complex, inclusive ziggurat. Human beings are members of the animal kingdom, the phylum of chordates, the subphylum of vertebrates, the order of mammals, the class of primates, the family of hominids, the genus of *Homo*, and the species *sapiens*. Remember that a system of classification is not a demonstration of evolution. It is, however, a revelation of organized, logical, perpetually creative intelligent design.

Remarkably, each level—each layer, each step—embodies a synthesis of the lower parts that is greater than the sum of all its synthesized parts. That synthesis, that addition, that integration, that something extra, is Creation.

Though we can imagine that social structures ziggurat upward—from family groups, to hunter-gatherer tribes, to self-sufficient domestic villages, to assimilating empires, to inter-dependent, codependent industrial states, to Everyman's communication network, the global commonwealth—these are changes within a discrete species (ours); they don't change the species type into a different order. Darwinian macroevolution of one order into another doesn't happen. Microevolution, on the other hand, does occur naturally within a discrete species. Our extraordinarily complex species is its own microevolution explosion that dwarfs the Cambrian; and our explosion blasts via innovations initiated via our own free will. Amazing! We humans are astonishingly odd, and perpetually so. Humanity is its own microcosmic Big Bang.

A fetus develops into a newborn which develops into a child which develops into an adult. At our fortieth class reunion we say we've evolved. We casually call developmental growth evolution, but it's not the same as the Darwinian premise that one species type becomes another. Even the class clown won't evolve into a chimp.

As the human body develops, other aspects like the mind and aesthetic microevolve from birth through childhood and on through adulthood, mirroring development of worldviews, from the primitive on up to the mystical. Self-realization comes through self-transcendence, which includes the lower as part of its "tradition," but which goes beyond, thereby giving that tradition new meaning. *Homo sapiens* literally means "man the wise." As always, though, a human can devolve, as witnessed by Darwin's aesthetic atrophy (to use his word), or civilizations reverting to barbarianism. Every devolution of one or more of our faculties is regression into stupidity and therefore into not-truth. But difference does not equal devolution. As we age we ripen; even cessation and death, far from stupid, are part of the maturation process of spirit moving beyond restrictions of space and time. Perhaps at the moment of death, we'll look back on this life as the placenta of our newborn Self.

Though body development is an example of smooth transition, a quantum leap of creative emergence can occur, as when, say, you have a sudden *aha* moment, a radical paradigm shift in perspective or feeling. Those shifts are like steps in that they involve an addition of something completely new. In a way, something like macroevolution takes place, but only within the parameter of microevolution, within the means of potential already programmed in your spiritual DNA, so to speak. You learn something that utterly changes you in some fundamental way, but you never cease being human. Your spirit is always a human spirit.

The simple solution to the conundrum of our origin, of course, is that the consistently surprisingly intricate universe, including life, was created by a transcending God. This God created space and time and space-time from a "place" and "time" beyond space-time. Being space-time bound, it's hard for us to wrap our brains around the concept of an "existence" that isn't anything like the universe where we live and think. But such a transcending God-Reality is the only smart conclusion we can reach.

So why is acknowledging a Creator so difficult?

Science is in the business of amassing facts. Facts are true, but facts are not truth. Facts are embodiments of truth, are representations of truth. But the older science becomes, the more aggressively it elbows its way into the sanctum of sage and saint, with the loudest prophets of science proclaiming the good news of atheism.

We boomers, a large segment of the population and the segment currently controlling the Darwinian meme, tripped into adulthood on the heels of Carl Sagan, whose famous *Cosmos* series each week reminded us, "The Cosmos is all that there is, or ever was, or ever will be." He punctuated his mantra with colorful examples of "all that there is," like the 1953 Miller-Urey experiment, contrived by a couple grad students, that showed life created in a test tube—showed off, really, the gleeful castration of the already impotent omnipotent God. No one informed us that the experiment was fraught with fallacies (today it's kaput). As I look back, I realize that a great many *Cosmos* facts were fraught with fallacies. But in those formative years, we trusted the great Carl Sagan, a regular guest on Johnny Carson and a name we read in the papers, to illuminate our savage brains with a radiance billions and billions of light years in the making. It's funny how time often somersaults. For instance, only recently did I learn that way back in 1997, Harvard geneticist Richard C. Lewontin admitted that during a debate, he and Sagan argued for Darwinism not because it was scientifically grounded. Rather, they would "take the side of science in spite of the patent absurdity of some of its constructs." Their goal was not to defend truth, or even to present the facts. Today I don't find their motive surprising: "We have a prior commitment," Lewontin declared, "a commitment to materialism," which "is absolute, for we cannot allow a

Divine Foot in the door."

That mini materialist manifesto appeared in the *New York Review of Books*, January 9, 1997, in his article, "Billions and Billions of Demons," which reviewed Sagan's book, *The Demon-Haunted World: Science as a Candle in the Dark*. Ponder the import of Lewontin's full disclosure:

> Our willingness to accept scientific claims that are against common sense is the key to an understanding of the real struggle between science and the supernatural. We take the side of science *in spite* of the patent absurdity of some of its constructs, *in spite* of its failure to fulfill many of its extravagant promises of health and life, *in spite* of the tolerance of the scientific community for unsubstantiated just-so stories, because we have a prior commitment, a commitment to materialism. It is not that the methods and institutions of science somehow compel us to accept a material explanation of the phenomenal world, but, on the contrary, that we are forced by our *a priori* adherence to material causes to create an apparatus of investigation and a set of concepts that produce material explanations, no matter how counter-intuitive, no matter how mystifying to the uninitiated. Moreover, that materialism is absolute, for we cannot allow a Divine Foot in the door.

Indeed, accepting a Divine Foot or even a Toe in the door requires a hit of caffeinated humility. The next sentence in his review reads: "The eminent Kant scholar Lewis Beck used to say that anyone who could believe in God could believe in anything. To appeal to an omnipotent deity is to allow that at any moment the regularities of nature may be ruptured, that miracles may happen." I believe in God, and I don't believe in "*anything*"—for instance, the preposterous Darwinian claims of common ancestry and macroevolution via random chance mutations guided by natural selection; and I don't believe in natural-law-violating miracles.

The ninety percent of us ordinary believers in a Whole Divinity wonder why on earth anyone, even a Harvard professor, A) would think picking the right answer violates the scientific method, and B) would assume that dishonest materialist bias trumps an honest, commonsense deduction that all the subtleties of this mindblowingly massively elegantly intricate universe, or even one of its complex components, like, say, a cell, necessitates an intelligent, transcending Designer. Isn't God the *materialist's* green Martian, the *Darwinian's* Satan?

It's not debatable: It's just plain common sense that the practically infinite ingredients of this deliciously exquisite space-time banquet called life are beyond a scientist's brainpower. Well beyond.

Amazingly, what's *not* beyond our ken is the blatancy of design. Why not just say Thanks. Too many scientists sit at the table picking apart the baklava like they were pulling an engine. Carping is not your job, sirs. Your job is to eat well and appreciate. Table manners required.

Why, I ask myself, are atheist scientists so aggressively unwilling to accept the most logical, the most obvious, solution to the "problem" of Creation? Why the stubborn ingratitude?

Perhaps they simply hate the Father at the head of the table.

Cultural patricide has long been considered one of the prime drivers of history. Each generation's sons must "kill" their fathers, or at least everything their fathers have created and stood for. Sons must "evolve" beyond. They must seize their fathers' property, intellectual and physical, and must convert that into a new form. War is assumed. Freud made it fashionable to seize even your own mother, or Mother Earth, it's all yours; if "girls" balk at the rape, cultural or physical, they're suffering from a common delusion called hysteria; the girls really want it.

Perhaps the tamer atheist scientists simply hate their own biological fathers. Given the track record of fathers in our society and throughout history, the chances of a scientist having had an abusive or absent father are pretty high. It makes sense that a scientist might project his loathing for Dad onto God the Father, especially if Dad made Son feel like the spawn of Satan. And isn't that what the Father-God of traditional sin-mongering makes him feel like? Father = Father: A valid equation.

But it's not the truth. Religious representations of God do not equal or even necessarily accurately represent God.

Some atheist scientists might have great dads. They might be rebelling against the representation of the warrior Father-God portrayed by the Judeo-Christian-Islamic-etc. tradition. It makes sense that they would want to kill the often unjust, violent, vicious, arrogant, jealous, selfish, fickle, slimy God of warrior tribes that created the serpent-spit Eden of the Bible. Even the softer side of God only insinuates himself in rare moments when the warriors are at peace or drunk. Even Jesus, they argue, exacerbates God's violence with each eschatological ultimatum.

But they're rebelling against a *myth* of God, not against a possible real God. The God of the Big Bang is not the God of Genesis, not even the God of the New Testament. At least not exactly. But some scientists hate the exact equating of the God of the Big Bang with the Genesist (Old Testament) anthropomorphic (New Testament) God. God and the biblical God are simply not the same entity. One is the reality, the other, taken literally, is a juvenile representation that should have grown up a few thousand years ago.

A critique of the biblical God is valid. But the spiritual patricide committed by contemporary atheists is misguided and harmful to the atheists, to culture, and to science. They've thrown out the baby with the bathwater. Have you ever noticed that atheists cry "Reality!" loudest when they're jousting with windmills?

THE PANTHEIST GOD

Because atheists doubt or deny the existence of a creator *other than nature itself* (sometimes referred to as *herself*, who *guides* natural selection), atheism is essentially closet pantheism rather than a flat denial of *any* creative force. Many scientists refer to the most primal component of existence—whatever that might be at the moment—as the mind of God, or to the universe as a whole as the body of God. Some assert that space-time existence itself is God evolving, learning, coming to be. We are nothing but sparks of the bonfire or droplets in the ocean of consciousness, and ultimately we return to the source—which mixes the metaphor, but as science these days becomes more and more science fiction, its articulation becomes more and more loosely metaphoric and less and less lucid.

The simple, literal, commonsense truth that most people know and have always known is that the source is God, that God is Creator, and that God is wholly other. God is not the universe, the process of the universe coming into being, or the most basic particle of the universe. We are not sparks in a universal bonfire or droplets in the ocean of divine consciousness. A learning, evolving God only restates all the problems. Because energy, like matter, is a component of space-time, not something that actually transcends it, science's cutting-edge theology—energy equals consciousness equals spirit—is really retro spiritualized materialism à la the pre-Socratic Greeks; it's materialism-lite.

But surely even the staunchest materialist realizes that the information that drives the universe—the enormously sophisticated software driving DNA, for instance—must come from somewhere. Even they admit that information is neither matter nor energy and that info software must be coded somehow. Only stubbornness blocks them from grasping that neither energy nor consciousness nor information is God. The "I-am-ness" of a "Big Self" like, say, Ken Wilbur, who claims that when he looks at a river, he *is* the river, when hiking a mountain he *is* the mountain, and concludes that "I am God," is the spiritual schizophrenia of hubris on steroids. Contrast that with a poet's metaphoric "I am a river" which is not to be taken literally.

These days, physics exists solely to perpetuate the Big Myth that there is no God. What else explains the ridiculous irrationality of its memes, not only the Me Meme of self-absorbed godlets, but also the meme of pure speculation parading as hard science. Many scientists still insist that science is by definition a process of establishing facts via observation and experimentation. But the grand conclusion of quantum mechanics, Heisenberg's uncertainty principle, says that at the quantum level, nothing can actually be "observed" in the normal sense of the word. The scientist doesn't see an object such as a quark; he only sees an energetic reaction to a procedure, the experiment, and he can never be sure that even this is an accurate description of anything substantial relating to the object itself. Furthermore, not only can a quantum object not be observed, intercepted, monitored, passed along, copied, or cloned—all consequences of scientific observation and experimentation—the very act of "observation," of setting up the experiment and measuring any action or reaction, disrupts the message, or flow of information from object to observer. Some interpret this to mean that the observer determines the outcome of the observation by becoming part of it—you don't just "look at" an object, you create it to some extent by becoming part of its wave-flow.

Scientists have gone so far as to assert that there are infinite Big Bangs firing up eternally; that there are many, perhaps even an infinite number of parallel multiverses where you are alive and where you are dead at the same time, where you are eating a ham sandwich and where you are not eating the ham sandwich; that due to Heisenberg's uncertainty principle, the observer actually creates the past, meaning all that happens in the present is in the future creating the past. And on and on it goes. All these theories are pure speculation conjured up to "explain" how existence came to be without resorting to a supernatural cause. It's like leaving by the back door and traveling around the world and then to Mars and parachute landing on reentry to get to your job down the block without running into your girlfriend who lives across the street who is really only a fantasy girlfriend who resembles the girl across the street.

Many scientists complain that much of New Age quantum physics, which can't be seen, which can't be tested, is a random ramble of equations that add up to nothing, not even good science fiction.

It's not that atheist scientists don't appreciate the amazing interactive complexity of the universe. Cosmologist Paul Davies even provides us with a theory of a designer universe that he says appears to be following a script, a pattern, a plan—which he equates with the laws of physics, mechanics, information processing. He doesn't speak for many of his fellow atheists, though, when he admits that the anthropic principle is valid: the universe seems carefully constructed according to a grand cosmic plan to culminate with the emergence of life on Earth. Like a biblical psalmist, he sings praises for a universe filled with meaning and purpose. The world is beautiful, and its construction, deeply ingenious. Even the parameters of the laws of physics are just right for life, and those laws complement each other perfectly due to their exact "coincidences," or "special factors." Clearly, he argues, there's a grand design to our bio-friendly universe.

His songs sound a bit tinny, though, to those of us schooled in music. Like his peers, Davies is adamant that the universe is not at all like an organism but is really basically a huge computer. It's an amazing machine, but it's not alive or even natural in the usual sense of those terms. A living universe would point to a living God, and Davies intends to steer clear of any, as he puts it, "cosmic magician," that dreaded Foot in the Door.

But Davies has an alternative, an idol to take the place of God. Unlike physicist Steven Weinberg, who laments, "The more the universe seems comprehensible, the more it also seems pointless," Davies wants to imbue the universe with meaning and purpose by brazenly creating God in his own image in a funhouse mirror.

According to Davies's creation myth, we human beings, through the sheer act of observation, helped shape the laws of physics that blasted into existence 13.7 billion years ago. You see, because the universe is a gigantic computer, we, like Neo in *The Matrix*, live in a fake, simulated virtual world of our own making. Of course this doesn't solve the problem of where we, the makers, or the materials and laws of virtual nature come from.

In Davies' world, a human-generated simulated universe resolves hard scientific/theological questions, like how did the laws of physics come to be? Why those laws rather than some others? Why were those exact laws embodied by the universe at its conception? Why those perfectly complementary laws rather than some others? Why does everything in the universe have a common set of physical laws? Why are the laws and conditions of the universe consistent with life?

"Because a transcending Creator made them" doesn't satisfy Davies. If atheists don't hate God outright, they certainly hate the God solution, as scientifically satisfying as it actually is. Raw materialism doesn't work for a species that intuitively senses a demand for a God; their best solution is to posit human consciousness as God.

In Davies' mind (which is God), this version of God corroborates the multiverse hypothesis, which, as he interprets it, means that our universe is just a bubble in a vaster, more elaborate system, the multiverse, which consists of many, possibly infinite, universes. Perhaps, he speculates (a bit out of character for a creator God), each universe is a huge bubble among other huge bubbles scattered throughout space (presumably a bigger space than any one universe), and each bubble comes with its own set of laws. I seem to recall some friends coming up with a similar theory years ago at a wedding reception overflowing with champagne.

Although Davies assumes that his bubbly solves the problem of a transcending God, it only widens the field of creation with all the same conditions and questions that can only be resolved by a transcending God.

Davies's solution is called the "strong anthropic principle," which places the observer—you and me—in the central creating position: We observers, who must inevitably arise due to the happy coincidence of fine tuning (the perfectly calibrated conditions required for existence as it is), are dictating how the universe is put together. In other words, the emergence of life and observers causes the "participatory universe," as physicist John Wheeler called it, to have the laws that it does. The future present creates the past. This "final anthropic principle" links all moments together into one "moment." Of course, one wonders how observers that don't yet exist create a universe that only at its very final stage of coming-into-existence creates observers.

Scientists like Davies are obsessed with establishing the cause of Creation as something within Creation itself. The Deist would ask how life today could cause or in any way affect the Big Bang. Davies and crew argue that because of the hypothesized underlying time symmetry in the laws of physics, the laws work forward and backward. Of course, it would be impossible to observe or test this hypothesis. They base their theory on their interpretation of Heisenberg's uncertainty principle, which in its original form simply means that there's uncertainty about how an atom is going to behave, or has behaved in the past, so you can't predict its in-the-moment behavior with certainty. Furthermore, you can't predict the past, present, or future behavior of anything you can't directly observe. Determinists have a problem with Heisenberg's principle.

Uncertainty really means that there is some flexibility, some freedom, some room for chance, within some immutable natural structures. Think of the laws of nature as the structural walls, floor, and ceiling of a house. Those "bones" of the universe as a whole, as well as the bones of smaller structures within the larger structure of the universe, don't change. But within the structure itself, as within the house itself, there is a lot of wiggle room for change. In fact, let's call the rooms in the house wiggle rooms. You move in, you arrange your furniture, you rearrange your furniture to accommodate decisions about how you will arrange your stuff. A few years in, someone moves in with you. More stuff. Rearrangement takes place again. A few more years in and you start having kids. You paint rooms, lay new carpet in some rooms, rip carpet and lay hardwood in other rooms. You sing, fight, make love, read textbooks, watch TV, change your philosophy, entertain friends, decorate for the holidays, teach your kids more things than you can remember, reminisce, pray, grow old, sit grieving as your spouse dies. These examples of wiggle room—wiggle rooms—within the structural house barely scratch the surface.

Within the immutable structures of existence there is room for change and freedom. You can predict events that conform to those structures. But you can't predict how your dog is going to behave in the next second or how you will behave every split second of your life, or even *any* split second with perfect accuracy. Even atheist scientists know that this wiggle room exists even in atoms and molecules. Just at that fundamental level alone, uncertainty disproves determinism.

Common sense alone shows us at least four determinate levels for what things are and how they happen. Level one is immutable structures, like the laws of gravity or 2+3=5. Materialists pile everything onto that level. The second level is wiggle room admitting chance; it's the realm of heads or tails. If the atom must move, all options being equal, it "just" moves. This is the level where neo-Darwinians live their flat, boring lives. The third level is a wiggle room where simple, two-dimensional choice can occur. A leaf scratches the window; your cat wakes, stares at the window, then either rouses enough to explore or yawns and falls back asleep: her choice.

The fourth level is a wiggle room reserved for humans. This room is the same "size" as the cat's room, but the human's wiggle room is where complex, multi-dimensional choice can—not necessarily must, but can—occur. Humans can hang out in the other three rooms. But when someone—you, for instance—retreat to the human wiggle room, you can make sophisticated choices that are the result of what we all know as free will. We think, we deliberate, we weigh the possibilities, their implications in the moment, consequences in the future, even causes in the past. We engage many or all of our many inherent faculties, not just reason, but conscience, intuition, emotion, experience, aesthetic sensibility, the judgments and desires of our physical and spiritual aspects, and of course, our powerful, self-defining will. Only in the human room does an organism experience true freedom.

Natural selection has failed to explain the perpetual waterfall of organic change. The neo-Darwinian solution, random chance, can't ever describe how anything random could contribute to the delicate, perfectly calibrated fine tuning of the universe. Random chance contradicts fine tuning, unless the fine tuning is tuned specifically to accommodate the wiggle room.

Davies trumps crap-shoot random chance with a different theory, and it's not Einstein's God who "doesn't play dice with the universe." No, in Davies' world (or worlds), atoms' past lives, aka "past histories," have led up to the present state of the universe. According to quantum mechanics—but contrary to science in general—because you can't put the universe in a lab to experiment on later like you can an atom, you can only infer backward in time; therefore, "you can make observations now that will affect the nature of reality as it was in the past" because "the nature of the quantum state in the past can't be separated from the nature of the quantum state in the present" because intelligent human beings are aware of the universe through the act of observation. This Matrix fantasy, Davies claims, is "just standard quantum physics."

Because there's an uncertainty about what an atom is going to do in the future or what it has done in the past, Davies concludes that "that uncertainty means there's a type of linkage," called "quantum nonlocality," by which two linked particles—think of them as codependently married— have separated and stand at opposite ends of the universe. Perform an experiment on one and the other instantaneously knows what the result is. "These experiments have been done many times," Davies explains. What he (dishonestly) doesn't mention is that there is no way to "see" particles even on a lab coat, much less at the other end of the universe.

Undaunted by this problem, Davies asserts that as we work our way back into the past, there are multitudes of "quantum histories that could have led up to this point. And the existence of observers today will select a subset of those histories which will inevitably, by definition, lead to the existence of life." He adds, "Now, I don't think anybody would really dispute that fact." In fact, almost everyone with a degree in science disputes it.

Because Davies can't stand the notion of a transcending God, he asserts that the immutable laws of physics—the Platonic-Newtonian universe governed by infinitely precise mathematical laws—themselves are subject to quantum uncertainty, "so that an observation performed today will select not only a number of histories from an infinite number of possible past histories, but will also select a subset of the laws of physics which are consistent with the emergence of life."

Davies has it all figured out: Mathematical and physical rules embodied by the active laws of nature are just information. The universe is a giant information processor, a finite-temporal computer—Wheeler's "it from bit"—of finite-temporal accuracy, hence the possibility of error—even in the laws of nature—that leads to evolution, both material and organic. The laws of physics that randomly come into existence from a primordial state of "vague and fuzzy" not-yet-laws become more and more law-like as time goes on, he says. The laws of physics as we know them—the bones of the house—are just adolescent laws that will continue to evolve into something different.

On the other hand, Davies asserts, the big computer simulation, the universe that we create, is only possible because we can program— essentially clone—our consciousness, or at least a simulation thereof, because after all, consciousness is only another physical process. Probably the universe is already the simulation, he notes. And if we're in the simulation, how would we know? (Author's clue: Plato's Cave.) This universe is a carnival funhouse of mirrors reflecting simulations of simulations of simulations...It can't be infinite and eternal, though, because there was that darn Big Bang.

Davies's circular argument is that the universe we create creates us who create the universe. He does admit that there are fundamental limitations to our becoming the God of simulation due to the way our brains have been put together. "Ultimately," he says, "it may not be living intelligence or embodied intelligence but some sort of intelligent information-processing system that could be omniscient and fill the entire universe." He adds, "That's a grand vision that I rather like."

A self-created simulated God is for Davies the only "logical" conclusion to an assertion made in his book, *God and the New Physics*: "It is hard to resist the impression that the present structure of the universe, apparently so sensitive to minor alterations in the numbers, has been rather carefully thought out...The seeming miraculous concurrence of numerical values that nature has organized to her fundamental constants must remain the most compelling evidence for an element of cosmic design." In *Superforce*, Davies adds that "The big bang was not, evidently, any old bang, but an explosion of exquisitely arranged magnitude."

To X the magician God from his universe and from science, over the next few decades following the publication of those books, Davies constructed a lobotomized cosmic mechanical magician that has "thought out" the structure of the universe. To protect the scientific method of reason, deduction, and empirical study, he explodes it into a crazy kaleidoscope of science superstition. A new religious myth is born. Ironically, the magician God never left the scene, because even Davies' explosion of the Big Bang explosion still needs a Fuse.

Science never has, never will, indeed *can't* prove that there is no God. But *everything* proves that there is.

One fundamental difference between "new science" and religion is that religion can imagine—not visually, but in an abstract, rational way—a Reality without space or time beyond space-time. Science tries. But religion knows better that human knowledge and understanding are extremely limited, and are most definitely finite and temporal. Standing amid the immensity of existence, registering the blatant lucidity of Nature, the spiritual person, humbled with awe, recognizes intellectually and/or spiritually the active Presence of its Creator. Religion has its myths and superstitions, and they must be re-viewed as representations rather than as literal facts. Both science and religion need to be critiqued. Truth must never be shunned. But religion trumps science with its ability to grasp transcendence as the necessary prerequisite of a rational universe.

It's odd that scientists of time and space are unable to imagine anything existing outside of time and space. They seem tangled in semantics. Yes, time and space came into existence at the moment of the Big Bang. But the Big Bang was a point in space and time even at the moment of space-time's conception. It's hard for atheist scientists to imagine something that's not space or time, something not bound by space-time. It's hard for their brains to imagine the possibility of Mind beyond anything we can know or experience. Space-time words representing space-time categories can't fully convey a reality that is not bound by space or time. Scientists like Davies don't get that "eternity" and "infinity" are not space-time concepts, they're only space-time representations of something transcending the categories of space and time.

Mind transcends brain; consciousness transcends the limitations of determinism. The spiritually inclined understand that there are realities that can be spiritually intuited that don't require convoluted convulsions like simulated multiverses that we created before we were born. In all good conscience, should we be letting that kind of mythmaking pass for hard science?

Most people agree that scientific concepts correspond to something that can be observed in the real world. We see gravity in the effects of gravity at work. We can attach things to concepts like 2+3=5. We observe very small and very large objects through microscopes and telescopes. We create devices that detect radiation, which is something we can't see that can kill us. We know love because we experience it. We know about post traumatic stress syndrome through case studies of people suffering it, if not through our own experience.

I know that God exists because the intelligent universe requires a transcending Creator. How is that more metaphysical, or less logical, than believing that a scientific experiment creates reality?

When Einstein noticed that light could exist in the form of particles as well as waves, he wasn't saying that a scientist setting up an experiment to measure light could somehow magically determine the light's "response" to shape-shift into either particles or a wave. Whether you see particles or waves depends on how you look at the beam of light; your perception is determined by your position relative to the light beam. A train a mile off looks like a speck, but barreling past me a few feet away it looks massive. A solid red brick wall consisting of a bunch of not-red subatomic particles bouncing off one another (red being wavelengths not absorbed by the wall but reflected off it out to, among other places, human retinas) is still a solid red brick wall to the kid on a bike crashing into it. But scientists want to tell the kid that he (or they?) determines the wall's being either particles or waves. Oh wait—this kind of appearance only happens during one of their scientific measuring experiments. Either way, it's another way of saying that their abstract theory transcends the kid's and even their own actual experience. Their theory is absolute; abstraction is their God. Being a meta-measurer, I've sized up the wave-particle measurers: they're scientific fundamentalists. We can all play this game.

What happens when the abstraction exists on its own, not just disconnected but in fact not at all connected to any concrete or even abstract *reality*?

Take for instance M theory (M code for membrane, aka "brane") and string theory. Branes and strings can't be observed in any way, not even in terms of observing reactions, though theorists ask you to picture strings as rubber bands. String theory (which encompasses brane theory) consists of *nothing* but equations (for some of us, that's "Plato's hell"). Even most scientists consider strings and branes to be fictions that only exist in the brains of their authors. Cleverly, one of those authors has transmuted fiction into "poetry" to win your respect.

Because string theory is unobservable and irrational—but then it only exists to confirm that God does not exist—it must be "proven" with mathematical glossolalia (speaking in tongues). Consider, for instance, this excerpt from physicist Machio Kaku's explanation of string theory circulated recently on Youtube:

> Subatomic particles we see in nature—the quarks, the electrons—are nothing but musical notes on a tiny vibrating string. What is physics? Physics is nothing but the laws of harmony that you can write on vibrating strings. What is chemistry? Chemistry is nothing but the melodies you can play on interacting vibrating strings. What is the universe? The universe is a symphony of vibrating strings. And then, What is the mind of God that Albert Einstein eloquently wrote about for the last thirty years of his life? We now for the first time in history have a candidate for the mind of God. It is cosmic music resonating through eleven dimensional hyperspace. So first of all we are nothing but melodies, we are nothing but cosmic music played out on vibrating strings and membranes. Obeying the laws of physics which is nothing but the laws of harmony of vibrating strings. Buy why eleven? It turns out that if you write a theory in fifteen, seventeen, eighteen dimensions, the theory is unstable. It has what are called anomalies, it has singularities. It turns out that mathematics alone prefers the universe be in eleven dimensions. Now some people have toyed with twelve dimensions....

Really, twelve? *Impossible!*

Here we have an example of a writing professor's worst nightmare: an essay that wants to be a poem and is neither. Kaku calls this mythological imagery "science."

First, he asserts that we "see" particles in nature; he says we "see" subatomic particles, specifically quarks and electrons, which we definitely can't *see*, or even "see."

Next, he sets up his first equation. I can't help but wonder if Kaku, a physicist and a mathematician, is a product of the "new math." He says that these subatomic particles equal nothing but musical notes on a tiny vibrating string. Particles = musical notes; particles = *nothing but* musical notes. If particles are nothing but musical notes, why isn't MIT just teaching its physicists music?

Please note (no pun) that Kaku isn't saying that these particles are *like* musical notes. He says that they *are* musical notes. He doesn't appear to mean this metaphorically. These notes are on a string. They aren't produced *by* a string, which he can't possible see (in any sense of the word). They are located *on* a string, a tiny vibrating string.

Really? Prove it.

Now he takes us beyond the subatomic realm of psychics.

Whoops, did I say psychics? I meant physics.

No wait, I did mean psychics. Because guess what? (And I do mean "guess.") String theory is based on a science fiction magical realism that can't be observed or subjected to experimentation *at all.*

Now we've entered the realm of subatomic chemistry. How this chemistry differs from regular chemistry or from subatomic physics he doesn't explain. But that doesn't matter. According to Kaku, all chemistry is nothing but the melodies you play on interacting vibrating strings.

I wasn't aware that I was playing any strings. I do play several string instruments of the not quantum brand in the real world, though I'm not playing them now. Do I have a parallel life in another musical universe, perhaps? I didn't know that chemicals weren't the substances we put in test tubes in high school. They're actually melodies. Literal melodies. If only I'd known that when I sweated through Chem 101. And to think that I got detention for humming!

Melodies, eh? Hmm. I'd better get my ears checked, because I'm not hearing the symphony of vibrating strings I'm supposedly plucking into a universe, this universe. Am I a God anyway? A fraction of God?

Am I the mind of God that Albert Einstein eloquently wrote about for the last thirty years of his life, the mind of the God that doesn't play dice with the universe, the transcending God that has established perpetually perfect order that can be observed and enjoyed? Is this the Albert Einstein that said, "My religion consists of a humble admiration of the illimitable superior spirit who reveals himself in the slight details we are able to perceive with our frail and feeble mind," the Einstein who said, "That deep emotional conviction of the presence of a superior reasoning power, which is revealed in the incomprehensible universe, forms my idea of God," and "Science without religion is lame, religion without science is blind"?

No, it seems, Einstein was wrong. He missed his entrance onto the stage where the symphony plays to a different violinist. The greatest scientist of our era missed a beat when he assumed, "One may say the eternal mystery of the world is its comprehensibility," then arrogantly shrugged at the conductor, "When the solution is simple, God is answering." It takes a real, post-Einstein genius like Kaku to discover for the first time in history that the mind of God is cosmic music resonating through eleven dimensional hyperspace.

How does he know this? He doesn't, not in any normal, real-world sense of knowing. He knows this in another dimension of a parallel universe in a past that does not yet exist.

Still, he knows that we are nothing—nothing but cosmic music played out (by us, he just said) on vibrating strings and membranes. Wait, where did the membranes come from? If the membranes are maybe the timpani, are they sitting out the symphony composed only of strings? I'm confused.

Now the strings and membranes are obeying the laws of physics— where did the laws of physics come from? Is that the composer? Who is the composer? Am I the composer? part of the composer? one of those pre-Socratic flames or drops of water in the fire/ocean of consciousness? I thought the laws of physics consisted of things like, if you dropped a big ball from a roof, gravity would pull it down and knock your gym teacher unconscious. Now I'm being told that the laws of physics are nothing but laws of harmony that I can't hear from vibrating strings that I can't see. Does harmony encompass the response of the gym teacher regaining consciousness? What is consciousness anyway? How do we know there's not a bigger consciousness out there stringing us along?

And what about that eleven dimensional hyperspace? Is that singular or plural? Hyperspace doesn't sound good. In my universe, hyper anything isn't a condition of harmony. Well, at least it's mathematics alone that prefers the universe be in eleven dimensions. What/who is this math? Is math God? That's a scary thought for a math-challenged person like me. Why would math prefer eleven? Why doesn't math like the other numbers, presumably his/her/its brainchildren (branechildren?).

We haven't even gotten to the real math, and I'm already lost. I thought there were four dimensions, three dimensions of space and a fourth dimension of time. Are these other dimensions space or time? spaces-time? spaces-times?

No, it's eleven dimensions. It turns out (via what wild weekend of chalks and blackboards I can't even imagine), if you write a theory in fifteen, seventeen, eighteen dimensions, the theory is unstable. In my opinion—and granted, I'm not a mathematician—eleven might also be unstable.

Forgive me, oh Lord Math, but why should I venerate a bunch of equations on acid? Even Plato would balk. It's hard to resist dubbing the M-string theory of God's space-time mind the Kaku Cuckoo. Oh for the simpler days of Paley's watch.

What kind of scientist would really expect smart people like me and you to believe that M-string theory doesn't have anomalous singularities appearing as traces of profound narcissism? If I'm nothing but a melody, he's nothing but a wannabe rock star in his fantasy rubber band. He's bandstanding: grandstanding.

No, I just don't buy that God lives in Kaku's back pocket. I'm siding with Einstein. Suffice it to say regarding "the mind of God that Albert Einstein eloquently wrote about for the last thirty years of his life" that Kaku's musical strings were neither plucked from Einstein's practiced violin nor from the mind of the God who "doesn't play dice with the universe." I agree with Einstein that "The man of science is a poor philosopher," and "There are two ways to live: You can live as if nothing is a miracle; you can live as if everything is a miracle."

Einstein once quipped, "Only two things are infinite, the universe and human stupidity, and I'm not sure about the former." The latter perhaps deserves a qualifying antithesis: "Intellectuals solve problems, geniuses prevent them."

I'm confused: the genius pop-mathematician Machio Kaku has certainly caused a big problem for me simply by violating the four Cartesian rules of mathematical procedure: accept nothing as true that is not self-evident; divide problems into their simplest parts; solve problems by proceeding from simple to complex; recheck the reasoning. Nor does Kaku clearly define all the key notions and limits of the problem he is supposedly solving. Clearly science has moved beyond this obsolete Cartesian requirement. Ironically, Descartes' first surviving work is *Compendium of Music*, written in his early twenties. I doubt that he would approve of the math riffs of Kaku.

Like other science fiction scientists, Kaku also disregards geologist Charles Lyell's principle of uniformity first adopted back in Darwin's day. Well, officially adopted by scientists; the rest of us had always already known this. Lyell's principle remains unchallenged even by science contrarians because it's just plain everyday common sense. Lyell's definition is as elegantly simple as the concept: "By the principle of uniformity is meant that the kinds of causes we observe producing certain effects today can be counted on to have produced similar effects in the past." If we drop a rock today, we assume it will fall to the ground because dropped rocks have always fallen to the ground. A volcanic eruption rather than an earthquake best explains a layer of ash in the rock strata. Based on our common experience that intelligent agents generate what has been clearly designed—the faces of Mount Rushmore, say, as opposed to a pile of rocks, or even the constant law of gravity—we can deduce that the clearly designed universe has been—well, clearly designed by an intelligent agent. God is the best—really the only—candidate for that agent.

It's ironic, isn't it, that Darwinian biologists rattling their cages have necessitated the reanimation of life. And now their quantum cronies, brazenly violating the scientific method, concoct irrational, not-provable myths simply to delete God from the scientific method. It's fashionable these days to hop on Dawkins' kill-religion bandwagon. The new science is a new religion that just like the old religion it criticizes disregards that old Keatsian axiom that "axioms in philosophy are not axioms until they are proved upon our pulses." Pulses not scored by Kaku.

Atheism and pantheism illustrate just how far people will go to avoid the most logical solution to the problems of design and consciousness—a transcending Creator. How are their solutions less mythological than other creation myths or less superstitious than any of the other religious superstitions that have gotten them in such an intellectual tizzy? None of their solutions eliminate the same old need for First Cause. The only truly logical solution is a transcending God. The sooner they accept that, the sooner they can get back to practical applications like Green cars, advanced communications technology, and cures for cancer. Clearly they're not up to the task of addressing ultimate concerns of meaning, purpose, value, or beauty. In fact, they waste precious time and grant money that should be spent solving real problems, like exploitation, poverty, violence, war, or just the basic rape and murder of Mother Earth. Kill the Father, kill the Mother. Freud must be rolling over in his grave.

How does the atheist differ from the pantheist? An atheist scientist is someone who describes the absolutely stupendously brilliant designs of existence and its clearly orchestrated preordained drive toward increasingly sophisticated complexity as emerging from a process absolutely devoid of intelligence or purpose, then smiles as you gauge him a genius in comparison to the brain-dead universe.

The pantheist shakes his head: *he's* not just a *genius*, he is God. The pantheist "I am God" is a reductionist's Holy Grail: I am part of the universe, which is God. The universe is one, and I am one with God, making me equal to God: I am God. Can't reduce much lower than that.

Who is the real genius here? The atheist? The pantheist? My candidate is Everyman.

In a radio interview with Steve Paulson, atheist Richard Dawkins commented, "I think the most powerful reason for believing in a supreme being is the argument for design. Living things in particular look complicated, look beautiful, look elegant, look as though they've been designed. We are all accustomed to thinking that if something *looks* designed, it *is* designed. Therefore, it's really no wonder that before Darwin came along, just about everybody was a theist."

And just about everybody still is a theist. Just about everybody is smart enough to put two and two together to get four. Just about everybody is smart enough to get that cosmic design requires a Designer. Design and consciousness are only *problems* for X-God pedants too preoccupied with God-poison to grasp this fundamental fact.

HOAXING, FORGING, TRIMMING, AND COOKING

As I mentioned in Chapter 3, academics politely disregard even the most preposterous theories put forth by their colleagues. Generally speaking, the ivory halls resound with wacky theories, as well they should. Toss creative ideas and critical thinking into the campus cauldron and you get civilization bubbling its best. Of course, every department has its cloak-and-dagger villain lurking in the wee-hour shadows with a vial of poison tucked in his vest.

Though the line between preposterous theory and lie is thin, crossing that threshold jeopardizes the liar's reputation and career. But despite this built-in deterrent, at times a lie explodes so shocking that some scandalized grad student squeals. But typically everyone just ignores the latest elephant stuffed in the file closet; even the snoopy poop scooper scoots.

Creative ideas and critical thinking. Ah yes, critical thinking, that nasty nag. Critical thinking is the lie cop; on campus or in the adjunct lab, the lie cop polices responsible methodology, valid conclusions, and that testy intellectual rectitude. Even sneaky lies tend to be recklessly stupid as well as dishonest. Unfortunately, stupid and dishonest can easily hide behind field jargon and research red tape.

But now and then, even professors whose busts have already been carved in marble get busted. Exhibit A: In the January 9/16, 2012 issue of *The Nation*, in his article "Disgrace," Princeton professor Charles Gross relates how after a four-year investigation by Harvard University authorities, research scientist Marc Hauser, professor of psychology, organismic and evolutionary biology, and biological anthropology, and author of over two hundred papers and several books, resigned his professorship a few months following the psych department's decision to not retain him as a teacher—in other words, after his being more-or-less fired. Already Harvard had charged him with eight counts of "scientific misconduct," academia's polite euphemism for research fraud, aka lying, which typically involves fabrication, falsification, and/or plagiarism, according to the National Institutes of Health (NIH) and the National Science Foundation (NSF), the major funders of U.S. research.

Hauser himself was originally outed by his own research assistant and subsequently investigated by three of his lab's researchers, then by Harvard, then by the federal Office of Research Integrity. Many student assistants are paid for their lab time, and whistle blowing could easily result in the student being fired, and much worse could ruin his career; Hauser's elephant must have been rank to rankle his brave student and researchers enough for them to jeopardize their futures.

Though a whole circus of elephants stink up plenty of research closets, Hauser's outing is not exceptional. During the last few decades numerous studies have documented rampant scientific misconduct in university-based research as witnessed or admitted by students and professors. The NIH very conservatively estimates that at an absolute minimum, 2,325 incidents of fabrication, falsification, and plagiarism occur each year. A meta-analysis of eighteen studies found that over fifteen percent of scientists are known to have fabricated or falsified data. With so much blatant lying going on, who has time to police lapses in critical thinking, much less energy to pick apart the esoteric, like the musical score of Kaku's Cuckoo or the strong anthropic principle of Davies' simulated Matrix multiverses?

Some academic crimes are easier to demonstrate. Hauser, who works primarily with rhesus monkeys, cotton-top tamarins, and human infants, stated on his website that his research focused on "understanding which mental capacities are shared with other nonhuman primates and which are uniquely human," and on determining "the evolutionarily ancient building blocks of our capacity for language, mathematics, music and morality." Gross points out that "A key motivation in Hauser's work has been to demonstrate that monkeys have cognitive abilities previously thought to be present only in the great apes and humans." He adds, "Darwin had tried to remove the human from the center of the biological universe, stressing its psychological and physical continuity with other living beings. Hauser seems to want to put humans and other primates, even the cotton-top tamarin, on a cognitive plane above other animals, like dolphins and crows, that have sophisticated cognitive skills but are not in the primate lineage."

Hauser skewed his research and outright lied to further the cause of neo-Darwinism. In the study that led to the Harvard investigation, Hauser interpreted and documented the presence of sound pattern recognition thought to be a necessity in language acquisition in the monkeys he and his assistants observed. But his students asserted, and the investigation concurred, that the studied monkeys' behavior displayed no sound pattern recognition at all. In a similar study in which a red dot was placed on the foreheads of study animals, Hauser declared that cotton-top tamarins could recognize themselves. But in fact, investigators concluded that Hauser's research materials not only did not support, but actually contradicted Hauser's claim. As it turns out, unlike Hauser's monkeys, many animals, such as dolphins, orcas, magpies, and elephants, share with humans the ability to recognize themselves. Also flying in the face of Hauser's evolutionary premise, research shows that jays and crows have cognitive abilities like tool use, foresight, and role-taking shared with great apes.

In the scholarly journal *Cognition*, Hauser claimed that like human infants, cotton-top tamarins could rapidly generalize "patterns that have been characterized as abstract algebraic rules," implying that monkeys could correspondingly process a similar symbolic system, language. As it turns out, even elderly tamarins will never be able to help me understand stings, branes, and strong anthropic multiverses. Following the Harvard investigation, Gerry Altmann, editor of *Cognition*, told the *Boston Globe* that the Hauser paper "reports data...but there was no such data existing on the videotape. These data are depicted in the paper in a graph. The graph is effectively a fiction and the statistic that is supplied in the main text is effectively a fiction." And "if it's the case the data have in fact been fabricated, which is what I as the editor infer, that is as serious as it gets." Altmann later commented on his blog, "The information I have received, when taken at face value, leads me to maintain my belief that the data that had been published in the journal *Cognition* was effectively a fiction—that is, there was no basis in the recorded data for those data. I concluded, and I continue to conclude, that the data were most likely fabricated (that is, after all, what a fiction is—a fabrication)." Scientists or any other academics that lie about the facts of their chosen field are—well, liars.

Another of Hauser's fabricated fictions is that chimps, rhesus monkeys, and cotton-top tamarins interpret human hand gestures and thereby understand the unspoken message, an ability possessed only by humans. But in fact dogs interpret human gestures better than chimps do. And no species but humans can understand complex meaning conveyed by a human being via physical gestures. Ideas Hauser presents in his book *Moral Minds* as his own original work and even some of their exact wording have been shown to have been plagiarized. Although Hauser does credit the work of some sources, for instance, John Mikhail, one of the accusing researchers from whom Hauser freely borrowed, writing presented as academic in the author's field of academic expertise requires strict citation following specific rules, unlike freer rules governing synthesized concepts and loose paraphrase presented to substantiate the opinions of trade book authors.

Hauser's "proof" of moral evolution simply continued an esteemed tradition of the Darwinian Noble Lie established when scientists first applauded Darwin's bogus "proof" of macroevolution. Ironically, Darwin's buddy Charles Babbage presented the first analysis of scientific misconduct, "hoaxing, forging, trimming, and cooking," in his 1830 book *Reflections on the Decline of Science in England and on Some of Its Causes.*

Studies examining the kind of typical scientist guilty of misconduct reveal a portrait that strikingly resembles Darwin himself: a bright, ambitious young man working among and mentored by the scientific elite, competing for recognition and status within the elite. Of course, research funding provides the means for research to continue, so a researcher might be tempted to skew his research to favor his lab's financial worth by presenting new information that profits the rewarding institution. Yes, scientists funded by a drug company say, your new drug works effectively with only a few small-print side-effects (that could kill you). Yes, scientists paid by corporate polluters claim, global warming is a myth (that could kill you). Sometimes, with one foot still firmly planted in the campus lab, a skewing scientist has already placed the other foot in the door of a lucrative corporate lobby. Corporations pump millions into universities to buy the right to skew; academic prostitution isn't yet as rampant as political prostitution, but it is on the rise.

But skewed research is probably most often the consequence of personal hubris fulfilling the universal university tenure requirement to publish work that contributes to one's field. Gross notes that in one interview, Hauser observed that psychopaths "know right from wrong but just don't care." Interestingly, Gross only vaguely implies that perhaps Hauser fits the bill. Hauser and many other neo-Darwinians and Darwinian science itself should really undergo psychological evaluation. (I am quite serious.)

In a very real sense, neo-Darwinian science has boxed itself into a corner. Scientists in most fields admit the obvious facts. How else can science proceed? How else can science justify its existence? Yet neo-Darwinians won't admit the truth—won't admit they're wrong—even to the point of looking ridiculous. Isn't that a clinical symptom of psychopathy?

What do neo-Darwinian scientists really know? How do they account for the perfectly calibrated complexity of our unfolding universe that, as one neo-Darwinian put it, looks as if it knew we were coming? How do they account for this tendency of the universe to go beyond itself, to transform, to transcend? How do they account for life? How do they account for intelligence, value, meaning, purpose; how do they account for consciousness and subjectivity? How do they account for our confidence in truth, goodness, beauty, God? How do they account for our talents, virtues, passions, quests? How do they account for our thirst for knowledge, our insistence for freedom, our demand for justice? How do they account for our sense of tragedy and ecstasy, our tears and jokes, our experiences of spiritual transcendence? How do they account for our persistent, even obsessive need to believe in something greater than ourselves? How do they account for our need to learn for its own sake, for our desire to codify unselfishness, for our drive to seek God? These are not tamarin tendencies.

Neo-Darwinian scientists appropriate the language and concepts of religion to explain natural phenomenon materialistically. Now they have an answer. But it's wrong.

Those scientists describe when they claim to explain. They know that when I'm thinking, my neurons are firing, the synapses are connecting, the lobes of my brain are activated, but they have no clue why I'm thinking what I'm thinking, or why I'm thinking at all. They don't know why I want to think, or why I want to think what I think, or even why they want to think what they think. They don't know what a thought is. They don't know what mind is, or how mind differs from brain. All this per neo-Darwinian scientists themselves.

Animals are conscious. Only humans are metaconscious. Only humans are self-aware in being aware that we are aware. We humans stand outside ourselves and look down on ourselves being aware. Only we humans are conscious of ourselves being more than material. We are aware of ourselves as beings in time, and can imagine ourselves as being outside of time. Each of us is the exact same being even while we are perpetually changing, growing, dying. Could we grow beyond death, we logically ask? We know intuitively that there is something about us that transcends the material. Nearly all of us know ourselves to be dual, mind more than body, spirit more than matter. How could we know this unless we had been created by something transcending body and matter, and even mind and spirit?

I get the feeling that for neo-Darwinians like Davies, life is a series of pasts they wish they could fix. They can. Even they know that the universe moves as a process of perpetual self-transcendence: That's simple growth; that's basic microevolution. We can taste an afterlife emerging out of life each time a moment sprouts fresh moments. Life is perpetually refreshing like a cool drink, or if you prefer, like your computer. Life is consciousness moving toward another dimension of consciousness, infancy to adolescence to adulthood to the afterlife. Life reaches out for the "Thou" in, through, and beyond the "It." Consciousness reaches to receive what the progress of the universe has promised. That's the intelligently designed consciousness reached via human microevolution and personal growth that neo-Darwinians despise.

Why do Dawkins &co hate God so much that they must kill him?

Why is it so hard for them to believe in God's existence? This selective blindness could simply be a negligible instance of son rebelling against Father. More likely, theirs is true blindness, an actual self-inflicted handicap tantamount to soul suicide.

Snipers of their own spirit, they pick off those faculties that most make them human: reason, conscience, intuition, emotion, and perhaps most decisively, aesthetic, the classic Mother of Invention. What happens to a soul riddled with bullet-holes? The whole being bleeds; the psyche suffers, and starts to die. Now that they're leaking life, they're really mad; now they want to exterminate any trace of God in us all. I think Dawkins &co would concur that neo-Darwinians are on a metaphysical murder-suicide rampage intent on spiritual extinction—though they might prefer a whitewashed "educational book tour" to the more accurate metaphor "murder-suicide rampage."

SPIRITUAL AESTHETIC

Perhaps most symptomatic of the soul's sickness unto death is the assassination of one's aesthetic, the faculty of aesthetic sensibility. Darwin confesses a diagnosis of his own impotence in his *Autobiography*, in the passage on his aesthetic atrophy that I quoted in Chapter 5:

> My mind seems to have become a kind of machine for grinding general laws out of large collections of facts, but why this should have caused the atrophy of that part of the brain alone, on which the higher tastes depend, I cannot conceive. A man with a mind more highly organized or better constituted than mine, would not, I suppose, have thus suffered; and if I had to live my life again, I would have made a rule to read some poetry and listen to some music at least once every week; for perhaps the parts of my brain now atrophied would thus have been kept active through use. The loss of these tastes is a loss of happiness, and may possibly be injurious to the intellect, and more probably to the moral character, by enfeebling the emotional part of our nature.

Darwin, you'll recall, was tone deaf and had no sense of musical rhythm; his taste in art was not subjective but was rather an objective reflex inculcated via friendly indoctrination; his love of poetry and metaphysical writings wilted in the jungle heat of his ambitious hubris. Yet Darwin suffered. At least he was that self-aware. He neither lied (about that) nor succumbed to pseudo-aesthetics a la Kaku or Davies. I think that here, as elsewhere, Darwin exposes, even if dryly (a form of bravado?), his worry for his soul.

Surely neo-Darwinians suffer as well, though few seem self-aware enough to realize that they have killed not God, but only their own God-given faculties that make them fully human. They want to be apes? They are. Not via natural selection, but by the unnatural selection of their own free will.

They must be blind to design to argue that the existence of a Creator God is not any more likely or provable than the just-happens-to-exist theory of Creation's genesis. Even they know that nothing in the space-time universe is self-created or self-sustaining, that everything that exists in the space-time realm necessarily must derive from something else. It makes sense to most of us that space-time itself must be created by a First Cause (but not cause in any space-time sense) that is "above" or "outside" space-time and that is likely of a "substance" so different from space-time that we space-time citizens could not imagine it. Most people call this entity God.

Neo-Darwinians counter that if there was no space or time before the creation of space and time, there was no space or time in which God could have created. Again, God necessarily transcends space, time, and space-time. If they can't grasp this simple concept, how would they understand incorporeal soul or transcendent spirit?

Just because aspects of the natural realm can be described scientifically doesn't preclude the possibility that they were and are divinely generated. Just because God can't be scientifically catalogued in humanity's little Book of Space-Time doesn't mean that a transcending God can't exist. Try as the atheist might to starve God in the dungeon of his brain, God frolics in a Reality far beyond his control.

Is it really such a quantum leap from faith in the awesomely exquisite "mindless" but rational laws of nature to the rational Mind who necessarily must create them? A primal particle just happened to explode out into this incomprehensibly diverse existence? Natural laws just happened to exist to make that possible? We just happen to be capable of pondering this? It doesn't take a genius to realize that there is no just happened; there's an infinity of just happens. Maybe it takes an artist to recognize that only a wildly creative Artist would design over 100,000 species of butterflies, a quarter million species of beetles. To those who complain with Bertrand Russell (who called mind and matter "logical constructions"—"logical" "constructions") that God hasn't produced sufficient evidence of his existence, or with Darwin, who equivocates, "I cannot look to the universe as the result of blind chance, yet I can see no evidence of beneficent design, or indeed of design of any kind, in the details," all I can say is, *Wow.*

In faith, some scientists believe that in the beginning of space and time, the cosmos was so densely packed together that the entire content of the universe—everything that would become atoms and galaxies and conscious human beings and blue jeans and computer games and unrequited love and all that is still to become—was a tiny chaos of subatomic particles no bigger than a pinhead, that behaved, in effect, like a single particle. In the violent birthing of this everything everywhere, an explosive flash of primordial light flared out into an accelerating expansion that has been occurring ever since.

"…and there was light." Well, not visible light; gamma rays. But in a hundred thousand years, when things had cooled down a bit, there was visible light. And more light. Space and time themselves are manifestations of light, as Einstein eloquently demonstrated. And this light of Creation is understood by almost everyone to be both literal and figurative.

According to the scientific experts, in the beginning, one collective point was all there was, is, and would become. All space and time in all its manifestations already existed at the Big Bang.

But in the *very* beginning, before there was light, even before there were particular angels dancing on the pinhead beginning of the space-time realm of perpetual beginnings, there had to have been *something*—a creator of some sort, or many creators. Where else could that primal particle, the laws of physics, empty space itself have come from? From other universes, parallel universes, eleven dimensional hyperspace? That is certainly not the shortest distance between two points. Where did those other universes come from? Again, nothing in the space-time realm is self-created or self-sustaining; the particular genesis of space-time could only have been conceived by something outside the space-time realm, by something not itself constrained by this universe's odd symmetry of beginnings and endings. Poems do not write poems; poets write poems.

Quantum physicists "watch" the sudden appearance and

disappearance of subatomic particles such as electrons and quarks "out of nothing" that result in small but measurable effects in the energy levels of atoms. This "nothing," quaintly called the vacuum, permits only certain entities to materialize. According to some interpretations of quantum theory, the nothing is a something where ghostlike potential universes wait to randomly leap into being.

In other words, there are things—entire universes of things—which are really nothing because they do not yet exist, that spring from a place outside the universe that is really no place because it does not exist either. Existence springs from an existent nonexistence, or a nonexistent existence, take your pick. Oddly, there are many today who believe *this* who cannot believe in anything "transcendent."

Another current theory posits that a steady-state universe just happens to have always existed, steady and eternal, the big bangs being local galactic phenomenon. Based on this theory, some have inferred that the universe itself is God, self-conceived within a whirlwind of opposites, and that we are as divine as a speck of dust.

Astronomers study photons that make up light that reaches the Earth from distant objects, analyzing the energy of individual photons and the direction from which they come. Photons carry very little information, yet almost everything scientists know about the distant universe is photon-inferences expressed as equations. Intriguing, those who revere these scientists of skimpy assumptions while ridiculing those of us who deduce, from the massive evidence of Creation, that there is a Creator.

At an ever-increasing pace, radically new entities spring into existence. Spring how? Only God can bring forth a completely new form, even form from a preexisting form. Again, the *potential* for change is a precondition already built into existence. Everything we humans create we create from preexisting potential. Potential itself is part of the blueprint drawn up by its Designer. Yet within that potential is free will, gift wrapped and tied with a big bow, which atheists, with the zeal of juvenile delinquents, rip to shreds.

Though each species is distinct, each is composed of the same source material, from light-driven primordial chemicals to amphiphiles to vesicles. All life on earth carries within every cell the metabolism and molecular genetics of one species of vesicle. The essential chemical processes within us and within all forms of life have remained the same for four billion years. Vesicles, pyrophosphates, keto acids, amino acids, nucleic acids—all of which *just happens to be* the genetic code.

Again, nature doesn't create itself out of itself. A painting doesn't generate itself out of its own canvas, paint, and concept. Nature is the *artwork*, not the *artist*. That we're all built of the same building materials doesn't prove that one species derived from another. God created the canvas and the palette of colors with which she perpetually paints the universe.

The only thing new about *neo*-Darwinism is its religious conversion from destruction to self-destruction. Today's worldviews are as entrenched in fallacies of scientific fundamentalism as in myths of other religious extremists.

The neo-Darwinian holds that in the beginning, a simple living organism (simpler than a single cell) arose by chance out of inert matter, reproduced, and evolved through random variation shaped by natural selection. As blind chance replaces cutthroat competition as the origin and purpose of species, we moderns are left at the mercy of forces completely beyond our control. No longer do we trust that we can survive, even temporarily, by our own efforts. Anxious "be on alert" has shifted to passive "why bother." Depression, suicide, drugs, mindless distractions from the pain of hopelessness and the stress of even more profound anxiety now define culture. The natural humanism of the Enlightenment, the force that drove our Deist Founders to create our democratic nation, has been subsumed by the new old natural: exploitation. People who have passively given up are more vulnerable to exploitation than people still struggling to survive.

Darwinism left us cutting each other's throats. Neo-Darwinism has us cutting our own throats. Sounds like fundamentalist Armageddon to me. Sounds like extinction.

Of course there's a better way, the Golden Mean of Deism, which teases the keys to the kingdoms of heaven and hell from the hands of fools and gives them back to God.

Humanity is an interconnected society, not a jungle of brutes jockeying for positions of superiority. If there's one concept that can save the world, it's that we're all in this together.

Humans are *fundamentally* and in a sense *infinitely* different from anything else in Nature, including apes (only humans grasp abstractions like *fundamentals* or *infinity*, or can compare and contrast humans and apes; even just show me an ape that lifts weights to gain strength).Yet we are completely natural, just like every other natural entity. Even so, we humans have always intuited that we aren't *just* natural. We aren't exactly *other* than natural; it's more that there's a part of us that is *in addition to* nature—some might even say in spite of nature. We intuit that there is something in us that is not quite natural in the space-time sense. Soul, spirit, afterlife are a few terms by which we, like our ancient ancestors, have tried to express this something "other," this "in addition to" the tiny box we have crammed ourselves into.

Humans experience in a way that transcends the practical. We don't just seek to learn how to better reach the banana; we want to know the meaning of life. Our desire for meaning is one of our most distinguishing features. It is an attribute that is super-natural, and by that I don't mean that it exists outside of nature; rather, it exists as a dimension of nature that transcends space-time nature-as-such: It is meta-natural, much like the symbolism of a poem or the quality of a painting transcends the sum of its material parts. To deny this transcendent dimension is to deny the distinctive humanity of humans.

A scientist could no doubt delineate myriad ways that a human being is like an ape, or even a tree, a molecule, or a speck of stardust—or for that matter, a truck, a cell phone, or a garbage disposal. A religionist, on the other hand, focuses on the ways humans are not animals, are not in fact like anything else in the material universe. Deism embraces the natural and the metanatural—the reality that humans are of this world but in ways that are different from the ways that other beings are of this world; in addition, we are not quite of this world.

Though we can't exactly define it, most of us understand the human spirit to be an aspect of *Homo sapiens* that exists beyond the merely primate. Our difference that makes us truly *other* is a quality of *spirit*. This intuition explains why some religions view human existence as a series of reincarnations that perhaps began as animal and transcended via a series of steps, or lifetimes, to the qualitatively different human, and then on up a series of qualitatively unique moral steps to enlightenment, and then ultimately to spirit transcendence into a qualitatively different life beyond space-time existence. (The evil, naturally, go the other way—eventually landing in hell, per religion, or perhaps worse, devolving toward ultimate death, extinction in the Darwinian sense.) It's not unreasonable, by this view, to represent humans as self-creating gods. In a sense, this view argues a case for Darwin-esque evolution but on a grander spiritual scale within an intelligently designed preprogrammed universe of exquisitely balanced continuities and potentialities. One can almost hear the harmony of the spheres.

The fact is that we now know that life does not emerge by chance, and species do not evolve due to survival of the fittest, though they might survive because they are in some way fittest or most suited. Surviving is one thing. Evolving is another animal altogether. If survival is not the sole purpose of an individual life, if evolution in the Darwinian sense is not the ultimate purpose of life, then what is the purpose of life—of all life, of any life? What is the purpose of distinctively *human* life in the vastness of an intelligently designed universe? Why couldn't the human spirit in space-time simultaneously survive and evolve and transcend on a not-material plane, "in the world, but not of it," as the proverb goes?

Humans are uniquely human precisely *because* we are driven to understand how and why we exist. We need to understand the objective purpose of things for its own sake but also for the sake of better understanding the subjective meaning of our lives. We understand the subjective by understanding the objective, and because we're specifically human, we understand the objective via our own subjective means of understanding. The way we understand and therefore what we can and do understand are *humanly* possible. Apes and cobras do not understand the way we understand, nor do they comprehend the qualities of things that we do. Cartoon personifications like pontificating puppies and philosophizing pandas tickle our funny bone precisely because animals representing the *human* are patently preposterous.

A human is animal but is also unique in being something *radically* more than animal. From this obvious fact comes our notion of mind/body dualism. Our vision of existence and of its various components assumes a quality and depth of understanding—and meta-understanding—that transcends that of any other animal. In a Disney moment, some scientist might chatter excitedly about talking apes, but I haven't seen evidence that apes can lecture on Aristotle or speculate about the essence of God. In some ways, the difference between humans and apes is greater than the difference between humans and human-created computers.

The classification *Homo sapiens* falls absurdly short of designating the quantitative and dramatic qualitative difference between humans and other animals. Humanity's engagement with the *meaning* of existence is that transcending quality that definitively separates us from every other form of material existence as we know it. The human spirit is the faculty that seeks and apprehends meaning, and the spirit's quest for meaning defines the most lofty aspirations and accomplishments of religion, philosophy, art, culture, civilization—in other words, humanity. Unlike any other creature on Earth, we *are* our meanings. And as the poets tell us, meaning is truth, and truth beauty. That's the beautiful truth that entirely escapes the neo-Darwinian.

CHAPTER 8

THE TINKERING WATCHMAKER: THE DEOLOGY OF INTELLIGENT DESIGN

God Is Awesome is the perfect motto for Deism. What could be more awesome than a brilliant Designer who perpetually refreshes the free gift of an elegantly designed universe graced by our intelligent consciousness?

It's odd that scientists like Dawkins and Davies and Kaku, who revere science as absolute and even absolutely awesome, in a sense to the point of worship, deny intelligent design—or rather, an intelligent designer. They don't seem to think that space-time existence is *un*intelligent. They don't *deny* that the intricate structural integrity of the universe, the complex yet precise organization of all existence, or the defining laws of nature that can be rationally apprehended are *rational*, are *intelligible*. Surely something as smartly articulated as nature can't be random. Surely there *must* be an intelligent designer that's smarter than those who deny the obvious existence of intelligent design or the necessity of its transcending intelligent designer.

Science and its inventions are simply descriptions of—and theories tentative guesses about—what things are and how things work. Even atheist scientists believe in their descriptions and theories via an act of *faith*. What is faith but allegiance to the best guess based on the best information? How is an atheist's "scientific" faith superior to faith in scientifically verifiable, entirely logical intelligent design? At the very least scientists *believe* in their own inherent faculties of apprehension and reason and in the validity of the scientific method, which requires absolute *trust* in the eternal rational laws of nature. Their faith in the higher power of reason and the reasonable structure of space-time existence is a religious conviction. By definition, reasonable structures are not random: They are purposely created by a transcending Creator.

Scientific explanations of how Creation came into existence never really satisfy the fundamental question of *how* the facts and principles of science could even be possible. Among scientists of "just the facts," *why* isn't even mentioned; just-fact scientists are cataloguers rather than investigators. (List-maker Darwin even tallied the pros and cons of taking a wife before marrying his cousin, Emma Wedgwood, of the rich family marketers of famous products bearing the family name.) Cataloguers miss the clearly exuberant *personality* speaking through Creation. They're the guys that squeeze the oranges but never taste the juice.

TASTING JUICE

Neo-Darwinian theory rests upon five major assertions: 1) A simple living organism arose by chance out of inert matter, 2) the original organism reproduced, 3) the organism developed through random variation, meaning by chance, 4) random variation, or chance, is natural— is part of the functional laws of nature, 5) life evolved randomly via natural selection.

The premise that a simple living organism arose out of inert matter can't explain *how* organized complexity emerged from simple matter; it can't explain how any greater arises from any lesser (logically, it can't). The coming into being of any one thing must be *generated* by something. Generation implies *desire* to generate plus an act of *will*, both attributes of a "person" in a general, non-human-specific sense. Any entity must be generated by something *greater* than the entity itself: A poem does not create a poet; a pigeon did not create the first pigeon. The greater must be a willing *mind*: A gear does not construct a watch, or vice versa.

Once generated, the thing—the complex orchestration of its complementary components—must be *sustained* by something beyond and greater than itself.

Nothing in our universe is self-created or self-sustaining. Even the profoundly simple, immensely complex, totally elegant laws of nature must have been designed by something of greater intelligence than the level of intelligence—much less intelligibility—of the laws themselves. The elegant laws of nature must have been designed by an intelligence of transcending elegance. The fact that we can deduce this indicates that the laws of nature were intelligently designed to be deduced by our intelligence.

Once the simple living organism just sort of leaked out of inert matter, the neo-Darwinian explains, it reproduced. But how would it know to do that? Why would it want to do that? How *could* it do that?

According to geneticists, each organism comes fully equipped/programmed with all the information/instructions needed to take it *to* the next step, which is to reproduce itself. The first organism didn't just say to itself one day, hmm, I think I'll reproduce myself. But *something* must have *decided* to make the organism reproduce.

There must have been an *impetus* to take the next step; something must have *wanted* it to take the next step to reproduction, or *motivated* it to want to reproduce. The first organism didn't just say, Wow, I'm gonna die, and to continue my line I need to reproduce myself, or at least something like myself. Something else made that *rational decision.*

But *how* can/does it reproduce? Where do the instructions on how to "do it" come from? Darwin himself admitted in *Origin of Species,* Chapter 14, that life began with a being that already possessed reproductive powers. It's absurd to think that the complicated, elegant, consistent principles of inheritance just appeared out of nowhere, as a blind, mindless "necessity," as if necessity were not itself an intelligible component of the grand design of life perpetuating itself.

Just like the first organism, each subsequent organism comes fully programmed with the info/instructions needed to *take* the next step, which is to reproduce. The organism comes equipped with the info/instructions needed *at* the next step. The organism comes equipped with the info/instructions needed to continue *beyond* the step; it has the info/instructions needed to reproduce.

The info/instructions needed to reproduce are far greater than an organism needs to simply exist without reproducing, and the info/instructions needed to *perform* the *process* of reproduction are far more complex and sophisticated than the instructional information the organism needs to simply exist.

Furthermore, the *field* of existence already exists into which the organism will reproduce itself. Even potential existence already exists as a kind of latent existence awaiting actualization within the possible rules or limits of existence, the laws of nature that describe our universe.

The immensely complex but highly organized information-rich instructions needed to *pass on* the information to another organism must have come from an informational programmer much smarter than the organism itself.

Again, how would the organism know it needed to reproduce? Why would it need to reproduce? Why would it want to reproduce? How would it reproduce? Reproduction of even the simplest organism is an immensely complex process involving a multitude of sophisticated functions. (You got a whiff of that from Darwin's description of orchids in Chapter 5.) Where did those functions come from? *How* do those functions *work*?

Some functions are decisional. Who or what decided that a function should exist? Who or what then knew that the function needed to be activated. Who or what knew how to throw the switch so the function could and would—well, function, and function only when needed, another decision?

Scientists now ask: How did the first eye—how does *any* eye—know *how* to see? How would an organism decide it needed to see if sight didn't yet exist? How would the sudden emergence of a wing explain the understanding of a need for flight, or explain the knowledge of the complex mechanism of flying? How could a wing evolve from a foot, as Darwinians assume, when any of the many intermediary evolutionary steps would be, in effect, impossible because it would serve no biological purpose. In fact, biologically the actual evolution of a wing would diametrically oppose the *purpose* of evolution in the Darwinian sense, which is to insure our survival. A half-foot/half-wing that neither runs nor flies well, if at all, would not only not benefit the organism, it would make it instant brunch.

How does life know how to live? Furthermore, what is the point of living for anything not yet living, or for anything already living? Why survive? And *why* survive comes before *how* survive.

I AM THAT I AM, OR, THE GENE POOL IN WHICH I PLAY

Have you ever doubted your own existence? Even if you have—say, in an intro philosophy class—you likely haven't for very long. Like the rest of us, you "just know" that you exist.

Not only do you know that you exist, you know that you exist as you, and that you couldn't be, or become, other than you.

Way back at your conception, you could only become you; you

couldn't become a duck or an oak tree. You had to become a human being, and a very specific human being determined largely—at least physically—by your DNA. Your coming into existence as you was far from random.

As a human individual you have been shaped by environmental forces, whether accidental or chosen by you or someone else. But no force could cause you to suddenly morph into a duck or an oak tree. Should you have children, they will be human, just like you are human, although each child will be—*must* be—uniquely him/herself, not exactly you, not even half you.

You know that you are human and that humans are not ducks or oak trees. You understand classifications, and you know the difference between a species and an individual.

But *how* do you know this? How do "you" as a collision of sperm and egg know to become *you*? How does a duck *know* to become a duck? How does a duck know *how* to grow into a duck and not into an oak tree? How do you know *how* to be you?

Contrary to what you might expect, your knowing the complicated process of *how* to exist comes before your knowing *that* you exist. That fundamental knowledge of *how* is not something you know via your conscious intelligence. There are things about you that you know only at a very primal level. You know to *be*. Your DNA knew how to make you *you* long before you knew about your DNA. Someone knew (can some*thing* be said to know?) how to orchestrate your astoundingly complex DNA into you before you even came into existence.

Your ability to "just know" *that* you exist and even more fundamentally *how* to exist serves as evidence not only that *you* exist, but also that a designing someone exists—God, the God of Nature, meaning the universe, the entire natural realm.

If you stop to think about it, it's clear that the fact of your existence is not imparted to you as knowledge via science, formal logic, or religion. Your own intrinsic common sense registers an awareness of you to yourself.

By common sense I mean a consensus of your innate faculties, including reason, conscience, intuition, experience, emotion, physical sensation, instinct, desire, will, and aesthetic sensibility, which registers the holistic elegance of truth—the *truth* of truth in the Keatsian sense (beauty is truth, truth beauty). Even the various functions that make up your body constitute a faculty. Your faculties are what *cause* you to know.

Spirit is the *essential* faculty, your core essence, the Self, the Boss, the fundamental, transcendental person *you*. Your spirit is that which directs you to manifest as the person you, to manifest you to yourself, to hold up the mirror. As with your built-in DNA, your spirit knows *how* to manifest you as you even before you know *that* spirit exists. Like your DNA, your spirit can adapt within a range of possibilities, but unlike DNA, your spirit can *choose* to adapt. God-given free will is no more impossible than—is just as miraculous as—life emerging from not-life.

How do we know humans have the free will to really *choose*?

Just ask any human. Any human not spellbound by the Darwinian meme, that is. Humans ask the question; machines and animals do not and cannot even think to ask the question because they have no awareness of free will or its absence. We self-aware humans *intuitively* "just know" we have free will; machines and animals (as far as we know) are not self-consciously *aware* of inherent free will. Humans can be aware of the limitations to our free will; our intellectual awareness and material experience of the absence of our free will is *painful*, sometimes so profoundly painful that the person limited will jump off a bridge; death is preferable to the (perceived) absolute shackling of free will, we are *that* aware of it. Do animals or machines choose suicide? No, only humans do that. Humans are so defensive of our freedom that the will must be murdered by ultimate programming, brainwashing, for freedom to be shackled.

I AM THEREFORE I THINK

In spite of multitudinous distractions, humanity is consistently self-aware to the extent that we all know that we exist—and that we exist in contrast to other entities that exist. It is at this point—a sharp point neither erased by Hume's skepticism nor smudged by Spinoza's pantheism—that any inference about the discrete existence of God or any other assumption (as opposed to any *other* assumption) must begin the case for its reality, its truth.

I think therefore I am is a truth so obvious to most of us that to challenge it is a ludicrous intellectual game. Postmodernism's anxious fretting about the legitimacy of our assumptions about thinking itself, not to mention what constitutes our thoughts, has failed to shake our inherent faith in our own existence and in our *ability to know* that that existence is a fact.

We all know that we exist, even if we disagree about what that existence actually is. Toy with Berkeley's notion that all things are the mind of God contemplating itself and still that mind exists if one can think that; and really, would God's mind mistake itself for you? The Taoist belief that ultimate reality is emptiness still assumes that that reality, that state of emptiness, exists, and exists in contrast to what is *not* emptiness; and really, is the ultimate *you* defined by what you are not? Despite Zeno's conclusion that to get somewhere you have to get half way there, and half of that half, and half and a quarter and a sixteenth of that, and so on infinitely so that you get nowhere because you can't traverse infinite subunits of space, we all know that we get there; we all know there's a there there and that we are here and that here is not there. People fiddle with space/time paradoxes regarding existence and self, but no sane person slits a wrist over them. Faith in our existence in contrast to other existences—faith in our *experience* of our existence—is more constant than the speed of light.

There are things we just *know*. The skeptic can argue till he's blue in the chops, but no quality of analysis, no quantity of existential doubt can move us one micrometer from our unshakable faith in our being here.

How do we know we exist? There is only one answer that makes sense: We are *designed* to exist and to know that we exist. And we are designed to exist as that which we are, within a specific range of possibilities. Again, humans are not ducks, no matter how loudly your kids might quack. You are you and not something or someone else, although environmental forces can stimulate changes within the range of possibilities that constitute your human framework. And you can *choose* to be a certain version of you—a truly extraordinary ability we humans tend to take for granted.

Because we understand that nothing in the universe is self-created or self-sustaining, common sense tells us that we mere mortals had to have been created by some force that transcends the myriad intricacies of our existence, which we have barely glimpsed, and of which we are scarcely conscious. Furthermore, that creating force by necessity must be more intelligent than the sum total of all the perfectly orchestrated forces of nature. And that creating force must necessarily be a sustaining force, since the universe is perpetually coming into existence as well as—well, existing. Something doesn't just exist; it continues to exist. Even actualized existence is never static. You are constantly changing, yet you remain entirely you.

Creation isn't an act as much as a process. All things are perpetually being created according to specific design plans. Despite environmental forces shaping you, despite your choices to change yourself, you are perpetually absolutely you. The fundamental structures of you and all other entities exist according to pre-drafted specifications. And all existing entities fit perfectly together according to a grand blueprint of the universe as a whole.

Deism posits this commonsense truth as its fundamental tenet: We are designed; there is a transcending designer, otherwise known as *God*. We can think this because we have been designed to think. Thinking is a profoundly sophisticated process created by an even more sophisticated thinker. Religion rests on this fundamental assumption: I am I because I think in the image of the Thinker, or at least in the image of the Thinker's thought about me. To believe otherwise would be, quite literally, non-sense.

Like Darwin, some scientists today seem dissociated from their aesthetic sensibility, that component of common sense that registers sublime elegance. How else could they miss all this beauty? Oh, they agree that beauty exists. They have opinions about what constitutes the beautiful and might display beautiful objects in their glass cases. But they experience beauty objectively, coolly from a distance, not subjectively like someone who lives passionately in his own skin, because passionate oneness with one's own being and with all life is an undeniably spiritual experience.

Those who agree with Keats that beauty is truth, truth beauty, know that the beautiful exists as *created* form. And form exists as cohesion. It's our aesthetic that viscerally spiritually grasps how amazing it is that all this beautiful flux gels, and continuously gels, so perfectly. Is it blind faith or simply common sense to assume that if the mindful Creator suddenly ceased perpetually actively creating us, the atoms of our material being would fly apart? How else do we, in spite of flux, remain whole?

God's Creation *is*, and the "is-ness" of Creation is impelled upon human consciousness, which is inescapably a fragment of that is-ness. Even scientists and philosophers who gripe that there is no evidence of God are spurred to discover *what* God creates, especially phenomena that are invisible or subtle, and are awed by what they discover even as they willfully refuse to acknowledge that *what* is created *is created*.

That God creates is self-evident fact clearly revealed to anyone exercising common sense. For the Deist, "God" simply means the creating Someone (the Creator of persons could not be a some*thing*). *How* God creates is a grand mystery we mere mortals will never grasp. *Why* God creates, even just why God creates us humans, is of course debatable. Some people argue that we can never know why God does anything. But because *why* probes for the meaning at the core of our existence, if there is no answer to *why*, there is for us humans no objective meaning of life.

Isn't it amazing that we can ponder the meaning and purpose of our existence? The Darwinian has no reason *why* or explanation *how* that would be. What irony. Seeking unity, he locates in his own heart a great dichotomy—his own separation from God; mundane matter torn from meaning; Cartesian subjectivity of consciousness *res cogitans* ("in here") forever estranged from objective existence *res extensa* ("out there"); even the Kantian hint of reality filtered through his senses and processed by his mind is deprived of direct experience of *Ding an sich* ("the thing as such"), existence itself. Even logic can't help him cross the bridge from "if" to "then."

Darwinian dualism is not the difference between contrasts, like hot and cold, good and evil, or even weak and strong; his dualism is existential schizophrenia of his own self from itself, that intellectual black hole of absolute negation into which all things perpetually tumble. There the observer observes himself finding the ultimate unification he seeks: Death.

In this era of postmodern Darwinism, the ivory towers teem with nihilists telegraphing their incongruous belief that each person dwells alone on a tiny island map of himself that he himself has drawn—incongruous in that the nihilists, far from being alone (except in their own fantasy), form a tight-knit group whose collective concepts and jargon codify codependence among themselves and their acolytes. Their catechized theology is that meaning beyond survival and reproduction is a mere existential construct. Like the religious hypocrites they glibly disregard, they stop their ears to any hypothetical alternative to their privileged ennui that can only end in suicide or escapism, coercion being a genus of escapism (unless it's psychopathic). Not exactly survival.

Deism, however, assumes that no man is an island, that we humans are constructed to ask why for a reason (even existential constructs are only possible because humans are constructed to construct), and that objective

Creation reveals nutritious answers and galvanic meanings that individuals and society need in this life. We even *need* for a reason.

Life is meaningful *because* it is inherently purposeful. We need meaning because it fulfills a purpose, a uniquely human purpose built into us as part of the functional structure of our human *being* right down to our DNA, right down to our soul and spirit.

If each of the myriad diverse components of existence exhibits its own discrete inherent perfection (an atom is perfectly an atom and is definitely not a molecule), and if those myriad components fit together in perfect natural symmetry—if each component serves its own discrete function, which manifests its own discrete coherence while contributing to the overall coherence of existence—isn't it reasonable to presume that God has a purpose in creating such a thoroughly exquisitely purposive universe, and that God perhaps even has a definite purpose for each of us conscious humans, and that the purpose involves individual growth within a growing cooperative community?

Faith is Knowledge is Naturally Consistent

Blind faith is no faith at all. Real faith is grounded in knowledge acquired in the pursuit of truth. Truth *is*; truth is reality. Knowledge is our interpretation and understanding of our perceptions of and reasoning about reality.

You believe that the sun will rise at a specific time tomorrow morning based upon knowledge. Knowledge is knowledge because God created Nature to be consistent and therefore knowable. Although Creation is a perpetual process of change, the fundamental structure is consistently coherent. All structures are perpetually what they are; all structures perform in perfect concert with all other structures. Gravity always acts the same way everywhere in the universe; gravity, being gravity, cannot suddenly morph into light. Gravity is gravity because it is gravity. 2+2 always equals 4; this equation, being what it is, cannot mutate into 2+2 equals 5; and 2+2=4 performs consistently harmoniously with all other equations. We know this—we believe this—because we experience, understand, and trust the consistency of existence. Our thoughts, feelings, intuitions, expressions, and all our other inherent faculties perform according to these harmonious structures, which, as we discern them, we call the laws of nature.

Natural law defines each structure. Abstractions express structural definitions. A four-legged table is not the same thing as a four-legged cow. We understand the difference because there is a difference. The concepts table, cow, and four-legged fit categories of many tables, cows, and four-legged things. From many examples of tables we derive the category table. Although no two tables are exactly alike, we know a table when we see one. The abstract category table is categorically different from tangible tables.

Understanding is a category of knowledge that differs from recognition knowledge, or recognizing a specific thing when we see it, and differs even from abstract recognition, or recognizing the category, such as table. Understanding is metaknowledge, and involves metathought, because it apprehends a thing in a way, or to a degree, that transcends the thing itself and even the abstract concept of the thing itself. We can imagine an ape recognizing a lion, any lion, both the individual thing and the category of the group, lions. But do apes understand the concept *thing* or the concept *category*? Do apes think about thinking? Do apes stand in awe of their own being? Do apes grasp the immensity of nature's complexity? Do apes contemplate the existence of God, or of anything?

Could an ape claim that all existence is itself miraculous? Even animal lovers would surely agree that only a human could understand that although it's impossible that something came from nothing, here it is. Only humans deduce that the something that is Nature came, and continues to come, from God. Only humans then ask: But where did God come from? Where did whatever was truly first come from? The miracle of The First occurred. Only a human could conceive such a concept.

As much as materialists deny it, metaknowledge and metathought can only be the province of that which transcends the material: the spiritual. The spiritual is simply that which transcends the material. Separating spiritual from not-spiritual is not as easy as it might seem. Is mind spiritual? Do humans have a spiritual nature, or a spiritual facet? If God is immanent in Creation, is the universe itself spiritual?

We call Creation miraculous because we understand that it is beyond our understanding of how things come into existence. In a sense, we understand that which is beyond understanding—and again, that level of "transglobal" or "extraglobal" understanding is spiritual. Existence coming-to-be out of nothing is impossible yet here it is. We understand this. Creation out of nothing (nothing we know, nothing as we know it) is impossible and therefore (subjectively) "miraculous."

But what Christians and most other religionists call a miracle is not the same thing. That kind of miracle is impossible within a context of God-given absolute consistency. Magical miracle contradicts the authentic miracle of existence as such. Magical miracle makes for entertaining and sometimes symbolically profound fiction, but again, representation is representation. Instantaneously changing water into wine transgresses the natural process of rain contributing to the natural growth of grapes that can be harvested by humans who then change them through a process of many specific steps over time into wine. The unnatural miracle of instant wine-making never happened. This is my opinion, but it is an opinion based on reason informed by experience. The opinion that the instant wine miracle occurred is based on far-fetched hearsay that originated in antiquity and was passed on by unknown people of unverifiable veracity. It is not only unreasonable, it is also unnatural and therefore, for a Deist like me, ungodly.

When I look at Nature I see a perfect balance of coming-to-be within a fixed structure of natural laws. Babies don't come from storks. Babies absolutely *cannot* come from storks, pray as you might that they can. Knowledge is based on our observation and experience of what can and cannot be. Babies coming from storks is as preposterous as the biblical Jesus being an actual person who was born of a virgin, performed miracles, and bodily rose from the dead.

A miracle in the mythic sense is a violation of knowledge, a transgression of obvious God-established laws of Nature that constitute existence, reality, truth. A miracle in the Christian sense is God contradicting himself.

If God as Creator contradicts himself, we have no firm basis for knowledge because there is no absolute truth, no trustworthy touchstone that we can depend on. If God contradicts himself, for our sake or for any other reason, God is contradictory, God is inconsistent, existence is not real in any definitive, absolute, or even concrete way. If we know that what we know could suddenly change, if 2+2 could suddenly equal 5, if the sun and moon could stop or move backward without any apparent natural cause and without any impact on the earth, if the very, very dead could resurrect a few days later and ascend into the clouds, if Jonah could live a few days underwater in the belly of a whale, if a man could break a single loaf of bread into the equivalent of dozens or hundreds of loaves, then anything could happen, and we could know nothing for sure. And if we can't trust Creation—if we can't trust the steadfast veracity of Creation, if we can't trust that Creation is what Creation is, if we can't trust that a loaf of bread is a loaf of bread—how can we trust the Creator? A thing not being what it is, a thing being what it is not, disintegrates reality into absurdity beyond insanity. Chaos is perhaps the only thing more terrifying than extinction. Fortunately, chaos does not exist. In my view, it never has, it never will. Reality being what it is and not something else (and not "nothing") is a beautifully self-exemplifying moral imperative: truth being true is truth being truth. For this reason, on old-world religious miracle presented as fact, especially in this day and age, is an unnatural, immoral lie.

Doesn't it seem that God indeed does want us to know something for sure, that God is allowing us to grasp something about his nature, that God wants us to learn to trust him as moral Creator by trusting the perfect stability of his Creation? Creation exists; and to exist, each component of Creation must be exactly what it is and only what it is. A loaf of bread cannot be a warehouse full of loaves of bread. If we can't trust Creation to be consistently what it is, how can we trust the Creator to be consistently what he is?

"Yes," one might argue, "but God wants us to know his absolute power through those miraculous transgressions of natural law." This reasoning doesn't make sense, because what kind of tyrannical God would put us into a state of extreme anxiety, fear, paranoia that would be the consequence of not knowing anything for sure? Consistency without stagnation, consistency that includes variation, that in us humans encourages creative freedom, instills peace in us that encourages goodwill from us. Happiness requires a balanced harmony of consistency and freedom.

It would only benefit inconsistent, illogical, and tyrannical priests (and priestly figures like abusive fathers and leaders) of any religion or denomination to perpetuate blind faith in an inconsistent, illogical, and tyrannical God. If miracles violate natural law, the God of anti-natural miracles is the God of chaos. Isn't Satan the supreme representation of the god of chaos?

GOD'S NECESSARY GOODNESS

At their primal core, most religions view God as good. A good God is consistent, like a good parent is consistent. If on Monday it's wrong to steal your dad's wallet or slash your neighbor's tires, consistent parents would let you know it's wrong on Tuesday. If God said, "This is Creation as I have created it," and then said, "Well, someday I might change my mind about gravity," how would that impact your sense of security, and what would that say about God?

If God is good, God is a consistent Creator. God consistently creates new things within a consistently fixed structure of natural laws. Nature, with all its new forms, its process of transformation, and its structure of laws—all of that is, in a sense, miraculous. But Nature is a consistent miracle, and is the only miracle. Violation of the miracle of nature, the nature that is what it is, could only be committed by a God that is not consistent, good, or loving.

Of course, God could be morally mediocre, or could be evil. Don't most of us instinctively believe that God is necessarily good? And because we believe that God is good, we believe that God is consistent. In fact, to some extent we believe that the Creator is good *because* he is consistent. God's consistency is evidence of God's goodness. God is good in being consistent; God is consistent because he is good.

Therefore, miracles, in the sense of transgressions of natural law, are preposterous (i.e., impossible). People believe in miracles because they want to believe that miracles are possible, that they or their priestly proxies can snap their fingers and materialize a pot of gold. People rub their Bibles hard hoping the magic genie will pop out to grant their every wish. They turn God into a man-god messiah—a human of their own rank, who is easier to persuade. Some people believe in miracles because they're naïve, some because they're passive. No doubt some believe because they're too tired or busy—or lazy or irresponsible—to think things through.

When God has given you the whole universe, doesn't begging for more, doesn't trying to coerce God into giving you more stuff, or even more solutions to problems you should solve on your own, doesn't treating God like your own personal gofer, or whining that God doesn't love or respect you, display a grotesque absence of humility, not to mention profound ingratitude? At the very least, it's childish. The God who created the universe shouldn't need to perform magic tricks for inattentive humans to prove his existence. Open your eyes; use your brains. Miracles in the mythic sense are impossible because God is consistent, good, loving, and *here*—right here creating and sustaining the true miracle, the natural realm. Nature is *that* it is because it is *what* it is.

The ancients wrote that God created the universe and saw that it was good. Unfortunately, most humans neglect to notice the goodness of existence because they're too busy complaining about what they don't have.

But the poets of the world sing psalms that ground us in gratitude. True poets are deist to the core. They appreciate the sensuous taste of Nature, the truly miraculous transfiguration of pollen into honey. Imagine: A hive of bees flies 60,000 miles to tap the two million flowers that make a pound of honey. In her whole lifetime, one bee makes 1/12 teaspoon of honey, less than what you have stirred in the cup of tea you hold warming your hands in your imagination as I suggest this moment which does not yet exist except in my imagination in this moment that I am writing this to you. Imagine: Standing perfectly still on a mountain of snow on a clear, moonless night, you are standing in the gravity of a planet moving 66,000 mph in orbit around the sun, and 45,000 mph through space with the rest of the Milky Way. The seasons change in your body. The snow melts, and life resurrects, burgeoning, drinking the water of life. You eat and drink that life, and it becomes your life; all around you this communion of transmutation called reading a book.

The Milky Way alone contains 250 billion stars, each a sun like our sun with its constellating planets. Earth is a million times smaller than the sun. 100 million other galaxies of hundreds of billions of stars burn above us, trillions of zodiacs under which we were born, galaxies upon galaxies of stars, stars mapped out overhead, searing seasons across your imagination. One dynamic Big Bang—*Boom!* this hydrogen/helium universe of voids and superclusters of matter expanding even as gravity pulls stars in on themselves until they've consumed their own hydrogen, then helium ashes—all that nuclear fusion energy released as starlight. Is it so irrational to divine from their poetry the essence of your existence? When the fuel runs out, gravity kills the stars, but their fusion reactions produce all other chemical elements, the calcium in your bones, iron in your blood, carbon and nitrogen in your tissues: Every atom of your being is composed of stardust—the dust of all that fire.

PURPOSIVE CREATION

Nature's consistency is itself good and indicates benevolence on the part of Nature's Creator. If God is consistent, and if existence is consistent, it seems reasonable to believe that because each and every component of the universe has a function, existence as a whole has a purpose. It's fair to assume that a human being conscious of purpose likewise has a purpose. This can't be proven. Neither can it be disproven. Most of us trust this (sometimes without consciously realizing it) based on a keen awareness of the inherent functional consistency of Nature.

If existence has a purpose, if life, if my life, if your life, has a purpose, the careful intricacy of the design suggests that it must be a *good* purpose. And a good purpose is designed and directed by a good designer—good both in the sense of skilled and moral. But how can I *know* this?

Self-evident truths can be deduced from Creation—noun and verb: Massive, elegant, perpetual coming-into-being held in perfect equilibrium within massive, elegant, perpetual structure serves as powerful evidence that God is good. Beauty is truth and truth beauty, and beautiful truth is good.

Some might argue that design does not prove good. But design does not suggest evil intent; it does not prove the absence of goodness. The case for design as good, first conceived well over a couple dozen centuries ago, when framed within the context of what's good for humans and other living beings, is inherently stronger than any case against it.

But of course you may disagree. For instance: Doesn't the fact that any life-form must eat—kill, destroy—another life-form to live argue against the designer's goodness, or at least the transcending goodness of the design? First of all, you don't have to kill the cow to drink its milk. But yes, point taken. And it is a good one. But it hinges on the assumption that the manifestation of goodness cannot include its contrast.

Yes, as animals, humans must kill to eat (though we don't have to kill and eat other animals; we could eat plants). But as a spiritual being, certainly as a Deist, I rationally conclude that humans are also more than animals. We Deists believe that humans experience the spiritual dimension of Nature. God, as Spirit, both transcends Creation and is immanent in Creation (which is not the same as *being* Creation) as its active Creator. Humans have that spiritual spark that ignites spiritual growth in those who willingly pursue that growth.

Humans perceive life as an amalgam of what many call blessings and curses. If God is good, the curse aspect of life, the kill to eat or be eaten animality, for instance, often becomes problematic. Centuries of great minds have concluded: Can we humans know what good is without experiencing both good and its absence? In this world, at least, evidently not. Whatever the reason, it appears that we're here to learn the difference, to see the contrast, to experience the profound consequence of the absence of the good and of the ultimate good that (in this life, at least) is life itself.

Can we appreciate life without the perpetual possibility of our own demise, or the extinction of all life? Again, in this world, at least, evidently not. I've seen people freak out contemplating their ceasing to exist, or more weird, their never having existed. There's a reason why our desire to live is so intense. All animals share this instinct for life. But whereas other animals want to live, we humans want to live forever. We are programmed to want, to deeply need, to live perpetually. For us humans, we also need quality of life—a good life. Suicide is an indication that the need for the *good* in life is for us humans more profound than the need for life itself deprived of that good.

We are here to freely, by choice, engage in a process of understanding and transcending—evolving, not in a Darwinian sense of morphing into another species type, but in the spiritual sense of growing into the highest version of ourselves. It's interesting, isn't it, that both religionists and Darwinians passionately assert the necessity of change, growth, evolution, transformation. Call it what you will, the deep intuitive, instinctual drive to transcend is inherent in us all, whether we choose to follow the call to transcendence or not.

Why would a good God cause, or even allow, good people to suffer?

Why assume that the good should not suffer, that allowing the good to suffer is a breach of justice, if not downright evil? You could argue that good people don't allow suffering, therefore why would God, who is presumably more good than we are. But good people do allow suffering. Parents allow their dependent children to suffer through the process of becoming independent. A teacher allows her student to suffer when he fails to turn in homework and receives an F and is turned down for college admission or scholarships. A doctor's patients suffer during and after the surgeries that save their lives.

Yes. But why do the innocent suffer? Of course, I don't know the answer. How could I? But I can guess, and my guess is a rational consensus of all my innate faculties: The good and the innocent suffer for two reasons. One is that a person is truly free only when he has the option to choose evil by victimizing the good and the innocent. The other is that we must see the consequences of harm, whether it be harm freely chosen or just seemingly random harm. This world wasn't meant to be the Hotel Paradise where your only purpose is to sit around the pool eating bonbons. Your task is (among other things) to do good, *in spite of*: Good tested proves to be ultimately good when it is painfully good *in spite of.*

All suffering ends, even if it ends in death—and why assume that death is a bad thing? It isn't a bad thing if some form of life—really, some form of our individual self as a person—continues after our material demise. Being comfortable with one's self simply dissolving into material dust is, in my view, a suicidal tendency that perhaps warrants professional psychological intervention. Most of us, though, want to survive our material demise. We accept the spirit/body dichotomy and are willing to let go of the body if our *self* can continue. I don't believe this is just wishful thinking or a purely animal instinct for physical survival. As a Deist who believes that purposive existence naturally extends beyond the material universe, my view is that our intense desire for the continuance of our self-as-person suggests that God is a Self-as-Person, though the form of that Person-Self is different than our own. We can't possibly know much about that Divine form; all we can surmise from our finite-temporal vantage is that such a "higher" Person-Self exists. We call our person-self spirit; God's Person-Self is Spirit, the originating Spirit of all spirits.

THE GOOD AND FREE WILL

But why suffer at all? Deists don't believe that we're here to be punished. I don't know why animals suffer. But the Deist answer for human suffering begins with the limitations of human knowledge and value judgments about something as monumental and inscrutable as Creation; it leads to the necessity of both good and evil for the true exercise of free will; it ends with the free, conscious transcending of spirit beyond the animal and the material as we experience them in this life. Freeing the spirit involves freeing the soul. I view soul as the immanent, "in-nature" experience of transcendent (be-ing), or perhaps transcending (coming to be), spirit.

For us Deists, liberty in this life is a moral imperative. Freedom is right for its own sake. And for free will to be truly free to do and to be good, it must be free to do and to be good *in spite of*—in spite of all obstacles to and all obstructions of that freedom.

Some argue that free will and the charge of liberty naively put humanity at the center of the cosmos, and we have evolved beyond that belief.

But really, have we? Even Galileo, telescope in hand, inquisitors at his back, believed that humanity will always stand at the center of the cosmos as experienced by humanity. We can't know much if anything about the experiences of other living creatures. We infer that most fear, suffer, procreate, enjoy a good meal. They, too, want to live and to be free of suffering. But what we truly know, we know as humans.

Many great souls have intuited that we are not here to just hang out with friends sipping martinis. We have a job to do. Within Creation, souls are fashioned, the self is manifested, and impossible though it seems, each of us is responsible for the final product that we ourselves co-design. We are accountable for what we are becoming. God has vested us with this godlike power. In this and (it seems) in only this way we are created in the image of God. Of course, comparing ourselves, who create with pre-created materials, with God, who creates everything from nothing, might seem a bit absurd. Still, at the lowly human level, we have the God-given, godlike free will to participate in our own creation. This right, this responsibility, is mindboggling. Yet I think it's fair to suggest that the vast majority of humans take this gift completely for granted. Ingratitude plus lack of insight equals our classic tragic flaw: hubris.

THE FUNCTION OF FREE WILL

Humans are free to *not* choose preprogrammed options and to create bizarrely unexpected new options. Humans seek deep truth, as demonstrated by sleuthing scientists, probing poets, and fretting philosophers. Humans engage in exploration for its own sake; machines can't and animals aren't interested in investigation beyond the exploitable given. Machines and animals exist on the plane of predictable bits and beeps, and so, to some extent, does the human animal, with its herd mobs and manias. But humans want to penetrate beyond the absolute depths of the given, which is one reason we relish creativity, intellectual prowess, and passion, and the primary reason we engender religion. Our emotional fervor corresponds to our sensation of freedom; whether we are actually free or not doesn't negate the point of sensate response to freedom. Nations are toppled with great sacrifice of human blood for the sake of freedom. Our inherent conscience registers the protection of our own freedom and the freedom of others as a moral imperative; slavery and exploitation are *just known* to be morally reprehensive, even evil. Humans have created a huge library of symbols representing protectors and destroyers of freedom. Humans revere the Programmer of freedom. Humans seek spiritual union with that Creator who creates our freedom to create. Humans seek freedom from that ultimate shackle: Death.

Yes, we "just know" we are free.

Yes, we "just know." We can demonstrate that 135+140=275. Information could make a human, an animal, or a machine mimic or even compute the right (or wrong) answer. But really knowing, really *understanding* the informational answer, transcends just *registering* the informational answer. Only humans can understand *Hamlet* or a Bach fugue. Human reason is entwined with other faculties, including intuition, conscience, aesthetic sensibility, and spirit. Spirit is that faculty that transcends and enlivens all the others. Spirit correlates with the Programmer, the true Creator. The core essence explicated through fundamental freedom, spirit registers understanding, meaning, purpose, and essential being that transcends material manifestation.

Darwinians fail to grasp that spirit is a *material* necessity. Without God-spirit, even the material could not materialize. The material is necessarily *programmed*. Spirit corresponds with programmer which correlates with meaning. Programmers code in order for the code to mean something. Code is meaning, represented via symbols, the code. The material manifestation of you represents your essence, your spiritual meaning. Perhaps your spirit partially preexists at conception and takes further shape as your live your material life, like a thought somewhat formed takes shape in the expressing of it in words.

Reason and other faculties transport—translate—information into meaning, the realm of highest spiritual *understanding*, in the sense that every faculty engages in its own form of "thinking" for the purpose of understanding. When it's working properly, every faculty, not just reason, in its own way thinks, realizes, and understands.

Although it appears to some that the mechanical universe is a meaningless machine, in truth the machine, like a computer, is the not-aware vehicle of its own transcendent meaningful message. But only humans can know this. Only humans are created in the image of the self-aware Programmer. Only meta-aware consciousness is aware that it's aware. Human *understanding* programs computers and builds the internet. Humans tinker with symbols. Poets create religion. Only creators both transcend and are immanent in creation.

What amazes me is that there are scientists who "just know" that the material is necessarily programmed who nonetheless deny this. Where I come from, that's called "lying."

Meaning embodies information; mind embodies brain; spirit embodies flesh. This is ancient, universal wisdom. And yes, wisdom places humans once again at the center of existence as we know it. With meaning as pinnacle and core of all that is uniquely human, wisdom embraces its awesome responsibility as protector of the Program. Hence, Deism.

As humans, we have the amazing capacity to understand. Even more remarkably, we have the freedom to understand or to not understand. Some fundamentalists don't believe in free will—predestined Calvinists, for instance, or determinists like Rev. Fred Phelps, who yells at gays through his megaphone, "God doesn't hate you because you're homosexual. You're homosexual because God hates you." Personally, I have never doubted my own free will or the free will of other humans. I feel sorry for people who do. Not every aspect of our being or our life is free, of course. Nobody asserts that. The question is whether humans are free at all, ever. The answer is—and you know this is true—*Yes!*

I can almost hear some stuffy Darwinian materialist sniffling that nobody is free. He wants us all to be as conflicted and miserable as he is. The Grand Scheme of the Universe, he snaps, and the smaller and smaller systems contained within it are so entwined and codependent that a sneeze in Alaska caused the hurricane in Florida on the day you chose to arrive there for vacation. Your choice to cancel your flight was not your choice at all. Even your choice to vacation in Florida was caused by your need for relaxation and your usual goose-stepping, in this case into a Disney/tropical paradise meme constructed by habits mimicking the habits of others whose "choice," like yours, was determined by advertising, fond childhood vacation memories, pressure from the kids, and a host of other forces and temptations. Cause and effect. You aren't choosing at all. It's called the butterfly effect. Get used to it. Thus saith the scientist.

Animals are "free" too, the shuffling, snuff-snorting scientist sneezes, if by free you mean that given the choice between banana A and banana B, both appearing equal, the chimp will "choose" one rather than the other. But that's just the random "freedom" of a coin toss, he sneers, and remember, you're just a chimp in a chair.

Even perfect Newtonian mechanical deterministic mindless material processes have the "freedom" to randomly "pick" heads or tails when the "choices" are equal and don't matter. Of course, all matter matters. So really it was some atom on Mars farting (tails won the coin toss) that caused the sneeze in Alaska that caused the hurricane in Florida that caused you to choose to cancel your flight to paradise. Ah, but what if you had three equal choices, not just this or that, not just yes or no?

What if you could get creative?

Even some neo-Darwinians realize that determinism that factors chance into the equation opens Pandora's Box of erasers and chalks of different colors. Physicists and mathematicians have recently proved that potentiality exists as an aspect of material existence. Potentiality trumps determinism. Determinism that is not absolutely deterministic is not determinism.

Yep, you're not a machine, and I don't think I've taken a huge leap here to state this as a valid claim. Well, you *are*, if you want to get technical. But you're a machine embodied with spirit, a machine with free will. You're not *just* a machine.

And that zombie demon, Richard Dawkins' so-called "selfish gene" that survives generation after generation possessing host after passive host just to replicate itself exponentially forever like a circus clown in a funhouse of mirrors, like a serial rapist?

Exorcised by the power of common sense.

And what is common sense?

If you have to ask, you will probably never know (or won't admit you know).

CONSISTENCY, COMMON SENSE, AND SPIRITUAL FREEDOM

All your eloquent faculties work amazingly well at communicating to you the truth of you and your world because they are *designed* to work well, individually and in concert. Common sense tells us humans that it would be mathematically impossible for all our elaborately interconnected faculties to come into existence fully functioning through random chance, as today's Darwinians assert.

But information is more than bits and beeps. Information contains meaning, value, and purpose, and we're the only creature to know this. We're self-aware machines, self-conscious animals. We humans and only we humans. You *know* this.

You are *self*-aware, and both self and awareness necessitate composite integration of your parts. All the faculties that make you a self and that make your discrete self aware are in agreement. If one of your faculties disagrees with the rest about any truth claim, you can no longer honestly trust the validity of that particular truth. I say "honestly," because often people bow to contradictions promoted by outside authority even when that authority's claims rub against innate common sense.

One thing you realize, perhaps without realizing that you realize it, is that truth is consistent. 2+2=4 is perpetually true for everyone. The force of gravity operates exactly the same way everywhere in the universe. There's a lot of comfort in knowing that the fundamental *you* are the same you that you were at your conception and will be at your death. Science has recently confirmed that the genetic message cannot be altered by information coming from events outside it. Evidently, whoever is designing the universe is eager to—perhaps even must (for the sake of honest truth)—maintain natural consistency among both discrete existences and their collective functions.

(Might there be a reason why you were constructed to *know* this? Clearly, God is communicating with you. Why is it that scientists who have all the technological advantages for hearing seem to be the last to hear?)

But within the consistent structure of the universe that we register as the laws of nature, there's a lot of wiggle room. The chimp can pick banana A or banana B, but that's not a lot of choice. The wiggle room is much bigger.

How big? And how do we know?

Our inherent common sense "just knows" we often have free will to choose from among many different choices. Recently, scientists have surmised this ancient truth, announcing it as a new scientific discovery.

They have puzzled out conclusions of non-determinism based on several key concepts centered on randomness. Chaos theory is its latest baby. The trajectory includes Gödel's incompleteness, Heisenberg's uncertainty, Turing's uncomputability, Shannon and Weaver's entropy as disorder, Chaitin's randomness and chaos, and now we're in the throes of the information theory revolution, which has led to a fattening smorgasbord of random chatter breeding a dearth of trifling tattle scattering over airwaves like weed seeds settling on neighborhood lawns.

The Big Conclusion? The universe is a cosmic computer existing as information in a perpetual flux of processing. Ancient concept, updated analogy: an old meme in a new shirt.

But unlike the heap of junk information churned out by humans, the natural universe only produces informational riches. Comparing the two, humans should be humbled.

MIT scientist Seth Lloyd calculates that given "every degree of freedom [his word] of every particle," the universe has already performed maybe 10^{120} "ops" and holds maybe 10^{90} bits of info. Not only is the universe humongous, so is its elegance.

Recent scientific discoveries simply restate ancient wisdom: The universe is elegantly structured; the laws of nature embody the essence of its consistency; within "absolute" structure is immeasurable potential: The pool contains water in which I can play.

No human genius programmer could accomplish such feats of computer wizardry even on a small scale. Human programmers simply cherry-pick from among the awesome array of the universe's predesigned, prepackaged hardware and software at their disposal. In other words, they learn. Personally, I think that if scientists would factor in the obvious reality of a Creator, they could do the math a lot quicker.

Like the rest of us, scientists learn by playing as they learn *to* play. Human creativity is a free play of imagination within consistent structure. Life is a sonnet, fourteen lines in rhymed iambic pentameter with a particular sequencing, but the choice of content is practically infinite.

Some scientists point out that individuals, human or otherwise, are temporal but that the animal form, human or otherwise, continues on due to perennial replication of the form's genetic information. Therefore, eat, drink, and be merry, because tomorrow you and every other poor sucker will be sucked down the cosmic Memory Hole.

In fact, do whatever you want. Determinist-Darwinist atheism justifies exploitation of expendable human beings, animals, and other living things. Don't worry; the form *Bos taurus* continues on no matter how many steaks you grill, no matter how you fatten and butcher the cows. The human form continues on no matter how many people you enslave, no matter how many children you molest, no matter how many throats you slit. Life continues on no matter how many pesticides you dump on the land, no matter how much water you slick with oil, no matter how many "foods" you lace with carcinogens.

Determinist-Darwinist atheists don't answer to any god but their own genetic propensity to survive well. Every lie, every selfish gesture, every act of violence is justifiable in the name of conquest, because nothing ultimately matters but the eternal life of the gene. Survive, spawn: That's the meaning of life as spawned by Darwin.

Therefore, why should atheist scientists themselves be above lying? All scientists, including Richard Dawkins, agree that a fact is a theory that is supported by all the evidence. After centuries of artificial breeding and lab experiments, nobody has ever observed type-jumping speciation through variation and selection. Not a single type has been demonstrated to have evolved according to Darwin's theory that all species evolved from a single ancestor via smooth transitional variation and selection, random or otherwise. Dawkins lies when he asserts that "the sheer weight of evidence, totally and utterly, sledgehammeringly, overwhelmingly strongly supports the conclusion that evolution is true." He not only means that "a tiny bacterium who lived in the sea was the ancestor of us all," but also that "macroevolution is nothing more than microevolution stretched out over a much greater time span." Even though he's been proven to be totally and utterly, sledgehammeringly, overwhelmingly wrong, Dawkins perpetuates the meme of natural selection in order to "kill religion." He said so himself. He is as guilty of lying as the dishonest fundamentalism he wants to destroy.

X-God hit men can be stubborn. But why? Absolute skeptic David Hume, who hanged epistemology in a tangled noose of impossible causation back in the sixteenth century, admitted that "since reason is incapable of dispelling these [philosophical] clouds, nature herself suffices to that purpose, and cures me of this philosophical melancholy and delirium...and when after three or four hours' amusement, I wou'd return to these speculations, they appear so cold, and strain'd, and ridiculous, that

I cannot find in my heart to enter into them any farther." Yet enter he always would.

Is the perennial entering anyway of atheistic philosopher and scientist the bravado of the intellectual sportsman or a symptom of psychosis? What irrational rationale drives a person ostensibly pursuing truth to shun obvious truth in order to—what? Enter an Inferno of absolute meaninglessness, absolute hopelessness with no Virgil or Beatrice to guide toward some sensible light? "Abandon hope, all ye who enter here."

("But here let poetry rise again from the dead.")

Rather than accept the Darwinian, Dawkins-ian view of a selfish, parasitic gene-machine ruthlessly cloning itself via stupid, worthless human hosts, most of us prefer to interpret the latest data as proof of a benevolent Creator who has built hopeful, meaningful choice into the universe for the benefit of our built-in free will.

Fundamentalists who subdue their wills and sacrifice their "natural man" and humble themselves into passive, submissive, unthinking puppets think they're honoring the God who blessed them with free will, the ultimate gesture of love. When they "crucify" their natural humanity, when they return unopened the gift of themselves that God has given them, aren't they in essence spitting in God's face? It's cause-and-effect that people who forfeit their free will are most easily deluded by predators.

Spiritual freedom is transgressed when common sense is not consulted. Consulting or not consulting common sense is a choice. Rubberstamp Darwinians and cookie-cutter Christians alike choose to contradict their own innate common sense.

Not just a truth but truth itself must be chosen. A truth is a fact, a bit of information. Truth is the higher field of reality in which a truth is true and known to be true. Plato called this realm abstract Ideas, or Ideals. Aristotle considered Ideals to be simply generalizations of concrete things. Truth was something else. No philosopher, no Plato or Kant or Berkeley or Russell, could describe or define truth itself in terms that didn't include the concrete examples. They all failed. Ironically, we all know what this truth is, just like, as Augustine noted, we can't really describe or define time but we know what it is. We know thanks to our common sense. And this commonsense knowing is part of our consistent nature that makes it possible for us to maintain the integrity of our freedom. Our common sense and our freedom are aspects of our nature, which are part of Nature.

Common sense and freedom are qualities that make us *not* automatons. They are transcendental features that make us more than matter, more than animal. They are human aspects that are simultaneously immanent and transcendent. What those dusty philosophers half-intuited and poets knew quite well was that humans are standing with one foot in this world and the other foot in another, the world of before- and afterlife that temporarily infuses this world like a taste of John Lennon's Strawberry Fields Forever. We know this because we know how to know—know how to know both directly and indirectly, concretely and abstractly, literally and metaphorically—though how we know how to know we don't know.

What can we know? Some truth is self-evident, like 2+2=4; this is evident at all because existence has been structured in such a way that 2+2 does =4 and because our minds have been structured to register this fact. Truth is a *creation* that we apprehend. We can apprehend truth because it is consistently what it is.

Obvious truth is registered almost instantaneously with little effort. But some truth must be learned. Learning involves absorption, interpretation, and revision. Learning requires the interaction with other humans that makes us consciously aware and self-aware. Most learning requires willful engagement.

We all know (but sometimes forget) that the process of adding new information often requires unlearning, or correction. It once made sense that the world was flat, but new information changed our vision of our world and its place in the cosmos. We took a quantum leap forward into a higher version of ourselves, our epiphany causing a major paradigm shift in consciousness. Even "small" personal leaps can be as earth-shattering for the individual as the Copernican worldview has been for our species. Whether personal or collective, these shifts define our growth as humans.

We evolve (i.e., microevolve) via natural revelations in much the same way that species evolve—by intelligent design and direction. Higher and higher dimensions of truth always add sophistication and clarity, which are aspects of intelligent design being manifested to intelligent minds. It's absurd to assert that consistent, sophisticated truth and the elegant functions of mind capable of apprehending that truth could possibly have arisen by chance via mindless, accidental forces of nature.

As amazing as it is that humans can *know*, we thoughtlessly take that ability for granted. Concentrated awareness is the prerequisite for knowledge, but we often passively sabotage our own consciousness with monotonous jobs, trivial TV shows, and repetitive activities like computer games, shopping, or idle chatter. Some sacrifice consciousness to an imposing meme, like Darwinism or fundamentalism.

Often consciousness is sabotaged by propaganda or violence. All willful destruction of consciousness involves dissolution of the Self for the purpose of exploitation. Free will is the power to make choices that equip us to resist, but it is also that faculty that chooses to exploit. Darwinian "survival of the fittest" and fundamentalist "it's God's will" justify and sanctify exploitation with equal vehemence. Concentrated awareness and critical thinking lead to the active participation in one's own evolution, personal and collective, which builds up the resilience to survive exploitation and to establish a humanist society that benefits all.

How the universe and life and humans came to be remains a mystery. Darwinism has failed to provide new answers to validate the atheists. Once again it appears that evolution only occurs *within* an organism type; thus far, there is no evidence that Darwinian evolution ever creates new types or orders. Of course, the connectedness among the remarkable diversity of living beings—and for that matter, non-living—leads us to suspect that some kind of evolution is taking place. We know that biologically, evolution is almost always adaptation triggered by environmental cues; non-living things, too, are altered by their environment because that's the way the universe is constructed. The organism can adapt because the means of adaptation is built-in, meaning it comes equipped with the information needed to change in a specific way. But how a completely new life-form type comes into being is as yet far beyond our ken. Even saying that a new species variety comes about due to adaptation or any other means of change doesn't really explain how or why those processes, those changes, would work. Zeno's paradox can never cease applying to biology as well as geometry. Scientists will never find the smallest indivisible unit of life or space. Yet life exists; the arrow hits the target. That's the miracle. Not just first cause but cause itself, which exists in a realm beyond human comprehension, services proof of God and intelligent design.

The Tinkering Watchmaker Winds a New Watch

Existence perpetually increases. New things are perpetually created. Newness emerges within preexisting systems. New attributes are added to organisms that already exist; the new emerges out of pre-given potential latent in the organism's molecular DNA/RNA structure. This is perfectly natural. Even so, there is a massive amount of addition during any adaptive moment. Addition is that impossible "going beyond" that only the reality of an active—I would go so far as to say *immanent*—Creator can explain. Not an absent Watchmaker who left the universe to tick on its own, the Watchmaker God perpetually tinkers at his workbench.

The Creator not only creates; the Creator perpetually creates, meaning perpetually creates newness. Addition is creation itself. Every split nanosecond a unique human or animal child is conceived out of the vast wealth of its inherited genetic raw materials. Every split nanosecond there's an almost infinite splurge of unique newborn—*something*s. And all those somethings exist within consistent form, so we can feel safe while we're being dazzled. Already the largest of four families of orchids consists of about 1,000 genre and 20,000 species of absolutely unique discrete orchids. (I can see three awesomely perfect orchids right now from the corner of my eye.)

Something can't come from nothing. So-called natural selection would prune away information to make a change. It would never add to, because a thing that exists can't create something beyond (greater than) what it is. A computer can't generate a human; a poem can't create a poet. But God can program human DNA with immense potentiality to create new details of itself within the parameters of *human*.

A new form must be an addition, a something from nothing that signals true transcending creation. A new order of species is an entirely new computer built and loaded up by a transcending geek. Even a new variety of species. Even a new version of a particular instance of a specific species at a specific moment contains that addition of something from nothing. The process of Creation, including the wiggle rooms where chance and freedom can occur, is the work-in-progress of an immanent transcendent Other.

The fundamental point deduced from recent genetics is that new information can't just "emerge" from lesser information. Truly *new* information must be pre-planted by a means or mechanism that transcends the previous information package. The process of increase, including the laws of nature that direct the increase, must be derived from a source that is greater than the process itself or the thing increasing.

We do evolve, but only within the parameters of the given—pre-given and being-given. There are latent potentials within all living things, but those potentials are latent in the sense of being present but not yet called upon. We evolve by calling up inner pre-given resources, inner pre-given information—installed software we haven't before used. Being used is a process being able to be used activated in the moment by the activating presence of God: Immanence

Plants and animals respond to needs created by the environment. Humans also respond to those needs. But humans also respond to needs and possibilities that far transcend material environmental cues. As an act of will, we humans probe deeply into the myriad types of possibilities that are latent within us. Humans search for meaning, truth, divine connection—profound interactions with the depths of soul and spirit. We search our own DNA even as we stretch for the farthest reaches of the cosmos. We search not just with our hands or eyes, but with imaginations and hearts spurred by our souls and spirits. Humans strive to create the new in order to enter the creative life-force inherent in all things, even things inanimate. The universe is infused with information. Existence overflows with the gift of tangible, not-yet-awakened possibilities. And then—awakened. Existence *is*, meaningful and purposeful.

It is in *being* that we evolve. But haven't we always known this? The universe fine-tuned for life; life fine-tuned for human life; human life fine-tuned for human understanding; human understanding fine-tuned to anticipate afterlife: Even atheist scientists admit that each fact statement is an *interpretation* of data, data fine-tuned for interpretative understanding. Life doesn't disprove God; life doesn't prove random chance mutation driven by natural selection. Aristotle claimed that knowledge—the "wisdom of the wisest of the wise"—gives the liveliest pleasure. Nature's pleasure principle—pleasure as cause—steers the purposive, directed, eschatological drive toward self-transcendence that is human evolution.

A paradigm shifts to a heliocentric solar system, to intelligent design, to Deism. We *become* as we probe, as we create, as we contemplate existence and its possibilities, as we appreciate the exquisite beauty of each unique hexagonal ice crystal, commonly known as a snowflake, while someone we love pins a florists' orchid to our lapel.

PART III

SLOUCHING TOWARDS DEISM

THE SECOND COMING

Turning and turning in the widening gyre
The falcon cannot hear the falconer;
Things fall apart; the center cannot hold;
Mere anarchy is loosed upon the world,
The blood-dimmed tide is loosed, and everywhere
The ceremony of innocence is drowned;
The best lack all conviction, while the worst
Are full of passionate intensity.

Surely some revelation is at hand;
Surely the Second Coming is at hand.
The Second Coming! Hardly are those words out
When a vast image out of Spiritus Mundi
Troubles my sight: somewhere in sands of the desert
A shape with lion body and the head of a man,
A gaze blank and pitiless as the sun,
Is moving its slow thighs, while all about it
Reel shadows of the indignant desert birds.
The darkness drops again; but now I know
That twenty centuries of stony sleep
Were vexed to nightmare by a rocking cradle,
And what rough beast, its hour come round at last,
Slouches towards Bethlehem to be born?

—William Butler Yeats, 1921

CHAPTER 9

HOGTIED

Turning and turning in the widening gyre
The falcon cannot hear the falconer...

"The devil made me do it," the world's second most perennial excuse for bad behavior (first being "I wanted to"), could be truer than the perpetrator suspects. A classic character in literature—usually antagonist, sometimes protagonist (as in *Paradise Lost*)—the devil represents human evil we fear in others and in ourselves. For people who accept religious literature as literal fact, the devil also serves as a projection. In the minds of naïve fundamentalists like your cousin's wife and the guy at work, the devil really does make them do it—*it* being whatever they want to believe (or want you to believe) they couldn't possibly do on their own.

Whether a representation or a projection, the devil is symbolic; yet even though the symbol always stands for evil, it can embody opposite *meanings*. The fundamentalist's "literal" devil often symbolizes the *absence of choice*; demonic possession negates freedom, responsibility, and inadvertently the God that designed humans with built-in free will as a given; needless to say, it demotes the human to a groveling moral wimp or predestined prey mesmerized by the almighty tempter, which gives the devil power to deposit both victimizer and victim in the same account, a devaluing, anti-humanist position closer to random-chance neo-Darwinism than to intelligently designed Creation.

The literary devil, on the other hand, symbolizes the *choice* of evil; the symbol functions as a warning that affirms human decision and personal accountability that God-given free will commands. Ironically, the literary devil of Deists and other humanists, not the literal devil of fundamentalists, facilitates contemplation of the spiritual *reality* of evil.

People like your cousin's wife and the guy at work tend to glare suspiciously at literature, if not all the arts and humanities, swayed no doubt by prominent evangelists like Pat Robertson and Jerry Falwell, who a few years ago ranted against the demonism of fantasies like *Harry Potter* and *The Lord of the Rings*—an interesting detour from the evils of Harlequin romance *Playboy* sex and other immoralities. Like the devil himself, prominent evangelists, inspired by the high priests of antiquity, insist on controlling the initiate's grasp of the dark arts. As always, religion presents spiritual evil as a spirit-incarnate not-human devil packaged as historical fact. Literature, though, assumes that spiritual evil is spiritual and evil and *human*, and its devil is a *representation* of human spiritual evil. By spiritual I don't mean otherworldly; I mean evil emanating from the individual's core spiritual essence, the Self. Religion assumes that there is a separate evil spiritual presence in the world not only tempting a human spirit to the dark side, but also possessing the spirit and controlling human destiny. To be fair, given the amount of wickedness in the world and the degree of its sophistication, it is reasonable to wonder whether pure evil as it actually exists, from atrocious butchery of a solo psychopath like Ed Gein (who ate people he didn't make into furniture) to the collective carnage of fascists, could possibly *not* be demonic.

The high priests of organized religion, who assume they must wield authority over a demonic archenemy to stay in business, have always erred on the side of the literal devil, unwittingly granting *projected* evil, real or fictional, more clout than it deserves. Religion even names its cloven-hoofed fiends and sometimes invests them with power equal to God's. The biblical Satan, for instance, made regular visits to heaven and tricked God into inflicting evil upon Job. And Jesus is portrayed as exorcising demons from the possessed when he isn't telling the tempter Satan to "get behind" him. The devil symbol becomes particularly convoluted when Jesus "makes" Satan possess Judas when he gives Judas the bread dipped in wine at the Last Supper, which gives Satan the green light to drive Judas to betray Jesus, by which Satan assumes superior strength by enabling Jesus' suicidal crucifixion for a purpose that, as many have shown (myself included, in *Born-Again Deist*), makes no sense. How would psychology interpret this biblical scene? Pretty much every religion except Deism includes in its repertoire a pantheon of demons. Deism asks directly (as literature asks indirectly) how the world might benefit if religion set aside its devil myths and superstitions and instead assigned responsibility for the evils of the world to their actual perpetrators.

Even when they know better, high priests, including religious scholars, refuse to relinquish their faith in demons. The devil slayers scoffed when Darwin's ape traded confession for psychoanalysis, which rendered Satan and his cohorts impotent and absurd. They gasped aloud when Carl Jung documented that the *shadow*, another version of the dark side, isn't necessarily evil, being simply a repressed content of the Self, appearing a bit darker when wearing a scary mask in nightmares, or in broad daylight acting out in tactless garb to grab the collar of consciousness. The Church is still sparring with the shadow, especially its own.

The shadow wants to tell the truth of itself, of its Self; the shadow wants to exit the dark and enter the light; it wants transformation. Though society has learned to differentiate motives of pure psychopathic evil from shadow neurosis and psychosis, popular culture still often paints evil as a devil figure. Unlike a Texas chainsaw psychopath or a maniacal Joker— evildoers who destroy the outward person—the devil *possesses* the person within, whether via a classic demonic spirit or an alien force or a Voodoo spell. The devil that possesses in essence becomes the person, becomes you: The devil makes *you* do it; you *are* the devil doing it. This is a representation, of course, but it exposes the shadow's truth: Your own evil projected outward onto the devil is projected back into you via possession. Wouldn't therapy be easier? Or even confession? Literature, even pop-lit, performs those functions in mainstream culture.

Literature wants to expose repressed evil whitewashed as projecting-religion—religion that projects its own evil onto others. Instead of healing our ailing soul—specifically, the moral faculty—religion further sickens us into spiritual schizophrenia: our own good side vs. our own bad side projected as us vs. them, them being gays, feminazis, Muslims, liberals— anyone excluded from the religious in-group. Meanwhile, the Church tries to reconcile its promotion of devil fear plus special role as exorcist with the biblical "Love casts out all fear"; in text, that's your love, not the Church's, but the Church has deemed all "real" love under its jurisdiction: In effect, religion has (in more senses than one) *possessed* love. Luckily, mainstream culture is in the repo business.

Evil, really, is superlative harm, but "harm" is too tame a term in a culture that consumes more drama than popcorn. We grown-up children like our antagonists demon-possessed. Even scarier than the murderer outside your window is the invisible, omniscient presence of evil chasing and attacking you *inside*, the evil that drags you to hell. Yes, we often represent that evil in bodily form, often a human already possessed, so the audience can *see* the spirit in the zombie-like, emotionless, soulless not-quite-person with an axe. For a moment we suspend our disbelief and think we fear evil spirits, but what really scares us witless is the relentless psychopathic stalker so cold, so intent on devouring the soul of us that there's nothing human about that human: We fear this spiritual evil in ourselves, we fear it in others as representatives of us collectively. The worst case scenario is everyone possessed except you and you being pursued by them. The most horrific monsters signify the terrifying presence of a quasi-human being devoid of even the semblance of anything humane: the devil: the deranged psychopath completely out of control yet utterly in control of our fate. Even in the real world outside the theatre, our deepest fear is of monstrous out-of-control control: slasher, child molester, rapist, Ponzi scheme accountant, public servant dutifully pushing the red button that blows up the world.

Culture likes to scream. Psychologically, this makes sense. Drama helps us *feel* when we recognize our true self in the mirror, be it victimizer or victim or the potential for either. Fear serves as a spiritual siren; fear spurs us to fix ourselves and our world. Empathy calls us to share in the feelings of others; empathy orchestrates the intimate oneness of humanity. In Aristotle's dramatic schema, fear plus pathos equals catharsis. At the very least it must be healthy to feel the safety in numbers. True fear isolates the one from everyone else but the predatory devil. The devil is the spiritual predator—the *human* predator. The worst in us is the devil—and by worst I mean most harmful.

The human drama and the literary drama of books, plays, and movies inform one another. When we write or view literary drama, we're examining ourselves under an aesthetic microscope. Because the aesthetic peers down to the core of our being, the lens is also spiritual.

But we can also use literary tools and techniques to analyze our actual lives. If you are the protagonist of your life story, who or what is your antagonist? I don't really think that any individual who survives into childhood has only one antagonist. On the other hand, I do believe that all of us have one grand perennial antagonist: Ourselves. Collectively, humanity is its own perennial antagonist. As an individual, your perennial antagonist, the one that likely causes you the most trouble and heartache and fear, is you yourself. You are victimizer of you; you are the victim of you. This doesn't mean that you can't also be the victim of other people or circumstances; if you haven't been, you will be. But in all likelihood your grand perennial antagonist, the one that shapes you, the one that stays with you, the demon that *possesses* you, is you yourself—your weaknesses, your attitudes, your beliefs, your obsessive memories. The process of self-victimization, the condition of you beating yourself up, the habit of you picking open your scabs, even your propensity for projection, is your life drama, the story of your life that you yourself create. But only until the protagonist—also you—musters the guts to save the day. Cape and laser-shield optional.

It might seem odd to think that you are making yourself your own victim (and potentially later your own savior), especially given the gift of psychopaths to victimize us—though really, they're just as adept in exploiting our proclivity for self-victimization. The truth is that the devil that made you do it is one of your own faculties taking the steering wheel and driving the rest of your faculties (including the body, which I consider a faculty) over a cliff. You pig out on potato chips that make you fat while your mind yells *No!* and your conscience weeps and your arteries collapse. Collectively, the rich one percent pigs out on the fat of the land while the rest of us weep and the economy collapses and society cries out for help from under the weight of irrational injustice. The whole world is a neurotic mess.

We've all heard the ancient proverb that a house divided against itself cannot stand. If your faculties are not in harmony, if you are divided into competing fragments, the harm (evil) in you (your "evil spirit") will plot to dominate (possess) the rest of you. Ditto us collectively. A little leaven leavens the whole loaf. You can make yourself thoroughly self-harming (evil). You can even leaven—make that fatten—your family, your church, your nation, the whole world. And you can frighten yourself into a frenzy, a group into a mob, and the planet into nuclear pandemonium.

Of course, you could resist evil. When you do resist, what in you is resisting? You might think your will. But why do you *will* to be or do something? (Isn't it amazing how little we really know of ourselves? Hence literature.) Why does America *will* itself fatter than a fatted calf slaughtered on an ancient altar of sacrifice? Is our fat fetish some atavistic ritual? An archetype of self-destruction? Spiritual laziness? Only the shadow knows.

In my view, the faculty ultimately in charge, the director, the boss, is spirit. You've heard the saying, the spirit is willing but the flesh is weak. Usually we think flesh means body; traditionally "flesh" has included pretty much everything that isn't spirit, everything considered to be "of this world." Of course, there's never been a consensus about what aspects of us are of this world. Is mind the same as spirit, or part of the flesh, the brain, for instance? Opinions vary. It's complicated. But most of us do understand that good and evil, benefit and harm, are driven by the spirit. The spirit, our core Self, directs our other faculties, including conscience and will.

Although the boss, your spirit, ultimately calls the shots regarding who and what you are, like many bosses, your boss might be a bit incompetent; your boss might have over-delegated to the point that a particularly bossy employee has assumed the responsibilities of running the business while the real you, the Self, the exec with the fancy title and corporate name and big pay check, snoozes in the lounge.

The spirit ultimately chooses good or evil, even if it sometimes chooses to vacation while the bossy body or mind or will moves into the front office (though will is usually just the dutiful gofer that gets blamed for whatever goes wrong). Sin, crime, despotism, psychopathy all name the same *symptom*; the *cause* is evil spirit, or Self, asserting itself through free will.

If you're reading this book, you probably assume that your spirit isn't evil. But remember that evil simply means harmful. Pure evil, the ultimate harm, is predatory and devoid of conscience; the shadow, on the other hand, can commit atrocities even if the innermost spirit isn't purely evil. A psychopath is purely evil, as far as the experts can tell. A psychopath might not be committing evil deeds at every moment, but he is capable of doing so, and he is *incapable* of authentically doing good. How and why this is so, nobody knows. The important point here is that you are not a psychopath. (I'm assuming, given Dr. Hare's description of psychopathy, that a psychopath would not have read this far into this book.)

You in a moment of weakness are not purely evil, even though those potato chips might be evil enough to kill you. Evil is like trans fats: the more you indulge in evil, the more you saturate yourself with evil. The more capitalists exploit and then lie about their motives, the more exploitive and dishonest they become, and the easier it is then to take a few more steps into the underworld. The more you shoplift, the easier it becomes to steal cash from your grandmother. The more you lie to yourself about being gay, the more aggressively your repressed shadow lashes out to proclaim its truth. The shadow often projects its repressed content onto others, which is why many people suspect that aggressive homophobes like thou-protesteth-too-much "god hates fags" Fred Phelps and "man on dog" Rick Santorum might well be repressed homosexuals (or worse; then gay-bashing serves as a red herring).

Evil manifests itself as itself; evil is what evil does. We represent this understanding all the time in literature. In Marlowe's *The Tragical History of Doctor Faustus,* devils manifest Faustus' evil self, which Faustus creates as he conjures them, knowing full well he destroys his own morality the way, say, a rapist imagines, commits, enjoys, and cultivates the habit of rape. In the Bible, the devil enters Judas, which is to say that at a particular moment, Judas resolves to make some big bucks busting the hideout of the man claiming to be God's Chosen. (In the Matthew version of the story, Judas then returns the thirty pieces of silver and commits suicide; in the Acts account, he buys some property and basically explodes there. You are free to choose the moral of the story.)

Humans bind themselves with and to their choices; the evil addict themselves to themselves. The gofer-will, then, intoxicated and perverted, assumes the role of boss until it *is* the boss: the spirit is gobbled by the will; the two have become one. In the many incarnations of the Faust myth, Faust's will repeatedly summons his inner demon. Dr. Jekyll drug-conjures his Mr. Hyde. Dr. Frankenstein constructs a high-tech simulation of his arcane "wisdom."

Humanity's most tragic flaw transcends Greek fate and Elizabethan hubris. Literature is steeped with shadowy protagonists warning us via their grand gestures of spiritual suicide. Shakespeare's Macbeth is a classic case study of demonic will-to-tragedy. Victimizers are victims of their own tragically flawed free will. Not just human individuals but also humanity as a whole willfully shackles itself to its pacts with the devil. Nazism and the

Inquisition serve as a couple reminders.

Or we can lay our path on higher ground. The alternative, the subtext, the deep point of *Nineteen Eighty-Four* and *Macbeth* and *Frankenstein* and every version of the Faust tale and even the lighter *Pride and Prejudice* and a whole host of literary dramatic and narrative texts is simply "Choose the Good." Without the Good, the Greeks persuaded us, there is no choice; without choice there is no Good.

Surpassing antiquated *religious* literature promoting hierarchies of control and submission (i.e., relinquishment of will) by exploiting projection, the perennial *literary* bottom line endorses individual integrity and societal liberation: Heroes choose the better angels of themselves; antiheroes choose the devil.

The insight of the Renaissance was that tragedy equaled the free choice of evil. The nineteenth century, deflated by Darwin and "death of God," realized that the greater tragedy equaled eradication of choice, not by fate or the gods or even oneself, but by other evil humans and their institutions. With a nod to the Greeks, the tragedy of protagonist choosing evil was consigned to an inferior margin beneath the true tragedy of the victim. Even so, the devil was still human, not some cosmic "fate."

Victimizers—psychopaths, the vampires of vulture culture—still stand in the literary spotlight, cloaked though they might be. Society today still suffers from acute victimization, which perhaps explains why popular culture craves Hollywood endings, complete with superheroes restoring justice and "real life" TV cops nailing the bad guys. Literary art gives us a powerful voice through which we vicariously shout down (or gun down) the devil. Even when it teaches utopia by analyzing dystopia, or heaven-on-earth by scrutinizing hell, great literature is a moral instructor, teaching as it delights. Even Hollywood happily-ever-after gives us hope that love—the ultimate Good—will prevail.

Morally, we are all free to choose good or evil. We are not tainted in our DNA by sins committed in some mythic Eden, human life is not a tangled jungle of selfish genes. Sometimes evil deeds are reenactments of evil deeds inflicted upon the perpetrator. Evil can breed evil. But not all victims of child molestation become child molesters; rape and battery victims do not typically become rapists or batterers or otherwise bad people. Good people choose to *not* succumb to evil.

Accepting the reality of our own free will (really, spirit acting through will) in this age of absolute determinism is a spiritual feat in itself. We are indeed the product of our environment. We are to a very large extent at the mercy of the material make-up of existence, including our very material selves. But we aren't *just* material any more than a symphony is just notes. Within the constraints of the given, perhaps even because of those constraints, we have tremendous creative freedom, like a great poet working within a rigid sonnet form can produce a great sonnet whose connotations far transcend the flat denotations of individual words or the form's tight structure.

Unlike some Deists who privilege reason as the core human faculty, I think the will is at least as close to spirit as reason is. We can know truth but choose to not do or be truth. We can be unclear about the conscious, intellectual reasons why and how something is good and true and still choose to side with the good and true. Reason is important because it helps us know; will helps us do and be. Yes, knowledge is part of being. But will is responsible for doing, for enacting what one knows and thereby making us become and *be* a certain person. A person can know that diet and exercise are essential to good health, but knowing this doesn't miraculously change him into a person with a level of health derived only via diet and exercise. Macbeth knew that to murder would be to forfeit his soul. Jekyll knew the drug he took was converting him into Hyde. Faust knew his pact with Lucifer was a one-way ticket to hell. One must do to be, physically and morally.

Some people choose to commit evil acts, some choose to do good, some prefer to passively sway to and fro with every passing breeze. Each act reveals and creates the person himself, be that Ted Bundy, Gandhi, or Mr. and Mrs. Couch Potato.

HOG HEAVEN

The "devil" that made you do it is you yourself, or rather the inner devil that you yourself nurtured into existence. Devil and angel are both present within you as potentials. You choose to *be*; then to manifest your being, you choose to *do* good or evil. I don't mean "good," the manufactured mask of good; I mean authentic good.

In my view, the root of all evil, the essence of evil itself, is selfishness. In any spiritual tragedy, the devil selfishness stands center stage. I think of evil as the Unholy Trinity: Selfishness is the father, greed the son, and hubris the unholy spirit. This of course is a representation. So is Hog, the name I've given to the triune god of selfish evil. I prefer Hog, because the devil is fraught with horns and tails and other clichéd connotations I'd like to avoid. In the real world of Hog, Eve wasn't fashioned from the rib of Adam; Adam was carved from the rib of Hog.

Too often in the world today, Hog worshippers, or Hogs, as I call them, excuse their harmful behavior with some version of the devil made me do it, which casts the blame out into a demonic Legion of swine they can push off a cliff. Classic projection. A Hog should say, "Hog made me do it," which is to confess the truth that the selfish god of himself, created in his own image, is his own narcissistic snout in the mirror.

Hog is representation. But Hog represents a real Hog, real human evil, freely chosen. Hog makes the psychopath rape and murder. Hog makes the terrorist blow himself up for revenge and a heavenly harem of virgins. Hog makes your ego smile at your sexy smile in the photograph. Hog makes you fire loyal employees to profit rich stockholders. Hog makes you call your lies "just part of the game of politics." Hog makes you strip children in your imagination. Hog makes you laugh when your rivals get the punishment you deserve. Hog makes you a thief, a hypocrite, a drug dealer, a porn addict, a fake, a murderer, a hedge fund con artist, a mega-church TV prosperity-evangelist. Hog helps you justify, sanctify, and glorify Hog. Hog guides you to pray in the spirit of Hog.

God is good. Hog is sometimes evil, sometimes just not currently actively good. Always, though, Hog self-righteously claims to be good, even if just good at being evil. God is a moral God. Hog is at times immoral, at times amoral, at times beyond good and evil. God had and still has a reason for creating our universe. Hog, too, has his reasons: In the beginning Hog created the heavens and the earth to fall down and worship Hog. God infused existence with meaning that can be mined by humans. Hog infused existence with commodities like oil and diamonds and gold to be mined by Hog's slaves. In God's universe, all and every human life has a purpose. In Hog's universe, the meaning and purpose of life is Hog. God's motive is love. Hog's obsession is selfishness. God's essence is truth. Hog's obsession is selfishness.

What sin or crime isn't driven by Hog's obsessive snatching for himself something that doesn't belong to him? From pollution to plunder of nature's resources, from gang rape to tax breaks for the rich, from manipulative advertising to vicious imperialism, from misogyny to homophobia, from rudeness to ingratitude, from tyranny to fraud, from child molestation to nuclear holocaust, Hog stops at nothing to get what he wants.

Think of all the great literature focused on Hog stopping at nothing to get what he wants, or on a hero preventing some Hog from succeeding. Our very survival depends upon our rehashing these same significant themes.

Beware of Hog's masks, in life as in literature. The all-American selfish who target money (the biblical "mammon," or wealth) and everything money can buy—I call them mammonites—are just as rapacious as serial rapists and just as eager to excuse their goals. The most cleverly costumed mammonites attribute their selfishness to God's will: God wanted them to act selfishly, or they acted selfishly on their own to please and glorify God.

Really?

Hog, not God, wants you to be rich when people are starving. Oh wait—God wants everybody to be rich. Okay, but what are you doing to equalize the world's wealth, to make the poor not poor? Oh wait, make that God wants every *Christian* to be rich. Okay, what are you doing to make every Christian not poor. Oh wait—that's not your job; that's God's job. Which makes God just as Hoggish as you are. And just as boorish.

Listening to the wisest of the wise, the "goodest" of the good among us humans, one would think that God doesn't want us to be rich; God wants us to be *unselfish*. Every religion agrees that you cannot serve God and mammon. Oh wait—you don't really *serve* mammon; mammon serves you, and you are a child of God, God the creator of everything, including mammon, to which you are entitled as "the King's kid," to quote a few pop-Christian authors. Great; but the wisest and goodest don't agree with you. Go ahead and take your chance; believe you're special. Move ahead with your plans to amass wealth and to keep the better portion for yourself.

The wisest and goodest call that greed, call that selfishness. Hog calls that a luau. Hog wallows boldly in his pig-out. Hog gorges proudly, while priggish piglets prance preciously in the palace of Pretend.

Many of the wisest and goodest don't think that God wants anyone to be poor any more than she wants anyone to be rich. Many of those wise and good prophets believe that life just might be a test of your fiscal integrity. Are you benevolent? How benevolent? Just enough so you can classify yourself as benevolent for your own sake, to make it easier to sleep at night or to chalk up brownie points for the Judgment Day or to impress cronies and minions? Some of those wise, good teachers do think that poverty has a redemptive quality, but most only believe this because one doesn't have the ability to equalize world wealth and therefore one should place oneself on a par with the least wealthy, or at least the less wealthy. Middle class would probably be okay for most of the wise good ones.

Middle class piglets and upper class Hogs excuse their mammonism on the same need for security. Darwinist and fundamentalist alike fear being trampled like pearls cast before swine. Any Hog worth his salt would tear you to ham hocks, would flip you like pork chops on the barbeque. Fight Hog with Hog, you think. Fear of losing your hide forces you to hoard everything, including the hides of your competitors. You've been Hogtied against your will; you've become your fear. What else can you do? You've seen the light. You're a worshipper of Hog now, and Hog wants you to stay strong; the worker is worthy of his hire; it's the free gift of Hog and it would be rude to just rewrap the Christmas present and put it under somebody else's tree.

In Hog's little ears, "prosperity" is a word uttered sweetly. Even Jesus wants us to be rich. That's right: Jesus died for our sins. The poor are still poor because they're sinners. TV evangelists, however, have been saved and therefore are prosperous. Send them money, and you too can be prosperous. Think positive; think prosperous. Prosper in Spirit means prosper in pocketbook for the rich saved from original sin by the power of Hog's re-mix of Jesus.

Hog knows perfectly well that Jesus himself, real or myth, never preached prosperity. Hog represses that knowledge. "Prosperity gospel," a classic oxymoron, is Jesus perversion perpetuated by Hogtied mammonites who call themselves Christians. Some of them run for President: The so-called Religious Right is a self-righteous front for obscenely rich predatory capitalists. In the actual Gospel, Jesus proposes a divine purpose for poverty: a test for both the poor and the rich that to pass with an A requires unselfish giving. The Gospel, you'll recall, is love—love God first, your neighbor and yourself second. That's the Good News meaning of life in a nutshell, according to that nutty pauper, Jesus. "But but but…" the put-put mammonites stutter.

Let's just look at a few facts.

THE GOSPEL OF JESUS ACCORDING TO HOG

Ironically, prosperity evangelists who legitimize their mammonism via Bible thumping don't know their Bibles very well. Either that or they're lying. The gospel literature depicts a Socratic protagonist, Jesus, who teaches against the evils of selfish greed and its worldly manifestations—money, riches, possessions, mammon, call it what you will. Nothing that Jesus said or did suggests that having wealth is okay, much less righteous. Many prosperity evangelists, who supposedly accept the Jesus literature as literal fact, have dispensed with the embarrassingly archaic Jesus to run simplified positive-thought workshops billed as church in order to avoid paying taxes.

Like the mythic Jesus—a literary motif that represents "light" foiled against the devil's (Hog's) "dark"—in arguing against obscene affluence I'm not arguing a case for poverty, I'm arguing against it. It's common knowledge that if the world's wealth were redistributed equally and wisely managed, every single person on earth would be rich for life by American standards. Wealth per se isn't the problem; the problem is Hogging wealth via exploitation.

I'm arguing here against poverty, but more to the point, I'm arguing against the blatant hypocrisy of prosperity fundamentalists and the rightwing politicians who pretend to be fundamentalist to protect mega-rich churches' tax-free status in exchange for votes.

The obscenely rich can only be so by forcing the rest of us into lower classes, the lower the better. Getting filthy rich Americans and their filthy rich corporations to contribute their fair share of taxes would greatly enrich this nation's lower, middle, and lower-upper classes. End government handouts for the rich, including rich churches that have benefitted the most from the Bush-instituted Faith-Based Initiative, which brazenly (still) violates the Constitution by handing out subsidies to rightwing "charities" paid for with taxpayer dollars. End corporate welfare. Poverty would disappear.

Yes, corporate welfare. For example, consider these facts about ten corporations highlighted by Vermont Senator Bernie Saunders in 2011: 1) Exxon Mobile's 2009 profits totaled $19 billion, yet according to its SEC filings, the company received a $126 million rebate from the IRS plus it did not pay any federal taxes. 2) Bank of America made $4.4 billion in profits last year after receiving a $1 trillion bailout from the Federal Reserve and

Treasury Department and a $1.9 billion tax refund from the IRS. 3) Though General Electric made $26 billion in profits in the United States over the past five years and received a $4.1 billion tax refund from the IRS, GE has cut a fifth of its American jobs in the past nine years and is boosting jobs overseas where tax rates are lower. 4) Chevron got an IRS refund last year totaled $19 million, but its 2009 profits came to a whopping $10 billion. 5) Boeing received a $30 billion contract from the Pentagon to build 179 airborne tankers; it also received a $124 million refund from the IRS. 6) Valero Energy had $68 billion in sales and received a $157 million tax refund check from the IRS; over the past three years, it has received a $134 million tax break thanks to the oil and gas manufacturing tax reduction. 7) Goldman Sachs paid 1.1% of its 2008 income in taxes, and though it made a profit of $2.9 billion, it got an $800 billion bailout from the Federal Reserve and Treasury Department. 8) Citigroup profits last year totaled more than $4 billion, but it paid zero dollars in federal income tax and received a $2.5 trillion bailout from the Federal Reserve and Treasury Department. 9) From 2007 through 2009 ConocoPhillips profits totaled $16 billion, but it was still awarded $451 million in tax breaks because of the oil and gas manufacturing deduction. 10) Carnival Cruise Lines profits over the past five years totaled more than $11 billion, but its federal income tax rate came to just 1.1%

Why stop with corporate welfare. Why not end welfare for filthy rich individuals, too. We could start by getting rid of the $42 billion per year tax cuts for the already mega-rich, for instance, and the $2.3 billion in tax loopholes for managers of hedge funds and private equity funds, the $11.5 billion per year tax cuts for millionaires' estates, the $6.7 billion in upper-class estate planning loopholes.

The rich think—or want the rest of us to think—that we 99%ers are responsible for our, and their, economic woes. Unfortunately, many 99%ers don't know the facts: for instance, that Bush wiped out Clinton's $5.6 trillion surplus in two years, or that the national debt hit $10 trillion during his presidency; that 82% of our current national debt (2012) was spent by Republicans; that the ratio of CEO pay compared to that of the average worker is 475 to 1 (Japan 11:1, France 15:1, Germany 12:1, Canada 20:1, Britain 22:1); that Cigna health insurance's CEO makes $19 million compared to the average Afghanistan deployed soldier's $38,000 a year, or seniors' $12,000 in Social Security; minimum wage is $7.25 per hour, while the average CEO makes $20,160 per hour. Republican politicians today are corporate gofers because they're owned and operated by the Tea Party, which is owned and operated by the corporate rich (like the Koch brothers). Of course politicians don't mind prostituting themselves because even if they lose the next election, they continue making their $174,000 salary for the rest of their lives, unless they're a majority or minority leader, in which case make that $194,000, or Speaker of the House, 223,500, or President, $450,000. Imagine, almost half a million a year to not work. Or those guys could keep on working as corporate lobbyists, in which case they'd get on average a 1,452% raise.

The rich think they're entitled to all that cash flow because they earned it, but their ability to earn anything is absolutely dependent upon an immense infrastructure—it's called *society*—paid for by the rest of us—it's called *social-ism*, a positive slurred into a negative by the hell-bent. It's only right that the clever, aggressive, ruthless, or lucky rich should pay much more tax than those of us who made wealth generation possible with our taxes and sweat, with our dutiful educating and protecting. The rich don't become rich in a vacuum, but isn't it true that most rich folk in their gated communities and their bullet-proof stretch Limos think their money is all about *them* and not about the bounteous gifts of opportunity provided by society as a whole? Hog isn't aware of the human community; the world of Hog is Hog.

People who are smart and talented and make lots of money producing goods or services have every right to accept the money people will pay for what they offer. Those people produce value for themselves and their consumers. But from him who has been given much, much is expected in return—isn't that a basic principle of reciprocity avowed by every mainstream religion? Isn't that just common sense? Isn't that good? Smart, talented people must also produce value for the social infrastructure that nurtures them, and that means, among other things, paying taxes—fair taxes, a higher tax the higher up the economic ladder you go. Even at the highest tax level, you'll still be filthy rich. You're able to be filthy rich because of the society you help sustain with your taxes.

Of course, there's a right and a wrong way to produce goods and services. Exploiting people, of course, is evil, right? You'd never know it, listening to TV prosperity evangelists or rightwing politicians. Isn't exploiting religion to make money an example of the spirit of antichrist that they throw in the faces of "socialists"? Besides enriching themselves, religionists and politicians provide a valuable service shrouding mega-rich corporate Hogs in smokescreens.

Poverty exists because of aristocratic selfishness. Poverty will persist until the unholy triune Hog is deconstructed abstractly and concretely dismantled. And that can only be accomplished via education, which the Right wants to control—to "privatize," meaning corporatize—to promote its Hoggish agenda. Better yet, home school the piglets.

Too late. Some doggone Deist opens the book and reads the words right off the page where Jesus, some author's or authors' vision of the Good personified as a perfect human being, the literary antithesis of Hog, said, "You cannot serve God and wealth," aka "mammon" (Luke 16:13). Then she leafs to the page where Jesus instructed point-blank, "Sell your possessions, and give the money to the poor" (Matt. 19:21).

(And all the piglets squeal, "But, but, but, oink.")

When Jesus sent his disciples out as missionaries, he told them to wear sandals and only one tunic and to take nothing on their journey except a staff, not even bread, a bag, or a little money in their belts (Mark 6:8-9).

(The prosperity evangelist explains, "What he *really* meant was…")

The directives of Jesus to his followers were not negotiable. "Sell your possessions, and give alms. Make purses for yourselves that do not wear out, an unfailing treasure in heaven, where no thief comes near and no moth destroys. For where your treasure is, there your heart will be also" (Luke 12:33-34).

(Of course, this doesn't apply to post-resurrection Hogs.)

How many possessions are enough? None, according to Matthew's version. "Do not store up for yourselves treasures on earth, where moth and rust consume and where thieves break in and steal; but store up for yourselves treasures in heaven, where neither moth nor rust consumes and where thieves do not break in and steal. For where your treasure is, there your heart will be also" (Matt. 6:19-21).

("Let me repeat," Hog assures his piglets, "This does not apply to us, the blessed ones, the faithful ones chosen to be prosperous.")

In Luke 16:10-13, Jesus claimed, "Whoever is faithful in a very little is faithful also in much; and whoever is dishonest in a very little is dishonest also in much. If then you have not been faithful with the dishonest wealth, who will entrust to you the true riches? And if you have not been faithful with what belongs to another, who will give you what is your own? No slave can serve two masters; for a slave will either hate the one and love the other, or be devoted to the one and despise the other." Again, "You cannot serve God and wealth."

(A piglet nods all-knowingly, light glinting from her gold tooth and diamond-studded nails, "We don't serve wealth. Wealth serves us.")

When Jesus was ridiculed by the Pharisees, "who were lovers of money," he responded, "You are those who justify yourselves in the sight of others; but God knows your hearts; for what is prized by human beings is an abomination in the sight of God" (Luke 16:14-15). Not gay lovers or women lovers packing contraceptives, but money lovers commit the great abomination. But, reader, be warned: Call a rich sexist homophobe a Hog to his face and he might just boot you.

All good Christians know that it's easier for a camel to go through the eye of a needle than for a rich man to enter the kingdom of God (Matt. 19:23; Mark 10:25, 27).

(Yes, Hog counters, but with God all things are possible.)

Hog's point being that it's possible for God to encourage selfishness. But Jesus wasn't saying that. Given that the "eye of the needle" was the name for the opening in the Jerusalem Wall where caravans entered, so named because it was so narrow that the camels had to be unloaded outside and the goods schlepped in later by hand, the parable doesn't mean that the rich can slip through without divesting themselves of their riches. Therefore, many who are "first" will be "last" (Mark 10:31). Certainly "none of you can become my disciple if you do not give up all your possessions" (Luke 14:33).

(Of course, Hog notes, blessings are not possessions. All I possess belongs to Hog. I mean God.)

Once, a rich man said to Jesus, "Good Teacher, what must I do to inherit eternal life?" Jesus answered, "Why do you call me good? No one is good but God alone." Jesus, being a man and not God, is not good like God is good. But he is nonetheless well-versed enough to give authoritative advice: don't murder, don't commit adultery, don't steal, don't bear false witness, don't defraud, and honor your father and mother. The rich man had done all that. Jesus advised him, "Go, sell what you own, and give the money to the poor, and you will have treasure in heaven." The rich man "was shocked and went away," Hogtied and "grieving" (Mark 10:17-22).

Jesus said that when we give a luncheon or a dinner, we should not invite our friends or brothers or relatives or rich neighbors; rather, when we give a banquet, we should invite the poor, the crippled, the lame, and the blind (Luke 14:12-14). Not just once with the cameras rolling, not just a few times as a guilt offering. Always.

He warned rich TV evangelists and talk-show hostesses just like the rest of us, "Beware of practicing your piety before others in order to be seen by them; for then you have no reward from your Father in heaven. So whenever you give alms, do not sound a trumpet before you, as the hypocrites do in the synagogues and in the streets, so that they may be praised by others. Truly I tell you, they have received their reward. But when you give alms, do not let your left hand know what your right hand is doing, so that your alms may be done in secret; and your Father who sees in secret will reward you" (Matt. 6:1-4).

Jesus never said that gays would go to hell, or even thought it necessary to mention homosexuality at all. Jesus never said that women were doormats or that they should stay barefoot and pregnant in the kitchen. But he did illustrate the important point that rich believers who leave the poor lying outside their gates will not enter heaven (Luke 16:19-31). No wonder Hogs keep harping on "terrorist agendas" instituting perversions of homosexuals, feminazis, and socialists. Red herring. *Hog* is perverted.

In the parable of the sower (Luke 8:14), the seed that falls among the thorns signifies "the ones who hear; but as they go on their way, they are choked by the cares and riches and pleasures of life, and their fruit does not mature." Piglets abound in the pigpens of spiritual infertility.

Luke 6:20-26 is Jesus' short list of blessings vs. woes. "Blessed are you who are poor, for yours is the kingdom of God. Blessed are you who are hungry now, for you will be filled. Blessed are you who weep now, for you will laugh. But woe to you who are rich, for you have received your consolation. Woe to you who are full now, for you will be hungry. Woe to you who are laughing now, for you will mourn and weep. Woe to you when all speak well of you, for that is what their ancestors did to the false prophets."

Prosperity fundamentalists try to wiggle out of this veritable truth about charitable unselfishness by arguing that this blessed/woe polarity is pre-resurrection. The future of blessing is already here, they assure themselves; just like the Pharisees, they are entitled to riches because they are divine-right children of the divine-right King, Almighty Hog.

Jesus himself responded to such faulty reasoning (Luke 6:29-31). "From anyone who takes away your coat, do not withhold even your shirt. Give to everyone who begs from you; and if anyone takes away your goods, do not ask for them again. Do to others as you would have them do to you." Now!

Twenty centuries later, post-resurrection, the poor are still among us.

Jesus warned, "Take care! Be on your guard against all kinds of greed; for one's life does not consist in the abundance of possessions" (Luke 12:15). Corporate dominionists should remember the parable of the rich man whose land "produced abundantly" (16), who said, "I will pull down my barns and build larger ones, and there I will store all my grain and my goods. And I will say to my soul, Soul, you have ample goods laid up for many years; relax, eat, drink, be merry.' But God said to him, 'You fool! This very night your life is being demanded of you. And the things you have prepared, whose will they be?' So it is with those who store up treasures for themselves but are [therefore] not rich toward God" (18-21).

"You cannot serve God and wealth" (Matt. 6:24).

Judas betrayed Jesus for a mere thirty pieces of silver. The chief priests who had bribed him took the returned money back, of course, but they didn't want to break any laws by restoring it to the treasury, where it could have been spent on things like food for the poor. Instead, they bought a field for burying foreigners, henceforth called the Field of Blood. Meanwhile, the chief priests gave the soldiers guarding the tomb of Jesus a large sum of money to tell people that the disciples stole Jesus while the guard was asleep. It's all right there in the Bible.

According to Jesus, a day of judgment will come when the goats on his left hand will be separated from the sheep on his right hand.

> Then he will say to those at his left hand, "You that are accursed, depart from me into the eternal fire prepared for the devil and his angels; for I was hungry and you gave me no food, I was thirsty and you gave me nothing to drink, I was a stranger and you did not welcome me, naked and you did not give me clothing, sick and in prison and you did not visit me." Then they also will answer, "Lord, when was it that we saw you hungry or thirsty or a stranger or naked or sick or in prison,

and did not take care of you?" Then he will answer them, "Truly I tell you, just as you did not do it to one of the least of these, you did not do it to me." And these will go away into eternal punishment, but the righteous into eternal life. (Matt 23: 41-46).

What dominionist Hog today really believes this? By its very nature, Hog dominionism contradicts the Parable of the Good Samaritan (Luke 10:25-37).

Jesus wasn't impressed by rich disciples tossing twenties into the collection plate. He was moved by the poor widow who put in two small copper coins worth a penny, which was "everything she had, all she had to live on" (Mark 12:41-44). Hers was an act of authentic charity. Imagine Warren Buffett and Bill Gates and Oprah Winfrey and Congress and the whole world's one-percenters tossing all their pennies into the collection plate.

Charity is perverted today by rich evangelists and their political Hogwash just as it was when the great teacher of unselfishness aggressively drove from the temple all those who by their selling and buying were converting a house of prayer into a den of robbers (Matt. 21:12-13; John 2:13-16).

Why is it that many of us who read Jesus as literary symbol honor his theology more than those claiming faith in the Bible as God-breathed literal truth? Only the shadow knows.

GOOD NEWS: MERCY, NOT SACRIFICE

Just like fat people know they have to forgo their daily pig-out to lose weight and get healthy, even atheists know they need to relinquish their money-grubbing to be emotionally happy and healthy. But there's good sacrifice and bad sacrifice. Replacing your quarter-pounders with Oreos is not going to work.

Spiritually, sacrifice of selfishness is really all that's needed. Most people, though, have been led to believe that to get something you want, even something spiritual, you have to sacrifice something material, like say those collection plate dollars. In fundamentalist circles, the principle of primitive sacrifice perverts charity by twisting it into an investment scheme requiring divine repayment with interest. Prosperity Christians today still tithe ten percent to temple robbers to bribe God for increased prosperity. It's tradition. Petitions to God became bribes and then "reminders" that God must "honor" his "promises." In effect, God was given orders to obey manmade directives masquerading as God's own Word. When God didn't obey the petitions, bribes, or orders, they were reissued toward humans, but only in distant myths could priests and tribal leaders miraculously erase calamity. The immediate cause and effect of sacrifice lost all credibility; sacrifice itself had lost its inherent efficacy. But humans continued to sacrifice in the name of tradition. The Law had become the means to its own end, like the yearly stoning of townsfolk in Shirley Jackson's *The Lottery*, or contributing to the "ministry" of prosperity evangelists like the charlatans I've deconstructed in *Born-Again Deist*.

Superstitious rituals of legalistic "sacrifice" are as hypocritical as they are fruitless, as Jesus eloquently exemplified (Matt. 12:1-8) in an encounter with some Pharisees who criticized him and his disciples for illegally breaking the sabbath by eating grain in the section of grainfield set aside by law for the poor, as per Leviticus 19:9. Jesus pointed out that there was nothing inherently evil about eating on the sabbath if the priests eating on the sabbath were guiltless. Jesus and his friends were just eating grain in a grainfield. David, he noted, wasn't held guilty when he and his comrades ate the forbidden temple bread of the Presence, which only priests were allowed to eat.

The Pharisees were condemning the guiltless, Jesus argued, because they took exception to the principle of love superseding primitive legalism. They didn't understand love's fundamental rule, "I desire mercy and not sacrifice," as he paraphrased Hosea 6:6: "For I desire steadfast love and not sacrifice, the knowledge of God rather than burnt offerings." David himself understood this: "Sacrifice and meal offering Thou hast not desired; my ears Thou hast opened; burnt offering and sin offering Thou hast not required." David had changed his mind about sacrifice. He had been enlightened. "Then I said, 'Behold, I come; in the scroll of the book it is written of me: I delight to do Thy will, O my God; thy law is within my heart" (Psalm 40:6-8). Moral law isn't a divinely dictated scroll of thou shalt, thou shalt not; the Bible isn't a book of magic spells; religion isn't ritual abracadabras. The higher law of love is articulated as moral principles registered by any human's inherent conscience, and moral religion embodies a group's effort toward enactment.

In Psalm 51, David added, "The sacrifices of God are a broken spirit; a broken and a contrite heart, O God, Thou wilt not despise." Contrary to the elaborate system of sacrifices established by exploiting high priests of church and state, all you have to sacrifice is your arrogance and your lack of steadfast love and mercy. Butcher and burn the unholy Hog trinity on an altar of love in the temple of your heart. There's something greater here than the religious institution ("temple") of antiquated legalism. It's the good news of lovingkindness embodied by the good teacher Jesus, who, as the nonstop ambassador of the law of love, thereby proclaimed anything good on any other day to be good on the sabbath.

No doubt feeding the poor would be a more legitimate use of the sabbath than, say, the Sunday morning money-groveling three-ring circus of TV evangelism.

Dominionists like, say, Pat Robertson or Rick Santorum or Ann Coulter who "strain out a gnat but swallow a camel" might be enlightened enough by perusing Matthew 23:12-28 to lighten up their bashing of everyone outside their country club.

The opposite of greed and aristocratic arrogance is unselfish love.

> If you love those who love you, what credit is that to you? For even sinners love those who love them. If you do good to those who do good to you, what credit is that to you? For even sinners do the same. If you lend to those from whom you hope to receive, what credit is that to you? Even sinners lend to sinners, to receive as much again. But love your enemies, do good, and lend, expecting nothing in return. Your reward will be great, and you will be children of the Most High; for he is kind to the ungrateful and the wicked. Be merciful, just as your Father is merciful (Luke 6:32-36).

Every major religion posits love and truth as fundamental tenets, but all versions of fundamentalism controvert love and contradict truth. Millions of Americans are exploited, preyed upon, and even left to die by policies implemented socially and politically by the so-called "Religious" Right.

In contrast to the flag-desecrating, pseudo-righteous Tea Party, Deism defines democracy as a society in which each and every person has the God-given freedom to do whatever he or she chooses as long as it does not directly harm another person, like say an exploited employee, or a victim of pollution or bankster greed. Cutthroat capitalism shows no mercy, hence regulation. Deism confutes the spiritual and practical lies of corporate-gofer politicians. In other words, in contrast to elitists, we Deists endorse the principles of Jeffersonian democracy preserved by government of, by, and for the people, not of, by, and for certain special people, or of, by, and for a corporate/religious oligarchy.

We believe that the role of government is to provide national security, to protect each and every citizen from harm, to preserve all civil and other natural rights, and to promote the public good, not to kowtow to the corporate elite sacralized by the religious elite. We believe that the government does not have the right to impose laws or restrictions or to favor values that deny freedom and civil liberties of individuals, hence separation of church and state, hence corporate regulation, hence laws that protect us from each other. Society does not have the right, either, to dictate values that deny individual freedoms and rights. Behavior that doesn't directly harm another should be allowed and legally protected, and any laws forbidding behavior harmless to others should be immediately overturned.

We Deists seek to uphold the spirit of our Constitution, as created by the genius of our Deist Founders. Hypocrites have the right to be hypocritical; the stupid have the right to be stupid; psychopaths have the right to be evil. But the hypocritical, stupid, or evil person, alone or in a group, has no right to harm any other person. He can *be* whatever he chooses; but he cannot *do* whatever he chooses if he chooses to harm someone else. It's a Deist's duty to expose the profound hypocrisy of Tea Party Christian-America control freaks whose pseudo righteousness smokescreens harm so severe it qualifies as evil even by their standards. Deist righteousness couples beneficence with justice; that's what we mean by love. Our only sacrifice is to the cause of that love. Our mercy is egalitarian and just, even toward Hogs.

WHEN HOG BRINGS HOME THE BACON

In *Criminology: Crime and Criminal Justice*, Criminologists D. Stanley Eitzen and Doug A. Timmer point out (quoting E. Currie's "Fighting Crime"), "Contemporary conservatives like those conservatives before them who 'have successfully posed as the guardians of domestic tranquility for decades' typically promote social and economic policies 'that bear a large part of the responsibility for the level of crime and violence we suffer today.'"

Let me offer Exhibit A: The pork pie known quaintly as America's economic meltdown gone global.

You've heard of America's economic meltdown, right? Do you know what that means? Sort of? Me, too. Oh, I knew bits and pieces picked up from snippets and snatches pitched by the news media. Of course, the big news, the facts, the truth about Wall Street corruption, was withheld from us for a long time because the mainstream "liberal" media was owned and operated by corrupt "conservative" Wall Street: Hog himself.

I had to work hard to understand the basics, because much of what it's important to know has been shrouded in secrecy. Much is opaque; it's not transparent. Let me share with you what I think I understand. I'll start with the house you or your neighbor recently lost to foreclosure.

In the old days before banks were deregulated in 1999-2000, you applied for a loan to buy a house; the bank checked your creditworthiness to make sure that you had a job and a good payback record (credit score) and that the house you wanted to buy was within your means; and the bank loaned you the money to buy the house, which you would pay back in installments over, say, twenty years, plus interest.

In the old days, the bank made money on the interest and simple investments it made with your monthly payments spread out over the twenty years. At any given time, you only owned the portion of your house you had thus far paid for. You and the bank were co-owners of your house until it was paid off at the end of the twenty years (or earlier, if you won the lotto or were otherwise able to pay off the rest of your mortgage ahead of schedule). If you defaulted on your mortgage loan, if you couldn't pay the mortgage plus interest on schedule, the bank still had your house as collateral. If you couldn't pay for an extended period, the bank foreclosed on your house. Your house could be sold and the bank paid the remainder owed on its remaining share in the house. In the old days, foreclosure was a rare event.

The Federal Deposit Insurance Corporation (FDIC) insured the bank so it wouldn't take a loss on its mortgaged houses and other loans and so money held in checking and savings accounts would be safe. The Fed insured loans to make sure that a good flow of capital funds were available to you and the rest of us to borrow, which kept your community and the rest of the country running. When you put money in a savings account, you got interest on some of that money, which the bank had invested in mortgages and other loans or in securities (stocks, bonds, and commodities). Local businesses could borrow bank money to start up, operate, and expand, and you got a job in one of those businesses or in an infrastructure institution (school, police department, post office, etc.) that supported the society within which those businesses could be grown.

Successful businesses paying back their loans made it possible for you to spend your paycheck on products and services provided by those businesses and to take out loans for large purchases like your house, car, boat, etc. In other words, all the money you borrowed from the bank made money for the bank, which paid bankers' salaries and allowed the bank to loan us all money to buy big purchases and pay for them over time, with interest, and even our small purchases at stores benefitted the banks that had loaned those stores money. The pool of cash, or capital, was continuously available to you and your neighborhood businesses.

The federal government, consisting of trusted people we elected to represent our best interests plus their trusted assistants and appointees, facilitated the smooth operation of this system of reciprocal benefit, collected taxes to fund itself and its agencies, aka the Fed (think of the Fed as the head of our household), and to provide a federal pool of money (the US Treasury, i.e., our tax dollars) available for infrastructure like roads and bridges and for services like schools, police departments, and post offices.

In the old days, you didn't drive on potholes and collapsing bridges, and your kids learned the facts and the cops threw the bad guys in jail. But after deregulation, especially after the capitulating deregulation of 2000, all that changed. A tumor began to bubble into the cancer that would eat away the body of America.

In the old days, if you personally wanted to invest money, you had to go through a broker, a special kind of banker who sold you a share, or stock, in a company; if the company did well, you got a piece of its profits, a dividend, a return. Bonds were sold to raise money for government projects, often local or state, but the yield, the amount of your profit, though guaranteed by the government, took longer to mature. Bonds were considered a safer risk, but the return was smaller and took time to mature. By investing in government bonds you were investing in America.

You the buyer didn't really have any way to know the actual worth of an investment. The broker sold you, say, a stock in IBM, jacked up the price to you a bit, then paid himself a commission plus the jack-up he skimmed from the actual price, which you weren't allowed to see; you only got to see the price you were charged, or maybe the jacked-up price plus the commission.

Once computers hit the scene, all the pricing and other data once only available to Wall Street brokers now became available to you. The information was now transparent. Not only could you see the actual value of an investment, making it harder and harder for brokers to skim from a jacked-up price, you could also buy from online companies that let you pay far less for your transaction. The middle man, the traditional broker, either made far less on transactions or was cut out of the process altogether.

It also got easier to shop around for better deals on loans. Left-behind traditional bankers suddenly needed to invent a new product. Voilá: the digital bond, aka blended bond, aka consolidated debt obligation (CDO), or what I call a glob. Banks bundled together lots of individual mortgages into a huge mortgage-bond glob, which they offered for sale to investment banks—big banks that invested in bigger, often riskier investments. An investment bank that bought a mortgage bond would now receive your and your neighbors' mortgage payments including interest. The investment bank gave the traditional bank, say, $800,000 for a million dollar mortgage. The traditional bank got instant cash and the investment bank got the payments plus interest over twenty or thirty years.

You might think the traditional bank got shorted, but remember that the actual house is only the means to an end; for the banker, your house's value is the money loaned and the return on the money plus interest. The traditional bank could now invest that immediate $800,000 and potentially make a profit that exceeded the $200,000 difference on the house. In effect, the bank took out a loan on your original loan for the purpose of its own investing. Because mortgage bonds were designer brands just getting hot, more and more banks began investing in them, driving demand and costs up even higher. Banks started lending money to just about anybody wanting to buy a house, because if you defaulted, your house would be worth more by then and they could resell your house for more than they would have collected from you. In other words, in that kind of housing bubble, investment banks could potentially make more if you foreclosed.

That kind of rotten dealing could not have thrived had the process been transparent. Here's where the devil made you do it.

If you, an investor (or the manager who handled your investments, including your pension funds), bought a mortgage-bond glob, you owned a share in the individual mortgages, meaning payback of various people's mortgages. Essentially, a "glob" of strangers from all over the world, strangers to you, strangers to each other, owned (and probably still own) your house until the final pay-off date. No longer was your house owned by your neighborhood bank, which was owned by neighborhood bankers you could look in the eye. Banking, and home ownership, had become surreally *glob*al. Ownership was now super opaque. So opaque that you, via your investment manager (say, of your 401k), could participate in ownership of a bond glob without even knowing it.

By the end of 2000, lenders had realized that if they could sell bundled mortgage globs, why not bundle other kinds of loans? A second type of glob bond was created, the "asset-backed security" bond, allowing investors to buy into ownership of payments on credit cards, college loans, car loans, and any other kind of membership or commitment to scheduled payments. The glob thickened.

Bankers thought, why not combine bundled mortgage bonds and bundled asset-backed security bonds into an even bigger bond? Enter the mondo-glob bond: A mondo-bond glob plus a mondo-bond glob equals a much larger mondo-glob bond—a glob bomb with its fuse already lit.

Remember that in the old days, investment banks and brokers were able to skim and make deals because people couldn't really know what the stock or other investment was actually worth. People had to trust the brokers. Computers changed that. Now people could "see." But because banks and brokers thrived on secrecy, on your not being able to "see," they decided to exploit those same computers to create a new level of secrecy. They blended together bunches of those existing mortgage bonds and asset-backed security bonds into mondo-glob bombs that were so humungous and complex that only the well-trained and very patient eye could "see," and they broke up those mondo-glob bonds into pieces to sell. Because there were so many obligations—potentially millions of individual mortgages, credit card accounts, loans, etc.—thrown into the mondo-glob pot, individual investors and even most brokers really couldn't "see" anything but a blur of miscellaneous data: Even they didn't know what the mondo-globs consisted of. They certainly didn't understand its risk—the probability of the glob losing money.

Secret, super opaque, risky mondo-glob bond bombs were a leading cause of the socio-economic meltdown that exploded into the Occupy Wall Street Revolt that flashed out into the current Occupy Revolution.

The mondo-glob bond controllers, the bank higher-ups who bundled and controlled and managed the whole mondo-glob bond, could easily skim and take commissions on all its thousands and even potentially millions of smaller pieces. If the pieces were sold and resold, and then repackaged and re-repackaged and then sold and resold again and again, the trader could make an even bigger killing than in the old days. The mondo-glob bond controllers were fast becoming the real owners of pretty much everything—our houses, our cars, our health care providers, our pensions, the businesses where we worked. They were intentionally buying up America. They, not we. We part owners, we owners of what we thought was our own stuff, we invested owners of the minute pieces of the mondo-glob pie, we had no clue what was happening.

OINK: IT GETS WORSE

Opaque overly-blended mondo-glob bonds muddied the transparency ushered in by computers. The digital revolution morphed into digital convolution, and then convulsion. Psychopathic predators shot us a toothy grin. They were poised to lure us through limbo into hell: They invented *deceptive blending*. The Hog predators didn't call it that; it got called that after they got caught. Deceptive blending is the glob gone viral.

The viral glob, investment banks' latest designer product to sell, was a bond consisting of blended high- and low-risk loans. And there were lots of high-risk loans to juggle. This fusion of high-low risk generated the nuclear blended-bond bomb. Because banks were insured by the Fed, i.e. FDIC, i.e. the Treasury, i.e. our tax dollars—because *defaults* were covered by *our* tax dollars, banks no longer had any motivation to be safe in their loans. In essence, they were gambling using *our* money. Risk became more lucrative than responsible loaning, because instant payback by the Fed on bad loans equaled more ready cash to invest right now on investments that could potentially yield much more than paltry sums collected on the loans over time. But there was yet another level to scam for profit.

Statistically, the blended bonds appeared to be medium-risk, making them attractive to potential investors and driving up their price, but in fact the high-risk loans made the blend far more risky than the viral blended-glob's statistical average. One reason is that statistics were based on the average credit scores of recipients of the loans, and those scores couldn't accurately predict real-life circumstances like deflated housing prices following a real estate bubble burst or growing unemployment and shrinking salaries due to off-shoring or any number of other factors. Another reason that the statistics were skewed was that the banks themselves hired the ratings agencies that rated the credit of the individuals whose debt was part of the blended bonds, and thus they (the banks) themselves rated the bonds. Plus those ratings agencies, like Standard & Poor's, including their guidelines and rules, were overseen by the banks themselves.

Then Hog belched. Picture a suit named John Paulson of the hedge fund Paulson & Co. holding a viral blended-glob. You might not have heard of hedge-Hog Paulson, but you've probably heard of Goldman Sachs and AIG. These three are an unholy trinity of deception; they are Hog on acid.

One of Paulson's sins against humanity was to create Abacus, a blended-glob consisting of 123 securities backed by mortgages in the overheated real estate bubbles of Arizona, California, Florida, and Nevada. In other words, Paulson's blended-glob bonds consisted of soon-to-be mortgage *defaults*; but because of his wizardry in deceptive blending, his glob was rated AAA, and because deceptive blends are opaque, investors couldn't "see" that this glob-bomb was ticking. Paulson hitched up with Goldman Sachs, which created a blended, synthetic CDO mondo-glob bond. Because Paulson knew the synthetic glob was explosive, in other words, because he knew the bond would go bust like a balloon filled with dynamite, he bought credit insurance from AIG. Once the mondo-glob bond failed, investors lost over a billion dollars, the same amount Paulson *made* in profit by collecting on the insurance from AIG. Goldman Sachs made around $25 million in fees. AIG was paid back the billion it paid to Paulson with *your* tax dollars in the bailout of 2008, because the mondo bank industry, the mondo-glob market, was "too big to fail"—meaning if one bank failed, a cascade of entities dependent on that bank would also fail. *Your* tax dollars bailed out all the other big-shot mondo-glob marketers luring investors like your pension manager into buying the $600 trillion in toxic, explosive bonds. Many deceptive-blended-mondo-glob marketers, devoid of conscience—psychopaths, in other words; in other words, the devil Hog—just reinvested the bailout money—*your* money—in more toxic bonds and offshore investments, which of course robbed you of your job, or it will. To help cover the $600 trillion, the government printed more money, which devalued the dollar along with all the stuff you had planned to buy with yours.

Insurance like that bought by Paulson used to be illegal. Well, it's still illegal. That's why the transaction is called by the whitewashed "derivatives," or credit default "swaps." You've heard of swaps, right? Swaps are deceptive insurance like that Paulson bought from AIG—shh, they don't call it insurance, because insurance is regulated by the government. (See why Hoggish politicians keep pushing deregulation and "free" market?) They call it swaps in order to pull the wool over the eyes of *American taxpayers* whose mortgages, credit accounts, pensions, etc. are used to make money for psychopathic predatory Hogs like Paulson, Goldman Sachs, and AIG—*American taxpayers* who foot the bill for a bailout of demonic companies who screw American taxpayers out of all this money and out of jobs, not only the actual jobs but the value of any existing jobs, meaning jobs still here in the U.S. bond-bomb nuclear winter of our discontent. Shakespeare couldn't have written a greater tragedy.

In the old days following the stock market crash and the Great Depression, regulations kept predator bankers and brokers under control. Some perfectly good people worked at some of those banks and brokerages. But mixed among those good people were selfish closet Hogs greedy for mega-mammon. The gluttons hired lobbyists to pay legislators to deregulate. And so it came to pass, beginning with deregulation of savings and loans in the 1980s followed by massive deregulation enacted by the Financial Services Modernization Act of 1999 and the Commodity Futures Modernization Act of 2000. Following deregulation, regulators no longer regulate. After 2000, being out of the loop, regulators couldn't "see" the Great Bank Robbery going on—couldn't see, for instance, the $600 trillion-plus in over-the-counter derivatives contracts by 2007—and therefore had no sense of the magnitude of risk metastasizing throughout the entire financial system, even though having a total sense was their job.

Following deregulation, the derivatives market, the swaps, the otherwise illegal insurance of defaulting mondo-glob bonds, was legal, sort of. Banks made more money on failed bonds than on those that succeeded, because bankers now sold insurance against our failure and even their own, the loss of our homes, the loss of our jobs, the loss of our credit, security, and happiness. Swaps markets—banks selling insurance against default— have devalued people, businesses, communities, and America. Greedy Hogs have transformed our fairly functional democracy into our present plutocracy ruled by the richest one percent. They cast an evil spell, putting the princess to sleep and turning the prince into a toad. The greedy traitors created the magical bubble of 2000-07, then made a killing when it popped. Dylan Ratigan calls these "bankster" Hogs "greedy bastards"; I read into that a bit more symbolism than he perhaps intended: The greedy bastards are not legitimate children of America. Maybe the Obama citizenship bigot bash is psychotic projection. Financial Crisis Inquiry Commission Chair Phil Angelides calls the driving force of our nation a sand castle economy. Because there have as yet been no prosecutions of greedy bastards, no deterrents put in place, no real payments of penalties to compensate for all the blatant instances of ethical irresponsibility, Angelides complains that Wall Street has escaped like a greased pig. Oink.

To put this in perspective, hold these facts in your hat: 1) In 2011, banks made record profits; 2) The ten biggest banks now control 77% of the country's banking assets; 3) The ten biggest banks made $62 billion in profits last year, thanks to the TARP bailout initiated during the Bush administration; 4) Wall Street compensation in 2010 rose to record levels— $135 billion to the rich hired hands employed by publically traded Wall Street firms; 5) 30 million people need fulltime jobs; 6) nine trillion dollars in wealth of American families has been vaporized; 7) four million families have lost their homes to foreclosure, and experts project that 8-13 million will have lost their homes before the current crisis is over.

Too bad, the Hogs snort. They just gave themselves millions in bonuses because their banks "turned a profit." In their dreams. Just a couple years ago they were teetering on the edge of the abyss. As a tax payer who contributed to the Treasury that gave these greasy Hogs the handouts that saved their bacon, am I and all my other taxpaying comrades not collectively those fat Hogs' employer? As their employer, I, on behalf of my fellow citizens, demand repayment of all that Hog stole from us. And I demand that all guilty Hogs get a sentence of life in prison—a *real* prison with bread and water, not the Gothic dungeon where they've dumped us.

But alas, Hogs sit poolside at their multimillion-dollar mansions sipping martinis and writing checks adding up to hundreds of millions—really, by now it's billions—to lobbyists and politicians to make sure their little crap shoot stays unregulated. Even the conservative Supreme Court Justices voted to keep it that way by ruling that banks and corporations are "people" who can give unlimited money to political campaigns supporting the special interests of banks and corporations. Screw "we, the people." *Real* people.

OINK, OINK: IT GETS EVEN WORSE

Wait, there's more. The Wall Street trader traitors have done far more damage than screwing us out of our cash and our homes.

To make even more money, the so-called "American" corporations, backed by Wall Street, subsidized by *our* tax dollars, have shipped *our* jobs overseas to places like communist China. "American" corporations aren't really American anymore. Mondo multinational corporations and the Wall Street banksters that stoke them and profit from them have become a separate nation unto itself. This Corporate Nation has successfully completed a covert coup d'état. The Corporate Nation now owns and operates the United States of America.

The Corporate Nation is Hog, self-righteous, arrogant, psychopathic worshipper of Almighty Hog. Hog, groveling lustfully before his own image (for that is what Almighty Hog is), grunts and squeals in the stench of his own mammon. That's right, piglets: Mammon is Hog poop, i.e., dinner.

Thanks to Hog, here in America more than one in four houses are underwater. Thanks to Hog, thirty million people need jobs, and laid-off workers who recently found new jobs have taken pay cuts of over twenty percent, the deepest cuts since the Great Depression. Thanks to Hog, almost half the population now lives in poverty. No generation alive has ever before seen that level of poverty in the United States of America. But the wealth of the Hoggish rich has exploded astronomically at the expense of the rest of us. In 2010, in the midst of economic catastrophe, CEOs paid themselves on average $10.8 million a year, a scandalous 23 percent more than the previous year. They gave themselves and their squires outrageously huge bonuses for successfully screwing us 99% of Americans out of our homes, our pensions, our health care, our industrial infrastructure, our tax dollars, and perhaps worst of all, our government. The government of, by, and for the people has been supplanted by a government of, by, and for "Wall Street," the Corporate Nation. It's disgraceful. It's terrifying.

Wall Street isn't just banks and their bonds pimps. Wall Street deals in bonds, commodities, and stocks, the paraphernalia of the corporate addict. Sweat shops, no longer legal in America, move the cogs and wheels of the Corporate Nation. Parading as "patriots," citizens of a Corporate Nation at war with the real America are moving offshore because they can make more money ripping off even more citizens of other countries, especially communist China. The so-called "American" elite colluding with the so-called "Chinese" elite have built a subsidiary of the global Corporate Nation made up of elites of many nations, including those that are technically enemies of the real America. Isn't that *treason*?

In the early 90s, China devalued its currency by about sixty percent, and other Asian countries followed China's lead. That meant we could get China's goods at bargain basement prices, but American goods now seemed twice as expensive. China imposed tariffs—the taxes countries charge on imports—of 25 percent, compared to America's 2.5 percent. That meant in China it was suddenly very expensive to buy American goods and much cheaper for the Chinese to buy their own goods. Because workers in China were basically slaves to the communist corporate elites, American companies could move to China or outsource to partner companies in China to produce their goods at a huge savings. At that point, over sixty percent of China's exports to the U.S. are actually goods produced in China by non-Chinese global corporations—the Corporate Nation.

Yes, we Americans could buy Chinese-made goods cheaper. But we did so by losing our jobs, because industries that had employed us were now largely or entirely based in China. The truth that Wal-Mart doesn't want you to know is that buying "cheaper" is very, very expensive. Low-paid Americans are manning the registers, but the products they ring up are not American-made, despite their "American" labels. Even products made in the U.S. are largely made of parts *not* made in the U.S.

Thanks to corporate deregulation, unemployment in this country has soared, people have lost their houses, loans have defaulted, and the Wall Street and communist China elite—the Corporate Nation—have gotten filthy rich. Surely this constitutes both an economic and a political partnership that by American standards constitutes high treason.

To make matters worse, so-called American corporations have so many tax loopholes, most amassed during the reign of "Dubya" Bush, that most multinationals pay little or no tax. Worst of all, several of those multinationals, even those making billions in profits, get subsidies. Let's be clear: A subsidy is government money, aka a handout, aka corporate welfare. That money is *our* tax dollars. Rich corporations and their rich owners and managers pay little or no taxes, they ship our jobs to someplace like China, they sell us cheap Chinese crap, take away our houses, put us in debt through no fault of our own, then steal from the US Treasury the tax dollars the 99% rest of us earned with our own sweat labor. On top of that, they have driven down the value of the American dollar while at the same time driving down worker pay, and then they have the Hog-balls to try to destroy unions. That's what I call a covert coup d'état. That's treason, people; let's take them to trial.

Well, right, they didn't technically steal our tax dollars from the Treasury. It was handed to them by politicians that they had bought. So basically they were just paying themselves back. A coup of collusion.

This shouldn't have happened. It did happen because in the era of deregulation, Wall Street lobbyists, squires in the Corporate Kingdom, swarmed to Washington to purchase one of their most valuable commodities: Congress. The majority of senators and house representatives we voted into office were candidates picked by their respective bought-off parties whose campaigns were fueled by Wall Street money, i.e., money controlled entirely by the Corporate Nation. There's now a population explosion of lobbyists, the corporate henchmen who tell our elected officials what to do. Shouldn't it be our job to support representatives who don't let the devil make them do it? Shouldn't we root out the bacon bits and toss them to the gutter? Instead we're stuck on an animal farm in nineteen eighty-four.

It could be worse. You could live in China, maybe in a labor camp like that run by Apple's partner corporation, Foxconn, aka "iPod City," an underworld that would have made Dickens balk. Here young people work twelve hours a day, six or seven days a week, doing the same task over and over all day long for seventy-five cents an hour. The workers live in "dormitories" no frat boy could imagine in conditions so horrible that workers kill themselves. One time, when Apple executives were touring the plant, yet another iSlave attempted suicide. Apple generously responded by increasing average wage to about a buck an hour and installed suicide-nets to catch jumpers. Remember that the next time you pull out your Americanese-made iPad or iPhone or iPod.

Yes, we're better off than Chinese slaves. But even here workers get screwed due to what has been dubbed "our shrinking economy." For instance, as Ratigan points out in *Dirty Bastards*, the Swedish company IKEA has a plant in Danville, Virginia, that makes furniture just like its plants in Sweden. Their minimum wage is about $19 an hour, and they get a government-mandated five weeks of paid vacation. But here, full-time workers start at $8 an hour and get twelve vacation days, eight of which are predetermined by the company. A third of the workers are temps whose wages are even lower; like most temps, they get no paid days off, no insurance, no benefits at all. Here in Florida our illustrious governor, Rick Scott, wants our state and the whole country to compete with China by deregulating altogether and creating our own labor camps. Oink, oink.

For those of you who have lived under a rock, it's us versus Wall Street, Hog incarnate. We the people are we the 99%. We the people are unions and workers and people who know that this nation is a society, not a jungle playground for ruthless psychopathic Hogs and their corporate toys. It's the United States of America vs. the Corporate Nation. God vs. Hog.

American corporations are not just shipping our jobs overseas; "American" corporations themselves are not just relocating to China. They are investing in China, merging with the communist elite, selling American technology to our enemies. They are becoming Chinese. And they want us to build an electric fence in Arizona? (Projection? Red herring?)

Corporate industrialists in China. Wall Street bondsmen. Political gofers. Don't even get me started on America's anti-American corporate health insurance/drug fraud.

These predators aren't just greedy. Their agenda is to form a Corporate Nation that can take over the world. Think of it: Hog will rule the Earth, with 99% of Earth's population as its personal slaves. Why wouldn't they?

That's where we're headed. The colossal coup d'état is underway.

Hog squeals and grunts.

HOGTIED, OR BONDAGE, IN LAYMAN'S TERMS

At the heart of the financial crisis is a fundamentally flawed worldview that is based on several fallacies: 1) the world is a jungle; 2) the fittest will survive; 3) as the survivor fittest thrive, the species evolves; 4) a nation is its economy; 5) only an unregulated economy thrives.

As demonstrated in previous chapters, the human world is a society, not a jungle. The predatory elite has made it appear like a jungle.

The jungle food chain consists of the rich 1% exploiting the 99%. Jungle exploitation takes many forms, including underpaying labor, overburdening the 99% taxpayers, off-shoring jobs, looting the Treasury via bailouts and subsidies (the whitewashed term for corporate Welfare), and buying-off politicians.

The jungle fauna consists of predators and prey. Psychologists tell us that approximately 1% of people are psychopaths; economic sociologists tell us that approximately 1% of people constitute the predatory financial elite. True, not all financial predators are psychopaths, and not all psychopaths are financial predators. You might think, then, that not all rich people are predatory. But all who derive great wealth from ownership of or investment in today's version of Wall Street and the corporations and banks of which it consists are guilty of fomenting predation. Some rich predators are not clinically psychopathic, they're just sociopathic. They're indirect predators. They're vultures that scavenge the carcasses left by the lions. They're the little Hogs following the crumb trail of the big Hogs.

The 1%, the big Hogs of the jungle, the economic psychopathic predators, insist that they and they alone be totally unregulated. They say it's good for the country because they have confused an economy for a nation. For them the nation is the playground of the 1%. The laws exist to benefit them. The 99% are their personal slaves—they wish; for now, the 99% are their personal servants. The Darwinian-libertarian Hogs want to be totally free to do whatever they want. Of course they want the 99% to be highly regulated, and the 1% to be entirely unregulated for the benefit of the 1% squealing about the absolute control that their jungle-pimp status demands.

Laissez-faire libertarians assert that the market will correct itself. Right. Just leave rapists alone and they'll do the right thing. That's the mental bubble that just popped. The financial crisis is a spiritual cataclysm, a catastrophic tragedy in which the hero is carried off by headhunters into the tangled undergrowth of nationalized greed.

Organized religion is no help. Fundamentalist Hogs live in the same jungle worldview as their Darwinian brothers, except the saints' jungle is a fallen world inhabited by wild animals and demons. Representing the devil as the Edenic serpent conflates the animal and demon into one convenient bugaboo. Like corporate Darwinians, fundamentalist high priests want absolute control to hyper-regulate others and to completely deregulate themselves. Their successes included the absence of court and law enforcement monitoring of priest child molesters, and zero-tax status for religious corporations, including mega-churches that pull in millions and even billions, and not for charitable purposes.

It's time to bust too-big-to-fail monopolies. It's time for restitution. I suggest starting with subsidized energy self-sufficiency—and by that I mean every house would be weatherized and retrofitted with made-in-America no-grid solar panels and windmills, paid for by housing meltdown banksters. And every other building would be likewise equipped, compliments of corporate suppliers of non-renewable energy. Meanwhile, the government would offer a large cash award to the automaker that could produce the first inexpensive energy self-sufficient car—and not a plug-in: a car that generates its own energy: a car that *is* a solar-wind generator. These three steps would reduce or eliminate pollution, global warming, pollution-related sickness and death, wars for oil, dependence on corporate energy providers, grids and their outages, and corporate control over politics. New jobs would be created to accommodate set-up and maintenance—jobs that would remain in America.

And it's time to transcend this absurd worship of jobs, jobs, jobs. Nobody wants a job. A job is something you don't want to do that you do anyway to survive. A career is a step closer to what you do want to do, or at least toward greater security, ideally in the form of more buck for your bang. Simple redistribution of wealth would allow every person on the planet to work far fewer hours for far bigger paychecks. Equalization would vastly reduce collateral damages like crime, war, neuroses, and laziness, and would grant people precious time to pursue their passions, which would add significant value to individual lives and to society. Eliminate elitist entitlement and we'd all take a quantum leap closer to Paradise.

And it's time to stop the poisoning of our food supply all the way up the chain, from GMO to pesticides to hormones to preservatives to sugar loading and nutrient stripping. Not only do we allow these practices, we subsidize them. An individual can be prosecuted for murder for poisoning another person, but a corporation can legally poison us sick or dead and lie about it via FDA pseudo-regulation and deceptive labeling, just for starters. In a true democracy, the *people* would vote to end such perverted transgressions against our intelligently designed bodies and Earth's body.

And politicians: If we must allow legal lying in order to protect freedom of speech, we should at least make it illegal for politicians to knowingly lie to the public, since by taking an oath of office our elected officials are technically under oath for the duration of their tenure in office. Though they seem to have forgotten it, politicians are the people's employees. If we the people can't fire them for lying, surely we could file class-action lawsuits for breach of contract or fraud or negligence or *something*. Surely a smart lawyer could prove that lying and other D.C. double-dealing violates the Constitution, i.e., *us*.

And violates the liar's constitution. Ah, of course; but he's untouchable; immortal, even. His flesh shall not corrupt nor his soul corrode nor his colossal stature crumble to dust like a statue of some mythic Ozymandias, he assures us, lighting up another fat cigar.

(…Fade to smoke.)

When Hog Has Had Enough

Then Adam awoke from his nightmare and found it truth: The meltdown was breakdown: his, his country's, his world's. Not just a mental breakdown; mental, moral, emotional, spiritual. How our protagonist longed for the community of humans! He aspired to humanness like theirs. No more the cloven hoof of a devil, no more the horns—how he had longed for horns, symbol of the alpha male. Now he recoiled from the adolescent lusts of Hogs. Revolted by his old taste for bacon, all he wanted now was one crumb of manna, even just a glimpse of the spiritual God. He loathed the word "dominance." He longed to read Keats.

Adam realized he couldn't just cash in his mondo bonds and give the money to the poor. Then he would be among those needy poor, he would be a burden to other people and to society. And what is society, he wondered, if not other people? How blind he had been, how foolish. His society was the jungle, his home the pen refuge where he plotted hunts of other beasts much like himself. No, not like himself: The old goat munching tin cans was his beloved uncle Joe. The lamb was Aunt Tina. The elephant and the tiger were neighbors just as sociable as the sparrow and the squirrel. They weren't even really animals; they were people. They weren't competitors, they were relatives, they were friends.

Adam straightened his tie. He took off his tie. He put on his blue jeans and took a walk in the park. A park paid for by the city, the community of "social-ists" who enjoy sharing nature. He walked past the county "social-ist" library—tempting, but it was such a beautiful day he hiked to the "social-ist" beach. How long it had been since he really looked at those waves. He couldn't remember the last time he stopped to listen, to smell, to feel the spot he once considered the most sacred place on Earth. Now he felt nothing but nostalgia. Not just for the past. He felt a longing to regain the paradise he had lost living in the kingdom of Hog.

He watched the buoys and gulls, embarrassed by the stupid Hog he had left sleeping in the body that had only last night been his. No, he wasn't dead. Well, maybe he was. But this was a good death, good like a shot of penicillin to stave off pneumonia delirium; yes, he thought, a tear slipping past his grimace—breathe, breathe—this was his last chance to slough the vulture culture, to drive a stake through his vampire heart, to recover the good health of just being human.

What to do? Nothing. Pray. Read Shakespeare, read Frost and Thoreau and Alice Walker. Give money to a worthy cause. Vote for humanity, for human values embodied by a government for the people. Vote against the corporate agenda that had made him rich, made him famous in the realm of pigpens. Listen to Bach; study jazz. Discuss the latest films with people who think. Care. He had almost forgotten how. *Had* forgotten how. How he hated his past! How he wanted out! But there was no escape from memories, only correction, only apologies and major changes of clothes and values.

He could do this. He had once been a good student, had played George in *Our Town*, had sung in Glee Club. His class, he remembered, had pondered Macbeth pondering the hellish consequences of enacting his "vaulting ambition." Lady Macbeth and the three Witches, he had argued, represent projections—prophesies—of his success, i.e., his failure as a human being and the loss of his soul. At the beginning, he had said, Macbeth carefully weighs every action in the spiritual balance. But Macbeth deteriorates into madness, finally losing his…

Eyes. Oedipus too had caused his own "fate." Oedipus the King gouged out his eyes to no longer "see" the world through the eyes of hubris, but like the blind prophet who had brought him knowledge of himself, his life, his choices at the crossroads, his true family, the king too would see by the light of the real world within. The dark without, the light within. Opaque, transparent. Like Oedipus, he would be Teiresias. He would turn himself inside out and expose the inner truth, the truth that sets you free. Like Oedipus he had acted blindly, had plagued his own country, had sullied his own mother, not knowing who or what he truly was. Oedipus received mercy: blindness instead of death, "blindness" that was insight, for enlightenment transcends punishment.

Love your neighbor as yourself. He had once loved. In college he had kissed an innocent princess awake. A few years later, he was a toad, and another princess kissed him into a prince. Then a great voice, a powerful brutish grunt, shattered the illusion: Realism was saved by the grace of Hog.

Riches followed him like toilet paper stuck to the heel of the first princess' flip-flop. Prestige was granted him as booty of the conquest. Nature sprouted computers and cubicles, offices and skyscrapers, private jets and gated pens in a magical kingdom devoid of oceans and humans and indigenous trees. Life distilled to its essence—a good deed, deed as in proof of ownership of property. The voice of the third princess blared in his brain: What does it profit a man if he gain the whole world but forfeit his soul? She was quoting a teacher he had once admired. But that teacher was a myth, the heady illusion of youth. Adam the Boss had gained a wealth of reality. That was all he wanted, all he needed following the divorce. Hog heaven.

Then he awoke and saw that it was a dream. A nightmare. A terrifying sweaty nightmare of suffocating, drowning, pursued by a zombie psychopath, skewered on the witchdoctor's spit, a child in flames on the altar of Hog.

Adam, literally "first man." The first great man frightened by his own shadow, the first great serpent.

Blake's Adam reaching through the cosmos.

What rough beast slouching towards Bethlehem to be born.

CHAPTER 10

LOGOS LOST

Things fall apart; the center cannot hold;
Mere anarchy is loosed upon the world...

In the beginning people created Creation myths. The world teemed with ancestors longing to grasp the origin of humanity, the earth, life, and the cosmos. The wise-ones looked, really looked, listened, smelled, tasted, touched; they approached nature with respect and wonder, sensing the presence of something transcendent. In time they learned to navigate by the star gods, and erected stone calendars to honor each goddess turning her pages of hours or seasons. Paying attention, the ancients distilled medicines from herbs, fashioned jewelry from smelted ores, sang and piped in caverns beneath portraits of neighborhood beasts. They mused and debated, they reckoned and rhymed. Being rational, the clever-ones concocted names as best they could to catch each glimpse of the essence lying (or was it moving) under the surface-flash of reality, and with special sacred words guessed at the rest. Thus were born concrete and abstract, literal and metaphoric, palpable and symbolic.

In the beginning humans were born loving stories and art, and with great aesthetic flair gave shape to the formless void of the earth and dispelled its darkness with haunting music and dazzling light painted over the surface of the deep. And because some nights were cold and some days dreary, the master wordsmiths, the shamans, the prophets, gift-boxed their glimpses and guesses in colorful narrations. Intuited understandings, articulated symbolically, translated into stories spiced with action heroes, divinities, dangerous adventures, cosmic romances, and gory battles, all laced with flasks-full of magical realism. Short stories evolved into epics. Over and over their tales, sprinkled with fairy dust, symbolized through monsters and champions and objects and creatures the human condition, the joy of passion, outrage toward injustice, and cathartic pathos toward suffering. If they could display their predicaments, perhaps they could fix them; if they could articulate the riddles of existence, maybe they could solve them. Why couldn't they see more, or understand all things? Were they unworthy, evil; demonic, fallen? Maybe they just needed to try harder, to learn more. At least they could cry and laugh together.

Myths bound people together into societies sitting around the fire munching popcorn. And here we sit still, dissecting nature, dancing and drumming, praying to grasp the meaning of life.

Creation myths represent our intuited understanding of the nature of Nature. Operative word, *represent*. Early on the philosophers among us noted that existence is coherent and logical. The word *logos*, meaning among other things the rational principle that generates, develops, and governs the universe, was a technical philosophical term already employed by the pre-Socratic Greeks. In the sixth century B.C.E, Heraclitus complained that most people live like dreamers with a false view of the world because they fail to understand the universal logos, or "reason," the source of all natural occurrences and the glue by which are things are interrelated. Heraclitus surmised that existence gels by means of an underlying tension between opposites. Binaries like good and evil, hot and cold, or sickness and health could only be grasped as relations of opposites. The universe is not-chaos because it is bound together—interconnected and organized—by the dynamic equilibrium of divergent elements. All things are both harmful and beneficial, Heraclitus believed. Seawater, for instance, is harmful to humans but beneficial for fish. It's not surprising that the philosopher who observed the persistence of unity despite change would emphasize the need for social harmony. No doubt today he would stress the benefits of diversity.

Heraclitus considered fire to be the primal element, perpetually kindling and burning out. "Fire" included fuel, flame, smoke, heat, eventually becoming air, and air becoming clouds of rain turning into ocean. Though philosophers today take his "fire" literally, perhaps more likely he used the image metaphorically. If so, what would fire represent?

Life is a river, Heraclitus said. "Upon those who step into the same rivers, different and ever different waters flow down." A few centuries later Plato interpreted this analogy to mean that all things are in constant flux. The dreamers Heraclitus complained about lived now in Plato's Cave, mistaking shadows of things, cast by firelight onto the cave wall, for the things themselves. They disbelieved even a peer who had escaped to observe the real world in pure sunlight outside the cave and had returned to proclaim the joyous tidings of reality beyond the darkened appearances of the senses. Plato's light and darkness were clearly metaphoric. But what exactly does the myth represent?

The myth represents myth itself. The Greek term *mythos*, from which the word *myth* derives, means word, saying, story, and fiction. Mythos, meaning "word," contrasts with logos, also meaning "word." Unlike myth, which is assumed to be true "just because," as when we suspend our disbelief while watching a movie and momentarily accept the fiction as "true," logos is valid truth that can be argued and demonstrated through inductive and deductive proofs and physical evidence. Religious narrative is myth believers have forgotten is myth; religious faith is like walking out of the movie theatre believing that the reality represented in the movie continues to be reality in the *real* world. Religious representation is perfectly valid if the believer remembers that the representation is *representation*. Superman and Harry Potter and King Arthur and Zeus and vampires are only true as fiction, and perhaps as symbolic representations. Like Heraclitus, Plato complained that far too many people live in a movie world of consecrated myth.

Aristotle first pointed out that the ability to make metaphor is the surest sign of genius. Many geniuses of his era and earlier—Aeschylus, Sappho, and Plato to name but a few—were generating many great literary representations in drama, poetry, and prose. Ancient geniuses generated many Creation myths that metaphorically personify the logos as God. In Genesis, God separates the light from the darkness, as do the Creators in other myths (mythmakers constantly borrow from each other). Because humanity is the genius species, light and darkness can be taken literally or symbolically. All religious motifs, being artistic literary representations, can be taken literally or symbolically.

Personifying the logos as God turns God into a metaphor that can be contemplated in order to better understand the transcending, ineffable reality of God. Some people do this instinctively, without consciously interpreting the metaphor. (Similarly, people often don't bother to interpret their dreams.) But the creators among us consciously construct specific meanings via metaphoric representations; they represent meanings symbolically; they make literature. Unfortunately, sometimes even the literati among us run into trouble when they forget that the metaphor is a metaphor. Representation is representation, not literally the thing represented. A painting of Queen Elizabeth is not Queen Elizabeth. The anthropomorphic "God the Father" is not God, and God is not a father in the animal, human sense.

The biblical Creation myth, like most Creation myths, evolved over time. The Bible's Old Testament opens, "In the beginning God created the heavens and the earth. And the earth was formless and void, and darkness was over the surface of the deep; and the Spirit of God was moving over the surface of the waters. Then God said, 'Let there be light'; and there was light. And God saw that the light was good; and God separated the light from the darkness."

In the New Testament, the Gospel of John opens, "In the beginning was the Word, and the Word was with God, and the Word was God. He was in the beginning with God. All things came into being through Him; and apart from Him nothing came into being that has come into being. In Him was life; and the life was the light of men." Christians equate the logos with Christ, which doesn't make sense, given that the logos event (Creation) is in past tense, when his life "was" the light of men. But did the writer of John mean for the word "word," or *logos*, to be taken literally? Rather than Jesus embodying logos, perhaps Jesus was meant as a metaphor for logos. After all, a human being can't *be* the logos. Not literally. Christians think that Jesus is God, and God is the logos. If God is logos, then Christianity is pantheism; if Jesus is God, then Christianity is polytheistic pantheism. Neither is monotheism.

If God is "other," then God is not logos. God employs logos; or God employs reason (logos) to produce the resulting reasonable order of existence (logos). But God isn't logos any more than mind is brain.

In John, the Greek word *logos* is rendered capitalized "Word" in English. The passage actually reads, "In the beginning was the logos..." *The Cambridge Dictionary of Philosophy*, *Webster's New Universal Unabridged Dictionary*, and *The HarperCollins Bible Dictionary* all define the Greek *logos* as "word," but they include other meanings such as statement, speech, discourse, thesis, argument, reason, reasoning, the rational faculty (Plato's logos as the intellectual aspect of the soul), abstract theory, discursive reasoning, explanation, reckoning, accounting, measure, relation, proportion, ration (Aristotle's logoi of musical scales), value, worth (Heraclitus's logos of humans being greater than that of other beings). In Stocism logos indicates divine order; Neoplatonism designates logos as the intelligible regulating forces displayed in the sensible world.

Logos forms the suffix of names of disciplines such as biology, psychology, and theology. All these disciplines rationally explore natural occurrences, origins, and interrelationships. All assume the necessity of reason. *Webster's* notes that the Greek *lógos* is akin to *légein*, to choose, gather, recount, tell over, speak. Reason distinguishes this from that, and necessitates the choice of this not that. By all definitions, divine logos separates the light from the dark. Heraclitus would approve.

The HarperCollins Bible Dictionary notes that the term logos "was taken over by Philo, the Alexandrian philosophical theologian of Judaism, who was roughly a contemporary of the apostle Paul." It's important to note that scholars date the writings of Paul as *earlier* than the Gospels, including John. "By means of the logos, Philo sought to reconcile Greek philosophical theories about the universe (cosmology) with the biblical accounts of God's creating the world by his spoken word. God's logos became a clearly identifiable entity, mediating between God and the world, the mode of the divine creativity and revelation." An equally important point is that the complex Greek term was used in John to translate the equally complex Hebrew word, which could mean, among other things, "word," "thing," or "event," and that the English translation "word," especially capitalized, brought its own connotations.

For Christians, logos is the divine word or reason incarnate in Jesus Christ, "the Word" who "became flesh" in the moment of Creation. In a brilliant stroke of genius, the author of John conflates *mythos*, i.e., "word," with *logos*, i.e., "word," and personifies the conflation as a human version of God. Jesus could well represent the intelligence of God displayed through intelligently designed Nature. The author of John (who might well have been Philo) seems to try to bridge the archaic tendency of religion to make gods human (or at least in the image of humans) and the modern inclination of philosophy to demarcate the distinction and the connection between God and rational Creation: Nature. It's interesting that Paul, the author of most of the books of the New Testament, doesn't discuss the historical life, works, or teachings of Jesus at all; Jesus is all mythologized logos.

In addition to logos, "wisdom," the Greek *sophia*, which Aristotle considered the highest knowledge of the wisest of the wise, also played a mediatorial role between God and creation. In *The Symposium* Plato addresses mediation as the province of those in spiritual pursuit of Beauty. Here Plato's character, Socrates, patterned after the actual person Socrates, quotes another character, Diotima, who expresses the view of the character Socrates who expresses the view of Plato (which itself represents the process of mythmaking). Diotima traces the interconnection of spiritual love, beauty, creativity, immortality, wisdom, truth, and virtue. "God is love" and Jesus as "the word of life" and "the word of God" are not original Christian concepts. These phrases are literary devices, specifically metaphor and personification, employed to represent an idea—opinion, guess—about the connection between God and Creation, and between Creation and us. The authors of John (the gospel) and I John (the letter) undoubtedly knew this passage from Plato in which Socrates recounts asking Diotima, "What could Love be?" She answers:

> A great spirit; for all the spiritual is between divine and mortal...power...to interpret and to ferry across to the gods things given by humans, and to humans things from the gods, from humans petitions and sacrifices, from the gods commands and requitals in return; and being in the middle, Love completes them and binds all together into a whole. Through this intermediary moves all art of divination, and the art of priests, and all concerned with sacrifice and mysteries and incantations, and all sorcery and witchcraft. For God mingles not with humanity, but through this comes all the communion and conversation of gods with people and people with gods, both awake and asleep; and she who is expert in this is a spiritual person, but the expert in something other than this, such as common arts or crafts, is vulgar. These spirits are many and of all sorts and kinds, and one of them is Love...Immortality is what all this earnestness to procreate and love pursue...for the immortal is what they love...those who are pregnant in

soul—for there are some who conceive in soul still more than in body what is proper for the soul to conceive and bear. And what is proper? Wisdom and virtue in general—to this class belong all creative poets, and those artists and craftsmen who are said to be inventive...A person with divinity in him, whose soul from his youth is pregnant with these things, desires when he grows up to beget and procreate...for by attaching himself to a person of [soul] beauty and keeping company with her, he begets and procreates what he has long been pregnant with; present and absent he remembers her, and with her he fosters what is begotten, so that as a result these people maintain a much closer communion together and a firmer friendship...by contemplating beautiful things rightly in due order...suddenly she will behold a beauty marvelous in its nature, that very Beauty for the sake of which all the earlier hardships had been borne: in the first place, everlasting, and never being born nor perishing, neither increasing nor diminishing...being by itself with itself always in simplicity...she sees the beautiful with the mind, which alone can see it, to give birth not to likenesses of virtue, since she touches no likeness, but to realities, since she touches reality; and when she has given birth to real virtue and brought it up, will it not be granted her to be the friend of God, and immortal if anyone ever is?

Socrates (i.e., Plato), of course, employs the literary device of metaphoric personification to represent his idea—his opinion, his guess—about the connection between two distinct entities: between God and everything else; between God and Nature. The intelligibility (rational logos) of Creation (manifest logos) and our ability to perceive and understand the Creation-logos themselves express God's love for us and for Creation.

In natural religion, logos indicates the immanence of God. Put another way, the transcendent Creator perpetually actively creates Creation. Creation isn't static; Creation perpetually comes into being, just as Heraclitus and Socrates and Plato and Aristotle and a host of other ancient philosophers assumed. Did God wind it all up just to walk away as the tension wound down? Or is God an artist perpetually creating art as an expression of love? If God is an artist, an artist representing something to us, then religion might best serve to explore aesthetically the interrelationship between God and us. Religious art and ritual serve this function, but only when their objects aren't deified; but usually they are, as is the case with religious elements ranging from magic potions to talismans to spells to baptisms. The Bible itself displays how Christian communion evolved from symbolic to literal body and blood (see especially John 6; in fact, try reading the entire Gospel of John as symbolic). If God's artwork is a manifestation of love, then religious people should probably think twice about defacing Creation for mindless pleasure and profit, and instead focus on honoring the delicate, sacred interrelationship, both material and spiritual, between us and Creation.

How would the authentically spiritual person respond to the logos, to Creation? Darwinians and atheists can justify dishonoring and desacralizing nature with anti-environmental agendas. But given that "religious" rightwingers are among the worst offenders, doesn't that suggest that their religion isn't an authentic religion of logos? Aren't anti-environmental fundamentalists, who advocate exploitation of nature as their special right, the heretics of natural religion honoring the Creator of Nature?

In the last chapter I quoted Eitzen and Timmer, who quote Currie: "Contemporary conservatives like those conservatives before them who 'have successfully posed as the guardians of domestic tranquility for decades' typically promote social and economic policies 'that bear a large part of the responsibility for the level of crime and violence we suffer today'." By supporting politicians that favor the rich and wealth-generating banks and corporations, the religious Right participates in the economic meltdown and the social ills that corrode the America envisioned by our Founders.

For the typical Genesist today, even though Nature is Creation created by a more-or-less benevolent Creator, even the post-Flood natural realm, including one's own body, is an evil enemy to be subdued, and once subjugated, it becomes a slave subject to exploitation by the high priests, the chosen ones. As ultra-rightwinger Ann Coulter put it a few years back, "God gave us the earth. We have dominion over the plants, the animals, the trees. God said, 'Earth is yours. Take it. Rape it. It's yours.'" (Updated, there's the equally fashionably phallic, "Drill, baby, drill.") The image of rape, hypocritically ironic because it is anti-Christ (antithetical to the ethics of Christ) and anti-women (also antithetical to the ethics of Christ), corresponds to the male-dominated, women-as-property tradition of elitist religion and the desacralization not only of human equality and freedom but also of sexuality per se. Snotty Coulter's snobbish myth is decidedly Darwinian pretending to be Christian.

Interestingly, Deism, which values all humans equally and accepts stewardship of the Earth as a sacred duty, has more in common with the "love God, love your neighbor as yourself" theology of Christ (actual or fictional) than with the elitism of either Darwinism or rightwing Christianity.

My calling Christianity "rightwing," a political term, needs no clarification. But many people don't realize that the corporate aristocracy, most notably corporate polluters, long ago appropriated religious fundamentalism for its own sinister purposes. Grating FOX News pundits like Coulter serve as lobbying gophers for corporate raptor CEOs. Ordinary fundamentalists, indoctrinated by pundits and preachers, have been shepherded into political serfdom. Groups like the Moral Majority, the Christian Coalition, and the Tea Party were created to rake in big bucks for their anointed chieftains and for pockets of politicians promoting cutthroat capitalism as an American ideal and to thwart environmentalism's efforts to protect real American values, like truth, justice, equality, security, and the well-being that constitutes happiness—in other words, freedom from poisoning tyrants. As kickback, even mega-churches raking in mega-millions (in some cases, billions) retain their tax-free status.

Pollution is a literal poisoning of our literal Earth. But pollution also symbolically represents the poisoning of the human body, soul, and spirit—human meaning collective humanity and the human individual.

In spite of steps taken to regulate pollution thus far during President Obama's tenure, the corporate polluter cartel continues to threaten our society and government. Occupy Wall Street and the broader Occupy and Get Money Out movements have targeted the global problem of corporate oligarchy. Corporate polluters are just one slice of the Wall Street pie. But looking closely at the process of religious appropriation by one class of corporate exploiters might help some trusting sheep grasp the magnitude of corporate-church collusion underlying the current crisis threatening America and the world.

Revolution can potentially establish the true democracy envisioned by our Founders. But to succeed, it must expose how organized religion is exploited to smokescreen corporate crimes. Much darker than a marriage of Church and State is its spawn: Hog. Democracy is really in trouble when religion is annexed by the mondo Corporate Nation.

THE RAPE AND MURDER OF MOTHER EARTH

Environmentalism is in many ways the poster child for old-fashioned American democracy. Everyone has the constitutional right to own property. Nature should not be the property of the aristocracy. The commons—land, air, water, crops, seeds, etc.—should not fall into the exclusive grip of the 1%, it should remain the trust of the whole society.

The most anti-humane segment of that 1% has managed to meddle its way into the Christian psyche via TV evangelists and their political patsies. Over the past few decades, millions of gullible Christians have absorbed the God's-elite Earth-raping perspective doled out by mean-spirited, unchristlike dominionists. Dominionists—Christian elitists who deem themselves the chosen elect who should rule the world—enjoy ridiculing those of us who care for the Earth and all God's creatures. Jerry Falwell, for example, once scoffed, "We're going to invite PETA [to "Wild Game Night"] as our special guest, P-E-T-A—People for the Ethical Treatment of Animals. We want you to come, we're going to give you a top seat there, so you can sit there and suffer. This is one of my special groups. Another one's the ACLU, another is the NOW—the National Order of Witches. We've got—I've got a lot of special groups." And right on cue, the grazing sheep bleated, "Amen."

Anti-environmentalism is a decidedly far-right Republican agenda. Former state representative Casey Emerson of Bozeman, Montana, commented during a panel discussion regarding the Endangered Species Act, "I think there are some species that ought to be killed off to subdue the Earth." According to Florida's Gainesville Humanists, "He wondered aloud whether 'so-called environmentalists' had read the Bible passage stating that people must subdue the Earth. It should be like getting rid of weeds in a wheat field, he said."

In January 2006, twenty evangelical leaders wrote a letter to the National Association of Evangelicals' President, Reverend Ted Haggard (who you'll recall was later outed as gay by male prostitute Mike Jones), asking him to not recommend any official policy on global warming.

According to the *New York Times*, one signer argued that "It is bad...that so many 'evangelical' environmental extremists have infected our churches, colleges, universities and evangelicalism with their liberal brand of Christianity but now they want to damage America's free enterprise system by making it difficult for business to compete in the world market place." Today Foxy fundamentalists swear that global warming is a myth even though October 2012 was the 332nd consecutive month with above average global temperatures thanks to big oil, big coal, and other pig polluters.

Is environmentalism anti-Christian? No, it's anti-polluting-corporate oligarchy, which is anti-Christian according to dominionist citizens of the Corporate Nation. The corporate oligarchy has so successfully exploited religion and programmed the sheep to regurgitate its sacred message of "free enterprise" that free enterprise now means the Corporate Nation's right to fleece the sheep who unwittingly ask and even pay to be fleeced. Remember why your teacher made you read *Animal Farm* and *Nineteen Eighty-Four*?

Those sheep also collude in their own poisoning. To get around this problem, some evangelicals maintain the biblical belief that the poisoning destruction of the Earth does not affect them directly. Abstract spiritual doctrine transcends actual physical being. If your kids drink the poison your company dumps in the water, it won't harm them, because you're special, you live in a bubble of God's care. Never mind that your company's poison is killing the rest of us (and your kids).

Polluters long ago realized, no doubt with a sadistic chuckle, that they could flaunt their Earth-raping. Fundamentalist nothing-can-hurt-me (because my God won't let it) blind faith quickly led to political snake-handling. Denigration of nature and Earth science that leads to harmful exploitation of our physical Earth has been sanctified biblically and presented so positively, so self-righteously, that for decades the Religious Right has used it as a core political platform.

"We don't have to protect the environment, the Second Coming is at hand," proclaimed James Watt, President Reagan's Secretary of the Interior. "My responsibility is to follow the Scriptures which call upon us to occupy the land until Jesus returns."

"Don't let anything like trees in the Clearwater National Forest get in the way of providing jobs and fueling the economy, even if that means cutting down every last tree in the state," warned Congresswoman Helen

Chenoweth (R-ID) during her 1994 campaign.

Representative Don Young (R-AK) stated on Alaska Public Radio, "Environmentalists are a socialist group of individuals that are the tool of the Democrat Party. I'm proud to say that they are my enemy. They are not Americans, never have been Americans, never will be Americans."

"Why is Earth Day, today, also Lenin's birthday?" insinuated Alan Caruba, former Bush-era public relations advisor for corporate and political anti-environmentalists. "Coincidence? Or does it signal the true intent of the national and worldwide environmental movement?"

Using tactics of deceit that range from sublime to outrageous, evangelical Republicans still work hard to eradicate church-state separation in order to benefit the Corporate Nation, which they claim is threatened by environmentalists. The abstract "religious" perspective justifies the irresponsible exploitation of the planet, though there is nothing authentically Christian about the exploitative, anti-environmental worldview.

Exploitative, anti-environmental dominionism masquerading as Christianity is the epitome of unnatural. If God is immanent, then what we do to Creation, what we do to one of the least of these His creatures, we do to Him, the Word, the Logos, according biblical Christian principles.

Although we Deists reject the mythic notion of Jesus-equals-Creation, we agree that protecting the environment created by God is a sacred responsibility. In our view, there is nothing more unnatural, nothing more perverted than the selfish, ruthless rape and murder of Mother Earth and her children in the name of the God who created them.

Toxic pollution, one of the primary human rights violations in the United States, has caused hundreds of thousands of unnatural deaths and perversely diminished the health of millions of Americans. Pollution doesn't rise naturally from nature. Pollution is the unnatural refuse of unnatural processes instigated by unnatural organizations of people with unnatural desires. Corporate polluters, master con artists, have successfully exploited religion as their smokescreen and brainwashed their religious minions to constantly throw out red herrings like "unnatural" homosexuals, feminazis, socialists, illegals, Muslim terrorists, etc. to keep even the smart media off the toxic trail. But of course, even the smart media is owned by the corporate oligarchy.

In his book, *Crimes Against Nature: How George W. Bush & His*

Corporate Pals are Plundering the Country & Hijacking Our Democracy, environmental lawyer Robert F. Kennedy, Jr. chronicles the ascendancy of corporate polluters to positions of unprecedented power. Back in the seventies, when the Right as we know it was solidifying its power, the major corporate polluters formed a coalition that would offer hundreds of millions in campaign contributions to politicians who would overturn environmental regulations and thwart law enforcement and litigation against the politicians' corporate sponsors, the big polluters. They wanted to pollute and they wanted the citizens to foot the bill for cleanup.

Things really got organized and nasty when Joe Coors (as in beer) founded the Mountain States Legal Foundation (MSLF) to file suits against environmentalists, unions, and minorities—any category of Americans that could disrupt the flow of corporate profits. Multinational polluters such as Chevron, Exxon, Texaco Shell, Amoco, Phillips Petroleum, and Ford Motor Company kicked in the needed funds to fuel MSLF.

Out of MSLF evolved the bigger rightwing Heritage Foundation, which stated its intention "to strangle the environmental movement…the greatest single threat to the American economy." Heritage Foundation was the waterhole where industrialists, joined by politicians, and later by evangelists, met to plot their mutual prosperity via the exploitation of the other 99% of us. The biggest polluters kicked in the biggest bucks—tens of millions—to support Heritage. The top five donors, five major polluters representing the automobile, coal, oil, and chemical companies—the "Gang of Five"—were the John M. Olin Foundation, maker of ammunition and toxic chemicals; Sarah Scaife Foundation, funded by arch-conservative Richard Mellon Scaife's industrial, oil, and banking fortune; Castle Rock Foundation, funded by Joe Coors; Charles G. Koch Charitable Foundation, funded by Koch, chairman of Koch Industries, the country's largest independent oil company and a mega-polluter; and Bradley Foundation, funded by electronics fortunes.

Other corporate polluters such as ExxonMobile, Chevron, and DuPont added to Gang of Five contributions to maintain Heritage's $34 million annual budget. Heritage spawned numerous facsimiles that piled up their own bankrolls for funding legal political bribes known as campaign contributions and lobbying. Groups like the Competitive Enterprise Institute, American Enterprise Institute, Reason Foundation, Federalist Society, Marshall Institute, Mercatus Center, and several other so-called "think tanks" were all greased by filthy rich industrialists.

Around 1980, the Coors cult staged the Sagebrush Rebellion to unite corporate and fundamentalist forces into a machine intent on taking control of the government. Ronald Reagan was its first willing victim. Heritage became Reagan's shadow government, conveniently housed in the Executive Office Building across from the White House. With Coors at the helm of a cabal of rightwing millionaires, Heritage deployed its 2,000 page manifesto, *Mandate for Change*, intended to dictate administration policy.

Coors picked several of Reagan's top administrators, for instance Anne Gorsuch for EPA. Gorsuch promptly slashed EPA's budget by 30 percent, demolished the Superfund, and appointed lobbyists from polluting industries to positions intended to protect the environment and its citizens from polluters. A timber industry lawyer became her chief of staff; Exxon provided her enforcement chief. Robert Buford, who vowed to destroy the Bureau of Land Management, became head of the Bureau of Land Management. James Watt, president of MSLF, the archenemy of the Department of the Interior, was appointed Secretary of the Department of the Interior.

A lot of people back then were laughing at "Lightbulb" Watt, so named for his bald head and long skinny neck. Probably most of us boomers remember his being unscrewed and canned. James Watt became synonymous for a classic religious nut, voltage one watt, as the joke went, one of those kinky apocalyptic fundamentalist dominionists so called for their insistence on man's metamisogynist duty to "subdue," i.e. exploit/rape, Mother Earth. He fulfilled this charge by relinquishing all notions of Christian stewardship and selling public lands to his rich industrialist cronies for next to nothing. Environmentalists, he warned, were "a left-wing cult which seeks to bring down the type of government I believe in." Which was dominionism, i.e., dominance of the Corporate Nation, the antithesis of democracy. Forced out of office in 1981, after 1.1 million Americans signed a petition calling for his removal, Watt was indicted on twenty-five counts of perjury, unlawful concealment, and obstruction of justice. Following closely in his wake, EPA's Gorsuch and twenty-three of her appointees faced congressional investigations of deals with Coors and other big polluters, forcing her resignation, along with that of her first deputy, Rita LaVelle, who was jailed for perjury and obstruction of justice.

Expedient sacrifices. Besides raking in billions, the big guys taught Reagan the meaning of deregulation. Big corporations grabbed at everything, including the press. Eradicating the Fairness Doctrine that had assured a balanced presentation of the news was a Sagebrush mission accomplished. Fat corporations got fatter gobbling up the media. Horrified Democrats and Republicans alike tried to preserve the Fairness Doctrine via legislation but were thwarted by Reagan's persistent vetoes.

Deflated by the numerous indictments and resignations, the Sagebrush Rebels pasted on a smiley face and in a flourish of Orwellian newspeak, renamed themselves "Wise Use." Timber industry press agent Ron Arnold, the official founder of Wise Use, reiterated, "Our goal is to destroy, to eradicate the environmental movement. We want you to be able to exploit the environment for private gain, absolutely." Hog squealed.

Naming themselves "Wise Use," the masked antithesis of themselves, deceived so well that other polluter front groups adopted their own antithetical disguises, their own "conterms," the term I use to mean a con word or concept or entity deceptively named to mean the exact opposite of what it actually is. Citizens For the Environment had no citizen membership, for instance; it represented corporate sponsors by lobbying *against* environmental regulations like the Clean Air Act. The Environmental Conservation Organization represented land developers and businesses opposed to conservation of wetlands. The Evergreen Foundation, representing the timber industry, advocated clear-cutting as pro-environment. The energy industry's Citizens for Sensible Control of Acid Rain opposed all controls of acid rain.

Wise Use did make wise use of one valuable American commodity: Religion. Ron Arnold headed up the Washington State chapter of the American Freedom Coalition, a political arm of Sun Myung Moon's heretical Unification Church (remember the Moonies?), which strove for anything but American freedom. It's fair to say that Wise Use itself was an arm of Reverend Moon's Church. Robert Grant's fundamentalist American Christian Cause in California had helped elect Reagan. He and others recruited Jerry Falwell to form the Moral Majority, which was neither moral nor a majority. When Wise Use later recruited Pat Robertson's Christian Coalition to the dominionist cause, the Right took a giant stride closer to their goal to control and exploit the American people. Robertson, the grand master of purposive deception, labeled environmentalists "communists," the evil priests of a New World Order of state mandated paganism intent on destroying Christianity and democracy. According to Robertson's paranoid worldview, the U.S. government was an alien nation, a kind of internal terrorist cult working to disarm citizens through gun control laws so they couldn't fight the alien government's insidious war against the family. The Corporate Nation, of course, was the real "government" doing that, so reeling in Robertson was a stroke of psychopathic genius.

In 1994, Robertson's Christian Coalition was fined for improperly funding then Representative Newt Gingrich (despite his much-publicized unchristian adulteries) and Republican Senate nominee Oliver North of Virginia. In 1995, the Christian Coalition formed an alliance with the National Beer Wholesalers to pass a Republican initiative that would restrict lobbying by nonprofit groups that get federal grants. Back then, nonprofits tended to be humanitarian and progressive rather than "Christian" like the tax-free mega-churches.

Despite public exposure of his criminal activities and sophomoric grasp of American jurisprudence, Robertson shamelessly created Regent University, funded by Coors beer via the Coors Foundation, much to the chagrin of MADD (Mothers Against Drunk Driving). In addition to its thriving ultra-right journalism department, Regent University houses The American Center for Law and Justice, a non-profit public-interest law firm that aggressively promotes the extreme Christian Right reconstructionist agenda demanding total integration of biblical law into society, the abolition of public schools, and "bringing the local media under the influence of a biblical world view." Robertson named his university Regent because a regent is someone "who governs in the absence of a sovereign." Regent university's purpose is to prepare its students to rule the millennial Kingdom. Needless to say, the reconstructionist agenda paved the way for a takeover by the wolf in sheep's clothing, the Hog Messiah, the Corporate Nation.

It's no surprise that the Christian Coalition's executive director, Ralph Reed, its aggressive and successful Wise Use greenwasher and media spokesperson/personnel trainer, became a Bush II campaign official. Reed symbolizes the merging of polluter industries, politics, and religion. Wise Use elevated mega-anti-environmentalist family values poster child Newt Gingrich, and later his ditto, Tom DeLay, to the influential position of

Speaker of the House, where together they gutted environmental law by slyly attaching riders to must-pass budget bills and promoting supermandates with conterm names. In 1995, as part of Gingrich's effort to enact Wise Use's anti-environmental manifesto, "Contract With America," DeLay asked 350 lobbyists for the biggest polluters to assist in drafting legislation that would dismantle federal health, safety, and environmental laws.

That same year, President Clinton shut down the government rather than pass a rider-riddled budget bill. Public outcry resulted with first Gingrich, then later DeLay being forced to resign and eventually indicted for their many crimes against nature. Is it any wonder that faux family values Gingrich and DeLay led the Clinton-Lewinsky lynch mob? Their version of revenge is yet another, almost humorous form of conterm. Gingrich was himself such a notorious adulterer that during his presidential campaign, his entire core staff resigned because of it. Gingrich and DeLay were each indicted for serious crimes committed against the American people and their laws, and both lost their jobs because of some of them. Some of the worst of those crimes were committed with the active support of prominent fundamentalists. Long live family values.

By the time Bush II ascended to the presidency, dominionists had germinated special interest domination into a seedling oligarchy. Dominionists upped the dirty politics ante by coordinating the new tactic of purposeful lying. Conterm became an important strategy to dupe the citizens who believed that America was still a democracy.

Wise Use dominionists were of course delighted when Bush picked as his running mate Dick Cheney, CEO and Chairman of Halliburton, the world's second-largest oil-drilling services company. Or perhaps, when Dick Cheney picked Bush. Between 1997 and 2002, Halliburton contributed over a million and a half purposeful dollars to the Republicans, primarily Bush. The energy industry kicked in over a hundred million and in turn reaped billions from Bush's handouts and axing of regulations and enforcement positions. Bush-era taxpayers shelled out over $65 billion a year in big oil subsidies, and another $35 billion-plus in subsidies to other energy big guys, subsidies given to corporations that were already making billions in profits at citizens' expense, subsidies, as Robert F. Kennedy, Jr. put it, that "helped create the billionaires who financed the right-wing revolution on Capitol Hill and put George W. Bush in the White House.

And now they have indentured servants in Washington demanding that we have capitalism for the poor and socialism for the rich...The free market has been all but eliminated in an energy sector dominated by cartels and monopolies and distorted by obscene subsidies to the filthiest polluters." Subsidies, remember, come from the Treasury, i.e., our tax dollars.

When those subsidized corporations move their headquarters to Bermuda and their operations to Taiwan, how does that benefit America? Isn't it treason to exploit one's own country by taking its tax dollars while inflating the cost of its products, cutting American jobs, and dumping toxic pollution that the American taxpayer has to clean up? Bush's "tax cuts" were cuts for the upper class at the expense of the rest of us, yet the FTC disclosed in March 2001 that tax-bled consumers had paid billions for gasoline those undertaxed and tax-exempt companies had hoarded to drive up prices. Each year companies violating environmental and labor safety statutes are awarded hundreds of billions in federal contracts. Thanks to Bush, big polluters saved hundreds of billions of dollars, and the public, not the polluters, must pay for the cleanup.

Dick Cheney facilitated the exchange of huge industrialist campaign contributions for much huger paybacks in the form of government appointments and government subsidies and tax breaks. Of Bush's forty-eight member transition team, thirty-one—including the six most powerful White House officials—had intimate professional ties to the energy industry.

With Cheney's guidance, Bush stuffed his cabinet with top officials and lobbyists from major polluting corporations, especially from the energy sector. Condoleezza Rice was a long-time board member of Chevron. Karl Rove was deeply invested in Enron, BP Amoco, and Royal Dutch Shell. Clay Johnson, director of presidential personnel, was heavily invested in El Paso Energy Partners; Lewis "Scooter" Libby, Cheney's chief of staff, Samuel Bodman, Kathleen Cooper, and many others were all deeply attached to corporate polluters. The energy industries had gained control of the government via a legally bribed—"lobbied"—elected official, the President. That's right: An enemy nation, the Corporate Nation, had elected one of its own as President to assist them in their covert coup d'état.

In a grand gesture of conterm, almost a fuck-you to the American people, the second Bush one-upped Reagan in the sheer number of top officials and lobbyists from the biggest polluters he appointed to top positions in government agencies that were supposed to oversee and protect America's environment and natural resources. Like Reagan, Bush filled specific agency positions with polluter advocates from the very corporate segments that were specific agencies' biggest violators. For head of the Department of Interior (which protects our natural resources) he picked Gale Norton, former attorney for Coors' MSLF under its director, James Watt. Norton not only expressly hates government and EPA regulations, she also opposes wheelchair ramps, asbestos removal from schools, the Fair Labor Standards Act, and the Violence Against Women Act. Norton advocates strip mining, clear-cut logging, and "raping the earth" by polluting industries. She allowed opening nine million acres of Alaska's North Slope to oil and gas developers, just for starters. She founded her own conterm pro-earth-rape organization, the Council of Republicans for Environmental Advocacy, which really means Advocacy for Mega-rich Earth-raping Industrialists Against Americans.

Mining lobbyist J. Steven Griles became Norton's second in command. Griles immediately arranged that the federal government would pay Chevron $46 million to not drill off the coast of Florida, to help Jeb Bush, the President's brother, get reelected governor. It didn't hurt veteran Chevron board member Condoleezza Rice, either. It was no surprise that near the end of Jeb's term, local news here in Florida reported that he now favored drilling. Griles has since been the focus of a criminal investigation for perjury and ethics laws violations, and for helping former clients secure government contracts. The Interior Department refused to release documents regarding a $1.1 million payment to Griles that were requested under the Freedom of Information Act. Griles was also implicated in federal payoffs to Shell and Chevron.

For EPA Director, Bush picked one of the nation's leading advocates of pollution-based prosperity, Christine Todd Whitman, who slashed EPA's budget, fired nearly all EPA's enforcement attorneys, and instituted "voluntary compliance" to replace enforcement of pollution laws.

To head EPA's Superfund, Bush appointed Marianne Horinko, a lobbyist and consultant to polluters, including mega-polluters Koch Petroleum and Koch Industries, the country's largest privately held oil company, owned by Wise Use funder and Bush megadonor, Charles Koch.

Bush installed former Alcoa CEO Paul O'Neill at the Treasury Department (who later quit, dismayed with obese Bush spending). Timber lobbyist Mark Rey became head of the Department of Agriculture. Mining lobbyist Thomas Sansonetti became Assistant Attorney General of Environmental and Natural Resources in the Justice Department. Linda Fisher, a lobbyist for Monsanto, one of the nation's largest polluters, became EPA Deputy Administrator. Jeffrey Holmstead, a utilities lobbyist and leader of a Wise Use front group, became Assistant Administrator of Air and Radiation. As Director of the White House Council on Environmental Quality, Bush appointed James Connaughton, a lawyer for asbestos polluters. And on and on.

Bush had a penchant for hiring just the right toadies to implement his agenda. He had a special mission for John Graham, director of the Office of Information and Regulatory Affairs, a nondescript agency within the Office of Management and Budget. Graham's cost-benefit analysis favoring Wise Use and his "long track record of ideological scorn for the public welfare," as Kennedy put it, made him the perfect gofer to make sure Bush's anti-environmental fiddling remained both secretive and, when outed, justified. Perhaps his most significant contribution was to fund media quack scientists who were industry insiders eager to contradict all the hard scientific environmental data documented by the very long list of real scientists and prestigious scientific organizations.

Bush continued the tradition of conterm naming. His "Healthy Forests," for instance, promoted destructive logging, and "Clear Skies" muddied the Clean Air Act.

EXIT THE SWAMP, ENTER THE QUICKSAND

Given Dick Cheney's deep involvement in Wise Use, it's not surprising that when he and Bush took office, the Justice Department kicked in its part of the $325,000 grant to study and report on environmental terrorism awarded to Wise Use founder Ron Arnold. Evidently, Arnold made no recommendations. Even though Attorney General John Ashcroft ranked environmental terrorism as the nation's top domestic terrorist threat, the Bush administration did nothing to secure the viable targets, such as chemical plants, nuclear power plants, or oil processing facilities. Even I can easily purchase at the local feed store enough ammonium nitrate to blow up the Capitol. But then, should we trust Ashcroft? You might recall that Bush snatched up Ashcroft for his cabinet right after Ashcroft lost his Senate seat. The good citizens of conservative Missouri voted for his deceased opponent, who had died the month before the election, rather than vote for Ashcroft. Ashcroft became even more infamous for ignoring critical information from U.S. intelligence sources warning that bin Laden was planning an attack on American soil using hijacked American planes. Ashcroft even refused to receive intelligence terrorist information; he said he was tired of getting it.

In the Bush White House, Church and State were sleeping together. Ashcroft resigned after Bush's first term and accepted a teaching position at Pat Robertson's Regent University. In January 2001, Bush issued an executive order establishing The White House Office of Faith-Based and Community Initiatives. John DiIulio, who was recruited to run the operation, quit in August, blaming the administration for caring more about politics than policy. According to former director Jim Towey, only Christian religious groups received funding. In 2005, more than $2.1 billion in grants were awarded. In effect, Bush illegally violated church-state separation by giving citizens' tax dollars to potential Bush supporters who could turn out Bush voters. It's like they stole money from your checking account to spend on scams that further ripped you off. Faith-Based Initiatives director Jay Hein was VP and CEO of the Foundation for American Renewal, whose stated goal includes: "America can be renewed only by returning to the nation's founding Biblical principles," which presumably includes raping the Earth, exploiting her children, and lying.

The Bush administration wasn't just the vector of Republican, corporate, and fundamentalist dominionists. There was a fourth player: neoconservatives, aka the "neocon." But the "new con" was the same old same old.

The nonprofit Project for the New American Century (PNAC), funded by the Sarah Scaife Foundation, John M. Olin Foundation, and Bradley Foundation (the same foundations that funded Heritage/Sagebrush/Wise Use), is perhaps the most prominent neocon think tank. Established in 1997, PNAC advocates U.S. global domination in all areas, including military, economics, space, and the new "international commons," cyberspace. When it suits them, PNAC neocons subscribe to the Kirkpatrick Doctrine, which originated as an anti-communist agenda that allowed for support of rightwing dictatorships that opposed liberalism but that has evolved into the super-inflated, mostly bogus "war against terror."

Neocons are credited with pressing for the Gulf War as an opportunity to rid oil-rich Iraq and neighboring Kuwait of Saddam Hussein's hold and to establish the U.S. military throughout the Middle East, including Saudi Arabia, ostensibly to "protect" our "ally," which happens to sit on the world's largest oil reserves but which lacks a strong military. Neocons, noted for their aristocratic disparagement of the United Nations, criticized Bush I for adhering to the U.N. agreement that the U.S. would simply oust Hussein from Kuwait rather than remove the dictator from the region altogether. The neocons pressed Clinton to finish the job; dictators got in the way of their plans to "extract," i.e. steal, Middle East oil and to assume domination of that strategic corporate/political market/territory—in other words, domination by the Corporate Nation.

In previous decades, the neocon Corporate Nation advocated a confrontational stance toward China and strong military support for Taiwan. More recently, money-grubby neocons seem only concerned with the oil-rich Middle East and decidedly unconcerned with China, Russia, or the North Korean nuclear crisis. PNAC cofounder Donald Rumsfeld compared Hussein with Stalin and Hitler. Hussein, of course, was sitting on oil. Demonize Hussein, "secure" his oil.

As payback for the enormous campaign donations that helped secure his election, Bush II appointed many PNAC members to key positions in his administration, including Vice President Dick Cheney; Donald Rumsfeld, Secretary of Defense; Elliott Abrams, National Security Council; I. Lewis Libby, Chief of Staff for Cheney (resigned October 2005; indicted by a grand jury on charges of obstruction of justice, false statements, and perjury in the Plame CIA leak controversy); Richard Armitage, Deputy Secretary of State (also implicated in Plame); John Bolton, U.S. Ambassador to the United Nations; Paul Wolfowitz, President of the World Bank; Peter Rodman, Assistant Secretary of Defense for International Security; Doy Zakheim, Department of Defense; Robert Zoellick, Deputy Secretary of State; Zalmay Khalilzad, U.S. Ambassador to Iraq; Seth Cropsey, Director of the International Broadcasting Bureau; Paula Dobriansky, Undersecretary of State for Global Affairs; Bruce Jackson (former Lockheed Martin VP for Strategy & Planning), President of U.S. Committee on NATO; Randy Scheunemann, U.S. Committee on NATO; and Francis Fukuyama, President's Council on Bioethics. Other members include Jeb Bush, Gary Bauer, William Bennett, Ellen Bork, Dan

Quayle, Richard Perle, and Jeane Kirkpatrick, to name but a few.

Extensive evidence has been surfacing that 9/11 and the invasion of Iraq could well have been orchestrated by PNAC members to further their stated and unstated goals (the subtext, of course, being expansionist/imperialist business opportunities). It has been suggested that Bush himself might have been exploited by PNAC. Though Governor Bush's tax cuts proved him to be pro-business, candidate Bush opposed military confrontation and the neocon's "nation-building" agenda, and early in his presidency, he lacked interest in supporting Israel and followed policies that neocon critics claimed were essentially the same as Clinton's.

Then came 9/11. Michael Moore's *Fahrenheit 9/11* suggests that Bush's lack of response to news of the attacks indicated not just his lack of decisive leadership; perhaps he had foreknowledge. But there's another possibility: Bush didn't know in advance but was processing the probability that PNAC could well have been involved. Maybe he was considering the possibility that he might be a target of assassination by one or more of *them*. They did, after all, blame 9/11 on Clinton's and Bush's lack of "ambition," meaning lack of aggressive involvement in neocon targets for exploitation. It seems awfully convenient that right when Bush was being buried under domestic pressures like accusations of voter fraud on his behalf and record unemployment, a *deus ex machina* dropped from the rafters.

Of course, Al-Qaeda also had its reasons for terrorist attacks. Of particular offense was U.S. support for "Muslim tyrannies" such as Saudi Arabia, Egypt, and Jordan, unqualified support for Israel, and manipulation of oil prices favoring Western consumers.

Regardless of who instigated and/or enabled 9/11, Bush's agenda took an instant about-face. The "threat of Communism" resurrected as immediate, graphic fear of "Islamic terrorism." Oil-ripe Afghanistan and Iraq were easily demonized as the source of terrorists and origin of terrorist attacks. The neocon-crafted Bush Doctrine that nations harboring terrorists were enemies of the United States, and then at war with the United States, furthered the neocon agenda and allowed them to repackage the puppet Bush as a skillful, heroic leader that would do their bidding and inspire every citizen to likewise obey. Now neocon expansive geopolitical avarice could run rampant. Their goal was in sight. PNAC aristocrats—the Corporate Nation—would rule the world.

Connect the dots and a frightening picture comes into focus. It's that same old agenda of domination via fear. In some circles, it's called playing God.

In his September 11, 2006, address to the nation, Bush asserted that the war on terror "will set the course for this new century and determine the destiny of millions across the world." Many throughout the world, certain that the terror has been staged by PNAC to justify a deceptive "war on terror," cite the organization's 90-page report, *Rebuilding America's Defenses: Strategies, Forces, and Resources For a New Century*, Chapter V, "Creating Tomorrow's Dominant Force," which discusses the Defense Department's need to aggressively upgrade the military with new technologies and operational concepts, while noting that the change they wanted would be a long, slow process "absent some catastrophic and catalyzing event—like a new Pearl Harbor." The 9/11-justified Iraq War would fulfill PNAC's strategy that America become the only world superpower, ensuring military-protected U.S. corporate expansionism and dominance, especially the mega-elite corporations and nations that make up the enormously wealthy Carlyle Group, a coalition of investors that includes Bush and his top cabinet members and associates and many of the world's richest oil barons, including Saudi royalty, including the bin Ladens.

Weigh both PNAC's desire to upgrade the military through significant increases in military spending and Carlyle's heavy investment not only in oil but also in defense. Neocons had everything to gain. Citizens, however, had thousands of lives (not counting tens of thousands of Iraqi lives) and billions of dollars to lose. Billions to lose immediately, directly in the war; trillions if the war dragged on (and it has), trillions more if you throw in all the ways Bush's war and other PNAC policies have enriched his neocon/corporate-welfare cronies. The scam is so blatant it smacks of the spoiled, conniving, historically classic aristocracy that it is. Spoiled nouveau riche Dick Cheney granted Halliburton multi-billion no-bid contracts for services that even his own government considered, in so many words, a rip-off. Prior to the invasion of Iraq, Halliburton was selling millions of dollars of supplies to Iraq for its oil industry via old subsidiaries of Dresser Industries under the corrupt UN Oil for Food Program. Former CEO and Chairman Cheney reportedly owned 433,333 Halliburton stock options worth about $8 million in addition to his enormous deferred compensation. In 2005, the Cheneys' gross income was about $8.82 million. Dick's net worth, derived mainly from his position at Halliburton, was between $30 million and $100 million. Such blatant conflict of interest could only be orchestrated by the VP himself. To spin a comment by the late Molly Ivans, electing puppet-king Bush was setting the fox to guard the hen house, but puppeteer Cheney as vice-president was a raccoon already in the hen house wrecking havoc.

Hussein's harboring of Al-Qaeda and development of weapons of mass destruction provided the concrete excuse to invade Iraq, but both excuses have proven to be blatant deceptions of enormous consequence. Many former Bush administrators, high-ranking military commanders, and CIA and FBI operatives have testified that the Bush team knew well in advance that a 9/11-type attack using hijacked planes was imminent yet the administration did nothing to secure the nation. Even after 9/11 they did nothing to secure the nation (they never did). But they did everything to scare the nation into backing their unwarranted overkill bombing of Baghdad, after warning Hussein to escape and despite the average Baghdad citizen's inability to flee. (And of course, the expended military firepower would need to be replenished, benefiting the Carlyle investors and fulfilling the neocon's demand for an upgraded military.) They did everything to terrify the nation into relinquishing its rights—rights that define us as Americans—under the conterms "Patriot" Act and "Homeland" "Security." Many critics believe that Cheney authorized the Valerie Plame CIA leak (which some point out *could* have led to her assassination) as revenge against her husband, Ambassador Joseph Wilson, who refused to substantiate Cheney's false claim that Niger was supplying Hussein with uranium-enriched yellowcake used to make nuclear weapons.

Benjamin Ferencz, a chief prosecutor at the Nuremberg trials, has argued that both Hussein and Bush should be tried for war crimes for starting aggressive wars. Under the Nuremberg Principles, because the U.S. was not defending against an imminent threat, its invasion of Iraq constituted the supreme international crime superseding all other war crimes. The world community agrees that the invasion, in the absence of authorization from the U.N. Security Council, is a crime against international peace in an era when cooperation is paramount.

One wonders why so many Americans have forgotten that when the first George Bush was head of the CIA, he gave weapons and billions of

American taxpayer dollars to religious fundamentalists known as Taliban under the leadership of Osama bin Laden so they could ward off the Russians and thereby protect Afghan oil for rich Carlyle Group oil barons and their expensive pipelines. Though it was compliments of American taxpayers, this wasn't American oil. No, this was privately owned oil that "American" oil barons would sell to Americans and the rest of the world at hugely inflated prices. When Bush I staged the Gulf War in 1991 as an excuse to invade Iraq, the price of oil soared from $13 to $40 dollars a barrel. Bush II invaded Iraq to finish the job of securing its oil for rich oil barons, many of whom just happened to be American, a few of them Bushes. Oil soared again. So did other commodities, and so did the hopes of venture capitalists like the Carlyle investors. It was all part of the Corporate Nation's coup of America.

Bush ties to bin Laden went way back. Even before Bush I reneged on his promise that Osama would rule Afghanistan, James Bath, a buddy of Bush II (they had been discharged from the Texas National Guard together for failing to appear for a medical exam), became the Texas money manager for the bin Ladens while Bush I was head of the CIA. Bath started his own aviation company after selling a plane to bin Laden. Bush II started a couple oil companies, distinguishing himself as a dry hole driller. An utter failure, Bush still had substantial cash flow, thanks to Bath investments in him. In other words, as Michael Moore points out, Bath used Saudi money to invest in Bush II. Which made sense, given that Bush II was the son of then-President Bush I, commander-in-chief of the military forces holding down the fort in Saudi Arabia. It didn't hurt that the President's son was on the board of directors of Harken when it came under investigation in 1990. Robert Jordon, attorney with James Baker's law firm, got Bush off and was subsequently appointed ambassador to Saudi Arabia. It didn't surprise me when I learned that during his first year in office, President Bush spent President Clinton's entire *surplus*—$5.6 trillion when Clinton left office, the largest surplus in American history. It didn't surprise me to learn that all that money, plus another $5 trillion, had been shifted from America's Treasury into the coffers of Bush's rich cronies. Stealing American money to fund an enemy nation, the Corporate Nation, is treason by American standards.

Given all this, it was perfectly natural that I, no doubt like many other informed Americans, blurted "Bush" when we witnessed with horror the collapse of the first Trade Tower.

It's significant that the Saudis had given $1.4 billion to the Bush family during the three decades preceding the election of Bush II. It's significant that the Saudis had invested $860 billion in America, making them the owners of 6-7% of America. It's significant that the Saudis had over a trillion dollars in our banks, which made our economy look "stronger." They had power over us, or rather, they had equalized "our" (Bush cartel's) power over them.

Shortly before 9/11, Bush had welcomed Taliban visitors, even though the Taliban had bombed the USS Cole and our African embassies. Bush had installed Afghanistan's new president, Harmid Karsi, a former advisor to Unicol—Unicol, as in big oil.

Immediately after 9/11, when all Americans (even Bush I) were grounded and stranded in airports, six private jets and two dozen commercial aircraft escorted 142 bin Ladens and other Saudis out of the country.

Why was Bush II doling out "we'll smoke out bin Laden" rhetoric at the same time he was protecting the bin Ladens, even preventing FBI and other investigators from questioning them? Bush tried to stop Congress from setting up its own 9/11 investigation, and he halted independent investigations. When Congress proceeded anyway with its investigation, the Bush administration censored twenty-eight pages of its report, most of it relating to Saudi Arabia. Saudi Prince Bandar, a bin Laden family member fondly called by the Bush family "Bandar Bush," was the most highly protected ambassador in American history, even though Al-Qaeda had been funded by Saudi money, even though most of the highjackers were Saudis. When 9/11 victims, ignored by Bush, filed a lawsuit against the Saudis, the Saudis hired Bush crony James Baker as their lawyer.

Of course the Bush cartel would blame Iraq, the second largest oil reserve in the world. They wanted to get at Iraq's oil. Ken Lay, CEO and Chairman of Enron, Bush's number one campaign contributor and part of Cheney's infamous insider "Energy Commission," would make a killing. (Before he could cash in, a grand jury convicted Lay of ten counts of securities fraud and other charges when Enron declared the largest bankruptcy thus far in U.S. history.) Unocal could get its pipeline through Iraq from Afghanistan. Informed Americans were outraged when Bush handed Cheney's Halliburton contracts to provide our armed forces' meals, clothing, communications, and other services at grotesquely inflated prices. And Cheney made sure that taxpayer-supported American troops provided guard services for private oil drillers even while Bush pushed for 33% pay cuts for soldiers and 60% cuts in assistance to their families, opposed veterans benefits, and supported closing Veterans hospitals. And American taxpayers (not the upper classes; they get all the tax breaks) would foot the bill for reconstruction.

"Dick Cheney!" my mind cried out as the second Tower collapsed. Was that cry a premonition?

After we bombed Iraq, it seemed logical to ask: If the Cheney-Bush administration could sacrifice the lives of thousands of Americans in Iraq—the largest number of military deaths since Vietnam—not to mention thousands of innocent Iraqi civilians, if they financially supported pollution that was known to kill tens of thousands of Americans each year, would they balk at sacrificing 2,973 American lives to a staged terrorist attack? It's not "liberal" but rather simply logical to consider Bush, Cheney, Carlyle, or other Bush-Cheney-Carlyle entities (neocon Rumsfeld, for instance) as possible suspects in the case.

Who really instigated the 9/11 attacks? What's utterly shocking is that it's not farfetched to think that high-ranking Americans could conceivably have been involved. "Nation building" is just a conterm for government subsidized infrastructure instituting corporate exploitation of foreign countries—and subsidized, of course, literally means at American taxpayers' expense. America's wars are corporate wars—wars advancing corporate interests. Wars are the Corporate Nation's most lucrative component of nation building. And soldiers naïvely die to advance this cause. Meanwhile, the poor get poorer, the Hog rich, richer.

MEANWHILE, BACK IN THE FERTILE FIELDS OF HOG SHIT

In January 2005, United Nations Chief Weapons Inspector Hans Blix announced that global warming dwarfs both war and terror as an international security risk. A multitude of the world's most prestigious scientists and scientific organizations concurred. The scientifically challenged Bush cartel disagreed. The Wise Use Bush cartel has always denigrated science, because science said there were no weapons of mass destruction in Iraq and that corporate pollution is destroying the world.

Blix hit a nerve. That corporate pollution causes global warming was something the Bush cartel didn't want gullible sheep known as Americans to ponder. Bush—who rejected evolution and stem cell research—evidently didn't care that the energy cartel jeopardizes the lives, health, well-being, and security of their own children and grandchildren. Even according to Bush's own hand-picked EPA, Bush's abolishment of key components of the Clean Air Act alone would result in the loss of 18,000 American lives each year—six times more than the 2,973 who died 9/11. Of course, air polluter industries contributed more than $100 million to Bush's campaign.

Most voting Americans don't know this. Thanks to Reagan's murder of the Fairness Doctrine and blanket deregulation, those same mega-rich polluting industries also own the media, whether outright or via advertising. When I last checked, NBC, for instance, was owned by the world's biggest polluter, General Electric, which held the world record with 86 Superfund sites. Until recently, CBS was owned by Westinghouse, the world's largest owner of nuclear power plants and third-largest manufacturer of nuclear weapons, besides having 39 Superfund sites. CNN belonged to AOL Time Warner, a major ultra-right dominionist campaign contributor. And the networks bring in over $15 billion a year in advertising from auto industry, auto as in oil, as in pollution.

You won't hear from the rightwing controlled media that in nineteen states, all fish are now unsafe to eat, or that one in six Americans have dangerous levels of mercury in their bodies. You won't hear that when Bush was governor of Texas, his anti-environmental policies allowed Houston to overtake Los Angeles as America's smoggiest city. Or that a quarter of Texas streams and rivers are so polluted that they aren't even safe for recreational use. Or that pollution-related health care costs of Houston residents range between $2.9 and $3.1 billion. Or that air pollution kills approximately 435 Houston residents each year.

If you got your news from mainstream sources, you probably didn't know that for the first time since the Clean Water Act was passed over thirty years ago, America's waters got dirtier under Bush, according to Bush's own EPA officials. Corporations are still strip-mining, logging, dumping toxins, waging war, and in every conceivable way raping and robbing America, but the wimp media would rather deaden your brain with movie star gossip and sensationalized crime sagas and political bickering than give you the real scoop, the real crime.

You did, however, hear the media blare in graphic detail the threat of the famous anthrax attacks, which killed a total of six people. The Wise Use dominionist-owned media used bullshit bullying to instill a home-front fear that could rally Americans around its war. Blind sheep that we are, we relinquished our rights to their cartel via the McCarthy wannabes' Patriot Act—yet another stroke of conterm genius. Even though the Patriot Act bill was submitted the night before the vote so no one had time to read it, the trembling Senate blindly voted overwhelmingly to pass it. The Senate voted like traitors of American democracy out of blatantly orchestrated fear. If you knew that, you likely got it from Michael Moore's *Fahrenheit 9/11* or some online liberal media; you certainly didn't hear it from the mainstream press.

Times had certainly changed. Back in 1979, you might well have heard about "corporate average fuel economy," or CAFE standards, established by President Carter to challenge the auto industry to design more fuel-efficient cars. I remember. Fuel economy rose 7.5 miles per gallon, turning an oil shortage into a surplus. Isn't fuel-efficiency a wise course of action? After all, the U.S. uses 25 percent of the world's oil but only houses three percent of global oil. 65 percent of global oil sits in the Persian Gulf states. In *Crimes Against Nature*, Robert Kennedy reminds us of this startling fact: "A 1-mile-per-gallon improvement would yield double the oil that could ever be extracted from the Arctic National Wildlife Refuge...A 2.6-mpg increase would eliminate the need for all Persian Gulf imports."

But in 1987, in order to benefit big oil and Detroit, President Reagan rolled back Carter's standards. Keep in mind that Joe Coors and his Sagebrush Rebels were calling the shots. Economist Amory Lovins reported that had the U.S. continued to conserve at the rate it did during the Carter era, we would have no longer needed Persian Gulf oil after 1986.

But rightwing Republicans "are" big corporations, especially big oil. Like psychopaths, so classified not just for the absence of good but for the presence of evil, these Republicans encourage polluter industries by deregulating, handing the already rich corporations giant subsidies, and giving them tax breaks (at the time Kennedy wrote his book a few years back, 61 percent of the largest corporations paid zero taxes on their huge profits). Thanks to Cheney-Bush, who rejected the tax deduction for gas-saving hybrid cars and implemented an obese $100,000 tax break for Hummers and the other thirty-eight thirstiest gas guzzlers, America had the worst energy efficiency in twenty years, which of course guaranteed huge profits for Cheney-Bush and friends. Little has changed, even with a Democratic president, thanks to Republican filibuster war-tactics.

Why can't we just say no to the oil pushers? Even now they're hoarding oil to drive up prices. They don't even care about polluting their own children's air and water, or fomenting terrorism, or waging wars that their grandchildren will pay for with their cash and their lives.

Blatant lying is one thing. But what psychopathic Faustian antichrist would commit the murder-suicide of his own species for momentary monetary gain?

Pollution and war are two faces of the same devil: Hog. Dominionists have not secured ports and power facilities because they want to be able to take them over. To control the country they need to take over our entire infrastructure. The quickest way to take them over is to make us first feel vulnerable, then threatened, then attacked by terrorists or assailed by catastrophe, such as a nuclear power plant meltdown or meltdown of arctic ice due to global warming. Dominionists realizing the importance of instigating fear would have realized the value of allowing terrorism. They might even have grasped the importance of appropriating terror. So-called conspiracy theories posit that dominionists fomented terrorism and orchestrated 9/11 to frighten us into sacrificing our rights and relinquishing our power to the Homeland Security Gestapo created by "our elected officials" to "protect" us. The Iraq War gave them increased control over the military. Cheney economic policies transferred the people's money, jobs, and well-being to dominionist corporations—the Corporate Nation—eradicating economic rights and creating an unbridgeable gap between the upper and middle classes. Threats, catastrophes, wars, and economic devastation escalate fear, and fear makes people reach frantically for rescue. People in need of rescue will grab any lifeline, whatever the cost. Dominionism becomes the religion of salvation and dominionists our saviors. Because of the failures represented by Iraq and Katrina, we see that these dominionist high priests are incompetent charlatans. Even so, most Americans haven't even glimpsed the sinister underbelly of the dominionist leviathan, the Corporate Nation: Almighty Hog.

UNITED WE STAND UP TO OUR NECKS IN POISON

What I've outlined above only scratches the surface. The Bush-Cheney era has ended. But the economic fallout from their reign will stoop our backs for many decades, and their greed will continue to literally poison the cells our bodies and their children's bodies are made of. The psychotic Earth-rape epidemic can't be easily controlled. We the people voted in President Obama, who promised change. We even gave him a Democrat Congress—sort of. Republican obstructionists kept Congress from doing its job. Change came, in miniscule doses. Pollution continued. So did other forms of exploitation and victimization.

We the people voted again, retaliated, really, on Obama's reneged promise. The Republican-controlled House just made things worse. And of course, there was the big BP oil spill—a media blitz that ranted and raved against BP while ignoring its multitude of typical smaller oil spills taking place at the same time. Given who owns the press, it makes sense that its reporters ignore polluters' massive crimes against nature committed every day. Nor do they report on, oh, the billions in tax breaks for offshore operations of U.S. financial companies, the billions in tax write-offs for oil companies' drilling and well costs, the hundreds of millions in special tax breaks for the timber industry, just for starters. But those media channels do subject us to commercials by the big polluter companies telling us about all the great Green-energy products and services they're providing to and for us. Ah yes, the Green smokescreen.

Maybe pollution seems too abstract, too remote from your own skin to scare you into action. But what if you were being secretly poisoned each and every day of your life? What if big agri-polluters that sicken Mother Earth to put bread on your table for a hefty profit sicken to death people like you with that bread?

Ah, you say, not all bread is created equal. You, a health nut, only eat old-fashioned good wholesome fiber-rich whole wheat bread, usually organic brands sold in your neighborhood health food store. What if I told you that medical doctors like William Davis, author of *Wheat Belly*, and Mark Hyman, author of *The Blood Sugar Solution*, point out that a slice of your good wholesome fiber-rich whole wheat bread, organic or otherwise, increases blood sugar as much as or more than table sugar? In fact, its glycemic index is higher than that for white bread and much higher than that of a Snickers bar. Chowing down on whole grain foods results in higher levels of glucose and therefore insulin. Just eliminating wheat from your diet can cure your diabetes, acid reflux, irritable bowel syndrome, brain fog, insomnia, rashes, rheumatoid arthritis, asthma, and of course obesity. Before you argue that you don't have any of these conditions, keep in mind that most people have some stage of at least some of these ailments that left untreated can become life-threatening. The gluten from wheat has been linked to heart disease, cancer, and of course celiac disease, among other conditions that make most of us shudder.

Always the skeptic you ask, if whole wheat bread is unhealthy, why is it being pushed as healthy? I'll give you a clue: Oink. (And "pushed" is exactly the right word.)

Hog agribusiness is as unregulated—i.e., as free to rape and plunder— as any other corporate colossus, thanks to gofer politicians that we ourselves vote into power. So agri-scientists dutifully customize wheat with even more mutant forms of even more addictive gluten so that you can get even fatter and sicker, which drives you to buy even more wheat products, including brands pretending to make you thinner and healthier. Needless to say, the big drug cartel, HMOs, and health insurance racket in which they're heavily invested *love* your inability to just say no.

You've heard of GMO, of course, but what you aren't being told by the government or big media is that GMO Frankenfoods such as real artificial wheat, corn, and soy are wreaking havoc on your carcass even as you're being sold that old snake-oil line: "healthy." Starting out in the mid-'40s as a noble agenda to reduce world hunger, hybridization and later genetic engineering metamorphosed into Dr. Frankenstein shoving monster after even scarier monster down an ever-accelerating assembly line that leads to your front door. But here's what's really scary: Frankenstein's monster isn't just Frankenfurters (processed with gluten) on your plate. That's just the means to an end. The real monster is you, the gluten glutton. And you don't even know it, because your psyche has been possessed by cutthroat corporate-owned advertisers, and those advertisers own the media and the government. Clearly conglomerate busting must be part of any fiscal diet plan for obese Hogs.

The neo-Darwinian might view conglomeration positively, as evolutionary transition of the super-fittest to survive. No more tame Mendelian breeding. In the mid-twentieth century, Dr. Frankenstein arrived, MBA in hand, to devise increasingly sophisticated ways to exploit the new science of heterozygosity and gene dominance. The staff of life harvested around 8500 B.C. by the semi-nomadic Natufians of the Fertile

Crescent, the bread broken by Jesus and his disciples, the amber waves of grain sustaining America's proud heartland, the toast hugging the ham in grandpa's ham sandwich—that bread of life no longer exists except on a few radically organic small preserves. Wheat that had naturally evolved very little over the centuries suddenly morphed in the hands of the gene gods into more than 25,000 freak-show varieties. Interesting that the religious right yelling about stem cell researchers playing God subsidizes hybridizing, crossbreeding, and truly grotesque genetic tampering that have given us the synthetic wheat, corn, and soy that are "strong" like a muscle-builder must have steroids and Viagra constantly administered by human hands, that are "potent" in that they genetically damage humans and their animals. Damaged meat on damaged bread spread with synthetic-laced condiments peddled as unprocessed are the health nut's ticket to blight in a land flowing with poisoned milk and funny money.

As if that level of perversion were not kinky enough, new strains of wheat, corn, and soy are bred to be part of a genetic package that includes specific fertilizers or pesticides with well-documented health risks. Mondo corporations like Monsanto, Cargill, and ADM patent their designer seeds to drive up their cost and the price of their brands of essential fertilizers and pesticides. Roundup Ready soybeans, for instance, bred so they won't be harmed when sprayed with the weed killer Roundup are special seeds sold with their complementing pesticide. It's bad enough that the mutant plants can't survive without constant human intervention; but they're also causing mutations in the animals and people who ingest them. No wonder folks think they've been alien abducted.

Even those corporate CEOs and their kids eat the same damaged food harvested from the same poisoned soil. Let's rename Dr. Frankenstein Dr. Jekyll and reinterpret the story.

The heart of the problem isn't really government, as rotten and impotent as it can be. The problem isn't a puppet media. The source of the problem isn't even the corporate oligarchy, the Corporate Nation—it's even bigger than that: It's the Corporate Nation disguised as God claiming to be a person.

Perhaps the revolution begun by our Deist Founders can still institute a real "change we can depend on." Perhaps the current Occupy Movement will "occupy God" so that natural democracy can prevail over aristocratic, dominionist perversion. But it won't happen without a concerted revolution against Hog Almighty.

The exploiter thinks that exploiting others makes him a superior person, but it only makes him a superior exploiter. A *person* is a member of a *society*. A person's innate faculties, his soul and physical self, his experiences, knowledge, loves, and dreams—everything that makes a person a person is the direct result of his living in a society. A person thrives by receiving the nurturance of a free society, not by imposing its enslavement, not by *poisoning* it. Dominionists don't understand that "dominion" domination is unnatural. Lording it over others violates natural personhood. A highly-functioning society is free of overlords. Aristocrats and other dictators are the real perverts of a democracy.

MOTHER LOVE

This is a test: Why are we here in this life, in these bodies in this world? Answer: This is a test.

The natural state of life is health and well-being. The body gets sick, yes, but then gets well, all by itself; the body's wounds heal without our intervention. But there are boundaries beyond which sickness and injury demand our attention; it is built into the natural scheme of life that sometimes health and well-being require our active participation. How and why we participate is the test.

The ancient query "Why would a good God permit evil?" or the more perplexing "Why would a good God *cause* evil?" deserves an answer. In fact it's one of the test's big-point questions. Unlike religions that assume we suffer as punishment to purge our inherent or fallen evil nature, Deism posits a different drama: We're here to prove our worth, to participate in our own self-creation, to become what we truly are. Unlike a butterfly pushing its way out of its cocoon, we unwrap a uniquely discrete self we ourselves shape with every choice we make. Life tests our mettle with a multitude of questions. How we answer defines who we have chosen to be. In order for the victimizer to become what he truly is, he must have the freedom to victimize the innocent. Justice isn't always served in this life. But if it's true that there's a God and that God is good, then the notion of a Judgment Day the day your leave this life makes perfect sense.

It makes sense, too, that the victimizing Right labels environmentalism "socialism," and socialism "sissy." Socialism protects society the way environmentalism protects the environment, and for the same fundamental reason: Benefit, i.e., health and well-being. Benefit is a pragmatic synonym for *philos*, meaning friendship, or brotherly love. Socialists and environmentalists are stewards of God's Creation. Stewardship protects and benefits Earth and humans. The Corporate Right with its predatory Earth-rape-and-murder agenda that includes pollution poison necessarily transgresses every version of authentic stewardship. Jungle brutes exercise their God-given right to kill us along with themselves. Destruction is ultimately self-destruction. The shadow knows this, which is why it belches and bellows its rhetoric of Armageddon and bribes universities with million-dollar grants in exchange for their hiring bogus scientists to promote among their students right-wing corporate lies like healthy gluten and harmlessly natural global warming.

Rape your Mother, upper class clown Ann Coulter proclaims. Rape your Mother: One wonders what bleeding past Coulter's shadow is pleading that she heal. Symbolically, rape your Mother exposes the shadowy misogynist pollution in which Hog gleefully wallows. Hog lusts for pollution. Pollution is the effect, the smoke spewed into the atmosphere. The cause is psychopathic evil, the great spiritual hunter, the classic devil, pitchfork in hand, stirring his smoldering little coals flaring into flames flashing high above the soot-swallowed roofs.

Psychopaths are marked not by the mere absence of good but by the transcending presence of evil. Pollution, which of course includes food poison, is not the absence of benefit but is willful predation that destroys the existing benefits that constitute God-given nature's nurturing bounty. Rape is not the absence of nurturing benefits of love but is a willful performance of pure selfish lust further perverted by hate.

Again, the natural state of life is health and well-being. The body of Earth and the human body are plagued with manmade sickness and injury of such catastrophic degree that survival requires our active doctoring. The bell tolls for thee, my friend. We must all become the Good Samaritan surgeon saving each other. Love thy neighbor.

Bah humbug, the Corporate Right grumbles. You vulgar liberals read too-earthy subtext into our godly text. It's just about money. No harm intended.

Really? What is your heavenly Mother's message to you if pollution, which violates her sacred Word of intelligently designed Nature, poisons you right down to the logos programmed in your DNA?

CHAPTER 11

SOROR MYSTICA

The blood-dimmed tide is loosed, and everywhere
The ceremony of innocence is drowned...

Why has humanity failed to establish the peaceable kingdom? Hog, of course. But what if Hog is a tiny minority; what if selfishness isn't inherent but is a defense mechanism; what if the hogwash could be hosed off? What if humanity could be deprogrammed, or if a simple paradigm shift could change the course of history away from oppression and toward utopia? What if the fruit of this shift could be instantly enjoyed?

The fact is, it can. The problem is simple and the solution just as simple—which doesn't mean it's *easy.*

The Hog problem began as an elementary mistake: Even before Heraclitus described logos as the interplay of opposites six centuries B.C.E., humanity had already recognized contrast and defined difference in terms of *conflict.* Sounds a bit Darwinian, doesn't it? Although statistically most people probably in principle agreed with Heraclitus that an ideal society *harmonizes* diverse elements, rather than get along with each other humanity chose to define itself in terms of oppositional dominance and submission: male vs. female; rich vs. poor; master vs. slave; young vs. old; white vs. not-white; victimizer vs. victim, etc. ad nauseam.

Well, okay, it likely wasn't humanity as a whole that made that choice. No doubt it was the predators—statistically about one percent of us, a very small minority—that recognized in polarities opportunities for exploitation. If young, rich males could naturally rule, then old, poor, and female described ideal victims. The "weaker" could only be defended by people in-between the oppositional extremes, or by people who chose to reject the master-slave categories as invalid. Assertions of superiority provoked resistance, revolt, revolution. Then superiors challenged each other, giving birth to war. All this occurred "naturally" only in the sense that humans had the natural facility to choose this rather than that: exploitation and conflict rather than harmony.

But who really was choosing? Even today "humanity" as a whole is largely defined by choices imposed by a predatory minority. Are you happy with that? I know I'm not. Isn't it time for majority rule of harmony to unseat elite rule of conflict?

Early on humans understood that binaries themselves fall into different categories. As Heraclitus noted, there is nothing inherently superior about hot over cold, light rather than dark, sweet instead of sour. Seawater is a good environment for fish but not for humans. Both day and night dazzle in every season, and each segment of time serves its own specific purpose. Some binaries complement each other, like male and female. Those contrasts are neutral, and only become good or bad in specific contexts. Superiority, in the sense of competition and conflict, is irrelevant.

Some binaries, however, are not neutral. For instance, snooty superiority defaces and perverts equality, freedom, justice, and truth, the cornerstones of any authentically harmonious society. The "superior" create conflict in order to challenge and conquer; the elite transgress against natural humanity by enforcing power-over. A repressed slave caste unable to revolt is not "harmonious." Deep down most people have always condemned assertions of superiority manifested as elite entitlement that includes ownership of people. Even pre-Civil War, most Americans considered slavery to be evil, or at least a grave social injustice.

But though most people even in antiquity understood that superior does not equal good, sometime in the Stone Age the superior decreed that it does. Eventually murder, rape, plunder, and every other form of power-over, legitimized as the necessary means to the end of superiority, sanctified evil as the just reward for achieving that end. Religion, too, was exploited to glorify the god-ordained rank and title and even supposed divinity of the elite. It's quite likely that the exploiting elite elevated religious myth to God-breathed fact in order to supervise the maintenance of elitist superiority.

But the human species was divinely programmed with an inherent conscience by which to distinguish between truth and fabrication, justice and injustice, good and evil. Human values emerged as a response to behaviors that struck the conscience as appropriate or inappropriate, as beneficial or harmful. Humans *naturally* understood that moral binaries were categorically different from neutral ones, and considered evil to be *unnatural*. Women were not naturally inferior to men, and the unnatural imposition of inferiority upon women by the cult of uppity men was unnatural and evil. Religions controlled by men codified misogyny. Women became property. "Inferior" men were reduced to the role of women; male slaves and serfs and hired hands and every other male in the rank of the ninety-nine or so percent were essentially property of the elite. Religions—or cultic subsets of most religions, the subsets that tended to become "organized"—further reduced women and everything womanly to the sub-status of evil: Eve was a mere rib of Adam consorting with the devil. Classic projection, contorted though the image might be.

Morality has always been deemed by almost everyone to be an inherent aspect of human nature, which is an aspect of truth—natural truth, truth embodied by Nature. If Nature embodies truth even by lowly human standards, and if Nature must be rational and therefore intelligently designed, then morality is rational by design, and the highest moral touchstone is truth rather than opinion.

Regardless what the atheist Darwinians assert, good and evil are not human "constructs" but are values (like numerical values) in a natural ethical dimension of human existence. Religion concerns itself with what makes us not-just-animal. Morality, along with creativity, free will, and reason, are qualities that distinguish humans from other animals. Humans know, evaluate, and choose in a way that is categorically, qualitatively "other."

Even atheist scientists keep exploring Nature, for some to the point of passionate obsession. What are they trying to discover? Cures for cancer, sure. But aren't they really looking for the sheer pleasure of *looking*? But why? Like many other ponderers, Aristotle believed that the knowledge of the "wisest of the wise," or what today we call philosophical, spiritual knowledge, "gives the liveliest pleasure." Aren't scientists and philosophers alike really seeking some quasi-conscious holy grail, the ultimate answer to some paramount question they don't even know they ask? Science is practical. But it isn't *just* practical. Fundamentally, science is metaphysically motivated. Scientists, like the rest of us, seek meaning. Deep meaning. Meaning that penetrates into and through and beyond space-time, meaning that touches the transcendent realm of eternity: Michelangelo's finger touching the finger of God. And like many statements about meaning, that's a *representation* used here as a *metaphor*.

Today, two thousand years C.E., the richly complex definitions of *logos* once again intersect at the core understanding that intelligently designed Nature embodies the Word of God to humanity. But even in our progressive era, exploration of sacred Logos is greeted with disdain by proponents of organized religious mythos on one side and scientific materialist mythos on the other. At least in a progressive nation like America, scientists and philosophers are free to express and publish their views. Even so, the metaphysical investigations into what is now popularly called intelligent design are oddly reminiscent of the situation of alchemists during the Inquisition, not because scientists and philosophers are overtly persecuted (at least not in America), but because they seek fundamental facts about reality that are steeped in levels of meaning that humanity seems only vaguely aware of, and because the facts they've discovered are taboo to both the religious and scientific establishments. Chemists today, like their forerunners centuries ago, stand at the crossroads where science and religion, philosophy and theology, knowledge and meaning intersect.

ALCHEMY: METAPHOR OF TRANSFORMATION

During the Inquisition many alchemists were burned at the stake, along with witches and other folk doctors and herbalists (pharmacists) who were forbidden to compete with church-sponsored guilds, which paid the Church dues and kickbacks. Though most European alchemists were Christians, alchemy was considered suspect by Church officials, partly because it was a secret society, partly because alchemists were early chemists working on, among other things, processes that would turn lead to gold, a commodity the Church wanted for itself. Not only was alchemy science, it had the audacity to be symbolic, creative, and mystical—all aspects of "mystery" the elite clergy controlled, interpreted, and exploited.

Similar to early Christians who used X and the rebus ICHTUS and the sketched fish as secret signs of their presence in the Roman Empire, medieval alchemists, the new Christian underground, shrouded "the word" with hermetic definitions to protect it from the Church. Alchemists viewed the Church as corrupt and heretical, and because it elevated symbols like Pope, Bible, and Holy Emperor to that status of God, it was guilty of idolatry. The great error of the Church was that it lifted up *representations* of God as God himself; believers had forgotten that the metaphors were metaphors. By transmuting the symbols back into *symbols*, the alchemists ritually enacted a radically subversive trans-figuration. These symbols located the fusion of science and art, and in a sense logos and mythos, in a transcendent, mystical synthesis.

Alchemy symbolizes that same kind of fusion taking place today. Religious heretics past and present have been involved in spiritual alchemy, in striving to transmute the lead of dead tradition into precious gold—a change as radically natural as life emerging from inert matter.

If Aristotle was right that the surest sign of genius is the ability to make metaphor/symbol, and if geniuses from Shakespeare to Jung are right that many of our symbols represent unconscious contents, and if unconscious contents unattended often emerge as a shadow (the shadow itself being a metaphor), and if life in all its richness is at least as deeply meaningful as a great literary work (subject to interpretation of its meaning), and if the meaningful life has a transcending purpose (like the *meaning* of a symbol), then it might be worth examining the work of alchemists as metaphorically representing the spiritual work we are currently engaged in as we pursue our passions in the sciences and arts. Certainly alchemy mirrors today's exploration of intelligent design.

AL-CHEMISTRY

The *opus*, or life work, of medieval and pre-medieval alchemists was transmuting baser into more valuable elements, like lead to gold, or weak materials into the philosopher's stone, the lapis lazuli, or mundane chemicals into the highly refined universal elixir of life. The *soror mystica*, "mystical sister," was the alchemist's assistant in her/his life opus of transmutation. An alchemist could be male or female, and the assistant, though referred to as the mystical sister, could also be male or female. Regardless of the gender of the players, the alchemist was symbolically male and the assistant female. The assistant was not a convenient gofer, but the essential provider of impetus and inspiration for the work at hand.

"She" was the alchemist's best friend, confidant, provider of insight and moral support; "she" represented the feminine aspect of the "he" performing the work. Figuratively, alchemist represented the soul (immanence), soror mystica the spirit (transcendence). Although in an "inferior" position as assistant, the mystical sister was in essence the alchemist's spirit guide.

Put another way, your spirit life in this world assists your soul in the process of transcendence. Designating spirit as female and soul as male is a cultural construct, a metaphor. Neither spirit nor soul is female or male or even a synthesis of the two. But that enlightened understanding, according to alchemy, only comes after the separation and reuniting marriage of soul and spirit during this life in the natural realm.

The *prima materia*, the original elements in the state of chaos, chosen from a schema organized in terms of opposites, were combined in the *vas*, the belief being that the attraction of opposites led to a conjunction giving rise to a new substance greater than the sum of original materials. After combining and regenerating these new substances many times in many ways, the final elements would be pure.

The *coniunctio*, or mating in the *vas*, was *hierosgamos*, the sacred marriage linking bodily and spiritual, which led to *impregnatio*, freeing of the soul from the material, which sounds pleasant enough. But the process of transformation involved *fermentatio, nigredo, mortificatio,* and *putrifactio,* moral struggle, psychic purges, wrestling with angels, dark nights of the soul. The alchemist's opus consisted of combining the separated elements to purify them so that a higher synthesis would emerge. The well-initiated adept was always conscious that his goal was transforming base matter into spirit and that he was working with the elements of his own being.

Since the alchemical mysteries were represented hermetically, or symbolically, to protect them from the exploitation of the selfish, one could learn alchemy only from another alchemist. The key to the symbols' meanings was only passed among fellow alchemists and soror mysticas who had proven trustworthy. Trust was an absolute essential aspect of alchemical relationships. A soror mystica could assist the alchemist only if she knew what the alchemist knew and kept her knowledge safe from outsiders. The spirit guarded and guided the soul during the process of transmutation.

The alchemists used artistic representations to depict every aspect of the alchemical process. The opus itself was represented by the *androgyny*, the synthesis of male and female, as opposed to their status-quo dichotomy. The opus was performed with material elements, but the goal was always spiritual—in Aquinas's view, mystical, in Jung's view, psychological (in a profound archetypal sense). The gender split represented a higher rift between matter and spirit. Symbolically the rift was synthesized through the alchemical process.

It might appear as if the soror mystica was an inferior in the alchemical hierarchy. But the soror mystica, who helped the alchemist in his work, could herself be an alchemist with a soror mystica, who might well be the other alchemist. The gender of the players could be either male or female, but the gender of the roles was clear-cut: alchemist male, soror mystica female. This represented the reality of the gender power dichotomy as it existed then, and which still exists today. The opus itself strove to transcend the limitations of the material with a genderless, or androgynous, transcendent spirit.

If this still sounds like hierarchical gender roles, keep in mind that the alchemist and "his" soror mystica could be two men, or two women. The point is that one person was working on "his" life and the other was there as close, nurturing friend/helper. In an ideal scenario, both would be alchemists also being each other's soror mystica, an arrangement that would embody the ultimate expression of androgyny and spiritual friendship. In an ideal relationship, the alchemist and soror mystica were in communion; they were one in the sense of being a complementary unity with each part retaining its differentiated integrity. When an individual's animus and anima, soul and spirit, are integrated into one, the person is in an ideal relationship (communion) with him/herself. Only then can the person find peace—because the opposite of peace is war, the *conflict* between the male/female (soul/spirit) binaries.

The alchemical opus brought to light the urgent need of our species to transcend the alienating male/female gender split that had ripped our civilization to shreds at every level: body, soul, and spirit. But the split between genders represented a psychological split within each of us as individuals. The opus completed through the ideal relationship between alchemist and soror mystica symbolized by the androgyny symbolizes the two aspects of an individual person working together to complete the integrated, unified opus of his/her transcending life. The alchemical relationship could in fact represent any symbiotic relationship, including harmonious society, or the process of human evolution and individual maturation.

In Jungian terms, the individual's desire for the unity of anima/animus into wholeness, represented by the androgyny, is repressed and therefore emerges as the shadow—i.e., neurosis, or worse, psychosis— meaning that the macho male or passive female is unwilling or unable to integrate anima and animus. Keep in mind that macho male characteristics are occasionally present in females, and passive female characteristics can be present in males. Played out in the socio-political arena, the psychological neurosis/psychosis of alienating gender polarization is at its core a spiritual infectious disease—an acute dis-ease. The need to harmonize the binary male/female gender split remains today. The gender gap is narrowing, albeit in slow motion, but not without repercussions via threatened males. This contagion requires potent medicine.

SOROR MYSTICA: THE HEALER

The elitist thinks his superiority is dependent upon the inferiority of his subjects. But in fact, the opposite is true. Friendly cooperation has been critical to our evolution and enlightenment. In *The Stone Age Present*, William Allman points out that "The way we behave today has its roots in the lives of our ancestors in the Stone Age; our large brains arose primarily to cope with the enormous complexity of dealing with each other; the primary adaptation of our species is not hunting, toolmaking, or language, but our ability to cooperate. Ultimately, my research revealed that our species' remarkable evolutionary success is due to a trait that most of us take for granted, but that is rare among other animals on the planet: We make friends."

Elites would argue that they have friends: other elites. But in a society constructed of manmade binaries, in a Darwinian world of cutthroat competition, how can the elitist know who his friends really are? At any moment he could be his best friend's next target. Even casual conversations would surely consist of little more than one-up bragging and cocky but very guarded revelations of each male's latest conquests. Fat egos are more dangerous than—well, fat. A plastic soul could never be authentically spiritual (unless evil could be considered spiritual) or genuinely friendly.

Though secretive, alchemical purification was not about elitist superiority. Hermetic isolation resulted from the need to protect the Self from predation and contamination. "Do not give dogs what is holy; do not throw your pearls to the pigs: they will only trample on them, and turn and tear you to pieces," as alchemists echoed Jesus' graphic warning. The Inquisition is a case in point. Good relationships draw good boundaries around themselves to protect what is holy.

When elites are brought down from their pedestals to live among us mortals, doors unlock and fling wide open to welcome a whole new world of friends. It's naïve to think that the new world will be perfect. As long as one percent of humans are clinically psychopathic, vigilance will remain a necessity. But wouldn't the world be ninety-nine percent perfect if we could know who our friends are and could be free of Hoggish selfishness, conflict, and exploitation that destroy every version of genuine friendship? Courage is the solution.

Today alchemy reminds us of the need to bridge the degrading "isms" in our culture—sexism, racism, classism, homophobe-ism, looks-ism, ageism—all of which represent the higher rift between our transcendent being and our present material being. Other kinds of rifts exist, but the ism rifts are human, personal, and impossible to ignore because they are a part of what we are as human beings. Each ism places one in a relative category: I am a particular sex, race, class, sexual orientation, look, or age; and even though some of these are subject to change, the point is that I am different than someone else, and that difference makes me conscious of what I lack or do not lack. Youth is coveted in our culture (as opposed to cultures that respect their elders), and when one grows old one becomes keenly aware of the lack of youth that one had and that now others have. The isms point to our separation, difference, and alienation, but more importantly they are humanly cultivated attitudes of inferiority and superiority; they are our choices to be separated, to not be one, and to dishonor difference. Isms foment conflict.

Not all isms degrade; some defend against degrading isms. Feminism, for example, defends against sexism. If there were no sexism, feminism would not exist. Androgyny is the symbolic, feminist expression of the need to reconcile the split between male and female by defying gender-specific roles/identities in order to deconstruct the male myth of "superiority." This is not an urge to create a gray from black and white; it is the demand that each aspect/individual be respected as an equal, not relegated to a position of inferior to be exploited. Mutual respect will give rise to a higher synthesized whole: a unifying Golden Mean represented by the androgyny.

In today's terms, the goal of alchemy is to overcome oppression and exploitation, the expressions of selfishness, with equality and mutuality, the expressions of transcendent friendship and love—in other words, communion. Clearly that includes making friends with the various aspects of ourselves. "Love your neighbor as yourself" includes "love yourself." Not Hoggishly. Love yourself as a person, not as a Hog. Communion with yourself is as critical as communion with friends, as communion with the society of humanity, as communion with Nature and with the God of Nature.

Alchemist and soror mystica work together much like the left and right brain. Because our mind (via body: brain) is the soul aspect that grasps and articulates spiritual truth, communion must involve the integration of what we have come to understand as the right and left hemispheres. The right hemisphere processes images, generates and integrates feeling states such as love, humor, and aesthetic appreciation, and grasps the input of all our senses simultaneously, giving consciousness its field of awareness. The left brain discriminates, analyzes, and dissects the world into pieces, objects, and categories through the symbolic linear expressions of language. Women's corpus callosum, the bridge of neuronal fibers that connects and synthesizes communication between the two hemispheres, contains ten to thirty-three percent more neuronal fibers than the corpus callosum of men. The unifying structure of the female brain is one reason women tend to be more nurturing than men. The alchemist can't achieve transformational wholeness without the unifying nurturance of the soror mystica.

Though polarization allowed our ancestors to successfully specialize as gatherers and hunters, our era requires a more mature, feminine paradigm. In the same way that we live not only in space and time but also in space-time, we are fulfilling the natural prepotency of integrating the feminine and masculine functions into a more unified surpassing whole. Every newborn brain is completely equipped for the full functioning of both modes of thought, the feminine (holistic, simultaneous, synthetic, concrete) and masculine (linear, sequential, reductionist, abstract). Our brain-sculpting necessarily involves creating a culture that is more androgynous, egalitarian, accepting rather than marginalizing, scapegoating, raping.

Whole-brain experience is like the complex music that arose from two traditions of instrumentation in ancient Greece. The kithara, a plucked string instrument used by the cult of Apollo, was characterized by clarity and simplicity of form and emotional restraint. A double-pipe reed instrument, the aulos, used by the cult of Dionysus, expressed emotional subjectivity. The integration of Apollonian and Dionysian experiences of music has given birth to symphony, jazz, and soul.

In the same way that we need to integrate right and left brain, we must integrate the hemispheres of our planet. Two hundred million years ago, Panegaea ("all earth") split into two smaller masses, Gondwanaland and Laurasia, then split further into our current continental masses. The splitting continues today. If the emergence of different continents had simply led us to develop a rich variety of races and cultures, that would have benefited us. But instead, our differences have also resulted in self-interested nationalism (which includes the mega-self-interested nationalism of the global Corporate Nation) and its fallout: competition, conflict and destructive, self-destructive war. Today, for the first time ever, the continents are truly "one" via communications technology and high-speed modes of travel. We take this new reality for granted, but it truly is a mindboggling evolutionary revolution unleashing tremendous potential for holistic integration—for communing community communication via high-tech commuting.

UNITY OF MIND

Whole-brain thinking isn't just a matter of utilizing the whole organ. Mind isn't just brain. Engaging the whole mind in balanced, eclectic thought that is both logical and creative is the primary objective of employing the whole brain. But can there ever really be an absolute "unity of mind" when we are constantly shifting our focus from one state of mind to another, not just between the male and female aspects?

In *A Room of One's Own* (1929), Virginia Woolf helps us notice that just maintaining a male or female perspective, that just thinking of one sex as distinct from the other, is an effort that requires a great exertion to keep unconsciously repressing the other; but a "unity of mind" can "continue without effort because nothing is required to be held back."

Once Woolf realized that the two sexes were designed to cooperate, she

> went on amateurishly to sketch a plan of the soul so that in each of us two powers preside, one male, one female; and in the man's brain, the man predominates over the woman, and in the woman's brain, the woman predominates over the man. The normal and comfortable state of being is that when the two live in harmony together, spiritually co-operating. If one is a man, still the woman part of the brain must have effect; and a woman also must have intercourse with the man in her. Coleridge perhaps meant this when he said that a great mind is androgynous. It is when this fusion takes place that the mind is fully fertilized and uses all its faculties. Perhaps a mind that is purely masculine cannot create, any more than a mind that is purely feminine

Woolf was quick to note that she was not privileging the female half of the mind.

> Coleridge certainly did not mean, when he said that a great mind is androgynous, that it is a mind that has any special sympathy with women; a mind that takes up their cause or devotes itself to their interpretation. Perhaps the androgynous mind is less apt to make these distinctions than the single-sexed mind. He meant, perhaps, that the androgynous mind is resonant and porous; that it transmits emotion without impediment; that it is naturally creative, incandescent and undivided. In fact one goes back to Shakespeare's mind as the type of the androgynous, of the man-womanly mind, though it would be impossible to say what Shakespeare thought of women.

In fact, when she turned from women's writing,

> Indeed, it was delightful to read a man's writing again. It was so direct, so straightforward after the writing of women. It indicated such freedom of mind, such liberty of person, such

confidence in himself. One had a sense of physical well-being in the presence of this well-nourished, well-educated, free mind, which had never been thwarted or opposed, but had had full liberty from birth to stretch itself in whatever way it liked. And this was admirable. But after reading a chapter or two a shadow seemed to lie across the page. It was a straight dark bar, a shadow shaped something like the letter "I." One began dodging this way and that to catch a glimpse of the landscape behind it. Whether that was indeed a tree or a woman walking I was not quite sure. Back one was always hailed to the letter "I." One began to be tired of "I." Not but what this "I" was a most respectable "I"; honest and logical; as hard as a nut, and polished for centuries by good teaching and good feeding.

Ah, yes, the male ego, which, she says, is "impeded and inhibited and self-conscious." It seems, she notes, that "virility has now become self-conscious—men, that is to say, are now writing only with the male side of their brains." But the female has an ego, too, and Woolf warns women of the risks of reading men's writing in order to find a true picture of themselves there, for no picture of woman objectified is ever true. "It is the power of suggestion that one most misses" in most male writing. It's true that the centuries have rolled out a large number of very able male writers, "acute and full of learning; but the trouble was, that his feelings no longer communicated; his mind seemed separated into different chambers; not a sound carried from one to the other. Thus, when one takes a sentence of Mr. B [a hypothetical male-minded writer] into the mind it falls plump to the ground—dead; but when one takes a sentence of Coleridge into the mind, it explodes and gives birth to all kinds of other ideas, and that is the only sort of writing of which one can say that it has the secret of perpetual life."

Woolf's complaint is a profound spiritual concern: "Do what she will a woman cannot find in them that fountain of perpetual life which the critics assure her is there. It is not only that they celebrate male virtues, enforce male values and describe the world of men; it is that the emotion with which these books are permeated is to a woman incomprehensible. [They] lack suggestive power. And when a book lacks suggestive power, however hard it hits the surface of the mind it cannot penetrate within."

Some male writers, though, are safe for women to read—Shakespeare, for instance, "for Shakespeare was androgynous; and so was Keats and Sterne and Cowper and Lamb and Coleridge. Shelley perhaps was sexless. Milton and Ben Johnson had a dash too much of the male in them. So had Wordsworth and Tolstoi. In our time Proust was wholly androgynous, if not perhaps a little too much of a woman. But that failing is too rare for one to complain of it, since without some mixture of the kind the intellect seems to predominate and the other faculties of the mind harden and become barren."

Woolf's advice to writers applies to us all: "It is fatal for any one who writes to think of their sex. It is fatal to be a man or woman pure and simple; one must be woman-manly or man-womanly." Woolf is not arguing that a man should cease being a man or a woman a woman; she isn't arguing a case for hermaphroditism. She simply stresses that "Some collaboration has to take place in the mind between the woman and the man before the act of creation can be accomplished. Some marriage of opposites has to be consummated. The whole of the mind must lie wide open if we are to get the sense that the writer is communicating his experience with perfect fullness. There must be freedom and there must be peace. Not a wheel must grate, not a light glimmer. The curtains must be close drawn."

Her critique of male domination extends even to academia, which in the 1920s was entirely male-privileged. "I do not believe that gifts, whether of mind or character, can be weighed like sugar and butter, not even in Cambridge, where they are so adept at putting people into classes and fixing caps on their heads and letters after their names."

Male privilege justified and sanctified by the power of the scientific method rests upon a fundamental fallacy: "All this pitting of sex against sex, of quality against quality; all this claiming of superiority and imputing of inferiority, belong to the private-school state of human existence where there are 'sides,' and it is necessary for one side to beat another side, and of the upmost importance to walk up to a platform and receive from the hands of the Headmaster himself a highly ornamental pot. As people mature they cease to believe in sides or in Headmasters or in highly ornamental pots."

Yes, yes, this is all very quaintly observed, the average half-brained citizen of the world sighs. Now let's just get back to men being men and women being their men's women. Or they argue that half-brained life doesn't exist anymore, now that feminism has elevated womanly-women to an equal status with manly-men.

But it's not that simple. The consequence of deeply-entrenched half-brained social organization is that when androgyny is shot, both man and woman are killed, and ultimately, civilization is destroyed. This is no slippery slope. This is the real world—a profoundly misogynist world.

RAPE AND MURDER OF THE SOROR MYSTICA

The opposite of communion is war. The actual war isn't the literal battles that butcher human bodies, nations, and cultures and could blow up the planet, triggering the extinction of all life in the known universe. The actual war is spiritual, and the battleground is each human spirit, each individual soul, each person with the free will to push the red button.

What happens when an individual refuses or simply doesn't know how to integrate the anima and animus into a unified whole? The person remains fragmented, spiritually schizophrenic. Families, institutions, nations, and cultures embody the fragmentation and operate schizophrenically. In a fragmented, schizophrenic world in which "other" is deemed the enemy, destruction of "other" justifies the red button and its thousands of manmade weapons of mass destruction and millions of subsets from switchblades to drones.

Conflict, or the split of isms, takes many forms. But misogyny is probably the original ism, likely going back at least to the bifurcating specialization of hunting vs. gathering/producing. Because men are physically larger and in some ways stronger than women, men could bodily overpower women to get her food, to get sex, to get her free labor. Overpower equaled hunt. Little has changed.

Once bodily power was equated with strength, and strength proven with violence, men assumed power over women and children, then over weaker men. Once a class controls power-over, it demeans and demonizes the "underlings." Might makes right continues as the prevailing attitude of the misogynist elite. The rest of us are the "women."

Women and "womanized" men are different in one critical fundamental way: women internalize their oppression; men externalize it. Women suffer; men take revenge. Unfortunately, exploited men take revenge not on oppressing superior males, who are beyond their reach, but on their inferiors, women and children.

Though perhaps physically smaller and less muscled, women are not naturally inferior to men; their inferiority is a male-generated construct based on physical prowess that has been internalized and over-generalized by both men and women. Millennia ago, religion proved most powerful in codifying demonization of women. Christian men still often quote the biblical Letter to Ephesians, in which its author, Paul, makes sure women know their place: "Wives, be subject to your husbands as you are to the Lord. For the husband is the head of the wife just as Christ is the head of the church, the body of which he is the Savior. Just as the church is subject to Christ, so also wives ought to be, in everything, to their husbands." Women are to men as men are to Christ, meaning women are to men as men are to God; the huge distance between God and men is equal to the huge distance between men and women; calculated, men are highly evolved and women are the equivalent of a single-cell organism in need of a humanizing savior husband. By the time of the Inquisition, women, called Eve, the mere rib of Adam, needed savior husbands because they were witches conjuring devils, as Eve had conjured the Edenic serpent (clearly a phallic-symbol projection), which made them responsible for all the evils of the Earth and therefore deserving of all the punishing violence, especially torture and rape, that men in their infinite strength could muster. And that goes for "women" as well: gays, slaves, hired hands, children, everyone beneath the chosen elite. It was a few small steps from Jesus to a Holy Roman Empire to modern dominionism and its gospel of elite prosperity.

Should a woman call the misogynist "Hog," a squeal of protest would rise as potent as the stench from a pigpen: a woman is a witch, a bitch, a feminazi. Female misogynist Ann Coulter calls women who use contraception physically ugly (not Aryan blonde like she is) and "communists."

What *is* true is that "misogynist" means, literally, a "woman-hater." Men will argue that most men aren't misogynist. Okay. Who exactly, then, is this man (or "man") who hates women? What would a typical misogynist mug shot look like hanging from a post office wall?

Though many a woman has fingered a real live misogynist in a line-up, "misogynist" as a category is harder to pin down. Let's start with an obvious forensic indicator of misogyny: rape. And I mean that literally.

According to government statistics compiled by the United Nations, over a quarter million cases of rape are recorded worldwide by police annually. Given that not all reported cases of rape are "recorded," given that according to official estimates between 75 and 95 percent of rapes are never even *reported*, and given that in some countries rape isn't recorded at all, that's a lot of women being raped every year. Using the ultra-conservative number of a quarter million, that means that over three million women are *recorded* as raped every dozen years. If even only twenty percent are reported, meaning eighty percent are not, that means that the number of women actually being raped annually is a million and a quarter, or fifteen million every dozen or so years.

Remember that each number from one to fifteen million represents an actual human being. Number 14,670,952 might be your mom, or your sister, or maybe your wife or Sunday school teacher or the person who bags your groceries. Maybe it's you. Maybe it *will be* you. After all, the Department of Justice reports, even here in civilized America a woman is raped every two minutes. That's literal women, which doesn't include men or children.

Let's add another statistic to the mix, just to help us see more clearly this single breed of havoc wrecked by the misogynist: rape of children, commonly referred to as the neutralized "molestation." Here in civilized America, one out of every three to four girls and one out of every six boys is sexually molested—raped—by the age of eighteen (though most molestations occur between ages seven and thirteen).

It's important to note that one-half of child rapes and one-fifth of rapes of adult women are committed by adolescent males, only a very small percentage of whom have been molested themselves. As with adult rape, victims of child rape rarely report the assault to police. In fact, only about one to ten percent of raped children tell anyone that they were abused; often someone else finds out and tells. Some victims only "confess" to the crime much later in life. And yes, many victims have been made to feel not just shame but also guilt, as if the assault were somehow their fault—one more level of internalized misogyny. Often we learn of a child's abuse via the abuser, once he's been caught. Statistically, the average molester of girls will rape 50 girls and the average molester of boys will rape 150 boys before being caught and convicted. As with other rapists, almost all molesters continue raping once they're released from prison. Of the nearly half a million registered sex offenders in the U.S., nearly a quarter of them are "missing," meaning law enforcement and parole officers don't know where they live and haven't bothered or been able to track them down.

Some rapists of women and children film their assaults and circulate them over the internet. There are millions of men—maybe your husband or preacher or son or senator—who are clinically addicted to watching porn that includes real or dramatized rape and molestation. This doesn't mean that all men are rapists, or fantasize about being rapists, or enjoy watching other men rape or pretend to rape. Not all men are misogynist, nor are most "normal" men "just" voyeurs of other men's misogyny.

In fact, some men are as horrified and disgusted with the misogynist rape mentality as women are. And some men, of course, have been rape victims themselves. But how many women commit this kind of evil against other women or children, or for that matter against men? Statistically, very few; so few it's pretty close to none. We know the name Lizzie Borden because she's an exception to the rule: unlike men, women almost never commit acts of horrific violence. Even today many men complain that military women don't have the balls for war—which perhaps explains why so many women are raped by their fellow soldiers: to prove that point.

Although it's true that a minority of men are committing rape and child molestation, overt physical rape isn't the only form of misogyny. Any attitude or gesture of male dominance, including voyeurism and objectification, is misogynist. Historically there have always been anti-misogynist men; but only recently has the issue of misogyny as a social evil been culturally normalized to include male feminists. Still, feminist males are probably a minority of men. They certainly don't protest when they get paid far more for doing the exact same job as a woman of equal or even superior skills, education, expertise, and experience. Even in progressive fields like academia, where male feminists are common, women are hired, paid, and treated inequitably, and I have personally never heard a male professor complain.

Along with male dominance in general, rape has been codified by male society—or rather, by the clique of dominant predatory males, many of whom are psychopathic. Scary, isn't it, to think that society might be controlled by an evil minority. If misogynists really are a minority, why has misogyny become entrenched in every nation on earth? How could minority misogyny *dominate* every society?

It's also critical to ask: Why does the predator always select a "womanly" other? Women are often not weaker or inferior. It's common knowledge that women are in some ways stronger and superior to men. Their perceived weakness has always been first on the physical plane. But today many women work out and some are faster and in some ways stronger than most men; and women can pull a trigger. Women are certainly not intellectually or in any other way inferior. Other kinds of weakness are sometimes but not always present in individual females (and males), though they are always *deemed* to be present in all females. In some eras, men have gone to great lengths to scientifically and religiously prove that women are morons, for instance, but today only an ignoramus in denial would believe that. Yet despite all the research, many men *do* believe that—or at least behave *as if* they believe that. Men have centuries of enculturation and practice at bravado. Misogyny is psychic murder of the anima projected onto women.

FEAR, COWARDICE, GANG RAPE

It's not rapacious males but *fear* of rapacious males that drives human civilization. Perhaps the best way to understand how this functions is to analyze how rape functions. Rape is a literal truth; it is also a metaphor for the cause and consequence of spiritual schizophrenia. Rape is the shadow manifesting the unresolved war between the individual male's anima and animus. (Women typically manifest this war as self-destruction. Even misogynist women like Ann Coulter are, obviously, woman-self destructive).

In one study cited by expert forensic psychologist Karen Franklin, women and men were asked what they most feared. Women feared being raped and murdered (hence, perhaps, misogynist women siding with misogynist men for protection), but men's greatest fear was being laughed at. Supposedly this "fear" explains why some men go along with gang rapes. When a dozen Cincinnati Bengals were indicted in 1990 on a gang rape charge, for instance, one implicated player whined that he went along because the alternative was to get ragged and teased about backing down.

A man who goes along with the vicious crime of gang rape because he doesn't want to get teased *is* backing down—from his morals. His going along, his backing down from doing the right thing, proves his passive weakness, not some manly strength. Centuries of chest pounding have turned men like that into spiritual wimps. Oddly, fear of being a coward motivates the most aggressive form of cowardice.

Typically, it is a more delinquent leader with previous convictions for solo rapes who concocts the plan to gang-bang a woman, or just any available target who happens to be vulnerable. For example, the mentally retarded girl who was lured to the basement hangout of a group of teenage athletes from Glen Ridge, New Jersey. As cited by Franklin, this young old-boys' club forced the girl to give them oral sex and then raped her with a broom handle and a bat. This kind of assault happens more often than moms bake apple pie.

Rape is not about sex. Rape is not even about domination. It's about domination for the sake of sadistic pleasure. Sadism is a spiritual crime against nature, spiritual in that it attacks the core being of someone who is absolutely innocent but who is fraudulently recast as a worthy victim in need of punishment, preferably in an arena where all the world can see, the world being the small sphere of comrades the sadist wants to impress. Staged sadism is the ultimate narcissism and the ultimate evil, indicating its motivation as psychopathic.

Experts like Franklin maintain that male sports stars are more likely to commit sexual assaults because of their sense of entitlement and superiority. But why would someone who already feels entitled and superior resort to the extreme act of rape to prove what needed no proving? Either participants in gang rape are cowards or they are sadists. What other fundamental reason could there be?

HOMOPHOBIA

Forensic and psychological experts have a theory: The fear of being teased is really fear of being gay. If you can't prove your masculinity, i.e. heterosexuality, you must be gay, the most extreme womanized male. It's easy to see how homophobic fear could motivate the male hysteria over contraception and abortion: Babies prove hetero-male potency. Just the homo insinuation is enough to push the "prove I'm a man" button—or in a few cases, to pull the avenging trigger.

Eric Harris and Dylan Klebold, the boys responsible for the Columbine High School shooting that killed thirteen and wounded twenty-one, took out their revenge not by raping women or otherwise proving their masculinity within the macho group, but by targeting the Columbine athletes who controlled it. Franklin cites a 1999 report by Adams and Russakoff:

The state wrestling champion, the leader of a clique of athlete bullies and the symbol of injustice for the school shooters, was allowed to park his $100,000 Hummer all day in a 15-minute parking space. The school indulged athletes' rampant sexual and racial bullying and physical abuse of others, including Harris and Klebold. For example, a sports coach did nothing when the athletes targeted a Jewish boy in gym class, singing songs about Hitler when he made a basket, pinning him to the ground and doing "body twisters" that left him bruised all over, and threatening to set him on fire. Like at Glen Ridge, the abuse was so severe that some students feared going to school...Where there is rampant sexual harassment of girls and women, there is usually antigay harassment as well. This was true at Columbine High School, where Harris and Klebold had endured repeated antigay harassment by the jocks, and persistent rumors that they were a gay couple. It was also true at many of the other schools where shootings erupted in the past decade.

Gays are targeted as "others" to be victimized like women because bullies need the womanized "other" to be their victims. Specific in and out groups are created to maintain a pool of victims and to justify victimization to others to alleviate their fear of being victimized. Bullies only need to justify victimization because the rest of us have set up structures to protect us from each other. The legal system, for instance. Educational and medical institutions, too, police victimization. The only way to bypass these structures is to create rationalizations for victimization, preferably with the sanction of the law and otherwise helping institutions, especially religion. "Gay" does the trick, just like "uppity woman."

Why does fear of being gay drive men to such extreme and violent overcompensation that they rape and murder to prove their manliness? Is being gay worse than the most heinous sins they commit against other human beings to prove they're not gay?

Why does homosexuality offend some people to such a deep level? One, the disgust for difference, i.e. weakness, is an unconscious excuse to be sadistic. Two, the person is afraid of actually being homosexual. Three, the person is afraid of being accused of being gay. Often the person's violent, physical fear-response is a primal reflex against potential physical violence against him. If he's mistaken for gay, someone might bash him, he might be the victim of a sadist. Better to be a faux-sadist than a victim. Better to send the message that you're a sadist, not a victim. Kids especially would often rather be dead than be victims of physical sadism, so many commit suicide when others taunt them with accusations of gay or threaten violence. Or they choose to participate in the sadistic drama.

Gang rapes by macho athletes don't have to involve a female or gay victim outside the macho group. Often athletes prove their superiority within their own pack. Weaker males, who represent the "womanly" other, serve the purpose. Franklin describes an example that involved three older players on the football team at Mepham High School in Long Island, New York, who repeatedly raped younger players during a weeklong training camp while other players watched. The sixteen-year-old leader had a long disciplinary record of assaulting schoolmates and threatening teachers. All three players were used to their entitled status as athletes. Franklin reports that Mepham teachers and administrators did not even intervene "against their rampant sexual harassment, which included pinning girls against lockers and grinding their bodies against them, or pulling out their penises and masturbating at girls in class (Lefkowitz, 1997). One of the group's favorite activities was so-called *voyeuring*, in which one boy would stage a sexual act with a girl while the other boys covertly watched; the boys bragged at school about these activities, and even passed around a videotape of one such dramatic production."

Franklin's account of the training camp rapes (following Henican, 2003) opens on the first night of camp

> when one of the young victims was taped to his bed…The next day, two assailants held down a boy while a third assailant sodomized him with a broomstick. This was done in front of other players, who laughed and joked about it. The broomstick assault was repeated the day after that…This time, the assailants applied duct tape to the victim's pubic area, buttocks, legs, and eyebrows, inflicting severe pain by pulling off the hair on these parts of his body. Again, other players witnessed the assault. In all, three younger players were sodomized with objects, including broomsticks, pinecones, and—in one case—a golf ball that was inserted into a boy's anus and rammed in further with a broomstick. Two players endured these assaults on multiple

occasions, and were also forced to assault each other in front of the other players. For example, they were forced to put Mineral Ice on their testicles and then alternately kick each other in the groin.

Another time, an assailant made one victim place a banana in his boxer shorts, after which the boy's friend was forced to eat the banana out of the shorts. Following this, a player was forced to lie naked with a potato chip on his buttocks, while another player ate the chip from that location. A victim was forced to make "degrading racial epithets" to an African American player. The younger players were also beaten with plastic bags of ice on their bare backs. Two of the victims later required medical treatment, including rectal surgery in one case…This case is an example of a not-unusual phenomenon in which the bullying of younger, weaker boys takes on a sexualized and/or antigay flavor; indeed, there is significant overlap among so-called hazings, group rapes, and antigay assaults.

Franklin further notes that

The Mepham case bears resemblance to both antigay assault and group rape in its ritualized enactment of masculine power. Older, physically stronger, and more prestigious players engaged in a public display of masculinity, celebrating their strength by violently emasculating their weaker—that is, less manly—teammates. The theatrical element is evident in the requirement of an audience; the laughing approval of this audience provided visible endorsement of the upperclassmen's gendered entitlement. That vilification of the feminine was a core component is illustrated by the emasculation of the victims, through forcing them to assume the female role in simulated sexual acts as well as through the depilation ritual in which one boy was feminized through painful removal of his body hair. This case illustrates both the heterosexist and misogynistic components of masculinity ideology. The boys were younger and weaker; therefore, they were treated like women or gay men. Masculinity ideology requires boys to be strong and tough, lest they be reduced to the status of women and dominated by other men. Thus, other players did nothing to intervene or to inform their coaches of what was transpiring in the cabins, either out of a belief that the victims deserved punishment for being weak, or out of fear of the consequences to themselves. Far better to be a ringside spectator than to play the role of victim in this drama.

A rapist pumping himself up to look strong among peers merely dons a costume that allows him to play the role of the sadist. Many gang rapes aren't even sexual. Often objects are used rather than the penis. The theory is that the play is about asserting male power dominance. But why invest and risk so much to prove dominance when your status is not even being challenged?

Gang rape transcends competition for dominance; it's a ritualized proclamation of dominance that merely sets a stage for the enactment of sadism. Showing off to an audience, or persuading others to participate, as in college hazing, increases the victim's experience of torture. Sexual violation tortures the victim's core being. It's not only physically painful; it's psychically/spiritually painful. It's an attempt to strip away some fundamental aspect of the other person's core being. It's spiritual rape, spiritual murder, committed slowly, painfully, via torture. It's not about sex; it's not about male domination or misogyny or enforcement of gender norms or ideology or power or survival of the fittest. It's about sadism—in gang rape, sadism assisted by cowardice, which displays yet another level of sadistic domination: power-over the coward. All the other conditions, including guys' "going along" (as the instigator's "soft victims"), simply describe a constructed stage upon which the psychopathic sadist plays out his desires.

This dynamic of sadist assisted by cowards is the converse of alchemist and soror mystica. Instead of nurturing the process of individual transcendence, cowardly participants collude in conflicted destruction. Rape is a black-sabbath perversion of sacred alchemical transmutation. Instead of integrating anima and animus into the androgyny, rape sadistically drives the wedge in deeper, separating man from woman (or "woman") and sadistic rape instigator from cowardly "go alongs," as well as each individual from aspects of himself.

Sometimes the rapist asks the victim to evaluate his performance.

Although this gesture is intended to prolong and "rub in" the victim's experience, it is also the case that the narcissistic rapist unconsciously lowers himself to the role of a stripper performing for an audience. He becomes the "she" he hates. Ultimately, then, the sadist is sadomasochistic.

Only a sadist could rape and/or murder a woman, a gay man, a black person, anyone at all. Bigotry exists not just to bolster a sense of entitlement to superiority. A person needs to be superior for two reasons: to guard against someone else's superiority, or to obtain "inferior" victims. Bigotry exists primarily as a source of victims, and secondarily as a justification for victimization. Sadism—which is malicious power-over, which is pumped-up elitism—is the core motivation of sexual violence. Secondary motivations—cowardice, revenge—derive from and partake in that primary cause.

Although all rape, physical or otherwise, is an enactment of sadism, certain catalysts can activate potential sadistic tendencies. Repressed homosexuality, for instance, can trigger sadistic shadow versions of denial, projection, and overcompensation, which many believe motivated sadosexual serial killer Jeffrey Dahmer, and some claim motivates verbal gay banger Reverend Fred Phelps (who famously said, "God doesn't hate you because you're homosexual. You're homosexual because God hates you.")

While it's true that Dahmer's sadistic streak was evident during early childhood—he tortured animals, for example—later his sadism targeted young gay men, the repressed "female" other within himself projected outward. Dahmer drilled holes in his victims' heads and administered acid as "an experiment," to make them "zombies," as Dahmer put it, to prolong his absolute power-over. Eventually, he brutally tortured and murdered them while raping them, then cut them in pieces, some of which he hid in a cellar, some of which he kept in his freezer for future fondling or feeding. Dahmer's cannibalism symbolically represents in concrete terms the sadist's destructive, self-destructive subduing and obliteration of the anima. His consuming, all-consuming obsession was symbolically self-consuming. He displayed mementos of his power-over, like skulls and penises, on an altar he constructed to honor Satan, the symbol onto which he projected his sadism.

Jeffrey Dahmer was likely gay. Ironically, experts point out that heterosexual rape, murder, and other forms of violence against women and children are motivated by what they call a perverse "negative homoeroticism." Think about it: Surely it seems odd that the person a macho heterosexual man would most want to impress sexually, a woman, is exactly the person he treats like dirt. He makes himself out to be a dickhead to impress other dickheads (pardon me, but "dickhead" is *really* accurate). For what purpose? Why are they impressed?

Most likely, they aren't impressed; they are simply caught up in shared sadomasochistic self-loathing that can only be kept alive by feeding the greedy animus the anima. Misogynist men can only relate to men, which explains why antigay violence and gang rape of women take place within male-exclusive groups like fraternities, military forces, street gangs, police departments, rock groups, and sports teams, according to forensic experts.

Negative homoeroticism explains several attributes common among group rapists. The drug-like high during the assault is experienced as a shared emotional orgasm. The sense of closeness, camaraderie, and bonding have nothing to do with the victim and everything to do with having "performed" sexually for the guys. It's that feeling commonly felt after having sex with an intimate, not a stranger, which is what the woman is to a rapist. The guys now know they would do anything and everything for each other. Oh, if only they could bang each other. But they must content themselves with discharging their pent-up frustrations in another dramatic performance. They are each other's voyeurs.

The irony of male-on-male rape of homosexuals to demonstrate heterosexual prowess is that it's a classic case of "thou protesteth too much." As psychologist Peggy Reeves Sanday points out, "The reframing of a homoerotic activity as a demonstration of heterosexuality is doubly ironic in that men who do *not* participate [in raping a man] are accused of being gay."

The woman the hyper-hetero male is jealous of is the woman he fears. The fearful, jealous male must destroy the "woman." The fearful, jealous animus must destroy the anima—a condition only possible in a narcissistic sadomasochist.

Rapists tend to engage in heterosexual sex without intimacy. That's because they don't love the woman (or even know her), they "love" other men and exclusively the male in themselves. Their pervasive cultural practices of misogyny and homophobia are additional examples of protesting too much. As psychologists point out, the sense of entitlement is bravado overcompensating for their fear of women. Their cooperation combined with risk-taking competition is homoerotic push-pull. They certainly aren't showing off for the women. Sexual violence is itself glorified, because the glorified animus that destroys the anima and the love of the anima has nothing but violence and self-violence left.

Sharing sexuality by the common practice of reporting their experiences to each other is the equivalent of phone sex with each other. Likewise the practice of voyeuring, or watching each other have sex. Hazing is a way to prove you're worthy of being in the man's man world of men, men, men by being, temporarily, a "woman" who takes it. All the dulling behavior, like drinking, drug use, and blasting music, and other behaviors like crudeness, sexual innuendos, cursing, and general uncleanliness (reported by Sanday and others) help put men in a state of "slipping into something more comfortable" and "letting go" with one another. They "share the girl" for the sake of circling up around their little campfire of burning dicks and savagely stimulating each other together as a group. According to researchers, including Sanday, the actual rape itself is strikingly nonerotic. Group rapists frequently don't ejaculate, and they often use objects in place of the penis. The simulated sexual acts are used to further emasculate and degrade.

Sanday suggests that "pulling train" is overtly homoerotic: "A group of men watch each other having sex with a woman who may be unconscious. One might well ask why the woman is even necessary for the sexual acts these men stage for one another." Sanday's study of fraternity gang rape noted a common ritual among the "brothers"—the "circle dance," described here by Franklin: "The 'brothers' circle around, arm in arm and sometimes naked, going faster and faster until they lose control and fall down atop each other; brothers periodically step into the middle of the circle and mime sexual and/or lewd acts, including homosexual intercourse. Similarly, she [Sanday] found the brothers to be preoccupied with oral sex, which one fraternity man acknowledged as containing 'more homoerotic potential' than heterosexual intercourse."

Franklin cites researchers (Mosher and Anderson, Scully, Sanday, Greenfeld, and others) who view male sexual performance as just that: a performance. Gay bashing and gang rape of women are both dramatic productions performed usually by young men for each other. The weakness of "female" victims is the symbolic prop used as the foil for demonstrations of masculine prowess.

A study by Mosher and Anderson found that 10% of college men reported "ritualistically" watching each other rape a "party girl" while waiting in line for their turn. Studies by Sanday, Scully, and others have revealed a recurrent theme of revenge-punishment with deployment of the penis symbolizing dominance, power, and social control over those who violate hierarchal rules. These days that list includes any successful college student who is not a white male.

Franklin reports that recent intensified aggression of group rape and gay bashing indicates an intensifying "expression of male contempt for women and femininity. The current popularity of *bukkake*, a symbolic group rape in which multiple men—up to 75 at a time—degrade a woman by squirting semen on her face, attests to the prevalence of such contempt. A Google search for this term in March 2004 met with 3.4 million hits, with web sites that glory in the degradation and objectification of women." Today there are millions of websites dedicated to obese women eating themselves to death for the erotic gratification of their male viewers; millions of sites devoted to "pro-ana" (pro-anorexia), where men can "get off" on women starving themselves to death; millions of sites glorifying titillating fetishes like chastity belts, foot-binding (and the modern version, stilettos), and S/M (sadomasochistic) sex toys like whips and chains and dog collars and far more sophisticated instruments of torture, not to mention the millions of digital peep shows starring clitoridectomies, forced prostitution, and the global sex slave market.

And don't forget snuff films. A: Who *are* these Hogs who so hate women? B: Who are these women who so hate themselves? A: victimizers; B: victims. There's a difference. Although many psychologists argue that gang rapes are homoerotic displays, the homoerotic contents could as likely be shadow expressions of repressed sadomasochism—not only the desire to participate in sadomasochism, but also the self-destructive annihilation of the rapist's anima by his animus. According to Jung's theory of anima/animus, psychological health requires equilibrium of feminine and masculine aspects. The ultramasculine male's misogynist behavior is intent on murdering—snuffing—his own anima: half his own self, the "woman" viewed as a threatening "other." Rape-murder, then, is a projection of what he is doing psychically to himself. This is at least as psychologically sick as it would be physically to cut off an arm and a leg and gouge a few organs.

It's psychic castration: Murdering the androgyny, the misogynist renders himself a deformed androgyny. *That's* unnatural. *That's* evil.

According to this model, the sadistic bigot is actually projecting his own self-loathing onto another. In victimizing the other, he both symbolically and literally damages himself. His is a classic example of a person unable to love another because he does not love himself. Sex for this man is "homo-erotic" not because he desires men but because he hates women because he hates the anima in himself. He is a negative homosexual. Let me repeat: This is evil. This is not an excuse for rape or sadomasochism; it's an explanation. And the condition of the individual male represents the condition of male-dominated culture: evil freely chosen.

THE PITIFUL IRONY OF MISOGYNY

If ultramasculine displays of superiority, like rape, battery, molestation, and murder, indicate weakness, not strength; if such performances flag vulnerability; if assertions of "superiority" inspire fear in the very people who can truly benefit the predator—wives, children, peers, members of one's own species; if the "superior" predator's allies—other aggressive males—are his strongest potential enemies; if the predator's greatest threat comes from other "equal" men, not from inferiors; if it's counterintuitive that males attack the weak to prove strength; if attacking those who could benefit him and would not harm him even contradicts the principle of survival of the fittest, then misogyny makes no sense. Or to put in the everyday vernacular, misogyny is stupid.

Humans are at the top of the food chain. There is no reason to assert superiority to survive. Cooperation contributes to survival better than competition does. The only time a person needs to make claims to superiority is when another person claiming superiority tries to make others look inferior and to prove it poses a genuine threat. Proving one's superiority means proving another's inferiority. But there's no compelling biological reason to do that, except in self-defense. Take away another's claim to superiority and there is no reason to make the claim oneself. Not even in our primitive past would it make sense for us to compete against ourselves. Proving another's inferiority for its own sake is a form of cruelty. Even proving inferiority for its own sake in a nonviolent arena like business or politics involves a cruel measure of callousness.

If misogynist violence is not sadistic, why all the hatred of "women"? Why this hatred of "other"?

Dominance? Strength? Gang rape doesn't prove strength. There is nothing impressive about a group attacking a single weaker person. Solo rapists choose someone weaker and strike unexpectedly when the victim is vulnerable. If this is a contest of strength, attacking a weaker contestant off guard would be cowardly cheating. The use of weapons makes an assault even less impressive. Your penis can't do it, so you have to use a phallic symbol, a mere prop. A man or a group of men raping a woman with a broom handle are not strong; they're socially and spiritually crippled. Raping at gunpoint is ludicrous. Even a four-year-old can pull a trigger. No proof of strength there. There's nothing impressive about a bully bellowing orders from a wagon train of "brothers," or hiding behind bushes, peeking in women's windows, shoving women around, forcing women to get in their place like a terrible-two kicking mommy's shin.

And they wonder why women aren't interested.

Macho men like to pose as the great protectors of women. But what are they protecting women *from* besides other macho men? "Protecting" macho men have generated a self-fulfilling racket that has made women more vulnerable, more in need of protection—a lot like lawsuit lawyers have turned states like Florida into lawsuit hell that exists solely to make money for lawsuit lawyers, whose ads feature them acting like movie stars in a commercial for a TV show: "Reality" TV at its best, i.e., worst.

"The world is a dangerous place to live," Einstein reminded us, "not because of the people who are evil, but because of the people who don't do anything about it." People who do nothing are culpable vultures who feed on the carcasses of victims. As more and more feminist men join feminist women in their global battle against misogyny, something will be done. It's the job of macho men to change. It's the job of feminist men to change them.

RECTITUDE, RECONCILIATION, RECIPROCITY, REVOLUTION

The times they are a'changin'. But though gender equality might be an ideal mainstreamed in America and abroad, true equality has yet to be accomplished. The age of male dominance is ending, but misogyny still rules much of the world and certainly most worldviews. But as the world progresses beyond attitudes of elitist superiority, sexism will cease along with other forms of bigotry.

Ending sexist mindsets is a spiritual agenda that starts by correcting antiquated text-based faith in the inherent superiority of the male. Many men will resist relinquishing power over women, but the time has already come when those men, who for millennia have objectified women, are themselves observed objectively through the lens of truth, and are found to be embarrassingly primitive life-forms parading in very expensive contemporary hats.

The misogynist struts around in an aura of the past so dusty it makes the rest of us sneeze. There's nothing more embarrassing than a shriveled old (or young old) patriarch in a toupee barking commands. People scurry when he pulls out his popgun; people duck when he phones in the heavy artillery. Even so, he's an embarrassing fool even to women in burkes obsequiously bowing as his henchmen march by. What choice do they have? Little do misogynists know that the burke often masks a woman laughing at the macho ass who makes her wear it, which perhaps ironically symbolizes poetic justice still to come for all women oppressed by religion—*any* religion, for what religion is not misogynist, despite "liberal" attempts to castigate its worst offenders? What better way to castrate the misogynist than to laugh at him?

Every religious text is misogynist, despite liberal or progressive or "neo-orthodox" attempts to mask its misogyny with rationalizations and ridiculous revisionist reassurance that what the Bible (or Koran, or other absolutely perfect text) *really* means is… The cost is not just a misogynist's dignity. What's ultimately at stake is the fate of his soul. What would he think would be the destiny of one who willfully relinquishes the power of his spirit to transcend? Could he figure out that the most powerful macho man is the most spiritually impotent?

Enforced forced power-over necessarily supplants true spiritual power—the power that ultimately matters. I'm speaking as a Deist, of course, for whom male and female are equally human in the sight of the Natural God of truth and love. Today some men and many women are exploring the female attributes of God, calling God *Goddess* to compensate for the entrenched macho fantasy of a bearded God with a huge rapacious penis swathed in holy garments of the purist white. Up close one can see through the priest's holey garments the God created in his own image. Of course God is neither male nor female, being not-physical Spirit. That's why male high priests must make their God-image part *human*: in order to make God male in order to elevate the status of the high priest' maleness to a rank equivalent with God's. It can be culturally and psychologically useful to exclude the machismo of our representation of God by including the feminine, as long as we don't forget that goddess is a *representation* of a non-material being that is neither male nor female. Deism views God as most logically a unified whole that from a human perspective includes perfectly integrated attributes that people have traditionally interpreted as male-ish and female-ish. And despite what fundamentalists and (ironically) atheists screech, God, the actual Creator God of the universe, isn't the sadistic, commandeering male "Father" of antiquated religions.

The image of humanity created in the image of God was shattered long ago by religion. We might see in a "glass darkly" a dim, dusty mirror image of our own faulty perception; we might see our shadows cast on Plato's cave wall. But humanity is not a shattered mirror image of God. Reality is a perfectly good mirror reflecting a fragmented human being whose vision of reality is as fragmented as he is. Really, any human being is more cubist than a Picasso portrait.

But unlike other religions, Deism doesn't accept that fractured humanity is "shattered" or that the world is "fallen." We live in a perfectly good world that exists in its present state for a perfectly good reason. Fragmented does not mean shattered. Picture a human being—you, for instance—as a work-in-progress, not the shattered, fallen wretch of religion. Your basic human form is given, right out of the box: The specific form of you yourself is the *you* of you. Many components are included in the package of your life. Some components, like the mother or mother-figure who nurtures your vulnerable baby-life, need to be activated immediately. Some are just there, like the time and space environment into which you are born. Many components are available like ripe fruit on a tree; you get to choose which fruit to pick and eat; you might climb high in the tree to pick the sweetest, juiciest fruit ripening in the sun closest to the top, for you a climb well worth the sweat and scratches.

Misogyny exists because misogynists *choose* to be misogynist and *choose* to perpetuate misogynist theology. People are born with free will and with tremendously multitudinous choices from which to choose this rather than that. The next time you feel inclined to complain, "Why did God let this happen to me?", or the more generalized, "How could a good

God permit evil?", remember that God has given us all amazing faculties, including the awesome gift of free will. How much bad in your life is the fallout of your bad choices, or the evil choices of your victimizers? Some people choose evil which harms (possibly you, directly or indirectly), rather than good which benefits. Sometimes the evil choice seems "good" because it benefits the choosing individual. Misogynists "benefit" pragmatically by owning women. The inherent faculty of conscience makes the misogynist individual aware that a choice that benefits him in some way harms someone else, making that choice a bad one. Ultimately, the most pragmatic choice is one that benefits the chooser but harms no one. What goes around comes around to bite the bad-doer in the butt, a bite that could prove practically and spiritually fatal. (Witness the dictators dethroned in recent months. "Where is the spirit of a dead dictator?" one who believes in God might wonder.)

Humans are not born "fallen." A person "falls" when he decides to choose a course of action that he knows will hurt another person. To justify his course, he must fabricate a rationalization. (I'm using the formal, grammatically correct "he" to represent "he" and "she." "He" is grammatically correct because *he* dominates grammar rules, language, cultural norms, and civilization. That some people use the updated "he or she" demonstrates some progress. To use "his and hers" still sounds patronizing, given that men still own/possess practically everything.)

Men (or whites, or straights, or Christians, or Americans) fabricate rationalizations for why they "had to" or why it was okay to exploit another person or a situation that harms another person. Men have relegated "weak," "needy" women to a position of property, which gives men the right to "take care of" women, i.e., to dominate and control them. "Women," of course, is a symbol that stands for any "inferior" *other*.

Deism transcends all other religions in being the only religion that seeks to reconcile differences like masculine and feminine into a harmonious whole. American democracy is an example of that desire to reconcile differences; the Declaration of Independence is a decidedly deistic document, and the Constitution reflects a deistic demand for equality and justice that thus far has been only partially fulfilled. I would remind the reader that the Declaration of Independence states up front that America was asserting its God-given right "to assume among the powers of the earth, the separate and equal station to which the Laws of Nature and of

Nature's God entitle them," and that Americans "hold these truths to be self-evident, that all men are created equal, that they are endowed by their Creator with certain unalienable Rights, that among these are Life, Liberty and the pursuit of Happiness." The grammatically formal term "men," of course, like "he," refers to all people, including members of both genders. Furthermore, Jefferson explained in his letter to the Danbury Baptist Association, dated Jan. 1, 1802, "Believing with you that religion is a matter which lies solely between man & his god, that he owes account to none other for his faith or his worship, that the legitimate powers of government reach actions only, and not opinions, I contemplate with sovereign reverence that act of the whole American people which declared [in the Constitution] that their legislature should make no law respecting an establishment of religion, or prohibiting the free exercise thereof, thus building a wall of separation between church and state." The whole American people, of course, includes women and men, blacks and whites, Muslims and atheists and Christians. "Adhering to this expression of the supreme will of the nation in behalf of the rights of conscience," Jefferson politely cautions, "I shall see with sincere satisfaction the progress of those sentiments which tend to restore to man all his natural rights, convinced he has no natural right in opposition to his social duties."

Critics might accuse Deists like Thomas Jefferson of promoting Deism as an *other* above all other *others*. True, we Deists today would promote Deist democracy above dictatorship, oligarchy, and rule of the Corporate Nation. And yes, I'm arguing that Deism is a better religion—more ethically honorable, more beneficial—than other religions, just like I would argue that a better answer to 2+3 is 5 rather than 7 or 9. Look at it this way: If feuding members of two gangs were sent to a detention center where a teacher would teach them how to overcome their gang mentality and to get along with each other in society, you wouldn't accuse the teacher of trying to recruit the gang members into his own gang, would you? Deism is that teacher; society is not a gang.

Nor would you allow evil to be "reconciled" with good. You don't try to "reconcile" cancer and health, allowing both to exist; you try to entirely rid the body of cancer. By definition health means absence of disease. You don't try to "reconcile" dictatorships with democracies, you try to purge dictators from the international community. You can't "reconcile" lies with truth; by definition, truth is the absence of lies, fallacies, and fictions presented as facts. Promotion of the good includes elimination of evil—evil, not "evil." Deists, being invested in rational truth rather than promotion of one's otherness for its own sake, are perhaps the best judges and teachers of what constitutes authentic good and evil. Certainly Deism is the religion most invested in seeking the actual truth about what constitutes good and evil. It's absurd to accuse Deists of elitism because we seek to establish and maintain maximum benefit for everyone—and maximum benefit by definition includes eradication of harm. Our MO is truth and love. And really, *truth* is the soul of love.

Deists are many, many different kinds of teachers all teaching the Good News of the one Creator God, the God of Nature, i.e., Creation. We Deists agree about that: that God is the Creator of Nature. Though we agree to disagree about many points, we don't usually disagree about very much, because Deism always relies on reason and common sense to guide us to the truth. This book presents aspects of my current version of Deism, but all Deists would agree with me about most of my points, because my points are rational, and many of my positions have been circulating without complaint among Deists for centuries. My personal definition of reason and common sense includes the inherently truth-focused functions of all our God-given faculties, including conscience, intuition, aesthetic, experience, free will, and spirit—spirit being the boss. This perspective perhaps expands the usual Deist conception of reason, but I don't think many Deists would quibble with adding species to the genus that most Deists call "reason." As I see it, learning to use all our faculties well is an alchemical opus, and the integration of our highly functioning faculties into a synthesized consensus is the alchemical androgyny.

Of course, like anyone, I could be wrong on some points. Deists don't mind being wrong. Because we trust each other to help us on our collective journey toward truth, because we are all alchemists undergoing transmutation and are all each others' soror mysticas, we willingly, even joyously, adjust to more rational positions. Education in truth, not ego, not indoctrinated tradition, drives our religion. My understanding of truth, my reason informed by my conscience, would never reconcile misogyny, or any other version of elitism that constitutes Hog selfishness or psychopathic evil.

The alchemical soror mystica of this chapter is a symbol pointing to the profound problem of misogyny (and by extension, any bigotry) and to its solution. Reconciling male and female into a higher, more beneficial whole is one step that must be taken immediately. That step represents other steps that are just as time-critical. The goal is never elimination of difference for its own sake. Nor is the goal inclusion of every difference. The goal is inclusion of any difference that is beneficial or that does no malevolent harm; the goal necessitates exclusion of every form of malevolent harm.

I'm contrasting malevolent with benevolent. Not every choice is a utilitarian addition of benefit; some choices just are, like the choice to paint your living room blue instead of white. If there is any benefit it is to your sense of well-being. But no one is helped or hurt by your selection of this rather than that. Furthermore, some benevolent choices include some harmful aspects, like surgery that "hurts" the body to get at the cancer, and hurts even after it's over, hence painkillers; and like chemo that causes you to throw up and lose all your hair, just for starters, but that thoroughly rids the body of cancer. The rich might experience their own special kind of pain when they have to cough up a little more tax on their billions, but the tax benefits society, which ultimately benefits the rich. If the rich Scrooge cares about his spiritual wellbeing, he could also benefit from a diet that lightens the flab of his Hog selfishness.

Throughout this book I've discussed some of the many specific beneficial choices that must be made if we humans are to heal our dis-eased species. So yes, Deism transcends other religions in being the only religion (that I know of) that seeks to reconcile beneficial differences into a harmonious whole while surgically removing the cancerous malevolent *other* like misogyny that harms the whole.

I realize how dangerous this perspective could be in the distorting hands of a TV evangelist or any other Hog or psychopath. High priests have already used perverted versions of the moral scalpel to persecute its enemies. The difference is that Deism and only Deism is focused absolutely on authentic truth and love. Deism does not seek to exploit others; it seeks eradication of all exploitation, and that means removing exploiters from their pedestals of power-over. Deism does not seek to destroy any beneficial other; it seeks eradication of all forms of malevolent harm, secular and religious.

Religion tries to paint worldviews like Deism as human-centered opposed to God-centered. Deism's perspective is that it is absolutely God-centered and therefore absolutely human-centered. Deist humanism is God-ism; it honors humans as creations of our intelligent Designer. Deism is the sacred marriage of alchemist and soror mystica, of male and female, into one unified humanist religion that honors God as Creator of us all. Male and female, of course, represent other others, like black and white, rich and poor, Christian and Muslim and atheist. (Isn't Woody Allen a truth-seeker when he claims, "To you I'm an atheist. To God I'm the loyal opposition"?) Deism excludes atheism that willfully distorts or omits truth to falsely verify its perspective.

Besides male vs. female, and human-centered vs. God-centered, other dichotomies that the world needs to reconcile include: reason vs. mysticism; utilitarian/pragmatic vs. compassionate/ethical; intellectual vs. spiritual; common sense vs. education via book learning and trained interpretation.

But some dichotomies must not and cannot be reconciled. Comprehensive study must always supersede indoctrination; literary study of the spiritual meaning of mythic texts always supersedes indoctrinated faith in the literal truth of myths. Nationalism, or love of country, must never be nationalism that exalts one's own nation above other nations or that denigrates, exploits, or seeks to destroy other countries to benefit itself; cultivation of an integrated, mutually benefiting global village must replace self-aggrandizing nationalism. Religious war must give way to religious pluralism, and all religions must foster truth rather than mythic tradition, fact rather than pretext.

Alchemy symbolizes the transformational process of integration we need to undertake together. We are all alchemists and each other's soror mysticas. Nature has built into us a pleasure principle that if functioning properly ensures that our loving our neighbors as ourselves is a joyous process. If the pleasure principle is diseased, love is perverted into Hoggish selfishness or psychopathic loathing of the other—other people, the other gender, even an "other" aspect of one's own self.

In a healthy human being, all her faculties are functioning to benefit the whole person. When a faculty isn't functioning well or at all, when an aspect of the person is diseased, the whole person suffers, degenerates, and ultimately dies. Ditto a healthy society, a healthy world. Ditto a healthy religion.

Many prominent Christian scholars are beginning to understand the need for religion to address problems within its own domain. In his book *The Remaking of Evangelical Theology*, religious scholar Gary Dorrien points out that "Evangelical theology is a product of the Protestant house of authority and is thus prone to biblicism. It is also prone to produce mean-spirited social movements that sacralize religious authoritarianism and male chauvinism." It is at this juncture of self-awareness and self-correction that Deism can join hands with Christianity: "In their resolve to rethink the basis and character of Christian faithfulness," Dorrien notes, "evangelical theologians such as William J. Abraham, Rodney Clapp, Stanley Grenz, Rebecca M. Groothuis, Henry H. Knight III, J. Richard Middleton, Nancey Murphy, Clark Pinnock, Miroslov Volf, and Brian J. Walsh are developing compelling understandings of the gospel as an open-ended communal message of saving grace, conveyed through the freedom of God's Spirit." While Deism does not accept the notion of the superior power of Christianity to bring about or administer saving grace, it could agree with an agenda of conscience correction and with a pluralistic theology of truth-based worship through the freedom of God's Spirit.

The chauvinist needs to be taught that free will is a gift for a purpose that is not selfish self-indulgence, is not power-over, is not the destruction of the *other* that culminates in self-destruction. And by chauvinist I mean by extension, of course, any aggressive elitist individual or group, including a church or other religious body, exercising malevolent power-over, even seemingly "harmless" malevolence touted as militant loyalty to infallible Scriptures of a religion or sect.

We're all in this together—in this extraordinary world in this astonishing universe. Being alive together on the same planet at the same time truly is coincidence of astronomical improbability. We're family. If everyone would share, there would plenty of everything for everyone. So why are certain people driven by a perverse obsession to enforce their mastery over others, when Earth is our shared home?

Habitat selection, aka home-making, is a behavior universal among all known organisms in the universe, all of whom happen to live here on Earth. A human home is a sacred place within a neighborhood of other homes of friends. The biophilia hypothesis posits that healthy human beings have a profound innate desire to enjoy affiliations with a wide diversity of life-forms. These are not master/slave affiliations but cohabitation. Biodiversity is not a liberal concept; it's tangible reality without which we would cease to exist. Physical spiritual well-being is rooted in this earthy planet's loamy, fecund nurturance. As a little leaven leavens the loaf, a little pollution pollutes the whole neighborhood, a little poison eats up one's whole being.

A master/serf hierarchy defaces a world where all of us are created equal in the sight of God. The American corporate pseudo-libertarian exploitation of women and "women" is treasonous travesty. Capitalist "free" enterprise is a conterm promoted to justify unregulated exploitation. Women have always been relegated to the role of brainless servant. But Mother Earth's genius can never be quashed. And she is teaching her daughters her ways lest life perish in a puff of misogynist hubris.

Earth's fragile biosphere is less than ten miles from ocean bottom to mountaintop. Trillions of lives in a wondrous multitude of life-forms swarm within this protective womb of blue amniotic fluid, thriving because of the mutual biological harmony of all our intricate collective variety. Our astronauts have brought home the vision that our bristling planet is floating alone in the forbidding black frigidity of outer space. We want to believe that somewhere in the vastness of the universe there's a global village alive like ours. But our probes have not found a single habitable planet. Most of the universe is made of hydrogen and to a lesser extent helium, elements not abundant on Earth, which is largely carbon, oxygen, nitrogen, silicon, iron, and other heavy elements that were forged in the interior of stars. Though space itself is not a rigid system of fixed stars but is a dynamic, expanding membrane hosting a vast archipelago of multitudinous galactic islands, our speck of a planet is alchemically peculiar, and our unique life we share here together in all its rich diversity, nothing short of miraculous.

Yet we are, like everything else, temporal forms of congealed energy. When our universe was one second old, its temperature was about 10 billion degrees. Today it has cooled to about 450 degrees below zero, about 3 degrees above absolute zero, the lowest temperature possible. Eventually the combined gravitational pull of all this cosmic material will slow the expansion of the universe until all its stars burn out, and the universe will collapse back into nothing, or the radiation background will grow colder and darker forever.

The reintegration of our fragmented Self by the freely willed power of our own spirit could well be life's greatest purpose for the individual and for the whole of humanity. It takes sperm and egg to make a human life. But the world isn't just half male, half female; humanity is a birthday party of balloons and presents, an alchemist's lab bubbling with chemicals all equally real and meaningful. The world is just now realizing that unity of diversity is the ruling principle of life. Love is the spiritual paragon—all love, not just love between a man and a woman, not just physical love. Holistic integration of our diverse parts is the path of love to peace, health, and survival for individuals and our species.

What is the Golden Mean between male and female? The alchemical androgyny? Is it not rather the transcending perspective of metagender? In an era when bombs proliferate recipes for extinction the high ground above us-vs.-them is the only path of survival. Throughout history among all peoples everywhere certain spiritual values have been cherished as sacred. In spite of norms imposed by the ruling class, values of truth, justice, benevolence, and yes, equality have prevailed. Misogyny represents any form of inequality, and every ruler enforcing subjugation deserves to be deposed with the fervor of revolution.

A new metagender meme could right now abolish the rule of the male. The spirit of fairness, freedom, and reciprocity always trumps chauvinistic, misogynist domination. Unity, union, oneness, communion—these are the ancient avant-garde ideals of the future shaping the present. The misogynist who refuses to grow up, to evolve, to transcend is already a relic of the past, a corpse an hour from complete rigor mortis. To resurrect, the aggressive misogynist male and his passive misogynist female must undergo a process of enlightenment that for some of them will require an alchemical trial through fire. But for many the paradigm shift entails nothing more than a sudden revelation of truth and subsequent adjustment of attitude.

Obviously, spiritual survival is not an attribute of spiritual extinction; it's a quality of progress, evolution, burgeoning life-force itself. After centuries, after eons of oppression, the smothered can breathe. The meaning of life always has been, always will be: We're all in this together; love your neighbor as yourself.

It's really just that simple.

CHAPTER 12

AESTHETIC TRANSFIGURATION

The best lack all conviction, while the worst
Are full of passionate intensity.

Surely some revelation is at hand;
Surely the Second Coming is at hand...

When I was a kid, for some years I had the annoying habit of saying about pretty much everything, "It's all symbolic." A dented stop sign, my mom dusting a rose bush with fungicide, a squirrel burying and reburying and re-reburying the same acorn under every tree in the yard. I learned early that a whole neighborhood tangle of humor and tragedy could be encompassed in one consistently wry, "It's all symbolic."

The mental tic of seeing everything as symbolic emerges naturally in most of us because everything *is* symbolic. We are all born with minds that soak up symbolism like a black hole sucks in light. It doesn't take much for us to spew it out the back door into a new universe—a new image.

If you doubt this "urge to symbolism," listen to kids name-calling with metaphors sharper than switchblades. And note how kids' metaphors evolve over time, sometimes into surprises. That car is cool became that car is hot, neither cool nor hot referring to the literal temperature of that car. When kids call another kid a turkey, that's metaphor; when they call the other kid a pig, metaphor takes a step closer to symbol (the kid is a pig: eats like a pig: is fat).

Symbol is typically far more incisive than metaphor. Metaphor implies that there's an intimate correlation; symbol suggests that the correlation is comprehensive and of consequence. In literature, metaphor isolates an instance of comparison; symbol displays a universe of interconnected meanings cohering as one grand unified purpose—ultimately, the complete work, the play, novel, or poem. Of all the arts, literature most thoroughly symbolizes life-as-such.

A clock is a metaphor of time; but then the clock is a *sign*—a representation of itself, of an aspect or function that belongs to itself—rather than a *symbol*—an image that stands for something other than or in addition to what it is. A stop sign is as a stop sign does—tells us to stop. A stop sign symbolizes more than itself in a poem in the voice of a mother whose drug-addicted teenager fails to stop and is killed when a Mack truck collides with his Beetle. (Maybe your mind associated Beetle with beetle with squashed bug, or maybe with drugs, 60s, Beatles?)

A clock shifts closer to symbol when we analyze the gears and springs that make the clock tick and explain how the functional parts of the clock are like the functional parts of something else. The clock becomes symbolic when the image represents an important complex of meaning that functions within a larger complex of meaning. Representation demonstrates analogy; it displays how one thing corresponds to another. Metaphor and symbol are both comparisons. Both metaphor and symbol are embodied by an image or image cluster, but symbol carries a bigger charge because it stands for a larger complex meaning of significance. Symbol, then, can be a microcosm of a macrocosm.

(Perhaps Paley's clock mentioned here and there throughout this book symbolizes my deconstruction of Darwinism and fundamentalism and my affirmation of intelligent design: I'm pulling the gears and springs out of an old rusted clock and reassembling them into a new clock. I might pun—puns can be symbolic, too—that some people will be "ticked-off" by my new clock. Perhaps the clock represents space-time; perhaps it represents the directional, though seemingly circular, passage of historical time. Perhaps the hands of the clock are wiping the sweat from its brow. Perhaps my clock has gotten a facelift and is now digital. You really have to stop a poet once she gets started.)

Symbol helps us contain complex meaning in a single image that stands for a complex whole. Literary symbol distills a whole complexity to its essence; in a literary work, symbolic images relate organically to each other as well as to the whole work. Though Dali's image of *Melting Time* might work conceptually in Dickens' *A Christmas Carol*, it wouldn't organically fit the overall style, tone, or meaning.

Literary symbol helps convey the deep meaning of the whole work. Meaning is deep when it explores profound dimensions where we face the meaning of life, of God, of existence, of humanity in a way that matters to us personally. Symbol can hurt (the kid called a pig), but its prick can be tipped with medicine no less potent than poison. Deep symbol, the variety employed by the arts, in particular literature (which includes religion), couples profound thought and emotion.

Well-developed literary symbol is something the spirit feels, a timelessness, a sense of immortal essence. As great artists have asserted, life is art, art is life. Through symbol a great artist teaches, at the very least, tangible salvation from the mundane. Have you ever felt, like Vladimir Nabokov:

> Through the smells of the bog, I caught the subtle perfume of butterfly wings on my fingers, a perfume which varies with the species—vanilla, or lemon, or musk, or a musty, sweetish odor difficult to define. Still unsated, I pressed forward…I confess I do not believe in time. I like to fold my magic carpet, after use, in such a way as to superimpose one part of the pattern upon another. Let visitors trip. And the highest enjoyment of timelessness—in a landscape selected at random—is when I stand among rare butterflies and their food plants. This is ecstasy, and behind the ecstasy is something else, which is hard to explain. It is like a momentary vacuum into which rushes all that I love. A sense of oneness with sun and stone. A thrill of gratitude to whom it may concern—to the contrapuntal genius of human fate or to tender ghosts humoring a lucky mortal.

Of course you have. You feel this all the time, though you might squelch the feeling because you're not a child. Pity. Perhaps you remember Augustine's query: "What is time? If no one asks me, I know what it is. If I wish to explain what it is to him who asks me, I do not know." Such is life. Unlike children, though, adults get stuck in the "I do not know," which is why Jesus told the grown-ups, "You must remain as children" to maintain your natural propensity not only for authentic goodness, but also for the sense of oneness with that extra something of spiritual presence so exquisite it ignites the thrill of gratitude.

It's odd that so many well-meaning religionists believe that their myths are literal fact rather than symbols awaiting participatory interpretation. Could it be that religious literature is so potent that people are stunned into forgetting that the symbolic, the metaphoric, the mythic, the aesthetic is representation? That doesn't mean it's not real. It is real, but in a way that's more like reality TV in those moments when the protagonist is caught on tape blurting, *whoops!,* the truth. Truth that emerges from religion in spite of its staging is like, say, a Freudian slip that pokes its head out almost unnoticed from an otherwise well-zippered speech. (Once noticed, though, a wry chuckle flutters across the stage.)

Or is it that the religious learn their myths by rote and recite their flat "factual" lines like parrot puppets sputtering first-grade equations? The habit of regurgitating catechism trains the mind to bow to the habit of scripted life. Symbol, on the other hand, engages the participant in the deep experience of interpretation. The dimension of symbolism infuses reality *as actually* as symbolism embodies alchemy or a great play.

WHAT'S LOVE GOT TO DO WITH IT?

In the symbolic Old World of Hog, the soror mystica serves as the alchemist's guide to the Promise Land of self-transcendence (which I've translated from the Middle Ages via Aquinas and Jung into this present book). To get to the Promise Land the alchemist has to escape the temptations and assaults of Hog. In effect, alchemy *is* that escape. The sacred marriage between alchemist and soror mystica concludes at the terminus where myth ends and the journey toward truth begins. Truth is found in myth when myth is recognized as myth aesthetically representing truth.

As per the last few chapters, for the alchemist (the "alchemist"), the myth left behind is that Hog is God; the truth approached is that God is God. How does something so simple become so complicated? The most accurate answer, it seems, is volition, the faculty most in need of a jump start if not thorough transmutation. The problem is that the dead-battery will must freely choose to start in order to start choosing, and must have already chosen in order to be able to choose to accomplish transmutation. The sticky point is that the will most in need of transmutation needs to undergo transmutation in order to be able to will transmutation. It's not (as we often assume) spiritual inertia that keeps us from driving on. It's a dead battery or misguided GPS—it's a malfunctioning will: "The spirit is willing but the flesh is weak." Enter the soror mystica to assist, first and foremost by helping to ward off the temptations and assaults of Hog.

Beyond the Old World of Hog, in the New World of God, specifically the Creator God of an intelligently designed universe, sacred marriage itself is undergoing the alchemical process of reinterpretation. People have begun to realize the benefit of unloading their baggage and resolving their neuroses together in an intelligently designed relationship before deciding to exchange rings in marriage. A ring symbolizes unity, love, and eternity, qualities that can only be truly attained and appreciated once the alchemical process has been completed. Religion wants you to tie the knot before you've really grown up, deeming it a sin to get seriously intimate before the wedding day. Ideally, though, there should be no "knot"; marriage should be a nurturing, creative union of two people who truly know and love the essence of each other, and essence takes awhile to manifest and love takes time to mature. Maybe marriage itself, or rather the institution of marriage, has become obsolete. Maybe the wedding should take place years or decades into the marriage.

Marriage is only one kind of union. Any close relationship involves a similar psychological and spiritual dynamic and produces the same kind of effect. The primary adult relationship is always with oneself. It's tragic how few people really get to know themselves. Besides the primary relationship to Self, most adults have important secondary relationships with partner, friends, relatives, coworkers, neighbors, and even pets and online acquaintances. It's tragic how few people really get to know others. Unfortunately, even among enlightened progressives, our most fundamental relationship—with God—is usually filed in an envelope labeled abstraction stuffed at the very back of the drawer. Many people feel uneasy even mentioning the word God. This doesn't mean, though, that people are "lost souls" destined for the fiery pit of losers. Most people commune with God without even realizing she's there. It's tragic how few people really get to know God.

But then, God is subtle. God is mysterious. God is hidden. You've heard all these somewhat accusatory, somewhat excusing descriptions before. Sometimes, though, creators who spend a lot of time "in flow" eventually realize they've been floating on their magic carpet in the Presence of a subtle, mysterious, hidden "something" that is in fact God. In a way that's remarkably humble, God has assumed the role of our *soror mystica*. (Once upon a time I thought: If Jesus had been born a woman, it wouldn't have been a miracle.) Communing with God via whatever medium—love, service, poetry, watercolor, the subtle perfume of butterfly wings on our fingers—engages the essential creative spirit within us. Which makes sense: God is the Creator of Creation; Creation is the manifestation of a perpetual process of Creation. If there's one thing we know for sure about the Creator it's that she's creative. It makes sense, then, that communion with God might be effectively facilitated through use of our creativity.

Like any relationship, alchemy (literal and figurative) is a creative process. The alchemist's goal of integration, resolution, and holistic transformation makes alchemy an art as well as science. The scientifically creative alchemical process represents a narrative of psychological spiritual progress. (The psychological is but one facet of spiritual transcending, i.e., growth, i.e., evolution.) Narrative is literary; meaning that transcends the material must be represented symbolically. Creators articulate essence via representation and meaning via symbol. So does God.

Creators utilize materials like paint and words and musical notes; God uses Nature, including human nature. Poets especially understand that stars and spider webs and chrysanthemums and diamonds and grains of sand are symbolic, that each and every star and spider web and chrysanthemum and diamond and grain of sand resonates with profound poetic truth. Poets intuit that poetic truth is spiritual truth because it distills essence and synthesizes both concrete and spiritual reality. Poetry's gift of incorporating micro and macro, and concrete (material) and spiritual, makes it prophetic in the old-fashioned literal sense—prophet meaning literally teacher, or spiritual guide.

Many agree with Wordsworth that "Poetry is the breath and finer spirit of all knowledge." No wonder so many religious texts are written in poetic forms. In *Biographia Literaria,* Coleridge maintains that Wordsworth's poetry creates a feeling analogous to the supernatural by directing our attention to the wonders of the natural world and imparting a kind of mystical union with nature. The religious sensibility of Wordsworth and Coleridge, like that of many poets before and after them, is essentially Deist.

Coleridge considers the primary imagination of the poet to be "the living Power and prime Agent of all human Perception, and a repetition in the infinite mind of the eternal act of creation in the infinite I am." What makes poetry poetry, he says, is the reader's delight in the unified whole and his distinct gratification with each harmonizing part—not the parts in and of themselves but their harmonization, like notes in a concerto or lines in a painting. The poet brings the whole soul into activity by diffusing a tone and spirit of unity that fuses the realms of all our faculties by the "synthetic and magical power" of imagination, which reveals itself in the balance or reconciliation of opposite or discordant qualities.

For Keats, "The excellence of every Art is its intensity, capable of making all disagreeables evaporate, from their being in close relationship with Beauty and Truth." Keats's beauty and truth exist in the realm of the soul, while the philosopher's thoughts remain stuck in the realm of mind, which Keats sees as a means to the soul and not an end in itself. The world, he said, is the place where the mind and heart act on each other to form the "soul or intelligence destined to possess the sense of identity." This, he believes, is a vision of salvation that does not affront our reason and humanity.

A poem provides a lesson via an experience of sensate intelligence—a process antithetical to the flattened didactic. Rather than being "above" a subject kept under control, poetry resonates with the same animating nature-force that it describes. Poetry translates nature's intelligent design— itself a volume of poetry—by building connections in the brain that convey to the mind an experience of the network of subjective meaning emanating from (through) objective data. Perhaps you've seen the famous side-by-side photos of a brain cell and a galaxy. What does it mean that they look almost identical? Poetry is composed of correlations because poets excavate correlations that compose the universe.

The connections transported from the brain to the mind are translated into mental meaning, which can then be transported to the spirit for transformation into transcending spiritual meaning. To then be *transported* on the magic carpet of spiritual meaning, the person must not simply "get" the concept but must also be "moved" spiritually, the destination being a change in the innermost Self, the spirit. That's alchemy. ("It's all symbolic.")

The difference between soul change and spirit change is like the difference between being intellectually moved by a tragedy like *Antigone* or

Hamlet and being so emotionally moved that you must *do* something, must change, must help, must get therapy or volunteer for a hotline. A changed *soul* might feel more compassion towards another or himself; a changed *spirit* must transcend: it's that classic relentless cathartic drive toward self-fulfillment coupled with empathy.

But there's another level of difference, the difference between changed and charged. A charged soul feels one with Nature or an aspect of her; a charged spirit feels one with the Creator of Nature, or feels a profound longing for that level of transcending oneness. A charged soul stands in a resonant Presence in this life; a charged spirit floats in an essential Presence that exists fully in the world but not quite of it. A charged life is a life of "oneness" accompanied by a profound sense of reverent awe and ecstatic gratitude, Nabokov's "thrill of gratitude to whom it may concern." Hog religion—religion shackled to its own mythic texts and self-righteous dogmas, to its selfish hubris and greed—fails to facilitate this shift to Presence, because Hog is only about Hog.

Static religion dies; creative religion thrives. Religious rituals that facilitate Presence are actually works of spiritual performance art. Many today sidestep religion altogether, claiming that art is the new (and true) religion. Certainly religion must be creative. One reason Deism is so appealing is that its focus is intrinsically creative, self-evolving, and Creator-honoring. Deism is an aesthetic work-in-progress, like Creation itself.

ALL THE WORLD'S A STAGE

All the world's a stage of development. Life evolves; humanity evolves; you evolve. A play represents a life—and by extension, your life—and the principles that make a life dramatic are paralleled by those that propel the dramatic representation.

Do we create meaning or discover it? Clearly both, but where do you draw the line? It's odd how mysterious one's own life really is. What's particularly interesting is that we seek the meaning of our discrete self along with the shared meaning of our species. One informs the other. It's hard to argue that human life *isn't* innately meaningful.

Humans seem peculiarly equipped to spot interconnections. Drama, for instance, parallels the process of alchemy; my life parallels your life. Why we bother to find ourselves, to work on ourselves, to seek religion and a good therapist and a life partner and a meaningful career expresses the same impulse that drives us to the movies and art festivals and bookstores and feasts.

Humans have always been attracted to dramatic representations of our quest for meaning. Then again, some people are just attracted to drama. Average people are so hungry for meaning they latch onto any cupcake of gossip as if it were manna. Drama queens are so desperate they whip up their own frothy soap operas; then when they're tired they plop on the couch and peep through the keyhole at reality TV. Pathetically fake, perhaps, but even the popularity of trivial sitcoms demonstrates how seductive meaningful—or "meaningful"—narratives can be. We're literally starving for significance, even by the thimbleful. So we shuffle the remotes controlling remote, vicarious "life" when we should really pull out our journals.

Aristotle understood this. He knew that people need drama and that the human drama needs to be understood. We create art to articulate "out there" the world "in here." Art is the mirror of the soul. What's amazing is that you can look in my mirror and see your soul. Every soul is on the same quest for meaning. Even Hog is on this quest, but Hog is penned-in by his pigheaded insistence that the quest is for Hog. In a way he's right. But instead of finding the truth of himself as a creation in need of a hose-down, he falls down and worships himself as God.

Aristotle understood both the frustration and the nobility of the quest away from Hog. The fragment of his *Poetics* that has survived and come down to us, which is specifically an analysis of tragedy (lost to us are the sections on comedy, epic, and lyric), explains dramatic principles that mirror our existential predicament. Art, including dramatic art, reflects life and *is* life, an aspect of life. An artwork of the highest quality and magnitude expresses the greatest universality through the most refined, particularized example. In other words, we need a very sharp, very high-resolution lens to see clearly and deeply.

Think of it this way: A pivotal event in your life, the kind that really shows your true metal in the moment, manifests your essence. At the same time, your life experience is an example of a more universal human condition. You're an individual but you're also part of the human family; you're a microcosm of the macrocosm. So, too, art.

Aristotle, the first person to really analyze/delineate/codify aesthetics, defines tragedy as "an imitation of an action that is serious, complete, and of appropriate magnitude." By imitation he means representation, not superficial copying. Any old snowflake is not any old snowflake when viewed through a microscope; art gives us the snowflake through a very special lens that allows us to actually *see* the snowflake in all its concrete glory and thereby to join in its resonating essence. At the very least you suspend your disbelief when you enter into a good movie's plot: You are "one" with that life portrayed on the screen. The play's plot is not action, but the *representation* of an action, by which Aristotle means not bodily movement on stage, but, as Dante explained it, "movement-of-spirit," or what we might call personal growth. Art mirrors life mirrors transcending spiritual life.

Thought and character, Aristotle says, are the two natural causes of action. Thought he identifies with reason, which is the active, conscious perception. Thought in this sense is the analytic, which involves 1) a process of discovery (empirical investigation and data collection) and 2) the demonstration (the proof; the correctness of this stage of the thought sequence being essential to the syllogism's validity). There's an objective *reason* (logos) for the plot.

There's a reason for your life, and yes, your tragedies, even your fake ones, which are simply shadows of your real ones. There's a reason for humanity's existence and struggles in this space-time universe. We discover our meaning as it is demonstrated through our life. Our life is its own logos. Our life is a work of art representing our core spiritual logos.

Character—the moral motivation, the unconscious and undefined feelings and emotions of pathos/passion—is embodied by the protagonist (the main character) and the antagonist (any character pitted against the protagonist). The antagonist in a narrative (play, movie, opera, novel, short story, narrative or epic poem) is typically a person, but could be a force (the sea in *Old Man and the Sea*), a creature (the whale in *Moby Dick*), or even the protagonist himself (Dr. Jekyll's Mr. Hyde). The juxtaposed antagonist provides a background foil against which the protagonist emerges in sharp relief. But the purpose goes beyond display; the protagonist manifests his true colors through his interactions—conflict—with the antagonist. The truth of our life is as much about what it is not as what it is. We are the product of our choices *to be* no more than *not to be*. Character employs the dialectic, which involves talking around a subject, approaching it from every angle until its intrinsic characteristic (general meaning) becomes manifest. Your essence, your core meaning, reveals itself through the myriad details of your life sculpted by your choices.

The complete action of a play has a beginning (or objective, conscious purpose, identified with thought), a middle (manifesting subjective, unconscious pathos), and an end (final perception: knowledge). Just like alchemy. Just like life.

All plot involves change, which is creation in action. Aristotle claims that the most important element of a play is the structure of incidents, and that the plot is "the first principle, and, as it were, the soul of tragedy." A good plot consists of acts that succeed one another in their probable and necessary sequence. The structure should be so tight that one event could not be interchanged with another; and anything that could be left out, should be. A good healthy plot evolves, a boring plot stagnates. Ditto your life.

Good structure depends not only on sequence but on unity. A beautiful object, like a living organism, must not only have an orderly arrangement of parts but must also have magnitude: "Beauty depends on magnitude and order." Magnitude must be that "which may be easily embraced in one view…easily embraced by memory." The longer the better, provided the whole be perspicuous. Magnitude is the opposite of boring, which leaves us mumbling, *So what?*

Does your life have good structure, or does it seem random? Does your life have unity, or does it seem fragmented, devoid of overall meaning and any sense of wholeness or feeling of oneness? Does your life have meaning of magnitude, or does it feel trivial, insignificant, boring? To find the meaning of life you must first find the meaning of yourself. Magnitude doesn't mean "big" like winning the Lotto. Magnitude consists of standing in a random landscape among rare butterflies and their food plants in a momentary vacuum into which rushes all that you love, of sensing oneness with sun and stone, of experiencing the ecstasy of Nature and the thrill of gratitude for your extraordinary luck in having been born.

The change of the best plots arises from their internal structure (following cause and effect) and is accompanied by reversal and recognition. Reversal means the action veers round to its opposite, and recognition is the change from ignorance to knowledge, which in the audience produces pity or fear that leads to a catharsis of those emotions;

pity and fear then give way to "a sense of wonder" (Aristotle) and "thrill of gratitude" (Nabokov).

If the universe is intelligently designed, if your life has been purposely created—Why? Everybody experiences setbacks and disappointments, irritating obstacles and tragic loss. Everybody has the freedom to learn from those experiences—or to not learn. What is learned? A sense of wonder? Is that it? Gratitude? What if it is? What if the meaning of life is simply standing fully alive in the midst of existence, filled with awe and gratitude? Embracing just *that* as your religion would certainly be cathartic, would it not? And isn't *catharsis* what religion calls *redemption*?

Unlike the protagonist who for the Greeks is at the mercy of fate and for the Elizabethans is possessed by his tragic flaw, we have the power to create out of the tragedy of our fall a life that is dramatic but not tragic. Tragedy warns us against taking the road of tragedy. Instead, we could follow Nabokov's "contrapuntal genius of human fate…to tender ghosts humoring a lucky mortal."

Life in our intelligently designed universe is rational, and so is the play mirroring life. The traditional five acts of a play follow our life's underlying pattern: thought, character, reversal, recognition, catharsis. In a broad sense, the play's unified structure embodying the protagonist's journey mirrors similar processes facilitated by alchemy, therapy, education, religion, and Kubler-Ross's stages of dying and grief. "It's all symbolic": Picture symbol as an image between two facing mirrors receding into infinite depths that give the image a sense of process of both going and being within and beyond while making us aware of the interconnectedness of all things.

Art and life embody each other in a state of perpetual communion. Finite/temporal material form expresses spiritual content; our particular life expresses the meaning of universal human life and existence. We contemplate, we create, we contemplate what we create and create ever new meaning.

Aristotle identifies two motivations for art: 1) the instinct for harmony and rhythm, or *form*, and 2) the instinct of imitation/representation, which is the work's intellectual and moral *content*. Central to Aristotle's philosophy is his belief in our capacity to know. The first principle or fundamental fact of the universe is "motion," or change, which today we call process, the fundamental structural juice of Creation. Aristotle views process in terms of each thing's internal function rather than, as materialists tend to view it, external mechanistic forces. Environment doesn't make an acorn become an oak, though it may inhibit or promote the process.

An acorn's becoming an oak is that thing's intrinsic function, and the process, or movement, is toward a particular end (oak tree). An acorn does not become a garbage can, gorilla, or grassland. But how different an acorn is from an oak tree! Who would have guessed they were the same *thing*? Oaks, grasshoppers, meteors, the universe—we all are evolving and sometimes taking broad-jumps of creative emergence into the better angels of ourselves.

Reality is a system of interrelated functionings culminating for us humans in the function of consciousness. Our pleasure in harmony and rhythm (and just think how many pleasures involve harmony and rhythm) stems from our intuitive recognition of patterns repeating throughout the structure of the universe which makes us feel linked to all things.

How miraculous that we are self-aware! I know I am standing in this material be-ing, expressing myself to myself and to you like a rose opening petal by petal on a rose bush in a garden in a galaxy in a universe. To *know* this spiritually is to love all roses, vegetation, stars, existence—which is to love "to whom it may concern" whom most of us call God.

Conscious knowing leads to the desire to create—to express, to rejoice, to shout from the rooftops the logos of our being. A higher pleasure than recognizing the repeating patterns of nature, says Aristotle, comes through our instinct for creative representation—a spiritual quantum leap beyond primitive imitation.

To learn gives the liveliest pleasure, he argues, and knowledge (wisdom/enlightenment), the end of learning, comes via contemplation, which requires language, which requires "society" (an audience). To say exactly what a thing is, is to know. Defining (saying exactly what a thing is) is the bridge between the world of particular/concrete things and the realm of universal concepts realized by reason. From the beginning is the Word that is spiritual articulation.

The quest for meaning is the motive of Greek tragedy. Aristotle believed motive is the impetus of function (self-manifestation). Meaning is revealed through subject (like the subject/noun in a sentence, so is the tragic hero), which is manifested through structure. The plot's essential structure—complication and denouement (unraveling) separated by a turning point—is echoed in all structures, even the most elemental: coming into existence, turning, ceasing to exist. As with all things in nature, the end of a great tragedy is tied back into its beginning. All things ultimately are whole. "All the world's a stage," Shakespeare put it in *As You Like It*, "And all the men and women merely players; / They have their exits and their entrances; / And one man in his time plays many parts... / Last scene of all, / That ends this strange eventful history, / Is second childishness and mere oblivion, / Sans teeth, sans eyes, sans taste, sans everything." The uroborus swallows its tail. "Mere oblivion" need not be tragic extinction. For some, it might mean transcending space-time constriction; it might mean waking up and walking out of the theatre.

Human beings, being rational and conscious, can *know* and can find meaning. Meaning includes beginning, middle, end; meaning is comprehensive; meaning is whole. Like the playwright's drama, any human life has meaning and an end purpose. We are motivated to express our core truth, which is revealed through our material self manifesting through our life. To borrow the religious paradigm, some macrocosmic fall from grace, played out in the myriad microcosms that constitute existence, unravels as our complicated predicament. We reach a crisis, which, if our life has quality and magnitude, becomes the turning point onto the narrow road back to transcendence.

In this life we need to make choices to be manifested, we need to freely prune away our own dead wood, we need to say *No, not this* for *Yes, this* to make sense. Creating art or life or anything demands that we make choices based on an evaluation of quality. The protagonist is like religion's fallen spirit wrestling with his angel; that dark angel represents the shadow aspects of our individual and collective material self; we are protagonist and antagonist. Becoming a unified whole involves winnowing away the antagonistic Hog. The protagonist performs the alchemy of life.

Tragedy gives us a model of human life as it is lived. But alchemy's soror mystica demonstrates that life need not be tragic. Rather than confrontation and conflict, life can be a serious, but not tragic, process of transmutation. Today, tragedy in life tends to play out as a war of "us" vs. "them." We can take the higher path by trading conflict with the "other," the antagonist, for a more mature and certainly more peaceful and mutually-benefiting process of spiritual self-fulfillment. It's called Love.

ALCHEMY AS SPIRITUAL PERFORMANCE ART

In ancient Greek drama the tragic hero is, Aristotle observes, "better than ourselves" yet is our highest self, our core essence. Art should "preserve the type yet ennoble it." Through contemplation of art we glimpse our core being, through creation of art we manifest it.

The process of distillation and synthesis is simultaneously a process of understanding and of articulating understanding. Human creation, like Creation itself, is a process. The alchemist uses chemicals the way the poet uses words to process/produce a product that is both literally true and symbolically meaningful. Similarly, I'm using the images of alchemist and poet to represent the alchemical and poetic processes, each and both of which represent any person's quest for spiritual truth; and one point I make throughout this book is that spiritual truth is embedded in Nature. Can you see how everything is connected, both concretely and symbolically? Deism considers the massive network of inter-correlation a powerful proof of intelligent design and testimony of the Creator's aesthetic engagement in human understanding.

Poets grasp the profound spiritual truth that everything, the whole of existence and its myriad particulars, all and each, is symbolically meaningful, and poets understand the connection between meaning and purpose. Poets use words to represent meaning; other artists are poets to the extent that they use their mediums to represent symbolic meaning. Art is literary when it refers to a myth or historical event; it is poetic when its references contain additional metaphoric meaning, when it connotes as well as denotes.

Humans' most fundamental materials are God-made; God's materials, Nature, are also God-made. Only God creates the fundamentals. The tendency of some humans to forget that they and all their raw materials are God-made is perhaps the great tragic flaw, and like all hubris, cosmic amnesia, really a snubbing of God, is the most absurd tragic flaw, a profoundly silly form of ingratitude. Tragedy is comedy without the laughs.

The levels of alchemical knowledge, the levels of understanding and meaning played out through the alchemical drama, are represented as symbols in drawings and other artistic renderings. The final knowledge, the embodiment of integrated anima and animus signified by the androgyny, uncovers the even deeper *meaning* of that knowledge: Love. Creation is an act of love in the book of alchemy.

The good chemistry of love between animus and anima (and alchemist and soror mystica, and scientific/aesthetic process and product) represented by sacred marriage, flies in the face of traditional Pauline wife subject (subjected, subjugated) to husband, and husband as head of the wife, and it defies the raping attitude of elitism, specifically as it foments gender schizophrenia and literal rape. On the one hand, sacred marriage frees men and women as groups (male and female), allowing them to commune as equals outside the jurisdiction of person- and relationship-as-property. On the other hand, it frees each individual man and woman by integrating anima and animus, allowing the person to resolve his or her neurotic inner conflict and to reside with him/herself in peaceful friendship.

Now that the alchemist unselfishly, not-narcissistically loves himself, he can love his neighbor as himself. Once Hog has been banished from the soul, the denigrated "feminine" faculties, such as emotion, intuition, and aesthetic, are released from the stranglehold of the privileged masculine "head" of reason, and all the faculties are unified into a healthy whole person. Ultimately, from all this healing flows a huge spiritual sigh of relief, both personal and collective. Then follows the drawing in of a deep breath of euphoria—exactly that classic "born-again" sense of Presence and feeling of joy to the world, peace on Earth, goodwill toward men and women, except that it's holistic, not specifically Christian (or Jewish, or Muslim, or...).

The process of arriving at love and the expression of love both employ the faculty of aesthetic sensibility. The union of anima and animus gives birth to art, art born free from the constraints of heterosexist traditions. The urge to art is the urge to religion—primal religion free from elitist encrustations. Art and religion are both narratives of spiritual quest.

In contrast, the rapist perpetually performs his nightmare role of Hog with the same musty props that have always represented the ultimate perversion of androgyny and love. Hog mates with hate to engender destruction. Art creates, Hog destroys. As the misogynist erases meaning, his final constricted knowledge emerges: destruction ending in self-destruction, a true spiritual murder-suicide. Love benefits and burgeons naturally: Love's spiritual life-force results in new life. Rape harms and self-destructs naturally: Rape's spiritual impotence results in death. The end of rape is extinction, its zombie marker, absolute alienation and loneliness.

The rapist drifts off into empty space like an astronaut who cuts the umbilical cord connecting him to the spaceship that can transport him home. One might pity a merely sociopathic rapist driven by tormenting shadows of cowardice rather than by psychopathic sadism—pity, perhaps, but not with the deep compassionate pathos reserved for his victims.

The hoggish rapist can only be saved by the grace of his own alchemical work. And of course I mean that symbolically. Put more directly, the repentant hoggish rapist can only be saved through the freely chosen work of alchemy facilitated by the grace of the soror mystica. And by soror mystica I don't mean necessarily women; perhaps the most effective soror mystica for the hoggish rapist is a former hoggish rapist saved by the grace of alchemy. Alchemy is an art; metaphorically, alchemy is art.

Alchemy is also science—the science of combining chemicals to discover their properties (truths) and to generate reactions (meaningful applications)—just like painters and poets and composers combine paint and words and notes to discover their properties (truths) and to generate reactions (meanings). The goal is the harmony of elements, even if that includes meaningful dissonance.

Alchemy integrates the functions of art and science; the alchemist treats Nature, including human nature, with the respect one naturally affords to God, the Creator, the Great Mother, Mother Nature, Mother Earth. Alchemy honors the feminine creative spirit that permeates Nature and her creative children: life, humanity. Science or art that treats Nature as an object to be raped (possessed, exploited) will not be effective science or art. Science and art of *value* express with exuberance the wonder of miraculous Nature.

The presence of the soror mystica puts a different spin on the usual image of alchemists and other artists (including scientists) working alone. Humans are social beings. The rugged individualist may have an advantage over being one of the herd, but no one was created to be alone. Even "without deep reflection," Einstein reminded us, "one knows from daily life that one exists for other people." Even when Thoreau was at Walden, his mother brought him cookies every day (his cabin being a short stroll from the main road). Picasso held some macho views, but during his formative decades he had dinner—respectfully—almost every night at the home of the famously androgynous couple, Gertrude Stein and Alice B. Toklas, whose friendship and Parisian home—a kind of wall-to-wall, floor-to-ceiling gallery of revolutionary friends' original art—and their expert art criticism, not to mention five-star culinary concoctions, made them jointly the perfect soror mystica to support Picasso's and many other artists' and writers' alchemical opuses.

Love that is not self-love requires an *other* to love. Lover requires lover, art requires audience. God, too, seems interested in getting our attention via awesomely aesthetic Nature in order to nurture some kind of relationship with the creature she created uniquely rational and conscious. Above all else, religion is about relationships, with oneself, with God, with one another. In a community of communicating communion, each communer is an alchemist and a soror mystica, and each opus is part of the larger opus: transcendence, or love-embodied truth. An actual utopia would be the representational paradigm of transcendent communion. The ultimate state of being is not all things equaling God, is not an isolated "God" narcissistically making love to himself, but all discrete beings, including God, loving one another.

Art articulates the meaning of something not just observed but actually *seen*. Unlike the rapist, who superficially observes a victim as an object to be manipulated, the artist is Nature's lover exploring her essence in order to know her. The more intimately he knows her, the better he knows himself. I'm using gendered pronouns, but the artist (and scientist), like the alchemist and soror mystica, can of course be male or female.

Buddha said, "The foot feels the foot when it feels the ground." Until you actually touch, until you truly feel another person, you can't be in touch with yourself. Similarly, you have to step barefoot through the layers of natural existence to really feel the essence within—within *it* and within yourself. As Heraclitus reminded us, "The hidden harmony is stronger than the visible." And because, as Heinrich Heine put it, "Nature is visible thought," we see that harmony is the product of thought, i.e., intelligent design. Ironically, as we really come to see the hidden harmony and exquisite thought behind it, we also begin to really *see* the layers that constitute the visible. Art helps us see multi-dimensionally. Many consider art to be the new religion because it helps us also *feel* the divine Presence and thereby *experience* the reality of existence—the kind of *seeing* that any religion should nurture.

NECESSARY AESTHETIC

Poet William Carlos Williams gave twentieth century aesthetics its most famous slogan: "Make it new." Already in the nineteenth century poets, composers, and especially Impressionist and Modern artists were exploding history into a kaleidoscope of new forms that created the world anew. It's no surprise that periods of spiritual renaissance accompany blasts of creative innovation in the arts: The gesture of authentic art itself symbolizes spiritual quest. The Greeks understood art to be representation, but what art represents, or what the best art should represent—or even if art should represent at all—has never ceased being debated, and the Modernists argued their new positions with passion.

Plato believed that reality consists of archetypal forms—Ideas, Ideals—beyond human sensation, and that the artist merely copies an experienced object, which represents the form (Idea), thus art can only be an imitation of an imitation. A sandaled elitist who busied himself classifying Nature objectively rather than subjectively experiencing her barefooted, Plato constructed the theoretical framework upon which Darwinism and religious fundamentalism have propped up their theologies. Darwinism is an abstract construct that supposedly represents concrete natural reality, but Darwinians have faith in Darwinism as if *it* were the concrete reality, not a theoretical representation. Fundamentalism is an abstract construct that supposedly represents concrete historical reality, but fundamentalists have faith in fundamentalism as if it *were* religion, not religious representation. The authority of Darwinism and fundamentalism are written texts that have been proven beyond any shadow of a doubt to be erroneous. Yet Darwinians and fundamentalists continue to revere their texts as absolute fact. Their authority has been debunked, so they are forced to dishonestly distort the text in order to maintain their meaning. Natural truth has been perverted into elitist dogma grounded in myth.

Artists, however, really *see* Nature concretely. They derive abstractions from concrete reality, and strive to represent her essential forms and symbolic meanings concretely via art. The artist looks into Nature, and through art makes the invisible visible.

The Darwinian myth and the fundamentalist myth and the misogynist myth are all equally myths upheld by mythic authority. A union of art and science that replaces conflict with cooperation, with working in concert like alchemist and soror mystica, helps us replace myths with reality and schizophrenia with sensible meaning.

Myths converted into abstract truths assumed to be literal fact clog the arteries of ape men and godlets. The problem is that they don't see what they're looking at. William James pointed out that "The greatest enemy of any one of our truths may be the rest of our truths." Darwinians and fundamentalists refuse to acknowledge that their "truths" have been thoroughly deconstructed by much more definitive truths. They refuse to *see*. In other words, they lie to themselves; they're self-blinded.

At their best, art and science help us really *look* to really *see*. Most artists, the ones actually doing the work of actually seeing, disagree with Plato's privileged Ideal; reality and meaning are equally real, and artistic creations serve a purpose and achieve a level of quality unmatched by the imitating capability of a photocopy machine. Artists tend to use the term *form* to refer to the material art object, or to a class of productions, such as poem or picture, or more specifically, Italian sonnet or watercolor, with the emphasis on the group of concrete objects, not their abstract classification. Form represents form, becoming itself another form: A cubist rendering of the spatial forms of Nature becomes a painting; many such paintings become Cubism.

Certainly the flux of the material realm, even if "immortalized" in art, is very much like shadows on Plato's cave wall. But Aristotle was right that abstract generalization is not ultimate reality; his theory of reality and art grounded form in the material realm. Instead of Nature representing form, form represents aspects of Nature. But "art partly completes what Nature cannot finish," per Aristotle, by representing—*not* merely imitating— "things as they *ought to be*." By suggesting that what we create transcends Nature—but as a category of reality, not an abstract reference to it— Aristotle began to explain the impetus of art, which is the desire to transcend the material realm by manifesting its depth, the deep spiritual truth immanent in reality, especially human existence.

The artist starts by separating form from one material object, such as a horse, and imposing it on another form, such as marble. Though the living horse is very different from the marble horse, both could be called a horse. What is often overlooked is that the movement of form from one state to an entirely different state is not the natural result of evolution or growth. Art, like alchemy, *willfully* enacts genuine transmutation. For Aristotle, representation does not merely copy, nor does it produce a symbol or analogy of the original. Like Plato, Aristotle intuited that reality transcends nature. Art represents a particular aspect that represents the essence of that thing, and by extension, the ground of essence binding together the universal whole. In Aristotle's view, the portrait of a great statesman could only represent his nobility and skills if it omitted the wart on the side of his nose, because the wart might make schoolchildren laugh—obviously not the response you'd want for a painting of a great statesman. Although modern art might sometimes privilege stark realism, photoshop still proves that everyday portraiture remains Aristotelian. Which leads one to ask: Is it real?

Aristotle would argue that what a person *should be* embodies what a person truly is within, or ultimately could be; the portrait of that person also should be what the person truly is within. Art gives both the artist and the viewer of art the potential to see and feel one's transcendent Self. Tragedy, for instance, provides catharsis by purging the viewer of pity (pathos) and fear (or awe), and it does so only by establishing a direct empathetic connection with the hero, who, Aristotle assures us, is ourselves though greater than ourselves. All great art, by giving us a taste of the sublime, enlivens within us a momentary intimation of our own transcendence.

But the experience of "what we ought to be" goes beyond the nobility of the tragic hero; it transcends even human *nature.* Great art provides those able to receive it a momentary experience of transfiguration. Plotinus thought that art manifests an object's form more clearly than common experience because it inspires the soul to contemplate the universal, and by losing oneself in aesthetic contemplation, one is led to a mystical union with the divine. Leonardo thought that "Where the spirit does not work with the hand, there is no art." And Michelangelo claimed, "My soul can find no staircase to heaven unless it be through earth's loveliness." These claims are decidedly deistic.

Anyone can experience spiritual union simply by *really seeing,* whether the vehicle is art, religion, love, nature, another person—any number of sources. Mystical connection, activated by the felt experience of depth, and by implication, the Mind that creates and beckons toward that depth, is available even to those who deny the existence of anything mystical. The Creator really is a generous and nurturing God.

It's one thing to be deeply aware to the point of feeling "one" with an *other*. It's quite a different thing to be changed as radically as inert matter into life. But it's that magnitude of cathartic change—transfiguration—that is any human being's deepest calling and desire. Such a charge can only be enacted freely by a true creator with true free will: a god. Seeing ourselves as gods in the process of becoming the gods we already (potentially) are through our own godlike will is outside the conscious scope of possibility for many, though it's no more impossible than anything else we deny unconsciously because it contradicts our prefab worldview or identity. The greatest tension in art and life is between our unconscious faith in our godness and our conscious hostility to faith. Godness is the term of choice rather than divinity, which is reserved for God. Being a god does not make us God. (Christians might best understand that here god is used the way Jesus meant it, quoting David in John, chapter 10.)

In a sense, transfiguration is becoming spiritually un-repressed. The spirit rises to the surface and into focus while the finite/temporal aspects of the self, having assumed their secondary role, are quickened with the spirit's numinous charge. Art inspires the soul *through* contemplation *beyond* the universal, beyond the inevitable constricted by the preexistent. By trans-form-ation, one enters the dimension of transpossibility. We are translated out of our material self into a deeper version of our self never before manifested. Like baptism of fire (lightning) and water evoked life from inert matter.

Longinus believed that the sublime in art participates in the "grand and harmonious structure" that constitutes existence, because in our souls is an unconquerable passion for all that is great and for all that is more divine than ourselves. "For this reason the entire universe does not satisfy the contemplation and thought that lie within the scope of human endeavor; our ideas often go beyond the boundaries by which we are circumscribed, and if we look at life from all sides, observing how in everything that concerns us the extraordinary, the great, and the beautiful play the leading part, we shall soon realize the purpose of our creativity."

Impressionists like Monet complained that most "art" didn't represent the nature an artist actually sees—surfaces of myriad colors and wavering shapes caused by the distorting play of light and shadow as the sun moves—but rather a Platonic idealization—Idea, Ideal—that the artist thought he should—ought to—see. But by truthfully *seeing* the outside, one could then look deeper, through the outside that represents, or masks, essence. By observing the flux of reality, the artist glimpses the truth of things.

At the turn of the twentieth century, artists anticipated scientific discoveries that would revolutionize our way of seeing Nature. Our looking via powerful optics allowed us to peer back through time to the Big Bang, and inward to subatomic particles and our own DNA. Scientists like Einstein expressed amazement that artists and poets always seemed to be at least one step ahead of scientists. Freud, too, commented, "Everywhere I go, I find a poet has been there before me."

Critics have claimed that Postimpressionists, Cubists, Expressionists, Fauves, and other movements of the early twentieth century were less interested in representing nature "out there" than in self-expression and the "at hand" structure of their painting. But the painters themselves disagreed. Their goal was to paint the essence of nature, really the obvious aspects that the eye has been trained to deny, a goal that could only be reached through many years of intense study of nature and practice of art. Their painting was an attempt to articulate their vision—vision both optical and mystical. They saw themselves as engaged in the profound alchemy of self-transformation, and they described the process in terms such as mysticism, spirit, spiritual vibration, rising toward God.

Even their descriptions of principles of art became themselves representations of their own mystical creative process. For instance, Cezanne claimed, "To achieve progress nature alone counts, and the eye is trained through contact with her. It becomes concentric by looking and working. I mean to say that in an orange, an apple, a bowl, a head, there is a culminating point; and this point is always—in spite of the tremendous effect of light and shade and colorful sensations—the closest to our eye; the edges of the objects recede to a center on our horizon."

In its long journey through a curved universe, the soul conforms to its purpose, its own and nature's convergence at a culminating point; the soul's journey has a point, one's "obvious" self, and reaches that point of no return, or there would be no need for art, no need to create or consider or discuss art or even look at those things that inspire art. Even art for art's sake doesn't mean art for no reason; it suggests that really looking includes really looking at one's own imagination, one's own creativity. Art always exists for our sake, for the sake of our transfiguration.

Some people might laugh to think of the artist's process as a spiritual quest or an act of love. The relentlessness of the true artist's love makes it appear selfish and strange. Not everyone understands an Indian miniature painter of the Kangra school who could apprentice for ten years before picking up a brush, then (at last) paints with a brush constructed of a single hair with colors concocted from crushed beetles, ground lapis lazuli, and blood. The true creator's love mines the deeper purposes of the self. Fulfilling the deepest self isn't selfishness; it's noble love for one's self as an essential part of the whole one/existence being actualized. The artist experiences the amazing grace of godlike participation in the creation of Creation.

Far from being mere copying, representation articulates deep concerns. "Art is the compulsion of man towards crystallization," as Edvard Munch put it. "Nature is the unique great realm upon which art feeds. Nature is not only what is visible to the eye—it also shows the inner images of the soul—the images on the back side of the eyes. A work of art is like a crystal—like the crystal it must also possess a soul and a power to shine forth."

Emil Nolde spoke of trying "to grasp the very essence of things." Describing a turning point in his approach to painting, he wrote," I doubt that I could have painted with so much power the Last Supper and the Pentecost, both so deeply fraught with feeling, had I been bound by a rigid dogma and the letter of the Bible. I had to be artistically free, not confronted by a God hard as steel like an Assyrian king, but with God inside of me, glowing and holy like the love of Christ. *The Last Supper* and *The Pentecost* marked the change from optical, external stimuli to values of inner conviction."

Kandinsky referred to creative necessity as the white, fertilizing ray that "leads to evolution, to elevation. Thus behind matter the creative spirit is concealed within matter. The veiling of the spirit in the material is often so dense that there are generally few people who can see through to the spirit," but when they do, the necessity to articulate the vision lends to the spirit "a new value...We are beginning to feel the spirit, the inner resonance, in everything," he claimed, but still lamented, "How many, who sought God, finally remained standing before a carved figure!"

How many, who sought God, rejected the natural Creator proclaimed by Deism and instead worshipped the graven idol of religion.

Kandinsky echoed many others in claiming that freedom is needed to clear the path for further revelations. "Contemporary art, which…is to be correctly designated as anarchistic, reflects not only the spiritual standpoint which has already been won, but it embodies the spiritual which is ripe for disclosure as a materializing force."

Oskar Kokoschka spoke of visions that "seem actually to modify one's consciousness…This change in oneself, which follows on the vision's penetration of one's very soul, produces the state of awareness, of expectancy. At the same time there is an outpouring of feeling into the image which becomes, as it were, the soul's plastic embodiment. This state of alertness of the mind or consciousness has, then, a waiting, a receptive quality." A writer as well as a painter, Kokoschka added, "We must harken closely to our inner voice. We must strive through the penumbra of words to the core within…One's soul is a reverberation of the universe. Then too, as I believe, one's perception reaches out towards the Word, towards awareness of the vision…Whatever the orientation of a life, its significance will depend on this ability to conceive the vision…It is the psyche which speaks…I myself become part of the world's imaginings. Thus in everything imagination is simply that which is natural. It is nature, vision, life."

Franz Marc commented that "the object is a negligible echo…The art to come will be…profound enough and substantial enough to generate the greatest form, the greatest transformation the world has ever seen."

Paul Klee believed, "Today we reveal the reality that is behind visible things, thus expressing the belief that the visible world is merely an isolated case in relation to the universe and that there are many more other, latent realities. Things appear to assume a broader and more diversified meaning, often seemingly contradicting the rational experience of yesterday…Art is a simile of the Creation." But even art does not exist in the highest circle of being or consciousness. "In the highest circle an ultimate mystery lurks behind the mystery, and the wretched light of the intellect is of no avail." Even so, "Art plays an unknowing game with ultimate things, and yet achieves them!"

Max Beckmann explained, "What I want to show in my work is the idea which hides itself behind so-called reality. I am seeking for the bridge which leads from the visible to the invisible…to make the invisible visible through reality…all important things in art since Ur of the Chaldees, since

Tel Halaf and Crete, have always originated from the deepest feeling about the mystery of Being. Self-realization is the urge of all objective spirits. It is this self which I am searching for in my life and in my art. Art is creative for the sake of realization...for transfiguration...it is the quest of our self that drives us along the eternal and never-ending journey we must all make."

Artists creating in the controversial new genre of photography—art photography, photography that *sees*—also laid claim to the deeper experience of vision. Ansel Adams echoes the sentiment of many painters: "The only things in my life that compatibly exist with this grand universe are the creative works of the human spirit...Deep resonances of spirit exist, giving us glimpses of a reality far beyond our general appreciation and knowledge...The subtle changes of light across a waterfall moved me as did a singular vista of a far-off mountain under a leaden sky. Others might well have not responded at all...The relatively few authentic creators of our time possess a resonance with eternity."

Van Gogh, a deeply religious man who before he embraced his calling as an artist had wanted to be a minister, claimed an ultimate need for art. "We artists, who love order and symmetry, isolate ourselves and are working to define *only one thing* [italics his]. Sometimes I know so well what I want. I can very well do without God both in my life and in my painting, but I cannot, ill as I am, do without something which is greater than I, which is my life—the power to create...I want to paint men and women with that something of the eternal which the halo used to symbolize, and which we seek to convey by the actual radiance and vibration of our coloring...representing the real man...portraiture with the thoughts, the soul of the model in it."

Creativity allows us to transcend ourselves by representing ourselves by representing each *other* (human or object). This is no more impossible than the sum of the universe still coming into being already existing in a few subatomic particles at the Big Bang, which scientists tell us was and is the case. To say that is rhetoric. To believe that is religion.

Cubism showed us blatantly what art of the past had implied—that there are facets or planes of being that can be uncommonly represented. Art gives us a glimpse of the potent potential of mystical transfiguration, of being utterly changed from one form "of this world" to another "not of this world," or at least not commonly apprehended within this world. Pure geometry as art seemed radically new, but really cubism was a continuation of the ancient problem of representing dimension and depth, in this case, in terms of volume.

Even the modernist avoidance of "realism" was nothing new. Realism has always been a depiction (of inner truth) conjured through illusion. A real landscape or human being is not exactly equivalent to the image presented on the small, flat, painted canvas or photographic paper. By trying to render an accurate *representation*, we learned ways that other dimensions besides the spatial could be represented via the spatial. In effect, artists have always been discovering that spirit could be manifested through flesh. Cubism, so radically new, reached back toward Euclid and the primitives in its quest for meaning. All artists of every age engage in the same agenda: to penetrate, to manifest, the mystery.

Limiting awareness to classic form and visible matter constrains even artists within the spatial dimension, whether the space is actual or abstract (extracting the form of a horse and imposing it on marble involves the same process of transmutation as classifying all marble horses as marble horses). This spatial bias explains why aesthetics until the last century focused on visual arts.

Cezanne was perhaps the first artist to attempt to incorporate the dimension of time, and with it the possibility of eternity, directly into painting, though many had painted time indirectly through suggestive narrative. By juxtaposing different planes, or views of a scene, in theory the viewer took in several moments from several places simultaneously. The painting represented—or ideally presented—space-time rather than simply space. The simultaneous view of several space-time planes was necessarily from a distance—above, beyond, transcendent. Though the painting represented the potential for a transcendent birds'-eye view, in actuality the viewer must take in the planes gradually, over time, as the eye moves over the spatial surface of the canvas.

In novels like Virginia Woolf's *Mrs. Dalloway* and James Joyce's *Ulysses*, the indefinite nature of space and time, embodied by individual experience and life, are demonstrated by juxtaposed, overlapping, colliding, and enmeshing scenes—a plot structure similar to Cezanne's arrangement of planes, though conveying more emotion due to the drawn-out descriptiveness of the literary facets or planes. (Despite efforts to represent a single, unified whole moment by presenting scenes nonlinearly, the linear nature of language syntax itself imposes time sequence that causes unfolding of characters' emotions and predicaments that evoke parallel emotional responses in the reader. Even so, the *effect* of scenes presented out of sequence registers wholeness intellectually.)

While modernist artists claimed to "make it new," their projects re-presented re-visions of Plato's archetypal forms and Aristotle's transcendent "ought to be" even as they rebelled against them. Impressionists challenged the academic version of what painting ought to be with their own version of ought, Cubists explored form as geometric Ideas, Fauves and other Expressionists uncovered the "greater than ourselves" unmanifested self and Dadaists, Surrealists, and Abstract Expressionists the "greater than our consciousness" unconscious and even willful-accidental and serendipitous.

What modern artists have done is expand the scope of aesthetic perception by legitimizing gauges such as intuition, emotion, individual vision, direct sensuous experience, psychic archetypes, dreams, will, imagination, and mysticism, dethroning the privileged gauge of reason and giving it a seat in the house of commons. After all, "A man is infinitely more complicated than his thoughts," as Paul Valéry reminded us. French surrealist poets performed experiments to tap the individual's infinite complication; theater of the absurd exposed it.

But really, all great artists have relied upon these same gauges, as modern artists have been quick to point out. Emphasis on *relied upon*, subjectively, concretely, as opposed to thought about, *impersonally*, abstractly. Art honors the essence of Nature instead of exploiting it superficially for the sake of validating a constricted theory. Throughout the ages, the greatest artists' concern has been the mystical process of self-creation via creation. The history of art and aesthetics is no exception in demonstrating the persistent balancing act that attempts to reconcile transcendental tensions that occupy so much human activity—tensions and activity that have not fundamentally changed since the Greeks.

At the same time that critics and philosophers were busy limiting gauges to realms legitimized by their respective PhDs, modern artists, writers, and composers were blasting apart conventional definitions of aesthetic by admitting any and every gauge imaginable, redefining the parameters of aesthetics by producing an explosion of statements, manifestoes, credos, criticism, and eloquent essays, not to mention lively discussions in cafes and salons and living rooms, about everything from art's living spirit to the mystical power of the line to the artist's status as true prophet. In an era moving progressively toward absolute Darwinian materialism, creators reacted with violent affirmations and impassioned justifications of their mystical process of creation. "Art is not the application of a canon of beauty but what the instinct and the brain can conceive beyond any canon," as Picasso put it. And his friend and fellow cubist Georges Braque famously added, "One must not imitate what one wants to create." It's no wonder the high priests of organized religion shuddered in the presence of this renewed ancient religion, art. Darwin's anxious lamenting of his aesthetic "atrophy" perhaps served as a confession of doubt concerning his theory: the new religion Darwinism.

While modernist artists were pouring out writings about creative process, their suspicion of philosophers of aesthetics, now collectively called critics, was growing hostile. Many echoed Keats, claiming that all we know and need to know is that beauty is truth and truth beauty. Unlike the critics, the artists didn't try to describe or define beauty, they were creating it, and instead of discussing beauty or art objectively, they rendered their experience of the profoundly subjective process of creation. This was a province the critics had no right to violate. Freud's insistence that creative eros is simply sublimation of the sex drive betrayed his impotence in the presence of artistic creativity. A frustrated writer (he claimed that he wanted to be a great writer, not a psychologist), he couldn't, i.e., wouldn't, penetrate beneath the superficial material level. Anything deeper than matter was fantasy, illusion—a view that still attracts an entourage of fellow atheist impotents.

Ironically, until postmodernism, artists continued to be less concerned with how we create than why we create. They continually tried to articulate art's deep spiritual motivations, to explain the sense of movement toward another level of being, to convey their experience of Presence both in and beyond this world. Philosophy tries to understand creative process indirectly, from the outside, through analysis of art's productions; it wants to stand outside the holiest of holies and report on what takes place within by examining scriptures that the prophets themselves admit can never truly convey a sense of the ecstatic experience of living Presence encountered within.

Just as literature, too, was becoming more experimental and radical in its attempt to represent Presence (what Virginia Woolf called "moments of being"), T.S. Eliot, feeling the dis-ease of the modern world, reached back toward the comfort of the Greeks, returning to the notion that poetry must be as impersonal as Plato's Ideal/Idea, and that criticism must grow within meaningful, purposeful tradition rooted in Aristotle's organic unity and catharsis. Ezra Pound, Eliot's mentor, took revolution and revolt to the extreme, spending a good part of his life in prison because of his political alliances. The crux, the "culminating point," of these two lives locates the synthesis of order and freedom, stability and free will, past and future, animus and anima. The resolution is transfiguration of the self into the integrated dramatic hero god who is ourselves yet greater than ourselves (which literature often represents negatively, through the absence of transfiguration in the antihero).

Round and round it goes, this need to come to grips with ourselves via one of our most fundamental instincts—the drive to create. But creating is not enough. We must know why, and how, and how best, and why not. Knowing is not enough. We must recreate ourselves. Recreating is not enough. The impetus of art is an eschatological drive toward self-fulfillment—transcendence out of ourselves, into ourselves, our deepest, truest *a priori* Self.

SLOUGHING OLD SKIN

Our knowledge, including our experience of beauty, is limited by our apparatus of detection and measurement. Philosophy's apparatus, as opposed to art's, is *reason* as philosophy currently understands it. If reason denies the existence of spirit, "its person" will deny spiritual experience even if he has it. The "objective" perception and apprehension of experts is confined within the scope of their given field. This privileging of specialized knowledge results in grand scale distortion. Experts cannibalize truth and give us one "authoritative" interpretation of one specialized facet of knowledge. This leads to perverted assumptions: You cannot think rationally unless you have a PhD in philosophy; you cannot understand art unless you specialize in aesthetics; you cannot properly feel unless you have a degreed therapist fixing you; you cannot obey your conscience unless it corresponds to manmade law; you cannot have an experience that cannot be corroborated by scientific consensus; you cannot intuit a truth that contradicts academic definitions of "reality," you cannot possess a thriving spirit unless it has been justified and sanctified within a recognized religion under the guidance of a legitimate priest. Our way of "seeing" has been limited by our "vision" of the material, spatial universe afforded by our material eyes.

Not unlike in other eras, today we live and create in an age in which the ultimate authority defining reality is inexact natural science positing hypotheses as facts, which are constantly bombarded by new data rendering them obsolete, or else we bow to religious fundamentalism, which demands allegiance to its facts even if they contradict common sense. This leads to conscious or unconscious skepticism about the "nature," or even the possibility, of truth. Faith is limited to belief that the material realm exists, but what we know about it is subject to momentary expert interpretations subject to revision. Even aware of this, we still assert "known facts" as facts. The universe has become so large, the data so immense, we fear thinking for ourselves; we stand on expert facts to feel solidly grounded. Imagination is an anarchist in this unstable world of flux we are struggling to control.

Though the great artists within every genre have stood outside the box—in that chiaroscuro surrounding finite/temporal "reality"—those artists complained that few others have the greatness of spirit to stand there with them. Vision for most people is reducible to objects subjected to the ordinary workings of the optic nerve limited by habitual excesses of tradition.

Rationalists fear new ways of thinking, but really, what's to fear? The conclusions based on other "detections" such as those employed by artists do not contradict reason, they expand its playground. Intuition is not really unreasonable. It only appears to be to those whose scope of reason is limited to what has traditionally been called reason. If you believe the world is flat, your scope of reason will have trouble "seeing" otherwise. If you know that the shortest distance between two points is a straight line, you will not accept the possibility that at the macro level, according to Einstein's relativity, the shortest distance between two points is a curve. In the realm of curved space, straight lines do not exist except as constructs in the mind—similar to Plato's forms, except that they do not refer to actual things but only to possibilities.

By now we are quite aware that material things are not as solid as we had thought. But then, the Greeks knew that. To conclude with postmodernism that because nothing is definite nothing exists is just reworking a common fallacy—which is not unexpected when scope and gauges are limited.

Art is definite content represented through definite form. Great art brings us awareness, or better yet, experience, of spiritual *Presence* immanent in the material realm. Paul Gauguin called this sense of Presence *sensation.* "For a long time the philosophers have considered the phenomena which seem to us supernatural and yet of which we have the *sensation* [italics his]. Everything is in that word. Raphael and the others were men in whom the sensation was formulated before thought, which allowed them, when studying, never to destroy the sensation and to remain artists. For me, the great artist is the formulary of the greatest intelligence; he receives the most delicate perceptions, and thus the most invisible translations of the brain."

Rather than talk *about* Presence, the best we can do, as Baudelaire understood, is create a correspondence, an analogy, a symbol—Eliot's objective correlative—of that Presence that will resonate for anyone who has had that experience or is sensitive to that potential within himself. The Symbolists attempted to represent the correspondence directly by bypassing "reality" (realism) that stalled one outside the door to deeper resonance. Their paintings attempted to stimulate mystical Presence directly, aggressively. At the same time, they acknowledged that the great masters had always done likewise. The consensus among artists was not that art should simply make something new, but that it should resonate, deeply, from the sensuous down through the symbolic down into the spiritual ground of being—a process as ancient as Creation itself.

In the intelligently designed New World of God, each great artist looks through the past into the future with the eyes of a prophet: He is Christ transfigured in the presence of his masters, who by surpassing them, fulfills his mission and theirs.

CHAPTER 13

THE BIG *OTHER*: SEX, DIVERSITY, AND THE MEANING OF LIFE

And what rough beast, its hour come round at last,
Slouches towards Bethlehem to be born?

One might think that psychopaths or Hogs are the biggest problem in the world. Together they do stir up a pretty big thick cauldron of poison. But in terms of sheer volume, the big problem award should really go to ordinary good people: The biggest problem in the world is perfectly good people doing bad things to other perfectly good people.

Perfectly good parents ostracize their perfectly good gay kids. Perfectly good young sons in gray uniforms kill perfectly good young sons in blue uniforms. Perfectly good white citizens suspect their perfectly good black neighbors of every crime in the neighborhood. Perfectly good German Christian Nazis gassed their perfectly good German Jewish friends and relatives. A perfectly good Baptist explains to his perfectly good Muslim colleague why all Muslims are going to hell. A perfectly good American guy pulled the lever that dropped an atomic bomb on tens of thousands of perfectly good residents of Hiroshima, as millions of perfectly good Americans cheered. The world swarms with perfectly good people judging each other quicker and more often than their remotes flip channels.

What the world needs now, as the song goes, is love, sweet love. What the world also needs now is truth, joy, security, happiness, freedom, creativity, opportunity—the list of basic human *needs*, codified in our country as natural God-given *rights*, goes on and on. What's really quite fascinating yet often entirely overlooked is the extent to which all these other needs are intimately conjoined with the love need. It could even be argued that love engenders all our needs and their genuine fulfillment.

The universe has been constructed in such a way that we need *in order that* the need can be fulfilled. No need can be fulfilled in absolute isolation. We need the world just to exist, and we need each other to be available to fulfill our basic human needs and to help us fulfill those needs by ourselves: We need Nature, and we need society, which is a natural aspect of Nature. If love engenders and fulfills our needs, Nature could be viewed as an expression of God's love that not only engenders and fulfills our needs directly in a multitude of ways both obvious and hidden, but that also gifts us with the freedom to love by fulfilling our own needs and the needs of others. Isn't the freedom to love one of life's great miracles, not to mention, if that love is authentic, one of life's consummate pleasures?

What most prevents fulfillment of our needs, what most destroys life's basic benefits to us, is a function of faulty morals of ordinary people no less insidious than the evils perpetrated by selfish Hogs and psychopaths. We would expect morally faulty Hogs and psychopaths to thwart the basic human rights of the rest of us to serve their own evil purposes. But we usually don't think it worth noting that denials of rights, and therefore suffering, can far more often be traced to ethics scratched and dented by the rest of us. Our other faculties serve as mere accessories to our crimes of defective conscience—conscience, of course, being the faculty responsible for checking our motives for doing bad things to perfectly good people.

What would be the incentive for depriving others of love, truth, joy, security, happiness, freedom, creativity, opportunity, etc.? Hog selfishness? Of course. But if everyone on Earth possessed all of life's so-called intangibles, if each person had all those basic needs met, it wouldn't deprive anyone, not even a Hog, of anything. Love isn't like money: You can't bank it; you can't steal it. If other people have a million dollars, that's a million you don't have. But if other people are rich in love, you are no less rich in love; potentially you could be even richer in love by being loved more and being part of a loving society that nurtures love, even yours. Why, then, are so many perfectly good people intent on depriving other good people of intangible benefits like love, truth, joy, security, happiness, freedom, creativity, opportunity, etc., that if allowed, deprive no one and even potentially add benefit for everyone else? It makes no *sense*. Even so, it's not faulty *reasoning* as much as misfiring *conscience* that squelches benefit and squashes potential benefiters. Isn't it clear that the squelch-and-squash MO of civilization or even a hamlet necessarily backfires? Still we drive that old tin can down the same old potholed freeway.

Consider how often in history or just your average workday Hogs and psychopaths frighten, threaten, intimidate, tempt, seduce, and confuse perfectly good people into executing some very dark deeds. Good people fold when the king trumps conscience. But good people also willfully succumb to bad behavior as a way to get back power robbed from them by victimizers. Good people resort to sins and crimes to survive. Good people sometimes just can't say no. Quite often perfectly good people commit profound evil believing it to be a sacred duty, and perfectly good people invent emblems like uniforms and holy books to prove that their duty to damage and destroy is sacred.

Selfish Hogs and psychopaths have taught even very good people how to rationalize bad behavior quicker than you can say, "Forgive them, for they know not what they do." Often good people justify doing bad towards other perfectly good people because they perceive those "others" to be bad people: They have *learned* to perceive those others as bad: They have learned to be bigots. But to accept that lesson, reason has to wobble with its twin, conscience, hobbling on flimsy crutches, even when it knows better.

Let's admit the truth: The infectious spiritual disease *bigotry* perpetrated by otherwise perfectly good people has destroyed more bodies and souls and civilizations than bubonic plague or even Hogs and psychopaths. Bigotry, though, is curable. But first the disease must be understood. Then we must take our medicine.

Disease manifests not just the presence of something harmful; harm thrives in the absence of something beneficial. We grow up taking our vitamins because nutritional deficiencies can lead to health deterioration resulting in sickness. Bigotry is the presence of hate (or one of its whitewashed permutations like disgust or self-righteous superiority or "love") cultivated in the absence of love and truth. Bigotry often grows like a cancer due to a misunderstanding of the facts. All bigotry, from Zionism to racism to sexism to redneck-ism, rests upon untruth, whether lie or fallacy; all bigotry contradicts love. Deism is a spiritually nutritional solution to any form of bigotry, including religious bigotry, because Deism is absolutely committed to authentic love and truth, the foundation of its worship of the Creator whose love and truth manifest through miraculous Nature, including human nature.

(It should be noted here that for a Deist like me, love does not include obligatory forgiveness. Victims never have the responsibility or even the right to forgive the victimizer. The moral foundation of Deism is truth, and for the sake of truth, the victimizer must assume accountability for his victimization. Because only God is privy to the innermost truth and motives of another human being, only God can forgive. But because love does not equal forgiveness, God can love even when she doesn't forgive. We, too, can love.)

Religious bigotry expresses hate, the antithesis of love posited as a core value of every religion. All religious people and even most not-religious people believe in the fundamental value of love. Why, then, do religious bigots focus on hate—on judgment, condemnation, rejection, persecution, "correction," and even eradication of people of other religions, or at least of the religions themselves? Because people's beliefs are not truly grounded in truth and love.

People all over the world have powerful spiritual experiences. People sense the numinous in places of worship within all religious traditions. People experience God's Presence outside the halls of worship, in spots grand and humble. People despair when they think God has abandoned them, or when they have abandoned God. People rejoice when this, too, has passed. People everywhere sacralize love and its meaning in marriage, birth, death, and many other of life's momentous moments, through ceremonies like weddings, baptisms, circumcisions, and funerals. But rather than celebrate that commonality among all human beings, religions isolate their differences (we pray in churches not temples, the ring goes on the left hand not the right, the deceased is buried not burned), elevate themselves to categories of superiority codified by myths and magical texts (my myth not yours is real, my text not yours is divinely revealed), and ostracize and at times even attempt to exterminate all *others*. More wars have been waged for ideological/religious reasons than for natural resources or political gain or any other reason. Even today all major religions and their multitudinous subsets engage in "spiritual" wars against all the other "infidels." Even on a small scale, Christians and Muslims, Jews and Buddhists, Catholics and Protestants forbid their children to marry or even to live peacefully together.

WHAT ON EARTH IS SPIRIT?

Millions of us recognize God's immanent Spirit in Nature—not just what we usually call "nature," but manmade aspects of nature as well, like particular places, music and literature, rituals and important events, etc. Many of us believe that in some way we can't really understand, God is Present in this space-time realm. Many of us realize that religion and spirituality are two very different things, and that actual spiritual experience is represented through many and possibly all religions but that representation is *representation*.

Spiritual experience, independent of religion, can manifest *through* religion. Religion can facilitate spirituality; it can serve as a door to spirituality. But religion is not spirituality itself. In my view, what is often interpreted as a "visitation" of Jesus or Mohammad or Buddha or a guardian spirit is actually an experience of God's Presence or Spirit—what Christianity calls the Holy Spirit and other religions call by their own designators. A born-again Christian interprets his initial "saving" experience as Jesus because he has been indoctrinated to believe that. A person of another faith has been indoctrinated to interpret his sense of God's Presence differently. We all translate our experiences using the conceptual language of the religion or philosophy in which we are currently saturated.

Though nobody really knows exactly what that Spirit is, nearly every faith agrees that people can experience some tangible, not-human manifestation of Spirit, and that that Spirit is God (by whatever name). Yet many religious people call the exact same Spirit experienced in any other religion the devil. Ironically, according to Christianity, calling the Spirit the devil is blasphemy, the one and only unforgivable sin. What motivates the claim that *your* Spirit is the devil but *mine* is God, or at least that *your* experience of Spirit is wrong and *mine* is right? Ignorant possessiveness. Just like love, there's plenty of Spirit to go around. People don't know that, because they neither think this through nor trust the Spirit. Their so-called faith displays an absence of faith in the God that loves all communers and that transcends manmade religion.

We're all groping in the dark, but some people have bigger flashlights than others. But even those bigger flashlights come in various colors, shapes, and sizes. When you're groping in the dark, you're going to follow the biggest flashlight on hand. No matter where you are or which biggest flashlight you follow, your tunnel ends in the same light of day as every other tunnel. We're all in this together, and we'll probably all be as wonderfully surprised as Plato's caveman by what the light of day reveals just beyond the tunnel of this life.

Like me, many people have experienced a classic spiritual high, often within the context of a religious fellowship. In my early twenties, not long after my Christian born-again experience at age nineteen, I realized that fellowship is not religion, at least not in the sense of any organized religion. Fellowship exists outside the religion, not within it, not because of it—at least not directly. Fellowship does, however, utilize the props of religion to set the stage for spiritual encounter.

Anything that symbolizes the spiritual, anything that focuses attention on Spirit, becomes, in the most accurate sense, religion. The true religion of Spirit can be entered via props of a specific religion, like Christianity or Buddhism or Islam—which in my fellowship included "breaking bread" (wine often included, which made it "communion"), reading the Bible, praying, discussion, and occasionally singing and washing feet, all often by candlelight. I joined and unjoined other Bible studies that used their own props. I explored many nontraditional Christian groups, events, and meetings—which sounds quaint, but they included things like psychic readings, "confessing miracles," praying in tongues—and an entire church *singing* acappella in tongues, randomly modulating in and out of keys in perfect harmonies for three-plus hours and doing absolutely nothing else, no preacher, no choir director, no nothing but people from many denominations singing together in tongues with fans whirring and nighthawks squawking along into the night out the open windows.

Though I maintained my skeptical squint when perusing the fringe, at that early stage I brushed aside my doubts about the Bible and dove in gleefully, splashing like a baby seal in the graces "the Word" offered me. I had already learned about the "problems" with biblical authenticity and infallibility, a sticking point that would later jolt me out of "born-again Christian," drag me through hell, and then gently deposit me back in the peaceful light of Deism. But at that born-again starting point I did what many people do: I fit the Spirit into my current indoctrination, like a lightning bug captured in a jar. At one point I went to an Inter Varsity Christian Fellowship youth conference at UI Urbana to investigate becoming a missionary, but was disillusioned by conference leaders that came across as arrogant, know-it-all money-grubbers and spiritual charlatans. At another point, a friend and I decided to quit college and hit the road with our witness—a plan short-circuited by a concerned professor; at another I gave away all my belongings and embarked on a disciple/Walden experience, a trip cancelled when I learned the cabin I was to occupy was infested with snakes (okay, occasionally visited by snakes).

What I've noted here is a short list of the multitude of engaging props supplied to me by my religion of choice that during my early twenties facilitated my settling down eventually in the true religion of Spirit.

What I realized was that organized religion itself is a prop contained within the broader religion that is fellowship, and fellowship is contained within the even broader, more universal spirituality that is being "in the Spirit." Being in the Spirit—being in communion with God, each other, and oneself—is perhaps the one true ultimate universal religion, which embodies all real truth and love. Not that anyone ever knows all truth or loves perfectly. Even so, the communion itself is perfect in being perfectly what it needs to be in the moment. Everyone who has been in such a fellowship knows what I'm talking about. Being one in the Spirit is an experience common across religions across eras across the globe, even though it is not an experience common to *all* or even necessarily most people *within* any religion. If all those communing people would find that common ground and commune as one, surely the whole universe would let out a huge sigh of relief.

THE THICK WALL OF INDOCTRINATION

It should be noted that Darwinism is also a religion of indoctrination. Because Darwinian atheism precludes any possibility of experiencing God's spiritual Presence because God does not exist, atheists don't, won't, and can't believe in such an experience even when it happens to them personally. I myself have witnessed that exact kind of denial in friends of mine.

It might seem unfair to accuse a thoroughly brainwashed Darwinian of spiritual laziness, though spiritual inertia seems reasonable. I think of atheists as spiritual couch potatoes.

Atheism is like physical deterioration of a body whose only form of exercise is moving to and from the refrigerator and whose diet not only doesn't add nutrients, it does add harmful substances like trans fats, sugar, preservatives, additives, and residual pesticides and other toxins and carcinogens; like mental deterioration and fuzziness of a brain that has stopped being exercised through new experiences, education, and challenges; like an atrophied aesthetic that views the world as a flat gray object instead of a living, pulsating organism that is a work of art in the process of being created Creation; like a conscience that grows lax and flabby through "exceptions" to what's right and true, and that ignores what's good and spouts off excuses while turning a blind eye to what's harmful, damaging, even violently destructive evil; like the intuition naturally mined by children squelched by an adult "impossible" staring right through creative solutions offered by insight staring him in the face; like widget makers living in prefab ticky-tacky houses all lined up in neat rows who move into ticky-tacky graves all lined up in neat rows somewhere on the flat plains of spiritual mediocrity.

But couldn't as much be said of fundamentalism? Aren't fundamentalists, too, guilty of spiritual inertia? Many prominent religious scholars believe so. In his book *The Scandal of the Evangelical Mind*, scholar Mark A. Noll analyzes the works of some of those scholars. He quotes Charles Malik's *The Two Tasks*: "The greatest danger besetting American Evangelical Christianity is the danger of anti-intellectualism," and Canadian scholar N. K. Clifford: "The Evangelical Protestant mind has never relished complexity. Indeed its crusading genius, whether in religion or politics, has always tended toward an over-simplification of issues and the substitution of inspiration and zeal for critical analysis and serious reflection." In his discussion of the works of scholars Ronald Numbers and Paul Boyers, Noll notes, "As the authors describe them, evangelicals— bereft of self-criticism, intellectual subtlety, or an awareness of complexity—are blown about by every wind of apocalyptic speculation and enslaved to the cruder spirits of populist science."

The central problem, really, is elitism. Every religion, every denomination, every sect within every denomination, every clique within every sect believes that its position and only its position is right and therefore divinely ordained. Yet all those contrary, competing sets of believers call themselves Christian, as if "Christian" had any specific meaning at all. As Gary Dorrien remarks in his book *The Remaking of Evangelical Theology*, "The evangelical impulse is to insist that only one religious tradition can be true, but evangelicalism itself contains several disparate traditions." One immediately thinks Protestant and Catholic—two very different Christianities. But within those Churches there are a multitude of subcategories: Roman Catholic and Greek Orthodox, for instance; Lutheran and Baptist and their subcategories, such as the Lutheran Wisconsin and Missouri Synod churches and the Southern Baptist Convention. There are born-again Baptists, Holiness-Pentecostals, Anabaptists, and Reformational-Confessionals. There are within denominations liberal, orthodox, and neoorthodox theologies and believers. There are Mennonites, Amish, and Church of the Brethren. There are Quakers and Puritans. There are Presbyterians, Methodists, Mormons, Christian Scientists. And so on. This list barely scratches the surface of the huge crucible of subsets of subsets of various Christianities.

Certainly the most contentious debate within the churches themselves is over biblical infallibility. Protestantism began when Luther elevated the authority of the Bible over that of the Pope. Once the Bible, closely scrutinized, was found to lack any definitive authority, by the late nineteenth century the Protestant Bible, which differed somewhat from the Catholic version (which included the Apocrypha), had to be elevated to its present status of a "God-breathed" book inspired by the Holy Spirit, making it, as scholar Charles Hodge put it, "infallible, and of divine authority in all things pertaining to faith and practice, and consequently free from all error whether of doctrine, fact, or precept." Charles's son A. A. Hodge, realizing that infallibility had already been publically disproven, taught that the original autographs of scripture—the books in their original form—were "absolutely infallible when interpreted in the sense intended, and hence are clothed with absolute divine authority." But a few decades later, in 1881, A. A. Hodge and his Princeton Seminary colleague Benjamin B. Warfield conceded that the biblical writers "were in large measure dependent for their knowledge upon sources and methods in themselves fallible," and that textual variations "embarrass the interpretation of many details." Since then, many theologians have adopted an "infallible teaching" model, which Gary Dorrian calls the neoevangelical position, "in which scripture is held to be infallible only in the affirmation of its message. This infallible message is variously construed as all matters of faith and practice, or all matters pertaining to salvation, or the overall message of scripture, or the essential message of scripture," depending on your religion, denomination, sect, and clique.

The same kinds of religious debates and factions exist within all religions. All have painted themselves into a corner with the bright color of divine authority resting in their religion's respective infallible texts. This is a corner from which there is no escape other than leaving footprints through the wet paint on your way out the door.

It makes sense, then, that another experience common across religions would be a spiritual dry spell, a classic "desert experience," a falling away from the faith. Doubt is an often excruciating symptom of false belief; truth can be as painful as surgery and chemo. But in the end, spiritual health is restored. In fact, truth brings with it new ways to believe that give the thinking doubter deeper insights about how to better take care of ourselves that lead us to even higher levels of spiritual health.

A different dis-ease results from experiences that make us doubt the truth and love of God. We rant at God, but really our negative emotions eat away at us from the inside out. Even more destructive in terms of sheer numbers of people affected are negative emotions projected onto others: I'm mad at God; therefore, I will hurt someone.

The most common symptom of unhealthy religion is that perennial trickster elitism—in the Jungian sense, where trickster takes on a life of its own. Serious problems arise when religious people try to protect *their* spiritual within *their* religion by excluding other spiritual people within other religions. That's perfectly natural; I myself have been there, done that. But now we need to learn to share our toys. Then we need to grow up and fix the planet.

In my view, religion isn't really myths and doctrines and hierarchies and man-made texts. Religion—authentic religion—is the sum of all that directly evokes, nurtures, and maintains God-centered spirituality. If true religion pivots on the core reality of God's Spirit, it might make sense to throw out the Bible and every other religious text; throw out Jesus, Mohammad, and every other guru; throw out religious institutions; throw out the high priests and all their games and tricks; throw out delusion and illusion: In other words, throw out organized religion and create a new religion focused on the truth of the Creator Spirit. Then go back and excavate from all you threw out whatever still rings true within this new religious context of Spirit. Throw out "religion"; focus on Spirit. This straightforward paradigm shift could transform the world.

PROBLEM: SOLUTION

It's really quite amazing how many problems can be solved with truth. Facts are one form of truth, 2+2=4, for instance. Facts led us to understand that smoking causes cancer; facts built upon facts will lead to an understanding of cancer that will provide a cure, or better yet, prevention. If some or even one of the facts is invalid, meaning not-true, if we have misunderstood the cause of cancer in smokers or some mechanism in the production of cancer cells, we will likely not find the cure. A cure depends upon our understanding all the pertinent facts—all the truth.

If somebody asserted that 2+2=6, and really meant it, we might respond, "That's crazy," or even "You're crazy." Craziness is a state of not-truth. If three people—say, a psychologist, a cop, and an official from the Health Department—walked into the room and told you that you were a Martian because your skin was as dark green as a pine tree and you assumed they weren't kidding or "pulling something," and if you looked in the mirror and your skin was not dark green, you would assume that either you or they were crazy. At the very least you would think that the situation was crazy, that there was something fishy going on that had a perfectly sane explanation.

Mental illness consists in large part of not-truths. Even a chemical imbalance indicates chaotic and crazy misalignment of mechanisms that maintain neurological health. Psychological imbalance reflects crazy chaos often resulting from distress or accident or violation no less deranging than a Mack truck crashing into a house. A mentally ill person emotionally believes something to be true that is to the rest of us clearly not true: All is *not* lost. Even moods can reveal an unconscious truth, or can manifest a not-truth. For instance, you might think you feel blue because you didn't get enough sleep last night, when really you miss your mother, who passed away six years ago; you might not know why you feel blue at that exact moment because you don't remember the dream you had last night about your mother, and don't recall the smell of fresh-baked bread you passed a few minutes ago at the grocery that at some semi-conscious level reminded you of your mother teaching you to bake bread. Or you might feel blue because you got fired from your job and you think you're a loser, when your being fired had nothing at all to do with your job performance or your character; your being a "loser" is a gross misrepresentation of the truth of you and of the situation. People kill themselves because of such momentary not-truths. Most of us have had our mental-illness moments. Tragically, one quick glitch in truth, one fleeting misinterpretation or brief miscalculation meltdown can kill.

People often cling to their invalid cherished assumptions—their "truths" that are not-true—because they are sewn into a fabric that is precious to them. A fundamentalist who refuses to give up his belief in an infallible Bible or historical Jesus when a multitude of contradicting facts have been laid out for him is "crazy," is he not? Yet because society has been thoroughly indoctrinated to believe that one's religious belief is sacred, and because freedom of religion has been codified by the Constitution, we Americans shut our eyes to religious craziness because the not-truths are threads in the fabric of their own, and by extension *our* own, lives. Your personal fabric's religious threads might include beneficial social relationships with fellow believers, pleasant church gatherings, a relationship with a mentor that transformed your life, religious holidays during which the whole family gathers for warm exchanges, and habits that help give your time coherence and meaning, like going to church each Sunday and saying prayers every night. Those practices are the opposite of crazy: They provide stability, focus, and order; they often provide love, and they can embody elements of truth.

The problem is that people keep the threads of not-truth for the sake of the overall fabric, even though the not-truths lower the overall quality of the fabric. What people like me are asking you to do is to tease from the fabric all the threads of not-truth and to replace them with truth. Is that such a bad idea? Society as a whole needs to do the same thing.

ONE DIFFERENCE IS LIKE ANY OTHER

Perhaps like me you've come to appreciate the differences in people. But wouldn't you agree that many religious people ostracize others even as they smile and lovingly assert "Thou shalt not judge"? Some believers have a knack for finding reasons to judge others who have *the same experiences as theirs* but who read their thou-shalt-nots from a different book of myths, or even from the true Logos of God's natural Creation revealed through anyone's common sense.

Shouldn't truth be the core value and reality in any religion? Isn't it crazy when people assert as truth what clearly is not truth? Doesn't lying contradict the Creator of ordered truth? Isn't a lot of not-truth crazy chaos;

isn't chaos the opposite of intelligent design?

Judgment passed by fundamentalists is often really indoctrinated prejudgment packaged as fact. In some cases it's easy for people to cling to not-truths as if they were truth because all their lives they've been hiding the truth, or hiding *from* the truth. Millions of people who were molested as children have been hiding that fact. Why? Victimizers often "train" victims via threats: If you tell, I will… Fill in the blank with your worst nightmare. Religion threatens with punishment and hell. Fear becomes a habit that becomes a way of life. Some molestation victims are persuaded that they are to blame. Most feel ashamed. All feel dirty, defiled, violated. Religion, too, often plays the blame-'n-shame game. Whatever the brainwash, the consequence for the victim is a learned skill at not-truth, especially hide-truth. Rape victims can experience this same process of denial. So can children and adult children of substance abusers. So can battered wives. So can many other categories of victims. Millions of victims suffer the shadowy pang of not-truth that is really not their fault.

Victimization that leads to denial in the lives of many individuals leads to incorporation of not-truth into the fabric of society. Ingrained denial explains why some people judge others: It's a projection of the shadow, the hidden; it's also a red herring tossed out to deflect attention away from one's own faults (perceived or actual) toward someone else's. Any form of bigotry that's not psychopathic sadism or elitist exploitation (sadism-lite) is projection rooted in denial. Truth sets us free of all bigotry.

Bigotry is big-box judgment. That entire group of people over there is *other*, which means inferior, which mean bad. Hell is the garbage can for inferiors invented by inferiors pretending to be superior. Infidel Muslims, unnatural gays, blacks not born into the Chosen Race are all hell-bound according to some born-again Christian.

How can good people be bigots? How can your friends and relatives who aren't in denial, who aren't projecting, cast other perfectly good people into hell? Fallacies and lies. Even clean-cut camaraderie with religious peers can rest upon not-truths fostered by the clique. Bigotry is tolerated when people won't or can't see their own not-truths. They don't see because there's a glitch in one of their faculties, often reason, often conscience, often aesthetic.

It might seem odd to blame the aesthetic faculty for the not-truth of bigotry. But misinterpretation of life can stem from the same aesthetic illogic as misinterpretation of literature. When a student misinterprets a symbol in literature, other students shake their heads and mumble, "That makes no sense," or "That's crazy." The symbolism in *Macbeth* has definite meaning. Though ferreting out *all* the meaning of a complex image might be difficult and even impossible, most of the meaning intended by Shakespeare is easily grasped by any literate reader. The literate are trained to recognize correspondences, and interpretation of symbolism is a skill as precise as interpretation of everyday speech. We easily understand even complicated sentences and paragraphs once we're trained to understand the language.

Bigots, and many anti-intellectual religious people in general, demonstrate an inability to grasp correspondences. This inability is perhaps the primary root of hypocrisy, which is two-way not-truth: the sum of the hypocrite's not-truth about himself and not-truth about the other. The bigot relegates a group of people to a position of not-true inferiority, but even the bigot could be relegated to an inferior position by another bigot. Christian bigots denigrate Muslims; Muslim bigots denigrate Christians. There are women bigots who denigrate blacks, and vice versa. There are bigots in every category: gays who denigrate blacks or women or Muslims; Hispanics who denigrate women or gays or Muslims; whites who denigrate blacks or women or blue-collar workers. What would the world look like if all the threads of bigotry were pulled out of the fabric of our lives and swept away?

When a bigot can't recognize a correspondence between himself and an ostracized other, he can't empathize with that other. Love is preached loudly to smokescreen his bigotry, which is a form of loathing, a version of hate. Every bigot loathes an other. *Everybody* is other. The problem is that some others only see the *other* others as other; the problem is correspondence blindness that results in unfair—not-truthful—judgment. Many straight people who judge gays for their gayness can't see the similarity between the otherness of being gay and the otherness of being female, or black, or old, or Baptist, or poor, or Southern, or uneducated, or spiritual, or straight.

Okay, let's face it, gays *are* different, as different as Neptune's moons, Triton and Nereid, which turn clockwise when the other planets and moons in our Solar System turn counterclockwise; one might say they turn forward rather than backward. Clearly human beings are not ticky-tacky automatons rolled off some lazy god's assembly line. Human differences are as relative as our perception of a rainbow's refraction, are as natural as the fireworks of burning chemical elements giving off their characteristic spectra of light.

Scientist Hans Christian von Baeyer commented, "It is the business of physics to find unity in the diversity of natural phenomena—and to discover analogies between the inaccessible realms of the universe and the immediate world of human experience." This is the business not only of science, but also of philosophy, theology, art, and every other activity of human consciousness. We are beginning to understand what many great minds of the past already knew: Survival, physical and spiritual, depends on unity in diversity rather than on inquisitions intent on destruction of difference.

CORRESPONDING DIFFERENCES

Gay, a symbol for *difference*, could stand for any *other*, be it women, blacks, Sufis, old people, or kids with autism. Any of those *others* could represent all the other *others*. Because everybody is *other* to somebody, everybody corresponds to every *other*. When will we realize that *other* is just us? Not while the diehard antisocial elitists, not while Darwinians and fundamentalists, reject the concept of strength in unity. Hog elitists want "others" to exploit; that's their means of survival. Darwinians want a world where only the strongest survive. Fundamentalists want a world where only *they* survive. What's their contribution to the survival of our species? War and all its concentric permutations: Attacks against the *other*.

The world has all the talents and resources needed to provide every person on earth with everything he or she needs. What we don't need is nuclear fallout, blown-out brains, or rat-race heart attacks. Isn't peace preferable to red alerts? Not for those who exploit war for power and profit. The goal of all their wars, battles, arguments, competitions is, of course, superiority. Elitists need war, and because they need bodies to fight their wars—they're certainly not going to do it themselves—they need to kick up some fear—fear of some *other*.

There's war and there's "war." Big literal wars, like corporate wars in Iraq and Afghanistan, like the corporate war on the middle class, blend fear of change with fear of difference. If the world embraced the radical concept of equality, there would be no exploitation, no power-lust, no war.

Libertarians like Ron Paul toss around "liberty" like a beach ball, but once you catch it, you realize it's filled with hot air. By "liberty" they mean an elitist's "freedom" to screw thy neighbor without consequence, which makes libertarianism another permutation of Darwinian/fundamentalist elitism sanctifying exploitation. Libertarians, like other Darwinian fundamentalists, think they live in a jungle, not in a society that survives because united we stand.

True liberty is the freedom to do as you chose as long as you don't hurt others. For liberty to be upheld, society does its best to protect its citizens from hurtful choices of others. Our legal system specifies behavior considered hurtful and assigns penalties for those crimes; though the legal system isn't perfect and needs tweaking, it's a principled necessity providing great benefit to a thriving democracy. Society also provides services for victims of victimizers, as well as services and aid for victims of harsh and destructive circumstances like poverty, sickness, fires, and natural disasters. Society provides public services that contribute to its own health and well-being, like government, education, libraries, the criminal justice system, and the military. The problem is not that these services exist, as libertarians assert, but that they are sometimes, but certainly not always or even often, misused and poorly administered. Libertarians—and Patriots, who are Libertarians dressed in eighteenth-century costumes— think these services should be privatized, meaning corporatized, meaning owned and operated by the Corporate Nation. Libertarianism is a conterm meant to smokescreen the Corporate Nation's agenda to trick America into trading its liberty for serfdom and slavery at the hands of multinational CEOs, the up-and-coming slave-drivers of the twenty-first century. In-house distortions of reality threaten liberty more than any terrorist threat. Reality-torquing Citizens United, the conterm for corporate CEOs united to bribe politicians and the Supreme Court into allowing unlimited anonymous campaign contributions to politicians, further the Tea Party libertarian agenda of unregulated cutthroat capitalism.

In the eighteenth century, American democracy radically departed from classist hierarchy and rule of the elite. We're still working on equality. Only recently have women and blacks attained equal status, at least theoretically. Like aristocrats of the Colonies, elites today fear departures from the status quo because it means they might lose their elite status, meaning their money and position and the power that comes with it. Their minions fear departures from the status quo because elites cunningly instill in them a fear of change, which is fear of difference, difference caused by *others* who are different, who want everybody else to change to be different the way they are different, like straights who want everybody to be straight and fear that gays want everybody to be gay.

Regardless of the concrete object of fear—gays, blacks, commies, terrorists, feminists—the abstract bottom line is always fabricated fear of difference. Fear of difference is the cause of intolerance, the source of a multitude of our sins and the majority of our problems. Brutes create fear of *other* to create intolerance, to exploit intolerance, to justify predation of both the feared other and of the fearful intolerant, who pay the brutes for protection from the terrifying other under the bed. Fear creates intolerance, which creates more fear, which creates more intolerance. It's a brilliant Ponzi scheme that lands Armageddon.

Suit-and-tie brutes today diversify, maintaining a thick portfolio of prejudices to choose from, an entire bigot bank ripe for investment. The homophobic war against the social "gay menace" and political "gay agenda," for instance, has become a cottage industry. Gays are perverted; gays are unnatural; gays are evil. Homosexuals are so loathsome that Reverend Fred Phelps of the God Hates Fags Church proclaims on his website, "God doesn't hate you because you're homosexual. You're homosexual because God hates you." The God of love in the hands of too many Christians is the God of hate. Oh, some of those Christians will say they love you, they just hate your sin, as if your "sin" is somehow removed from "you." Their hate takes the deceptive form of judgment passed down from on high, which of course places them atop the same pedestal of superior elitism they share with their "chosen" brother in Christ, Reverend Phelps. Self-righteous judgment is just a not-physical form of violence against an actual person being treated like an abstraction. Objectification of gays is just as prevalent as objectification of women. Christians often murder *other* and rarely embrace *correspondence.* Not-truth always eventually sacrifices love.

Not-truth even sacrifices love of *oneself* in the guise of "saved by grace" (Lord knows it's not by good works). Any degree of hate is covered up by the vicarious love of Jesus. Classic rationalized projection in action. Repression aggression unites strange bedfellows praying under the same steeple: rightwinger goody-goodies and bad boys—you know, the NRA boys with the facsimile balls dangling below their tailgates who smack girls on the fanny with their Bibles on their way out from church on their way to chase blacks and Muslims back past the tracks. These are righteous acts, according to real-men interpretations of the Bible, which real-men haven't actually read, at least not in detail. I've met many of these guys. Some of them are quite nice. And quite repressed. I'm not saying they're all gay, there are other ways to be repressed, though perhaps you, too, have thought at least once: Thou dost protest too much. Macho is fast becoming threadbare even in their neck of the woods. It's starting to look downright suspicious. At the very least a queer-fear bully bash is as juvenile as red-faced Rush bouncing on his heels like a terrible-two in a highchair. Roles are not people. Though some people are donuts—all white flour and lard and sugar with a big hole in the center. Fresh baked: tempting. But not good for you.

The ultimate sacrifice of not-truth is hate. For instance (to stick with gay as symbol of *other*), as we saw in earlier chapters, criminal psychologists point out that early ultramasculine socialization and rigid enforcement of gender norms result in a propensity toward aggression that can lead to violent crimes against gays, for predators the male version of women. Hate crimes against gays tend to be committed by males with violent tendencies who have been influenced by an anti-gay ideology, which could consist of religious or moral values, or beliefs that gay people spread AIDS or are sexual predators. Society's cultural message that gays are second-class citizens because they're deviant makes legalized discrimination acceptable. Perpetrators of gay violence feel entitled to punish gay men and women who do not adhere to their respective gender roles. They appoint themselves judges and cast *others* into hell, literal hell if they're fundamentalist, figurative hell if they're not.

Though the need to control difference, or deviance from the norm, is rooted in brute self-righteousness, psychological and social motivations don't explain violence and aggression, they merely describe the way violence and aggression function. Underlying violence and aggression are more profound motivations of elitism on the one hand and psychopathic sadism on the other—sadism bashes, elitism judges: judging is sadism-lite.

To suggest that enculturation engenders homophobia puts the cart before the horse. The cultural message doesn't cause homophobia. Homophobia causes the cultural message, which gives the sadist an excuse to gay bash. Homophobia is simply one of many sadistic props, like misogyny, like any version of bigotry. It gives the elitist the right to exploit, and the victim the means to blame someone, anyone other than him- or herself, in order to take back power. In every case, homophobia, like any other brand of bigotry, unjustly executes power-over.

People gay bash because it's socially acceptable? Perhaps. But more to the point, it's socially acceptable because people do it and get away with it. Some people do it because there has to be a plot for the sadistic play. Sadists group together to enslave "weaker" groups of people they can mutually exploit. Throughout the ages, grand coliseums, literal and figurative, have staged great public displays for sadistic voyeurs. Hands-on sadists prefer do-it-yourself. Nazis, inquisitors, even just your average rapist all want a more immediate experience of sadistic pleasure.

According to many fundamentalists, it's not sadists, it's not even terrorists, but the well-planned and executed homosexual agenda that is responsible for the destruction of the nation, terrorist bombs, earthquakes, tornadoes, meteors, the destruction of the elements, the devastation of war, economic disaster, totalitarianism, Nazism, communism, the decay of the family, and the collapse of civilization (Pat Robertson alone has made all those specific accusations). The solution? Send the fear-mongers money to hire an exorcist. Covering all the fear bases has made Robertson a billionaire.

Remember, gay here is a symbol for *other*. If it's not the gay threat, it's the black threat, the feminazi threat, the Muslim terrorist threat, the Hispanic ("immigrant") threat, the liberal socialist threat. Though this moronic attitude is fading, every five seconds a far-right fundraising plea shrieks like a terrible-ten trick-or-treater. This, too, shall pass. Humanity is stumbling into adulthood.

Meanwhile, among adults, understanding of nature, including human nature, has evolved dramatically over the last century. Because of this expanding consciousness, our species is being transformed—I say "is *being* transformed" rather than "is transforming" because the transformation process takes a huge effort of will by those who care. As we microevolve, we enlarge our universe of discourse. Nature never lies, but humans must seek in order to find—and then interpret—her truths. Facts are not simply facts; they are jets of meaning. Our means of getting at the truth, our very definitions of what we mean by truth, are maturing, as they must, now that we've reached the age of realizing that more than 99% of the mass of the universe is invisible to our telescopes and is a type of matter "different" from anything on Earth.

New, more inclusive definitions of our human family to include, for instance, biracial and gay families are no more radical than warped space or the constant of gravitation that modern science discovered by noticing they manifest in a multitude of different ways. Closed-mindedness lessens our chances of survival. We need one another no less than the equal and opposite forces of each unique planet and the Sun dancing by mutual gravitational attraction around the barycenter of the Solar System.

Sexual Taboo

What is it about gay that is so unacceptable? For the average good religionist, isn't sex really the problem? Sex has always been part of our world's survival tradition. Sex that expresses more than the animal instinct to procreate is a fairly new adaptation, possibly uniquely human. Sex that expresses genuine spiritual love that transcends the constraints of the material realm is so new-fangled that many members of the herd are mooing against it.

Even for most Christians, the modern view is that at its best, physical intimacy expresses spiritual communion, or at least passionate emotional oneness. To deny this is to say that we are nothing more than animals that only have sex to conceive progeny, and that the foundation of marriage boils down to the Darwinist-sanctioned insertion of the male sex organ into female sex organ. And this is exactly the view of Christians insisting that the sole purpose of sex is to procreate.

It is interesting that the more puritanical the worldview, the more *focused* it is on sex, zooming in on "doing it" the right way. Some web sites of fundamentalist organizations like the Family Research Council (FRC) describe homosexual sex in graphic detail (public outrage convinced FRC to remove its oblique porn). Such constricted peering seems downright voyeuristic. One wonders if the authors and readers of these articles are themselves repressed homosexuals. That might explain their frenzied condemnation of contraception, too: it's a way to avoid having sex with a member of one's own gender, who might get pregnant. If they're not repressed homosexuals, maybe they're victims of rape who find the whole idea of sex distasteful. Or maybe they're trying to hide the fact that they're just poor performers.

Ironically, many Christians call interracial or homosexual or female-generated love unnatural when all occur naturally and all benefit the lovers and harm no one. Yet those same Christians never consider that what they call "miracles" are perversions of God's natural law and that "sacred duties" can lead to tragedies, for instance when believers pray for miracles instead of seeking critical medical attention, or "rely on God" instead of paying their bills, or "bear their cross" instead of blowing the whistle on good-Christian Dad's child molesting.

Some old-timers still insist that homosexuality is wrong because it never results in producing a child. If procreation were our sole, ultimate purpose in life, then those with other ultimate purposes who did not produce offspring, among them priests, nuns, and the infertile, as well as those who died young or whose children died young, and those who prioritize career or relationship over childrearing, could be viewed as biological failures. Jesus himself would be a failure. If procreation were the sole, ultimate purpose of marriage, then failures would include those who marry late in life, those who will not bear children for medical reasons, and those who responsibly choose not to add to the population explosion and instead adopt.

Heterosexual love can give rise to life, an actual physical life to be loved, but rape can give rise to that same life. Is that natural? Is that good? Everybody knows that sex can be anything from rape to transcendent passion. What makes it one or the other or anything in between has nothing to do with the gender of the people involved or the begetting of children. What makes it transcendent is the connection, the spiritual communion between the two *persons.*

Most of us understand that there are other purposes than baby-making for living, loving, having sex, and getting married. Ironically, squeamish fundamentalists are manifesting their under-evolved animal/material priorities. Their vision of fulfillment consists of a nest with a male, a female, and a brood of chicks. But this arrangement is not the absolute transcendent reality. Nor is it the practical reality of daily life—even a good daily life. We are more than noble savages. We are not just animals. It's a crazy contradiction that the religious who have sacrificed their humanity to abstract "transcendence" are satisfied to lower themselves to be just animals.

Though conservative Christians seem peculiarly unnaturally hung-up over anything having to do with sex, including gender issues, our whole civilization is hung-up with sex. One reason sex is super-charged is that biologically it is equated with our species' survival. Food, shelter, sex—there is nothing more charged for us. No doubt our insatiable lust for money is obscenely intense because it is the modern means of obtaining this trinity of basic survival needs—troglodyte survival needs embedded in the primitive limbic regions of the brain. Sex is the most charged of the primal big three because it involves not just material/physical needs, but deeper/higher emotional, psychological, and spiritual needs as well. And those higher concerns all involve love—eros, philos, agape. Love is the essence of life, the deeper spiritual life and the material life. For humans, love is life-force.

Perhaps what most opposes life-force and love is fear of death. It's fair to argue that much evil is life-force perverted by the fear of death. Perhaps homophobia is nothing more than overzealous "basic biology" enforcing mandatory propagation so that everyone procreates to insure the survival of our species. Again, it's ironic that those prescribing spiritual transcendence and trust in God are so anxious about physical perpetuation. Homophobia is motivated by fear of death and extinction, not by love as expressed in the Christian text, I John: "Perfect love casts out all fear."

Equally ironic is the fact that this overzealous basic biology has led to a population explosion that actually threatens rather than promotes the survival of our species. Way back in 1797, Thomas Jefferson wrote to James Madison:

> In truth, I do not recollect in all the animal kingdom a single species but man which is eternally and systematically engaged in the destruction of its own species. What is called civilization seems to have no other effect on him than to teach him to pursue the principle of *bellum omnium in omnia* [war of all against all] on a larger scale, and in place of the little contests of tribe against tribe, to engage all the quarters of the earth in the same work of destruction. When we add to this that as to the other species of animals, the lions and tigers are mere lambs compared with man as a destroyer, we must conclude that it is in man alone that nature has been able to find a sufficient barrier against the too great multiplication of other animals and

of man himself, an equilibrating power against the fecundity of generation.

Many argue that homosexuality is one of nature's peaceful equilibrating powers against the overzealous fecundity of generation. Make love, not war; and not babies. Certainly homosexuality is the most foolproof birth control. Many people, including many psychologists, think that except for the one percent of misogynist sadists, most aggressive homophobes and heterosexist opponents of women's reproductive rights are likely repressed homosexuals.

THE DARWIN FACTOR

Less than a century after the ratification of the Constitution (1788) and certification of the Bill of Rights (1791), and in the midst of the Civil War era, culminating in the slavery-ending Thirteenth, Fourteenth, and Fifteenth Amendments and Lincoln's edict, the Emancipation Proclamation (1863), Darwin's *Origin of Species* (1859) and *Descent of Man* (1871) came to the rescue of the average white male by offering a scientifically proven worldview that effectively erased every vestige of noble equality and responsible free will as envisioned by our Founders. According to Darwin, humans are not motivated by sacred moral imperatives bestowed by the Creator but are impelled by blind mechanisms of natural selection. Even while denigrating apish atheism, Christians appropriated Darwinian survival-or-the-fittest elitism by proclaiming Christian dominion. Other religions also proclaimed dominion, and wars among those competing religions still claiming to own God will quite possibly end in our extinction.

By the end of his life, Darwin placed sex—sexual selection—at the top of the survival hierarchy; food was still a close second, and anything else that allowed one to survive came in third. Competition replaced humanist cooperation as the impetus of civilization. It's easy to see how we evolved into a physically and psychologically dis-eased world of sex and food and gadget addictions, chased with a few drugs, exploited for corporate profits. Wasn't that inevitable?

But Darwin's view wasn't really new, it simply codified what we already knew existed just under the surface-flash of civilization: Sex makes the world go round. If sex equals survival, the aristocracy mused, we must control sex. And for at least two-plus millennia they have, whips and chains optional. Every aspect of sexuality that ensures white male dominance is still corralled and packaged today like merchandise displayed in a sex emporium.

Feminism, reproduction rights, gay rights, racial equality, labor equity, and all social institutions and programs have been labeled with the warning "cooties" because they threaten aristocratic entitlement. Inferior is equated with womanly. Real men transcend sissy socialism, the cootie catchphrase of the hour. Real men are proud to be predators in pinstripes puffing Cuban cigars in boardrooms controlling the Corporate Nation. Real men are sons of God. Women and "women" were shaped from Adam's rib as an afterthought to service the needs of real men.

Power-lust is as ancient as leprosy, greed as archaic as the Flood. For the America of our Founders to be truly established, power-lust must be cured and greed swept away. Wealth is a good thing that needs to be shared by the hands that create it. Hubris can only be checked by a universal spirit of cooperation. Unions, collectives, cooperatives, equal pay for equal work—these aren't radical constructs but are practical moral imperatives that ensure economic growth. Do elitists *really* not know that justice and equality issued not from Adam or apes but from the Creator of intelligently designed and enormously diverse Nature?

Our Founders made concessions to elitists to get their signatures on the Constitution. Slavery usually comes to mind first. And although white women had had an equal right to citizenship from the moment the Constitution was ratified, they were nonetheless deprived of many of their just rights and in effect remained slaves even after slavery had officially ended. In many states, women had little or no property rights and were deprived of any rights over their own children. Only in 1920 did the Nineteenth Amendment grant women the right to vote.

In Darwinian terms, this is not surprising. Although according to Darwin the female generally controlled the salient mating ritual, men needed to believe that the weaker sex could not survive without them, and women fulfilled their subservient role of providing sustenance to men by being owned and controlled by men. Perhaps more importantly, by subjugating women, men could confirm that their offspring were really their own. This ancient male-dominated weaker-sex worldview survived the rancorous debates of Independence Hall and still dictates fundamental social norms today. In reality, the weaker sex has always been stronger in determining male heirs, the ultimate form of survival for chest-pounding brutes. Therefore, warped though the logic might be, brutes force women to be sex slaves, to wear chastity belts, to fill in for a blow-up doll by having forced clitoridectomies, to name a few of their solutions.

Much of the world's violence reflects the elitist's refusal to grant equality and freedom to those who serve him. Ironically, this refusal displays the elitist's weakness—his inability to do things for himself—rather than strength. He flaunts his greed and hubris as if they were virtues rather than self-indulgent addictions. He never realizes that his destructive exploitation is spiritually self-destructive, if the Creator is mindful and just. Even practically, cooperation produces greater benefits than does anti-social competition.

In the reactionary Darwinian world of the late nineteenth century, when superiority among competitors defined human values as it defined values of all organisms, if organisms could be said to have values at all, moral values were nothing more than lines drawn in the sand demarcating one person's power from another's. The deepest sand lines were property lines. Humans' obsession with kinship was nothing more than a kind of natural system of property bookkeeping without which we would kill off everybody, everybody being everyone not holding the banana (euphemism intended, since after all, we are discussing Darwinism).

By the twentieth century, values—the kind of values that emerged from our God-given conscience—had been relegated to the last chapter in the chronicle of debunked myths. New values had to be—indeed, could *only* be—constructed. Existential angst replaced any version of moral certainty. Darwinian obsession with sexual selection morphed into a collective Freudian psychosis exhibited especially by the explosion of sexual and sexualized violence.

Of course, many religionists and just as many humanists fought the good fight for moral decency as a defining quality of humanity. Many thinkers argued that humans are the apex of the animal kingdom because of intangible qualities like rectitude, justice, and compassion.

Other thinkers begged to differ. But it wasn't really the monkey mind as much as human frailty that allowed Darwinian kill-or-be-killed look-out-for-number-one incentives to annex society. Masters of Orwellian doublethink, Americans can claim to value liberty for all even while valuing cutthroat capitalism, obscene materialism, and prosperity-fundamentalist dominionism. Very few apple-pie Americans balk at selfishness, narcissism, hubris, and greed marketed by corporations and their political spawn as fulfillment of the American Dream. Yet even many mom-and-pops hoping to make it big decry these vices of sanctified power-mongering, and enlightened religionists condemn the rich-and-famous operating as a whitewashed socio-political version of sadomasochism.

Slavery is a hiccup in today's dominionist boardrooms. Some of those boardrooms seat uppity broads. New inferiors must take their place. Practically, serfs have replaced slaves. And though many good wives still pander to their husbands, these days a real man needs a whipping boy to confirm his masculinity. Corporate real men also need red herrings to deflect attention from their whipping, and scapegoats to raise money to bribe politicians.

Gays. Though the stereotype is not the reality, it's close enough. Gays are the last great hope for male domination. Gays equal womanly men and manly women. Perfect. Gays embody perversion of the superior male role and the inferior female role, all wrapped up in one: Ideal target. Gays are the ultimate challenge to masculinity, and that makes them intimidating, evil, and frightfully weird. Mardi Gras is downtime when guys get wasted with hookers, but a gay parade strikes terror in the loins of real men.

A fundamentalist arguing that gays are children of the devil asks, "Why would God create gays?" Well, why would God create anything? Not to mention *everything*!

SHIFTING GEARS

Even when a paradigm shift is a matter of free choice, the shift is ignited by an addition of new knowledge and understanding building up new meaning and purpose.

What if the tooth fairy was really your dad? What if Santa Claus was actually your mom, and the Easter Bunny your godparents? What if they were simply roles in elaborate games of myth and ritual designed for the pleasure and edification of children? But of course you know that already: You *learned* that as a child.

What if the numinous sense of Presence you thought was Jesus or Mohammad or Krishna was really God? What if members of other religions have experienced the same Presence of God but attribute it to their own messiah or god? What if challenges to your primitive beliefs are really your own growing pains? What if what you perceived to be macroevolution is the creative flourish of an intelligent Artist? If you got new information that contradicted your cherished assumptions, would you stubbornly clutch your juvenile catechism, or would you willingly embrace the new knowledge as a step toward broader truth?

Human life is full of choices, and full of paradoxes. It's interesting, isn't it, that we can only see a whole person when that person's whole life has ended, a bit like when we haven't really heard a whole symphony until it's over. Yet we *do* see the actual person even as the person is evolving. We *hear* the symphony as it's playing, as it's being played. Yet, we haven't really heard the symphony in its entirety, we haven't heard "the symphony," until it's completed: we've heard the symphony when it's over. Yet we don't *hear* the symphony when it's over; we *hear* it as it's being played, in progress. Yet—and what a mystery—we haven't entirely *heard* it until we stop hearing it.

Perhaps death is that moment when the music stops and something in you lets out a huge sigh, wipes a tear, and lifts you to your feet applauding. All the way home the music stays with you. The essence of that symphony, composed by an *other*, performed by other *others*, is now a part of you. Even when you can't consciously remember it, it's still filed in the database of your brain. Who says you can't take it with you—not only your life, but the lives of others. Reading a book, really looking at paintings, listening to a close friend or birdsong, every taste of chocolate mousse, every time you took the time to smell the gardenias—every minute aspect of your life all incorporate a part of the *other* into *you*—the entire, integrated Self that is the final whole *you*. If the parts of our life did not exist, if our DNA and our social diplomas and our brain libraries did not exist, we would not exist. Surely this is the awareness that leads people to create representations of oneness like communion, marriage, and other religious rituals. Really, religion itself: At its best, organized religion is, more than anything else, spiritual performance art representing socio-spiritual unity, or fellowship. But it needs to be better, to incorporate corresponding *others* into its communion.

Humans are profoundly dependent creatures. What would we be without each other? If humans vanished from existence, cells, molecules, and atoms would continue to exist just fine. But if those components vanished, humans would vanish, too. Those parts are not dependent upon us; but we kings of the jungle are utterly dependent upon them. Even selfish narcissists understand the necessity of protecting our diverse environments—not just land, air, and water, but emotional, intellectual, social, and all our other not-physical environments as well. Wholes are dependent upon parts, but the existence of parts is not dependent upon wholes. Even if we blew up the Earth, atoms would continue rocking out to their favorite drummer as if nothing had happened. But within wholes, parts need other parts. Life needs other life to thrive and reproduce. When a family member suffers, the family unit suffers as well.

Everything is exactly what it is: A tree is a tree, a star is a star. Yet within this constant, change perpetually dazzles our consciousness. Difference abounds: blue eyes and brown eyes (and contact lenses), red hair and blonde (and purple and green), harpsichord and saxophone, prose and poetry, plastic Barbie and plaster Madonna, stone tablets and the Web. Human inventions evolving naturally in Nature's wiggle rooms are often called "co-creation": Divine generosity created our creation to be part of a shared Creation, where weird becomes the new familiar, subatomic particle becomes explosion becomes universe, *then* becomes oddly unique *now*. Queer is the stuff of life. Indeed, queer is the miracle of all existence.

DIFFERENCE EQUALS CREATION

So yes, homosexuals are different. But homosexuality is unnatural because it's an aberration? Nature *is* aberration. Creation is, after all, *creation*, the perpetual process of coming into existence and of change from one form to another form of itself within the parameter of its own form's continuity. A fetus changes into a baby that changes into an adult; each form of that person is the same person; that change of form proceeds naturally within the constant parameter of the overarching form. But sometimes change is for its own sake, for the sake of being creative. We can't really say that primitive art was less advanced than the primitive-inspired artworks of Picasso, or that Baroque art was less sophisticated than Abstract Impressionism. It's all equally creative, for the sake of creating a creation, i.e., just 'cuz.

Difference means change. A computer geek rock star could not have been imagined by Caesar. Adaptation isn't the only thing that keeps any species evolving and surviving. So does creativity. Whether adaptive or creative, nature *is* change—an infinite variety of having-changed in a state of still-changing. Survival is microevolution via adaptation and replication of beneficial changes. Our species is adjusting to the new truth that our democracy ideally embodies: Harmony, not war, ensures survival. Harmony embraces burgeoning difference that is life-force itself; war imposes uniformity deformity that begets the stasis of a corpse.

Different does *not* mean unnatural. Homosexuality is the perfect symbol of *natural* human difference. On this point, old-world religion got it wrong. Considering how many people (not to mention how many animals and other organisms) are homosexual or bi-sexual, considering how persistently homosexuality has existed throughout the ages, considering how adamantly honest people refuse to give up the behavior even when threatened with death, one thing we can*not* say about it is that it is unnatural. It is more natural than genius, mysticism, or perfect love, and far more natural than any nature-violating miracles ascribed to Jesus or Mohammad or Moses or Krishna.

Followers of the biblical evangelist Paul who insist that homosexuality is evil because it's unnatural should ask themselves: What does the natural world look like? Clearly all homosexual human beings are not inherently evil except in the minds of those who don't really look with their God-given eyes but instead judge on the basis of prior indoctrination. Many homosexuals are warm and loving; many are good Christians, Jews, Buddhists, or Muslims. Statistically, the accomplishments of homosexuals have contributed just as much good to civilization as accomplishments of heterosexuals.

True, natural does not necessarily mean good. The millions of psychopaths in North America occur naturally within the big pool of humanity, but their psychopathic deeds are never good, not even ultimately for the psychopath. Psychopaths are driven to do evil. Gays are no more driven to do evil than are straight people.

I like a little straight. Every time I'm at the beach I see the straight line of the horizon, I assume the sunlight striking my sunscreen is actually beaming down in straight lines from the sun. But scientists tell me that a straight line doesn't exist anywhere in nature. Almost nothing in nature is straight; almost everything, if not everything, is naturally curved, curled, coiled, twisted, arched, rounded, warped. Look at nature's kaleidoscopic arabesques, its art nouveau embellishments, its salads of surprising greens and reds and fragrances of wildly exotic petals along intricate honeyed pathways of butterflies and bees.

Now look at everything manmade. Squares, rectangles, cubes—straight lines everywhere. Walk around your house; look at its floors and walls, floorboards and tiling and pictures and their frames; the furniture and cabinets and their arrangements; the TV and stereo components and their remotes; the rooms; their doors and windows; rugs and closets and bookcases and their books. Even the boards behind the walls, the pipes and electrical wires and nails and staples. Straight edges everywhere. Bricks, stones, shingles, shutters. Your yard; your garden; your neighborhood and its sidewalks. The grid of city streets. Cars, trucks, buildings, city blocks, football fields, hot dog stands, newspapers, briefcases, graph paper, dollar bills, billboards. In the white male universe, it's straight lines, straight edges, straight. One could argue that it's unnatural, even perverted, certainly as boring as the control-freak's closet of white shirts and black ties neatly lined up by the butler.

CREATED IN THE IMAGE OF THE CREATOR

But the rich diversity of natural life is intelligently created by a far more creative intelligence. Even Darwinian evolution, could it exist, would be necessarily far more creative that the Darwinian creator, natural selection. Even if by some mysterious micro-evolutionary process, ancient apes led to man-apes, Australopithecus, who gave rise to *Homo habilis,* supposedly the first man-ape to use stone tools, who became *Homo erectus* (no pun intended), supposedly the first to use clubs, stone blades, and fire; even if by some micro-evolutionary mechanism the first fully modern tribe, Qafzeh Hominid 9, who lived (depending on which expert you consult) 90,000 or 115,000 years ago just south of Nazareth, gave rise to Neanderthals, Peking man, and *Homo sapiens* ("man the wise"), all that painting of forms on the canvas of life must still exemplify a process of pure *creation*, a going *beyond*, that could only be accomplished by a transcending Artist. Creation is by definition creation of *difference.* "In the beginning, God created the heavens and the Earth." In the beginning, God created differences, one thing differing from another ad infinitum.

If species creation cannot be explained by minute mutations in DNA, and even if it can, if it is the coming into existence of a unique form that has never before existed, if even the existence of a wing or an eye or life itself or all matter represents a creative quantum leap *ex nihilo*, out of nothing-as-yet, whose meaning transcends quaint definitions, then this much is true: Due less to adaptive or random mutations in DNA than to the aesthetic intentions of the Creator, we are here. *All* of us, each and every one.

No matter how you look at it, the universe was created by a transcendently intelligent Creator. Operative words: Intelligent; Creator.

How can we not be awed by the sheer immensity? The star Alpha Herculis is twenty-five times larger than the circumference of the earth's revolution around the sun, and the diameter of the star Betelgeuse is more than a quarter the size of our entire solar system. One single quasar emits more light than a thousand galaxies, 100 trillion stars; and its light illuminating our telescopes left its source billions of years ago; the quasar is extinct, but its light still radiates, like the spirit-energy said to leave the human body at the moment of death. And our tiny brain contains awareness of it all.

For that matter, what is space when the faster an object moves the shorter it becomes? The speed of light is the maximum speed that matter, energy, or information can be transferred from one place to another. If an object could be accelerated to the speed of light, its length along the direction of its motion would collapse to zero. It would vanish; one might even say it would "transcend." This the scientists have witnessed, even though they "know" that nothing made of matter can exceed the speed of light—as certainly as they know that if the universe does not reach the speed of light it will collapse back into its original generative particle.

Self-conscious civilizations of minds asking ourselves about the meaning of life—that's not a product or function of random chance or adaptation. It doesn't really matter to me or probably to most people whether we're descended from apes or not. Humans are not apes, regardless of where we come from. Like many people, I don't accept Darwinian evolution because science has persuaded me that there is no definitive proof that the random-mutation natural-selection version of evolution is a fact, and plenty of data that suggests that it is not.

The Darwinist is persuaded by similarities between humans and apes; proponents of intelligent design are just as persuaded by the differences between the species. Are we really that different from apes, the Darwinist asks? Well yes, we are.

Humans ask *why*. *All* of us—gay, female, black, uneducated, poor: Humans seek truth for its own sake. Humans desire transcendence, not just in terms of evolving, but in the sense of transmuting into a completely different form of existence beyond space-time. We contemplate; we conceive possibilities based on intuition; we imagine. We laugh and cry. We are passionate in our aesthetic engagements. We agonize over our own existence; we suffer through identity crises and self-consciousness. We crave knowledge of God. We crave knowledge of each other, ourselves, all existence. We seek wisdom. We understand the concept *truth* and grasp the connections between and among seemingly disparate things. We feel guilt and shame. We experience ecstatic love. We hate. We feel joy, depression, compassion, righteous anger. We ponder our experiences, and we carry our cherished memories with us into the present and on into the future. Our complex language, our poetry of metaphors, expresses such a high degree of depth and complexity that to compare it to the mutterings of a "schooled" ape is ridiculous. Why some people seem eager to equate the elegance of literature or music or even everyday speech to the level of chattering chimps is frankly beyond me. But it's even worse to cast a fellow human being into hell for being *different*, meaning inferior, less than human, evil.

If you listed in column A the ways we are like apes, and in column B the ways we are different, the vast gulf between the family of apes and the family of man would impress even the apes. Column A would consist almost exclusively of physical characteristics. Column B would begin with differentiating physical features but would then tumble down the page, down pages and pages and volumes of pages logging our unique qualities and accomplishments. *All* humans share the multitude of characteristics unique to the human species.

Some people define that mass of marvels as extensions of physical attributes. Is mind the same as brain? Is spirit the same as mind? Is it possible to prove that mind or spirit exists?

Far from being not-derivative like God the Creator who necessarily exists outside Creation, we humans have been placed in a position of needing to nurture and sustain Nature, because Nature isn't just our environment "out there," it also constitutes the very fabric of our being. Nature includes environments in addition to natural resources, such as home and school spaces, emotional and psychological situations, spiritual settings, and cultural atmosphere. It is ancient wisdom that at the practical level, human survival and compassion seem to be oddly one and the same thing. But compassion appears to include a purpose that leads beyond mere survival toward a higher, transcending goal.

What's really strange, especially for a Darwinian, is that the direction of Creation is toward increasing complexity plus greater vulnerability (which counteracts survival), toward increasing autonomy plus greater dependency (remember the ziggurat: humans need molecules, but molecules wouldn't be fazed if we ceased to exist), toward increasing differentiation plus greater integration, toward increasing individuality plus greater unity. The movement of the cosmos is toward simultaneous differentiation and unification.

God, of course, is not undergoing this process; God, the Creator of process and of this process of space-time, transcends this or any process we could conceive. As distasteful as it might be to the human ego, the universe is not God, and we are not God or a drop in the ocean of God.

God is wholly other—which doesn't mean we can't commune with that Other. Even though we can't fully comprehend God's transcendence, being ourselves space-time bound, we can grasp the conceptual reality. There's a fundamental difference between the historical details and the essence of a person. Even though we can't fully *know about* another person, we can *know* that person, even to the point of feeling "one" with that wholly other person. In a similar way, we can know—feel one with—God. This doesn't mean that you are God, but that you are intimately connected with God. You can know this by experiencing spiritual oneness.

Metaphysically, the *telos* of Creation moves toward love, creativity, morality, and spiritual communion with the Creator. This is the Deism that I ascribe to: theism with a conscience, theism with soul and spirit, theism of, by, and for creative freedom. Love is the creative impetus of existence: Creators love *to* create and love *what* they create. Love experienced as affectionate loving-kindness for our fellow human beings—eros, philos, or agape—is the felt and fully articulated ethic of supreme mutual benefit. The structure of existence, the very essence of reality, embodies and emanates an overarching transcending principle of movement toward mature autonomous beings united in love.

No doubt Darwinians would balk at this interpretation—a leap of faith almost as far as the leap from inert matter to life. But even they know that humanity is a wondrous diversity of unique individuals contributing a multitude of useful, meaningful functions. Our diversity defines our unity.

Adaptive steps are *instinctively* chosen from a menu of preprogrammed options, like a bird's choice of larger or harder seeds cause its beak to become stronger with use. Humans are notoriously odd in their preference to freely innovate in ways that aren't just adaptive. Exhibits A through D, museums and retail malls, thesauruses and libraries, illustrate that humans are outrageously *creative*. Creative are the minds that made up quarks and the lyrics of Sappho burned into hides of crocodiles. We've been created in the image of God's creativity.

Creation seems constructed with a kind of egalitarian poetic justice in mind. Humans need particles, but particles exist happily without humans. Our survival depends on the survival of other creatures lower down on the food chain. Ironically, it's our big dependence that inspires our big responsibility that ignites the revelation of big gratitude and its progeny, big love. Despite this ancient wisdom, we moderns, who take such pride in being so advanced, actively destroy the very means of our survival—not only the world "out there," but our inner resources as well. We are what we eat, be that apples or doctrines or sitcoms. Our very being is composed of the beings "beneath" us, all the way down to our DNA. Even for the Darwinian, this would be analogous to all we have been. But we "rational" humans have no problem exterminating aspects of nature that remain the original, continuing means of our existence. Destruction then is ultimately self-destruction. Humanity is surely mentally deranged if we destroy each other and thereby ourselves. What's more insane than bigoted destruction of difference that for the sake of "survival" of "one's own" begets human extinction?

Sanity is natural progress: creation, change, transcendence. We live to die. When we die, our material being will de-compose downward through the levels. Picture an imploding ziggurat. What starts out as the body of a highly functioning beautiful brainy human being disintegrates down to atoms and quarks. Yet the thrust of creative development advances upward toward adulthood, literally and figuratively. When even the moment it takes to read a book is a mini transfiguration, could it not be, as many have believed, that the spirit, too, self-transcends? Perhaps some people disintegrate into oblivion. But the deep intuition of most of us is that disintegration can be an alchemical process of distillation, and that the distilled elements are reintegrated in a new way into a new form.

Death is present with us every moment of our lives. In its fiery kiln, death distills life to its essence, finally reintegrating the clarified spirit in a refined realm of existence, the natural light at the end of the tunnel, the fresh light outside the cave. The symphony is heard; the translated text is understood and loved. Being unfolds meaning. Meaning divulges purpose. The Creator loves us! Isn't it a sign of God's love and evidence of afterlife that *having had existence*—a kind of transcending cosmic memory—is a condition of the present reality even of something that no longer exists?

Divine intervention isn't a series of discrete creative acts that transgress the jurisdiction of nature. Creation (noun) embodies an ongoing process of Creation (verb) within a set of stable, permanent natural boundaries, the so-called laws of nature, the expanding borders of space-time created "in the beginning." Divine intervention locates the process of not-yet-existing coming into existence: Creation, the marriage of noun-verb, space-time. God isn't Creation itself. God is *other*: the Creator creating Creation. Though transcendent in being Creator, God is immanent in being perpetually actively engaged in creating Creation, which includes both creating newness and sustaining its existence.

We are created in the image of the Creator in that we, too, can choose to freely create newness—can co-create, can "intervene"—within the natural boundaries. And this zone of freedom where creation can take place is the realm where God can intervene to guide us and to answer prayers. Creation is, in more ways than one, an intervention.

Obsolete Darwinist and creationist conceptions shrivel in this green age of the consciousness of eternally unfolding miracle. What, then, is time? What is space? The means of the miracle of existence remains a Divine mystery unraveling its denouement. But despite what we don't and can't know, we immortal mortals have inched closer to what it means to *be*: To be, that is the miracle. Even death, natural and smart, is part of that miracle of be-ing.

Meanwhile, as you've read this book, as you've lived your life, time has passed, the space of each moment that constitutes the universe has come and gone. Yet here it is, the same universe, full and concrete.

A little transformed.

And it's expanding.

.

SELECTED BIBLIOGRAPHY

Omission of footnotes and citations is an aesthetic choice. This book is not a research work but rather a presentation of some of my ideas and experiences that might be useful or of interest to Deists and to others exploring Deism. When referencing critical sources, I have tried to distinguish between my own ideas and information I obtained from others. Most current information mentioned is common knowledge to those who keep up with the news and popular culture, and quotes and data not cited have circulated widely on the internet and can be accessed via a simple online search; some concepts and examples cited in this book have been used by other writers. This bibliography is by no means a complete record of all the works and sources I have quoted or consulted; it indicates the substance and range of reading upon which I have formed the ideas put forward in this book, and I intend it to serve as a convenience for those who wish to pursue further study.

Achbar, Mark and Jennifer Abbott and Joel Bakan. *The Corporation.* DVD. 2005.

Allen, Col. Ethan. *Reason, the Only Oracle of Man; or a Compendius System of Natural Religion.* Kindle edition. Boston: J. P. Mendum, Cornhill, 1854.

Allen, Brooke. *Moral Minority: Our Skeptical Founding Fathers.* Chicago: Ivan R. Dee, 2006.

Allman, William. *The Stone Age Present: How Evolution Has Shaped Modern Life— From Sex, Violence, and Language to Emotions, Morals, and Communities.* New York: Touchstone, 1995.

Anderson, J. N. D. *Christianity and Comparative Religion.* Downers Grove: Inter-Varsity, 1971.

Aristotle. *Aristotle's Poetics.* Edited by Francis Fergusson. New York: Macmillan, 1961.

——. *Introduction to Aristotle.* Edited by Richard McKeon. New York: Random House, 1947.

——. *Metaphysics.* New York: Columbia, 1952.

Aristotle, Horace, and Longinus. *Aristotle, Horace, and Longinus.* Translated by T.S. Dorsch. Baltimore: Penguin, 1965.

Armstrong, Karen. *The Battle for God: A History of Fundamentalism.* New York: Random House, 2000.

Art After Modernism. Edited by Brian Wallis. New York: The New Museum of Contemporary Art, 1984, 1992.

Art and its Significance: An Anthology of Aesthetic Theory. Edited by David Stephen Ross. Albany: State University, 1987.

Bambrough, Renford. *The Philosophy of Aristotle.* New York: Penguin, 1963.

Barnes, Jonathan, ed. *The Cambridge Companion to Aristotle*. Cambridge: Cambridge University, 1995.

Behe, Michael J. *Darwin's Black Box: The Biochemical Challenge to Evolution*. New York: Free Press, 1996/2006.

——. *The Edge of Evolution: The Search for the Limits of Darwinism*. New York: Free Press, 2008.

Behe, Michael J., William A. Dembski, and Stephen C. Meyer. *Science and Evidence for Design in the Universe*. San Francisco: Ignatius, 2000.

Berlinski, David. *The Devil's Delusion: Atheism and its Scientific Pretensions*. New York: Basic Books, 2009.

Berlinski, David. *The Deniable Darwin*. Seattle: Discovery Institute Press, 2009.

Bernstein, Jeremy. *Cranks, Quarks, and the Cosmos: Writings on Science*. New York: Basic, 1993.

Blaker, Kimberly. *The Fundamentals of Extremism: The Christian Right in America*. New Boston, MI: New Boston Books, 2003.

The Book of the Goddess Past and Present: An Introduction to Her Religion. Edited by Carl Olson. New York: Crossroad, 1992.

Boorstin, Daniel J. *The Creators: A History of Heroes of the Imagination*. Toronto: Vintage, 1992.

Borg, Marcus J. *Jesus: Uncovering the Life, Teachings, and Relevance of a Religious Revolutionary*. New York: HarperOne, 2006.

Bosanquet, Bernard. *A History of Aesthetic From the Greeks to the 20th Century*. New York: Meridian, 1957.

Boston, Rob. *The Most Dangerous Man in America: Pat Robertson and the Rise of the Christian Coalition*. New York: Prometheus, 1996.

Bowker, John. *World Religions: The Great Faiths Explored & Explained*. London: Dorling Kindersley, 1997.

Brooks, Jim. *Origins of life: From the First Moments of the Universe to the Beginning of Life on Earth*. England: Lion, 1985.

Bulfinch, Thomas. *Mythology: The Age of Fable, The Legends of Charlemagne, The Age of Chivalry*. New York: Dell, 1959.

Bush's Brain. Directed by Michael Shoob. Based on the book by James C. Moore and James Slater. DVD. Tartan, 2004.

Butcher, S. H. *Aristotle's Theory of Poetry and Fine Art*. New York: Dover,1951.

Callahan, Tim. *Secret Origins of the Bible*. Altadena: Millennium, 2002.

Campbell, Joseph with Bill Moyers. *The Power of Myth*. New York: Doubleday, 1988.

Charlesworth, James H. *The Historical Jesus: An Essential Guide*. Nashville: Abingdon, 2008.

Chipp, Herschel B. with Peter Selz and Joshua C. Taylor. *Theories of Modern Art: A Source Book by Artists and Critics*. Berkeley: University of California, 1968.

Colenso, John William. *The Pentateuch and Book of Joshua Critically Examined [1870]*. Cornell University Library Digital Collections. Originally published: London: Longsmans, Green, and Co., 1870.

Conway, Flo and Jim Siegelman. *Holy Terror: The Fundamentalist War on America's Freedoms in Religion, Politics and Our Private Lives*. Garden City: Doubleday, 1982.

Croce, Benedetto. *Aesthetic: As Science of Expression and General Linguistic*. Boston: Nonpareil, 1909, 1983.

Crossan, John Dominic. *The Birth of Christianity: Discovering What Happened in the Years Immediately After the Execution of Jesus*. New York: HarperOne, 1998.

——. *God & Empire: Jesus Against Rome, Then and Now*. New York: HarperOne, 2007.

——. *The Historical Jesus: The Life of a Mediterranean Jewish Peasant*. New York: HarperOne, 1991.

——. *Jesus: A Revolutionary Biography*. New York: HarperOne, 1995.

Crossan, John Dominic and Jonathan L. Reed. *In Search of Paul: How Jesus's Apostle Opposed Rome's Empire with God's Kingdom*. New York: HarperOne, 2004.

Csikszentmihalyi, Mihaly. *Creativity: Flow and the Psychology of Discovery and Invention*. New York: HarperCollins, 1996.

Daly, Mary. *Beyond God the Father: Toward a Philosophy of Women's Liberation*. Boston: Beacon, 1973, 1985.

Darwin, Charles. *Autobiography* (1887). Project Gutenberg, 1999.www.gutenberg.org/dirs/etext99/adrwn10.txt.

——. *The Autobiography of Charles Darwin: 1809-1882*. New York: Classic Books International, 2009.

——. *The Autobiography of Charles Darwin: 1809-1882*. Edited by Nora Barlow. New York: Norton, 1958/2005.

——. *The Descent of Man, and Selection in Relation to Sex*. London: Penguin, 2004.

——. *The Origin of Species By Means of Natural Selection of the Preservation of Favoured Races in the Struggle for Life*. New York: Signet, 1958.

Darwin's Dilemma: The Mystery of the Cambrian Fossil Record. DVD. Illustra Media Presents, 2010.

Davies, Paul. *The Mind of God: The Scientific Basis for a Rational World*. New York: Simon & Schuster, 1992.

Davis, William. *Wheat Belly*. New York: Rodale, 2011.

Dawkins, Richard. *The Blind Watchmaker: Why the Evidence of Evolution Reveals a Universe Without Design*. New York: W. W. Norton, 1996.

——. *The God Delusion*. New York: Mariner, 2006/2008.

The Dead Sea Scriptures. Translated by Theodor H. Gaster. New York: Anchor,

1956.

Dembski, William A. *The Design Revolution: Answering the Toughest Questions About Intelligent Design*. Downers Grove: InterVarsity, 2004.

———. *Intelligent Design: The Bridge Between Science & Theology*. Downers Grove: InterVarsity, 1999.

Dembski, William A. and Jonathan Witt. *Intelligent Design Uncensored: An Easy-to-Understand Guide to the Controversy*. Downers Grove: InterVarsity, 2010.

Dembski, William A. and Michael Ruse. *Intelligent Design*. Minneapolis: Fortress, 2007.

Dembski, William A. and Sean McDowell. *Understanding Intelligent Design: Everything You Need to Know in Plain Language*. Eugene: Harvest House, 2008.

Denton, Michael. *Evolution: A Theory in Crisis*. Bethesda: Adler & Adler, 1985.

Denton, Michael. *Nature's Destiny: How the Laws of Biology Reveal Purpose in the Universe*. New York: Free Press, 1998.

Dorrien, Gary. *The Making of American Liberal Theology: Imagining Progressive Religion 1805-1900*. Louisville: Westminster, 2001.

———. *The Remaking of Evangelical Theology*. Louisville: Westminster, 1998.

Dourley, John P. *The Psyche as Sacrament: A Comparative Study of C.G. Jung and Paul Tillich*. Toronto: Inner City, 1981.

Edinger, Edward F. *Ego and Archetype: Individuation and the Religious Function of the Psyche*. Boston: Shambhala, 1992.

Ehrman, Bart D. *Jesus, Interrupted: Revealing the Hidden Contradictions in the Bible (and Why We Don't Know About Them)*. New York: HarperOne, 2009.

———. *Misquoting Jesus: The Story Behind Who Changed the Bible and Why*. San Francisco: HarperSanFrancisco, 2005.

Einstein, Albert. *Ideas and Opinions*. New York: Crown, 1954, 1981.

———. *Relativity: The Special and the General Theory: A Popular Exposition*. New York: Crown, 1961.

Estés, Clarissa Pinkola. *Women Who Run With the Wolves: Myths and Stories of the Wild Woman Archetype*. New York, Ballantine, 1992.

Expelled: No Intelligence Allowed. DVD. Starring Ben Stein. Premise, 2008.

Fabricius, Johannes. *Alchemy: The Medieval Alchemists and their Royal Art*. Copenhagen: Rosenkilde and Bagger, 1976, London: Diamond, 1994.

Franklin, Benjamin. *Benjamin Franklin: Autobiography and Other Writings*. Edited by Ormond Seavey. Oxford: Oxford University, 2008.

Franklin, Karen. "Enacting Masculinity: Antigay Violence and Group Rape as Participatory Theater." *Sexuality Research & Social Policy* 1, no. 2 (2004).

Frazer, James George. *The Golden Bough*. New York: Macmillan, 1922, 1963.

Freeman, Charles. *The Greek Achievement: The Foundation of the Western World*. New York: Viking, 1999.

Freud, Sigmund. *New Introductory Lectures on Psychoanalysis*. New York: W. W.

Norton, 1965. Originally published in 1933.

——. *An Outline of Psycho-Analysis*. New York: W. W. Norton, 1949, 1969.

Fromm, Erich. *The Art of Loving*. New York: Bantam, 1956, 1967.

——. *Psychoanalysis and Religion*. Clinton, Mass: Yale, 1950, 1958.

Frontline. WGBH. "Money, Power, and Wall Street." April 24, May 1.

Galileo. *Discoveries and Opinions of Galileo*. Translated by Stillman Drake. New York: Anchor, 1957.

Gardner, Howard: *Creating Minds: An Anatomy of Creativity Seen Through the Lives of Freud, Einstein, Picasso, Stravinsky, Eliot, Graham, and Ghandi*. New York: Basic, 1993.

Gaustad, Edwin S. *Benjamin Franklin*. Oxford: Oxford University, 2006.

Gay, Peter. *Deism: An Anthology*. Princeton, N. J.: Van Nostrand, 1968.

Gitt, Werner. *In the Beginning was Information: A Scientist Explains the Incredible Design in Nature*. Green Forest, AR: Master Books, 2006.

Gleick, James. *The Information: A History, a Theory, a Flood*. New York: Pantheon, 2011.

Goleman, Daniel. *Emotional Intelligence: Why It Can Matter More Than IQ*. New York: Bantam, 1995.

Gross, Charles. "Disgrace." *The Nation, January 9/16.*

Hamilton, Edith. *Mythology: Timeless Tales of Gods and Heroes*. New York: Warner, 1942.

Hare, Robert D. *Without Conscience: The Disturbing World of the Psychopaths Among Us*. New York: Guilford, 1999.

HarperCollins Bible Commentary. Edited by James L. Mayes. With the Society of Biblical Literature. New York: HarperCollins, 2000.

HarperCollins Bible Dictionary. Edited by Paul J. Achtemeier. With The Society of Biblical Literature. New York: HarperCollins, 1996.

Haught, James A. *Holy Horrors: An Illustrated History of Religious Murder and Madness*. New York: Prometheus, 1990.

Hawking, Stephen. *A Brief History of Time: From the Big Bang to Black Holes*. New York: Bantam, 1990.

Helminiak, Daniel A. *What the Bible Really Says About Homosexuality*. San Francisco: Alamo Square, 1994.

Hill, Jim and Rand Cheadle. *The Bible Tells Me So: Uses and Abuses of Holy Scripture*. New York: Doubleday, 1996.

Hillman, James. *The Soul's Code: In Search of Character and Calling*. New York: Random House, 1996.

The Historical Jesus: Five Views. Edited by James K. Beilby and Paul Rhodes. Downers Grove: Intervarsity, 2009.

Holmes, David L. *The Faiths of the Founding Fathers*. Oxford: Oxford University, 2006.

Homosexuality and Christian Faith: Questions of Conscience for the Churches. Edited by Walter Wink. Minneapolis: Fortress, 1999.

Hordern, William E. *A Layman's Guide to Protestant Theology.* New York: Macmillan, 1955, 1972.

House, H. Wayne, ed. *Intelligent Design 101.* Grand Rapids: Kregel, 2008.

Houston, Beth. *Born-Again Deist.* Bradenton, FL: New Deism Press, 2009.

Huberman, Jack. *The Bush-Hater's Handbook: A Guide to the Most Appalling Presidency of the Past 100 Years.* New York: Nation Books, 2003.

Hyde, Lewis. *Imagination and the Erotic Life of Property.* New York: Vintage, 1983.

Hyman, Mark. *The Blood Sugar Solution.* New York: Little, Brown, 2012.

The I Hate Ann Coulter, Bill O'Reilly, Rush Limbaugh, Michael Savage, Sean Hannity...Reader. Edited by Clint Willis. New York: Thunder's Mouth, 2004.

The I Hate Dick Cheney, John Ashcroft, Donald Rumsfeld, Condi Rice...Reader: Behind the Bush Cabal's War on America. Edited by Clint Willis. New York: Thunder's Mouth, 2004.

Isaacson, Walter. *Benjamin Franklin: An American Life.* New York: Simon & Schuster, 2003.

In Our Own Voices: Four Centuries of American Women's Religious Writing. Edited by Rosemary Skinner Keller and Rosemary Radford Ruether. Louisville: Westminster, 1995.

Ingersoll, Robert. *The Best of Robert Ingersoll: Selections from his Writings and Speeches.* Edited by Roger Greeley. New York: Prometheus, 1977, 1993.

Isaacson, Walter. *Benjamin Franklin: An American Life.* New York: Simon & Schuster, 2003.

Ivans, Molly. *Bushwhacked: Life in George W. Bush's America.* New York:Vintage, 2003.

Jacobi, Jolande and R.F.C. Hull. *Jung, C.G. Psychological Reflections: A New Anthology of His Writings 1905-1961.* Princeton: Princeton University, 1953, 1978.

Jaffé, Aneila. *The Myth of Meaning in the Work of C. G. Jung.* Zürich: Daimon Verlag, 1984.

James, William. *The Variety of Religious Experience.* Middlesex: Penguin, 1987. Originally published: U.S.: Longmans, Green, and Co., 1902.

Jefferson, Thomas. *The Quotable Jefferson.* Edited by John P. Kaminski. Princeton: Princeton University, 2006.

——. *The Writings of Thomas Jefferson.* Edited by Andrew A. Lipscomb and Albert Ellery Bergh. 20 vols. Memorial Edition. Washington, D. C.: Thomas Jefferson Memorial Association, 1903-04. Also available: Project Gutenberg, 2007. www.gutenberg.org/ etext/21002.

——. *The Writings of Thomas Jefferson.* Edited by Paul Leicester Ford. 10 vols. Ford Edition. New York, 1892-99. Etext.virginia.edu/jefferson/quotations/.

Johnson, Donald D. *Probability's Nature and Nature's Probability: A Call to Scientific Integrity*. Charleston: Booksurge, 2009.

Jung, C.G. *Aspects of the Feminine*. Princeton: Princeton University, 1982.

——. *Man and His Symbols*. New York: Dell, 1964.

——. *Memories, Dreams, Reflections*. New York: Vintage, 1965.

——. *Modern Man in Search of a Soul*. San Diego: Harcourt, 1933.

——. *Psychology and Alchemy*. New York: Princeton/Bollingen, 1953, 1968.

——. *Symbols of Transformation*. New York: Princeton/Bollingen, 1956, 1976.

——. *Two Essays on Analytical Psychology*. New York: Princeton/Bollingen, 1953.

Kee, Howard Clark, Franklin W. Young, and Karlfried Froehlich. *Understanding the New Testament*. Englewood Cliffs, N. J.: Prentice-Hall, 1965.

Kennedy, Robert F., Jr. *Crimes Against Nature: How George W. Bush & His Corporate Pals Are Plundering the Country & Hijacking Our Democracy*. New York: Harper, 2005.

Kirsch, Jonathan. *The Grand Inquisitor's Manual: A History of Terror in the Name of God*. New York: HarperOne, 2008.

Lambert, Frank. *The Founding Fathers and the Place of Religion in America*. Princeton: Princeton University, 2003.

Leeming, David with Margaret Leeming. *A Dictionary of Creation Myths*. Oxford: Oxford University, 1994.

Levinson, Horace C. *The Science of Chance: From Probability to Statistics*. New York: Reinhart, 1939, 1950.

Locke, John. "A Letter Concerning Toleration" (1689). www.oregonstate.edu/instructphl302/texts/locke/locke2/locket/locke_toleration.html.

——. "Second Treatise of Government" (1690). Project Gutenberg, 2005. www.gutenberg.org/etext/7370.

Macquarrie, John. *Twentieth-Century Religious Thought*. London: SCM, 1963, 1988.

Mapp, Alf J., Jr. *The Faiths of Our Fathers: What America's Founders <u>Really</u> Believed*. New York: Fall River, 2003.

Marcuse, Herbert. *Eros and Civilization: A Philosophical Inquiry into Freud*. New York: Vintage, 1955.

Marsden, George M. *Understanding Fundamentalism and Evangelicalism*. Grand Rapids: Eerdmans, 1991.

Maslow, Abraham H. *Religions, Values, and Peak-Experiences*. Columbus: Ohio State, 1964.

May, Rollo. *Man's Search For Himself: How We Can Find a Center of Strength Within Ourselves to Face and Conquer the Insecurities of This Troubled Age*. New York: W. W. Norton, 1953.

Meyer, Stephen C. *Signature in the Cell: DNA and the Evidence for Intelligent Design*. New York: HarperOne, 2009.

Miles, Jack. *God: A Biography.* New York: Vintage, 1996.

Moore, Michael. *Capitalism: A Love Story.* DVD. Starz/Anchor Bay, 2010.

——. *Fahrenheit 9/11.* DVD. Culver City: Westside Productions, 2004.

Moring, Gary F. *The Complete Idiot's Guide to Understanding Einstein.* Indianapolis: Alpha, 2000.

Murphy, Catherine M. *The Historical Jesus For Dummies.* Hoboken: Wiley, 2008.

Mysteries of Life and the Universe: New Essays from America's Finest Writers on Science. Edited by William H. Shore. Orlando: Harcourt, 1992.

Narby, Jeremy. *The Cosmic Serpent: DNA and the Origins of Knowledge.* New York: Tarcher/Putnum, 1998.

Newberg, Andrew and Mark Robert Waldman. *How God Changes Your Brain: Breakthrough Findings from a Leading Neuroscientist.* New York: Ballantine, 2009.

Noll, Mark A. *The Scandal of the Evangelical Mind.* Grand Rapids: Eerdmans,1994.

The Oxford Bible Commentary. Edited by John Barton and John Muddiman. New York: Oxford, 2001.

Pagels, Elaine. *The Secret Gospel of Thomas.* New York: Vintage, 2003.

Paine, Thomas. *The Age of Reason.* New York: Citadel Press, 1988. Originally published: Paris: Barras, 1794.

——. *The Thomas Paine Reader.* Edited by Michael Foot and Isaac Kramnick. London, England: Penguin Books, 1987.

Palmer, Elihu. *Principles of Nature.* Kindle edition, Mobile Lyceum, 2011.

Paulson, Steve. *Atoms & Eden: Conversations on Religion and Science.* Oxford: Oxford University, 2010.

Pert, Candace. *Molecules of Emotion: The Science Behind Mind-Body Medicine.* New York: Touchstone, 1997.

Plato. *Great Dialogues of Plato.* Translated by W. H. D. Rouse. New York: Mentor Books, 1956.

Plato. *Plato: Complete Works.* Edited by John M. Cooper and D. S. Hutchinson. Indianapolis: Hackett, 1997.

The Politics of Women's Spirituality: Essays on the Rise of Spiritual Power Within the Feminist Movement. Edited by Charlene Spretnak. Garden City: Anchor, 1982.

Poole, Michael. *The "New" Atheism: 10 Arguments That Don't Hold Water.* Oxford: Lion, 2009.

Price, Robert M. *The Incredible Shrinking Son of Man: How Reliable is the Gospel Tradition?* Amherst: Prometheus, 2003.

Rana, Fazale. *The Cell's Design: How Chemistry Reveals the Creator's Artistry.* Grand Rapids: Baker, 2008.

Reimarus, Hermann Samuel. *Reimarus: Fragments.* Edited by Charles H. Talbert. Eugene: Wipf and Stock, published with arrangement with SCM-Canterbury,

1970.

Remsberg, John E. *The Christ: A Critical Review and Analysis of the Evidence of His Existence*. New York: Prometheus, 1994. Originally published: New York: The Truth Seeker Company, 1909.

Ruether, Rosemary Radford. *Christianity and the Making of the Modern Family: Ruling Ideologies, Diverse Realities*. Boston: Beacon, 2000.

——. *Sexism and God-Talk: Toward a Feminist Theology*. Boston: Beacon, 1983, 1993.

——. *Women and Redemption: A Theological History*. Minneapolis: Fortress, 1998.

Sanders, E. P. *The Historical Figure of Jesus*. London: Penguin, 1993.

Sanford, J. C. *Genetic Entropy, and the Mystery of the Genome*. Waterloo: FMS, 2008.

Schweitzer, Albert. *Out of My Life and Thought: An Autobiography*. Baltimore: Johns Hopkins, 2009. Originally published: New York: Henry Holt, 1933.

——. *The Philosophy of Civilization*. New York: Prometheus, 1987.

——. *The Quest of the Historical Jesus*. Mineola: Dover, 2005. Originally published under the title *The Quest of the Historical Jesus: A Critical Study of Its Progress from Reimarus to Wrede*. London: Adam and Charles Black, 1911.

Singer, Margaret Thaler. *Cults In Our Midst: The Continuing Fight Against Their Hidden Menace*. San Francisco: Jossey-Bass, 2003.

Smith, Huston. *The Religions of Man*. New York: Harper & Row, 1958.

Spetner, Lee. *Not By Chance: Shattering the Modern Theory of Evolution*. New York: Judaica, 1997.

Spitzer, Robert J. *New Proofs for the Existence of God: Contributions of Contemporary Physics and Philosophy*. Grand Rapids: Eerdmans, 2010.

Strauss, David Friedrich. *The Life of Jesus, Critically Examined*. Lexington: Filiquarian, 1835, 1846 (digital copy of the original).

——. *The Life of Jesus Critically Examined*. Translated from the German by George Eliot (1892). Reprint: Sigler Press, 2002.

Thomas, Lewis. *Late Night Thoughts on Listening to Mahler's Ninth Symphony*. New York: Bantam, 1984.

——. *The Lives of a Cell: Notes of a Biology Watcher*. New York: Bantam, 1974.

——. *The Medusa and the Snail: More Notes of a Biology Watcher*. New York: Bantam, 1979.

Tripp, Edward. *The Meridian Handbook of Classical Mythology*. New York: Meridian, 1970.

Von Franz, Marie-Louise. *Alchemy: An Introduction to the Symbolism and the Psychology*. Toronto: Inner City, 1980.

——. *On Divination and Synchronicity: The Psychology of Meaningful Chance*. Toronto: Inner City, 1980.

Wells, Jonathan. *The Politically Incorrect Guide to Darwinism and Intelligent*

Design. Lanham: The National Book Network, 2006.

Wenger, Win and Richard Poe. *The Einstein Factor.* Rocklin, CA: Prima, 1996.

Westfall, Richard. *The Life of Isaac Newton.* Cambridge: Cambridge University, 1993.

Wilson, Edward O. *Consilience: The Unity of Knowledge.* New York: Vintage, 1998.

Woolf, Virginia. *A Room of One's Own.* New York: Harcourt, 1929.

World Scripture: A Comparative Anthology of Sacred Texts. A Project of the International Religious Foundation. St. Paul: Paragon House, 1995.

Made in the USA
Lexington, KY
02 May 2014